Persuasion

Reception and Responsibility

Tenth Edition

CHARLES U. LARSON

Northern Illinois University, Emeritus

THOMSON
™
WADSWORTH

Australia • Canada • Mexico • Singapore • Spain
United Kingdom • United States

THOMSON

WADSWORTH

Publisher: *Holly J. Allen*
Editor: *Annie Mitchell*
Assistant Editor: *Breanna Gilbert*
Editorial Assistant: *Trina Enriquez*
Technology Project Manager: *Jeanette Wiseman*
Marketing Manager: *Kimberly Russell*
Marketing Assistant: *Alanna Kelly*
Advertising Project Manager: *Shemika Britt*
Project Manager, Editorial Production: *Mary Noel*

Print/Media Buyer: *Doreen Suruki*
Permissions Editor: *Sommy Ko*
Production Service: *Melanie Field, Strawberry Field Publishing*
Copy Editor: *Thomas L. Briggs*
Cover Designer: *John Odam*
Cover Image: *car and jet, Artville; woman at microphone, Craig McClain; similing young man, RubberBall Productions; microwave tower, PhotoDisc; man whispering to woman, PhotoDisc*
Compositor: *TBH Typecast, Inc.*
Text and Cover Printer: *Webcom*

For more information about our products, contact us at:
Thomson Learning Academic Resource Center
1-800-423-0563

For permission to use material from this text, contact us by: **Phone:** 1-800-730-2214
Fax: 1-800-730-2215
Web: http://www.thomsonrights.com

Library of Congress Control Number: 2003108596

ISBN 0-534-61902-9

Wadsworth/Thomson Learning
10 Davis Drive
Belmont, CA 94002-3098
USA

Asia
Thomson Learning
5 Shenton Way #01-01
UIC Building
Singapore 068808

Australia/New Zealand
Thomson Learning
102 Dodds Street
Southbank, Victoria 3006
Australia

Canada
Nelson
1120 Birchmount Road
Toronto, Ontario M1K 5G4
Canada

Europe/Middle East/Africa
Thomson Learning
High Holborn House
50/51 Bedford Row
London WC1R 4LR
United Kingdom

Latin America
Thomson Learning
Seneca, 53
Colonia Polanco
11560 Mexico D.F.
Mexico

Spain/Portugal
Paraninfo
Calle/Magallanes, 25
28015 Madrid, Spain

*To the memories of my mother, Elsa Viola Larson,
and my youngest sister Sandra Larson Wright,
both of whom we lost this past year.*

Brief Contents

Contents

Preface

When I wrote the first edition of *Persuasion: Reception and Responsibility* more than thirty years ago, the United States was on the verge of a national nervous breakdown. The anti–Vietnam War movement sparked highly emotional unrest in the streets. The assassinations of Martin Luther King, Jr., and Bobby Kennedy within the space of two months shook the nation like an earthquake. National Guard soldiers shot and killed four college students at Kent State University in Ohio during an antiwar demonstration. Race riots left most major cities smoking. For the first time since the Civil War, the Capitol and the White House required guarding by military troops, who aimed .50-caliber machine guns at their fellow Americans. And for differing reasons, the public caused two presidents to withdraw from office.

These dramatic and dangerous times frightened us to the core, and when I faced teaching my first college class in persuasion, it seemed as if we were on the brink of anarchy. It was a large class—fifty or sixty students, as I recall. Given the tenor of the national mood, I didn't feel there was any way I could simply teach these students to speak persuasively. Instead, I decided to teach the course from the perspective of the receiver, the consumer of persuasion who was faced with thousands of persuasive appeals every day—some of which seemed benign, others malignant. At the time, many persuasive messages distorted or invented "facts," used fallacious reasoning, and paid little heed to ethics.

Finding an appropriate textbook to use in this new course was my major teaching problem. Everything on the market at the time focused on training the producers, not the consumers, of persuasion. So I decided to write a book specifically for the consumers. The result was the first edition of *Persuasion: Reception and Responsibility,* and with the help of my friend and colleague Dick Johannesen and my risk-taking editor at Wadsworth, Becky Hayden, we discovered a need for the book among teachers of persuasion. During the first convention at which the book was displayed, the *New York Times* declared it "a runaway hit." Adoptions came in slowly at first but then more rapidly, and soon Becky asked me to begin work on another edition. The rest is history.

And what a history this book has seen over the past few decades! Consider the enormity of just a few events: Foremost was the collapse of the Soviet Union, the subsequent democratization of its satellite countries, and the spread of market economies. The AIDS virus resulted in the tragic deaths of millions of persons, especially in Third World countries. The invention and popular adoption of personal computers, videotapes, and DVDs were topped by the introduction of the Internet. The greater availability of pornography—especially on the Web—forced parents and others to reconsider the use of television and the Internet. Today, there is the increasing frequency of identity theft and other, related forms of fraud. And the growth of China as a world-class economic power surprised us, as did the suddenly stagnating economy of Japan. All of these issues, and others yet to come, relate to persuasion and the need for critical consumers and receivers.

In the years since that first edition was published, my colleagues and students at Northern Illinois University have helped me revise and update the book. They have led me to examples I'd overlooked. They have pointed out issues, media, and technologies that needed to be addressed. They have proofread my work and given me the support I needed when necessary. With their help and that of a series of editors, editorial assistants, and others at Wadsworth/Thomson Learning, we have arrived at a tenth edition that is far better than that first edition.

FEATURES NEW TO THIS EDITION

The goal of the tenth edition remains the same as in the previous editions: to help train you to be a critical, questioning, and somewhat suspicious consumer and receiver of persuasive messages. Here's what is new to this edition:

- A single persuasion theory, the elaboration likelihood model, binds the various theoretical perspectives into a unified whole.

- Chapter 2 has been thoroughly revised by Richard L. Johannesen and now includes the ethics of ends and means and the process of moral exclusion.

- A new Chapter 3, "Traditional and Humanistic Approaches to Persuasion," written by Joseph Scudder of Northern Illinois University, covers persuasion research methods from the Aristotelian tradition to humanistic approaches, including the women's movement and radical movements.

- A new Chapter 4, "Social Scientific Approaches to Persuasion," also by Joseph Scudder presents the empirical study of persuasion—including reinforcement and learning theories, attitude change, cognitive approaches such as the elaboration likelihood model, compliance gaining in the interpersonal context, and per-

suasion and mass media theory and research—as a complement to the traditional, rhetorical approaches presented in Chapter 3.

- All chapters have been revised with an eye to keeping up with the breathtaking changes we've seen in recent years, including the terrorist attacks of September 11, 2001, business scandals, current political and advertising issues, and technological innovations.

- Completely revised InfoTrac® College Edition items throughout the book provide a wealth of material with which to expand text discussion and classroom learning.

- The book offers detailed discussion of the difference between persuasion, influence, and coercion.

ACKNOWLEDGMENTS

This edition would not have happened without the help of my colleagues and students at Northern Illinois, and the staff at Wadsworth/Thomson Learning, beginning with Annie Mitchell, editor; Holly Allen, publisher; Breanna Gilbert, assistant editor; Sommy Ko, permissions editor; and many others.

Additionally, I would like to thank my colleagues across the country who provided feedback on the ninth and earlier editions, and especially those colleagues who did in-depth reviews of the ninth edition and provided me with much appreciated insights, suggestions, and references for this new edition. They are William N. Denman, Marshall University; Sharon E. Jarvis, University of Texas–Austin; Kevin T. Jones, Chapman University; Melanie R. Trost, University of Montana–Missoula; Clay Warren, George Washington University; and Gwen M. Whittenbaum, Michigan State University.

And finally, I offer special thanks to you, the students and teachers, who will use and hopefully profit from adopting, reading, and discussing the tenth edition of *Persuasion: Reception and Responsibility*.

Charles U. Larson

PART I

Theoretical Premises

Persuasion rocks. It rocks not only our individual worlds but the whole world around us. Persuasion both changes our world and represents a way that our world changes us. Persuasion is about choice. Understanding persuasion helps us make better choices and is essential to live in our ever-changing world. It is clear that persuasion can make the world a better place just as Martin Luther King, Jr., made it clear through persuasion that society could be a better place.

Unfortunately, persuasion also has a dark side. We live in a period of reconstruction in the United States. In the aftermath of the events of September 11, 2001, we face a different kind of enemy—and, perhaps, a different kind of *influence,* one that previously was not known in this country. It is now clearer than ever that persuasion is much larger than the United States and the Western world—persuasion is global. But the enemies are not all from other countries. The more difficult task of reconstruction may be the restoration of trust in our major institutions. The loss of trust in the political establishment became evident in the years following the resignation of President Richard Nixon, but it has been reinforced by the poor example of other politicians like Bill Clinton. Trust in business leadership has also been shaken. It is now evident that persuasion was used on Wall Street to cover up years of corporate deceit. The accounting scandals at Enron (which also brought down one of the nation's elite accounting firms, Arthur Andersen) were only the tip of the iceberg of what was to become a cascade of bookkeeping scandals that brought other mighty corporations such as WorldCom to ruin. Trust also has been eroded in religious institutions, which are fighting for their survival after repeated revelations of sexual improprieties by priests with minors. Ethical violations have even touched Martha Stewart and her homemaking enterprises.

Another challenge to our understanding of persuasion involves the introduction and rapid adoption of new, high-impact technologies such as personal computers and the digitization of many older technologies. And we have the ongoing development of virtual realities of all sorts. Easy and instant global communication affects us as never before. Traditional ways of doing business, conducting national and international politics, interacting with others, and even building cultures became obsolete following the globalization of virtually every aspect of human endeavor. Examples include the ability to buy, sell, trade, and bid online and to communicate continuously with a host of entities like the stock and commodities markets, airlines, friends, relatives, strangers, and even entire governments across the globe. And we do this twenty-four hours a day, seven days a week. Underlying all of this change, however, is a constant—persuasion from all sides. In fact, persuasion has been the great common denominator in the arenas of economics, politics, religion, business, and interpersonal relations ever since humans began to interact. Never before, however, has persuasion had such potential as a tool for affecting our daily lives, as a means to many ends—both good and bad—and as a presence in every moment of our waking lives. The world we face in the new millennium rests on the power of various kinds of persuasion.

We need to approach this profusion of persuasion in our everyday lives with an awareness that, at its core, persuasion is a symbolic act for both persuaders and receivers. We use symbols—usually words or images—in our commercial interactions and even our family life. Persuasion basically represents a democratic and humanistic attempt to influence others, to convince them to take certain actions—purchasing, voting, cooperating with one another—instead of forcing or coercing them to do so. For the most part, persuasion uses either logical or emotional means to accomplish desired ends, instead of force. Recent research and theory suggest that we process logical persuasion carefully and critically, but we process most emotional persuasion far less critically. In either case, the logical or emotional persuasion seeks to give us "good reasons" for acting. These good reasons must be delivered to the receivers via an appropriate medium, whether "one-to-one" interpersonal communication or "one-to-many" forms of communication, such as contemporary electronic and print media. And the good reasons must be acceptable in terms of the dominant norms and values of culture and society.

As you read this book, I hope that you change in important ways. We live in a world in which persuasive messages of various types continually compete for our attention, our beliefs, and our actions. What's more, the exciting times in which we live depend heavily on successful persuasion. Persuasion affects consumer behavior, interpersonal behavior, and intrapersonal behavior (self-persuasion). And most importantly, we spend far more time receiving persuasion than sending persuasion—we are predominantly in the role of the persuadee, or receiver and consumer, of persuasive messages. Therefore, the primary goal of this book and class is to make you more critical and responsible consumers of persuasion.

In some ways, you are already a critical receiver, but you can improve your reception skills. You need to identify how critical a receiver you are at the outset. How easily are you persuaded? How does persuasion work on you? What tactics are most effective with you? With others? Which are least effective? Part I investigates these questions and establishes a perspective.

In Part II, we search for fundamental persuasive premises that usually sway most receivers and examine the foundations on which persuaders build their arguments. We need to understand how and why persuaders appeal to these premises, and why we respond to certain psychological appeals and not to others. Why are some lines of reasoning more convincing than others? Why do persuadees in some cultures respond in one way, but not in others? Why does some successful persuasion seem almost knee-jerk while other persuasion must provide a myriad of evidence, reasoning, and rational consideration? Why do certain appeals work to persuade me but not you? These are the key questions to be addressed in Part II.

Finally, in Part III, we explore some of the contexts in which persuasion operates —political campaigns, social movements, public speeches, interpersonal relations, mass media, propaganda, and advertising. Again, we will see some persuasion that occurs in knee-jerk fashion while other persuasion must rely on careful and rational mental processing.

In Chapter 1, we examine how persuasion dominates our lives. We look at several definitions of persuasion, ranging from those rooted in ancient Greece to those derived from the contemporary media age—especially one that has answered many questions about contemporary persuasion. Our discussion also focuses on a useful model of persuasion suggested by Hugh Rank, a scholar of persuasion, advertising, and propaganda. The model grew out of Rank's work with the National Council of Teachers of English (NCTE) and their concern with the increase in "doublespeak"—the attempt to use words to confuse and mislead. In Chapter 2, Richard L. Johannesen discusses a variety of approaches to the ethical issues that arise whenever persuasion occurs. Keep in mind that these approaches and issues involve both persuaders and persuadees—senders and receivers, advertisers and consumers, politicians and their constituents, governments and citizens. In Joe Scudder's Chapter 3, we explore the traditional roots of persuasion and humanistic approaches to persuasion. It is remarkable how many of the principles articulated long ago remain as good practice today. We also see the importance of understanding how persuasion is grounded in human experience and society. In a marked departure from Chapter 3, Scudder's Chapter 4 focuses on social scientific methods and what they have revealed to us about persuasion. In Chapter 5, we examine the raw material of persuasion—human symbolic behavior—especially as it occurs in language and in images. Finally, Chapter 6 describes and demonstrates several alternative ways receivers analyze, interpret, decode, and critique persuasive language. It is not important that you find one theory or approach that you prefer, but rather that you consider the various alternatives.

In Part II, we begin a deeper investigation of persuasion and its applications. The study of persuasion goes back to the ancient Egyptians and then the Greeks, especially to Aristotle and his investigation of persuasion in Greek democracy. He knew that by establishing common ground (or a sense of emotional or logical identification between speaker and audience) persuaders usually achieved their aims. So, persuaders first needed to find areas of common beliefs and preferences. Aristotle believed that having identified this common ground, persuaders then succeeded by developing logical or emotional "arguments" or syllogistic discussion points in which the audience participated by providing a part of the argument—usually a widely held major premise. He called these participative arguments enthymemes (or abbreviated syllogisms), which were either emotionally, logically, or culturally based. Our search in Part II for those premises that persuade large numbers of persuadees thus reflects Aristotle's teaching.

When you finish this book and course, I hope you find that you have changed from a somewhat uncritical persuadee to a responsible and analytical receiver, ready to face the persuasion blitz of the twenty-first century.

1

✳

Persuasion in Today's World

The first edition of *Persuasion: Reception and Responsibility* came out in 1973 in a world so different that most of you know it only through movies and reruns. Bands like Led Zeppelin, Creedence Clearwater Revival, Steppenwolf, Grand Funk Railroad, and Crosby, Stills, and Nash were the mainstays of the younger generation. President Nixon was in hot water over the Watergate scandal. The Vietnam era was winding down, but the changes it had ushered in were evident. For example, television had changed, bringing grisly images from the war into homes across the nation on a nightly basis. The tragic events at Kent State University, where protesting students were shot by the National Guard, still haunted the national consciousness. Revolutionary rhetoric had emerged to protest not only the war but also the plight of persons of color. The urban riots of the mid-1960s and the assassinations of Dr. Martin Luther King and Bobby Kennedy in 1968 were still on people's minds. The music had changed as well. The feel-good songs of the early sixties of the Beatles and the Beach Boys had given way to a darker, more

complex genre, with the Beatles leading the move to embrace a style reflecting major issues of the times. Jim Morrison, Janis Joplin, and Jimi Hendrix were major cultural icons who had died too young from drug overdoses. Many people challenged traditional values at home, school, church, and the workplace. Drugs and free love became common. Few would have predicted that change would continue to accelerate over the next thirty years.

But it did. We abandoned a major war in Vietnam at the cost of over 50,000 American lives. Gasoline prices went from around 40¢ per gallon to prices approaching $2 per gallon. The national debt passed $2 trillion, and the age of the personal computer dawned. Americans were forced to directly address questions of health care, deficit reduction, and the end of the Cold War. We witnessed the transition of U.S. presidential power from a veteran of World War II to two veterans of the Vietnam era, and we saw the rise of militias willing to engage in urban terrorism. Then, in a surprising turnaround, vast projected budget surpluses induced the federal government to enact sweeping tax cuts, only to have a minirecession quickly turn the surpluses into deficits. And as we found on September 11, 2001, the United States is vulnerable to new enemies—enemies most of us didn't even know existed. They used new and horrifying ways to try to "influence" us.

We also incorporated a host of technological innovations into our daily lives. We adopted the use of personal video cameras and recorders, cable and satellite television systems, wireless telephones, automatic teller machines, universal price coding (to delve deeply into the minds of consumers), and two totally new media—the Internet and email. Meanwhile, the Soviet Union crumbled from within, leaving the United States as the only superpower. However, on the political front, the nation found itself unable to dictate its will in Latin America, Europe, the Middle East, or anywhere else. And, equally important, a new age of plentiful and easily obtainable electronic global information dawned. This made it easier for the "little person" to say his or her piece. At the same time that these new media seemed to offer us the opportunity to participate in important decision-making processes, however, they also "dehumanized" us. They turned us into statistics—ratings numbers for advertisers, public opinion numbers for politicians, and return-on-investment numbers for businesses.

Yet some things remain the same. We still have to respond to persuasive appeals from advertisers, politicians, and ideologues. We still esteem traditional institutions such as the family and values such as success, effort, and optimism; and we still play politics on campus, on the job, in our organizations, and in our families. Unfortunately, we also continue to face an energy shortage, even as we pollute our environment and gleefully use up resources. And, of course, world peace still eludes us.

PERSUASION IN AN INFORMATION AGE

In one way or another, everything just cited relates to persuasion. The past decade persuaded us that, although the United States is a superpower politi-

cally, it might not be the world's number-one economic power in the near future. China and India are emerging intellectual and economic forces that will change the world as we know it. Advertisers persuaded us that we dearly needed items such as ATM cards, remote control devices, personal computers, home pages, and cellular telephones, and we learned how to "surf the net," among other things. As voters and consumers, we were persuaded by politicians and advertisers to support various candidates or to buy products that we probably don't need. After all, given the energy shortage and environmental problems, who *really* needs an SUV? The car-buying public was somehow persuaded that a macho vehicle has "authority" and so was a must. The persuasion must have been emotional rather than logical, given that very few persons really use four-wheel drive. Interestingly, tow truck operators report that SUVs are the most common type needing to be towed. They say that drivers of these vehicles get an emotional "high" out of trying to drive through the biggest snowdrifts or in the muddiest terrain. As another example, take politics in my home state—Minnesota—where Jesse Ventura was elected governor for the most irrational and emotional reasons. There is nothing logical about a governor having a background as a professional wrestler or a Navy Seal, yet Jesse "the Body" Ventura swept away his quarrelsome Democratic and Republican opponents in the 1998 election. Then he went on to effectively paralyze normal government by waging a running battle with the state legislature for four years. He also made numerous outrageous statements. For example, he once said that St. Paul's streets were so confusing because they had been laid out by drunken Irishmen. And when being interviewed by *Playboy* magazine, he was asked what he would prefer being if reincarnated; he responded, "a 38DD brassiere" (Alter, 2002, p. 37).

Do these brief examples of emotional, knee-jerk forms of persuasion mean that we need to automatically reject the persuasive appeals of advertisers, politicians, and others? Absolutely not—in fact, it's essential that we consider *all* persuasive appeals made to us simply to sort out the wheat from the chaff. Whether as individuals, corporations, or governments, we need to be persuaded to do our part on a number of fronts. Take, for example, the need to preserve and restore our environment while moving toward energy independence. This means we need to decide whether we support drilling for oil in the Alaskan Wildlife Reserve. There are logical and emotional arguments on both sides of the issue. What are the potential costs and benefits? What are the alternatives? Or consider the logical and emotional reasons to choose the occupation we want to pursue or the major we take in college. For these and other reasons, it is more important than ever to train ourselves to become responsible and critical receivers of persuasion.

Let's consider just a few of the areas in which we need to become better persuadees. Researcher Jamie Beckett (1989) reported in the *San Francisco Examiner* that the average U.S. adult is exposed to 255 advertisements every day. That figure actually seems low to me when I consider how many ads I see while I'm reading the morning newspaper or hear on the radio while driving to work. *Advertising Age* magazine may be closer to the truth when it estimated that the average American sees, reads, or hears more than 5,000 persuasive advertising messages a day. And semiotician Arthur Asa Berger (2000) reports, "Some estimate that the total number of impressions one processes in one day is as high as 15,000" (p. 81). These persuasive messages appear in many formats. Take the ubiquitous television spot, with its high-tech artistry utilizing computer graphics, sophisticated special effects, and digitally sweetened sound. Even as these ads become more and more sophisticated, they are shrinking in duration. Instead of 30- and 60-second spots, long the staples of television advertising, we now see the 15-second spot and even the 10-second reinforcement spot dominating television advertising. And it looks like the 7½-second spot is coming.

Other formats contain persuasive messages including newspaper and magazine advertisements in all their artistic and nonartistic forms, billboards and signs along the roadside, radio spots, T-shirts with product names imprinted on them, home pages, faxes, and public relations releases. Even the packaging of the various products we use persuades us to consider the brand. The "shelf talkers" (that is, signs urging the purchase of brands) in the supermarkets and the coupons or rebate forms that accompany products today reinforce this packaging.

Most recently, we find ourselves deluged with direct-marketing messages, ranging from catalogs and direct-mail appeals to telephone solicitations, direct-response television ads, and Internet direct offers. And the persuasive appeals go beyond the realm of mere branding. Politicians use these various media (practically all of them have Internet home pages), and they employ most of the advanced techniques utilized by modern advertisers. These many media also carry messages of social importance. For example, the Illinois Department of Public Health uses billboards and other out-of-home media to help people quit smoking. Some churches now use direct-marketing techniques and public relations to recruit new members. In fact, my church has a marketing "task force." Another local church invites guests to "Come and break bread with us" and follows up by delivering two miniloaves of bread to guests' homes the day after their visit. Other persuaders use the new media as well.

Even as you read these words, ad agencies are designing newer and more sophisticated forms of advertising. For example, persuaders now use digitally produced billboard images, and soon all television networks will digitize their appeals. The interfaces between home computers, electronic mail, and computer-generated graphics and filing systems not only persuade us but also make it possible for individuals to receive their own personalized "newspaper" (which includes only subjects of interest to that individual) or to hyperlink to still more information. Will people simply reject these appeals made via the new media? I hope not—we need information to make wise political, consumer, and personal decisions.

The answers to such questions relate to how we process information. Do we accept or reject persuasion without much thought simply because it is easier that way? We need to critically and rationally decide whether to accept or reject persuaders' messages. And persuaders know more and more about what makes each of us tick—they target a segment of one. Although the thought of receiving totally individualized information and services is appealing, few persons or institutions give serious consideration to the implications of this kind of deep segmentation. How much information about ourselves should we give away? A primary concern is that we divulge much of our individual and group identities—interests, age, political and sexual preferences, religion, income, media habits, and a host of other "private" information—too freely. This process begins with the census, extends to warranty cards and drivers' licenses, and threatens to expand through exploitation of email, Internet tracking, cell phone eavesdropping, and other means. As a result, governments, advertisers, editors, and other persuaders get "into our heads" more deeply and effectively than ever before.

In fact, from the advertising industry's perspective, this relinquishing of intimate data has already been achieved. In brand-scan marketing research, consumers are given a "consumer card," similar to a credit card, which entitles them to "special" prices on selected products. When their purchases are rung up at the computerized cash register, they are compared with information the consumers have previously volunteered (television viewing habits and demographic and psychographic information, for example). In this way, for the first time, advertisers have a direct link between advertising exposure and actual product purchase. So, although the world of persuasion is expanding, it is also shrinking—ultimately to a segment of one person. And what do we guinea pig consumers get in return for giving away large chunks of our private selves? A small discount on our groceries. In short, we are rapidly losing our privacy and our individuality as we are "packaged" into market segments or potential consumer groups. Nowhere has this sort of information been so cleverly and completely exploited as in the casino industry. Here, "brand-scan type" room keys and special casino cards can be used to charge anything from food and drinks to gambling chips and shows. This information combined with results of customer surveys, hotel registration information, and other databases allows the casinos to track customers' gambling and eating behavior and even the paths they take through the casino.

In an information society, we lose a significant degree of privacy, and there is little we can do about it. This information age will not go away, so as persuadees we need to learn to deal with it. We can't afford to be like the horse-and-carriage lovers of yesteryear, who refused to throw away their buggy whips because the horseless carriage "just wouldn't catch on."

This is a good time for you to become familiar with your InfoTrac® College Edition. Access the Web page at http://www.infotrac-college.com/wadsworth, and type the password you received on the card that came with your free subscription. Type "persuasion" in the subject search engine, and click enter. How many entries are listed? Examine one of the psychology and one of the rhetoric journal articles or "see also" items. (In later links, you can use the "Related Subjects" items.) Browse some interesting titles in both the academic and popular press to see the kinds of academic research being done in persuasion and to determine how the popular press approaches topics related to persuasion.

PERSUASION IN A TECHNOLOGICAL WORLD

Today, more than ever before, we are in the midst of what Alvin Toffler famously called "the Third Wave" of great change experienced by humanity—the technological revolution (Toffler, 1980). Persuasion was very useful in instituting change in the first two "waves" of great innovation—the agricultural and the industrial. Today, persuasion is essential in inducing people to try, accept, and finally adopt the many new ways of thinking, believing, and behaving that come with the global shift to the technological age. We are seeing but the first vague dimensions of a few of the changes that will be facing us. Children no longer take their parents' word as law—they need to be motivated to avoid drugs, to take core subjects at school, or to turn down the volume of their Walkmans to avoid damage to their hearing. The U.S. government discovered that it needed to make increasing use of persuasion to convince citizens to conserve energy, to "find themselves" in the Army, or to be honest when filling out their income tax returns. Social institutions such as churches, schools, and community groups find it more necessary than ever to use persuasion to gain or even to maintain membership levels and financial support. Meanwhile, marketers must convince consumers that a given product will add excitement to their lives—that it will make them more successful or secure or sexy. In education, we find persuasion becoming more important in motivating students to listen, participate, and achieve. All these persuaders vie for our attention, loyalties, and support.

The world around us tells us that we need to be persuaded, if only to reduce our alternatives before making choices. At the same time, we need to be prepared for the many potent and perhaps mistaken —even negative—things persuasion can do to us. Noted communications expert Neil Postman (1981) called attention to just one aspect of persuasion and its potency in shaping our values: the television commercial. According to Postman, by the time you're twenty you're likely to have seen about a million commercials—an average of a thousand a week. Imagine what we would think if a propaganda artist were pumping persuasion down our throats that often every week. What impressions do we get from these commercials? Here is Postman's analysis:

> This makes the TV commercial the most voluminous information source in the education of youth. . . . A commercial teaches a child three interesting things. The first is that all problems are resolvable. The second is that all problems are resolvable fast. And the third is that all problems are resolvable fast through the agency of some technology. It may be a drug. It may be a detergent. It may be an airplane or some piece of machinery. . . . The essential message is that the problems that beset people—whether it is lack of self-confidence or boredom or even money problems—are entirely solvable if only we will allow ourselves to be ministered to by a technology. (p. 4)

How often have we been affected by this simple little belief? How often have we bought Obsession, or Ban, or those Hanes stockings, because we subconsciously feel that the brands make us more attractive to the opposite sex and boost our love life, or help us land a job or impress a teacher? How many of us believe that the environment will be

saved by technology? Postman (1985) also warned nearly two decades ago that we are "Amusing Ourselves to Death" by allowing television to occupy more and more of our daily lives and to dictate more and more of our beliefs about the world in which we live. He noted, "There is no more disturbing consequence of the electronic and graphic revolution than this: that the world as given to us through television seems natural, not bizarre. . . . We have so thoroughly accepted its definitions of truth, knowledge, and reality that irrelevance seems to us to be filled with import and incoherence seems eminently sane" (pp. 79–80). The title of this book suggests both its purpose and your job as a persuadee. *Persuasion: Reception and Responsibility* aims to make you at least aware of what is happening in the logical, emotional, and cultural persuasive appeals targeted directly at you. The book focuses on you and on your responsibility to engage your "response-ability," or your ability to wisely respond to the persuasion you encounter every day.

Of course, persuasion is hardly a recent phenomenon, and it would have been good in past times for people to have been aware of the persuasion going on around them. If they had been, many tyrants might not have risen to power, some wars might have been avoided, and some diseases might have been cured or avoided. But today, in a technological age in which the means through which persuasion is designed and disseminated are extremely sophisticated, being an aware and cautious persuadee is more essential than ever. The National Council of Teachers of English (NCTE) recognized this need when it instituted its regular conferences on "doublespeak" and began to announce an annual "doublespeak award," to be given to the persuader(s) whose language was most "grossly unfactual, deceptive, evasive, confusing, or self-contradictory."

DOUBLESPEAK IN A PERSUASION-FILLED WORLD

Even in a persuasion-riddled world such as ours, you would not need defensive training if all persuaders were open and honest. Too many, however, try to persuade you in doublespeak. Doublespeak is the opposite of straightforward language: It purposely tries to miscommunicate; it tries to conceal the truth and to confuse its audiences. The word is related to "newspeak," a term George Orwell coined in his chilling description of the world he anticipated in his novel *1984*. Newspeak tried to shift meanings for words and concepts to confuse the citizenry. For example, "war" meant "peace," and "freedom" meant "slavery." Although Orwell's full frightening vision has not come to pass, enough of it has come true to make us all take a second look at the doublespeak of our times. Consider the "peacekeeping" military missions engaged in around the world by our government. Or consider Bill Clinton's insistence that he had never "had sex with that woman" (referring to Monica Lewinsky); his doublespeak negated fellatio as an act qualifying as sexual relations. The term "ethnic cleansing" as used in Serbia, Croatia, Macedonia, and other parts of the former Yugoslavia provides a key example of doublespeak—the term was used to camouflage the existence of concentration camps and the slaughter of thousands of innocent victims. The concept is not very far from Adolf Hitler's "Final Solution," in which millions of people lost their lives.

If you find the words "Final Solution" disturbing, access InfoTrac College Edition under the subject index option, and enter them in the search engine. You will find many articles that elaborate on the development of the term and the policy of genocide that followed. Which did you find most surprising?

Of course, doublespeak isn't confined to the world of politics. A real estate ad indicating that a house is "convenient to the interstate" probably means that you will hear cars whoosh by day and night. College administrators who refer to "more liberal admission standards" when they mean "falling enrollments" are using doublespeak, as are used-car ads that contain the words "good work car," which really means a "junker." And, more recently, doublespeak was used by Enron, World-Com, and other companies to confuse investors

into believing that liabilities were in fact assets— that "spending" meant "earning."

For some good examples of doublespeak here and in other countries, access InfoTrac College Edition, and enter the word "euphemism" in the search engine. Which of the items is the most entertaining?

Start identifying examples of doublespeak as you encounter them. You'll be surprised how often persuaders try to miscommunicate. One of the most humorous examples, which received the NCTE award for doublespeak from a foreign source, belongs to General Joao Baptista Figueiredo, then president of Brazil. He told reporters, "I intend to open this country to democracy, and anyone who is against that I will jail; I will crush!"

DEFINING PERSUASION AND RELATED TERMS— FROM ARISTOTLE TO ELABORATION LIKELIHOOD

Definitions of Persuasion

Persuasion has been defined in many different ways over the centuries, and no single definition can reconcile the various versions. This book will present the major approaches to persuasion—both their strengths and their limitations. Several definitions of persuasion and related terms are provided in this chapter as a starting point, but many of them will be revisited in later chapters in more detail.

The formal study of persuasion traces its roots to the ancient Greeks, who were the first to systematize the use of persuasion, calling it "rhetoric." They studied it in their schools, applied it in their legal proceedings, and used it in implementing the first democracies, in their city-states. Primary among the ancient theorists was Aristotle, who defined rhetoric as "the faculty of observing in any given case, the available means of persuasion." According to Aristotle, persuasion is made up of artistic and inartistic proofs, both of which we will explore in more depth. Persuasion, according to Aristotle, can be based on a source's credibility (ethos), emotional appeals (pathos), or logical appeals (logos), or a combination of them (Roberts, 1924). Aristotle also thought that persuasion is most effective when based on the common ground existing between persuader and persuadee. This common ground permits persuaders to make certain assumptions about the audience and its beliefs. Knowing these beliefs, the persuader can use the enthymeme, a form of argument in which the first or major premise in the proof remains unstated by the persuader and, instead, is supplied by the audience. The task of the persuader, then, is to identify common ground—those major premises held by the audience—and to use it in enthymematic arguments (see Figure 1.1).

Roman students of persuasion added specific advice on what a persuasive speech ought to include. The Roman orator Cicero identified five elements of persuasive speaking: (1) inventing or discovering evidence and arguments, (2) organizing them, (3) styling them artistically, (4) memorizing them, and (5) delivering them skillfully. Another Roman theorist, Quintilian, added that a persuader has to be a "good man" as well as a good speaker.

Those early definitions clearly focused on the sources of messages and on the persuader's skill and art in building a speech. In the communication discipline, they would be considered "rhetorical" approaches to the study of persuasion. Later students of persuasion reflected the changes that accompanied an emerging mass media world. Winston Brembeck and William Howell (1952), communication professors, described persuasion as "the conscious attempt to modify thought and action by manipulating the motives of men toward predetermined ends" (p. 24). In their definition, we see a notable shift from the focus on the centrality of logic in persuasion toward a focus on the more "emotional" means of persuasion—the internal motives of the audience. By the time Brembeck and Howell wrote their second edition, in 1976, they had changed their definition of persuasion to simply "communication intended to influence

choice" (p. 19). In the mid-1960s, Wallace Fotheringham (1966), another communication professor, defined persuasion as "that body of effects in receivers" caused by a persuader's message (p. 7). By this standard, even unintended messages, such as gossip overheard on a bus, could be persuasive if they caused changes in their receivers' attitudes, beliefs, or actions.

Kenneth Burke (1970), literary critic and theorist, defined persuasion as the artful use of the "resources of ambiguity." Burke believed that the degree to which persuadees feel that they are being spoken to in their "own language" is critical to creating a sense of *identification*—a concept close to Aristotle's "common ground." In Burke's theory, when true identification occurs, the persuaders of the world try to act, believe, and talk like the audience, a process discussed in depth in another chapter.

In the first edition of this book, I defined persuasion as "a process that changes attitudes, beliefs, opinions, or behaviors." In that definition, the *process* of persuasion gets the attention. Following Burke's lead, it is more and more evident that persuasion occurs only through cooperation between source and receiver and that it is a symbolic process. So, the updated definition used in this edition is this: "Persuasion is the process of cocreating a state of identification between a source and a receiver that results from the use of verbal and/or visual symbols." Once you identify with the kind of world a huckster wants you to like—say, Marlboro Country—persuasion occurs. You may never smoke a single cigarette, but your view of the world is altered. The world of Marlboro Country is now attractive to you. Your response to the appeal of the Marlboro attitude may cause you to value ruggedness and individualism. Maybe you buy a pickup truck with gun racks in the back windows, or try emulating the Marlboro Man's dress and demeanor, or decide to vote for a candidate who projects a "Marlboro" image. It is important to recognize that the outcomes of a persuasive attempt may not be the exact outcomes desired or expected. Thus, in the Marlboro example, you might not decide to smoke but still form a strong impression of the cowboy. There are multiple levels at which change may occur. In this definition, the persuasion focuses

FIGURE 1.1 The Lincoln Financial Group establishes common ground in this advertisement between the company and any person of any race or ethnicity who is approaching retirement. Note the satisfied and happy looks on both of the faces and the healthy appearance of both persons. This resonates with the desire to have a happy, healthy retirement and helps build the common ground. Note also the examples referred to in the ad copy—"40 years building," "30 years paying off," and "20 years saving," each of which would probably resonate with any retiree, and the idea that "Now I want to LIVE." These words continue building common ground between the company and the potential customer.

(Used by permission of the Lincoln Financial Group.)

not on the source, the message, or the receiver as single entities, but rather on all of them, collectively. They all cooperate to make a persuasive process. The idea of *cocreation* means that what happens inside the receiver is just as important as the source's intent or the content of the message. In one sense, all persuasion consists of self-persuasion. We rarely act in accordance with the persuasion unless we participate in the process, whether logically or emotionally. The words "process," "cocreated," and "identification" are central in this discussion. Persuasion results when source and receiver combine to create a sense of Aristotle's "common ground."

Perhaps the elaboration likelihood model (ELM) has been most responsible for the significant change in the way persuasion is viewed since this book's first edition. Suggested by two social psychologists, Richard Petty and John Cacioppo, in 1986, the ELM is a cognitive model in which persuasion takes one of two routes. In the *central route,* the person one is attempting to persuade is consciously and directly focusing on the communication and is mentally elaborating on the issues. This is an effortful process. When central processes are fully engaged, the target of the persuasive message searches out the issues, supporting evidence, alternatives, respective costs and benefits, and other potential outcomes. Sometimes, however, the central route involves only a momentary period of concentration on an issue. In contrast, some persuasion occurs through the *peripheral route,* where information is being processed by the senses, but the target is not directly focusing upon it. At any given moment, there are millions of pieces of information within our view, but we are attending to only a few of them. The peripheral route is like a sponge: The person is soaking up information but is not focusing on it in a direct and effortful way. The person may be able to answer questions about this information at a later time even though it was not the main consideration at the moment. The peripheral route may be a shortcut for making decisions that we call heuristics. Sometimes we respond with little mental effort to common situations because we have these patterns stored in our memories—as when we add cream to our coffee or drink a certain

brand of soda. We will look at this model in depth in Chapter 4 and examine how it applies to many forms of persuasion in other chapters as well. Let's now turn to that which most can agree on regarding persuasion.

Persuasion and Other Forms of Influence

Do not be discouraged by the many definitions of persuasion. It is probably more important to focus on how persuasion usually operates than to seek a definition that will apply across time, for every person and in every situation, whether by a mass communication or at a personal level. Several points of agreement provide a foundation for the contemporary student of persuasion. First, most communication scholars agree that persuasion usually involves communication that attempts to change another in some way, whether by verbal or nonverbal means. Many suggest that the attempt also has to *succeed* to be considered persuasion. Second, nearly universal acceptance exists for the proposition that persuasion involves participation by a sender and a receiver— though they do not have to be aware of each other. The receiver of the persuasive attempt must participate in some way for the desired change to take place. Thus, a sender cannot impose her or his will on another without some participation by the receiver. Third, by adapting to the world of the intended receiver, the sender's attempts to persuade others are more likely to succeed. This includes adapting to the situation, the context, the culture, and individual motivations. Finally, the outcomes of a persuasive attempt may not be those that are desired or expected.

Several related, overlapping terms often are confusing to the new student of persuasion. Figure 1.2 should help you understand the relationships among these terms. Note that the diagram doesn't accurately depict the relative importance of each form of influence. Rather, the importance of each form probably varies substantially from person to person and according to the context. The central point of this diagram is that many forces other than persuasion may bring change to the lives of individuals.

Just as there are differences of opinions regarding the best definition of persuasion, not all agree

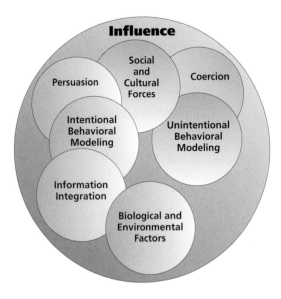

FIGURE 1.2 The relationship of persuasion to other forms of influence.

about the relationships of the terms in Figure 1.2. For example, in this diagram, "influence" is equated with all the forces that bring about change in a person. Those who study persuasion (see, for example, Simon, 1976, p. 19) don't always distinguish among these terms, and in many discussions, "influence" and "persuasion" are interchangeable. This imprecise use of language is unfortunate. To build a foundation for later discussion, we need to distinguish among several terms related to persuasion, including *influence, coercion, compliance-gaining, acquiescence, behavioral modeling,* and *information integration.* Influence, the most general category, refers to one person's behavior resulting in a change in the attitude or behavior of another person. Although persuasion is a kind of influence, not all influence is persuasion. There are several ways that attitudes or behaviors can change for an individual, and not all involve persuasion. For example, many young fans adopted the styles or behavior of their pop idols. Although most of these behaviors are harmless, some, such as the Goth look, appear quite dangerous to some observers. This represents influence through unintended behavioral modeling. Similarly, many adults are embarrassed when their young

child emulates a parent's behavior in public by using profanity that the child overheard at home. There is no question that influence can lead to a change in behavior, but these are not examples of persuasion as we understand it, because no cocreation was involved. In contrast, persuasive attempts are being made when parents consciously model positive behaviors for their children.

At its core, persuasion is a communicative process whereby persuaders seek to get receivers to change. Thus, persuasion involves choice. In contrast, coercion uses some degree of force to gain compliance. The use of force raises ethical questions, but what constitutes force is open to interpretation. Further, in practice, this distinction between persuasion and coercion is not that simple. Later in this book, we will consider Sally Miller Gearhart's statement (1979) that all persuasion involves violence. Many types of power may be used to influence other people. For example, when friends use the relational power of their friendship to get a friend to do something they do not wish to do—commonly known as peer pressure—some degree of coercion occurs. As we will see in a future chapter, certain uses of emotional appeals constitute coercion. Consequently, persuasion and coercion should probably be seen as two ends of a continuum that ranges from choice with few constraints to forced choice. Although cases of terrorism such as we saw on September 11 or the taking of hostages appear to be acts of coercion instead of persuasion, the cocreation of states of identification results. That is, hostages begin to identify with their captors. And some innocents even embrace the terrorists' cause, as was the case for one young American man who enlisted in the Taliban in Afghanistan. He was later prosecuted on the grounds of treason, which certainly suggests that he cooperated with the enemy. And the fact that air travel decreased following the events of 9/11 demonstrates that the audience (the general public) changed their behavior by identifying with the potential harm that Al Qaeda could deliver. Individuals may never accept the legitimacy of the central issues advanced by terrorists, but they may fear the actions of terrorists and so change their normal practices. Thus, even in bizarre and potentially coercive situations, persuasion may operate at some level.

Gerald Marwell and David Schmitt, social psychologists, published the first compliance-gaining study in 1967. Since that time, over a hundred compliance-gaining studies have been completed, many of them by communication researchers. By their own admission, Marwell and Schmitt were not interested in communication (see Marwell & Schmitt, 1990, pp. 3–5). Rather, they were concerned with how people seek to gain the compliance of others. They believed that successful appeals target a common behavioral repertoire. On the surface, compliance gaining seems to be merely another name for persuasion. Yet some compliance-gaining tactics, such as threats, at times seem more appropriately viewed as coercion. We will return to a discussion of the ethics of using threats and other negative influence techniques in Chapter 2. When compliance gaining involves mere acquiescence, the issue is what type of persuasion took place. Behavioral compliance has been obtained, but consensual attitude change has not followed. An agreement may be formed whereby a person votes for a certain action in return for concessions on a different issue, without being convinced that the proposition under discussion is a wise course of action. This frequently happens in politics. Persuasion probably occurred in the making of the deal because some common ground was reached, but no one changed his or her mind based on the merits of the actual issues. Thus, it is important to note that the outcome of a persuasive attempt may be far different from the objective of the original attempt. Acquiescence may accomplish the immediate objective, but it is rarely a satisfying outcome.

Information integration and analysis is another route to influence that may not involve persuasion. For example, the attitude of a manager may change after she or he views factual information about whether quarterly sales were up or down. Many of these reports are computer-generated, without direct human intervention. The discovery of new information or evidence from these data may bring about a change in attitudes. Something that is overheard in the conversation of others may lead to changes in behavior, but it is not persuasion because no cocreation was involved. A difficult issue is whether all teaching should be considered to be persuasion and whether all learning that occurs as a

result of this teaching as persuasion. It is probably safe to conclude that all persuasion involves learning, but not all learning is persuasion. Not all persuasive attempts, however, result in positive outcomes. Sometimes negative influence develops after an adverse reaction to a message or to the person delivering the message.

VARYING CONTEXTS FOR PERSUASION

As the discussion of compliance gaining showed, the persuasive context may be at an interpersonal level, featuring one-on-one communication. Persuasive contexts extend beyond public-speaking situations. There is a growing recognition that the nature of persuasion changes as the context changes. For instance, protest marches, decision-making get-togethers, staff meetings, sales presentations, and mass media events all require consideration of additional dynamics in the persuasive process. Although contextual differences will be considered in more detail in later chapters, it is important to recognize that successful persuaders adapt to the relevant context. What works in one context may not work in another.

CRITERIA FOR RESPONSIBLE PERSUASION

How does cooperative and cocreative persuasion happen? What makes it work? Although persuasion sometimes occurs under the most unlikely circumstances (for example, in the midst of an emotional argument, during a riot, or even in a death camp), three circumstances seem to increase the chances that responsible receivers can be rationally and ethically persuaded.

First, persuasion is most likely to occur in a responsible and fair way if all parties have an equal opportunity to persuade and if each has approximately equivalent ability and access to the media of communication. If a gag rule is imposed on the proponents of one side of an issue while advocates of the other side have freedom to persuade, then receivers get a one-sided and biased view of the issue. In one way, the events of 9/11 gave Osama Bin Laden and Al Qaeda somewhat equal access to the media. Parts of the Muslim world *identified* with their cause, and many cheered at the blow that Bin Laden struck that day. But persuasion of a different sort also occurred through the cocreation of meaning that resulted from verbal and visual mediated symbols. Examples few of us will forget include the images of the airliners crashing into the towers of the World Trade Center (a visual symbol of American capitalism) and the media commentary that accompanied the horrifying scenes as they were replayed over and over again. Many people were persuaded to avoid air travel, especially with individuals appearing to be of Middle Eastern extraction. Then there were the "news release" videotaped speeches and commentary distributed by Bin Laden and Al Qaeda. In this sense, responsible persuasion implies equal access to the means (and media) of persuasion.

Second, in an ideal world, persuaders reveal their agendas to the audience—their ultimate aims and goals, and how they intend to achieve them. Hitler did this in his book *Mein Kampf.* Similarly, political candidates need to tell us how they will improve the schools, how their tax proposal will work, and so on. Auto manufacturers need to tell us that they build reliable cars, not oversized, unsafe gas guzzlers. Of course, if we knew the hidden agendas of many persuaders, we would quickly be put on guard against their messages. Certainly, in the case of 9/11, knowing that Al Qaeda intended to use airliners as missiles might have prompted heightened security at airports. In many cases, this criterion of revelation of agendas is met only partially. But even having a hint of the real goals of a persuader can make us more responsible receivers.

Third, and most important, receivers must be critical—they must test the assertions and evidence presented to them. This means looking for information from all sides in the debate and withholding final judgment until they have sufficient data. The passengers of the fourth airliner on 9/11, who initially assumed they were simply being taken hostage, soon learned of the real intent of the hijacking and took action, with the resulting failure of

the terrorists' plan. With critical receivers, the importance of the first two criteria is minimized, and responsible persuasion can still occur. In the presidential elections of 1992, 1996, and 2000, many candidates used negative advertising and brief sound bites, just as they had in years past. When the press pointed this out, many pulled their negative and incomplete ads. As campaign critic and communication researcher Kathleen Hall Jamieson (1992) observes, "All forms of campaign discourse were becoming alike. . . . assertion was substituted for argument and attack for engagement" (p. 212).

Access InfoTrac College Edition, and enter the words "negative political advertising" in the search engine. Explore some of the articles that are referenced.

Because the receiver is central to persuasion, it's a good idea to study the process of persuasion from that point of view. You need to observe yourself being persuaded and try to see why and how persuasion happens. This knowledge will enable you to be more critical and therefore more effective in rejecting persuasive messages when appropriate—and in accepting others when that is wise.

THE SMCR MODEL OF PERSUASION

The simplest model of communication, and the one most widely referred to, is Shannon and Weaver's (1949) SMCR model (see Figure 1.3). The model contains these essential elements:

- A source (S) (or persuader), who or which is the encoder of the message. The code can be verbal, nonverbal, visual, or musical, or in some other modality.

- A message (M), which is meant to convey the source's meaning through any of the codes.

- A channel (C), which carries the message and which might have distracting noise.

- A receiver (R) (or persuadee), who decodes the message, trying to sift out channel noise and adding his or her own interpretation.

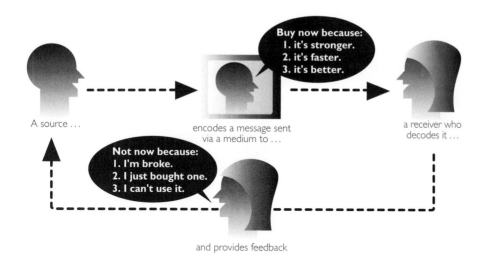

FIGURE 1.3 The SMCR model.

As we shall discover in Chapter 4, these four elements of the model have served as the focus of numerous studies conducted from the social science research perspective as opposed to the rhetorical perspective.

To illustrate the components of the SMCR model, suppose you tell a friend that a TV ad for the GEO Tracker is misleading because the camera angles used make it seem larger than it really is. In this case, you help your friend to make or not make a purchase decision by explaining a source-related aspect of persuasion. Then you alert your friend to the doublespeak in the ad—the product "virtually guarantees" popularity. You ask what the word "virtually" means in this advertising claim and thus focus attention on the message itself rather than on the motives of the persuader. You also point out that skillful editing makes the vehicle seem almost indestructible when, in reality, it is composed of flimsy plastic. Here, you focus on the persuasive impact of the medium of transmitting the message, the channel. Finally, you might ask your friend whether there is some internal or unstated reason he or she wants to be popular and thinks that owning a Tracker guarantees such popularity, thus focusing on the receiver element of this model.

These elements are also part of the persuasive process that is the focus of our definition of persuasion. Being a critical receiver involves being prepared for all four elements. That is, we must be alert to the motives of the source, whether they are obvious or disguised. We must pay attention to the message—its verbal and visual symbolic meaning(s). We must think about the channel, or medium, being used to send the message and the kinds of effects it has. Finally, we must be aware of our own role in persuasion—what we are adding to the source's argument(s).

A number of tools can be used to try to determine a source's motives. For example, language choice often tips us off to the source's intent. The ideas that the source thinks are persuasive to the audience are always expressed in the words, sentences, and metaphors the source uses. Are they questions? Exclamations? Are they short and punchy? Long and soothing? What might these words indicate about the persuader's intent? For example, several years ago, Schick came out with a "cosmetic" razor called Personal Touch. What do the words "cosmetic," "personal," and "touch" tell you about Schick's view of their potential customers? Are they aiming at a "macho" man? A business tycoon? A

FIGURE 1.4 Ad encouraging people to boycott fish sandwiches to stop the killing of harp seals.

(Used by permission of IFAW.)

sports enthusiast? Or are they aiming at women who feel they deserve special attention and haven't been getting it lately?

Analyzing the source yields two benefits. First, it alerts us to the persuasion aimed at us. Second, it tells us things about the source that can help us when the source becomes the target of our own persuasion. If you hear a friend trying to persuade you by using statistics, for instance, you can bet that the use of statistics will help when you are trying to persuade that person.

Other tools also help us to analyze the intent of the message. In later chapters, we will explore the organization of the message, its style, and the appeals it makes. We will look at the evidence contained in messages and at how it relates to the persuasive goal. And we will look at the nonverbal as well as verbal elements or codes in the message to see which of these yields what kinds of effects.

For example, consider the layout, graphics, and wording of an ad placed in newspapers across the country by the International Fund for Animal Welfare (IFAW), which was opposing the harvest of baby seals in Canada—a highly emotional issue because the young seals are clubbed to death. As shown in Figure 1.4, the ad reads:

Do you really know what can go into a simple fish sandwich?

Fish caught by Canadian Fishermen who also kill the baby seals. Your purchase of a McDonald's or Burger King Fish Sandwich could help buy the boats, hard wooden clubs, and guns used by the seal hunters as they turn from fishing to the cruelty of killing adult and baby seals.

The images and words such as "hard wooden clubs" alert you to the underlying emotional persuasion being used and prompts you to investigate more fully. Such an investigation would reveal that only a few Canadian fishermen are also seal hunters, that clubbing the seals is actually the least painful, most humane means of killing them (a claim made by the hunters), or that the flesh of the seals is not used in the fish sandwich as the visuals suggest. Looking at the message carefully prompts you to get other sides of the story or identifies places where the full story is not given or even where the argument is deceptive.

It's also important to be alert to the kinds of effects that various channels have on persuasion. Does the influence of TV, for example, make a message more or less effective? TV makes us more vulnerable to certain types of messages, such as humorous ones, exaggerations, comparisons, and before/after appeals. Do media such as radio or the Internet affect the message or even other media, like signs or billboards? Are certain kinds of ballyhoo more useful or persuasive than others? Why do some media use certain techniques and others use different ones? Would the baby seal message have had more or less impact if billboards had been used as the channel? What about television or the Internet? By looking at the persuasive effects of this element in the SMCR model, receivers begin to understand how a persuasive message works—what its goals are.

Finally, it's important to look at ourselves, the receivers in persuasive transactions, to determine what kinds of motives, biases, and perspectives we bring to the given situation. What fascinations, needs, and desires do we add to the persuasion? The answer, of course, is continually being sought by persuaders, whether they are politicians, ideologues, advertisers, propagandists, or simply our co-workers, friends, and colleagues. Knowing even a part of the answer makes us more critical and responsible receivers.

Think of persuaders simply as persons who want to achieve certain goals. These goals are directed by one or more strategies and are put into action by specific tactics. Communication researcher Patricia Sullivan (1993) describes these steps in her analysis of a keynote speech given by Reverend Jesse Jackson at the Democratic National Convention. Jackson had a goal of uniting the party in his speech. One of his strategies was to stress the common ground among the various factions of the party; another was to get the audience involved in the message. He used several tactics to put his strategies into action. For example, he titled his speech "Common Ground and Common Sense," thus making the issue of unity central and supportable by all because it made logical sense. Jackson also used a call–response format for parts of the speech (uttering a phrase or sentence that the audience then repeated in unison) to involve and unite the audience.

RANK'S MODEL OF PERSUASION

The NCTE asked several persons to suggest ways of teaching students to be critical receivers of persuasion. Hugh Rank (1976), a researcher in the group, put the challenge this way: "These kids are growing up in a propaganda blitz unparalleled in human history. . . . Schools should shift their emphasis in order to train the larger segment of our population in a new kind of literacy so that more citizens can recognize the more sophisticated techniques and patterns of persuasion" (p. 5). Rank outlined a simple but insightful model of persuasion, called it the intensify/downplay schema, that helps teach people to be critical receivers. He tried to make it easy to use, even on the spur of the moment.

The basic idea behind Rank's model is that persuaders usually use one of two major strategies to achieve their goals. Persuaders either (1) *intensify*

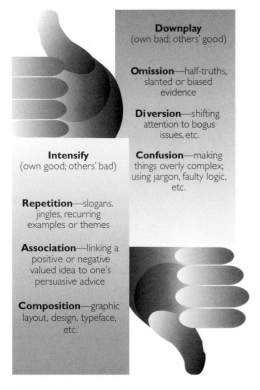

FIGURE 1.5 The intensify/downplay schema.

(Adapted by permission of Hugh Rank.)

certain aspects of their product, candidate, or ideology or (2) *downplay* certain aspects. Often, they do both. Like a magician, they draw attention away from some things and direct attention toward others, and thus pull off the illusion. Figure 1.5 illustrates this model.

On the strategic level of the model, persuaders can choose from four courses of action:

1. Intensify their own good points.
2. Intensify the weak points of the opposition.
3. Downplay their own bad or weak points.
4. Downplay the good points of the opposition.

On the tactical level, persuaders can use repetition, association, and composition to intensify their own good points or the bad points of the opposition, and they can use omission, diversion, and confusion to downplay their own bad points or the good points of the opposition. And any one of these tactics can be utilized either logically or emotionally.

Persuasive strategy, then, is the overall step-by-step program for reaching some goal. Strategy relies on tactics, which are the specific kinds of arguments or points the persuader tries to make. For example, if a candidate wants to persuade voters to support her (her goal), she tries to make them feel good about her candidacy (her strategy of intensifying her own good). She accomplishes this by taking forthright stands on the issues. She also repeats her campaign slogan on signs, buttons, bumper stickers, and advertisements, and she places an image of the state capitol building in the background of all her ads and photos. In other words, she uses the tactics of repetition, association, and composition. Let's explore the strategies and tactics of the Rank model in more depth.

Intensification

The first strategy in the Rank model is intensification. This strategy has two substrategies: either (1) intensifying one's own strong or good points or (2) intensifying the weak or bad points of the opposition. All persuaders want to look good in the eyes of the audience—be they voters, joiners, or purchasers. This goal can be achieved by using either processing route—central or peripheral—in the ELM. For example, some tactics intensify our own good points ("He's always been a willing and honest servant for good causes"), and others intensify the bad points of the other guy, thus making us look good by comparison ("He's got shifty eyes—I wouldn't trust him").

The tactics of repetition, association, and composition are all effective in implementing the strategy of intensification of our own good or others' bad points.

Repetition. One way to intensify good or bad points about a product, person, or candidate is by repeating them over and over. That's what slogans, jingles, and logotypes are doing—intensifying good elements about the product over and over again. The Energizer battery "just keeps going and going," whether in TV spots or in magazine ads or on the packaging for the batteries. But does this make "cognitive" sense? The harp seal advertisement repeatedly intensifies the bad aspects of the seal hunt through its brutal images and language and through the helpless and innocent-looking baby seal. It also repeatedly puts you, the reader, into the story. Notice the words "Your purchase," "If you made a pledge today," and "You have it in your hands to save the baby seals today." This repetition intensifies the IFAW's good aims and emphasizes that their ultimate success depends on each individual reader making an effort to end the slaughter of the seals.

Both sides of the debate used all of these tactics during the impeachment hearings of President Bill Clinton and in his subsequent trial in the U.S. Senate in 1999. The U.S. representatives who directed the hearing and trial used repetition when they quoted the same parts of grand jury testimony over and over again. They wanted to convict Clinton, and they used the strategy of intensifying his badness by repeating what they thought to be evidence of his perjury and his sexual misconduct. For their part, Clinton's supporters repeated the contention that the charges weren't "high crimes and misdemeanors."

A fascinating discussion of repetition in advertising can be accessed on InfoTrac College Edition by entering the words "slogans and jingles" in the search engine. Read the synopsis of "Of Tang and Little Mikey." Can you identify some of the same things in advertising presently occurring? Would they be processed in the central or the peripheral route?

Association. Another tactic for intensification suggested by the Rank model—association—relies on a three-part process: (1) A cause, product, or candidate is linked (2) to something already liked or disliked (3) by the audience. Thus, the cause, product, or candidate is identified with the thing liked or disliked. In the harp seal ad, the hunters are associated with cruelty and brutality. When we first see the ad, most of us are shocked by the thought that baby seal meat might be mixed into the fish sandwich. The sandwich is pictured next to the baby seal, and the clubbing scene provides negative association. Some of the minor details drive home the point—for example, 15,000 seals clubbed to death in twenty-eight days.

Persuaders engage in careful audience analysis to identify the fears, wants, and biases of their target audience. They then mesh their goals with this set of alignments. For example, politicians know that we have fears about privacy in cyberspace, so they tie these fears to their own causes by stating that, if elected, they will enact strict controls over the use of information communicated through cyberspace. Or an advertiser might associate a product—say, a certain kind of athletic shoe—with a well-known professional athlete who uses them. The ad might also associate the shoe with everyday people who are athletic—joggers, tennis players, or, as Nike did, a person in a wheelchair. This set of associations intensifies the good aspects of the shoe and demonstrates that one doesn't have to be an athlete to benefit from its features.

In a rather bizarre use of association, a snack chip company underwrote Pope John Paul's 1999 trip to Mexico and then associated their product with him by printing his picture on packages of the chips. What an endorsement!

Composition. The third and final tactic of intensification is composition, which means emphasizing one's own good characteristics or the other guy's bad characteristics by changing the physical makeup of the message. This change frequently comes across through the use of nonverbal or visual means and can take several forms. For example, the makeup of the printed word can be altered, as in changing "U.S.A." to "U.$.A." or "America" to "AmeriKa," to send the message that the nation is only interested in money or that it is racist (the substitution of the letter "K" sparks association with the Ku Klux Klan). The composition of a candidate's publicity photo also can be manipulated. For example, using a low camera angle makes the candidate look larger than he or she really is and tells us to look up to him or her. The layout of an advertisement can also be used for purposes of intensification. For example, the upper-right and lower-left corners of a magazine page or a poster are "fallow," or less likely to get the reader's full attention. The eye only glances at them momentarily, so that's where the cigarette manufacturers usually put the health warning. All of these cases exemplify the use of affective or peripheral persuasive appeals.

Composition also allows persuaders to compare and contrast in various media. Marshall McLuhan (1964) called this technique the "brushing of information against information." For example, one bit of information about a candidate for political office may be the candidate pictured against some dramatic setting—say, the Vietnam War Memorial in Washington, DC. To intensify the incumbent's bad points, the ad superimposes his or her image on a picture of a polluted river or harbor in his or her district, thus creating negative identification using an emotional image. To emphasize the negative identification, perhaps a muted version of "America the Beautiful" accompanies a voice-over talking about the incumbent's lack of social responsibility. The ad might end with a disclaimer: "This ad is paid for by thousands of dedicated Americans for Jones—Vote for Jones on November 3 and you vote for dedication." Or, to intensify the incumbent's bad points, the image of the polluted river or harbor might be accompanied by sinister-sounding music and a voice-over saying, "He says that he's protected our streams and harbors. Does this look like protection?" In both ads, the background, the music, the voice-over, and the printed words of the disclaimer combine to "compose" the ad's meaning, which is accomplished through the cooperation of source and receiver.

As noted earlier, juxtaposing the baby seal with the fish sandwich in the harp seal ad creates a dramatic effect—an innocent victim becomes part of your meal. Of course, this is not the case, but the initial association and the headline make the point emphatically enough to gross out the average McDonald's or Burger King customer. In the lower right-hand corner of the ad, the "Save the Seals" logo also uses composition by superimposing an image of the killing of a seal with the words "NØ to Canadian fish." Further, the letter "Ø" with the slash through it looks like the road sign we frequently see warning us not to turn left or not to park in a certain place. The composition of both the logo and picture, as well as the altering of the print, creates negative feelings toward Canadian fish. Similarly, in the Clinton impeachment case, the accusers used composition when they reminded the public that the "inappropriate relationship" took place in the White House and perhaps even in the Oval Office. Both places are sacred symbols for most Americans.

Using Rank's model for intensification as a starting place in becoming a critical receiver, you can gain insights into how a particular piece of persuasion works. Let's do the same thing with the other component of the Rank model—downplaying.

Downplaying

Sometimes persuaders want to avoid intensifying or calling attention to something (their own shortcomings or another person's strong points, for example) because doing so undermines their persuasive purpose. Likewise, marketers avoid advertising the strong points of the competition. With this strategy, then, persuaders downplay their own bad points and at the same time downplay competitors' good points.

For example, when the media discovered that information uncovered in August 2001 indicated that airliners might be used as missiles, the Bush administration found it necessary to downplay the report. Thus, officials claimed that it wasn't clear a month before the events of 9/11 that Al Qaeda would actually use the tactic of crashing planes into highly symbolic sites such as the World Trade Center, the Pentagon, or the White House (which is where the fourth airliner is thought to have been heading). As another example, both Ford and General Motors initially downplayed a number of industry innovations introduced by Chrysler. Specifically, Chrysler "invented" factory rebates, 7/70,000 warranties, the minivan, front-wheel drive, and the driver's (and later passenger's) airbag. Chrysler also reintroduced the convertible and promoted the four-wheel-drive Jeep Cherokee as a vehicle for upscale owners as opposed to macho outdoorsmen, the initial target for the vehicle. Although both Ford and GM subsequently tried to match Chrysler's efforts, the initial downplaying left the two latecomers with a "me too" image that had to be downplayed because Chrysler's preemptive innovations forced the issue.

Let's now at the specific tactics for implementing the strategy of downplaying: omission, diversion, and confusion.

Omission. With omission, persuaders simply leave out critical information to avoid highlighting their own shortcomings. For example, the Claussen pickle company intensified its own good points when it advertised that its pickles are refrigerated rather than cooked and are therefore much crisper than Vlasic pickles, its major competition. They did this in a TV ad that showed two pickles—one a Vlasic and the other a Claussen—being bent in half. The "snap!" of the Claussen pickle and the burst of juice from it really intensified Claussen's good points. However, Claussen omitted telling consumers that, in order to extend the shelf life of the pickles, they contain more sodium than Vlasic pickles (their own bad point) and that refrigeration isn't necessary for Vlasic pickles (the other's good point). In the 9/11 case, the Bush administration left out of its defense the fact that the FBI neglected to follow up on a suspect in Minnesota who had taken flying lessons.

Diversion. Diversion, another downplaying tactic, consists of shifting attention away from another's good points or one's own bad points. The basic purpose is to provide a substitute issue—sometimes called a "stalking horse"—that draws fire from the opposition and diverts attention from one's own bad points or issues or from the opposition's good points or issues. For example, in the presidential primary campaigns of 2000, diversion was used in several ways. To divert attention from Pat Buchanan's surprising popular appeal, the Bush camp provided information about Buchanan's statements of admiration for Hitler—a clearly emotional or affective and peripheral appeal. This drew attention away from Buchanan's refusal to use negative ads and hence away from his failing campaign.

Persuaders also use humor to divert attention. For instance, the Energizer battery ads use humor by depicting a toy bunny that "keeps going and going" to divert attention from the fact that all alkaline batteries wear out in about the same period of time. In the Clinton impeachment trial, a key defender used humor to make the point that no one is perfect. He told a joke about a minister's sermon. During the lesson, the preacher asked the crowd if they had ever heard of any person who, given his suffering, even approached the level of perfection of Jesus. A little man in front raised his hand and said, "I know such a man." "Who is he?" asked the

minister. "My wife's first husband." The joke diverted attention from the seriousness of the charges.

Using highly emotional appeals that focus on an opponent's personality or appearance (sometimes called the ad hominem argument) can divert attention from the real issue. Advertisers frequently use this tactic to divert attention from the competition's good features or away from one's own bad characteristics. A good example was Ford Motor Company's use of emotional appeals to divert attention away from its own shortcomings in the design of the Explorer. The vehicle had a dangerous tendency to roll over, and a number of deaths and injuries resulted. When the victims and their families began to file large lawsuits, Ford's defense was to redirect blame to the Firestone tires. Splitting hairs can divert attention from the major issues of the debate and siphon valuable time from discussion of the central issues. For example, a recent governor of Illinois was linked to a "driver's licenses for sale" scandal that occurred during his term as secretary of state. The scandal became emotionally charged when the press discovered that one of these illegal licences belonged to the driver of a truck that had crashed into a school-bus full of children; many of the children were killed. The governor's defenders split hairs over whether the governor ever truly knew that his aides had received campaign funds from kickbacks generated by the sale of the bogus licenses. This helped to divert attention from the governor. The fact that several aides were convicted also helped.

Confusion. A final tactic in downplaying one's own weak points or the competition's strengths is to create confusion in the audience's mind. Using highly technical terminology or jargon that the receiver doesn't understand creates confusion, as does weaving an intricate, rambling answer that evades the real issues. Another device for downplaying one's own weaknesses or the competition's strengths through confusion is the use of faulty logic. "She's Beautiful! She's Engaged! She Uses Earth Balsam Hand Creme!" is one example. The supposed logical progression is that, because "she" uses the hand cream, she is beautiful, and because she is beautiful, she met and won the man of her dreams. Not even fairly naive consumers are likely to buy this whole package, but the idea that the hand

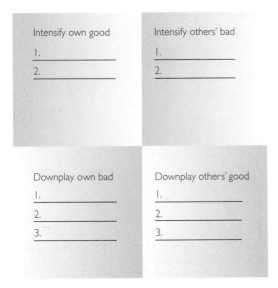

Intensify own good	Intensify others' bad
1.	1.
2.	2.

Downplay own bad	Downplay others' good
1.	1.
2.	2.
3.	3.

FIGURE 1.6 Intensify/downplay scorecard.

(By permission of Hugh Rank.)

cream will make users more attractive to men is fairly likely to stick. Rank (1976) cited a number of other ways to confuse, including being inconsistent, contradicting, and talking in circles—for example, "V.O. is V.O." or "So Advanced, It's Simple."

SELF-PROTECTION: A METHOD

In his discussion of doublespeak, Rank (1976) offered some advice on how to detect the flaws of persuaders who use various tactics to intensify or downplay: "When they intensify, you downplay." That is, when we recognize a propaganda blitz, we should be cool, detached, and alert not only to the inflated promises of the barrage, but also to intensified attack propaganda—the threats and exploitation of fears by a demagogue or government agent, elected or appointed. Rank also says, "When they downplay, you intensify." A way to do so systematically is to divide a sheet of paper into quarters, as shown in Figure 1.6, and then enter the kinds of downplaying and intensifying being practiced. Simply by seeing these items, you can become more alert to what kind of manipulation is going on.

Try using the self-protection method on an advertisement or political speech. When the ad or speech downplays something—its own shortcomings, for instance—you intensify its shortcomings. And when it intensifies something—the side effect, for instance—you downplay it.

We will discuss a number of other tools of analysis as we proceed, but Rank's intensify/downplay tool is a useful general one to employ initially. Try it with a variety of persuasive messages that you encounter.

REVIEW AND CONCLUSION

If you now feel more alert to the possible ways persuaders can manipulate you, you have made progress on your way to becoming a critical receiver. You are ready to arm yourself with some tools of analysis that make for wise consumers, and there is a bonus for learning them. Learning how you are persuaded and exploring the tactics that other persuaders use will help you become a more skillful persuader yourself. Seeing what works—in what circumstances, with what kinds of people—helps you prepare to become a persuader. Skillful consumers of messages learn to be more effective producers of messages. As we move ahead, you can apply the tools of persuasion on your own and in the study questions at the end of each chapter. You can also explore the InfoTrac College Edition sites sprinkled throughout the text.

It is useful to examine the ways in which you are persuaded on the interpersonal level. Every day you make decisions in nonpublic settings. You decide to heed or reject your parents' advice on the basis of your interpersonal communication with them. They may try to persuade you to major in a certain field, to seek a summer job, or to continue or cease dating a certain person. Rank's model helps here, too. Identify what your parents intensify and downplay. Do the same thing with other interpersonal relationships in which persuasion is used—with roommates, friends, colleagues, or your boss. Determine whether identification or alignment is occurring between you and the other individuals, and try to spot the kinds of symbols that lead to or discourage identification.

Critical analysis of interpersonal persuasion helps you make decisions and improves your critical reception skills in many situations. People are persuaded daily in the public arena through advertisements, speeches, radio and TV programs, and newspaper and magazine articles; remember that significant persuasion also takes place in your personal life. Try to determine if the appeals being made to you are being processed in cognitive or affective ways.

QUESTIONS FOR FURTHER THOUGHT

1. If you or someone you know recently made a major purchase (for example, an auto, a CD player, or a digital camera), identify the context in which persuasion occurred. Where did the persuasion take place? In the showroom? Through a television ad? Interpersonally, such as in discussing the purchase with a friend? What kinds of appeals were made? What characteristics were intensified? Downplayed? Was the persuasion emotional or logical, or both? What did you learn from the careful examination?

2. Much persuasion occurs in interpersonal contexts. Examine one of your interpersonal relationships, such as that between you and your parents, your roommate, a teammate, or a fellow member of an organization or church. Describe how, when, and where persuasion has been used in the relationship. What characteristics about yourself have you intensified? Downplayed? What characteristics has the other person intensified? Downplayed? Was repetition used? Association? Omission?

3. Beginning with the definition of persuasion offered in this chapter, attempt to create a model that reflects all the important elements of the definition.

4. Identify three types of persuasion you recently observed (such as advertisements or speeches), and analyze each according to the definition offered in this chapter and the ELM. What verbal and/or visual symbols were used? What was the persuader's intent? Was the peripheral or the central route being used? What did the message say about the persuadee's probable frame of reference? What did the persuader do to create identification? What was intensified? Downplayed? What tactics were used? Repetition? Association? Composition? Omission? Confusion? Diversion?

5. What are the tactics of intensification? How do they work? Give examples of their use on television, in print, on radio, by politicians, and by advertisers.

6. What are the tactics of downplay? How do they work? Give examples of their use on television, in print, on radio, by politicians, and by advertisers.

7. What is a "propaganda blitz"? Identify one currently going on in media coverage of an event or in regard to some political issue. Do you think it is being processed by the audience in the central or the peripheral route? Give an example of one now being used on your campus.

8. What are some current examples of the strategies of intensification and downplaying being used in the war on terrorism? Where are some of the tactics of intensification and downplaying being used in regard to environmental issues?

 For online activities, go to the Web site for this book at http://communication.wadsworth.com/larson.

2

✸

Perspectives on Ethics in Persuasion*

RICHARD L. JOHANNESEN
Northern Illinois University

The recent financial scandals at Enron, World-Com, Arthur Andersen, and other large corporations in part involved unethical communication—the giving of false or misleading information to clients, stockholders, and prospective investors. According to a June 2002 poll by the *Chicago Tribune* (July 28, pp. 1, 14), 66 percent of respondents believed that the ethical standards of business executives have changed for the worse in the past several decades; only 4 percent felt the executives' ethical standards have changed for the better. Evidence abounds of public concern with the decline of ethical behavior, especially by persons in positions of significant public or private responsibility. "What Ever Happened to Ethics?" asked a cover story of *Time* (May 25, 1987). "A Nation of Liars?" inquired *U.S. News & World Report* (Feb. 23, 1987). According to *Time*, "Large sections of the nation's ethical roofing have been sagging badly, from the White House to churches, schools, industries, medical centers, law firms and stock brokerages."

Political commentators and private citizens debated the issue of "character" as it applied to ethics in the public and private lives of President Bill Clinton and other political leaders. Magazine articles explored the decline of an appropriate "sense of shame" as a norm in American culture (*Atlantic Monthly*, Feb. 1992, pp. 40–70; *Newsweek*, Feb. 6, 1995, pp. 21–25). A national survey of 3,600 college students at twenty-three colleges (*Washington Post National Weekly Edition*, Dec. 7–13, 1992, p. 36) revealed that one in six college students had lied on a résumé or job application or during a job interview; two out of five had lied to a boss, one out of three had lied to a customer during the past year; and one out of five had cheated on an exam. *Time*

---

*For a much more extensive exploration of the perspectives, standards, and issues discussed in this chapter and identification of relevant resource materials, see Johannesen (2002). My personal view of ethical persuasion is rooted in the political perspective of American representative democracy and in Martin Buber's conception of dialogue.

magazine devoted seven pages to the topic of "Lies, Lies, Lies" (Oct. 5, 1992). A 1998 national public opinion poll, reported in the *Washington Post National Weekly Edition* (Jan. 11, 1999, pp. 6–7), found that 71 percent of Americans interviewed felt that, in general, people today are not as honest and moral as they used to be.

Access InfoTrac College Edition, and enter the word "lying" in the search engine. Access the item "Lying on Top: Many Are Up in Arms About the Enron Scandal—But Our Political Leaders Are Just As Disgraceful As Their Corporate Counterparts," published in *Dollars & Sense* (March 2002). How do the examples and arguments raised in the article relate to ethical issues in persuasion?

Imagine that you are an audience member listening to a speaker—call him Mr. Bronson. His aim is to persuade you to contribute money to the cancer research program of a major medical research center. Suppose that, with one exception, all the evidence, reasoning, and motivational appeals he employs are valid and beyond ethical suspicion. However, at one point in his speech, Bronson consciously uses a set of false statistics to scare you into believing that, during your lifetime, there is a much greater probability of your getting some form of cancer than is actually the case.

To promote analysis of the ethics of this hypothetical persuasive situation, consider these issues. If you, or society at large, view Bronson's persuasive end, or goal, as worthwhile, does the worth of his end justify his use of false statistics as one means to achieve that end? Does the fact that he consciously chose to use false statistics make a difference in your evaluation? If he used the false statistics out of ignorance or a failure to check his sources, how might your ethical judgment be altered? Should he be condemned as an unethical person or an unethical speaker, or, in this instance, for use of a specific unethical technique?

Carefully consider the standards, and the reasons behind those standards, that you would employ to make your ethical judgment of Bronson. Are the standards purely pragmatic? (In other words, should he avoid the false statistics because he might get caught?) Are they societal in origin? (If he gets caught, his credibility as a representative would be weakened with this and future audiences, or his getting caught might weaken the credibility of other cancer society representatives.) Should he be ethically criticized for violating an implied agreement between you and him? (You might not expect a representative of a famous research institute to use questionable techniques, and so you would be especially vulnerable.) Finally, should his conscious use of false statistics be considered unethical because you are denied the accurate, relevant information you need to make an intelligent decision on an important public issue?

As receivers and senders of persuasion, we have the responsibility to uphold appropriate ethical standards for persuasion, to encourage freedom of inquiry and expression, and to promote public debate as crucial to democratic decision making. To achieve these goals, we must understand their complexity and recognize the difficulty of achieving them.

In this chapter, I do not intend to argue my own views regarding the merit of any one particular ethical perspective or set of criteria as the best one. Rather, my role here, as in the classroom, is to provide information, examples, and insights and to raise questions for discussion. The purpose is to stimulate you to make reasoned choices among ethical options in developing your own positions or judgments.

Ethical issues focus on value judgments concerning degrees of right and wrong, and goodness and badness, in human conduct. Persuasion, as one type of human behavior, always contains potential ethical issues, for several reasons:

- It involves one person, or a group of people, attempting to influence other people by altering their beliefs, attitudes, values, and actions.

- It involves conscious choices among ends sought and rhetorical means used to achieve the ends.

- It necessarily involves a potential judge—any or all of the receivers, the persuader, or an independent observer.

As a receiver and sender of persuasion, how you evaluate the ethics of a persuasive instance will differ depending on the ethical standards you are using. You may even choose to ignore ethical judgment entirely. Several justifications are often used to avoid direct analysis and resolution of ethical issues in persuasion:

- Everyone knows the appeal or tactic is unethical, so there is nothing to talk about.

- Only success matters, so ethics are irrelevant to persuasion.

- Ethical judgments are matters of individual personal opinion, so there are no final answers.

Nevertheless, potential ethical questions exist regardless of how they are answered. Whether you wish it or not, consumers of persuasion generally will judge your effort, formally or informally, in part by their relevant ethical criteria. If for none other than the pragmatic reason of enhancing chances of success, you would do well to consider the ethical standards held by your audience.

ETHICAL RESPONSIBILITY

Persuaders' ethical responsibilities can stem from statuses or positions they have earned or have been granted, from commitments (promises, pledges, agreements) they have made, or from the consequences (effects) of their communication for others. Responsibility includes the elements of fulfilling duties and obligations, of being accountable to other individuals and groups, of being accountable as evaluated by agreed-upon standards, and of being accountable to one's own conscience. But an essential element of responsible communication, for both sender and receiver, is exercise of thoughtful and deliberate judgment. That is, the responsible communicator carefully analyzes claims, soundly as-

sesses probable consequences, and conscientiously weighs relevant values. In a sense, a responsible communicator is "response-able." She or he exercises the ability to respond (is responsive) to the needs and communication of others in sensitive, thoughtful, fitting ways.★

Whether persuaders seem intentionally and knowingly to use particular content or techniques is a factor that most of us consider in judging communication ethicality. If a dubious communication behavior seems to stem more from an accident, a slip of the tongue, or even ignorance, we may be less harsh in our ethical assessment. For most of us, it is the *intentional* use of ethically questionable tactics that merits the harshest condemnation.

In contrast, it might be contended that, in argumentative and persuasive situations, communicators have an ethical obligation to double-check the soundness of their evidence and reasoning before they present it to others; sloppy preparation is no excuse for ethical lapses. A similar view might be advanced concerning elected or appointed government officials. If they use obscure or jargon-laden language that clouds the accurate and clear representation of ideas, even if it is not intended to deceive or hide, they are ethically irresponsible. Such officials, according to this view, should be obligated to communicate clearly and accurately with citizens in fulfillment of their governmental duties. As a related question, we can ask whether sincerity of intent releases persuaders from ethical responsibility concerning means and effects. Could we say that if Adolf Hitler's fellow Germans had judged him to be sincere they need not have assessed the ethics of his persuasion? In such cases, evaluations are probably best carried out by appraising sincerity and ethicality separately. For example, a persuader sincere in intent might use an unethical strategy.

What are the ethics of audience adaptation? Most persuaders seek to secure some kind of response from receivers. To what degree is it ethical for them to alter their ideas and proposals to adapt to the needs, capacities, desires, and expectations of

---

★This discussion of responsibility is based on Pennock (1960), Freund (1960), Niebuhr (1963), and Pincoffs (1975).

their audience? To secure acceptance, some persuaders adapt to an audience to the extent of so changing their own ideas that the ideas are no longer really theirs. These persuaders merely say what the audience wants to hear, regardless of their own convictions. At the same time, some measure of adaptation in language choice, supporting materials, organization, and message transmission for specific audiences is a crucial part of successful communication. No ironclad rule can be set down here. Persuaders must decide the ethical balance point between their idea in its pure form and that idea modified to achieve maximum impact with the audience.

THE ETHICS OF ENDS AND MEANS

In assessing the ethics of persuasion, does the end justify the means? Does the necessity of achieving a goal widely acknowledged as worthwhile justify the use of ethically questionable techniques? We must be aware that the persuasive means employed can have cumulative effects on receivers' thoughts and decision-making habits apart from and in addition to the specific end that the communicator seeks. No matter what purpose they serve, the arguments, appeals, structure, and language we choose do shape the audience's values, thinking habits, language patterns, and level of trust.

To say that the ends do not *always* justify the means is different from saying that the ends *never* justify means. The persuader's goal probably is best considered as one of a number of potentially relevant ethical criteria from which the most appropriate standards are selected. Under some circumstances, such as threats to physical survival, the goal of personal or national security may *temporarily* take precedence over other criteria. In general, however, we can best make mature ethical assessments by evaluating the ethics of persuasive techniques apart from the worth and morality of the persuader's specific goal. We can strive to judge the ethics of means and ends *separately*. In some cases, we may find ethi-

cal persuasive tactics employed to achieve an unethical goal; in other cases, unethical techniques may be used in the service of an entirely ethical goal.

Although discussed in the context of journalistic ethics, the six questions suggested by Warren Bovee (1991) can serve as useful probes to determine the degree of ethicality of almost any means–ends relationship in persuasion (see Figure 2.1). Here are the questions in paraphrased form:

1. Are the means truly unethical/morally evil or merely distasteful, unpopular, unwise, or ineffective?

2. Is the end truly good, or does it simply appear good to us because we desire it?

3. Is it probable that the ethically bad or suspect means actually will achieve the good end?

4. Is the same good achievable using other, more ethical means if we are willing to be creative, patient, determined, and skillful?

5. Is the good end clearly and overwhelmingly better than the probable bad effects of the means used to attain it? Bad means require justification whereas good means do not.

6. Will the use of unethical means to achieve a good end withstand public scrutiny? Could the use of unethical means be justified to those most affected by them or to those most capable of impartially judging them?

THE IMPORTANCE OF ETHICS

"A society without ethics is a society doomed to extinction," argued philosopher S. Jack Odell (in Merrill & Odell, 1983). According to Odell, the "basic concepts and theories of ethics provide the framework necessary for working out one's own moral or ethical code." Odell believes that "ethical principles are necessary preconditions for the existence of a social community. Without ethical principles it would be impossible for human beings to live in harmony and without fear, despair, hopelessness, anxiety, apprehension, and uncertainty" (p. 95).

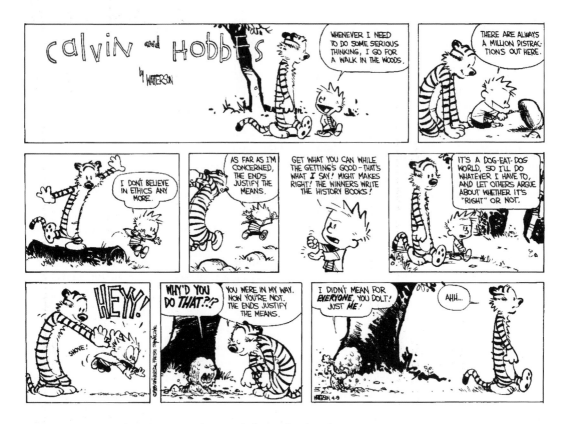

FIGURE 2.1 How might Bovee's questions apply for evaluating the justifications here?

A societal or personal system of ethics is not an automatic cure-all for individual or collective ills. What can ethical theory and systematic reflection on ethics contribute? One answer is suggested by philosopher Carl Wellman (1988):

> An ethical system does not solve all one's practical problems, but one cannot choose and act rationally without some explicit or implicit ethical system. An ethical theory does not tell a person what to do in any given situation, but neither is it completely silent; it tells one what to consider in making up one's mind what to do. The practical function of an ethical system is primarily to direct our attention to the rele-

vant considerations, the reasons that determine the rightness or wrongness of any act. (p. 305)

ETHICAL RESPONSIBILITIES OF RECEIVERS

What are your ethical responsibilities as a receiver of or respondent to persuasion? An answer to this question stems in part from the image we hold of the persuasion process. Receivers bear little responsibility if audience members are viewed as passive and defenseless receptacles, as mindless blotters uncritically accepting ideas and arguments. In contrast, persuasion can be seen as a transaction in which both persuaders and persuadees bear mutual responsibility to participate actively in the process. This image of persuadees as active participants suggests several responsibilities, perhaps best captured by two phrases: (1) reasoned skepticism and (2) appropriate feedback.

Reasoned skepticism includes a number of elements. It represents a balanced position between the undesirable extremes of being too open-minded or gullible, on the one hand, and being too closed-minded or dogmatic, on the other. You are not simply an unthinking blotter "soaking up" ideas and arguments. Rather, you exercise your capacities actively to search for meaning, to analyze and synthesize, and to judge soundness and worth. You do something to and with the information you receive: You process, interpret, and evaluate it. Also, you inform yourself about issues being discussed, and you tolerate, and even seek out, divergent and controversial viewpoints, the better to assess what is being presented.

As a receiver of persuasion, you must realize that accurate interpretation of a persuader's message may be hindered by attempts to impose your own ethical standards on the persuader. Your immediate, gut-level ethical judgments may cause you to distort the intended meaning. Only after reaching an understanding of the persuader's ideas can you reasonably evaluate the ethics of his or her persuasive strategies or purposes.

In this era of distrust of the truthfulness of public communication, reasoned skepticism also requires that you combat the automatic assumption that most public communication is untrustworthy. Just because a communication is of a certain type or comes from a certain source (for example, a government official, political candidate, news media figure, or advertiser), it must not automatically, without evaluation, be rejected as tainted or untruthful. Clearly, you must always exercise caution in acceptance and care in evaluation, as emphasized throughout this book. Using the best evidence available, you arrive at your best judgment. However, to condemn a message as untruthful or unethical solely because it stems from a suspect source is to exhibit decision-making behavior detrimental to

our political, social, and economic system. Any rejection of a message must come after, not before, evaluation of it. As with a defendant in a courtroom, public communication must be presumed to be ethically innocent until it has been proved "guilty." However, when techniques of persuasion do weaken or undermine the confidence and trust necessary for intelligent public decision making, they can be condemned as unethical.

As an active participant in the persuasion process, you need to provide appropriate feedback to persuaders. Your response, in most situations, should be an honest and accurate reflection of your true comprehension, beliefs, feelings, or judgment. Otherwise, persuaders are denied the relevant and accurate information they need to make decisions. Your response might be verbal or nonverbal, oral or written, immediate or delayed. A response of understanding, puzzlement, agreement, or disagreement could be reflected through your facial expressions, gestures, posture, inquiries, and statements during question-and-answer periods and through letters to editors or advertisers. In some cases, because of your expertise on a subject, you may even have an obligation to respond and provide feedback while other receivers remain silent. You need to decide whether the degree and type of your feedback are appropriate for the subject, audience, and occasion of the persuasion. For instance, to interrupt with questions, or even to heckle, might be appropriate in a few situations but irresponsible in many others.

Disagreement and conflict sometimes occur in intimate and informal interpersonal settings. In such situations, when at least one participant may be emotionally vulnerable, individual personalities often affect each other in direct and powerful ways. When you as a receiver in such a situation decide to respond by expressing strong disagreement, you should avoid "unfair" tactics of verbal conflict because they are irresponsible (Ross & Ross, 1982). For example, avoid monopolizing the talk with the intent of preventing others from expressing their position. Avoid entrapment, in which you lure someone into saying something that you intend to use later to embarrass or hurt him or her. Avoid verbally "hitting below the belt" by taking unfair advantage of the other person's psychological vulnerability. Avoid stockpiling or accumulating numerous grievances so that you can overwhelm others by dumping the complaints on them all at once. Finally, avoid dragging in numerous irrelevant or trivial issues and arguments in order to gain an advantage.

SOME ETHICAL PERSPECTIVES

We will briefly explain six major ethical perspectives as potential viewpoints for analyzing ethical issues in persuasion. As categories, these perspectives are not exhaustive, mutually exclusive, or given in any order of precedence.

As a receiver of persuasion, you can use one or a combination of such perspectives to evaluate the ethicality of a persuader's use of language (such as metaphors, ambiguity) or of evidence and reasoning. You can also use them to assess the ethics of psychological techniques (such as appeals to needs and values) or the appeal to widely held cultural images and myths. The persuasive tactics of campaigns and social movements can also—indeed must—be subjected to ethical scrutiny.

Religious Perspectives

Religious perspectives on communication ethics are rooted in the basic assumptions of a religion about the relation of the divine/eternal to humans and the world, and vice versa. In light of such assumptions, various world religions emphasize values, guidelines, and rules that can be employed as standards for evaluating the ethics of persuasion. Religious perspectives are reflected in the moral guidelines and the "thou shalt nots" embodied in the ideology and sacred literature of various religions. For instance, the Bible warns against lying, slander, and bearing false witness. Taoist religion stresses empathy and insight, rather than reason and logic, as roads to truth and right living. Citing facts and demonstrating logical conclusions are minimized in

Taoism in favor of feeling and intuition. These and other religiously derived criteria can be used to assess the ethics of persuasion.

To illustrate the relation between religion and ethical persuasion, consider the following case. On two weekends in January 1987, evangelist Oral Roberts recounted on his nationally syndicated television program an encounter he had had with God the previous year. God told Roberts that he would not be allowed to live beyond March 1987 unless he raised $8 million to fund sixty-nine scholarships for medical students at Oral Roberts University, to enable them to serve in medical clinics overseas. In an emotion-laden plea to his viewers, Roberts asked, "Will you help me extend my life?" Roberts' chief spokesperson, Jan Dargatz, defended Roberts' motives to reporters but conceded that his "methods have hit the fan." Dargatz said that Roberts sincerely believed, "from the very core of his being," that the fund drive was a "do-or-die effort." The Reverend John Wolf, senior minister of Tulsa's All Souls Unitarian Church, condemned the appeal as "emotional blackmail" and an "act of desperation" (Buursma, 1987). Another news report revealed that in 1986 Roberts had made a similar appeal. Roberts told a Dallas audience that his "life is on the line" and that God "would take me this year" if he did not raise necessary funds to finance "holy missionary teams." "Because if I don't do it," Roberts said, "I'm going to be gone before the year is out. I'll be with the Father. I know it as much as I'm standing here." Roberts failed to raise the necessary money (*Chicago Tribune,* Feb. 26, 1987).

To assess the ethicality of Roberts' appeals, you might bring to bear an ethic for Christian evangelism developed by Emory Griffin (1976). For example, to what degree could Roberts' persuasion be condemned as that of a "rhetorical rapist" who uses psychological coercion to force a commitment? Intense emotional appeals, such as to guilt, effectively remove the element of conscious choice. Or was Roberts' persuasion more that of a "rhetorical seducer" who uses deception, flattery, or irrelevant appeals to success, money, duty, patriotism, popularity, or comfort to entice an audience? What other ethical standards rooted in Christian doctrine or scripture might be used to evaluate Roberts' appeals, and how might those standards be applied?

Human Nature Perspectives

Human nature perspectives probe the essence of human nature by asking what makes us fundamentally human. They identify unique characteristics of human nature that distinguish us from so-called lower forms of life. Such characteristics can then be used as standards for judging the ethics of persuasion. Among some of the suggested characteristics are the capacity to reason, to create and use symbols, to achieve mutual appreciative understanding, and to make value judgments. The underlying assumption is that uniquely human attributes should be promoted to enable fulfillment of maximum individual potential. A determination could be made of the degree to which a persuader's appeals and techniques either foster or undermine the development of a fundamental human characteristic. A technique that dehumanizes, that makes a person less than human, would be unethical. Whatever the political, religious, or cultural context, a person would be assumed to possess certain uniquely human attributes worthy of promotion through communication.

In 1990 in Florida, a U.S. district court judge declared obscene the album *As Nasty As They Wanna Be* by the rap group 2 Live Crew. But in a local trial in Florida that same year, three members of the group were acquitted of obscenity charges for performing the songs. These incidents are part of a larger controversy concerning lyrics that explicitly refer to the sexual and physical abuse and debasement of women and that attack ethnic groups. For example, lyrics on the *Nasty* album vividly describe the bursting of vaginal walls, forcing women to have anal or oral sex or to lick feces, and such acts as urination, incest, and group sex. Similarly sexually violent lyrics can be found in songs by such individuals and groups as Judas Priest, Great White, Ice-T, and Guns n' Roses. And bigotry against immigrants, homosexuals, and African Americans surfaces in the Guns n' Roses song, "One in a Million."

Regardless of whether such lyrics are judged obscene or whether they are protected by the freedom-of-speech clause of the First Amendment, many would say that they should be condemned as unethical (Johannesen, 1997). Such lyrics treat women not as persons but as objects or body parts to be manipulated for the selfish satisfaction of males. Thus, they dehumanize, depersonalize, and trivialize women and celebrate violence against them, and they reinforce inaccurate and unfair stereotypes of women, homosexuals, and ethnic groups. How do you believe a human nature perspective on communication ethics might be used to assess such lyrics?

Political Perspectives

The implicit or explicit values and procedures accepted as crucial to the health and growth of a particular political system are the focus of political perspectives. Once these essential values are identified for that political system, they can be used to evaluate the ethics of persuasive means and ends within that system. The assumption is that public communication should foster achievement of these basic political values; persuasive techniques that retard, subvert, or circumvent the values would be condemned as unethical. Different political systems usually embody differing values leading to differing ethical judgments. Within the context of U.S. representative democracy, for example, various analysts pinpoint values and procedures they deem fundamental to the healthy functioning of our political system and, thus, values that can guide ethical scrutiny of persuasion therein. Such values and procedures include enhancement of citizens' capacity to reach rational decisions, access to channels of public communication and to relevant and accurate information on public issues, maximization of freedom of choice, toleration of dissent, honesty in presenting motivations and consequences, and thoroughness and accuracy in presenting evidence and alternatives.

In the late 1980s and early 1990s, the issue of "hate speech" on college and university campuses illustrated the tension between the right of freedom of speech and the ethically responsible exercise of that right. On one campus, eight Asian American students were harassed for almost an hour by a group of football players, who called them "Oriental faggots." On another campus, white fraternity members harassed a black student by chanting, "coon," "nigger," and "porch monkey." On yet another campus, a white male freshman was charged under the school's speech code with racial harassment for calling five black female students "water buffaloes."

In response to hate speech incidents, many colleges and universities have instituted speech codes to punish hateful and offensive public messages. Among the forms of expression punishable at various schools are these:

- The use of derogatory names, inappropriately directed laughter, inconsiderate jokes, and conspicuous exclusion of another person from conversation

- Language that stigmatizes or victimizes individuals or that creates an intimidating or offensive environment

- Face-to-face use of epithets, obscenities, and other forms of expression that by accepted community standards degrade, victimize, stigmatize, or pejoratively depict persons based on their personal, intellectual, or cultural diversity

- Extreme or outrageous acts or communications intended to harass, intimidate, or humiliate others on the basis of race, color, or national origin, thus causing them severe emotional distress

To see the variety and intensity of hate speech Web sites on the Internet, go to www.stormfront.org. Read some of the hate literature of this organization, and then click on various links to Web sites of other hate groups and read some of their literature. What ethical issues are raised by the language used and actions urged by these groups?

Whether hate speech is protected by the First Amendment and whether campus speech codes are constitutional, specific instances of hate speech should be evaluated for their degree of ethicality (Johannesen, 1997). Hate speech can be assessed according to various ethical perspectives (such as

human nature), but how might values and procedures central to a U.S. democratic political perspective be used to judge hate speech?

Access InfoTrac College Edition, and enter the words "hate speech" in the search engine. Access the item "Hate Speech and Constitutional Protection," published in the *Journal of Social Issues,* 58 (2002). Consider how the arguments concerning the First Amendment and the Fourteenth Amendment relate to ethical judgments about hate speech.

Situational Perspectives

To make ethical judgments from a situational perspective, it's necessary to focus *regularly and primarily* on the elements of the specific persuasive situation at hand. Virtually all perspectives (those mentioned here and others) make some allowances, on occasion, for the modified application of ethical criteria in special circumstances. However, an extreme situational perspective routinely makes judgments only in light of *each different context.* Criteria from broad political, human nature, religious, or other perspectives are minimized, and absolute and universal standards are avoided (see Figure 2.2). Among the concrete contextual factors relevant to making a purely situational ethical evaluation are these:

- The role or function of the persuader for receivers

- Expectations held by receivers concerning such matters as appropriateness and reasonableness

- The degree of receivers' awareness of the persuader's techniques

- Goals and values held by receivers

- The degree of urgency for implementing the persuader's proposal

- Ethical standards for communication held by receivers

From an extreme situational perspective, for instance, it might be argued that an acknowledged leader in a time of clear crisis has a responsibility to

Berry's World

"It's exciting to be part of a firm that's on the cutting edge of 'MORAL FLEXIBILITY.'"

FIGURE 2.2 How might situational ethics apply here?

(© 1987 by Jim Berry, NEA, Inc.)

rally support and thus could employ so-called emotional appeals that circumvent human processes of rational, reflective decision making. Or a persuader might ethically use techniques such as innuendo, guilt by association, and unfounded name-calling as long as the receivers both recognize and approve of those methods.

Legal Perspectives

From a legal perspective, illegal communication behavior also is unethical, but that which is not specifically illegal is viewed as ethical. In other words, legality and ethicality are synonymous. Such an approach certainly has the advantage of

enabling simple ethical decisions: We need only measure communication techniques against current laws and regulations to determine whether a technique is ethical. We might, for example, turn for ethical guidance to the regulations governing advertising set forth by the Federal Trade Commission (FTC) or the Federal Communications Commission (FCC). Or we might use Supreme Court or state legislative criteria defining obscenity, pornography, libel, or slander to judge whether a particular message is unethical on those grounds.

However, many people are uneasy with this legalistic approach to communication ethics. They contend that obviously there are some things that are legal but are ethically dubious. And some social protesters for civil rights and against the Vietnam War during the 1960s and 1970s admitted that their actions were illegal but contended that they were justifiable on ethical and moral grounds. Persons holding such views reject any conception of ethicality and legality as synonymous, view ethicality as much broader than legality, and argue that not everything that is unethical should be made illegal.

To what degree, then, can or should we enforce ethical standards for communication through laws or regulations? What degrees of soundness might there be in two old but seemingly contrary sayings: "You can't legislate morality" and "There ought to be a law"? In the United States today, very few ethical standards for communication are codified in laws or regulations. As indicated previously, FCC or FTC regulations on the content of advertising, and laws and court decisions on obscenity and libel, represent the governmental approach. But such examples are rare compared with the large number of laws and court decisions specifying the boundaries of freedom of speech and press in our society. Rather, our society applies ethical standards for communication through the more indirect avenues of group consensus, social pressure, persuasion, and formal-but-voluntary codes of ethics.

Controversies surrounding computer communication on the Internet and Web illustrate not only the tension between freedom and responsibility but also pressures for legalistic approaches to ethics and the creation of formal codes of ethics. Should you be free to say or depict anything you want, without restriction, on the Internet or Web or in email? The freedom–responsibility tension is underscored by Frank Connolly, a professor of computer science at American University: "With the Internet, we are in the situation where there are no controls, no cyber-cops, no speed limits. The other side of these freedoms is that individuals have to exercise responsibility for their actions" (*Washington Post National Weekly Edition,* Oct. 30–Nov. 5, 1995, p. 36). But there are pressures for controls and for formal rules of responsibility. In February 1996, Congress passed the Communications Decency Act to punish the publishing of "indecent" or "patently offensive" material on the Internet—material that could be available to children as well as adults. But in June 1997, the U.S. Supreme Court declared the Communications Decency Act unconstitutional, as violating the freedom-of-speech clause of the First Amendment to the Constitution.

University officials have debated whether to apply existing campus speech codes that prohibit hate speech and harassment to the Internet and email activities of students or whether to formulate special codes of computer communication ethics to guide student use. Virginia Tech University, for example, instituted a student code that prohibited conduct, in words or actions, that "demeans, intimidates, threatens, or otherwise interferes with another person's rightful action or comfort," both online and elsewhere on campus. The dean of students at Virginia Tech said the university's position was that, "if you use our server, then you have some responsibility because you associate the name of the institution with what you say." (See, for example, *Washington Post National Weekly Edition,* Oct. 30–Nov. 5, 1995, p. 36; Nov. 6–12, 1995, p. 27; *Chicago Tribune,* Nov. 24, 1995, p. 30.) What is your view on how ethical responsibility for computer communication on the Internet should be promoted? On your campus, what official policies (set how and by whom?) govern ethically responsible

communication on the Internet and Web? How adequately and appropriately do these policies speak to specific issues of communication ethics? Do these policies actually seem to address matters of legality more than of ethicality?

Dialogical Perspectives

Dialogical perspectives emerge from current scholarship on the nature of communication as dialogue rather than as monologue.* From such perspectives, the attitudes toward each other among participants in a communication situation are an index of the ethical level of that communication. Some attitudes are held to be more fully human, humane, and facilitative of personal self-fulfillment than are others.

Communication as dialogue is characterized by such attitudes as honesty, concern for the welfare and improvement of others, trust, genuineness, open-mindedness, equality, mutual respect, empathy, humility, directness, lack of pretense, nonmanipulative intent, sincerity, encouragement of free expression, and acceptance of others as individuals with intrinsic worth regardless of differences over beliefs or behaviors.

Communication as monologue, in contrast, is marked by such qualities as deception, superiority, exploitation, dogmatism, domination, insincerity, pretense, personal self-display, self-aggrandizement, judgmentalism that stifles free expression, coercion, possessiveness, condescension, self-defensiveness, and the view of others as objects to be manipulated. In the case of persuasion, then, the techniques and presentation of the persuader would be scrutinized to determine the degree to which they reveal an ethical dialogical attitude or an unethical monological attitude toward receivers.

How might ethical standards rooted in a dialogical perspective be applied to political campaign persuasion? Consider the face-to-face, question-and-answer citizen forums held by Bill Clinton with voters during the 1992 and 1996 presidential campaigns. For any particular forum, you could as-

---

*For a more general analysis of communication as dialogue, see Johannesen (1971, 2000) and Stewart and Zediker (2000).

sess the degree to which the communication of participants reflected and promoted dialogical rather than monological attitudes. How might a dialogical ethical perspective apply to intimate interpersonal communication situations such as between friends, family members, lovers, and spouses? Earlier in the section on responsibilities of receivers, some unfair tactics of verbal conflict in interpersonal communication were summarized. How would you assess those tactics from a dialogical perspective?

With knowledge of the preceding ethical perspectives (religious, human nature, political, situational, legal, dialogical), we can confront a variety of difficult issues relevant to ethical problems in persuasion. As receivers constantly bombarded with verbal and nonverbal persuasive messages, we continually face resolution of one or another of these fundamental issues.

ETHICS, PROPAGANDA, AND THE DEMAGOGUE

Is propaganda unethical? The answer to this question partly depends on how the term is defined. As emphasized in a later chapter, numerous, often widely divergent, definitions abound. Originally, the term *propaganda* was associated with the efforts of the Roman Catholic church to persuade people to accept the church's doctrine. Such efforts were institutionalized in 1622 by Pope Gregory XV when he created the Sacred Congregation for Propagating the Faith. The word *propaganda* soon came to designate not only institutions seeking to propagate a doctrine but also the doctrine itself and the communication techniques employed.

Today, one cluster of definitions represents a neutral position with regard to the ethical nature of propaganda. A definition combining the key elements of such neutral views might be: Propaganda is a campaign of mass persuasion, an organized, continuous effort to persuade a mass audience, primarily using the mass media (see Kecskemeti, 1973; Qualter, 1962). Propaganda would thus include ad-

vertising and public relations efforts, national political election campaigns, the persuasive campaigns of some social reform movements, and the organized efforts of national governments to win friends abroad, maintain morale at home, and undermine opponents' morale in both "hot" and "cold" wars. Such a view stresses communication channels and audiences and categorizes propaganda as one species of persuasion. Just as persuasion can be sound or unsound, ethical or unethical, so, too, can propaganda.

Another cluster of definitions takes a negative stance toward the ethical nature of propaganda. Definitions in this cluster probably typify the view held by the average American. A definition combining the key elements of such negative views might be: Propaganda is the intentional use of suggestion, irrelevant emotional appeals, and pseudoproof to circumvent rational decision-making processes (see Chase, 1956; Werkmeister, 1957). In this view, the emphasis is on communication techniques, and propaganda as inherently unethical.★

Are traditional propaganda devices always seen as unethical? This book's accompanying Web site discusses the traditional list: name-calling, glittering generality, transfer, testimonial, plain folks, card stacking, and bandwagon. Such a list, however, does not constitute a surefire guide for exposing unethical persuasion. The ethics of at least some of these techniques depends on how they are used in a given context. For example, the plain-folks technique stresses humble origins and modest backgrounds shared by the communicator and audience. The persuader emphasizes to the audience, although usually not in these words, that "we're all just plain folks." In his whistle-stop speeches to predominantly rural, Republican audiences during the 1948 presidential campaign, Democrat Harry Truman typically used the plain-folks appeal in introductions to his speeches to establish common ground and rapport; he did not rely on it for proof in the main body of his speeches. If a politician relied primarily on the plain-folks appeal as pseudoproof in justifying the policy he or she advocated, such usage

---

★For a philosophical and ethical analysis of propaganda, see Cunningham (2002, pp. 97–178).

might be condemned as unethical. Further, Truman was the kind of person who could legitimately capitalize on his actual plain-folks background. A politician from a more privileged and patrician background, such as Ted Kennedy, could be condemned for using an unethical technique if he were to appeal to farmers and factory workers by saying, "you and I are just plain folks."

Access InfoTrac College Edition, and enter the word "propaganda" in the search engine. Access the item "Propaganda: Remember the Kuwaiti Babies?" published by United Press International (Feb. 26, 2002). What ethical judgments, and why, would you make about some of the examples of propaganda described?

Today, the label "demagogue" is frequently used to render a negative ethical judgment of a communicator. Too often, however, the label is only vaguely defined—the criteria used to evaluate someone as a demagogue are unspecified. In ancient Greece, a demagogue was simply a leader or orator who championed the cause of the common people.

Consider the following five characteristics collectively as possible appropriate guides for determining to what degree a persuader merits the label "demagogue":*

1. A demagogue wields popular or mass leadership over a number of people.

2. A demagogue exerts primary influence through the medium of the spoken word—through public speaking—whether directly to an audience or by means of radio or television.

3. A demagogue relies heavily on propaganda defined in the negative sense of intentional use of suggestion, irrelevant emotional appeals, and pseudoproof to circumvent rational decision-making processes.

4. A demagogue capitalizes on the availability of a major contemporary social issue or problem.

5. A demagogue is hypocritical; the social cause serves as a front or persuasive leverage point, but the actual primary motive is selfish interest and personal gain.

Several cautions are in order in applying these guidelines. A persuader may reflect each of these characteristics to a greater or lesser degree and only in certain instances. A persuader also might fulfill several of these criteria (such as characteristics 1, 2, and 4) and yet not be called a demagogue; characteristics 3 and 5 seem to be central to a conception of a demagogue.

Access InfoTrac College Edition, and enter the word "demagogue" in the search engine. Access the article "The Sincere Demagogue," about former Democratic presidential candidate Bill Bradley. Note that it is published in a politically conservative journal and is about a politically liberal candidate. Given the information and judgments in the article, use the criteria for determining a demagogue described in this section, and develop your own argument (citing evidence in the article or a lack thereof) to explain why you think Bradley is or is not a demagogue.

ETHICAL STANDARDS FOR POLITICAL PERSUASION

Directly or indirectly, we are daily exposed to political persuasion in varied forms. For example, the president appeals on national television for public support of a military campaign. A senator argues in Congress against ratification of a treaty. A government bureaucrat announces a new regulation and presents reasons to justify it. A federal official con-

---

*The basic formulation from which these guidelines have been adapted was first suggested to me by Professor William Conboy of the University of Kansas. These five characteristics generally are compatible with the standard scholarly attempts to define a demagogue; see, for instance, Reinhard Luthin (1959) and Barnet Baskerville (1967).

tends that information requested by a citizen action group cannot be revealed for national security reasons. A national, state, or local politician campaigns for election. A citizen protests a proposed property tax rate increase at a city council meeting. What ethical criteria should we apply to judge the many kinds of political persuasion? We will consider several potential sets of criteria in the hope that among them you will find ones useful in your own life.

Traditional American textbook discussions of the ethics of persuasion, rhetoric, and argument often include lists of standards for evaluating the ethicality of an instance of persuasion. Such criteria often are rooted, implicitly if not explicitly, in what we previously described as a political perspective for judging the ethics of persuasion. The criteria usually stem from a commitment to values and procedures deemed essential to the health and growth of our system of representative democracy. Obviously, other cultures and other political systems may embrace basic values that lead to quite different ethical standards for persuasion.

What follows is a synthesis and adaptation of a number of traditional lists of ethical criteria for persuasion.* Within the context of our own society, the following criteria are not necessarily the only or best ones possible; they are suggested as general guidelines rather than inflexible rules, and they may stimulate discussion on the complexity of judging the ethics of persuasion. Consider, for example, under what circumstances there might be justifiable exceptions to some of these criteria. Also bear in mind that one difficulty in applying these criteria in concrete situations stems from differing standards and meanings people may have for such key terms as *distort, falsify, rational, reasonable, conceal, misrepresent, irrelevant,* and *deceive.*

1. Do not use false, fabricated, misrepresented, distorted, or irrelevant evidence to support arguments or claims.

2. Do not intentionally use specious, unsupported, or illogical reasoning.

3. Do not represent yourself as informed or as an "expert" on a subject when you are not.

4. Do not use irrelevant appeals to divert attention or scrutiny from the issue at hand. Among the appeals that commonly serve such a purpose are smear attacks on an opponent's character, appeals to hatred and bigotry, innuendo, and god or devil terms that cause intense but unreflective positive or negative reactions.

5. Do not ask your audience to link your idea or proposal to emotion-laden values, motives, or goals to which it actually is not related.

6. Do not deceive your audience by concealing your real purpose or self-interest, the group you represent, or your position as an advocate of a viewpoint.

7. Do not distort, hide, or misrepresent the number, scope, intensity, or undesirable features of consequences or effects.

8. Do not use emotional appeals that lack a supporting basis of evidence or reasoning or that would not be accepted if the audience had time and opportunity to examine the subject themselves.

9. Do not oversimplify complex, gradation-laden situations into simplistic two-valued, either/or, polar views or choices.

10. Do not pretend certainty where tentativeness and degrees of probability would be more accurate.

11. Do not advocate something in which you do not believe yourself.

During the 1980s, political analysts in the mass media often criticized President Ronald Reagan for misstating and misusing examples, statistics, and illustrative stories. They charged that he did this not just on rare occasions but with routine frequency in his news conferences, informal comments, and even speeches (Green & MacColl, 1987; Johannesen, 1985). The glaring misuse of facts and anecdotes in

---

*For example, see the following sources: Buehler and Linkugel (1975), Oliver (1957), Minnick (1968), Ewbank and Auer (1951), Thompson (1975), Bradley (1988), Nilsen (1974), and Wallace (1955).

ethically suspect ways continues in the national political discourse. For example, syndicated columnist Joseph Spear took to task former House Speaker Newt Gingrich for this habit ("Third-Wave Newt Comes Unglued," [De Kalb, IL] *Daily Chronicle,* March 17, 1995, p. 4). Spear observed:

> We know that Newt doesn't care that his facts are often not factual. He spoke about a ten-year-old student in St. Louis who was suspended for asking God's blessings on his cafeteria meals. It was not true. He told how the FDA refused to approve an innovative heart pump. It was not true. He rattled on and on about a federal shelter in Denver that was outperformed by a private facility down the street. It was not true.

Spear's judgment was that "Newt is a prattler, a careless accuser, an irresponsible teller of tales." An editorial in the *Washington Post National Weekly Edition* (March 13–19, 1995, p. 27) contended that trying "to get the story straight, whether you're in our business or Speaker Gingrich's, is not a luxury, but a responsibility." To assess the ethicality of such misstatements in current political discourse, you are encouraged to apply our previous discussions concerning intention, sincerity, responsibility, the political perspective, and suggested standards for political persuasion.

ETHICAL STANDARDS FOR COMMERCIAL ADVERTISING

Consumers, academics, and advertisers themselves clearly do not agree on any one set of ethical standards as appropriate for assessing commercial advertising. Here we will simply survey some of the widely varied criteria that have been suggested. Among them you may find guidelines that will aid your own assessments.

Several writers on the ethics of advertising suggest the applicability of perspectives rooted in the essence of human nature. Philosopher Thomas Garrett (1961) argued that a person becomes more truly human in proportion as his or her behavior becomes more conscious and reflective. Because of the human capacity for reasoning and because of the equally distinctive fact of human dependence on other people for the development of their potential, Garrett suggested several ethical obligations. As humans, we are obliged, among other things, to behave rationally ourselves, to help others behave rationally, and to provide truthful information. Suggestive advertising, in Garrett's view, is that which seeks to bypass human powers of reason or to some degree render them inoperative. Such advertising is unethical, not only because it uses emotional appeal, Garrett believed, but also because it demeans a fundamental human attribute and makes people less than human.

Advertising scholar Theodore Levitt (1974) used a human nature position to defend advertising techniques often viewed by others as ethically suspect. While admitting that the line between distortion and falsehood is difficult to establish, he argued that "embellishment and distortion are among advertising's legitimate and socially desirable purposes; . . . illegitimacy in advertising consists only of falsification with larcenous intent" (p. 279). Levitt grounded his defense in a "pervasive, . . . universal, characteristic of human nature—the human audience demands symbolic interpretation of everything it sees and knows. If it doesn't get it, it will return a verdict of 'no interest'" (p. 284). Because Levitt saw humans essentially as symbolizers, as converters of raw sensory experience through symbolic interpretation to satisfy needs, he could justify "legitimate" embellishment and distortion:

> Many of the so-called distortions of advertising, product design, and packaging may be viewed as a paradigm of the many responses that man makes to the conditions of survival in the environment. Without distortion, embellishment, and elaboration, life would be drab, dull, anguished, and at its existential worst. (p. 285)

Sometimes advertisers adopt what we previously called legal perspectives, in which ethicality is equated with legality. However, advertising executive Harold Williams (1974) observed:

> What is legal and what is ethical are not synonymous, and neither are what is legal and what is honest. We tend to resort to legality often as our guideline. This is in effect what happens often when we turn to the lawyers for confirmation that a course of action is an appropriate one.
>
> We must recognize that we are getting a legal opinion, but not necessarily an ethical or moral one. The public, the public advocates, and many of the legislative and administrative authorities recognize it even if we do not. (pp. 285–288)

Typically, commercial advertising has been viewed as persuasion that argues a case or demonstrates a claim concerning the actual nature or merits of a product. Many of the traditional ethical standards for truthfulness and rationality have been applied to such attempts at arguing the quality of a product. For instance, are the evidence and the reasoning supporting the claim clear, accurate, relevant, and sufficient in quantity? Are the emotional and motivational appeals directly relevant to the product? The techniques that will be discussed in Chapter 14 as "weasel words" and as "deceptive claims" might be judged unethical according to this standard of truthfulness.

The American Association of Advertising Agencies' code of ethics was revised in 1990. As you read the following standards, consider their level of adequacy, the degree to which they are relevant and appropriate today, and the extent to which they are being followed by advertisers. Association members agree to avoid intentionally producing advertising that contains the following:

- False or misleading statements or exaggerations, visual or verbal
- Testimonials that do not reflect the real choices of the individuals involved

- Price claims that are misleading
- Claims that are insufficiently supported or that distort the true meaning or practicable application of statements made by professional or scientific authority
- Statements, suggestions, or pictures offensive to public decency or to minority segments of the population

What if ethical standards of truthfulness and rationality are irrelevant to most commercial advertising? What if the primary purpose of most ads is not to prove a claim? Then the ethical standards we apply may stem from whatever alternative view of the nature and purpose of advertising we do hold. Some advertisements function primarily to capture and sustain consumer attention, to announce a product, or to create consumer awareness of the name of a product. What ethical criteria are most appropriate for such attention-getting ads?

Finally, consider advertiser Tony Schwartz's (1974) resonance theory of electronic media persuasion, which is discussed in detail in the chapter on modern media and persuasion. Schwartz argued that, because our conceptions of truth, honesty, and clarity are products of our print-oriented culture, they are appropriate in judging the content of printed messages. In contrast, he contended, the "question of truth is largely irrelevant when dealing with electronic media content" (p. 19). In assessing the ethics of advertising by means of electronic media, Schwartz said, the FTC should focus not on truth and clarity of content but on the effects of the advertisement on receivers. He lamented, however, that "we have no generally agreed-upon social values and/or rules that can be readily applied in judging whether the effects of electronic communication are beneficial, acceptable, or harmful" (p. 22). Schwartz summarized his argument by concluding that

> truth is a print ethic, not a standard for ethical behavior in electronic communication. In addition, the influence of electronic media on print advertising (particularly the substitution of photographic techniques for copy to achieve an

effect) raises the question of whether truth is any longer an issue for magazine or newspaper ads. (p. 22)

What ethical evaluation of effects and consequences would you make of an advertisement for Fetish perfume in *Seventeen* magazine, a magazine whose readers include several million young teenage girls? The ad shows an attractive female teenager looking seductively directly at the readers. The written portion of the ad says, "Apply generously to your neck so he can smell the scent as you shake your head 'no.'" Consider that this ad exists in a larger cultural context in which acquaintance rape is a societal problem, women and girls are clearly urged to say "No!" to unwanted sexual advances, and men and boys too often still believe that "no" really means "yes."

THE ETHICS OF INTENTIONAL AMBIGUITY AND VAGUENESS

"Language that is of doubtful or uncertain meaning" might be a typical definition of ambiguous language. *Ambiguous* language is open to two or more legitimate interpretations. *Vague* language lacks definiteness, explicitness, or preciseness of meaning. Clear communication of intended meaning usually is one major aim of the ethical communicator, whether that person seeks to enhance receivers' understanding or to influence beliefs, attitudes, or actions. Textbooks on oral and written communication typically warn against ambiguity and vagueness; often, they take the position that intentional ambiguity is an unethical communication tactic. For example, later in this book, ambiguity is discussed as a functional device of style, as a stylistic technique that is often successful while ethically questionable.

Most people agree that intentional ambiguity is unethical in situations in which accurate instruction or transmission of precise information is the acknowledged purpose. Even in most so-called persuasive communication situations, intentional ambiguity is ethically suspect. However, in some situations, communicators may believe that the intentional creation of ambiguity or vagueness is necessary, accepted, expected as normal, and even ethically justified. Such might be the case, for example, in religious discourse, in some advertising, in some legal discourse, in labor–management bargaining, in political campaigning, or in international diplomatic negotiations.

We can itemize a number of specific purposes for which communicators might believe that intentional ambiguity is ethically justified: (1) to heighten receiver attention through puzzlement, (2) to allow flexibility in interpretation of legal concepts, (3) to allow for precise understanding and agreement on the primary issue by using ambiguity on secondary issues, (4) to promote maximum receiver psychological participation in the communication transaction by letting receivers create their own relevant meanings, and (5) to promote maximum latitude for revision of a position in later dealings with opponents or with constituents by avoiding being locked into a single absolute stance.

In political communication, whether from campaigners or government officials, several circumstances might justify intentional ambiguity. First, a president or presidential candidate often communicates to multiple audiences through a single message via a mass medium such as television or radio. Different parts of the message may appeal to specific audiences, and intentional ambiguity in some message elements avoids offending any of the audiences. Second, as political scientist Lewis Froman (1966) observed, a candidate "cannot take stands on specific issues because he doesn't know what the specific choices will be until he is faced with the necessity for concrete decision. Also, specific commitments would be too binding in a political process that depends upon negotiation and compromise" (p. 9). Third, groups of voters increasingly make decisions about whether to support or oppose a candidate on the basis of that candidate's stand on a single issue of paramount importance to those groups. The candidate's position on a variety of other public issues is often ignored or dismissed. "Single-issue politics" is the phrase frequently used to characterize this trend. A candidate may be intentionally ambiguous on one emotion-packed issue in order to get a fair hearing for his or her stands on many other issues.

In his *Law Dictionary for Non-Lawyers,* Daniel Oran (1975) warned against use of vague language but also noted:

> Some legal words have a "built-in" vagueness. They are used when the writer or speaker does not want to be pinned down. For example, when a law talks about "reasonable speed" or "due care," it is deliberately imprecise about the meaning of the words because it wants the amount of speed allowed or care required to be decided situation by situation, rather than by an exact formula. (pp. 330–331)

In some advertising, intentional ambiguity seems to be understood as such by consumers and even accepted by them. Consider the possible ethical implications of the Noxzema shaving cream commercial that famously urged (accompanied by a beautiful woman watching a man shave in rhythm to strip-tease music), "Take it off. Take it all off." Or recall the sexy woman in the aftershave commercial who says, "All my men wear English Leather, or they wear nothing at all."

THE ETHICS OF NONVERBAL COMMUNICATION

Nonverbal factors play an important role in the persuasion process. In a magazine advertisement, for example, the use of certain colors, pictures, layout patterns, and typefaces influences how the words in the advertisement are received. A later chapter provides examples of "nonverbal bias" in photo selection, camera angle and movement, and editing in news presentation. In *The Importance of Lying,* Arnold Ludwig (1965) underscored the ethical implications of some dimensions of nonverbal communication:

> Lies are not only found in verbal statements. When a person nods affirmatively in response to something he does not believe or when he feigns attention to a conversation he finds bor-

ing, he is equally guilty of lying. . . . A false shrug of the shoulders, the seductive batting of eyelashes, an eyewink, or a smile may all be employed as nonverbal forms of deception. (p. 5)

Silence, too, may carry ethical implications. If to be responsible in fulfilling our role or position requires that we speak out on a subject, to remain silent may be judged unethical. But if the only way that we can successfully persuade others on a subject is to employ unethical communication techniques or appeals, the ethical course probably will be to remain silent.

Another example of potentially unethical nonverbal communication via photographs occurred in the political arena. In *Harper's* magazine, Earl Shorris (1977) condemned as unethical the nonverbal tactics of the *New York Times* in opposing Bella Abzug as a candidate for mayor of New York City:

> The *Times,* having announced its preference for almost anyone but Mrs. Abzug in the mayoral election, published a vicious photograph of her taken the night of her winning the endorsement of the New Democratic Coalition. In the photograph, printed on page 1, Mrs. Abzug sits alone on a stage under the New Democratic Coalition banner. There are three empty chairs to her right and five empty chairs to her left. In this forlorn scene the camera literally looks up Mrs. Abzug's dress to show the heavy calves and thighs of an overweight woman in her middle years.
>
> While the editorial judgment may be right, in that Bella Abzug is probably not the best choice or even a good choice for mayor of New York, the photograph is an example of journalism at its lowest. (p. 106)

Similarly, television coverage of the 9/11 terrorist attacks on the World Trade Center yielded many vivid images that were burned into our memories. An Associated Press photographer produced one especially emotional image—of a man plunging headfirst down the side of the still-standing North Tower. Although no captions identified the man, the photographer's telephoto lens was powerful enough that, in versions enhanced for clarity, the man's face was recognizable to persons who knew him. With regard to ethics, this photo generated criticism of the media that used the photo and praise for the media not using it. On what ethical grounds might you condemn the use of the photo? On what ethical grounds might you justify its use? Consider the likely emotional trauma for persons who knew the man. Did the ends of selling papers or crystalizing the personal dimension of the attack justify using it as a means that intensified the grief and violated the privacy of family members and friends? How does the photo feed into the public's seemingly unlimited appetite for glimpses into the intimate details of the grief of others—a process that some scholars refer to as the "pornography of grief"?★

To further explore ethical standards for nonverbal communication, you are urged to read several sources that are especially rich in extended case studies. The entire issue of the *Journal of Mass Media Ethics, 2* (Spring/Summer 1987) is devoted to ethics in photojournalism. Some contributors suggest concrete ethical guidelines (pp. 34, 71–73); others discuss photos as claims and the nonobjectivity of photos (pp. 50, 52). A photo as a reflection of the photographer's formed ethical character is probed (p. 9). Two books by Paul Martin Lester—*Photojournalism: An Ethical Approach* (1991) and *Visual Communication* (2003)—are rich sources on the topic. Also thought-provoking is Thomas H. Wheeler's, *Phototruth or Photofiction? Ethics and Media Imagery in the Digital Age* (2002).

THE ETHICS OF MORAL EXCLUSION

Moral exclusion, according to Susan Opotow (1990), "occurs when individuals or groups are perceived as outside the boundary in which moral values, rules, and considerations of fairness apply.

Those who are morally excluded are perceived as nonentities, expendable, or undeserving; consequently, harming them appears acceptable, appropriate, or just." Persons morally excluded are denied their rights, dignity, and autonomy. Opotow isolates for analysis and discussion over two dozen symptoms or manifestations of moral exclusion. For our purposes, a noteworthy fact is that many of them directly involve communication. Although all of the symptoms she presents are significant for a full understanding of the mind-set of individuals engaged in moral exclusion, the following are ones that clearly involve persuasion:

- Showing the superiority of oneself or one's group by making unflattering comparisons to other individuals or groups

- Denigrating and disparaging others by characterizing them as lower life forms (vermin) or as inferior beings (barbarians, aliens)

- Denying that others possess humanity, dignity, or sensitivity, or have a right to compassion

- Redefining as an increasingly larger category that of "legitimate" victims

- Placing the blame for any harm on the victim

- Justifying harmful acts by claiming that the morally condemnable acts committed by "the enemy" are significantly worse

- Misrepresenting cruelty and harm by masking, sanitizing, and conferring respectability on them through the use of neutral, positive, technical, or euphemistic terms to describe them

- Justifying harmful behavior by claiming that it is widely accepted (everyone is doing it) or that it was isolated and uncharacteristic (it happened just this once)

An example may clarify how language choices function to achieve moral exclusion. The category of "vermin" (mentioned in the second item in the list) includes parasitic insects, such as fleas, lice, mosquitoes, bedbugs, and ticks, that can infest

---

★For one insightful discussion, see Jane B. Singer, "The Unforgiving Truth in the Unforgivable Photo," (2002). A superb general analysis of ethical issues in media treatment of victims of tragedy is Cooper (2002).

human bodies. In Nazi Germany, Adolf Hitler's speeches and writings often referred to Jews as a type of parasite infesting the pure Aryan race (non-Jewish Caucasians or people of Nordic heritage) or as a type of disease attacking the German national body. The depiction of Jews as parasites or a disease served to place them outside the moral boundary where ethical standards apply to human treatment of other humans. Jews were classified or categorized as nonhumans. As parasites, they had to be exterminated; as a cancerous disease, they had to be cut out of the national body.

Now consider a more recent example. The headline "An Eskimo Encounters Civilization—and Mankind" appeared in the Tempo section of the *Chicago Tribune* (May 29, 2000). Can you identify two ways in which the words in the headline reflect a process of moral exclusion? How do these words place people outside the categories where human ethics normally apply? Hate speech, as discussed earlier in this chapter, and racist/sexist language, examined in the next section, also illustrate the process of moral exclusion.

THE ETHICS OF RACIST/SEXIST LANGUAGE

In *The Language of Oppression,* communication scholar Haig Bosmajian (1983) demonstrated how names, labels, definitions, and stereotypes traditionally have been used to degrade, dehumanize, and suppress Jews, blacks, Native Americans, and women. His goal was to expose the "decadence in our language, the inhumane uses of language" that have been used "to justify the unjustifiable, to make palatable the unpalatable, to make reasonable the unreasonable, to make decent the indecent." Bosmajian reminded us: "Our identities, who and what we are, how others see us, are greatly affected by the names we are called and the words with which we are labeled. The names, labels, and phrases employed to 'identify' a people may in the end determine their survival" (pp. 5, 9).

"Every language reflects the prejudices of the society in which it evolved. Since English, through most of its history, evolved in a white, Anglo-Saxon, patriarchal society, no one should be surprised that its vocabulary and grammar frequently reflect attitudes that exclude or demean minorities and women" (Miller & Swift, 1981, pp. 2–3). Such is the fundamental position of Casey Miller and Kate Swift, authors of *The Handbook of Nonsexist Writing.* Conventional English usage, they argued, "often obscures the actions, the contributions, and sometimes the very presence of women" (p. 8). Because such language usage is misleading and inaccurate, it has ethical implications. "In this respect, continuing to use English in ways that have become misleading is no different from misusing data, whether the misuse is inadvertent or planned" (p. 8).

To what degree is the use of racist/sexist language unethical, and by what standards? At the least, racist/sexist terms place people in artificial and irrelevant categories. At worst, such terms intentionally demean and put down other people by embodying unfair negative value judgments concerning traits, capacities, and accomplishments. What are the ethical implications, for instance, of calling a Jewish person a "kike," a black person a "nigger" or "boy," an Italian person a "wop," an Asian person a "gook" or "slant-eye," or a thirty-year-old woman a "girl" or "chick"? Here is one possible answer:

> In the war in Southeast Asia, our military fostered a linguistic environment in which the Vietnamese people were called such names as slope, dink, slant, gook, and zip; those names made it much easier to despise, to fear, to kill them. When we call women in our own society by the names of gash, slut, dyke, bitch, or girl, we—men and women alike—have put ourselves in a position to demean and abuse them. (Bailey, 1984, pp. 42–43)

From a political perspective, we might value access to the relevant and accurate information needed to make reasonable decisions on public issues. Racist/sexist language, however, by reinforcing stereotypes, conveys inaccurate depictions of people, fails to take serious account of them, or even makes them invisible for purposes of such decisions. Such language denies us access to necessary accurate information and thus is ethically suspect. From a human nature perspective, such language is ethically suspect because it dehumanizes individuals and groups by undermining and circumventing their uniquely human capacity for rational thought or for using symbols. From a dialogical perspective, racist/sexist language is ethically suspect because it reflects a superior, exploitative, inhumane attitude toward others, thus denying equal opportunity for self-fulfillment for some people.

SOME FEMINIST VIEWS ON PERSUASION

Feminism is not a concept with a single, universally accepted definition. For our purposes, elements of definitions provided by Barbara Bate (1992) and by Julia Wood (1994) are helpful. Feminism holds that both women and men are complete and important human beings and that societal barriers (typically constructed through language processes) have prevented women from being perceived and treated as of equal worth to men. Feminism involves a commitment to equality and respect for life. Feminism rejects oppression and domination as undesirable values and accepts that difference need not be equated with inferiority or undesirability.

"My indictment of our discipline of rhetoric springs from my belief that any intent to persuade is an act of violence." Thus, Sally Miller Gearhart (1979) opened her attack on rhetoric as persuasion as reflecting a masculine-oriented, "conquest/conversion mentality." According to traditional views of rhetoric, "it is a proper and even a necessary function to attempt to change others." The conquest/ conversion model for persuasion is subtle and insidious, said Gearhart, "because it gives the illusion of integrity. . . . In the conversion model we work very hard not simply to conquer but to give every assurance that our conquest of the victim is really giving her what she wants." Gearhart contended that the rational discourse of traditional rhetoric actually is a "subtle form of Might Makes Right." Teachers of rhetoric, she argued, "have been training a competent breed of weapons specialists who

are skilled in emotional maneuvers, experts in intellectual logistics."

Working from feminist assumptions, Gearhart offered a particular version of "communication" as a more desirable and ethical alternative. This view of communication involves "deliberate creation or cocreation of an atmosphere in which people and things, if and only if they have the internal basis for change, may change themselves; it can be a milieu in which those who are ready to be persuaded persuade themselves, may choose to hear or choose to learn." Participants in this kind of interaction (1) try to develop an atmosphere in which change for all participants can take place, (2) recognize that participants may differ in their knowledge of the subject matter and in basic beliefs, (3) look beyond these differences to attempt to create a sense of equal power for all, (4) are committed to working hard to achieve communication, and (5) are willing at a fundamental level to "yield [their] position entirely to the other(s)." This view of communication, Gearhart suggested, moves away from a maledominated model that assumes that all power is in the speaker/conqueror. Instead, the "womanization of rhetoric" focuses on improving the atmosphere, on listening and receiving, and on developing a "collective rather than a competitive mode."

Although they accept much of Gearhart's critique of a speaker-centered rhetoric of conquest, conversion, domination, and control, Sonja Foss and Cindy Griffin (1995) believe that such persuasion should remain one among several rhetorics available to humans for selection in varying contexts. They do not want to characterize such a view of rhetoric as inaccurate or misguided. But as one alternative, Foss and Griffin develop an "invitational rhetoric" rooted in the feminist assumptions that (1) relationships of equality are usually more desirable than ones of domination and elitism, (2) every human being has value because she or he is unique and is an integral part of the pattern of the universe, and (3) individuals have a right to self-determination concerning the conditions of their lives (they are expert about their lives).

Invitational rhetoric, say Foss and Griffin, invites "the audience to enter the rhetor's world and to see it as the rhetor does." The invitational rhetor "does not judge or denigrate others' perspectives but is open to and tries to appreciate and validate those perspectives, even if they differ dramatically from the rhetor's own." The goal is to establish a "nonhierarchical, nonjudgmental, nonadversarial framework" for the interaction and to develop a "relationship of equality, respect, and appreciation" with the audience. Invitational rhetors make no assumption that their "experiences or perspectives are superior to those of audience members and refuse to impose their perspectives on them." Although change is not the intent of invitational rhetoric, it might be a result. Change can occur in the "audience or rhetor or both as a result of new understandings and insights gained in the exchange of ideas."

In the process of invitational rhetoric, Foss and Griffin contend, the rhetor offers perspectives without advocating their support or seeking their acceptance. These individual perspectives are expressed "as carefully, completely, and passionately as possible" to invite their full consideration. In offering perspectives, "rhetors tell what they currently know or understand; they present their vision of the world and how it works for them." They also "communicate a willingness to call into question the beliefs they consider most inviolate and to relax a grip on these beliefs." Further, they strive to create the conditions of safety, value, and freedom in interactions with audience members. Safety involves "the creation of a feeling of security and freedom from danger for the audience," so that participants do not "fear rebuttal of or retribution for their most fundamental beliefs." Value involves acknowledging the intrinsic worth of audience members as human beings. In interaction, attitudes that are "distancing, depersonalizing, or paternalistic" are avoided, and "listeners do not interrupt, confront, or insert anything of their own as others tell of their experiences." Freedom involves the power to choose or decide, with no restrictions placed on the interaction. Thus, participants may introduce for consideration any and all matters; "no subject matter is off limits, and all presuppositions can be challenged." Finally, in invitational rhetoric, the "rhetor's ideas are not privileged over those of the audience."

In concluding their explication of an invitational rhetoric, Foss and Griffin suggest that this rhetoric requires "a new scheme of ethics to fit interactional goals other than inducement of others to adherence to the rhetor's own beliefs." What might be some appropriate ethical guidelines for an invitational rhetoric? What ethical standards seem already to be implied by the dimensions or constituents of such a rhetoric?

From her stance as a feminist teacher and scholar of communication, Lana Rakow (1994) spoke to an audience of students and teachers of communication at The Ohio State University. She employed the norms of "trust, mutuality, justice, and reciprocity" as touchstones for communication relationships. As part of a wide-ranging address on the mission of the field of communication study, Rakow contended that we must develop a communication ethic to guide "relations between individuals, between cultures, between organizations, between countries." She asked, "What kind of 'ground-rules' would work across multiple contexts to achieve relationships that are healthy and egalitarian and respectful?" She suggested these:

- Inclusiveness means openness to multiple perspectives on truth, an encouragement of them, and a willingness to listen. Persons are not dehumanized because of their gender, race, ethnicity, sexual orientation, country, or culture.

- Participation means ensuring that all persons must have the "means and ability . . . to be heard, to speak, to have voice, to have their opinions count in public decision making." All persons "have a right to participate in naming the world, to be part of the discussion in naming and speaking our truths."

- Reciprocity means that participants are considered equal partners in a communication transaction. There should be a "reciprocity of speaking and listening, of knowing and being known as you wish to be known."

In what respects, and why, do you agree or disagree with the positions advocated by these feminist scholars? What contributions do their viewpoints make to our better understanding of the process of persuasion as it functions and as it ought to function?

ETHICAL STANDARDS IN CYBERSPACE

What ethical standards should apply to communication in cyberspace—in the realm of the Internet, the Web, listservs, newsgroups, and chat rooms? We can get guidance and suggestions from several sources. Some of the "Ten Commandments of Computer Ethics" formulated by the Computer Ethics Institute are particularly relevant. For example, "thou shalt not: Use a computer to harm other people; interfere with other people's computer work; snoop around in other people's computer files; use a computer to steal; use a computer to bear false witness against others; [or] plagiarize another person's intellectual output" (reprinted in Ermann, 1997, pp. 313–314).

In *Communicating Online: A Guide to the Internet,* John Courtright and Elizabeth Perse (1998) define acting ethically as simply "doing the right thing, even when no one is looking" and as "behaving properly, even when there is no chance of being caught" (p. 16). Concerning communication via email, they propose that we ask ourselves, "Would I be embarrassed or ashamed if I read my own words in tomorrow's newspaper?" It's important to never, intentionally or unintentionally, harass someone with email, or to send "flames" or messages that contain strong language and are meant to provoke or criticize. "Just like any other form of communication, don't email in anger. Give yourself a chance to cool down before you send your message" (p. 33). Whenever you use the ideas of another person from an Internet source, give that person credit by using a proper citation (p. 64). With email, listservs, and newsgroups, avoid "shouting," or routinely typing in all capitals, which generally is considered inappropriate if not rude. Also avoid

"trolling," or posting messages designed simply to agitate a group to "bite back" with an extreme response (p. 82).

A more philosophically grounded source is James Porter's *Rhetorical Ethics and Internetworked Writing* (1998). Porter adapts traditional sources such as Aristotle and Kenneth Burke but also draws heavily on postmodernist, critical theorist, and feminist sources such as Foucault, Lyotard, Benhabib, and Irigaray. In focusing on how ethical rules are created and changed, Porter condemns static, decontextualized, universal rules. He also explores how competing ethical principles can be reconciled in concrete contexts. He provides no absolute and specific answers to issues of persuasive ethics but does offer provocative questions and guiding principles for exploring what ethical judgments might be reasonable in a given case. Porter's critical rhetorical ethics examines how individuals' communication is situated in and influenced by a web of class, economic, racial/ethnic, and gender relationships and limitations. Porter thus gives special priority to the concerns of marginalized, oppressed, or silenced persons. As ethical guidelines to structure both our stance toward the audience and our choice of persuasive techniques, Porter offers the following: (1) Respect the audience and audience differences, (2) care for the audience and for concrete others, (3) do not harm or oppress the audience, (4) consult dialogically with diverse sources, (5) focus on contextualized elements and the situated moment, and (6) recognize the complexity and ambiguity of most ethical judgment (pp. 151–162).

What kind of a code of Internet ethics might you propose as appropriate, clear, and workable?*

ETHICS AND PERSONAL CHARACTER

Ethical persuasion is not simply a series of careful and reflective decisions, instance by instance, to persuade in ethically responsible ways. Deliberate

---

*A number of excellent books focus on standards and issues for ethics in cyberspace. You are urged to examine, for example, Robert Baird et al., *Cyberethics* (2000); Cees J. Hamelink, *The Ethics of Cyberspace* (2000); Deborah G. Johnson, *Computer Ethics* (2000); and Duncan Langford, ed., *Internet Ethics* (2000).

application of ethical rules is sometimes impossible. Pressure for a decision can be so great or a deadline so near that there is insufficient time for careful deliberation. We might be unsure what ethical criteria are relevant or how they apply. The situation might seem so unusual that applicable criteria do not readily come to mind. In such times of crisis or uncertainty, our decisions concerning ethical persuasion stem less from deliberation than from our formed "character." Further, our ethical character influences what terms we use to describe a situation and whether we believe the situation contains ethical implications (Hauerwas, 1977; Klaidman & Beauchamp, 1987; Lebacqz, 1985).

Consider the nature of moral character as described by ethicists Richard DeGeorge and Karen Lebacqz. As human beings develop, according to DeGeorge (1999), they adopt patterns of actions and dispositions to act in certain ways.

> These dispositions, when viewed collectively, are sometimes called *character*. The character of a person is the sum of his or her virtues and vices. A person who habitually tends to act as he morally should has a good character. If he resists strong temptation, he has a strong character. If he habitually acts immorally, he has a morally bad character. If despite good intentions he frequently succumbs to temptation, he has a weak character. Because character is formed by conscious actions, in general people are morally responsible for their characters as well as for their individual actions. (p.123)

Lebacqz (1985) observes:

> . . . when we act, we not only do something, we also shape our own character. Our choices about what to do are also choices about whom to be. A single lie does not necessarily make us a liar; but a series of lies may. And so each choice about what to do is also a choice about whom to be—or, more accurately, whom to become. (p. 83)

In Judeo-Christian or Western cultures, good moral character is usually associated with habitual embodiment of such virtues as courage, temperance, wisdom, justice, fairness, generosity, gentleness, patience, truthfulness, and trustworthiness. Other cultures may praise additional or different virtues that they believe constitute good ethical character. Instilled in us as habitual dispositions to act, these virtues guide the ethics of our communication behavior when careful or clear deliberation is not possible.

In what ways does the issue of ethical character apply to the 1992 and 1996 presidential campaigns of Bill Clinton and to his communication during his presidency? Consider the arguments in some of the national press commentary. During the 1992 campaign, political columnist Paul Greenberg (1992) wrote:

> The character issues just won't go away no matter how many times Bill Clinton assures us, word of honor, that his is fine. His stock response to questions about his character or absence of same is to say that nobody's perfect, admit he's not, and therefore imply that he's no better or worse than anybody else." (p. 25)

Economist and syndicated columnist Robert J. Samuelson (1994, 1995) was especially critical of Clinton's communication as it reflected his character. Samuelson argued that Clinton routinely exaggerates, fibs, and misstates on both foreign and domestic policy. In 1996, a *U.S. News & World Report* survey (Borger & Kulman, 1996) concluded, "Yet character remains the president's Achilles heel. The poll found that while 70 percent of voters describe [Republican party nominee Bob] Dole as moral, only 41 percent describe Clinton that way." Although respondents in the poll could not identify concrete "best aspects" of Clinton's character, they included "deceptive, cheater, and indecisive" among the "worst aspects" of his character (p. 36).

The period from 1997 to 1999 found Clinton's character to be a primary focus of media scrutiny because of his sexual improprieties with White House intern Monica Lewinsky, because of independent counsel Kenneth Starr's investigation into alleged Clinton and Clinton administration misdeeds, because the House of Representatives voted two articles of impeachment (indictment) against the president, and because the Senate acquitted Clinton on the two charges of perjury to a grand jury and of obstruction of justice. Public opinion polls during the period reflected a paradox: Clinton's job performance approval ratings ranged between 60 and 70 percent, but significant numbers of citizens doubted his personal ethical character and trustworthiness. For example, a CNN/*USA Today*/Gallup Poll released in mid-January 1999 (*Washington Post National Weekly Edition*, Jan. 25, 1999, p. 12) found that 69 percent of those surveyed approved of Clinton's job performance as president, and 81 percent said his presidency had been a success. In contrast, only 25 percent said he was honest and trustworthy, and only 20 percent said he provided good moral leadership. In the summer, fall, and winter of 1998–1999, Clinton gave four speeches of apology (August 16, September 11, December 11, February 12) in which he admitted engaging in sexual improprieties and lying about it and in which he progressively expressed regret, remorse, sorrow, and shame. You are urged to analyze the arguments and appeals in these four speeches to judge their degree of ethicality (see the *Weekly Compilation of Presidential Documents*).

Columnist Robert Samuelson (1998) continued to condemn Clinton for "routine and unending deceptions"—not only about personal behavior but also about public policy: "What inhibits most people from routine lies is a sense of shame. Clinton seems to lack this" (p. 17). Other political analysts contended that the issue of personal ethical character should be of crucial importance in selecting future presidents. John Kass (1998) concluded, "Character is the only thing that matters. And we're responsible for forgetting" (p. 3). And Joan Beck (1998) urged, "And next time we should pay more attention to character issues, to understand that character can't be divided into public and private sectors, and that the presidency can, indeed, be weakened by such discussions as whether oral sex counts as adultery" (p. 19). In what ways, and why, do you agree or disagree with the judgments of the various critics cited in these sections on Clinton's ethical character?

Columnist Stephen Chapman (1987) suggests three reasons that media scrutiny of the character issue is so intense for presidential candidates. First, voters are imposing increasingly higher ethical standards. Second, "personal integrity is one of the few matters that lend themselves to firsthand judgments by the voters. Most voters may feel unable to judge whether a politician is right about the defense appropriations bill. But they are able to consider evidence about a politician's ethics and reach a verdict, since they make similar evaluations about people every day." Third, voters "tend to vote for general themes, trusting candidates to apply them in specific cases. A politician who creates doubt about his personal honesty doesn't merely sow fear that he will steal from the petty cash. He creates doubt that his concrete policies will match his applause lines" (p. 3).

To aid in assessing the ethical character of any person in a position of responsibility or any person who seeks a position of trust, we can modify guidelines suggested by journalists. We can ask, Is it probable that the recent or current ethically suspect communication behavior will continue? Does it seem to be habitual? Even if a particular incident seems minor in itself, does it fit into some pattern of shortcomings? If the person does something inconsistent with his or her public image, is it a mere miscue or an indication of hypocrisy (Alter, 1987; Dobel, 1999; Johannesen, 1991)?

Access InfoTrac College Edition, and enter the word "ethics" in the search engine. Access the item "Do As I Say, Not As I Did," published in *Time* (July 22, 2002). What ethical judgments could you make concerning the described comments and actions by President George W. Bush and Vice President Dick Cheney?

IMPROVING ETHICAL JUDGMENT

One purpose of this book is to make you a more discerning receiver and consumer of communication by encouraging ethical judgments of communication that are specifically focused and carefully considered. In making judgments of the ethics of your own communication and the communication to which you are exposed, your aim should be specific rather than vague assessments, and carefully considered rather than reflexive, "gut-level" reactions.

The following framework of questions is offered as a means of making more systematic and firmly grounded judgments of communication ethics.★ At the same time, we should bear in mind philosopher Stephen Toulmin's (1950) observation that "moral reasoning is so complex, and has to cover such a variety of types of situations, that no one logical test . . . can be expected to meet every case" (p. 148). In underscoring the complexity of making ethical judgments, in *The Virtuous Journalist,* Klaidman and Beauchamp (1987) reject the "false premise that the world is a tidy place of truth and falsity, right and wrong, without the ragged edges of uncertainty and risk." Rather, they argue, "Making moral judgments and handling moral dilemmas require the balancing of often ill-defined competing claims, usually in untidy circumstances" (p. 20). How might you apply this framework of questions? (Also see Figure 2.3.)

FIGURE 2.3 How might the guidelines for ethical judgment help to evaluate this situation?

(© Creative Media Services, Box 5955, Berkeley, CA 94705.)

1. Can I specify exactly what ethical criteria, standards, or perspectives are being applied by me or others? What is the concrete grounding of the ethical judgment?

2. Can I justify the reasonableness and relevancy of these standards for this particular case? Why are these the most appropriate ethical criteria among the potential ones? Why do these take priority (at least temporarily) over other relevant ones?

3. Can I indicate clearly in what respects the communication being evaluated succeeds or fails in measuring up to the standards? What judgment is justified in this case about the degree of ethicality? Is the most appropriate judgment a specifically targeted and narrowly focused one rather than a broad, generalized, and encompassing one?

4. In this case, to whom is ethical responsibility owed—to which individuals, groups, organiza-

tions, or professions? In what ways and to what extent? Which responsibilities take precedence over others? What is the communicator's responsibility to her- or himself and to society at large?

5. How do I feel about myself after this ethical choice? Can I continue to "live with myself" in good conscience? Would I want my parents or mate or best friend to know of this choice?

6. Can the ethicality of this communication be justified as a coherent reflection of the communicator's personal character? To what degree is the choice ethically "out of character"?

7. If called upon in public to justify the ethics of my communication, how adequately could I do so? What generally accepted reasons or rationale could I appropriately offer?

★For some of these questions, I have freely adapted the discussions of Goodwin (1987, pp. 14–15), Christians, Rotzoll, and Fackler (1991, pp. 21–23), and Perelman and Olbrechts-Tyteca (1969, pp. 25, 483).

8. Are there precedents or similar previous cases to which I can turn for ethical guidance? Are there significant aspects of this instance that set it apart from all others?

9. How thoroughly have alternatives been explored before settling on this particular choice? Might this choice be less ethical than some of the workable but hastily rejected or ignored alternatives? If the only avenue to successful achievement of the communicator's goal requires use of unethical communication techniques, is there a realistic choice (at least temporarily) of refraining from communication—of not communicating at all?

REVIEW AND CONCLUSION

The process of persuasion demands that you make choices about the methods and content you will use in influencing receivers to accept the alternative you advocate. These choices involve issues of desirability and of personal and societal good. What ethical standards will you use in making or judging these choices among techniques, contents, and purposes? What should be the ethical responsibility of a persuader in contemporary society?

Obviously, answers to these questions have not been clearly or universally established. However, we must face these questions squarely. In this chapter, we explored some perspectives, issues, and examples useful in evaluating the ethics of persuasion. Our interest in the nature and effectiveness of persuasive techniques must not overshadow our concern for the ethical use of such techniques. We must examine not only how to but also whether to use persuasive techniques. The issue of whether to is both one of audience adaptation and one of ethics. We need to formulate meaningful ethical guidelines, not inflexible rules, for our own persuasive behavior and for use in evaluating the persuasion to which we are exposed.

QUESTIONS FOR FURTHER THOUGHT

1. What standards do you believe are most appropriate for judging the ethics of political persuasion?

2. What ethical standards do you think should be used to evaluate advertising?

3. When might intentional use of ambiguity be ethically justified?

4. To what degree is the use of racist/sexist language unethical? Why?

5. Do the ethical standards commonly applied to verbal persuasion apply equally appropriately to nonverbal elements in persuasion? Should there be a special ethic for nonverbal persuasion?

6. What should be the role of personal character in ethical persuasion?

7. What ethical standards do you believe should guide communication on the Internet?

8. How does hate speech illustrate the process of moral exclusion?

 For online activities, go to the Web site for this book at http://communication.wadsworth.com/larson.

3

✴

Traditional and Humanistic Approaches to Persuasion

JOSEPH SCUDDER
Northern Illinois University

Permanence and change exist in the world of persuasion, and the same holds true for research in persuasion—some ancient theories and concepts have current validity and usefulness even as new theories and concepts emerge as explanations for persuasive events. Knowledge of these established and emerging theories should help you to become a more critical persuadee and hence a more effective persuader. This chapter considers a wide range of approaches from traditional approaches in the Aristotelian tradition to humanistic approaches that focus on persuasion in terms of the totality of human experience.

ARISTOTLE'S INSTRUCTIONAL APPROACH

As mentioned previously, the formal study of persuasion has its early roots in ancient Greece. The Greek city-states valued the right of their citizens to speak on issues of the day and required them to speak on their own behalf in legal disputes, without the help of lawyers as we have today. Greek philosophers like Aristotle tried to describe what happened when persuasion occurred. Much of what Aristotle said on the subject of persuasion has relevance today. Of course, his principles must be adapted to fit contemporary society, in which the stresses and habits of a developing technological world will determine which premises are important.

Aristotle was a remarkable person. His father had been the court physician to Philip, the king of Macedonia, so Aristotle received the finest education. He studied for twenty years with Plato and was then selected by Philip's son, Alexander the Great, to be what we might call the secretary of education. Not only did Aristotle develop schools using the methods of Platonic dialogue, but he also set a thousand men to work cataloguing everything known about the world at that time. He was thus the first great librarian and researcher of Greece. He also wrote up the findings of his researchers in more than four hundred books covering a variety of topics, including his *Rhetoric,* considered by many to be the single most important work on the study of persuasion (see Golden, Berquist, & Coleman, 1989, p. 30). The basic processes by which we are persuaded, however, have remained amazingly constant. A few of the most relevant features from the *Rhetoric* are briefly summarized here.

Adaptation to Context and Purpose

Aristotle recognized that one approach to persuasion did not fit all situations. He proposed that a persuasive speaker must adapt to the context. Three contexts dominated his thinking: (1) Forensic discourse considered allegations of past wrongdoing in the legal arena; (2) epideictic discourse treated present situations in which praise or blame was leveled; and (3) deliberative discourse dealt with future policy, with special attention to the political realm. It should also be recognized that adaptation was not just to the place or setting but also to the purpose of the activity that would happen there. These three types of discourse remain very important today. In today's world, however, we deal with many other persuasive contexts—particularly those that deal with selling, advertising, and other forms of commerce. The important point here is that Aristotle recognized that persuasive tactics had to be matched to the context.

Let's look at an example of how complex the process of understanding the context can be. Senator Paul Wellstone of Minnesota died in a plane crash on October 25, 2002. The *New York Times'* description of Senator Wellstone, reprinted in Figure 3.1, is an example of epideictic discourse that praised him while describing the uniqueness and quirkiness of the man. Although some may take offense at how politics is mixed in at the end of the article, it is an appropriate statement overall that most associated with Senator Wellstone could respect. The televised, public memorial service for Wellstone, however, contained one of the most controversial eulogies delivered in recent history (see Figure 3.2). The family chose Rick Kahn to deliver the main eulogy for Senator Wellstone. It was controversial because Kahn shifted from praising Wellstone to encouraging support for his legacy by voting for the yet-to-be-named Democratic can-

didate. Kahn used statements like "We can redeem the sacrifice of his life if you help us win this election." Marked backlash resulted from the perceived inappropriateness of mixing a eulogy at a funeral with political purposes. Republican William F. Buckley (2002) wrote:

> There was even speculation about how Paul Wellstone would have reacted to his own memorial service. The first hour was reverential, but the world knows what then happened, namely a frenetic political rally. One television executive was quoted as saying the three hours —which is how long it stretched out—should not have been broadcast but that it would have been "disrespectful" to tune off when the frenzy began. So, on it went into however many millions of television receivers. (n.p.)

Mixing a service honoring a deceased senator with a political rally clearly offended many who attended, as well as many television viewers. Part of the violation of appropriateness also involved poor audience adaptation. Many who attended the public memorial were prominent Republican colleagues and state officials. This leads to a consideration of Aristotle's perspective on adaptation.

Audience Adaptation and a Common Universe of Ideas

Aristotle assumed that listeners in different contexts would hold ideas in common. That is, one could assume that it was likely that certain types of appeals would be effective in gaining the attention of many audience members. In Book I, Chapter 5, of the *Rhetoric* (pp. 37–38), Aristotle makes one of the earliest statements about the approach–avoidance tendencies of individuals. He proposed that speakers should promote things that bring happiness and speak against those that destroy or hamper happiness. Aristotle's popular appeals included having one's independence, achieving prosperity, enjoying maximum pleasure, securing one's property, maintaining good friendships, producing many children, enhancing one's beauty, attending to one's health, fostering one's athletic nature, and promoting one's

Paul Wellstone

Hardly anyone knew his name when he began his campaign for the Senate in 1990. He had no money to speak of, no experience in politics. He traveled the state in a rickety green school bus, wore a work shirt and jeans, wrote his own speeches and stayed in people's homes rather than hotels. Twelve years later, everyone in Minnesota and everyone of importance in Washington knew who Paul Wellstone was: a principled fighter for liberal causes, a maverick in a Senate known more for collegiality than fierce independence, a sworn enemy of big-money politics—he championed a ban on gifts to lawmakers by special interests, much to the annoyance of many of his colleagues—and a reliable friend of the dispossessed and the environment. He voted against giving two presidents named George Bush the authority to wage war against Iraq. His was a consistent voice for the poor and against what he regarded as adventurism, the kind of voice that seemed to have gone out of style more than 30 years ago.

The Senate lost that voice yesterday when a twin-engine private plane carrying Mr. Wellstone and seven others went down in freezing rain and light snow in northern Minnesota. All eight were killed. That the dead included Mr. Wellstone's wife and daughter made the loss all the more searing. Yesterday's events were similar to those that claimed the life two years ago of Mel Carnahan, the Missouri governor and Senate candidate who was killed in a light plane crash just three weeks short of Election Day. Mr. Carnahan's name remained on the ballot and he outpolled the incumbent, John Ashcroft. His widow, Jean Carnahan, was then appointed to the Senate seat, and Mr. Ashcroft became President Bush's attorney general.

Mr. Wellstone's death just 11 days before the election threw the battle for the Senate into uncharted territory. Before yesterday, Democrats held control by a single seat, and Mr. Wellstone's re-election was not a sure thing. His opponent is a popular and moderate former mayor of St. Paul, and Mr. Wellstone had not helped himself by retreating from repeated pledges not to seek a third term. In characteristically blunt fashion, however, he said he had broken his promise because, with a Republican president and the Senate up for grabs, "now is not the time for me to walk away."

It was not immediately clear what the Democrats would now do to mount a campaign. They have until four days before the election to name a replacement. The only clear outcome was that the Senate had lost a decent and compassionate man.

FIGURE 3.1 This *New York Times* editorial is an excellent example of epideictic discourse praising Senator Paul Wellstone's contributions after his tragic death in a plane crash.

fame, honor, and virtue. A majority of these appeals remain effective today. (Aristotle would have done well in making infomercials!) Most elements of more modern needs approaches, such as Maslow's hierarchy of needs, are found here. Aristotle clearly recognized that many of the things in this list are external and that others are internal.

In later parts of the *Rhetoric,* Aristotle provides examples of persuasive devices with broad appeal to audiences. In Book II, Chapter 21, he introduces a maxim that is much like one of our common sayings today: "Fool, who slayeth the father and leaveth his sons to avenge him" (p. 138). He advocates the use of the maxim for listeners who love to hear universal truths in which they believe. In essence, Aristotle is advising the persuader to reinforce what the audience already believes. He says, "The orator has therefore to guess the subjects on which his

Minneapolis Star-Tribune guest editorial:
The Wellstone funeral
Friday, November 1, 2002

Before Minnesota's Senate campaign truly gets restarted, there's the matter of Rick Kahn to clear up. Kahn, described as Paul Wellstone's best friend, gave a speech at Tuesday night's memorial that has Republicans enraged and people of every political stripe shaking their heads.

Minnesotans need to think clearly about what happened, then try to put it aside. They need to focus on the few days of a campaign that should be respectful and tightly focused on issues of substance. What happened had nothing to do with either Norm Coleman or Walter Mondale, and the controversy should not be allowed to overshadow their short but crucially important campaign.

In the second half of his speech, Kahn strayed from memorializing Wellstone. For 10 to 15 minutes he turned the gathering into a political rally for the Wellstone legacy. It was inappropriate, but more to the point, it was irrational. Kahn appeared so caught up in grief, loss and anger that he lost his way. What else can explain his implor-ing Republicans, whom he individually named, to lay down their political swords and join in keeping the Wellstone legacy alive in Tuesday's election? The idea is such an emotional fantasy—and so *not* in keeping with the actual Wellstone legacy—that it could only have come from a person wracked with grief and pain.

However they were intended, Kahn's words were an affront to the Republican candidate, Norm Coleman, and those who support him. We can understand Kahn's state of mind, but we must repudiate his message. There can be no capitulation in this race. Coleman and Mondale owe Minnesotans a vigorous contest of ideas. Then, come Tuesday's election, those who believe Coleman would be the superior U.S. senator from Minnesota should proudly cast their votes for him. The same holds true for those who believe Mondale would do the best job. As for those who have lost a champion in Paul Wellstone, only they can decide their course.

FIGURE 3.2 This guest editorial in the *Minneapolis Star-Tribune* demonstrates how inappropriate use of epideictic discourse may result in considerable backlash.

hearers really hold views already, and what those views are, and then must express, as general truths, these same views on these same subjects" (p. 139). This section of the book causes many contemporary readers of the *Rhetoric* to question whether all of Aristotle's talk about morality is merely a cover for how to manipulate others.

Types of Proof

Aristotle developed his theory of persuasion by observing many persuaders at work in Athens—in the law courts, the government, and the marketplace. In the *Rhetoric,* Aristotle focused on what he called the artistic proofs or appeals that the persuader could create or manipulate. For example, persuaders can create emotional moods by their choice of words and images and can heighten the mood by varying their vocal tone, rate, and volume. Inartistic proofs reflect elements that are not under the control of the persuader (for example, situational factors such as the place where the persuasion occurs or the speaker's height or physical attractiveness). Recall from Chapter 1 that Aristotle identified three major types of artistic proof—ethos, pathos, and logos—which remain remarkably current in today's world. It is useful to explore them more closely.

Ethos and Credibility. The first element in Aristotle's theory of persuasion, ethos, has several dimensions. Before actually making a persuasive presentation, a persuader is perceived in some way by the audience. Even if the persuader is totally unknown to the audience, members will draw certain conclusions about him or her based on what they see—the speaker's body type, height, complexion, movements, clothing, grooming, and so on. In cases in which the persuader is known, he or she may have a reputation for, say, honesty, knowledge, experience, or a sense of humor. The same kinds of observations about ethos can be made regarding various political candidates and even products and/or services.

Additional characteristics become apparent as the speech is delivered that add to or detract from ethos—for example, vocal quality, cleverness of argument, word choice, eye contact, and gestures. More recently, researchers have added other dimensions including sincerity, trustworthiness, expertise, and dynamism or potency. Press releases, image makeovers, flattering photography, and a host of other devices can be used to develop a speaker's ethos to an audience. The speaker might deliberately make eye contact with various audience members or might make direct eye contact with the television cameras because eye contact can be an important element in whether a person is believed. And trust and credibility are particularly big issues today in the wake of the Wall Street accounting scandals. There is not only a crisis in trust involving any financial information coming from corporations but also a loss of confidence in what the heads of corporations have to say (see Figure 3.3).

At times, one element in an individual's ethos may outperform the others. Sometimes the person's reputation can be the critical factor. For example, Bill Clinton's long-standing reputation as a womanizer dogged him throughout his political career. Yet many questioned the credibility of his accusers Gennifer Flowers and Paula Jones because each of these women had much to gain from the publicity. The account of state trooper Danny Ferguson, who

FIGURE 3.3 The loss of public trust in corporate financial information is illustrated here. All numbers cannot be believed.

(© 2002 Tribune Media Services, Inc. Redistribution in whole or in part prohibited.)

recalled advances toward Jones made by Clinton when he was governor of Arkansas, was more believable for many. Even more potent was an interview with Kathleen Willey, a former White House volunteer, on *60 Minutes,* in which she discussed the details of an alleged sexual advance made by President Clinton in 1993. Perhaps her credibility was enhanced because she was a reluctant witness in the Paula Jones lawsuit. The remarkable thing is that Clinton continued to be popular and won two terms as president even with many of these allegations circulating. His charisma still attracted people to him despite his apparently overactive libido.

Ethos, however, comprises many complex elements that are not always predictable. For example, former Speaker of the House Newt Gingrich was unfaithful to his wife even as he was criticizing President Clinton for being immoral; the same was true of Robert Livingston, who was to become speaker of the house following Gingrich. Neither of these men was able to sustain his political career after the damaging information became known. A bizarre aspect of the story is that much of the information about the sexual escapades of these conservative Republicans was brought to the public's attention by the publisher of *Hustler,* Larry Flynt—

hardly a credible character. Yet much of the information could be independently verified. Even the *National Enquirer* has been the source of breaking news such as the affair of Jesse Jackson, evidence that helped solve the murder of Ennis Cosby, and shoe print evidence in the O. J. Simpson case. In sum, even those with questionable reputations can be convincing when they have facts that withstand scrutiny. When a person's ethos is in question, it rarely happens without also creating an emotional reaction. This leads to the next type of artistic proof.

Pathos and the Virtues. Pathos relates to the emotions and involves appeals to the passions or the will. In today's terms, pathos equates with psychological appeals and is aimed at our emotional hot buttons. Persuaders assess the emotional state of the audience and design artistic appeals aimed at those states.

The following list describes several of the deep-seated values, or virtues, cited by Aristotle as appeals to the emotions. As you consider them, try to think of contemporary examples for each.

- Justice involves respect for laws, people's right to have what belongs to them, tolerance, and related attributes.

- Prudence relates to how a person gives advice or demonstrates good judgment. For example, former baseball star Pete Rose seemed to lack prudence, or good judgment, whereas a seemingly humble star like Nolan Ryan is thought of as having good judgment—as being prudent.

- Generosity involves having an unselfish attitude at home, at work, in the community, in government, or in international relations. This virtue helps inform the ongoing debate about America's role in the world. Are we to be the world's police force? How much leadership can we give to efforts to save the environment?

- Courage means doing what is right even under pressure—not backing away from unpopular issues or positions. An example might be the president's veto of a popular bill because it runs against some principle of fairness or wisdom.

- Temperance includes self-restraint and moderation in all areas of human conduct. The temperate person is in control of his or her emotions and desires. Such people are open-minded and willing to consider all sides of a situation, and they try to empathize with the other person's point of view.

- Magnanimity reflects a willingness to forgive and forget, a desire to seek ways to better the world, and an ability to rise above pettiness. The ability to be as gracious in losing as in winning is a sign of magnanimity. Politicians, athletes, and others must appear magnanimous; that is, when they win, they compliment their opponents, and when they lose, they congratulate and vow to support the winner.

- Magnificence is the ability to recognize and be committed to the better qualities in human beings and to encourage them. History abounds with examples of magnificent persuaders— Washington, Lincoln, Eleanor Roosevelt, Crazy Horse, Martin Luther King, Jr., and others—whose magnificence came from the ability to encourage the best in themselves and others.

- Wisdom is more than mere knowledge or intelligence; it is also associated with good judgment, character, and experience.

This list of virtues is hardly exhaustive, but it points to the potential kinds of emotional arguments. It also shows that this "artistic" form of proof still works in our current technocracy.

Logos and Places of Argument. Logos refers to appeals to the intellect, or to the rational side of humans. It relies on the audience's ability to process statistical data, examples, or testimony in logical ways and to arrive at some conclusion. The persuader must predict how the audience will do this and thus must assess their information-processing and conclusion-drawing patterns. Aristotle and others frequently used reasoning called an enthymeme. Aristotle describes it as following the form of what the study of logic would call a syllogism (see Book II, Chapter 22).

Syllogisms begin with a major premise such as this:

The chemical PCB is dangerous to humans.

This major premise is then associated with a minor premise:

Cattle raised near chemical plants absorb PCB.

This, in turn, leads to the conclusion:

Cattle raised near chemical plants are dangerous to humans.

Of course, the persuader then offers a course of action for consumers, such as identifying the origins of the meat they eat or perhaps avoiding beef altogether. In any case, to use this kind of proof, the persuader must predict how the audience will logically assemble the information. In Book II, Chapter 22, Aristotle also recommends that the persuader be an expert on the facts in order to use such reasoning effectively:

The first thing we have to remember is this. Whether our argument concerns public affairs or some other subject, we must know some, if not all, of the facts about the subject on which we are to speak and argue. Otherwise, we can have no materials out of which to construct arguments. (p. 140)

Clearly, being able to identify these patterns of information processing, design arguments, and use evidence effectively will result in artistic proofs. You can find logical appeals operating in your daily life. Your parents, for example, might use data about the cost of tuition, living in a dormitory, and travel to and from college to persuade you to attend one school as opposed to another. Politicians use statistics and examples to persuade you to believe in a certain view or to vote in a certain way. Advertisers use graphs and tables to persuade you to smoke their cigarette, drive their car, or add a new appliance to your home. In each case, the persuader is betting that you will process the information logically and predictably. In each case, as well, there has been a cocreation of meaning using the syllogistic form of reasoning. Yet the form of the argument

may not appear to you to be exactly like the one in the previous example. Consider a syllogism that Aristotle quotes: "Thou hast pity for thy sire, who has lost his sons: Hast none for Oeneus, whose brave son is dead?" (p. 145). Sometimes the language does not follow the format exactly. Let's consider this example again in contemporary language:

You have pity for a father whose sons have died. (major premise)

The brave son of Oeneus is dead. (minor premise)

You should have pity for Oeneus. (conclusion)

So, syllogisms may leave out one of the premises or have parts in slightly different order. Nevertheless, the pattern of reasoning is there.

Much contemporary market research attempts to identify consumers' major premises. With these in mind, marketers design products, packaging, and advertising that effectively develop "common ground" and hence the cocreation of persuasive meaning. Knowing how effective appeals to common ground are and, equally important, how disastrous not knowing it can be crucial. For example, the lead author once worked for an agency that was advising a client about a new contact lens. The client manufactured contact lenses that could change the wearer's eye color. The agency asked several questions: Who are the typical customers for this product—males or females? Which media would you choose to reach these customers—cable television or radio or . . . ? On what programs would you advertise—health and exercise shows or . . . ? The agency advised the client to conduct some market research to learn about the current users. The research revealed that the largest portion of the customer pool was made up of black males. An intuitive guess about users would probably have overlooked this market segment and thus would have resulted in wasted advertising dollars and a failed advertising campaign. The client decided to use black radio stations and direct mail based on lists of subscribers to magazines such as *Jet* and *Ebony,* which target black readers.

The ancient concept of the syllogism remains a foundation of persuasion, especially when coupled with audience involvement—the cocreation of proof or meaning. This shared creation forms what Aristotle called "common ground." Aristotle thought that a good way to find such common ground was to categorize the places or topics of argument *(topoi).* Persuaders identify these "places" and try to determine whether they will work for a particular audience. Let's look at a few of these places as Aristotle saw them. Again, you will probably find them remarkably contemporary.

- *Arguments as to degree, or "more or less."* For example, will it profit me more or less to sell my inventory at reduced rates rather than to store it? Will candidate A be more or less trustworthy than candidate B? Are Guess jeans more or less durable than Levis? Are they more or less fashionable than Levis? Is durability more or less important than style or brand?

- *Arguments of possibility versus impossibility.* For example, is it possible for Third World countries to live in ecologically sound ways? Will the Internet and email cause the U.S. Postal Service to go out of business?

- *Past fact:* Has an event really occurred? This tactic is very important in the courts, where it must be proved that a crime actually occurred. Similarly, a corporation that is trying to decide whether it should close a factory needs to look at past facts: Was the factory profitable? Was it efficient? Was it environmentally sound?

- *Future fact:* Is something likely to occur in the future? This differs from the argument of possibility versus impossibility in that it focuses on probabilities, not possibilities. For example, how likely is it that we will be able to shop for clothing (including trying on various articles) using "virtual reality" in the near future? Is it wise to invest in that technology?

- *Size:* Is something important or unimportant? Will it result in a significant or insignificant change? For example, will a large or a small amount of our leisure time be consumed by surfing the net? To what degree will email be integrated into college instruction?

Yet Aristotle recognized that it was not simply the structure of the syllogism, but the language used within it. His focus on language merits our attention.

In the search box of InfoTrac College Edition, using the key word option, type in the title of the article "Attorney Persuasion in the Capital Penalty Phase: A Content Analysis of Closing Arguments" by Mark Costanzo and Julie Peterson. Do you think the use of pathos is equally appropriate for the prosecution and the defense in the summation of a criminal trial?

The Potency of Language

Aristotle recognized that carefully chosen language is part of a successful persuasive strategy. He promoted the use of emotional expression because it makes the audience share feelings with the speaker (Book III, Chapter 7). Yet emotional language has to be appropriate to the context and situation. Moreover, he understood that more emotionally charged language can be used when the audience shares similar feelings about the topic. He emphasized the importance of metaphors and similes in conveying new ideas and facts through images of the familiar: "It is from the metaphor that we can best get hold of something fresh" (p. 186). However, not just any metaphor would do for Aristotle; rather, the metaphor needed to be so lively or active that it made those hearing it actually see things. Of course, metaphors can be overdone. Like any other form of language, Aristotle would maintain that the metaphor must be appropriate.

Locate the article "The Arctic Persuasion" by William Powers by typing the title in the search box of InfoTrac College Edition and checking key words for the search. How are the potent powers of language emphasized by Aristotle being used by both sides of the Arctic controversy?

In sum, Aristotle's principles of persuasion are remarkably contemporary and provide the foundation for modern persuasion research. Granted, there are portions that have little relevance today and that reflect values that our society does not embrace.

Nevertheless, there are few books over a hundred years old that remain so relevant. Other issues raised by Aristotle will be addressed at the appropriate points. Now we must turn to other points of view.

DIALECTICAL AND EPISTEMOLOGICAL APPROACHES

Although the contemporary practice of persuasion owes a large debt to Aristotle, there are other perspectives on how we come to know things that guide our decision processes. Frankly, Aristotle makes some people uncomfortable. To illustrate a central problem with Aristotle, let's start with a story based on a true experience:

> Having forgotten a hat to keep off the rain, a certain professor visited an amazing hat store in New Orleans called Meyer the Hatter. As he was trying on a reasonably priced Stetson, the salesperson said to him, "Boy, that hat sure looks good on you." He dismissed the comments because he thought that the salesperson would say anything to make the sale. The professor was not sure if others would think the hat looked good. The professor recalled a conversation with his stepdaughter, a retail salesperson, who said she usually told customers whatever she thought they wanted to hear—regardless of whether they actually looked good. A female customer at the hat store then commented that she also liked the way the hat looked on the professor. The professor asked, "Why?" She said, "I like how that hat brings out your eyes." The professor bought the hat.

What was the ambivalence that the professor faced? He did not know whether the comments of the salesperson were genuine because the salesperson had something to gain through the sale of the hat. He considered the comments of the other customer

to be more genuine or authentic because that person didn't work there and had nothing to gain. But he was skeptical of whether the salesperson was being genuine and truthful or was being manipulative. This is a central issue for the way many people interpret Aristotle. His discussion of ethos often makes it seem that he was more concerned about the *appearance* of being believed than with what the person actually believed. Thus, Aristotle's advice regarding the adaptation of messages to the audience can be seen as involving manipulation. The *Rhetoric* does not give as much consideration to establishing truth as Aristotle's mentor, Plato, did through the dialectical method. It is difficult to know whether Aristotle made a conscious break with his mentor or whether the *Rhetoric* simply should be considered in a larger context. One could interpret Aristotle's opening line, "Rhetoric is the counterpart of dialectic," to mean that his advice in the *Rhetoric* needs to be considered in conjunction with the pursuit of truth through use of dialectics. We simply cannot know which interpretation is correct, but the issues raised by Plato's dialectical method remain important today.

Surprisingly, many people have more trouble with Plato's approach to truth than with Aristotle's lack of attention to it. Plato believed that as humans we do not see absolute truth directly, but only glean indirect images, glimpses, or shadows of the truth. So, we do not see the whole truth. Through dialogue with others, truth becomes clearer. Discovering truth through dialogue, however, is not sufficient for those who believe that truth is absolute.

Plato devoted a lot of attention to the concept of truth. In one of his Socratic dialogues, the *Gorgias,* he expressed little respect for rhetoric as it was commonly used because he viewed it as a skill used more to flatter, appease, disguise, or deceive than to discover truth and identify the important things in life. Plato presented the ideal speaker, in Socrates' dialogues with Phaedrus, as one who seeks the best interests of his listeners rather than advancing his own self-interests. Plato clearly articulated that the facts of the situation do make a difference. Consider one dialogue between Socrates and Phaedrus. Socrates asked Phaedrus to assume that he had convinced Phaedrus to buy a horse and take it to war. But assume that neither Socrates or Phaedrus really knew what a horse looked like, though Socrates did know that Phaedrus believed a horse was a tame animal with long ears. Yet a donkey also has long ears and could be very functional in a war. So imagine that someone took that donkey to war instead of a horse, and the donkey performed well. Then imagine that after the war Socrates made a speech detailing the merits of the donkey, but instead called it a horse. Socrates pointed out that merely calling a donkey a horse does not make it a horse (Plato, 1937, p. 263). So, Plato did not believe that all truth was relative. There were material facts that one simply could not ignore.

Plato used dialogue instead of the public speaking model articulated by Aristotle. His dialogues begin with a question in which terms are defined. Hypotheses are then introduced through answers to these questions, and the answers are cross-examined. In the end, there is typically some resolution resulting in changes, with each side of the issue demonstrating increased understanding of each position. Clearly, Plato's dialectical approach involved closer relationships in which ethics cannot be separated from the techniques communicators used. Moreover, it promotes discovery, community, and increased emphasis on the human experience.

SCOTT'S EPISTEMIC APPROACH

Although Plato's voice has not been silenced entirely in discussions of persuasion, contemporary persuasion texts give more consideration to Aristotle. Some, however, do uphold the notion that rhetoric is a major way we come to know about our world. Rhetorician Robert L. Scott (1993) bemoans the dominance of the Aristotelian tradition: "In general what may be called 'Aristotelian instrumentalism' has dominated thinking about rhetoric and the teaching of it. . . . I am suggesting that the dominant attitude . . . should be drastically altered" (p. 121). Scott objects to truth being presented as an

objective package, as if it were a possession or commodity. He suggests that truth is never certain, whether in the realm of science or public affairs. For Scott, rhetoric is a process of constant discovery in which truth is seen as moments in "human, creative processes" (p. 133). This perspective is known as epistemic. In other words, rhetoric is a way of coming to know about things. Although truth can be stable at times, it cannot be static in an ever-changing world. Many of these discoveries come during our rhetorical encounters with others. These instances when we see something in a new way are often called epiphanies or "eureka moments." Scott's perspective has many similarities to that of existential thinkers, who argue that truth is experienced in the lived moment and it cannot be "possessed" forever. Think about the happiest times in your life. How long did you experience those feelings of happiness? Such moments are often short-lived even for athletes winning a championship. When a sports team wins a major championship, obnoxious journalists dampen the elation of the moment by immediately asking whether the team can repeat.

Seeing persuasion as a process of constant discovery is a key principle for students of persuasion to learn. This perspective clearly shows us why simply learning a set of tactics of persuasion is not enough. It seems as if this more personal approach to persuasion should have prevailed as the preferred method. Why, then, has Aristotle's influence on persuasion been greater? That question cannot be answered with certainty, but with regard to persuasion in the modern era, many mass communication media such as television, radio, newspapers, and direct mail do not permit much interaction. Aristotle's methods can be adapted more readily to marketing and advertising, which are more efficient methods for reaching consumers. Beyond the efficiency issue is the issue of certainty. It is much harder to explain or sell an approach that cannot speak with certainty. That is why sound bites are so important for the presentation of political candidates in the media. This does not mean, however, that we should ignore the lessons from Plato and Scott. Truth and trust are clearly in vogue in the aftermath of some of the biggest ethics scandals we have ever seen in corporate life. Sound bites will not be sufficient means to promote trust. Alternatives such as narrative theory, however, offer tangible ways to develop such trust.

Search for Robert L. Scott's article titled "Response to Lyne, Hariman, and Greene" by typing the author's name and the title in the search box of InfoTrac College Edition and checking key words for the search. Have his views about the epistemic nature of rhetoric changed much over the years?

FISHER'S NARRATIVE APPROACH

In recent years, narrative approaches have been gaining support as an alternative to traditional Aristotelian thinking. At the core of such perspectives is the belief that the drama or story is the most powerful and pervasive metaphor that humans can use to persuade and explain events. In his particularly comprehensive narrative theory, communication theorist Walter Fisher (1987) suggests that all rational (and perhaps some irrational) behavior can be understood using the story, drama, or narrative as an analytical device by casting the persuasive event in narrative terms: Who are the persons in the narrative? What do they do in it? Why do they do what they do? What are the results? For example, in an advertisement, a slightly balding man is told that Rogaine can stop hair loss and even regrow hair in four out of five cases. He responds, "With my luck, I'll be the one out of five where it doesn't work." The advertiser then tells the man that if Rogaine doesn't stop his hair loss to his satisfaction within a certain period Rogaine will totally refund his purchase. We see the man some time later with a full head of hair, saying, "Boy! Am I ever glad I at least tried!" Is the narrative believable, and if so, is the story persuasive?

Fisher maintains that narratives succeed (that is, persuade), or fail depending on whether they have coherence and fidelity. Coherence refers to the way the story hangs together and thus has meaning or impact. Fidelity relates to the probability or believability of a story.

With a coherent story, almost everyone understands its premises or the points it tries to make. The story is told artistically, and it is believable. Coherence relies on the degree to which the story is consistent. Consistency means that the story is logically organized or told. In other words, we generally don't know the outcome of the story or the fate of the characters until the story is complete (that is, it has a beginning, middle, and end in the most traditional cases). In consistent narratives, the characters have good reasons for doing what they do, and the impact of the situation or setting of the story also makes sense. For example, the narratives told by tobacco company officials regarding their lying when testifying about the known effects of nicotine and the industry's manipulation of the substance boomeranged because of a lack of narrative coherence. The narratives about battery life acted out by the Energizer bunny succeeded because they had consistency—he always kept going and going. Successful political candidate "stories" are usually consistent, whereas unsuccessful (and hence unpersuasive) stories or narratives aren't because the characters in them wouldn't act that way in real life.

Coherence also refers to the degree to which the narrative matches, "fits" with, or resonates with other, similar narratives that we have heard, believed, and remembered. It seems complete; there are no loose ends. This means that a candidate's video biography matches or is similar to the story or stories of prior nominees. A fund appeal to provide food and medicine to starving refugees from a war or natural disaster fits with similar appeals made in other circumstances. The narrative or story used in a shampoo advertisement shows the characters having problems or experiences similar to those in the "real world." For example, in a shampoo ad, a boy meets a girl in an elevator; the girl notices dandruff on his blazer and ignores him; the boy's boss tells him about Head and Shoulders; he uses the brand that night; the boy sees the girl in the elevator the next day, and this time she notices him. How typical is this kind of event in the real world?

Characterological coherence refers to the degree to which the characters in the narrative are believable. The portrayal of Hannibal "the Cannibal" Lecter by Anthony Hopkins in *Silence of the Lambs* is a good example—he is bone-chillingly believable. In looking at TV advertising, we might ask how often the person giving the endorsement actually uses the product.

Fidelity in a narrative is similar to coherence but focuses more on the reliability or truthfulness of the story—does the story "ring true"? It presents a rationale or "logic of good reasons" (Fisher, 1987) for the setting, plot, characters, and outcome of the narrative. Fisher gives us some benchmarks of narratives that have good fidelity: (1) They deal with human values that seem appropriate for the point or moral of the story and for the actions taken by the characters; (2) the values seem to lead to positive outcomes for the characters and are "in synch" with our own experiences; and (3) the values form an ideal philosophy or vision for our future.

Persuasive narratives cut across a broad expanse of human behavior. For example, they can be applied to topics as lofty as religious values and as sordid as child pornography. They can be applied to both logical and emotional causes. They appeal to our native imagination and feelings. Further, they have an easy access code in that, like silent movies, they are easy to understand.

Narratives can also form communities of identification that together lead to a common worldview. Because of this, narratives have been a central part of most if not all ideological movements throughout history. For example, America's founding fathers promoted a narrative of freedom, and pro-life advocates tell a narrative of the sanctity of life and of the viciousness of the villain—the abortionist—who is never depicted as having any redeeming characteristics. Thus, he (and in the narratives, it is always a he) uses his forceps to crush the skull of the fetus and then snips it from the mother and sucks the remains out, tossing them into the garbage. Such images solidify the pro-life community of understanding. In contrast, pro-choice advocates tell narratives of the situation before abortion was legal in all states, when women were maimed and killed in back-alley abortions.

Narratives are one of the most powerful persuasive tactics available. At times, good stories may counter a lot of facts. Fisher's narrative theory helps us understand this, and Kenneth Burke's work, which is considered in a later chapter, makes many of these points as well. The narrative form of persuasive strategy will likely continue to pervade human affairs in the future. As we proceed with our study of persuasive reception and responsibility, we will encounter other narrative theories. The key point here is that you should never underestimate the value of a good story that resonates with its hearers.

Access InfoTrac College Edition, and enter the words "narrative theory" in the search box using the key word option. Also include the name "Padgett" in the search box to find the entry by Dan Padgett and Douglass Allen in the *Journal of Advertising,* and discover how narrative theory is used to create ads for service-related brands.

POWER-ORIENTED PERSPECTIVES

Challenges to the authority and power of the dominant culture is the central theme running through the final group of perspectives covered in this chapter. These approaches allow us to look at a persuasive situation from the position of groups who are not in power. This group of theories has great utility in constructing defensive strategies against positions that are considered abusive. These perspectives also offer reasons why some persuasive campaigns have failed with groups who are not in the majority.

Many people do not understand why traditional perspectives on persuasion are being attacked. After all, many of the forms of persuasion we use today have been in use for centuries. Some groups believe that they have been ignored or silenced by the dominant culture, which in the United States has been a white male power structure. Some variation of the following argument is usually articulated: Traditional forms of persuasion have been the tools of the powerful to maintain control over those without power. At the surface level, there is little question that the foundations of persuasion were established among the privileged class. Aristotle was a member of the privileged class and encouraged the use of wealth. In Book I, Chapter 5, he says wealth comprised "plenty of coined money and territory; the ownership of numerous, large, and beautiful estates; also the ownership of numerous and beautiful implements, live stock, and slaves. All these kinds of property are our own, are secure, gentlemanly, and useful" (p. 39). A lifestyle such as Aristotle describes is out of the reach of many in society—and it was in his day as well. Part of the critique of traditional persuasion is that people (or groups) of privilege who attempt to persuade others who have been pushed to the margins of society cannot meaningfully engage those who are not privileged. The argument is that most of the elite cannot really understand what it is like to live in poverty or to suffer the humiliation that the disadvantaged feel. Despite the substantial progress effected by civil rights legislation, it is very difficult, if not impossible, for those who are white to fully understand the constant assaults on the dignity of persons of color, for whom advantage is usually assumed to be due to preference given because of their skin color rather than their competence. Similarly, white males in positions of power find it hard to identify with the struggle of women to be respected for their intelligence and competence. We now turn to several perspectives on ways to challenge the dominant culture.

Social Movements
and the Rhetoric of Protest

The perspectives in this chapter have focused on situations in which the rules of society promote reason and choice. Social movements, however, play by different rules, with confrontation as a key strategy. Persuading people to make a major social change is an extremely difficult task—particularly when it forces them to admit that they hold beliefs that are wrong. Political systems create and enforce rules and laws that tend to favor keeping the systems as they are. Years after African Americans and other persons of color were given the right to vote, they

still were not allowed to vote in many states. Stewart Burns (1990) details how African Americans in the early 1960s accounted for nearly half of the population in Mississippi but for only 5 percent of registered voters. African Americans who wished to register to vote were often given difficult tests that they failed and so were deemed unqualified to vote. Such systems are more likely to act to maintain the status quo than to change things radically. This means, for instance, that it is increasingly difficult to unseat incumbents in Congress, with incumbents winning reelection over 90 percent of the time in recent years. Moreover, things like constitutions and bylaws of governments and organizations are highly resistant to change. For example, changing the U.S. Constitution by proposing an amendment is very hard to do—no amendment has been ratified since 1971, when the right to vote was given to those who were as young as age eighteen. Thus, forces outside of the government often act as a catalyst for societal change.

Traditional Movement Studies

In 1952, rhetorical scholar Leland Griffin proposed that a shift was needed in the study of communication to focus on movements rather than merely important individuals. He suggested that a movement study should examine a situation in which people have become dissatisfied with their environment, desire change, and seek to alter their environment—preferably through persuasion rather than by force. It is beyond the scope of this chapter to detail the various approaches of the hundreds of movement studies, but it is useful to look at a few issues relevant to the challenge to the perspectives of those in power by those who are not in power.

First, the issue of identity emerges throughout the discussion of social movements. Public address scholar James Andrews (1980) argued that "a collective must first be conscious of itself. . . . Groups must define themselves in a positive manner before they can truly become a collective" (p. 279). Further, he suggested that a strategy that denounces "the enemy" may actually serve to bring a protest group together. Second, abstract and complex ideas can often be simplified into potent terms. In this vein, rhetorical critic Michael McGee (1980) discussed the ideograph (ideogram), whereby ideology is communicated through such terms, perhaps using metaphors. The key is funneling a lot of meaning into a few words that define the movement. For example, the term *black power* said a lot about the struggles of many African Americans in the 1960s and is still used today. Yet the core of the movement involves the confrontation and agitation of those in positions of power by those who are not.

Do two separate searches in InfoTrac College Edition. Type "black power" in the search box using the key word option. Do the same for "rethinking black leadership." How is the term "black power" changing, and why are some leaders less willing to embrace it now?

A concise but excellent description of the agitation process is presented by conflict scholars John Waite Bowers and Donovan Ochs (1971). They argued that the power available to agitators is usually much less than that held by those in power. Although the fear created by race and antiwar riots in the 1960s was great, ultimately, those in power were able to use force to quell them, as Mayor Richard Daley did during the Democratic National Convention in Chicago in 1968. Although the threat of violence can be used strategically, Bowers and Ochs maintained that agitators must rely on the power of expertise to get their message out and on referent power to attract people to the cause. Ultimately, a movement must attract a significant mass of people who identify with the cause. Yet some movements, like the American Indian Movement (AIM), achieved significant momentum but never could attract enough of a mass to be a major force. The small number of Native Americans in the United States is probably a limiting factor on a national level, but AIM continues to have influence at the state level in North and South Dakota.

Type the name "Leonard Peltier" in the search box of InfoTrac College Edition using the key word option. Who is Leonard Peltier, and what were people trying to persuade President Clinton to do regarding him? Why do Peltier and

AIM remain so controversial for law enforcement officials today?

A key decision confronting those addressing the need for social change is whether the focus should be on a political solution, with the hope that changes in the political structure will trickle down through society, or whether the focus should be on cultural change, so that the minds of people are transformed to see the world in a different way. For example, there historically was much debate over whether women should invest major effort to obtain the right to vote or whether their energies should be devoted to transforming the minds of people about the place of women in society so that they have equal access to things like education. The right of women to vote became law seventy-two years after it was first seriously proposed at the Seneca Falls Women's Rights Convention in 1848. Choosing a persuasive strategy is complex for a social cause. A focused, clear, and confrontational ideology may draw more dedicated individuals, but fewer individuals overall, to the cause. Less confrontational approaches may draw more individuals but discourage the most ardent. Not all confrontation, however, has been a direct confrontation of words; music played a major role in the anti–Vietnam War protests.

The Anti–Vietnam War Movement

Music was not new to protests in the 1960s, but it was a centerpiece of the antiwar movement. Bob Dylan's "Blowin' in the Wind" became a classic, and Peter, Paul, and Mary's "If I Had a Hammer" was commonly sung by groups of protesters. Such songs built solidarity among the protesters. Antiwar and civil rights sentiments were often joined together in the music of the peace movement. For example, Barry McGuire's 1965 hit "Eve of Destruction" raised several issues with the war. McGuire pointed out that many soldiers were not old enough to vote, but they were placed in the position to kill. He raised the issue of hypocrisy by drawing parallels between racism in the United States and hating communists in Red China. The song proclaimed that people maintained the trappings of religion through their prayers, but practiced hatred against those in their own country. The song clearly articulated that issues regarding the war were linked to other societal issues. Artistically, "Eve of Destruction" was widely criticized, but it was remarkable because it reached beyond college audiences to much of the population. Several songs, however, focused solely on the war.

Using the key word option in InfoTrac College Edition, type in the search box the article title "The Sixties Between the Microgrooves: Using Folk and Protest Music to Understand American History 1963–1973" by Jerome L. Rodnitzky. In addition to providing an excellent introduction to the topic of protest music, he argues that music was also used to support the war. What major type or genre of music generally supported the war?

One of the most pointed protest songs was Country Joe McDonald and the Fish's "Feel Like I'm Fixin' to Die Rag," released in 1965. Verse 4 drove home the message to mothers and fathers:

> You can be the first one on your block
> To have your boy come home in a box.

This song was featured at Woodstock. No musical event has matched the original Woodstock in 1969, where the music and message of protest came through loudly to the nation. Woodstock was billed as three days of "Peace and Music." Jimi Hendrix, Janis Joplin, Joan Baez, Arlo Guthrie, and Santana were among the more than 50 musical acts featured there. Also in 1969, John Lennon provided a popular chant with his "Give Peace a Chance" in addition to his famous "bed-in for peace" with Yoko Ono. Lennon put a fitting end to this era in 1971 with his song "Imagine," in which he concluded, "I hope some day you'll join us, and the world will live as one."

Using the key word option in the search box of InfoTrac College Edition, type in the article "Pop and Avant-Garde: The Case of John and Yoko" by Jon Wiener. What do you think about the way John and Yoko tried to persuade the public?

Music continues as a medium for protest today, but not with the magnitude of impact it had in the Vietnam era. Gangsta rap shares many characteristics of the protest music of the 1960s, but violence against the so-called oppressors is probably more prominent today in works like Ice-T's "Cop Killer":

> I'm bout to dust some cops off!
> COP KILLER, it's better you than me.

Whether such lyrics actually inspire violence against the police is hard to assess, but the hostility toward the establishment is unmistakable. At the same time, as Ice-T demonstrates in his role metamorphosis into a TV actor portraying a police detective, co-optation is always a danger to sentiments of protest found in music.

The use of music as a persuasive tool crosses many contexts today. Large-scale political events and rallies frequently use music to aid persuasion. Major musical benefits such as Farm Aid have attracted hundreds of thousands to the cause of the family farm. The campaign against AIDS and HIV has featured several musical benefits as well.

Other persuasive uses of music have received little attention, such as the singing of slaves before they were granted their freedom. One of the most frequent contexts for music as persuasion is the religious service. Religious movements often use music as a persuasive tool. For example, many Protestant denominations still use music as a means to bring persons to conversion. The use of music in social movements and religious movements does illustrate that there are paths to persuasion that involve the senses and not reason. In this vein, Aristotle's view of pathos is relevant to the discussion of social movements as involving the raising of emotions.

The Women's Movement

Although activism waned after the Vietnam conflict ended, it hardly disappeared. Perhaps the current movement involving the most individuals is the women's movement, which has been very critical of the dominant culture that has suppressed women. Feminist criticism represents one part of the women's movement that attempts to better the lot of women. Feminist scholar Sonja Foss (1996) argues that "feminist criticism has its roots in a social and political movement, the feminist or women's liberation movement, aimed at improving conditions for women" (p. 165). So, feminist theory fits well with the prior discussion of social movements. The term *feminist* does not have one single meaning, but Foss suggests that the different varieties of feminism do share a commitment to end sexist oppression and to change the existing power relations between women and men.

A central issue for feminist theory is that traditional considerations of rhetoric and persuasion have focused on the discourse of males and been dominated by male perspectives. Feminists clearly articulate that history is "his story" and not "her story." Feminist theory questions the exclusion of the consideration of women and the issue of whether women have approached communication situations differently. Important questions are raised about how women are represented—particularly through language, but increasingly through other forms of imagery in mass media. Although feminist scholars do not all agree on the causes of and the remedies for oppression, many American feminists approach the issue as one of emancipation or liberation from female oppression, with a goal of obtaining the power necessary to create their own reality. Feminist scholar Karen Foss and her colleagues (1999) suggest that feminists also generally agree that women's experiences are different from men's, due to differences in socialization and biology. Foss et al. claim that feminists' values of self-determination, affirmation, mutuality, care, and holism are part of a world that is superior to the traditional culture dominated by male values. Finally, says Foss, women's perspectives are not incorporated in our culture, which means that the culture has silenced women. Sonya Foss and Cindy Griffin (1995) attack traditional notions of persuasion and propose an invitational rhetoric that promotes understanding rather than change. Invitational rhetoric resembles Plato's dialogical approach and is clearly not Aristotelian. It also bears a strong resemblance to Scott's proposal that rhetoric is epistemic. There are feminist activists such as rhetorical scholar Karlyn Kohrs

Campbell, however, who reject the assumptions of invitational rhetoric.

Type the name "Karlyn Kohrs-Campbell" in the search box of InfoTrac College Edition using the key word option and read her article "Inventing Women: From Amaterasu to Virginia Woolf." How does her perspective stand in contrast to invitational rhetoric?

Whether or not such feminist values can ever become the dominant values of society, it is important to hear some of the points being made about traditional practices of persuasion. Consider a real event that happened to one of our female neighbors who was looking to purchase a new van. By all accounts, she is very competent at her job and has been in the workforce for twenty years. She is no stranger to managing financial assets. She is married and is doing a great job of parenting two sons. One day she visited a local car dealership to buy a van to replace their old one. She found the male salesperson to be very condescending. He did not want to negotiate price with her and suggested that her husband stop by to talk. This condescending attitude led her to purchase a vehicle from another dealership. Males in sales positions can often be very condescending to women, assuming that women know very little about items like cars and computers. Such insensitive persuasive tactics make little sense because women drive the consumer economy through their purchases much more than do men. On the bright side, we are seeing increasing use of gender-free or gender-equitable language, especially with pronouns—some organizations are getting the message. For example, many see the financial potential of professional women and are directing advertising toward them (see Figure 3.4). Those crafting persuasive messages for women must be attuned to all of the possible meanings being sent. Organizational scholar Gail Fairhurst and consultant Robert Sarr's (1996) recent work on framing demonstrates how our communication can change to be more friendly to women. It is quite possible that future research will more clearly define a style of communication that women prefer. It is already evident that a chauvinistic style is not a wise choice

FIGURE 3.4 Phoenix Wealth Management recognizes the importance of appealing to the intelligence of professional women.

for attempting to persuade women. Bringing about change through understanding does have one very clear implication: Understanding requires a lot of listening. Whether one fully embraces the feminist approach to change or not, persuaders can learn the valuable lesson that change begins with *listening* rather than *telling*.

Recent offerings by the mass media have had a mixed record in terms of fostering a more progressive view of women. Strong images of women are found in prominent news personalities like Barbara Walters, Diane Sawyer, and Leslie Stahl, but the primary anchor jobs on the major networks continue to go to men. Further, the image of women is hurt by such persons as Vanna White on the highly popular, long-lived, but simple-minded game show *Wheel of Fortune*. In addition, questionable persuasion practices in the media may be creating poor ideals for girls and women. The recent book *Deadly Persuasion: Why Women and Girls Must Fight the Addictive Power of Advertising,* by author and filmmaker Jean Kilbourne (2001), details the problematic influence of advertising on the development of the female image. She calls into question many of the poor habits of our culture and the ways in which the media reinforce them. For example, she observes that only thin models are used in TV ads, and breasts are used to sell anything. She refers to an ad with a well-endowed female wearing only a bra, one side of which is held up by a string of monofilament fish line. The caption reads, "Stren—the strongest fishing line in the world." Kilbourne's earlier film *Killing Us Softly* (1979) visually illustrates these problems in advertising.

Type "Jean Kilbourne" or "Killing Us Softly" into the InfoTrac College Edition search box using the key word option. What ethical issues with advertising are raised by her that affect females in particular?

Marxist Theory

Some feminists also embrace a form of Marxist critique because they believe structural changes must be made in society if feminist goals are to be more fully realized. A major feature of Marxist theory is a focus on the inequitable economic system. Marxist theorists address the issue of economic power as it exists in capitalistic countries such as the United States, Japan, and Germany. They believe that those who control the means of production (the bourgeoisie, or power elite) also control and determine the nature of society. Such elite circles were as prominent in Plato and Aristotle's time as they have been in U.S. society. At the time of the Civil War, for example, only 5 percent of those in the South actually owned slaves. And an even a smaller group of these slave owners, numbering about a thousand persons, controlled about 60 percent of the wealth in the South. Such patterns of unequal distribution of wealth are mirrored today in most nations around the world.

The major economic motive in capitalism is profit. Profit is naturally tied to the production and consumption of goods and services. The elite achieve production and profit by exploiting the abilities of the workers (the proletariat), dominating and oppressing them in a variety of ways. For example, the workers are enticed to produce so they can earn wages, which then permits them to purchase the essentials (and later the nonessentials) of life. This produce-earn-purchase cycle creates a never-ending and ever-increasing necessity to work in order to produce and, in turn, earn wages in order to buy products.

How does this all relate to our study of persuasion? Some ways should be fairly obvious. Because political power is needed to maintain economic power, the bourgeoisie must find members willing to run for political office and support their campaigns with money, volunteers, and other things necessary for political persuasion. Marxist critics note how the profit motive and its resulting cycle of consumption are instilled in the citizenry through subtle forms of persuasion. The value of earning money begins in childhood (having a lemonade stand, taking out the garbage to earn an allowance, and so on). This focus continues throughout adulthood (getting a well-paid job, accumulating wages to purchase products, and so on) and is constantly reinforced in the media. As consumers, we should be aware of the persuasive push to obtain material goods supporting this type of culture.

Marxist critics also identify news reporting as promoting the prevailing political and economic ideology. They argue, for instance, that the mass media depict terrorists as outlaws when a perfectly valid argument could be made that terrorists represent the proletariat and that terrorism is merely a strategy to dramatically state an opposing ideology. Moreover, it is increasingly difficult to separate the news from entertainment in current TV programming. Marxist critics of mass media note that news programs contain advertising that fosters capitalism and lends legitimacy to materialistic values. And the media focus on celebrities persuades consumers that financially successful persons (such as Michael Jordan, Serena Williams, Spike Lee, Madonna, and Donald Trump) lead the most interesting lives and that such success should be everyone's goal. The poor are rarely the focus of the news even though the world is filled with them. Television programming is controlled by the power elite, who make certain that the content of entertainment programming reinforces the dominant ideology (capitalism). It is therefore not surprising that the popular reality genre emphasizes glamour and money.

The Marxist critic's role is to unmask the forces of control and to reveal the dominant ideology. To Marxist critics, the mass media in general communicate a view of reality that supports the status quo. Naturally, such critiques are controversial; however, they may be useful if only to alert us to potential persuasive strategies that we as receivers may face.

Radical Movements

Verbal and physical confrontations are used to gain attention for special causes. A key question is whether moving from verbal to physical confrontation is justifiable. Physical confrontation means crossing the line from persuasion to coercion, and the ethics of physical confrontation are currently being debated. Take, for example, groups of radical environmentalists such as Earth First! Is it ethical for such groups to drive spikes into trees knowing that loggers may be seriously injured when their chainsaws hit the spikes? Was it ethical for a radical envi-

ronmental group calling itself ELF to set fire to Two Elks Lodge in Vail to protest the actions of a company they believed to be environmentally unsound? Is it ethical for pro-life extremists to go to residential neighborhoods to harass the families of doctors who perform abortions? They suggest that millions of babies have been murdered and that this justifies such tactics. The question of the use of intimidation, harassment, force, and violence has no easy answer. This tension was reflected in the different philosophies embodied by Dr. Martin Luther King, Jr., and Malcolm X. Dr. King promoted nonviolence as the means for change, whereas Malcolm X advocated armed self-defense and revenge against the Klan and other white terrorists. It is easy to understand Malcolm X's point about not taking abuse from white people any more when we consider that over four thousand black people were lynched in the South in the decades following Reconstruction (see Burns, 1990). These tactics, however, are not persuasion.

Type the article name "Earth First Re-Evaluates Tactics After Activist's Death" in the InfoTrac College Edition search box using the key word option. Are their tactics justifiable?

REVIEW AND CONCLUSION

Aristotle's *Rhetoric* created the dominant pattern of persuasion for centuries, but alternative models in the tradition of Plato view persuasion in a different way. Traditional forms of persuasion have many limitations including the impression that those using them often do so in manipulative ways. Alternatives to the traditional approaches include processes of discovery in which the best interests of all parties are identified. Narratives represent an alternative way of seeing the world—the persuasive nature of a good story should not be underestimated. Power also plays an important role in persuasion. For example, in social movements, persuasion is used by those who have less power in society to address those that have more power. Examples of social movements include the antiwar movement and the women's movement, with the latter informed by feminist critiques of the dominant power structure. The more general Marxist critique represents another way of thinking about the abuse of power in society. Overall, the message of these latter perspectives is that greater attention must be paid to situations in which the interests of some groups are ignored by more powerful others.

QUESTIONS FOR FURTHER THOUGHT

1. Compare President Bush to former President Clinton. In your opinion, which one rated higher on pathos? Logos? Ethos?

2. When you are persuaded, do you tend to pay more attention to people's personal experience with a product or to the product's specifications and performance statistics?

3. What are possible explanations of the failure of AIM to convince most U.S. citizens that great injustices continue to be leveled against Native Americans?

4. Was there a time when African Americans could have used violence legitimately? Was the burning of Two Elks Lodge at Vail by radical environmentalists justified?

5. What is your overall impression of so-called feminists? In your world, is feminism a good or a bad thing? Are the opinions of women really ignored?

6. Can you name any recent music containing lyrics you would label as protest music?

7. Did Ally McBeal represent a positive example of how a feminist would desire women to be portrayed in the media?

8. How is feminism at odds with our traditional understanding of persuasion?

 For online activities, go to the Web site for this book at http://communication.wadsworth.com/larson.

4

Social Scientific Approaches to Persuasion

JOSEPH SCUDDER
Northern Illinois University

A half century ago, a group of Yale researchers drew serious attention to the empirical study of persuasion, thereby changing persuasion theory and practices forever. Not only did *Communication and Persuasion,* by Carl Hovland, Irving Janis, and Harold Kelley (1953), stimulate the study of persuasion in the 1950s, but the personnel associated with this research continue to have an impact on studies of persuasion today. So, the empirical investigation of persuasion is a much younger field of study than the traditional approaches presented in Chapter 3. In contrast to the approaches considered in Chapter 3, these studies often use experimental methods to answer questions about how persuasion works under controlled conditions. Variables are controlled, measured, and analyzed in an attempt to explain how persuasion works in certain circumstances and to predict how it might work in the future. "Empirical" refers to the practice of validating knowledge by experience or ob-

servation. Observation involves watching actual behaviors or gathering self-report information about persuasive experiences. Many of these studies use statistical methods to analyze experimental results, but some use systematic descriptions of persuasive behaviors.

In this chapter, we consider this initial set of ground-breaking studies and trace the unfolding of social scientific study of persuasion up to its most recent empirical developments. Researchers use very different empirical approaches to study persuasion in different contexts. We group theories according to their general orientation rather than by a strict chronology. Most of these orientations have a central theme applicable to persuasion today. Thus, they may contribute to your ability to evaluate the many persuasive messages aimed at you every day by family, friends, advertisers, politicians, government, and mass media.

REINFORCEMENT AND LEARNING THEORIES

In one way or another, much of the persuasion research conducted in social science relies on the assumption that people continue to maintain attitudes, beliefs, and behaviors that they find rewarding and to avoid those that have negative consequences. Some call this the hedonistic principle or the pleasure–pain principle. More generally, this group of theories falls under the umbrella of reinforcement theories. On the surface, reinforcement sounds like a straightforward proposition, but many varieties of persuasion theories have some form of reinforcement at their foundation. Often this reinforcement is simply viewed as learning, with persuasion being a specialized kind of learning. We learn to use symbols associated with language early in life to get things we want. As children, we learn that certain behaviors may get us things we want while other behaviors will often lead to punishment. There are many learning theories, and most contemporary ones are rooted in the behavioral tradition. Their goal is to predict, and ultimately to control, behavior through such methods as conditioning.

In InfoTrac College Edition, using the key word option in the search box, find the article "'I' Seek Pleasures and 'We' Avoid Pains: The Role of Self-Regulatory Goals in Information Processing and Persuasion" by Aaker and Lee. How does this article tie into reinforcement theory?

Skinnerian Behaviorism

Although classical conditioning was well known from the work of Edward Thorndike, John Watson, and Ivan Pavlov before him, B. F. Skinner became the name most identified with behaviorism, beginning in 1938 with his book *The Behavior of Organisms.* Much of Skinner's work remains applicable to the study of persuasion (Skinner, 1957). For example, Skinner identified what he called schedules of reinforcement (see Lefrançois, 1980), which refers to how frequently and for what kinds of behavior positive or negative reinforcers (or rewards or punishments) are presented. When a positive reinforcer is presented for every instance of a specified behavior, Skinner called it a continuous reinforcer. We all behave in conformity with such schedules in our everyday lives. Vending machines, for example, regularly give us items whenever we deposit money (unless they are not functioning properly).

Skinner called his second kind of reinforcement intermittent reinforcement, reflecting the fact that not all correct responses result in reinforcement. Skinner further suggested that these intermittent schedules could occur on either a ratio or an interval basis and that the ratio or interval could be fixed or variable (see Figure 4.1). With a fixed ratio schedule, a correct response is reinforced after a given number of responses; sales based on a flat commission is an example. With a random, or variable, ratio schedule, you cannot predict the number of correct responses resulting in reinforcement (a behavior might be reinforced after the 5th, then 19th, then 50th response, and so on). For example, those who play slot machines do not know how long it will be until their next jackpot. With a fixed interval schedule, reinforcement happens at predictable time intervals (such as every 5 minutes). With a random (variable) interval schedule, the length of time between reinforcements is not predictable (after 5 minutes, then 20 minutes, then 1 minute, then 28 minutes, and so on). Giving verbal rewards to employees for answering the phone within two rings, for routing deliveries efficiently, and for packaging items carefully, Skinner obtained significant improvements in a short time. We could say that he used praise to *persuade* the workers to improve. With regard to education, he demonstrated that rote learning in subjects like mathematics is inferior to doing a problem and learning immediately whether the solution is correct or not. He even developed learning machines that assisted in this process long before computers were widely available for the classroom (see www.bfskinner.org).

Let's look to the world of advertising for an example of how schedules of reinforcement are used or appealed to in order to persuade. Consider the ad for Chivas Regal scotch in Figure 4.2. The six pan-

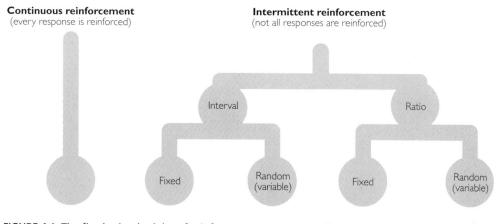

FIGURE 4.1 The five basic schedules of reinforcement: continuous, fixed interval, random interval, fixed ratio, and random ratio. These may be combined in a variety of ways.

(Reprinted by permission of Guy R. Lefrançois and Wadsworth Publishing Co.)

els depict a repeated gesture—the giving or receiving of Chivas on special occasions. The ad is intended for the person who gives Chivas. The advertisers are attempting to create the perception that Chivas is the gift that will always please the recipient, who, in turn, will regard the giver highly. That is the positive reinforcement. In contrast, if viewers or readers see a character, say, being rejected because he or she has bad breath, they will try to avoid this negative situation by using the mouthwash product advertised that cures this problem.

In politics, the persuader's task is to determine voters' patterns of reinforcement. This is why candidates engage in so much polling: to determine whether their speeches, ads, position papers, and so forth make a difference with the voters. As receivers/voters, we need to evaluate the reinforcements politicians offer us: Are the campaign promises positive or negative stimuli? What will we have to do to get the positive reinforcements and to avoid the negative ones? Unlike many other theories, traditional learning theory places less emphasis on the receiver than on the source. In fact, Skinner would not admit to the testing of any black-box constructs—that is, mental states such as drives, motives, instincts, attitudes, values, or beliefs. All of these were unknowable to Skinner because they are

all internal to a person's mind and body—they are inside the black box. Skinner believed that correlation of the subject's behavior with the researcher's manipulation of the environment was the only real observation that mattered.

Social Learning Theory

Albert Bandura's (1977) social learning theory is not as restrictive as Skinnerian behaviorism and does permit concepts at work inside the so-called black box to explain how change occurs. Bandura suggested that humans respond to the continuous interaction between their internal state and the social reinforcements that follow from their behavior toward others. Thus, when we perceive that a certain behavior is not socially rewarding or perhaps even leads to social punishment, we learn to cease it. The reinforcers come from two major sources: (1) external information, in the form of direct or vicarious experience, and (2) internally developed, self-reinforcing systems such as our self-concept.

From the external world, we might get direct rewards or punishment for our behavior and, as a result, discover a social rule and behave accordingly. We learn most of the social rules we follow through

FIGURE 4.2 What reward does this ad imply that purchasers of
Chivas Regal will receive? What is the reward for the recipients?

(Used by permission of General Wine and Spirits Corp.)

direct experience, and, although we acquire many of them in our early years, we continue to discover new social rules throughout our lives. For example, it does not take long for those new to the Internet to discover what is inappropriate and what is not because they will be flamed—that is, sent nasty messages by others—for inappropriate communication. For instance, in moderated discussion groups, it is inappropriate to post content on topics not related to the focus of that group. Similarly, it is usually inappropriate to try to sell others something unless that is the purpose of the discussion. It is also inappropriate to send personal messages to only one member of the group. So, these social rules soon alter the behavior of newcomers. If flaming a person doesn't alter behavior, she or he may be kicked off the list.

Another external source through which we learn acceptable social behavior is role-playing. This is a popular activity for children that many of us carry into adulthood. As adults, we may call this perspective taking, whereby we try to put ourselves in the positions of others to determine what they would do. It is a way that we can try out alternative courses of action. Its value as a decision-making tool is well demonstrated. With regard to the definition of persuasion used in this book, it is a productive way of getting others to see our own viewpoint.

A final external source of reinforcement identified by Bandura is role models. We all admire certain individuals—sports figures, successful businesspersons, spiritual leaders, and others. Because we admire them, we emulate their behavior or take their advice. We get many examples of acceptable behavior from our family and peers. We model our behavior after theirs and in so doing persuade ourselves to value that kind of behavior. Many of these models come to us through the mass media and can persuade large groups to behave in similar ways.

Role models also seem more important at some times in our lives and less important at others. Junior high school is a time when peer role models heavily influence behavior; early adulthood, the much-talked-about "midlife crisis" at age thirty-five or forty, and retirement are others. During each of these periods, we may alter our behavior in conformity to, or sometimes in defiance of, socially approved patterns.

If you want to learn more about role models, access InfoTrac College Edition, and enter the words "role models" in the search engine. Select any of the periodical articles listed.

Activity Theory and Cultural Learning

By 1924, psychologist Lev Vygotsky had produced a developmental perspective of behavior in Russia. This was still a form of reinforcement, but it represented a marked departure from the route behaviorism took in the United States. Vygotsky said that knowledge is mediated; that is, infants begin learning through the association of symbols with the external world, aided by connections that parents or caregivers help them make. In Vygotsky's perspective, the community has a large role in what children learn. For example, when an infant points at something, people say a word associated with the object. Now known as activity theory (see Vygotsky, 1978), Vygotsky's formulation was one of the first developmental explanations of how culture helps shape individuals as they mature. Although his work is not yet well known in the United States, it emphasizes the importance of the symbolic nature of how we come to understand—something often ignored by much of the persuasion research in the behavioral tradition. A very important connection to see in activity theory is that meaning, and in particular the meaning of a symbol, develops not just as an individual issue, but as a cultural one.

Students of persuasion should not overlook the importance of culture in the use of symbols. Take, for example, the symbol of the Confederate flag in the South. Many whites in the South still see the Confederate flag as an integral part of southern heritage—as something important to retain. Some schools, however, have banned clothing bearing this flag. In the letter in Figure 4.3, the Dixie Outfitters clothing company claims that the right to wear the flag is guaranteed by the First Amendment to the Constitution. In contrast, the statement made by the NAACP, shown in Figure 4.4, contains a very different interpretation of the symbol. Suppose you

An Open Letter To Schools
Considering Banning Dixie Outfitters Shirts

We at Dixie Outfitters have been contacted by many students and parents advising us of the banning and/or considered banning of shirts featuring the Confederate Flag and in particular Dixie Outfitters brand shirts at their school.

School Boards and Principals, please be advised that there are currently over 36 lawsuits filed upon school boards for banning confederate flag clothing. Your actions to ban Southern Heritage from your schools put you at risk of similar lawsuits.

We have responded to students/parents requests by putting them in touch with the Southern Legal Resource Center (www.cheta.net/slrc), Black Mountain, N.C. and the American Civil Liberties Union (www.aclu.org), both of which specialize in cases of discrimination against Confederate Americans under the Civil Rights Act of 1964 and freedom of speech as guaranteed by the First Amendment to the Constitution. We are also advising them to stand up for their rights and to fight back at school attempts to deny them of their rights and freedoms.

We understand that your intentions to prohibit the Confederate Flag from being worn at your schools may be to prevent controversy or incidents involving racial issues. There are other remedies available to prevent such incidents or controversy and we respectfully disagree with denying your students their rights as guaranteed by law.

The demonization of the meaning of Confederate flag by special interest groups such as the NAACP and the KKK have little or nothing to do with the real history of the flag. The real truth is that 260,000 Southern men and women died for this flag. The real truth is that the War for Southern Independence had little or nothing to do with slavery or racism.

It is the responsibility of our schools to educate its students about the true history of the War for Southern Independence and the Confederate Flag and not to succumb to those who make trouble because they are uneducated about the facts. Schools should not punish the innocent for being proud of their heritage while upholding ignorance, misinformation and unruliness caused by propaganda disseminated by radical special interest groups for their own purposes.

We hope that your school will reconsider your current policy in regard to the Confederate Flag and allow your students the rights and freedoms enjoyed by all other Americans.

Best Regards,

Dewey Barber
Dixie Outfitters

http://www.dixieoutfitters.com/open_letter.html?
PHPSESSID=6b67434d06b4a8d7be0aaa011ed6c3dc

FIGURE 4.3 The Dixie Outfitters challenge the constitutionality of banning the Confederate flag from the apparel of students.

(Used by permission of www.dixieoutfitters.com.)

are a politician running for office in the South, and several Confederate flags appear in the background as you speak at a rally. What issues arise for you if images appear on television showing you with these flags in the background? Even though you had nothing to do with the presence of these flags, what questions might the media ask about your support for the presence of these flags? It is a no-win situation. Clearly, the deep cultural sentiments associated with some symbols can evoke very mixed responses that persuaders must consider carefully. Outside of the South, most people do not understand the diffi-

Confederate Flag Symbol of Evil and Hate

Kweisi Mfume, President & CEO, the National Association for the Advancement of Colored People, today said the Confederate flag today represents evil in much the same way as the German Swastika.

"The NAACP believes it is time for Mississippi to have a flag that all of its citizens can support. This means one without the symbol of the confederacy," Mfume said. "Confederate flag supporters who are proud of the heritage it represents should understand that this includes the support of slavery and the belief that African Americans are not entitled to all of the protections of the Constitution."

Mfume said Confederate vice president Alexander H. Stephens made this clear in his famous Cornerstone speech in 1861 in Savannah, Georgia. Stephens said: "Our new government is founded upon exactly the opposite idea [in the U.S. Constitution that all men are created equal]; its foundations are laid, its corner-stone rests upon the great truth, that the Negro is not equal to the white man; that slavery—subordination to the superior race—is his natural and normal condition."

Furthermore, Mfume said, defenders of the flag should closely read the Confederate constitution that says: "The citizens of each state shall be entitled to all the privileges and immunities of citizens in the several states, and shall have the right of transit and sojourn in any state of this Confed- eracy, with their slaves and other property; and the right of property in said slaves shall not be thereby impaired."

The NAACP Board of Directors has passed three resolutions condemning the display of the Confederate flag "in or on any public site or space, building, or any emblem." In the resolution passed last year, the Board of Directors noted that the Confederate flag and emblem is often displayed to make a "statement of public policy that continues to be an affront to the sensibilities and dignity of a majority of Americans."

The resolution also noted that groups that advocate white supremacy and opposition to the federal government often use the Confederate symbols.

The NAACP resolutions make no mention of the use of Confederate symbols on private property for private use. Founded in 1909, the National Association for the Advancement of Colored People (NAACP) is the nation's oldest and largest civil rights organization. Its half-million adult and youth members throughout the United States and the world are the premier advocates for civil rights in their communities, conducting voter mobilization and monitoring equal opportunity in the public and private sectors.

http://www.truthout.org/docs_01/0148.NAACP. Flag.htm

FIGURE 4.4 The NAACP sees the Confederate flag as a symbol of evil and hate.

(NAACP 2001 Press Release www.naacp.org.)

culties people in the South are experiencing in trying to reconcile their heritage—whether those individuals are black or white. It is hard for many whites in the South simply to forget about the quarter million lives lost in their secessionist cause. Yet it is equally difficult for those whose ancestors were enslaved to view this flag as a positive symbol of southern heritage. These cultural forces are im- portant considerations for those mounting campaigns in the South. The management of these cultural tensions was very difficult for Democratic Senator Mary Landrieu in her close 2002 race for reelection in Louisiana. Despite being a Democrat, she wanted no part of the symbolism associated with being a liberal candidate. To show that she was not a liberal, she stated that she had voted with

President George W. Bush in over 70 percent of Senate votes. By emphasizing her more conservative voting record to attract more white voters, however, she alienated many persons of color who previously had supported her. Thus, the visits of President Bush and his staff to Louisiana to campaign against her may actually have helped her with some voters. So, politicians do much thinking about the symbolic nature of labels such as liberal, conservative, and moderate. The same symbol can help in one cultural context, but be a detriment in another.

Using the key word option in InfoTrac College Edition, enter the term "Confederate flag." There are several articles about the controversy over students wearing clothing showing the flag. Why is it controversial for students to display the Confederate flag? Now add "NAACP" to the search for "Confederate flag." What is the NAACP, and why is it upset about the Confederate flag?

PERSPECTIVES ON ATTITUDE CHANGE

Despite the impact of Skinner's work, World War II was the catalyst that prompted researchers to question some of the simplistic explanations for complex behavior. The war showed the awesome power of persuasion and propaganda, particularly when conveyed to the masses via the radio and special short-feature films that showed moviegoers how they could contribute to the war effort. After the war, mass persuasion reached the marketplace as well. In politics, religion, and commerce, effective persuaders tapped mass audiences in unprecedented numbers and kinds, thanks to the new media of the postwar years. During the war, psychologist Carl Hovland had investigated the relationship of communication to attitude assessment. The assumption that attitudes could *predict* behaviors was a major break with Skinner's brand of behaviorism. According to research on attitude change, human behavior is guided by many constraints, but among the most important are attitudes. Moreover, contemporary persuasion re-

search still views attitude change as one key to changing behavior. The question for researchers then becomes: What factors in the persuasive process are most important in changing people's attitudes?

The Variable-Analytic Approach

Hovland attempted to isolate many of the factors leading to effective persuasion through an ambitious program of research. Most of this research was collectively done under the auspices of what is now known as the Yale Communication and Attitude Change Program, which included an impressive group of collaborators such as Irving Janis, Harold Kelley, and Norman Anderson. Later, all became major researchers of attitude change in their own right. Instead of attempting to develop a general theory of persuasion, Hovland studied persuasion by systematically considering the main variables related to persuasion through a number of studies focused on single issues—much like the approach used in the natural sciences (see Hovland, 1957). The Yale group assumed that people would change their attitudes if provided with sufficient reinforcement for or evidence in support of the change. In other words, people need motivation to process information that will change their existing attitudes and the actions that flow from those attitudes. The researchers maintained that persuasion passes through a chain of five steps or stages, summarized in Figure 4.5 and detailed below:

1. *Attention:* If persuadees do not attend to a message, they cannot be persuaded by it.

2. *Comprehension:* If persuadees do not understand or comprehend a message, they cannot be persuaded by it.

3. *Acceptance:* If persuadees reject the message after attending to and comprehending it, they will not be persuaded.

4. *Retention:* Most of the time, persuadees have to withhold action for some time after comprehending and accepting the message. They therefore must retain or remember the message until the time comes to act on it.

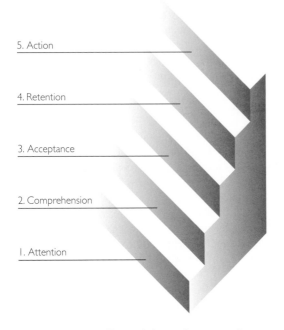

5. Action

4. Retention

3. Acceptance

2. Comprehension

1. Attention

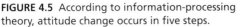

FIGURE 4.5 According to information-processing theory, attitude change occurs in five steps.

5. *Action:* The specific behavioral change or action requested in the message must be in accordance with the accepted and retained appeals. The Yale approach assumes that people act in logical ways that are consistent with the argument of the persuader.

Although each of these elements in the persuasive process is important to the success or failure of a message, most of the researchers conducting studies in the Yale tradition focused on the third step—the acceptance stage. In other words, they tried to discover what factors most powerfully lead to acceptance or rejection of a message.

Source Effects. Acceptance depends on two factors: (1) the source's credibility or believability, which we touched on in our discussion of ethos, and (2) the source's attractiveness to the receiver. Much of the early credibility research relied on the Aristotelian notion of reputation. In source-varied studies, the same message was attributed to persuaders having various kinds of reputations. A message about smoking and lung cancer, for example, was attributed either to a college sophomore or to a doctor from the surgeon general's office. Not surprisingly, greater attitude change occurred when the audience believed the message was coming from the doctor as opposed to the student. But the critical point here is that the effect of speaker credibility may decline over time if the content of the message becomes separated from the source in the memory of the hearers. This is a particular problem with messages that are heard only once.

Hovland and his colleagues called this delayed effect the "sleeper effect." The sleeper effect can work to a speaker's disadvantage when the speaker's credibility is initially high. That is, the high credibility of the speaker is often lost over time—it decays. This, however, may work to the speaker's advantage when initial speaker credibility is not particularly high but very strong arguments are offered, because people may remember the strong arguments and forget about the credibility factor. Although subsequent research on the sleeper effect has yielded mixed outcomes, communication researchers Mike Allen and James Stiff (1998) suggest, in their review, that the research does support the existence of a sleeper effect. But many questions remain about how it works. For instance, research is not conclusive as to whether information is not even stored in memory when the credibility of the speaker is very low or the relevance of the information is low. The possible occurrence of the sleeper effect means that framers of messages should keep speaker credibility high, reinforce the connection of the speaker to the content—perhaps through repetition of the message on different occasions—and have high-quality arguments in case the link dissolves between the content and the speaker. For credibility to remain important, listeners must remember the connection of the speaker to the content.

The recent corporate and church scandals demonstrate that credibility is important for both organizations and their leaders. The images of several organizations have been tarnished in recent years by unethical behavior of key leaders. Now many of these companies are attempting to persuade customers to place new confidence in them because "things have changed." For instance, WorldCom has placed full-page ads in the *Wall Street Journal* that specifically address the enforcement of an expanded code of ethics. Other companies that were not involved in the scandals have used their traditional, conservative values to boost their credibility in the eyes of potential investors (see Figure 4.6).

Other source studies focused on such questions as whether the height of a source leads to more or less attitude change, whether the rate of delivery has effects, and whether eye contact has effects. Researchers found that perceived height is a factor in source attractiveness, with taller persuaders rated as more believable and more trustworthy than shorter ones. Also, if persuaders deliver their messages in halting or introverted ways, they exert less effect on attitudes than do those who deliver their speech in smooth and extroverted ways. Gender also influences acceptance, with attractive same-sex persuaders rated as having less credibility than attractive opposite-sex persuaders.

An important factor in determining the attractiveness of a source apparently is the degree to which the source is similar to us. For a persuader, similarity is a very convincing appeal to build trust for a proposal. Yet appeals to similarity can be used unethically to deceive by building unwarranted trust. Those committing the fraud pose as group members or enlist the help of actual group members to spread the word. They exploit the trust and friendship existing in groups whose members have much in common. Many of these frauds are never reported because members of these groups often try to work out the problem within the group. Many of these scams involve Ponzi (pyramid) schemes in which new investor money is used to pay off earlier investors. Many of the earlier investors may actually be making a very good return on their money and so unwittingly convince other potential investors that it is a good deal. The Securities and Exchange Commission lists several examples of big losses from these scams. One scam used a sales pitch that was loaded with biblical references to sell nonexistent trading programs to 125 church members who lost

a total of $7.4 million. Another affinity scam involved a group of 100 Texas senior citizens who had $2.5 million stolen from them when they were asked to switch safe retirement savings to securities promising a higher investment return. So, consumers from close-knit groups or communities must be especially wary of deals that look too good to be true.

Message Effects. The Yale studies also focused attention on the nature of the message. For example, researchers investigated one of the oldest findings of persuasion research, presented by psychologist F. H. Lund (1925), claiming that the most important piece of evidence should come first (the primacy effect) rather than last (the recency effect). Reconsideration of the primacy effect came after studies such as communication researcher Harvey Cromwell's (1950). Hovland and his associates (1957) reported that the primacy–recency issue is a complex one, with the first speaker not necessarily having an advantage over the second speaker. However, the primacy of negative information has an important role in impression formation—it is particularly difficult to overcome negative information presented first. Motivation also plays a role in the processing of information. Specifically, the order of the content makes little difference to those with a high need for cognition, or the tendency to be motivated to process information. However, it makes a substantial difference to persons not motivated to process information. These studies indicated that more opinion change happens when information desirable to the recipient comes first—before less desirable information.

These studies were among the first to establish "face needs." That is, recipients of a message publicly endorsing an opinion are less likely to change their minds than those that do not endorse a position. More recent research has not clearly refuted the work of Hovland and his associates on the impact of order of materials on persuasiveness, but it has demonstrated that the time frame is important in predicting whether primacy or recency effects prevail. It appears that recency effects decay over the longer term but may be relevant in short-term situations.

FIGURE 4.6 This Southern Company ad emphasizes to investors how they are changing to meet todays values while also maintaining their traditional values.

Related to the placement of arguments and evidence is whether the persuader should present one side or two sides of an issue. Obviously, persuaders need to ask about the prevailing attitudes of the target audience, and sometimes they must address people who hold views likely to be contrary to their own. Hovland (1957) suggested that when controversial issues arise it may be wise to introduce the negative arguments that people are already considering first. Consider United Airline's *Wall Street Journal* ad dealing with its filing for bankruptcy, shown in Figure 4.7. The ad addresses several major issues that might lead travelers to avoid flying on United. The ad establishes that travelers need not fear flying with United and promotes the company's new beginning.

More recently, Allen's (1998) metanalysis of seventy studies of message-sidedness considered combined results from over 10,000 people. The analysis indicated that two-sided messages are most effective across conditions when they contain a refutation of the opposition's arguments. Even those holding similar values are likely to benefit from two-sided messages. Such messages inoculate those whose belief systems are not yet mature by forewarning them of the dangers out there. They may also generate more support against the opposition, much like a pep rally. However, it is not enough merely to mention the positions of the other side; those positions must also be refuted.

Fear Appeals and Drive Reduction. Hovland, Janis, and Kelley (1953) proposed that the use of fear appeals increases the likelihood of persuasion. They suggested that complying with a persuasive attempt using fear appeals seems to reduce emotional tension. The drive-reduction model is a more specialized version of the pleasure–pain principle discussed previously. Janis (1967) summarized the use of fear appeals and the drive-reduction model:

> Whenever fear or any other unpleasant emotion is strongly aroused, whether by verbal warning or by a direct encounter with signs of danger, the person becomes motivated to ward off the painful emotional state and his efforts in this direction will persist until the distressing

cues are avoided in one way or another. Thus, if the distressing threat cues do not rapidly disappear as a result of environmental changes, the emotionally aroused person is expected to try to escape from them, either physically or psychologically. (pp. 169–170)

Hovland and his associates suggested that the fear appeal will be effective only if it is sufficiently intense to create a drive state that recipients believe can be effectively countered by the recommended action. This perception that the threat can be handled is now called "efficacy." If the negative outcome seems insubstantial in terms of the perception of the threats or warnings, then its effectiveness is likely to be negligible. Likewise, if the credibility of the person issuing the threat or warning is low, compliance levels suffer. Subsequent research in twenty-eight studies involving over 15,000 individuals found significant and consistent links between the use of fear appeals and attitude change (see Mongeau, 1998). In sum, fear appeals work.

Controversy exists over whether using more fear is better. In the most famous fear appeal study of all time, Janis and Feshbach (1953) studied fear appeals in a dental hygiene context. They found that too much fear arousal can be less effective than more moderate fear arousal. Janis (1967) attributed these effects to an inverted U-shaped reaction to fear appeals. That is, high levels of fear (the top of the inverted U-curve) lead to defensive avoidance but low levels of fear lack sufficiency to induce attitude change. Thus, Janis maintained that using moderate levels of fear produces optimal results. The superiority of the use of moderate fear appeals has not received general support from subsequent research (see Mongeau, 1998). Aware of the failure of many studies to support this curvilinear effect, Janis (1967) responded by charging that contrary results could be attributed to the failure to arouse high levels of fear.

It is easy to be confused by the various findings pertaining to fear appeals. Although support for other models of fear arousal such as Leventhal's (1970) parallel response model, Rogers' (1975) protection motivation theory, and Witte's (1992) extended parallel process model is mixed, this does

CHAPTER 1

There's one thing we all feel very strongly about at United.

Our future.

Sure, it's been a hard time for us, and we'd rather not have been in the position of having to file for bankruptcy protection.

But that doesn't mean we have any less conviction in our ability to successfully overcome our current situation and emerge a stronger company.

And we will not be distracted from serving our customers at the highest level.

We are still flying. We still accept the same tickets. Our global network remains intact. Of course, all your miles are still valid. Most importantly, safety will continue to be our top priority in everything we do.

And you can still count on us putting you first. The same focus that resulted in United being ranked number one among major airlines for on-time arrival performance in two of the last four reported months.*

That's just one of many things we have accomplished.

We believe adversity presents an opportunity. An opportunity to renew our commitment to making travel just a little easier.

When you step on-board a United plane, you will feel the difference. You will feel the new energy and the new optimism.

You will feel the new beginning.

WE ARE UNITED

A STAR ALLIANCE MEMBER

united.com

FIGURE 4.7 This United Airlines ad attempts to build trust while announcing the company's new beginnings.

(Reprinted by permission of United Airlines. All rights reserved. Visit united.com.)

not mean that fear appeals are ineffective. The significant impact of fear appeals on attitude change is supported by communication researcher Paul Mongeau's (1998) metanalysis. Moreover, these studies suggest that fear appeals are more effective with people as they grow older and less effective with people already prone to anxiety. Mixed results simply mean that more complex explanations of why some fear appeals work and others don't need further refinement. Most of them have important ideas to consider when framing fear appeals. Collectively, the many studies on fear appeals over the past five decades suggest that an effective fear appeal must (1) pose a significant threat to the recipient's world, (2) be perceived as likely to occur, and (3) have a remedy that can be realistically implemented by the recipient.

Why so much attention to fear appeals? Fear appeals are one of the most common persuasive devices encountered by consumers today. In a class lecture at our university, a product manager at a telecommunications giant acknowledged that one of their most common sales techniques is to use fear, uncertainty, and doubt—also known as FUD. Although the precise origin of the term is not certain, it is most often attributed to Gene Amdahl, who claimed that salespeople at IBM tried to instill fear, uncertainty, and doubt in the minds of potential customers who were considering Amdahl computer products. The tactic plays up the security of staying with the tried-and-true product while avoiding the risk of the competitor with a less proven product or history. Such is the case with the major telecommunication companies, which emphasize the importance of dependability and reliability and the fact that, unlike their competitors, they own and control their own phone lines and equipment nationwide. Power companies use similar tactics to retain customers in states where consumers now have the right to choose which company they wish to supply their electricity and natural gas.

Technology is an area that seems particularly suited to the use of FUD tactics, because technology is always emerging and uncertainty is a natural consequence. Some companies emphasize their strengths in uncertain environments (see Figure 4.8),

but other companies use FUD to disparage their competition. For example, Linux supporters accuse Microsoft of engaging in the use of FUD (see FUD-Counter, 2001). Linux is a rival operating system to Microsoft that is free or has a low initial cost. Their claim finds support in a twenty-two-page document distributed by Microsoft (see Microsoft, 2001) for the retail environment revealing serious flaws with Linux. These include limited device driver support, limited technical support, high maintenance costs, lack of available software, untested waters in retail, uncertain future development, lack of standards, increased labor costs, and questionable response time. The Microsoft report also lists examples of companies using Microsoft operating systems products effectively. Of course, such warnings may be legitimate and important when danger does exist.

The financial investment market is another area in which FUD tactics are common. The huge losses in many investor portfolios have made people receptive to FUD tactics. A scan of financial investment ads in 2002 reveals the common themes of the risks of investment and the stability of established firms. Clearly, FUD tactics will not disappear any time soon, but the ethics of FUD tactics need more debate, especially with regard to senior citizens.

Social Judgment Theory. The book *Social Judgment* (Sherif & Hovland, 1961), the final volume of the Yale Studies in Attitude and Communication, marked the end of an era with Hovland's death that year. Social judgment theory focuses on how we form reference points, or what Sherif and Hovland called "anchors." The anchor is an internal reference point with which we compare persons, issues, products, and so on that we encounter. In this perspective, every issue has an anchor at any given time. Research compares the original anchor to an anchor established by a persuasive communication at a subsequent time. Perhaps the most important contribution of this theory is the idea that the anchor really represents a range of positions rather than one single point. Thus, "the individual's stand on a social issue is conceived as a range or a latitude of acceptance" (pp. 128–129). It is a range of posi-

FIGURE 4.8 This ITT Industries advertisement emphasizes the strength of the company in uncertain times without criticizing its competition.

tions that are acceptable to persuadees, including the most acceptable one. Yet the position also includes the latitude of rejection, which is the range of positions that persuadees find objectionable, including the most objectionable one. Moreover, this research indicates that highly ego-involved individuals have a very narrow latitude of acceptance and a very broad latitude of rejection. According to this research, the likelihood of changing the minds of highly ego-involved people is very small. The best chance of persuasion involves a message advocating a position that is only a small distance away from the position held.

One of the more important tasks, according to this theory, is determining whether various groups of people have firmly set anchors on positions that relate to the issue at hand. It is extremely hard for those who are publicly committed on an issue to consider changing, but it can happen over time. Many brand-loyal consumers have high ego-involvement with their *favorite* brand. The latitude-of-acceptance component of the theory has important implications for sales of branded goods. Consider what happens to Oldsmobile customers as General Motors phases out that division. Early in its history, GM developed a strategy aimed at moving customers from its basic Chevrolet car line to its more expensive lines as customers could afford more luxury. Moving customers to slightly more expensive lines over time fits social judgment theory well. As Oldsmobile ends production, however, the loyal Oldsmobile customer must change brands when buying a new car. GM thus is already offering additional incentives for Oldsmobile drivers to buy a new GM car. For many Oldsmobile owners, their latitude of acceptance probably includes other GM choices, as opposed to switching to the models of another company. For instance, a person could switch from an Oldsmobile 98 to a Buick Park Avenue easier than to a Ford.

Again, we see that the receiver is central in the explanation of persuasive effects in social judgment/social involvement theory. An important difference here, however, is that social commitments to particular groups are especially important if the receiver is highly involved in the issue because of a public commitment made to the issue.

Mere Exposure Hypothesis

Psychologist Robert Zajonc's (1968) mere exposure hypothesis is quite simple—repeated exposure to a stimulus results in more favorable evaluation of that stimulus. In a classic study, Zajonc asked participants to pronounce a series of Turkish nonsense words. In varying the frequency of times each word was pronounced, he found that more frequently pronounced words were evaluated more favorably. He reported the same pattern for different photographs of men and for Chineselike characters. Favorability increased substantially up to about ten exposures and continued to increase at slower rates until twenty-five repetitions were performed. Other studies suggest a point of diminishing returns whereby more repetitions yield no benefit and sometimes become counterproductive, with people getting bored with overexposure. Bornstein's (1989) metanalysis of over two hundred studies indicated that the mere exposure phenomenon appeared reliably across many different types of stimuli and objects. Psychologist Robert Bornstein's analysis demonstrates that the effect is stronger when (1) more complex stimuli are used, (2) exposure is brief, (3) gaps between repetitions are longer, and (4) varied kinds of stimuli are presented. Moreover, Bornstein found that the mere exposure effect tended to be larger when stimuli occurred in a subliminal manner—too quickly to be consciously recognized. So, there is little doubt that the mere exposure phenomenon occurs, but there is much disagreement as to *why* it occurs. Zajonc used these findings time and again to argue against the primacy of cognition—that is, that everything begins with cognitive thought processes.

The mere exposure principle is a central concept that persuaders cannot ignore. Today's media regularly use mere exposure with the masses. The implications for politics are especially worth noting. Psychologists Joseph Grush, Kevin McKeough, and Robert Ahlering (1978) examined political campaigns for political newcomers and low-visibility of-

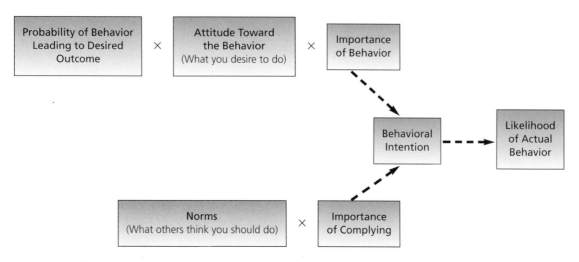

FIGURE 4.9. The Fishbein and Ajzen model for the prediction of intentions and behavior.

fices. They found a significant connection between increasing the exposure of unfamiliar candidates due to greater campaign spending and winning the election. Although it is frustrating to those who want voters to base their decisions on the issues, the use of short commercials with sound bites makes sense for candidates unfamiliar to the masses.

Brand awareness is another area of persuasion that benefits tremendously from the mere exposure principle. Pharmaceutical companies regularly launch new drugs by heavily promoting the brand names to consumers. This is a controversial practice because many people believe a doctor should prescribe the best medication based upon the condition of the patient rather than through pressure from the patient for a particular drug seen on television or in magazine advertisements. In reality, many doctors prefer certain brands of drugs, too. One of the first prescription drugs to heavily advertise to consumers was Claritin—the most popular allergy medication in history. For many allergy sufferers, this drug works all day long without causing drowsiness. Now it is available without a prescription. The commercials that originally introduced Claritin showed cheery outdoor scenes and the brand name Claritin, but the commercials did not

tell what the drug was intended to control. Some people remarked that they didn't know what it did but they still wanted it. After a few weeks of the commercials building brand awareness, the company finally released commercials that told what kind of drug it was. It will be interesting to watch how advertising is conducted for the more powerful prescription drug Clarinex.

Theory of Reasoned Action (TORA)

Researchers find it difficult to consistently demonstrate attitude–behavior relationships. In the theory of reasoned action (TORA), psychologists Martin Fishbein and Icek Ajzen (1981) suggest that attitudes have been defined so generally that it is no surprise that there are mixed results for the attitude–behavior relationship. Instead, they propose measuring the effects of persuasive variables on persuadees' behavioral intentions, and not on their attitudes. Instead of asking people to rate their attitude toward recycling, for example, Fishbein and Ajzen asked them to rate their intentions regarding actually engaging in recycling and how important that activity was to them (see Figure 4.9).

As the model indicates, the behavioral intention is the result of two assessments: (1) a person's attitude toward a behavior, and how important that behavior is to the individual, and (2) the normative influence on an individual, and how important that influence is judged to be by the individual. Normative influence is a person's belief that important individuals or groups think that it is advisable to perform or not perform those behaviors. In other words, a person intends to do something because he or she desires to do it or because that person believes others want him or her to do it. In reality, some combination of the two probably makes the difference. The same principles generally apply to an intention *not* to perform a certain behavior. It follows that, in testing the effects of a certain advertising or public relations campaign, it's necessary to test behavioral intentions, not broader attitudes. This means asking consumers, "Do you intend to try the new brand?" instead of asking, "How positive or negative do you feel about the new brand?" Even the act of saying, "Yes, I intend to try the brand," or clipping a coupon is a kind of symbolic commitment to actually purchasing the brand.

Brand behavior seems to be a simple process, but attempting to form the desired behavioral intentions is highly complex because so many components come into play. This is especially true for parents trying to foster appropriate behavioral intentions in their children. It is also difficult for teens making the transition to adulthood. For example, all sorts of difficulties arise for a sixteen-year-old living with his parents. Consider a situation in which this teenager receives a new car for his birthday, and he picks up his friends for a trip to the amusement park. The teen knows that sixteen-year-olds have several times the likelihood of dying in a car crash as older persons. One of his friends brings along a six-pack of beer. The teen driver weighs whether he should illegally drink an alcoholic beverage; that is, he weighs doing what his peers want him to do against refraining because the law and his parents say he should not drink. Furthermore, he knows it is not a smart thing to do from a safety standpoint. It is difficult to know which forces will win out for this teen.

We do know that many persuasive campaigns successfully use norms to demonstrate that individuals selecting the recommended behavior are in the majority. One such campaign to fight alcohol abuse is used at our university to show that the majority of students do not participate in binge drinking. Another normative approach being used at our university involves showing that females do succeed at calculus and are actually better at it than their male counterparts. No model has been better at predicting behavior than TORA, but it is far from perfect. It does, however, provide us with some basic strategies for designing persuasive campaigns.

COGNITIVE APPROACHES

Cognitive Consistency

Cognitive consistency theories rest on the assumption that humans want to reduce inconsistencies in their lives. Social psychologists Marvin Shaw and Philip Costanzo (1970) described this group of theories: "The term *cognitive consistency theories* refers to a host of proposals based upon the general proposition that inconsistent cognitions arouse an unpleasant psychological state which leads to behaviors designed to achieve consistency which is psychologically pleasant" (p. 190). For instance, an inconsistency arises when you like a person, but that person behaves badly toward someone else you like. Conversely, you may like a political candidate from another political party that you typically vote against. Various cognitive consistency theories address situations in which our lives are conflicted.

Fritz Heider's p-o-x theory (1946, 1958) is now more than a half century old, yet it still offers a simple yet elegant explanation of the tension reduction formulation. Now better known as balance theory, it was originally called the p-o-x theory because a person (p) was oriented toward another person (o) and an object (x) that was connected or belonged to the other person (o). It was later understood that (x) could be another person as well. It is important to recognize that one person is connected or seen as being a unit with the object or the third person. Balance happens if the two persons like each other and both hold either positive or negative evaluations of the object (or another person).

In the simple situation, inconsistencies arise when one person holds a certain belief or opinion about the topic and the other person holds a different position. Such disagreements are common—you probably experience this type of recurring but never-resolved argument frequently. The discomfort that arises provides the human dynamics for the Heider explanation of balance theory. When tensions arise either between or within individuals, they try to reduce these tensions by changing beliefs or trying to persuade others. Here is where balance theory offers strategies for persuasion.

Let's look at how such instances of balance or imbalance might be diagrammed. The attitudes of two persons (the persuader and the persuadee) are represented by positive (+) and negative signs (−). Thus, the two persons like (+) or dislike (−) each other. They could agree that the issue they are dealing with possesses bad (−) or good (+) values. One person could feel good (+) about the topic and the other feel bad (−) toward it. Notice in Figure 4.10 that both the receiver and the source have good feelings about each other. Because they agree on the topic and relate positively toward each other, they feel comfort—or, in Heider's word, balance.

A person feels this balance in one of three ways:

1. The source and receiver hold a negative attitude toward the object or idea and a positive attitude set toward each other, as in Figure 4.10. (You and I both dislike politics and like each other, so we experience comfort and balance.)

2. The source and receiver possess a positive attitude toward the object or idea and maintain good feelings toward each other.

3. The source and receiver disagree about the idea or object and dislike each other. (You and I dislike each other, so it is comforting to know that we don't agree on the topic. Or it is nice to know that those we respect and like have the same values and ideas as we do. It is also nice to

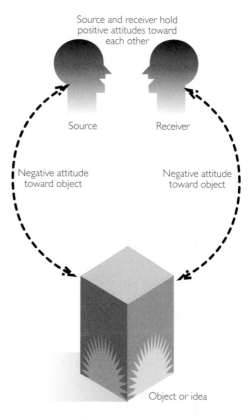

FIGURE 4.10 The Heider-Newcomb model of balance.

know that those nincompoops we dislike don't agree with us.) (See Figure 4.11.)

Theodore Newcomb's (1953) a-b-x theory is very similar to Heider's p-o-x theory. Newcomb differed in his proposition that communication plays the critical role in transmitting information about the relations between persons and objects of their attention. Newcomb (1959) made adjustments to balance theory and adapted the process more to the real world by suggesting that relationships are more a matter of degree than merely positive or negative. For example, Newcomb suggested that balance theory considers the degree of perceived differences, the degree of attraction among persons,

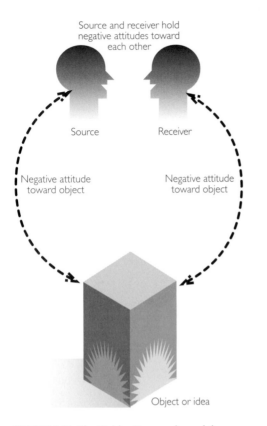

Source and receiver hold
negative attitudes toward
each other

Source

Receiver

Negative attitude
toward object

Negative attitude
toward object

Object or idea

FIGURE 4.11 The Heider-Newcomb model
of imbalance.

and the importance of the object under evaluation. This allows people to have different levels of liking individuals. It also recognizes that people may not even care about trivial issues.

Support exists for balance theory (see Eagley & Chaiken, 1993), but it is difficult to construct conditions that falsify the theory. In particular, problems exist for measuring shifts in the strengths of relationships. In laboratory situations, it is difficult to expose participants to people and issues that matter. Nevertheless, the theory clearly has utility for the construction of certain types of persuasive campaigns.

Consider how balance theory explains the following persuasive situation. Many readers are prob-

ably unaware that considerable conflict has existed between the Southern Baptist Convention (SBC) and more moderate Baptist groups in the South for several years. One of the more moderate groups, Texas Baptists Committed, heightened the conflict when they mailed a letter written by former President Jimmy Carter to 75,000 Baptists nationwide. In this letter of October 19, 2000, Carter announced that he was officially breaking ties with the SBC. Although his dissatisfaction had been known for several years, he took this opportunity to voice his displeasure with the rigid nature of the SBC and several other issues including their unwillingness to recognize that women could be in leadership positions with men subordinate to them. The mailing of Carter's letter was accompanied by a videotape of Charles Wade, executive director of the Baptist General Convention of Texas (BGCT), addressing issues surrounding the BGCT's upcoming vote to reduce funding to the SBC by $5.3 million. Carter encouraged the readers to listen carefully to Wade's tape.

It is interesting to consider this persuasive attempt by moderate Baptists in light of balance theory. How would you predict the question marks would be completed in Figure 4.12 (that is, + or −)? If the letter reader holds a favorable opinion of former President Carter, what is the predicted relationship to the tape of Charles Wade? Based on the letters to the editor in the *Atlanta Journal Constitution* following Carter's letter, it appears that Carter's letter led some readers to hold a more negative evaluation of the SBC. However, consistent with balance theory, some readers apparently developed even stronger ties to the SBC and devalued their opinion of Carter.

A persuader could also introduce a disliked person into a persuasive attempt to throw our view of the world out of whack by creating imbalance, in which our beliefs are shaken. Consider Figure 4.11. In this situation, someone I do not respect dislikes the same thing I dislike. I am bound to feel uncomfortable, or in a state of imbalance, in such a case. How can I agree with a person I do not respect?

Persuaders who want to get receivers to change their minds about an idea or object create feelings of psychological imbalance, or discomfort. When

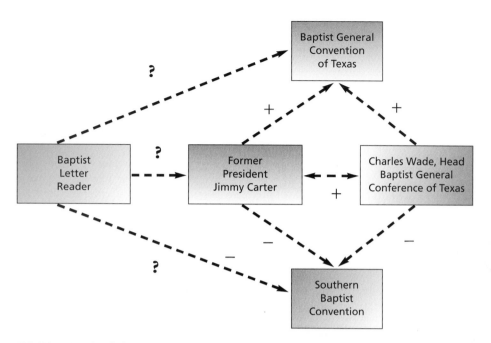

FIGURE 4.12 Using balance theory to predict attitudes in a conflict over religious values, what values should replace the question marks?

persuaders try to destroy your beliefs (for example, with a message stating that joining a fraternity will detract from your studies), you ought to realize that they are creating imbalance for you. They want to change your opinion by relying on your need for psychological balance, or comfort.

Other, more complex and powerful dissonance reduction theories have been put forward since Heider's model, including Festinger's (1962) theory of cognitive dissonance, which we will examine later. All of these theories show how persuaders use cognitive tension to reinforce or change our attitudes and behaviors.

Dual-Process Theories

According to social psychologists Shelley Chaiken and Yaacov Trope (1999), dual-process theories propose that there are two qualitatively different modes of information processing that operate in making judgments and decisions. The first is a "fast,

associative, information processing mode based on low-effort heuristics," and the second is a "slow, rule-based information processing mode based on high-effort systematic reasoning" (p. ix). Two dual-process theories command the most attention and are discussed here: (1) the elaboration likelihood model and (2) the heuristic-systematic model.

The Elaboration Likelihood Model (ELM). As discussed in Chapter 1, social psychologists Richard Petty and John Cacioppo (1986) formally detailed a dual-process theory that they called the elaboration likelihood model. The notion of two distinct routes for processing information had been developed by Petty a decade earlier. The ELM revitalized researchers' interest in persuasion. The term *elaboration* refers to a continuum of the conscious scrutiny used in making an evaluative judgment. Elaboration involves both the motivation and the ability to process information. Even though you possess exceptional ability to process information, that ability goes to waste if you are not motivated to process the information. Thus, it is important to consider both elements in devising a persuasive strategy.

This elaboration continuum is represented on each end by one of two routes of information processing. The high end of the elaboration continuum is defined by the central route of information processing, which occurs "as a result of a person's careful and thoughtful considerations of the true merits of the information present" (p. 3). It is a slower, more deliberative, high-effort mode of information processing that uses systematic reasoning. When persons use the central route, it is clear that they are consciously involved in thinking. Petty and Wegener (1999) maintain that not only is the greater amount of thinking being done at the high end but elaboration at the high end involves a kind of thinking that adds something beyond the original information. At the high end of this continuum, people are making the best-reasoned judgments they can make based on scrutiny of the information available. On the low end of the elaboration continuum, people use the peripheral processing route, which involves much less cognitive effort. It may also involve simple classical conditioning or the use of mental shortcuts known as heuristics, which we will discuss later. It definitely involves a lot less effort and often occurs "as the result of some simple cue in the persuasion context (for example, an attractive source)" (p. 3). Processing in the peripheral mode often simply happens, like a sponge soaking up water, perhaps outside of our conscious awareness. It involves a low-effort scrutiny of the available information and may involve surveying less information than in the central route.

Using the key word option in InfoTrac College Edition, enter "Michael Pfau" and "presidential debates" in the search box. Do you agree with Pfau about presidential debates? Do the debates have more impact on your central or your peripheral processes?

Yet even small decisions may require central processing. For example, a recent visit to Wal-Mart revealed that it was not so obvious which type of Crest toothpaste my wife needed because so many types of Crest are now available. After carefully looking at all of the varieties, I chose mint-flavored Crest with peroxide and baking soda because it most closely resembled the tube at home. What a mistake! Upon arriving home, I learned that the correct toothpaste was mild mint Crest with sensitivity protection.

The decision to buy a computer is more complex than buying toothpaste because we have more criteria to consider. We might compare memory capacity, processor speed, software, warranty, service, and other factors. Our thinking will involve reasoning, scrutiny of evidence, price comparisons, and an evaluation of our computing needs, to name a few. This information will be centrally processed. Many people, however, simply do not have the ability to evaluate which computer is best for their needs. So, they may not even try to process all of the features of the computer themselves. They may call a friend or relative who knows a lot about computers for a recommendation. Relying on the recommendation of an expert means that only a small amount of central processing was used.

In contrast, some decisions are almost automatic. For instance, when asked at a fast-food restaurant what you want to drink, you may respond automatically, "Diet Coke." This is peripheral processing: You did not evaluate all of the choices carefully or even ask what they were. Brand preferences often lead us to process information peripherally. For instance, many people prefer Heinz ketchup and will buy no other. Heinz is the world's number-one ketchup, with annual sales of more than $1 billion and a 50-percent share of the U.S. retail ketchup market—twice the market share of its nearest competitor. Strong brand preferences reduce the central processing necessary in grocery shopping. The ELM, however, does not provide much help in determining which people will rely heavily on brands as opposed to making purchase decisions based on price.

Petty and Wegener (1999) acknowledge this limitation of many of the experiments conducted at a single point in time. They also acknowledge that stronger attitudes develop over time due to many repetitions in a peripheral mode. For example, strong attitudes toward a brand of toothpaste often develop over years of exposure in one's family. In many cases, brand preferences for cars form over many years through peripheral processes, and children growing up in families that are brand loyal often maintain those preferences into adulthood. Consider one professor's family, which has owned five Mazdas in the past twenty years. Not surprisingly, the first new vehicle the daughter purchased on her own after college was also a Mazda.

Using the key word option in InfoTrac College Edition, in the search box find the article "The Application of Persuasion Theory to the Development of Effective Proenvironmental Public Service Announcements" by Bator and Cialdini. What do they have to say about central and peripheral processing in the construction of public service announcements for environmental causes?

Peripheral processing covers a large set of behaviors. For example, the speech rate of individuals influences how we perceive them, with some evidence suggesting that we prefer rates as fast as or faster than our own. The use of physically and socially attractive persons in advertising also reflects an appeal to peripheral processes. They are features of persuasive messages that we usually don't think about consciously. Sometimes, appeals to peripheral processes are more useful in drawing our attention to the message than in altering our perception of the content of the message.

Enter the term "speech rate" into the InfoTrac College Edition search box to see the many ways speech rate affects perceptions. In particular, read the abstract of the article on speech rate by Buller, LePoire, Aune, and Eloy.

Petty and Cacioppo's (1986) ELM rests on the assumption that people are motivated to process information because they want to hold correct attitudes, or at least those perceived as being correct. They may arrive at their perceptions of correct attitudes by doing social comparisons and considering norms. Some people even conduct original research and investigate issues fully on their own.

Petty and Cacioppo also believe that various factors can affect the direction and number of individuals' attitudes and can enhance or reduce argument strength. For instance, if an attractive or highly credible source opposes flag burning, that factor could increase or decrease the weight you might give to the Supreme Court's decision that flag burning is legal. The ELM also suggests that as people increase scrutiny through the central processing route, this lessens the impact of peripheral cues, and vice versa. This controversial proposition represents a marked difference with our other dual-process model, the heuristic-systematic model.

The key ethical issue raised by the ELM involves determining when children develop the ability to centrally process persuasion at a level that allows them to make informed choices. The inability to make informed choices is one of the reasons so much concern exists about advertising aimed at children. The advertising of alcopops (for example, Mike's Hard Lemonade) is a major concern because the product is so appealing to children who are not of legal age to drink these products. Yet the Supreme Court recently overturned a ban on advertising alcohol near schools in California, ruling that states cannot ban speech intended for adults in the interest of protecting children. As Figure 4.13 illustrates, concern exists for the inability of children to recognize messages about potentially harmful products—particularly from the alcohol and tobacco industries.

Enter the term "alcopops" in the InfoTrac College Edition search box to see how popular alcopops are and what the advertising controversy is.

The Heuristic-Systematic Model (HSM). Similarities are apparent between the ELM and the heuristic-systemic model (Chaiken, Giner-Sorolla, & Chen, 1996). The HSM proposes a systematic processing route that represents a comprehensive treatment of judgment-related information. It is a slow, high-effort reasoning process that bears a strong resemblance to the central processing route in

TRUE! *by Daryl Cagle*

FIGURE 4.13. Young persons are more susceptible to the influence of advertising.

(© Daryl Cagle; www.cagle.com/art.)

the ELM. The other route in the HSM is the heuristic processing route, which is a fast, low-effort process that relies on the activation of judgmental rules or heuristics. Heuristics are knowledge structures stored in our memories that help us deal with common situations; they are adaptive strategies that help us reduce the time it takes to make decisions. Grounded in the assumption that humans have limited information-processing capabilities and interest in cognition, the HSM proposes the sufficiency principle whereby people attempt to strike a balance between minimizing cognitive effort and satisfying their goals.

Heuristics are mental rules of thumb. In photography, for example, we have the sunny-16 rule for cameras that have manual time and aperture settings. It tells us that on sunny days we should open our aperture (which regulates the amount of light let into the camera) to 16 and set the time closest to the speed rating of our film. This rule works quite

well most of the time, but it is not infallible. For most of you, of course, this is useless information and so would not be a valuable heuristic. As another example, instead of trying to remember the rules of right of way when two people come to a stop sign at the same time, many people simply wave the other person through the stop sign—a heuristic to avoid having to think too much. Many heuristics are useful only in specific contexts. And some heuristics can be very misleading, like the moss grows on the north side of the tree. If you are lost in a forest, this heuristic is unreliable because moss is often found on the other sides of the tree. Yet many heuristics are understood widely. For example, in gift giving, the reciprocity heuristic often works when we do know that a gift might be expected of us. We do not want to embarrass the recipient of our gift by making it much larger than the gift they give us, but we don't want it to reflect poorly on our generosity. Heuristics may also explain why women process some information differently. Falk and Mills (1996) propose that sexist language inhibits the persuasion of women but not men.

Using the key word option in InfoTrac College Edition, search for the article "Why Sexist Language Affects Persuasion: The Role of Homophily Intended Audience, and Offense" by Falk and Mills. Do you buy their argument that sexist language leads women to ignore certain types of information?

In the HSM, systematic processing and heuristic processing occur simultaneously. In the ELM, there is an inverse relationship between the use of the central and the peripheral routes—as one rises, the other falls. In the HSM, the systematic use of evidence may be considered at the time people are using heuristics. Unlike the ELM, the two systems in the HSM operate more independently. Thus, the rise in the use of the systematic route does not directly limit the use of heuristics. There can be *additivity* when the systematic evidence and the heuristics lead in the same direction, so that the impact on attitude change is enhanced. But there can also be *attenuation* when the evidence and the heuristics disagree, so that attitude change is lessened. Thus, it is important to discover the kinds of heuristics that people hold when you are trying to persuade them.

PERSPECTIVES ON COMPLIANCE GAINING

Compliance gaining considers how one person can get another to do something. Compliance gaining is a task that parents and bosses face every day. Compliance gaining is usually examined in the interpersonal context rather than in situations in which mass media are used, but this distinction is not hard and fast. Most point to sociologists Gerald Marwell and David Schmitt's 1967 article as the beginning of compliance-gaining research. They focused on the ways people seek to gain the compliance of others, but communication per se was not part of their agenda (see Dillard, 1990, pp. 3–5). Interestingly, they believed that compliance-gaining appeals could be made from a common behavioral repertoire—a very Aristotelian idea. They generated a typology of sixteen compliance-gaining strategies, clustered into groups of positive and negative strategies. Kellermann and Cole (1994) detail over sixty types of compliance-gaining messages that were identified across numerous studies, and this list is far from complete (see Kipnis, Schmidt, & Wilkinson, 1980; Rule, Bisanz, & Kohn, 1985; Schenk-Hamlin & Wiseman, 1981). The value of research into compliance gaining, however, rests not in developing more comprehensive lists of strategies, but in understanding the dynamics of their use.

One important dynamic is the situational nature of compliance gaining, as revealed in the classic study by communication researchers Gerald Miller, Franklin Boster, Michael Roloff, and David Seibold (1977) that brought compliance gaining to the attention of communication researchers. In this study, people reported the use of different Marwell and Schmitt compliance-gaining strategies in different interpersonal situations. This is an important factor to consider when planning influence messages. The

persuader has to ask, "What special considerations need to be made for this particular situation?"

A related dynamic is the matching of appropriate tactics to the intended goals. Communication researchers Michael Cody, Daniel Canary, and Sandi Smith (1987) reported that college students use different tactics depending on what their goals are and who they are trying to influence. Not surprisingly, the students use different tactics when they believe others have some obligation, such as a landlord making repairs, as opposed to when they are asking favors of friends. Cognitive goals in the compliance-gaining situation are a current focus of communication researchers (see Wilson, 2002). The consideration of multiple goals is one of the most important lessons from this recent research. So, the persuader may need to consider a multilevel strategy instead of assuming that there is only one objective. The goals of the receiver have not received much attention, but it seems that good audience analysis should address this issue as well.

The final dynamic is the episodic nature of compliance gaining, That is, compliance gaining is often an episode that involves a series of attempts rather than just one message. Some consideration has been given to which tactics follow prior unsuccessful attempts (see Cody, Canary, & Smith, 1987). Apparently, compliance-gaining attempts move from positive tactics to more negative ones as more resistance is encountered. In many of these episodes, making simple, direct requests is the preferred approach. Using reasoning to make basic arguments is another popular approach. Yet the situation, the goals, and the power relationship all play a role in which strategy is most effective. One of the limitations of compliance-gaining research is that it usually focuses on short-term results. In contrast, solicitors at major nonprofit institutions view large donations as the result of long-term efforts. They realize that building relationships is a strategy that leads to people wanting to give.

Although many people view compliance gaining as merely another form of persuasion, this is not totally consistent with how persuasion was defined in Chapter 1. Return for a moment to Figure 1.2. Where should compliance gaining be placed on this chart? Certainly, compliance-gaining tactics are forms of influence. Some of these tactics, such as making a request of an individual, probably fit within the realm of persuasion, but not all requests truly involve free choice. Other tactics, such as threats, probably do not respect a receiver's freedom to choose, and so should probably be placed within the coercive domain. There is no consensus over the appropriateness of negative compliance-gaining strategies.

The themes of power and choice are central issues in the compliance-gaining literature. Knowing many of the common sources of power can aid you as a framer of compliance-gaining messages and as a consumer. John French and Bertram Raven (1959) identified five sources of power that remain remarkably relevant today:

1. *Referent power:* Based on the personal liking one person has for another whereby one individual identifies with another. The two parties do not have to be acquainted. Other researchers have expanded this source to include relational power.

2. *Expert power:* Grounded in the specific knowledge an individual has about a topic and limited to that area of knowledge.

3. *Legitimate power:* Vested in an individual as part of being in a certain position. Thus, a boss has expectations that workers are responsible for certain tasks and can hold them accountable.

4. *Coercive power:* Rooted in the ability to punish and the belief that an individual may level consequences if expectations are not met.

5. *Reward power:* Rooted in the ability to reward an individual for positive performance or behavior.

This list is not exhaustive. In fact, information power was later added by Raven and Kruglanski (1970) when it became apparent that the control of information was a source of power. Although there can be overlap with expert power, in organizations persons such as secretaries have a great deal of power because they are repositories of information. The use of information power also can be an invaluable way to empower consumers—particularly women. For example, people have a lot more power when they go into a car dealership with information about specific models and dealer costs in hand. In personal conversations with several car salespersons, I learned that they hate the Internet because potential buyers come in with printouts of what the dealership paid for a given vehicle. This tactic works. The issue often becomes what is considered fair markup for the dealer—particularly when the vehicle is not on that dealer's lot. Knowledge is power. Yet some dealerships, such as those selling BMWs or other hot models, will not retreat much from the retail price. Knowing this also helps. In addition, having a firm alternative from another source provides leverage. Still, many female car buyers prefer to buy at dealerships like Saturn, which advertise no-haggle pricing and emphasize relationships with customers. In reality, some bargaining may be possible at such places, but men and women are more likely to pay similar prices.

Beyond the marketplace and workplace, these types of power are used daily in our interpersonal relations with friends and family. It is easy to overlook the coercion that many of us use in an attempt to get those close to us to do something. Coercion is not used solely with those we consider adversaries or enemies! Relationships often involve many trade-offs. We may agree to something that we really do not want to do to reach a goal that we desire. When we control the outcomes of others in some way, or when they control our outcomes, power is involved. Thus, when friends use the relational power of their friendship to get friends to do something they do not wish to do—commonly known as peer pressure—some degree of coercion is present. Guilt, debt, and obligation are short-term motivators, but resentment builds over time.

A difficulty for compliance gaining from a persuasion perspective is that behavioral compliance often reflects mere acquiescence, without the development of mutual understanding. For example, employees frequently express displeasure about certain rules but abide by them as part of the terms of employment. When behavioral compliance is obtained, consensual attitude change may or may not follow. Agreements are often formed whereby a person votes a certain way in return for consideration on a different issue, without being convinced that the proposition under discussion is a wise course of action. This frequently happens in politics. Persuasion occurs in political deal making because some common ground was reached, but no one changed his or her mind based on the merit of the actual issues. Thus, it is important to note that the outcome of a persuasive attempt is often far different from the objective of the original attempt. Acquiescence may accomplish the immediate objective, but it is rarely a satisfying outcome.

PERSUASION AND MASS MEDIA THEORIES

Although we will be looking at the mass media, especially electronic media, in detail in a later chapter, some mass media theories have importance for the way persuasive communication is distributed through the media. Familiarity with these theories can aid in the design of persuasive campaigns. As new forms of mass media were developing in the early twentieth century, it was assumed that media messages would be received in a uniform way by audiences and that the media would have immediate and direct effects on those processing them. This perspective was called the hypodermic needle theory because persuaders believed that the media could directly inject or transfer ideas into people's minds. They assumed that the audience was passive and did not actively process the information they were receiving. As the power of the media became apparent, better explanations of how media affected people were needed. Thus, by the 1940s, more systematic studies of the media were being undertaken. Diffusion studies were some of the first conducted.

Diffusion and Voter Choices

Diffusion studies consider how new information, ideas, practices, or goods are accepted or rejected by targeted groups. Many of the early diffusion studies looked at media, while others focused on how new agricultural products such as hybrid seed corn were accepted. We will start with the consideration of how information was spread through the media. The "people's choice" (Lazarsfeld, Berelson, & Gaudet, 1944) study of the impact of the media on

voting behavior was a landmark diffusion study that began to challenge the assumptions of the hypodermic needle model. Paul Lazarsfeld and his associates considered the impact of the media on voting behavior in a 1940 election in Erie, Ohio. This was an intensive study even by today's standards. It introduced the panel design and longitudinal research to mass media studies. Interviews were conducted with 2400 voters each month from May through November.

According to Katz (1957), the people's choice study provided three major conclusions that challenged the thinking about mass media effects at that time. First, the most important factor was personal influence. That is, people reported that they were more likely to make their voting choices based on the personal influence of family and friends than any other source. More people reported having a personal discussion of the election than having heard a campaign speech or read a newspaper editorial. Second, there was a flow of information from opinion leaders to others around them. That is, some people were more influential, and they distributed information to others around them. The opinion leaders were found on every level of society— they were not just part of the elite. Finally, the opinion leaders were more exposed to radio, newspapers, and magazines during the months before the election than were the rest of the population. Thus, the concept of the two-step flow of information was born. In the first step, opinion leaders garnered information from the media; in the second step, they shared this information with others around them. Several studies support the two-step flow of information model (see Weimann, 1994).

The Diffusion of Innovations

Interest in the spread of innovations developed at the same time in the agricultural world as Lazarsfeld was exploring the impact of media upon voter choice. Ryan and Gross (1943) studied how farmers adopted hybrid seed corn over the open-pollinated varieties that they had planted previously. Interestingly, these researchers found that neighbors were the most frequently cited channel of information leading to their change—even though they heard of hybrid seed corn from a salesperson first. So, the

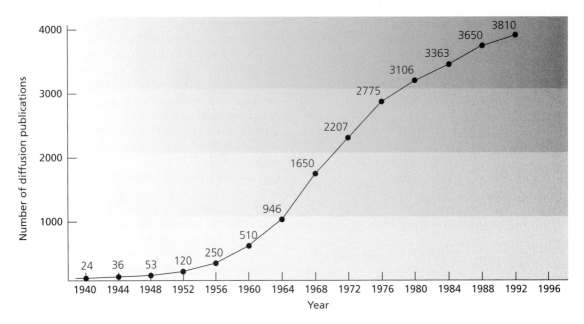

FIGURE 4.14 Cumulative number of diffusion research publications, by year

(Reprinted by permission of E. M. Rogers. From *Diffusion of Innovations,* 4th ed., p. 45.)

importance of personal relationships in persuasion was noted by the two independent groups of researchers studying very different types of diffusion. Sociologists Bryce Ryan and Neal Gross, however, found additional factors that really were not relevant to the voter studies. They reported the occurrence of the S-shaped adoption pattern. This very important concept suggests that something that is successfully adopted initially takes off very slowly. Then, at a certain point of critical mass, when a substantial number of people have adopted it, the rate of adoption begins to accelerate more rapidly. This is followed by a period in which the rate of adoption begins to level off. Interest in the study of the diffusion of innovations followed this same S-shaped adoption pattern, as shown in the graph of the number of publications regarding diffusion (in Figure 4.14). The curve may be much steeper for things that are adopted rapidly, but the curve may never happen for innovations that are not successful when introduced to the market. The other important finding from Ryan and Gross was that farmers often started by planting a test plot of hybrid seed

and increased their acreage over a three- or four-year period before planting all hybrid seed. Many farmers still follow this pattern of trying out new varieties of seed.

Many seemingly good innovations fail. Rogers (1995) discusses the failure of the implementation of modern drinking water systems to Egyptian villages. We know that pure drinking water is one of the most important factors in improving people's health. Yet, despite attempts to provide safe drinking water to villages in Egypt, most villagers continued to go to their traditional source of water in polluted canals. Thus, innovations that seem reasonable, rational, and beneficial to those proposing them may run into cultural and social roadblocks.

For those designing persuasive campaigns targeting large groups of people, the findings from these two traditions of diffusion studies are very important. First, they highlight that people are greatly influenced by information provided through relationships with those around them. We are more likely to trust those who are close to us. Second, cultural and social values must be considered.

Third, opinion leaders are more influential in changing the minds of others, and persuading those individuals first may make the persuasion of others in the group easier. There are many other elements of diffusion, and we will return to this perspective later in the book.

USES AND GRATIFICATION THEORY

A very different approach to the investigation of the persuasive effects of mass media is uses and gratification theory. It focuses on receivers of communication, on the assumption that "the audience is actively utilizing media contents rather than being passively acted upon by the media" (Blumler & Gurevitch, 1974, p. 11). This is another perspective that counters the hypodermic needle of media effects. As active receivers of mass communication, people have basic needs that can be satisfied or gratified through the media. Simply put, the theory assumes that receivers have various needs, ranging from low-order, basic needs, such as food, shelter, or sex, to high-order, complex needs, such as self-identity. There are many ways by which to meet those needs, and receivers make choices from among them. Some of these choices—in fact, many of them—involve using the mass media. As a result, a particular mass medium competes with other mediated and nonmediated methods to gratify needs.

Jay Blumler (1979), one of the originators of uses and gratification theory, outlined four kinds of needs that motivate us to turn to media. The first is surveillance—the need to keep track of our environment. We look to media to find out what's happening that might be of use to us. Even though you might think your college newspaper has little news value, you probably still glance through it to find out what is going on.

The second kind of need is curiosity—the need to discover new and previously unknown information. We frequently see appeals to this need in sensationalist publications like the *National Enquirer.* Usually, the story doesn't live up to the promise of the headline, but apparently this doesn't matter to the curious reader. Of course, there are less dramatic examples of curiosity at work. For example, most direct-mail marketing appeals have a "teaser" printed on the envelope—something like "Cashier's Check Inside!" to prompt what direct marketers call an "open up." Other curiosity-arousing tactics in direct-mail marketing reflect application of the "Cracker Jacks" theory by putting something lumpy in the envelope. The assumption is that, just as everyone who opens a Cracker Jacks box immediately looks for the "prize" even though they know that there has never been a good prize in a Cracker Jacks box, they will open the lumpy package to discover the contents. Curiosity lies at the heart of this kind of behavior.

The third kind of need identified by Blumler is diversion. We need relief from our day-in, day-out routines and use media to escape. The need for escape is met in many mediated and nonmediated ways, such as by reading novels, watching TV, or going to the movies.

Finally, Blumler identified the need for personal identity, which is closely related to Rokeach's (1973) self-concept. Media help us identify who we are, through our reading, listening, or viewing. Blumler and his colleagues found a fascinating difference between print and electronic media. For example, persons who are sure of themselves and are outgoing, social, and interactive tend to get a sense of who they are through reading, whereas less socially interactive and perhaps less self-assured persons rely on television to get a sense of who they are or to find a substitute for social activities. This sense of identity may come from role models we see on television, from political views reported in newspapers, or from a certain type of music that we listen to and identify with our own lifestyle.

The uses and gratification approach to mass media persuasion brings to light some human needs and desires that have not been highlighted elsewhere. And media gratification is much more extensive than the brief descriptions presented here make it appear. For instance, the appeal of nostalgia can be powerful. Even college students often look back fondly at certain movies or music from their high school days. Why are old shows popular on TV channels like Nickelodeon? For students of persuasion, it is useful to consider why Elvis still sells—the Elvis Presley estate earned $37 million in 2001 ((Schiffman, 2002).

Indeed, the power of nostalgia should not be under-estimated. Many other forms of media uses and gratification remain to be defined in light of the growing merger between computers and entertainment. The popularity of video games probably tells us something about players' needs for mastery and control. Although the uses and gratification perspective is not used widely by those interested in persuasion, it is an area that deserves more consideration.

REVIEW AND CONCLUSION

Most of the perspectives introduced in this chapter retain relevance for application in today's world, but no single theory addresses every persuasive situation. Some address larger issues of strategy while others are useful concurrently to address particular tactics at the micro level. So, you as the persuader need to understand the full range of options provided by these perspectives. Reinforcement theories suggest that change is fostered by providing those things that are rewarding. Several perspectives on attitude change provide a broad range of factors to consider. Various cognitive theories are relevant to persuasion, especially dual-process explanations. Finally, the media have important implications in relation to persuasion. These theories are only representative of the many approaches to explaining the process of persuasion, but they should give you some idea of the varied ways that researchers study this phenomenon. We will revisit many of these perspectives throughout the remainder of the book.

QUESTIONS FOR FURTHER THOUGHT

1. How might an advertiser use knowledge of reinforcement theory to make their advertising more effective?

2. Consider the symbol of the American flag and the cultural meanings that it might have in an activity theory perspective. What are the pluses and minuses of using the flag in advertising or commercials?

3. Give an example of how friends or family used coercive tactics to get you to do what they wanted. Were you aware of the coercion?

4. How might Sherif and Hovland's notions of the latitude of acceptance and rejection be applied to political campaigns?

5. Consider a campaign from PETA advocating that you become a vegetarian. From the TORA perspective, map how you see your behavioral intentions being formed. If you are a vegetarian, use the TORA to map how your behavioral intentions would be formed in response to a message advocating eating more beef.

6. If you were working for a group trying to get a new school bond issue passed by voters, how might Lazarsfeld's two-step flow of information help you plan your strategy?

7. How could you use an image of Elvis in a persuasive campaign?

8. Suppose you are a satellite television salesperson in a community that has previously had no satellite service available. Which perspectives in this chapter could help you sell your product?

 For online activities, go to the Web site for this book at http://communication.wadsworth.com/larson.

5

✳

The Making, Use, and Misuse of Symbols

Author and language critic Richard Lederer (1991) observes:

> The boundary between human and animal— between the most primitive savage and the highest ape—is the language line. The birth of language is the dawn of humanity; in our beginning was the word. We have always been endowed with language because before we had words, we were not human beings. [Words] tell us that we must never take for granted the miracle of language. (p. 3)

Throughout history, the uniquely human ability to create symbols has made possible all major cultural advances. Before the development of the spoken word, humans weren't very different from the beasts, but the ability to use symbols for communication enabled them to live cooperatively. Tribes were formed using the communicative power of symbols. Communication facilitated the specialization of labor and allowed humans to create cultures. As with the opening of Pandora's box, however, the use of visual and verbal symbols to communicate also al-

lowed humans to engage in less constructive behaviors, such as teasing, breaking promises, deceiving, scolding, demeaning, lying, and propagandizing. And with the development of the written word and movable type, people found that treaties could be both made and broken, legal contracts could destructively bind people for years, and laws could be used for evil as well as good. As the title of a recent book, *Deeds Done with Words,* indicates, language is a frequent surrogate for action—"Sticks and stones can break your bones, but words can really hurt you!" Neil Postman (1992), professor of media ecology, maintains that language is what he calls an "invisible technology" in that it is a kind of machine that can "give direction to our thoughts, generate new ideas, venerate old ones, expose facts or hide them" (p. 127). Perhaps language theorist Kenneth Burke (1966) put it best when he said that humans are "symbol making, symbol using, and symbol misusing" creatures.

This ability to use symbols—verbal, pictorial, gestural, and musical—lies at the heart of persuasion and so deserves our attention. As receivers, we need to get to the bottom of persuasive meanings; carefully analyzing the symbols used or misused by persuaders can help us get there. We need to ask whether the symbols prompt logical or emotional conclusions. For instance, imagine a TV advertisement for a brand of beer. It probably uses verbal, visual, gestural, musical, and other symbols to indicate that truly "in" people consume the brand, enjoy a certain lifestyle, and live happily ever after.

By examining the various kinds of symbols used in persuasion, we can accomplish several things:

1. Discover the persuader's use or misuse of symbols.

2. Discover the persuader's stylistic preferences and what they may reveal about his or her motives.

3. Anticipate the kinds of messages likely to come from this source in the future.

How can a careful examination of a persuader's symbols reveal so much? The answer is that the making of symbols is an ego-involving creative act that reveals a good deal about the persuader's modes of expression.

Lederer (1991) offers many examples to help us avoid taking the English language for granted. Consider just a few of them:

- Of almost 3000 languages in existence today, only 10 are the native language of more than 100 million people, and English ranks second in the list only behind Chinese, which has more native users (pp. 19–20).

- Users of English as a second language outnumber native users (p. 20).

- English is the first language of forty-five countries (p. 20).

- One out of every seven people alive today speaks English (p. 20).

- Most of the world's books, newspapers, and magazines are written in English, and two-thirds of all scientific publications and 80 percent of all stored computer texts are written in English (pp. 20–21).

- English has one of the richest vocabularies—615,000 words in the *Oxford English Dictionary* (which doesn't include slang, many technical and scientific terms, and newly invented words) compared with French, which has about 100,000 words; Russian, which has about 130,000; and German, which has about 185,000 (p. 24). And at the same time that it is so rich in vocabulary, English is remarkably economical (for example, it requires far fewer syllables to translate Mark's gospel in English than it does in any of the Romance, Germanic, or Slavic languages) (p. 29).

- English is now the international language of science, business, politics, diplomacy, literature, tourism, and pop culture—for example, Japanese pilots flying Japanese airliners over Japanese air space must communicate with Japanese flight controllers in English, not their native Japanese (p. 30).

- It would take 10 trillion years to utter all the possible English sentences that use twenty words (p. 17).

- English is a hospitable language—more than 70 percent of our words come from other languages (for example, boss, kindergarten, polka, sauna, canoe, zebra, alcohol, jukebox, camel, tycoon, tundra, ketchup, pal, vodka, sugar, tattoo, and flannel, to name a few) (pp. 24–25).

- English is probably the easiest language for nonnative speakers to learn (p. 28).

Lederer also demonstrates a powerful permanent element of the English language by asking students to arrange five words—"Lithuanian," "five," "scholars," "Shakespearean," and "old"—so that they make syntactical sense. Try this exercise, and you will discover that you and most, if not all, of your classmates come up with "five old Lithuanian Shakespearean scholars." Our language use is also very sophisticated. For instance, consider the following:

InwritingandreadingtheEnglishlanguage, weneedvisualcuestodeciphermessages.

There are two visual cues in that string of syllables—the comma and the capital E—and both of them shout out, "Here is a word break!" In written English, those cues really help, but in spoken English,

FIGURE 5.1 Compare these statistics with the fact that the King James version of the Bible uses only about 8000 words, the entire works of Homer contain about 9000, and all of Milton has only about 10,000. Other words coined by Shakespeare include "amazement," "bump," "clangor," "dwindle," "fitful," "majestic," "obscene," "pious," "road," and "useless."

(Used by permission of Wide World Photos.)

we don't have visual cues and consequently might be baffled when trying to hear words. In spoken English, what is the difference between "no notion" and "known ocean," between "buys ink" and "buys zinc," between "meteorologist" and "meaty urologist," and between "cat's skills," "cats' kills," and "Catskills"? So, as persuadees, we need to consider whether the persuasion is coming to us in written or spoken language—the channel plays an important part in meaning.

In addition, Lederer calls attention to how creative each of us is when using language: "Incredible as it may seem . . . practically every sentence that you speak and write during your lifetime has never been spoken or written before in human history," with the exception of stock phrases like "have a good day" (p. 16). Probably each of us "invents" words, though not as prolifically as Shakespeare did (see Figure 5.1).

LANGUAGE AND ITS ROOTS

Eloquent persuasion is unique and fresh. It strikes us as having captured the moment; it may even prophesy the future. The speech made by Martin Luther King, Jr., the night before he was assassinated had elements of prophecy. He said that God had allowed him "to go up to the mountaintop," that he had "seen the Promised Land," and that he doubted that he would get there with his followers. He concluded, "And I am happy tonight! I'm not fearing any man! Mine eyes have seen the glory of the coming of the Lord!" Although the words were drawn from the Old Testament and Julia Ward Howe's "Battle Hymn of the Republic," King's use of them was unique in the context of the movement he was leading. They certainly were emotional and probably were processed in the peripheral channel. After all, there is nothing "logical" about the use of those words. And, after King's assassination, they seemed eerily prophetic.

When we think about persuasion and eloquence, then, we are inevitably faced with the artistic process of making symbols. There are some symbolic acts—like burning the flag or spitting in holy water—that express rejection of authority, outrage at capitalism or Catholicism, or some other objection. But these are not the usual stuff of influence—in fact, they may not even qualify as persuasion or influence. Language is the real stuff of persuasion.

By age two, children acquire language and begin to talk ceaselessly, along the way discovering two very powerful words: "No!" and "Why?" They

FIGURE 5.2 As this cartoon demonstrates, language used in its spoken form can be quite different from its use in its written form.

(Reprinted by permission of Aaron Johnson.)

call this age the "terrible twos" because the power of language, the power of the negative, and the power of the question have been unleashed almost simultaneously. This "word power" or "magic" that humans possess can kill or cure, as we know from the voodoo spell or the chant of the medicine man. Modern-day witch doctors of language include advertising copywriters, radio talk show hosts, politicians, and televangelists.

Today we find many groups responding to symbols in dramatic ways. Some people use buttons, badges, or bumper stickers to make their symbolic point: "Think Globally; Act Locally," "Guns Don't Kill; People Do," or "Da Bulls." Others use their license plates to make declarations about themselves and their philosophies: "IM N RN," "REV BOB," "COACH," "I M SX C," "MR X TC," or "TACKY." There was even a joke plate supposedly owned by a congressman who had an affair with a fifteen-year-old assistant: "ID8 JLB8." Each of these messages is a symbolic act that makes a revealing statement about its user. Researchers know that persons displaying bumper stickers, wearing T-shirts with product labels imprinted on them, or sporting campaign buttons will be far more likely to vote for a candidate, buy the products, or join the cause they are promoting. This is because, by making their symbolic "statements," they have already "acted,"

and their words have become deeds. (See Figure 5.2.) As Burke (1966) observed, "Language is symbolic action."

Language can also be misused, as we discovered in looking at doublespeak and euphemisms in Chapter 1. The deaths of Afghani civilians in Operation Rolling Thunder became "collateral damage," while "surgical air strikes" made the enormous damage sound neat and clean. The title of the largest-circulation magazine in the United States is another example of euphemism at work. Doesn't *Modern Maturity* make the "senior citizen" sound special?

The symbols and language used in advertising frequently border on misuse. Market researchers decided to use the words "Recipe for Success," for example, to assure working women who use Crisco that they are indeed "cooks" and not merely "microwavers" who thaw and reheat meals. "Budget Gourmet" is a great pair of words to use to describe a prepackaged meal that is not very inexpensive and not quite of gourmet quality.

Another reason language requires careful analysis is that we can learn a lot about a persuader's motives by paying careful attention not only to the overall message but also to its particular verbal and visual symbols. Consider the language used by Hitler and other Nazis in the 1930s in referring to the Jews: "vermin," "sludge," "garbage," "lice," "sewage," "insects," and "bloodsuckers." Visual images of the Jew were posted in German cities and towns. Inevitably, he was a money changer with a beard and mustache dressed in a long robe and sneering at the viewer. Those words and images were red flags signaling Hitler's march toward a "final solution"—concentration camps, gas chambers, and genocide. Words became deeds, and as a result more than 6 million Jews were treated exactly like vermin or lice—they were simply "exterminated." The words even bamboozled Adolf Eichmann, one of the architects of the Holocaust. At his trial, he insisted that he had never killed any Jews—"I simply exterminated them." Lest we think that such a possibility is ancient history, we need to remember that "ethnic cleansing" is still occurring in many places in the world. The major weapon for instigating dehumanization is language. Words seem to blunt the edge of their true meaning when put into action; they seem to sanitize the brutality lurking behind them. After all, "ethnic cleansing," in and of itself, doesn't sound so bad, does it? Rather, it sounds sort of sanitary and healthy. It makes an emotional and horrific deed almost seem logical— the peripheral path of information processing transformed into the central one. We will certainly encounter such terms in the future, so I offer a warning to receivers: Linguistic camouflage can be dangerous stuff.

Even in less dramatic settings, we find that words create emotional responses and can demean people. Consider the term "lady doctor." What does the person using those words imply? That the doctor is not as good as a male physician? That the doctor is in the business only for the fun or sport of it? Why does the use of "lady" convey so much meaning and evoke such an emotional response? Communication scholar Dan Hahn (1998) points out how language is used to depict males as sexual aggressors and females as stalked prey or as passive entities. Consider a few of his examples in which the language of seduction is turned into the language of stalking: "He's a real animal" and "He can't keep his paws off her," while the female is "a real dish" or "a real piece of meat" who can be "turned on" or "cranked" like a mechanical toy.

On my campus, the word "greasers" sparked a heated debate in an email chat group. Persons familiar with the prejudicial use of the word in referring to Hispanics were naturally outraged that the word was used. Other group members, however, thought the word was harmless. They were familiar with a meaning for "greaser" that equated it with tough, cocky, and arrogant high-school-aged males during the 1950s and 1960s who wore leather jackets, rode motorcycles, smoked cigarettes, and had long hair combed (and greased) back into what were called "duck butts." Only recently have we become sensitized to the use (and misuse) of Native American references in athletics—the Braves, the Redskins, the Chiefs, "the Fighting Illini," and so on. These examples show how word usage can outrage people as well as persuade them.

For an interesting peek into how emotionally involved people can get over language issues, access InfoTrac College Edition, and enter the words "language style" in the search engine. Read a few of the items dealing with language and religion, language and feminism, and language and marketing/salesmanship.

The world of marketing provides many examples of the persuasive power involved in language choice. Brand names often reveal producers' attitudes toward their customers, or even toward the public in general. For instance, Oster Corporation markets a "food crafter" instead of a "food chopper," which tells us that Oster is taking a gourmet approach. (Chopping sounds like work. Crafting? Now, that's art.) Smoking certain brands of cigarettes was a way of making a gender statement— Eves and Virginia Slims, for example. What self-respecting man would smoke those brands? At one time, the brand names of American-made automobiles suggested status, luxury, power, and speed: Roadmaster, Continental, Coupe de Ville, and Imperial. Later, new brands coming on the market suggested technology, speed, and economy: Rabbit, Colt, Fox, Jetta, Laser, and 6000 LE. When the baby boomers started hitting midlife in the 1990s, auto brand names suggested wealth, quality, durability, and long lives: Sterling, Infiniti, Sable, Probe, and Cadillac's 1999 addition to the sport utility vehicle category, the Esplanade. In the world of food, fast, easy preparation is suggested by names like Lunchables, Handy Meals, and Bagel Bites. Indeed, the language of brand names is a critical element of persuasion for a variety of product lines.

By understanding the many ways in which language can be manipulated, persuadees can look beyond the surface to delve deeper into the meaning of messages and motives of the sources. Persuaders, for their part, can analyze receivers and craft their words and phrases to appeal to them. They can "listen" to their audience for clues to what they need and want to hear.

How can we learn to identify the uses and misuses of symbols, especially in the language used by politicians, advertisers, employers, and other persuaders? One way is to investigate how language scholars view the power and use of words. A useful approach to the study of language is based on the work of philosopher Suzanne K. Langer.

LANGER'S APPROACH
TO LANGUAGE USE

Langer (1951) recognized the power of language symbols. Like Lederer and others, Langer believed that the ability to create symbols is what distinguishes humans from beasts. In addition to being able to experience feelings, events, and objects, we can talk and think about them, even when the actual feelings, events, or objects are not present. Two concepts are associated with this capacity: signs and symbols.

Signs indicate the presence of an event, feeling, or object. For instance, thunder is a sign of lightning and usually of rain. That's why my dog goes into a panic at the sound of thunder—having had lightning strike close to her as a pup, she frantically tries to hide from it. If she could process symbols, I could talk to her about thunder and explain the futility of trying to hide from it. Only the comforting tone of my voice (another sign) seems to calm her down.

Another sign might be the red light at an intersection, indicating potentially dangerous cross traf-

fic. Leader dogs can recognize the red light by its location on the top of the traffic signal and can even be taught to stop the person they are leading, but they cannot be taught to recognize the symbolic link between the red light and danger (dogs are color-blind). That is a much more complex notion. As Langer (1951) put it, "Symbols are not proxy of their objects, but are vehicles for the conception of objects" (p. 60). Because of our ability to use symbols, you and I can understand the presence of danger by such means as the color red, the word "danger," or the skull and crossbones on a bottle of poison. Further, Langer maintained, the power to use symbols is a basic need; even persons unable to write or speak can't avoid making symbols—they revert to visual symbols.

Some symbols have a common meaning that most agree on. Langer called such symbols "concepts," in contrast to "conceptions," which she used to refer to any particular individual's meanings for the concept. All human communication (and hence persuasion) involves concepts and conceptions. So, naturally, the possibility of misunderstanding is always present. Recall how some persons' conception of the symbol "greaser" differed vastly from others' conception of the same symbol. Because of the possibility of misunderstanding what other persons mean, Langer introduced three terms to be used when discussing meaning: "signification," "denotation," and "connotation." Signification is what the thunder means to my dog and what the top (red) light on the traffic signal means to a leader dog. Denotation is the common and shared meaning we have for the concept of danger. Connotation is my or your private and emotional conception of danger. Langer also maintained that meaning is either "discursive" or "presentational." *Discursive* meaning is the combination (usually sequential) of smaller bits of meaning (usually language). *Presentational* meaning occurs all at once and must be experienced in its entirety (looking at a painting or statue, or experiencing a ritual or a piece of music, or watching the images of September 11 replayed over and over again). Thus, some of the "meaning" in any advertisement is discursive (the slogans, jingles, and ad copy), and some is presentational (the graphic layout, fonts, and pictures). Similarly, some of the meaning of a political campaign is discursive (the speeches, press releases, and interviews), and some is presentational (the way the candidate looks, his or her "image," and the pictorial and musical elements in spot ads). Responsible receivers of persuasion try to identify the common meanings or concepts being communicated, their individual conceptions of those meanings, and the difference between their individual connotation and the unique connotations of other receivers.

THE SEMANTIC APPROACH TO LANGUAGE USE

Beginning with the landmark work *Science and Sanity* by Count Alfred Korzybski (1947), scholars known as general semanticists began a careful and systematic study of the use of language and meaning. Their purpose was to improve understanding of human communication problems and to encourage careful and precise uses of language. They wanted to train people to be very specific in sending and receiving words, in order to avoid such pitfalls as stereotyping. For instance, the general semanticists believed that an effective way to prevent the rise of cruel dictatorships would be to teach people to be aware that the appeals of demagogues were "maps" (inner perceptions) and not "territories" (realities).

Access InfoTrac College Edition, and enter the word "psycholinguistics" in the search engine. Go to the subdivisions options and select the analysis option. Examine the items referring to "Fatal Words" (which concerns the crash of ValuJet flight 592), "Words, Words, Words," "Linguistic Virtual Reality," and the language used by schizophrenics. How do the items heighten your awareness of the power of language and word choice?

Even when based on observed traits, stereotypes are unreliable, simply because no member of a class or group is exactly like any other member. As Kor-

zybski suggested, "the map is not the territory." In other words, our internal perceptions or conceptions of other persons, groups, things, and ideas are likely to be different from the real persons, groups, things, and ideas. Like Langer, Korzybski and his colleagues recognized the difference between an event, object, or experience and an individual's conception of it. In their scheme, the word "map" is equivalent to Langer's "conception," and the word "territory" is equivalent to "objective reality" and close to Langer's "concept." Our faulty maps are usually expressed through the language we create to convey them, and they usually miscommunicate in some way.

For the general semanticists, the real problems occur when people act as if their maps do a good job of describing the territory and so turn the map into the territory. For example, my image of Alaska was quite different before I actually visited there. I thought of it as a place of towering mountains, endless snow and ice, magnificent animals, huge salmon, and mainly native Inuit inhabitants living as they had for thousands of years. But when I got to Alaska, I saw what the territory was really like— dusty roads, lush forests (in fact, much of it is a "coastal" rain forest), and vast emptiness. Most of its inhabitants outside of the five major cities (the fifth largest of which only has 7000 inhabitants) seem to live in shacks, cabins, or run-down trailers. They maintain a subsistence economy depending on the killing of game; the $2000-per-year oil money that each man, woman, and child receives; and what I call "ding-donging around." This equates to doing odd jobs, working at tourist attractions, or growing marijuana as a cash crop. Quite a difference between the map and the territory! Korzybski believed that we all carry thousands of maps around in our heads that represent nonexistent, or at least unreal, territories. To demonstrate this concept for yourself, write down the name of a food you have never eaten, a place you have never been, and an experience you have never had. Associated with these names are maps for unknown territories. For example, you may think that fried brains would feel slimy and gooshy in your mouth when, in reality, they have the texture of well-scrambled eggs. What is your map for skydiving? For being a rock star?

FIGURE 5.3 What would a semanticist think of this cartoon? The words "reproach" and "beneath contempt" might be likely to prompt a signal response. Why?

(*Frank and Ernest* reprinted by permission of NEA, Inc.)

How do these maps match up with the real territories? In some aspects, the territory will agree with your map, which is probably a result of the media exposure you have had to other countries, foods, and activities. But in most cases, your maps will be very different from the territories as they really are.

Our mental, visual, and word maps represent a real problem in communication, especially in persuasion. Just as persuaders have to discover the common ground of ideas so they can persuade us to adopt their point of view, they also have to identify the maps we carry around in our heads. Then they must either play on those maps, using our misperceptions to their advantage, or try to get us to correct our faulty maps. Only then can they persuade us to buy, vote, join, or change our behavior. And most maps are probably emotionally constructed, just as Alaska was for me or the prospect of driving an SUV is for many purchasers. Sometimes, however, the maps might be logically constructed, as they are for a lawyer building a summating statement in a trial or for a financial advisor who suggests a certain investment plan or strategy.

Our faulty maps are usually expressed through language; that is, we create and use words to communicate our maps. We react to them as if they are true representations of the territories we imagine. To the semanticists, this "signal response" is equivalent to my dog trying to hide from lightning whenever she experiences the "sign" (also "signal") of

thunder. Signal responses are emotionally triggered reactions to symbolic acts (including language use), and these responses play out as if the act were actually being committed. For example, in the congressional debate over a proposed constitutional amendment to ban flag burning, one side argued that flag burning (the "map") was equivalent to destroying the country. The other side felt that the "territory" (the ideas behind the flag—the Constitution, the Bill of Rights, freedom of expression, and so on) was more important than the flag itself. Those who opposed flag burning often exhibited violent signal responses, such as physically attacking flag burners. In a recent example of the signal response, an official in the Washington, DC, City Council and aide to the mayor was removed from the council because he used the word "niggardly." Now, the dictionary definition of the word is "unwilling to give, spend, or share . . . stingy, scanty, or meager" (Berube, 1985). But because the word sounds similar to a racial epithet—the "N" word—it prompted a signal response among members of the council, even after a definition of the word was given. The semanticists were certainly accurate about the power of the signal response (National Public Radio, 1999).

The semanticists' approach to language is to train senders and receivers to be continually alert to the difference between signals and symbols. As Figure 5.3 demonstrates, symbols (such as the words Frank uses in the job interview) can even be self-effacing. Semanticists also try to isolate meaning in concrete terms. For example, suppose I tell you that "Gen X college students are conservative, selfish, and lazy." Your response will probably be negative because of the connotations of some of the words used—"selfish" and "lazy" for sure, and maybe "conservative" as well. You might well respond that "ancient, ivory tower, egghead professors are spaced-out, vindictive, and uncaring!" In this case, neither of us has much chance of establishing common ground and persuading the other; the words have moved our information processing into the peripheral or emotional channel.

Semanticists would advise both of us to use what they call "extensional devices," or techniques for getting outside of the emotional connotations that often accompany words. One extensional device I could use to modify my language would be to identify the specific college students I have in mind. This is called "indexing." In this case, I would alter my statement to something like "Gen X college students who have everything paid for by their parents are conservative, selfish, and lazy." That would calm down some of you—at least a little—because you probably know fellow students who have everything paid for, including lots of extras you don't get. But I still would not be as clear as I could be, according to the semanticists.

They would further urge me to use an extensional device called "dating," or letting you know the time frame of my judgment about college students. Using dating, I would alter my sentence further by saying something like "Gen X college students of the nineties who had everything paid for by their parents were conservative, selfish, and lazy." That might cool you down a little more—unless, of course, you are one of those college students whose parents pay for everything. Here is where the extensional device semanticists call "etc." comes into play. This device is meant to indicate that I can never tell the whole story about any person, event, place, or thing. Using this device, I would alter my sentence to something like "Gen X college students of the nineties who had everything paid for by their parents were conservative, selfish, and lazy, among other things." Now I have suggested that conservatism, selfishness, and laziness

aren't the students' only attributes. For example, they also might be "societally concerned about environmental issues," "worried about honesty," or any of a number of other positive attributes.

Finally, the semanticists would advise using an extensional device called "quotation marks," which is a way to indicate that I am using those flag words in a particular way—my way—that isn't necessarily your way. For example, my use of the word "selfish" might relate to the students' unwillingness to help other students succeed in class. Or it could mean their unwillingness to volunteer in the community or to do any of a number of other things that wouldn't necessarily match your meaning for the word "selfish." My sentence might now read, "Gen X college students of the nineties who had everything paid for by their parents were 'conservative,' 'selfish,' and 'lazy,' among other things." Now how would you react to the statement? You would probably probe for my meanings for the emotional words, or you might even agree with me if your meanings for those words were similar to mine.

Using extensional devices in decoding persuasion helps us make sure the maps in our heads more closely resemble the territory to which we are responding. Persuaders should design specific, concrete extensional messages, especially when using emotionally charged words or abstract words for which there can be many meanings—but frequently they don't. More importantly, persuadees need to consider whether they are being appealed to via their maps or the territory. Abstract words such as "power," "democracy," "freedom," "morals," and "truth" are particularly vulnerable to misunderstanding. Unethical persuaders often intentionally use abstract or emotionally charged language to achieve their purposes. It is our task to remember the map–territory distinction and to use extensional devices as we attend to symbols. We must remember that as receivers we, too, have "response-ability."

To learn more about the power of words, access InfoTrac College Edition, enter the word "newspeak" in the key word option, and explore the item titled "Pomobabble" by Dennis

Arrow. Make a list of your top ten examples, make copies for your classmates, and pass them out.

BURKE'S APPROACH TO LANGUAGE USE

Perhaps no language theorist or critic wrote as many treatises in as wide a variety of fields, nor with as broad a knowledge of human symbolic behavior, as Kenneth Burke, who died in 1993. A self-educated intellectual who once said he was merely footnoting Aristotle, Burke focused on language as it is used to persuade people to action. The word "rhetoric" was very important to him, as was the word "motives." His books *The Grammar of Motives* and *The Rhetoric of Motives* are central both to this book and to this discussion. Burke (1950) defined persuasion as "the use of language as a symbolic means of inducing cooperation in beings that by nature respond to symbols" (p. 43). This active cooperation is induced by what he termed "identification," a concept tied to Aristotle's common ground.

According to Burke, the development of identification occurs through the linguistic sharing of what he called "sub-stances." (He liked to divide the word into its prefix *sub,* meaning "beneath," and *stances,* which in the Latin refers to "grounding" or "places.") In other words, identification is based on the raw material of our self-concepts—those bedrock foundations on which our beliefs, values, and views of the self are based. Burke noted that these "sub-stances" or "places" that undergird our most fundamental beliefs and values also emerge in the words we use to define things, persons, and issues. So critical receivers of persuasion need to pay particular attention to the words, images, and metaphors that persuaders use to create (or undermine) identification based on the presence or absence of common ground or "sub-stances." Think of how exorcised people become over gender and language or other issues involving political correctness.

Our self-concepts are made up of various kinds of symbolic and real possessions including physical things (clothing, cars, books), experiential things (work, activities, recreations), and philosophical possessions (beliefs, attitudes, values). Identification with others develops to the degree that we symbolically share these possessions. In other words, we identify with persons who have a similar view of life, who enjoy the same kinds of activities, who have similar physical possessions, who have similar lifestyles, beliefs, and attitudes, and so on. If we identify with persuaders, we naturally tend to believe what they say and probably will follow their advice. Thus, the job of persuaders is to call attention to those "sub-stances" that they share with receivers. The receivers' job, in turn, is to critically examine these "sub-stances" to see whether they truly are shared values and beliefs or whether the persuaders are merely making them appear to be shared.

In other words, persuadees need to decode persuaders' messages to see if they are authentic or bogus—if they reflect their real beliefs and values or are merely convenient concoctions. For example, in 2003, President George W. Bush condemned the CEOs of several major corporations for lining their own pockets by purchasing stock and stock options using money borrowed from their own companies. That is they borrowed from the "seller" to buy what was sold and what they could then resell, often with advance notice of good or disastrous earnings reports. At the same time Bush condemned such actions, however, the press learned that he had utilized the gimmick to line his own pockets. The shared "sub-stance" of condemning such behavior was, apparently, not really all that "shared."

Think of the word *substance,* which the dictionary defines as "the essential part of a thing—its essence." The definition is especially meaningful with regard to identification. We identify with others because we share their essential beliefs, values, experiences, and so on. I am like you and you are like me to some degree; hence, I will believe you when you try to persuade me. For example, in the movie *Natural Born Killers,* Mickey and Mallory, the two serial killers, forge a powerful identification with each other via shared "sub-stances." They share the experience of being abused by parents. They share the murder of Mallory's father and later the murders of many other persons. They share physical belongings such as each other's blood, each other's bodies, and identical rattlesnake rings, to cite a few. Most importantly, they share a lifestyle—from the first scenes in the movie, in which they go on a killing binge in a small restaurant, to the final scenes, in which, after a bloody escape during a prison riot, they roam the country in a motor home with their children. They identify with one another in a particularly horrific way.

Burke argued that the sharing of "sub-stances" or "identification" is equivalent to persuasion. To Burke, most persuasion attempts to describe our "essential parts," and this description is always revealing. All words have emotional shadings and reveal the feelings, attitudes, values, and judgments of the user. Examining persuasive language can tell us about ourselves *and* the persuaders who solicit our interest, support, and commitment.

Burke also suggested that symbolic activities (such as the use of language) inevitably lead people to have feelings of guilt. He reasoned that from the beginning language automatically led to rule making and moralizing, and because we all break the rules or don't measure up to moral standards at some time, we all experience some degree of guilt. Burke argued that all human cultures exhibit patterns that help explain guilt, and the development of language in each of us is foremost. As noted previously, one element of language that emerges early is the invention of the negative, or what something is not. Obviously, the word "puppy" is not an actual puppy, so language that names what something is inherently leads to the idea of what something is not—the negative. The negative then leads to sets of "Thou shalt nots" (whether supernatural, parental, spousal, or societal). Inevitably, we fail to obey some of these negatives and experience shame and guilt. "No" is one of the first things we learn as children, and we realize that it means we have displeased someone. Our own use of the negative usually emerges at about age two, when we start to take control of our own lives. We have heard "No, no, no," but now we begin to use it ourselves. It gives us power, and we go about testing the extent of that power during the "terrible twos" and, in fact, throughout life. The second pattern that con-

tributes to guilt involves the principle of hierarchy, or "pecking order." It happens in all societies and groups, and it leads to either jealousy of others higher in the pecking order or to competition among members. We rarely (perhaps never) reach the top of the pecking order, and we feel guilty about that. A third source of guilt is our innate need to achieve perfection. Unfortunately, we all fall short of our goals and so feel inadequate and ashamed for not doing our best. This shame makes us feel guilty about not living up to our own or others' expectations.

How do we rid ourselves of guilt? In most religions, guilt is purged symbolically—we offer up a sacrifice or engage in self-inflicted suffering, penance, and so on. And these "cures" are used in our self-persuasion as well—for example, "I'll be good, God, if only I get out of this dilemma." But the handiest and most flexible, creative, artistic, and universal means to whip guilt is through language. We usually try to get rid of guilt by talking about it —in prayer, to ourselves, to a counselor or authority figure, or to someone with whom we share sub-stances and with whom we identify. Consider how frequently persuaders offer us symbolic ways to alleviate our guilt. The mother who feels imperfect gets rid of her guilt by having Betty Crocker refrigerated cookie dough on hand. The imperfect-feeling dad takes his family on a vacation to Disney World or coaches his kids' baseball team. The imperfect child tries to do better at school by using the Internet *Encyclopaedia Britannica*.

Persuasion through identification works because we all share sub-stances and because we all experience guilt. In processing persuasion, try to recognize that persuaders create identification by referring to shared sub-stances—preferred beliefs, lifestyles, and values. They motivate us by appealing to our internal and inevitable feelings of inadequacy or guilt. Examine the language and images in advertisements, sermons, political appeals, and other persuasive messages, reminding yourself of the strategies being used to create identification, as well as feelings of imperfection and guilt.

To see how critics have used Kenneth Burke's theories, go to InfoTrac College

Edition, and select the Powertrac option. Enter the words "Kenneth Burke" in the search engine. Read the "Kenneth Burke—R.I.P." item to get a feel for the importance of his work. Access any of the items listed to learn how others have applied Burke's theories in language analysis. Report your findings to the class.

THE SEMIOTIC APPROACH TO LANGUAGE USE

Like other approaches to language use, semiotics is concerned with the generation and conveyance of meaning. A number of scholars are associated with this "science" of meaning including Ferdinand de Saussure, Charles Sanders Peirce, Roland Barthes, and Umberto Eco. Semiologists apply the tools of linguistics to a wide variety of "texts." Viewing almost anything as a text, a semiotician can talk about the "meaning" of a doctor's office, a meal, a TV program, a circus, or any other verbal or nonverbal symbolic event. According to semiotic theory, all texts convey meaning through "signs" or "signifiers" that refer to objects, concepts, or events called "signifieds." These signifiers interact with one another in meaningful and sophisticated, but not obvious, relationships, or sign systems, which make up the "language," or "code," of the text.

These codes can be inferred from a text. For example, consider your classroom as a text having its own signifiers and signifieds—some linguistic and some visual, some logical and some emotional. The room usually has an institutional "meaning," signified by the type of walls, lighting, boards, and so on. Blackboards and plaster walls usually signify that the building is an old one. Green or white boards and cinder block walls signify a younger building. The kinds of student desks (with or without arms), the arrangement of the room (for example, desks in rows versus groups), and the physical objects (an overhead versus a video projector) are all signifiers that tell us about what to expect when entering this "text." There may be a clock on the wall signifying that time is important here, and it may be in view of the students or only to someone facing the back of the room (usually the teacher).

Consider several of the codes embedded in various texts. For example, a simple code is the use of black and white hats in old cowboy movies to indicate the good guy and the bad guy. Pages being blown off a calendar signify the passage of time. What meanings are conveyed by drinking out of mugs as opposed to Styrofoam cups or fine china? Each type of cup is a signifier, and each coffee drinker, consciously or unconsciously, is conveying a different message. Yet words aren't even involved. In a semiotic approach to the study of meaning, we try to "read" each message from several perspectives: (1) the words that are or are not spoken, (2) the context in which or from which they are spoken, and (3) the other signifiers in the message—visuals, colors, tone of voice, furnishings, and so on.

Indeed, the semiotician approaches any communication event as if it were a "text" to be "read" by the receiver/analyst. Language scholar Arthur Asa Berger (1989) cites Sherlock Holmes' unique ability to infer meaning from minute clues as an example of semiotics at work in the "real world." In the story "The Blue Carbuncle," for example, Holmes explains a series of meanings that he infers from several signifiers identified in a hat left behind by a crime victim. Though the hat is of the best quality, it is in disrepair, thus signifying that its owner has had a decline in his fortunes. House dust versus street dust on the hat signifies that the man doesn't go out much and that his wife doesn't love him anymore. Holmes explains that if she did love him she would clean his hat (of course, this story predates the recent feminist movement in Western culture). And a wax spot on the hat indicates that the man still lights with candles versus gaslights. Holmes' sidekick Dr. Watson's skepticism notwithstanding, his semiotic analysis proves to be quite accurate.

More and more marketing and advertising research is being conducted from a semiological approach, according to Curt Suplee (1987) of the *Washington Post*. He quotes advertising/design celebrity George Lois as saying, "When advertising is great advertising, it fastens on the myths, signs, and symbols of our common experience and becomes, quite literally, a benefit of the product. . . .

As a result of great advertising, food tastes better, clothes feel snugger, cars ride smoother. The stuff of semiotics becomes the magic of advertising" (p. 3). In a recent commercial for a bank (described by one of its ad agency creators), "An oddly modern-faced caveman is running across a barren rockscape. He is breathing hard, glancing around as if fearing pursuit. Finally he comes to a ledge and leaps . . . to become a snugly space-suited astronaut floating above the earth." The voice-over for these actions says, "You don't need a bank that keeps pace. You need a bank that sets it. Perpetual. What your bank is going to be" (Suplee, 1987). Compare your reading of the ad/text with what its designers have to say about it. In order to suggest that the bank is forward looking and pace setting, they explain, "we show early man—by analogy the viewer and his 'primitive' banking system—and the various things he has to react to. Then we show him taking a literal leap of faith into the future with Perpetual as his bank" (Suplee, 1987, pp. 1–3).

For an excellent discussion of how semiotics can be applied and for insight into how the worlds of advertising and marketing use semiotics, access InfoTrac College Edition, and enter the word "semiotics" in the search engine. Select the analysis option, go to the item drawn from the *Journal of Advertising Research,* and learn how agencies like Saatchi and Saatchi use the tool to market entertainment products. Now go to the research option, and select the article from *The International Journal of Market Research* to learn how Guinness beer uses semiotics in designing its advertising.

Semiotics also can help us understand where a persuader is coming from and what his or her agenda might be. What is the semiotic meaning of the following letter sent to the communication studies chair of my department?

Dear Professor Jones,

I am interested in directives as to how one may proficiency out of the speech requirement. Having been advised to seek counsel from you "specifically"—I sincerely hope you will not be displeased with my enthusiasm by asking this indulgence. There is a basis for my pursuing this inquisition as I am an adept speaker with substantiating merits. I will be overburdened with more difficult courses this fall—at least they will be concomitant with my educational objectives in the fields of Fine Arts and Languages. It would be a ludicrous exercise in futility to be mired in an unfecund speech course when I have already distinguished myself in that arena. I maintained an "A" average in an *elite* "advanced" speech course in High School. I am quite noted for my bursts of oratory and my verbal dexterity in the public "reality"—quite a different platform than the pseudo realism of the college environs. There is a small matter of age—I shall be twenty-two this fall. I am four years older than the average college freshman. I am afraid that I would dissipate with boredom, if confined with a bunch of *teenagers.* Surely you can advise something that would be a more palatable alternative?

Yours sincerely,

P.S. Please do not misconstrue this "inquiry" as the enterprise of an arrogant student, but one who will be so immersed in *serious* intellectual pursuits that the "speech" requirement will be too nonsensical and burdensome.

If ever a student needed to learn about communication, it was this individual. But what does the language usage here tell you about the writer of the letter? She (yes, it's written by a female) uses sixty-four-dollar words—perhaps a code for insecurity—but she seems unsure about her choice of words. Several times she puts words into quotation marks, a code for her own "special" meaning. She uses *italics* to signify the same thing—this word has a special meaning. She also misuses some words. For example, she says that she is pursuing an "inquisition" when she means an "inquiry." (An inquisition is a tribunal for suppressing religious heresy.) She says she has "substantiating merits" when she probably means that she has "substantial reasons" for being excused from the course. These and other signifiers add up to the semiotic meaning of the letter. (See Figure 5.4.)

FIGURE 5.4 As this cartoon illustrates, language is fun to experiment with as well as being important in persuasion.

(*Frank and Ernest* reprinted by permission of NEA, Inc.)

To explore the fascinating work of Berger on the semiotics of cartoons (he is a cartoonist himself), go to InfoTrac College Edition, and select the Powertrac option. Enter the words "Arthur Asa Berger" in the search engine. Then access the item titled "Scratches from a Secret Agent," and enjoy.

REVIEW AND CONCLUSION

This chapter should give you a deeper appreciation for human symbol making, use, and misuse and for the power of language as a tool of persuasion—especially the English language. Perhaps you are beginning to realize how much meaning you can discover when you critically analyze the various verbal and nonverbal symbols in persuasion. It takes time and effort to discover discursive and presentational persuasion, to identify the means being used to create a state of identification, to determine the difference between the map and the territory, and to learn the many codes operating in various kinds of texts. To be a responsible persuadee, you need tools to assist you in analyzing the many persuasive messages targeted at you. Chapter 6 focuses on tools for analyzing language and other symbols.

QUESTIONS FOR FURTHER THOUGHT

1. Why is symbol making such a powerful human activity? Give several examples of how symbols create high involvement in people. Are symbols logical or emotions? Are they processed centrally or peripherally?

2. What is meant by Burke's phrase "symbol misusing"? Give some examples of the misuse of symbols.

3. Why is the English language so powerful?

4. Why is a red stoplight a sign to a leader dog, and how is that "meaning" different from the words "red stoplight" or "dangerous cross traffic"?

5. What did Suzanne Langer mean when she said that symbols are the "vehicles for the conception of objects"?

6. What is the difference between signification, denotation, and connotation?

7. What is the difference between a presentational and a discursive symbol?

8. What is the difference between a "map" and a "territory" according to the general semanticists? What is an example of one of your food maps? One of your geographic maps? One of your experience maps?

9. What is a "signal response"? Give several examples.

10. What are the extensional devices recommended by general semanticists? What purpose do these devices serve? Give examples.

11. What did Kenneth Burke mean by "identification"? By "substance"? By the "need for hierarchy"? By "guilt"? How do these concepts explain why language is so important in persuasion and in living life?

12. What is the difference between a signifier and a signified? What is a code? Give examples of simple codes from the worlds of sports, politics, and advertising.

13. Were the attacks on the World Trade Center and the Pentagon discursive or presentational messages?

14. What did Burke mean by the statement "Language is symbolic action"?

 For online activities, go to the Web site for this book at http://communication.wadsworth.com/larson.

6

✴

Tools for Analyzing Language and Other Persuasive Symbols

Now that you have some perspective on the making, use, and misuse of symbols and a greater appreciation for the power of the English language, we can consider several ways to analyze both verbal and nonverbal persuasive symbols. We begin by looking at several dimensions of language.

The cube in Figure 6.1 represents three major dimensions of language: (1) the semantic dimension (all the possible meanings for a word), (2) the functional dimension (the various jobs that words can do, such as naming, modifying, or activating), and (3) the thematic dimension (the feel and texture of words). For example, consider the feel of the word "swoosh"—it sounds or feels like its meaning. Imagine that this cube consists of many smaller cubes, each representing a word or set of words having its own unique semantic, functional, and thematic dimensions or meanings. Then consider this line of ad copy: "Sudden Tan from Coppertone Tans on Touch for a Tan That Lasts for Days." On the functional dimension, the words "Sudden Tan" name a product. Semantically, however, much more is involved. The word "sudden"

indicates an almost instantaneous tan, and, indeed, the product dyes skin "tan" on contact. The ad's headline—"Got a Minute? Get a Tan"—is superimposed over before-and-after photos of an attractive blonde who has (presumably) been dyed tan by the product. On a textural, or thematic, level, the words that name the product do even more. The word "sudden" sounds or feels like the word "sun," so the product name sounds like the word "suntan." The "s" and "t" sounds are repeated in the line of copy, reinforcing the notion of a suntan.

Here are some more examples of the thematic or textural qualities language can have:

- The Presto Corporation named its new corn popper "The Big Poppa!" in the hope that your mind would establish a thematic link with the sounds of popping corn while you chuckle at the takeoff on the familiar "Big Daddy" cliché and the popper/poppa play on words.

- The "Kero-Sun" heater burns kerosene and warms your house like the sun.

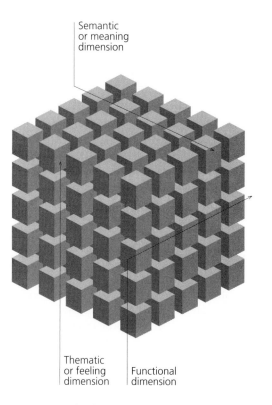

Semantic
or meaning
dimension

Thematic
or feeling
dimension

Functional
dimension

FIGURE 6.1 This figure showing the dimensions of language is based on a description of a model for meaning suggested by Charles E. Osgood, George J. Suci, and Percy H. Tannenbaum.

- You can have a "Soup-erb Supper" with a package of Hamburger Helper's beef-vegetable soup.
- There is a product that will make every woman "Smooth, Soft, and Sexy."

THE FUNCTIONAL DIMENSION: WHAT DO THE WORDS DO?

Examine the following language used during a trial in which the accused—an abortionist and the woman who had the abortion—faced charges of manslaughter because the abortion was performed late in the pregnancy. The defense attorney referred to previous attempts to abort the fetus by saying, "After two unsuccessful attempts . . ." The prosecutor, however, used active verbs and identifying nouns, saying, "They tried twice . . . they were unsuccessful," to focus the blame on the woman and the doctor. In the one case, the function of the words was to blunt the accusation; in the other, it was to focus blame. The functional dimension has powerful persuasive potential; if nothing else, it can simply shift our focus (Andrews, 1984).

As communication scholar Dan Hahn (1998) observes, "Definitions are like blinders on a horse: They focus attention on some aspects while blinding us to others" (p. 53). For example, consider the naval encirclement of a country to stop shipping into and out of its ports. You could call such an action a "blockade," which is generally considered an act of war against the country. But what if you called the action a "quarantine," as the United States did when it surrounded Cuba in 1962 to prevent Soviet missiles from getting to the island nation. Hahn claims that this naming had at least three functions. First, it signaled the Russians that we weren't interested in all-out war. Second, it gave them a way to honor the blockade without losing face. Finally, it created the sense that importing the missiles would be akin to importing an infectious disease (p. 58). In another example, Hahn points out the various meanings associated with the label "middle class." For some, the term means those earning between $17,000 and $64,000 per year—quite a range—and yet 93 percent of the American population think they are in the middle class (pp. 61–62). What does the term mean if almost all of us are included in it? So an important dimension of persuasive language is the functions, tasks, or jobs that the words perform.

Communication researcher Robert Cialdini (2001) observes that some language use functions to compensate for our personal feelings of insecurity or low self-worth. He notes that "the persistent name dropper is a classic example. So too is the rock music groupie who trades sexual favors for the right to say that she or he was 'with' a famous musician" (p. 173). Sometimes, words function to create fear. Consider the following "canned" sales pitch that I learned when I started my own advertising agency after retirement in 2001:

> We've been talking with businesses in the area, and they tell us that <u>they're afraid</u> of three things. The area is growing so fast that <u>they fear</u> that <u>they'll miss out</u> on the new movers coming into the area. Twenty percent of the country is on the move at any one time and <u>they worry</u> about the competition getting to these folks first. Then <u>they tear their hair out</u> when they hear that people who have lived in the same area for years don't even know where their business is located. And finally <u>they're terrified</u> that their brand loyal customers will go to the competition.

Notice the underlined words. Supposedly, they function to develop fear in the business owner, and then the advertising vehicle that will save them (a cooperative coupon mailer) is introduced. Sound gimmicky? I use it—and believe me, it works! The familiar and successful "Got Milk?" ads do the same thing with the ad copy that reads, "One in five osteoporosis victims is male. Luckily, fat free milk has the calcium bones need to beat it." The words clearly function to create fear in the male reader.

Cialdini (2001) identifies several functions, other than fear building, that language can perform. These include directed deference or blind obedience to authority figures when their use of language seems to suggest that they are superior in some way (p. 182). For example, in Ken Follett's historical novel *Jackdaws* (2001), a German officer dressed in civilian clothing encounters a Gestapo sergeant in a restricted area. The sergeant asks, "What are you doing here?" The officer responds, "I am Major Franck. Your name?" The sergeant immediately becomes deferential and replies, "Becker, sir. At your service" (p. 47). Cialdini says that titles can also convey authority (p. 188). For example, we no longer hire a "secretary" for our businesses; we hire an "administrative assistant." Yet another function that Cialdini identifies is the power of language and symbols to create a sense of perceived scarcity; he calls it the "scarcity principle" (p. 205). We can see language creating a sense of scarcity in the fa-

mous advertising use of the words "Price Good Only While Supplies Last!" In the trade, we refer to that function of ad language as "creating a sense of urgency," but in reality, the words represent the scarcity principle at work. Undoubtedly, there are many more functions that language can perform and that you may want to include in your list of "tricks to look out for."

THE SEMANTIC DIMENSION: WHAT DO THE WORDS MEAN?

The semantic dimension explains the various shadings of meaning that can be given to certain words. For example, in the abortion case, the defense won a ruling censoring the prosecution's use of the terms "baby boy" and "human being" and allowing the word "fetus" to be substituted throughout the trial. What is the difference in the meaning or connotation of these words? Clearly, choosing words with the proper semantic meanings can be critical for the persuader, so persuadees need to focus on word choice. Word choice can provide clues about the source's underlying intentions and, perhaps, believability.

Consider the following language used on the first page of a four-page foldout ad for the Chevrolet Camaro: "Laser Cameras. Hotlight Inspections. Robogates. Sonic Tests. What Are We Building Here, a Cruise Missile?" Unfolding the ad reveals the answer: "You Might Say That." The first quote clearly demonstrates the power of the naming function of nouns by citing the various tests performed on the vehicle. And three of these noun names are modified by adjectives, each of which semantically suggests state-of-the-art technology: "Laser," "Hotlight," and "Sonic." In light of the recent revelations regarding the actions of corporate bigwigs "dishonestly" getting rich at the expense of stockholders and employees—for example, Enron, WorldCom, Global Crossing, and Adelphia—it is not surprising that naming words like "embezzlement" and "insider trading" were replaced. Take a look at the high-power semantic naming boosts in words and phrases like "looting the company's pension fund," "robbing employee security," "CEO sharks drawn by blood," and "auditing flimflams."

Then there was Bill Clinton's statement that he "had never had sex with that woman!" He defined sex as intercourse, and so the fact that Monica Lewinsky had performed fellatio on him in the process of "earning her presidential kneepads" was not considered to mean "having sex." The linguistic naming kept prosecutors, politicians, and media busy investigating the affair for months, ultimately leading to Clinton's impeachment—only the second presidential impeachment in our history. The impeachment trial itself produced many examples of carefully chosen language. Much focus was placed on Clinton's statements under oath that he had not had sex with Lewinsky. Clinton used a very narrow semantic interpretation of "sex" by defining it as intercourse. Article 1 of the impeachment document stated:

> In his conduct while President of the United States, William Jefferson Clinton, in violation of his constitutional oath faithfully to execute the office of President of the United States and, to the best of his ability, preserve, protect, and defend the Constitution of the United States, and in violation of his constitutional duty to take care that the laws be faithfully executed, has willfully corrupted and manipulated the judicial process of the United States for his personal gain and exoneration, impeding the administration of justice, in that:
>
> On August 17, 1998, William Jefferson Clinton swore to tell the truth, the whole truth, and nothing but the truth before a Federal grand jury of the United States. Contrary to that oath, William Jefferson Clinton willfully provided perjurious, false and misleading testimony to the grand jury concerning one or more of the following: (1) the nature and details of his relationship with a subordinate government employee; (2) prior perjurious, false and misleading testimony he gave in a Federal civil rights action brought against him; (3) prior false and misleading statements he allowed his attorney to make to a Federal judge in that civil rights action; and (4) his corrupt

efforts to influence the testimony of witnesses and to impede the discovery of evidence in that civil rights action.

> In doing this, William Jefferson Clinton has undermined the integrity of his office, has brought disrepute on the Presidency, has betrayed his trust as President, and has acted in a manner subversive of the rule of law and justice, to the manifest injury of the people of the United States.
>
> Wherefore, William Jefferson Clinton, by such conduct, warrants impeachment and trial, and removal from office, and disqualification to hold and enjoy any office of honor, trust or profit under the United States. (The Democracy Project, 1999)

The votes against Clinton were not very close ones. On the charge of perjury leveled in this first article of impeachment, only 45 senators voted for his conviction, with 67 votes needed to prevail. It is interesting, however, to examine the semantic aspects of the language used in relation to this charge. Note the use of terms applied to Clinton like "subversive," "corrupted," and "betrayed." Senator Arlen Specter was very aware of the implications of his no-conviction vote as a Republican—he noted that the charges were "not proved" instead of declaring a belief that Clinton was "not guilty." Despite much evidence that Clinton had not been entirely truthful, many senators were looking for ways not to convict him. Close scrutiny of the language provided a rationale for some to acquit him. As the impeachment process progressed through Congress, several investigations of Republican members' personal lives revealed that they had a lot of explaining to do about their own indiscretions. Many of these members carefully chose their language to minimize the relevance and importance of that information to the Clinton case. One of the most common strategies was to distance themselves through the use of time by claiming that many of these incidents took place long ago.

You might want to experiment with how words can be used and how subtle differences in meaning can occur through word choice and the semantic dimension of language. Such practice can help keep you alert to what persuasive appeals might *really* mean.

THE THEMATIC DIMENSION: HOW DO THE WORDS FEEL?

In addition to having functional and semantic meanings, some words also have a feeling, texture, and theme to them. You can almost sense them. Onomatopoeic words (words that sound like their meaning, such as "shush," "whir," "rustle," "buzz," "hum," "ding," or "boom") are obvious examples of the theme or texture of language.

Somewhat less obvious thematic examples rely on assonance, or the repetition of vowels or vowel sounds—for example, "the low moans of our own soldiers rolled across the battlefield like the groans of the doomed." Alliteration is similar except that it relies on the repetition of consonants. For example, a *Sesame Street* cartoon about the letter "w" had the text "Wanda the wicked witch washes her wire wig in a wishing well on windy Wednesdays." An advertising example might be, "Make me meatloaf like my mother used to make—get Mom's Meatloaf Magician!" Both alliteration and assonance are favorite tools of the advertising copywriter. Once you are attuned to these techniques, you will find many examples in print and electronic ads.

Sometimes, the style of the persuader has a texture or theme to it. For example, after boasting that he was "going to kick a little ass" in his vice-presidential debate with his opponent Geraldine Ferraro, then–vice president George H. W. Bush appeared in a highly publicized 1988 interview with Dan Rather, in which Bush let slip that Rather "makes Leslie Stahl look like a pussy!" The comment was accidentally recorded on tape and then leaked. Bush was forced to apologize to numerous women's groups, explaining that he had only meant that Stahl was as harmless as "a pussy-cat." What do you think he really might have meant?

Thematic meaning or texture can also be created by the use of powerful metaphors. According to communication researcher Michael Osborn (1967), one of the best-known persuaders of the twentieth century, British prime minister Winston Churchill, repeatedly used what Osborn termed archetypal "light" metaphors to characterize the British military and citizenry and "dark" metaphors for the Nazi leaders. In a radio speech during the Battle of Britain, Churchill said,

> If we stand up to him [Hitler], all Europe may be free and the life of the world may move forward into broad, sunlit uplands. But if we fail, then the whole world, including the United States, including all that we have known and cared for, will sink into the abyss of a new Dark Age made more sinister, and perhaps protracted, by the lights of perverted science. . . . Good night then: sleep to gather strength for the morning. For the morning will come. Brightly will it shine on the brave and the true, kindly upon all who suffer for the cause, glorious upon the tombs of heroes. Thus will shine the dawn. (pp. 115–126)

By carefully considering the functional, semantic, and thematic dimensions of any persuasive message, we can exercise our "response-ability" as receivers. Even if our interpretation of the message doesn't match that of its creators, the process of identifying the symbols and trying to interpret what they mean is a positive step in preparing us for responsible reception of persuasion. Our interpretation can alert us to the uses and misuses of persuasive symbols.

THE POWER OF SYMBOLIC EXPRESSION

Symbolic expression has the power to affect us mentally and physically. For example, the kinds of symbols people use and respond to can affect their health. People who use expressions such as "I can't stomach it" or "I'm fed up" or "It's been eating away at me now for a year" tend to have more stomach ulcers than do others. Symbolic days such as birthdays can also have dramatic effects. In nursing homes, for instance, more persons die during the two months after their birthdays than during the two months before. Thomas Jefferson and John Adams both died on the Fourth of July, a date of tremendous significance for both of them. Jefferson is even reported to have awakened from a deathlike coma on the third to ask his doctor if it was the fourth yet. Some people die soon after the death of a loved one—and sometimes from the same disease. In other words, symbolic sympathy pains can become real (Koenig, 1972). In this sense, many survivors and family members of victims of the 1995 bombing of the Federal Building in Oklahoma City experienced such serious physical and psychological malaise that they required prolonged medical and psychological treatment. The words we say to ourselves can also cure disease and even stop hemorrhaging (Seigel, 1989).

Not only do symbols deeply affect individuals, but they also serve as a kind of psychological cement for holding a society or culture together. Traditionally, the central symbol for the Lakota Indians of the Dakotas was a sacred hoop representing the four seasons of the earth and the four directions from which weather might come. In the center of the hoop were crossed thongs that symbolized the sacred tree of life and the crossroads of life. Shortly after the hoop was broken during the Wounded Knee massacre of 1890, the tribe disintegrated. A Lakota wise man named Black Elk (1971) explained the symbolic power of the circle for his tribe:

> You have noticed that everything an Indian does is in a circle, and that is because the Power of the World always works in circles, and everything tries to be round. In the old days when we were a strong and happy people, all our power came to us from the sacred hoop of the nation and so long as the hoop was unbroken the people flourished. . . . Everything the Power of the World does is done in a circle. The Sky is round and I have heard that the Earth is round like a ball and so are all the stars. The Wind, in its greatest power, whirls. Birds make their nests in circles, for theirs is the same religion as ours. The sun comes forth and goes

down again in a circle. The moon does the same, and both are round.

> Even the seasons form a great circle in their changing and always come back again to where they were. The life of a man is a circle from childhood to childhood and so it is in everything where power moves. Our tipis were round like the nests of birds and these were always set in a circle, the nation's hoop, a nest of many nests where the Great Spirit meant for us to hatch our children. (p. 134)

Black Elk believed that his tribe had lost all their power or "medicine" when the whites forced them out of their traditional round tepees and into square houses on the reservation.

What symbols serve as the cultural cement for our way of life, and how do persuaders use them when they appeal to us? A good place to identify some of the central symbols in our culture is in advertisements. Consider the verbal and nonverbal symbols in Figure 6.2, such as the words "Quadra-Drive™," "maximum power," "revolutionary," "most capable," and "most advanced," as well as the football "chalk talk" imagery and the picture of the Jeep taking a corner. How do they reflect the central values of our culture?

We can also look to political rhetoric to find symbolic evidence of our cultural values. In the context of the breakup of the communist world, two important words used by politicians were "freedom" and "equality." As columnist David Broder (1984) noted, "Words are important symbols, and . . . 'freedom' and 'equality' have defined the twin guideposts of American Democracy" (p. 41). The words have the thematic qualities to stir patriotic emotions. Interestingly, however, they are not rated the same by all persons. As several sociological researchers have observed, "Socialists rank both words high, while persons with fascist tendencies rank both low; communists rank 'equality' high but 'freedom' low, and conservatives rate 'freedom' high but 'equality' low" (p. 41). What do these word preferences tell us about their users?

It is easy to see that the power of symbols in their functional, semantic, and thematic dimensions is considerable. Not only do symbols reveal motives,

IN LOW TRACTION CONDITIONS, QUADRA-DRIVE™ FINDS AN ELIGIBLE RECEIVER AND SENDS ALL THE POWER† TO IT.

(AND YOU THOUGHT QUARTERBACKS HAD TO THINK FAST.)

Now there's a revolutionary new four-wheel drive system that does the thinking, and the work, for you. Introducing Quadra-Drive,† our most advanced four-wheel drive system ever. If only one wheel has traction, Quadra-Drive seeks that wheel out, then transfers all the power* to it. And, unlike some other systems, it works both front-to-rear and side-to-side. In fact, Quadra-Drive is the only system in the world that delivers maximum power all the time. So Jeep® Grand Cherokee can pull you out of situations other 4x4s just couldn't handle.

For further information about our newest, most capable sport utility ever,** please visit us online at www.jeep.com or call 1-800-925-JEEP.

THE ALL-NEW JEEP® GRAND CHEROKEE
THE MOST CAPABLE SPORT UTILITY EVER**

*Sends 100% of the developed engine torque. **Based on AMCI overall on- and off-road performance tests using Grand Cherokee with available Quadra-Drive™ and V8 engine. †Optional. Jeep is a registered trademark of DaimlerChrysler.

FIGURE 6.2 Consider the cultural values underlying this ad.

(The marks JEEP® and QUADRA DRIVE™ are trademarks of DaimlerChrysler and are used with permission from DaimlerChrysler Corporation.)

but they also affect our self-image and express our cultural ideals and national character.

We now examine tools for analyzing the functional dimension of language in persuasion. Let's keep the power of the semantic and thematic dimensions in mind because no single word can be charted in semantic space without reference to all three dimensions.

TOOLS FOR ANALYZING PERSUASIVE SYMBOLS

Being aware of the functional, semantic, and thematic dimensions of language and nonverbal symbols is helpful in our roles as responsible receivers of persuasion. However, these dimensions are broad and somewhat general. Various tools for the analysis of persuasion help us focus our critical eyes and ears on more specific aspects of language symbols. Following are several such tools.

Tools for the Functional Dimension

Two tools for analyzing the functional dimension of language symbols in persuasion are language critic Richard Weaver's grammatical categories (especially regarding sentence types) and consideration of the effects of word order, or syntax, in sentences.

Weaver's Grammatical Categories. Language theorist and critic Richard Weaver (1953) suggested that the type of sentence format preferred by an individual can offer clues as to that person's worldview, the way he or she uses information, and the process by which he or she comes to conclusions. Weaver discussed the implications of a persuader's preference for simple sentences, compound sentences, or complex sentences.

Simple sentences usually express a single complete thought or point, and they must have at least one subject or noun and one action word or verb (for example, "He hit"). They sometimes have objects or words that receive the action ("He hit the ball"). They might even have several subjects ("Juan and Kim hit the ball") or several verbs ("Juan and

Kim kicked, screamed at, and pointed at the ball"). Examples of incomplete simple sentences might be "Behind the ball" and "And ran fast," neither of which expresses a complete thought. There are a variety of other possibilities involving modification of both subject and verb.

Persuaders who prefer simple sentences do not perceive the world as a very complex place. As Weaver put it, such a person "sees the world as a conglomerate of things . . . [and] seeks to present certain things as eminent against a background of matter uniform or flat" (p. 120). The simple sentence sets the subject off from the verb and object; it sees causes that have effects on objects. When a persuader uses this form, the persuadee ought to look at what is being highlighted, at what affects what, and at how action occurs. Listen to the way the sample sentences operate in the following excerpt from a letter to the editors of *Newsweek* magazine regarding the magazine's 1999 story on Salt Lake City's scandalous "purchase" of the 2000 winter Olympics:

> I am sure your article . . . will prompt responses from other citizens of Salt Lake City too. . . . You need look no further than personal greed to find the motivation [for bribing Olympic Committee officials]. The Olympics are merely a potentially profitable business venture for them. In reality, that has little to do with the nearly 840,000 residents who call this valley home. Salt Lake City and its residents are embarrassed by the acts of these individuals. *Newsweek*'s statement doesn't reflect our lives. . . . Frankly we do not need the Olympics to tell us that we have it good here. (Marshall, 1999, p. 20)

There is a clear foreground and background in most of these sentences. Subjects are set off from verbs and objects, and cause and effect are highlighted.

Compound sentences are made up of two or more simple sentences joined by a conjunction (for example, "She ran, and she jumped"). Weaver observed that the compound sentence sets things either in balance ("He ran, and he ran fast") or in opposition ("He ran, but she walked"). The compound sentence expresses some kind of tension—

whether resolved or unresolved. According to Weaver, it "conveys that completeness and symmetry which the world ought to have, and which we manage to get, in some measure, into our most satisfactory explanations of it" (p. 127). Persuaders who use compound sentences see the world in terms of polar opposites or distinct similarities—totally against one another or in concert with one another. For example, the union leader who says, "You are against us, or you are with us!" oversimplifies a complex world by using a compound sentence. Each of the two elements (simple sentences) in the example is complete and could stand alone. Though ungrammatical, the first two sentences in Mark Twain's classic novel *Huckleberry Finn* are compound ones:

> You don't know about me, without you have read a book by the name of The Adventures of Tom Sawyer, but that ain't no matter. That book was made by Mr. Mark Twain, and he told the truth, mainly.

The elements before and after the conjunctions "but" and "and" could stand alone as single complete thoughts. Notice how both sentences convey a sense of resolved tension, completeness, and symmetry (you wouldn't know who Huck is, but that's okay—Mark Twain wrote the book, and he was basically truthful). When you encounter compound sentences in persuasion, it is important to try to identify the tension (resolved or unresolved), the completeness, and the symmetry.

Complex sentences are similar to compound sentences in that they may have two or more distinct components, but not all the components can stand alone as complete simple or compound sentences. That is, some of the elements in the sentences rely on (or are dependent on) another element in the sentence and cannot stand alone. Once, in speaking about word choice, Mark Twain used a complex sentence: "Whenever we come upon one of these intensely right words in a book or a newspaper, the resulting effect is physical as well as spiritual and electrically prompt" (Lederer, 1991, p. 128).

The complex sentence features a more complex world—several causes and several effects at the same time. Weaver (1953) said that it "is the utterance of a reflective mind" that tries "to express some sort of hierarchy" (p. 121). Persuaders who use complex sentences express basic principles and relationships, with the independent clauses more important than the dependent clauses. For example, consider the following paragraph describing an ex-Olympic athlete's feelings about the bribery, steroid, and hormone scandals:

> But after having represented the United States in five Olympic track and field teams—from 1980 to 1996—I certainly have a feel for what the next class of Olympians is doing now. For world-class athletes, the Olympic cycle is as eternal as the Olympic flame: First comes years of intense physical and mental preparation. . . . And finally, if you are lucky enough to make it, there is the singular drama of Olympic competition. The ultimate joy comes from performing one's absolute best, no matter the order of finish. (Lewis, 1999, p. 56)

Look for elements that depend on others to express a complete thought (such as "For world-class athletes" and "And finally, if you are lucky enough to make it"). In all likelihood, they rank lower in importance than the independent elements do.

Weaver (1953) also had some observations about types of words. For example, because they are thought of as words for things and as labels for naming, nouns are often reacted to as if they were the things they name. They "express things whose being is completed, not whose being is in process, or whose being depends upon some other being" (p. 128). Thus, when people call police officers "pigs," they make the enemy into an object—a thing. It is easy to spit on a pig; the pig is an object. Looking at persuaders' nouns can give us clues to their perceptions of things. When persuaders reduce persons to the level of things or objects, they do so for a reason: to deal with the people as objects, not as human beings.

The function of adjectives is to add to the noun, to make it special. For Weaver, adjectives are second-class citizens. He called them "question begging" and said that they show an uncertain persuader. If you have to modify a noun, Weaver would say that you are not certain about the noun. In Weaver's opinion, the only adjectives that are not uncertain are dialectical (good and bad, hot and cold, light and dark). Examining adjectives used by persuaders may reveal what the persuaders are uncertain about and what they see in opposition to what.

Adverbs, to Weaver, are words of judgment. Unlike adjectives, adverbs represent a community judgment—one with which others can agree and that reflects what the persuader thinks the audience believes. For example, adverbs such as "surely," "certainly," and "probably" suggest agreement. When persuaders say, "Surely we all know and believe that thus-and-such is so," they suggest that the audience agrees with them.

Syntax. In addition to, or in lieu of, using grammatical categories and sentence types to analyze persuaders' messages, we can look at the syntax. *Syntax* is defined in the *Random House College Dictionary* as "the pattern or structure of the word order in sentences or phrases." How can that have a persuasive effect? Word order can either alert or divert the reader/listener. Consider the difference between these pairs of sentences:

- Before bombing the terrorist headquarters, we made sure the target was the right one.
  We were sure the target was the right one before bombing the terrorist headquarters.

- After thinking the proposition over, I've decided to buy another brand.
  I've decided to buy another brand after thinking the proposition over.

In the first sentence in each pair, the dependent element occurs at the beginning of the sentence ("Before . . ." and "After . . ."). This alerts the reader/listener to the conditions that need to be satisfied before taking or not taking the action (checking the target or thinking over the proposition). The main point of the sentence is expressed in the independent element. In the second sentence in each pair, the action comes first, and the dependent element diverts the attention of the listener/reader to the justification for taking the action or to the action itself (changing the brand or bombing the target). Some persuaders use emotional or surprising words by placing them at the beginning of a sentence to reduce the impact of the evidence to follow—the audience is alerted by the emotionality of the claim to focus on the details of the evidence. For example, the speaker might say, "There is no greater hypocrite than the animal rightist who opposes use of animals in research labs during the day and then goes home and has beef, fish, or chicken for dinner!" The reader/listener knows beforehand that the claim or theme is about hypocrisy, and he or she then focuses on the reasons for making the claim. The sentence is dramatic and creates a puzzle for the reader/listener, thus focusing his or her attention. The other side of the coin is the speaker who diverts the audience from the evidence by hiding the claim at the end of the sentence, making the reader/listener wonder where all this evidence is leading. For example, the speaker says, "The animal rightist who opposes the use of rats in the research lab and then goes home to eat beef, fish, or chicken is the kind of hypocrite this country doesn't need and who causes more than their share of trouble." Not only is the drama of the sentence reduced, but the power of the evidence is also overlooked because the audience is in search of the speaker's destination.

Communication scholar L. H. Hosman (2001) notes that language variations affect one of three elements of the persuasion process: "judgement of speaker, message comprehension and recall, or attitude toward the message" (p. 372) and that these effects are crucial in the information-forming process. This, of course, brings us back to the elaboration likelihood model (ELM) and the old debate over the comparative effectiveness of emotional versus logical persuasive appeals. Other interesting persuasive effects of syntax have been discovered by researchers looking at advertising. For instance, Hosman also reports findings that active versus passive sentence structure affects perceived believability, clarity, appeal, and attractiveness in print advertisements. As he observes, "The nature of a sentence's grammatical construction or of a narrative's construction has important persuasive consequences" (p. 374). Sentence structure is important and often indicates a persuader's goals and state of mind.

The impeachment trial of President Clinton produced many examples of carefully chosen language. As discussed previously, much focus was placed on his statement under oath that he had not had sex with Monica Lewinsky. Clinton used a very narrow semantic interpretation of sex by defining it as intercourse.

To learn more about how sentence structure is used in evaluating such potentially important messages as hate letters, access InfoTrac College Edition, and enter the words "sentence structure" in the search engine. Read the article titled "More Than a Figure of Speech" by Jerrold Post. Report to the class what you discover about using sentence structure to evaluate threats. Also enter the words "hate mail" in the search engine, and examine a few of the articles listed there. What do you think about the use of language in them?

In addition to using sentence structure to identify a persuader's motives, as with hate mail, sentence structure and word choice as indicators of information-processing modes meld well with the ELM and probably affect which information-processing path will be used in decoding the persuasive appeal.

Tools for the Semantic Dimension

Although the functional dimension of language bears important verbal and nonverbal meanings, the semantic dimension carries the bulk of meaning for most messages. Thus, it has been one of the most studied dimensions of language and meaning. Let's examine some tools for analyzing this dimension of language symbols.

Strategic Uses of Ambiguity. It may seem like heresy for persuaders to intentionally be ambiguous in designing their persuasive messages, but they often do just that—they try to be somewhat unclear, vague, and general. They do so to allow for the broadest possible degree of common ground or identification. In other words, they want each potential persuadee to fill in his or her own private meanings or connotations for the particular word or symbol. This strategy results in the largest number of potential interpretations and thus creates the largest potential audience for the persuader's brands, candidates, or causes. It also provides the persuader with an "escape hatch" if questioned on the way a word or other symbol is being used, which helps the persuader please as many and offend as few persons as possible. As a receiver, you need to identify such cases of intentional ambiguity and analyze the reason(s) for the lack of clarity.

Persuaders use several methods to create strategic ambiguity. One method is to choose words that can be interpreted in many, often contradictory, ways. For example, a politician may support "responsibility in taxation and the education of our youngsters." Those who think teachers are underpaid and need substantial raises might hear this as a call for spending tax dollars. Those who hold a reverse view could as easily interpret the statement as meaning that educational spending needs to be cut. There are other possible interpretations as well. The key word, the one that increases the ambiguity, is "responsibility"—it sets up the rest of the sentence. Another ambiguous word is "astronomical," as in "The budgetary implications of engaging Iraq in an all-out war are astronomical." Does this mean millions of dollars or billions of dollars or hundreds of billions of dollars? Depending on one's position regarding military action, several meanings could be imagined. Another way to create strategic ambiguity is to use phrases like "noted authorities on the subject seem to concur that . . ." Some researchers have labeled such strategic uses of ambiguity intentional vagueness or equivocalness. Communication scholar E. M. Eisenberg (1984) held that strategic uses of ambiguity can help persuaders win agreement especially on things like mission statements and at the same time allow individuals to interpret the statement as they wished.

Ambiguity can also be created by juxtaposing or combining words or phrases in startling ways or by presenting issues in a new light. For example, the term "born again" became familiar in the 1980s and was persuasive to many people. It referred to people who claimed to have been converted to Christianity, even if they were already members of Christian denominations before their conversion. The term "born again" suggests that the earlier beliefs were forgotten or incorrect and that the conversion caused them to be re-created and revitalized. Some born-again lobbyists labeled their political group the "Moral Majority," creating highly persuasive and intentional ambiguity. The term was ambiguous because the group did not constitute a majority but actually was a minority. The term also implied that, because most people try to behave morally, almost anyone could be a member. This ambiguous term had great persuasive appeal. Media preachers created what political researchers Dan Nimmo and James Combs (1984) called "the Electronic Church." "Moral decay" became another highly persuasive, but ambiguous term. We respond to "moral decay" in the same way we respond to tooth decay. Rush Limbaugh coined a term that juxtaposes meanings to create a powerful kind of ambiguity about a group of persons whom he calls "feminazis." The positivity of "feminine" clashes with the negativity of "Nazis" and shocks the audience into a new way of thinking.

How can we defend ourselves against ambiguous language? The semanticists advise using more specific and concrete elaborations on any ambiguous term. The semioticians advise us to seek the full meanings in persuasive "texts" by delving into various verbal and nonverbal "signifiers" to determine what is really being "signified." In fact, there is even a "toolkit" for doing such analysis marketed to the advertising industry, and semiotics is being used to devise global marketing and advertising strategies (Domzal & Kernan, 1993).

Examining the denotations and connotations of persuasive symbols is another tool for studying the semantic dimension of language. There are other tools for approaching the semantic dimension of language. Among the more useful is the dramatistic approach suggested by philosopher and literary critic Kenneth Burke.

To learn more about the uses of strategic ambiguity, access InfoTrac College Edition, and type the words "strategic ambiguity" in the search engine. Select one of the periodical references by Jim Paul, and learn how business uses strategic ambiguity.

Burke's Dramatism. In addition to his theoretical ideas on language discussed in Chapters 1 and 5, Kenneth Burke offered students of persuasion a theory and a tool for analyzing the semantic dimension of language. He called his method "dramatism," and his tool of analysis the "dramatistic pentad."

Like the other theories discussed in Chapters 3 and 4, dramatism maintains that the basic model that humans use to deal with and to explain various situations is the narrative or story. Burke (1960) thought of it as "a philosophy of language" capable of describing and analyzing a wide variety of human motivations as they are expressed in symbolic acts such as human language use. Burke maintained that a central concept in this approach to language and motivation is the idea of action (which is motivated) as opposed to motion (which is not motivated). Basic bodily functions, such as sweating or digestion, that occur without our willing them to occur are nonsymbolic acts. Action, in contrast, requires motivation and the ability to use language symbolically—we must will it into being. In other words, language use is a kind of symbolic action because it is motivated.

Burke believed that when we communicate we choose words because of their dramatic potential and that different individuals find some elements in the drama more potent than others. Some, for example, may believe that so-called great people affect the outcome of historical events. When persuading, such persons give examples of individual effort winning the day. Burke described their persuasion as based on the agent, or actor. For other persons, the scene, or setting, may be the motivating element; thus, they choose scenic words and phrases to persuade. Burke's model, the dramatistic pentad, has five central elements, as its name implies: scene, act, agent, agency, and purpose (see Figure 6.3).

Scene is simply the place where action occurs. It includes not only physical location but situation, time, social place, occasion, and other elements of the setting. The scene could be something like "Campaign 2004," "the Oval Office," "a Web site," "an inauguration," or *The Oprah Winfrey Show.* People for whom this is a key element are likely to believe that a change in the scene will cause other

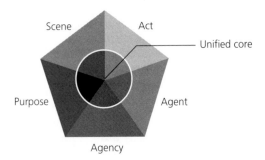

FIGURE 6.3 The five elements of dramatism ultimately affect one another, and each emerges from a common unified core—the drama itself.

things to occur. They might believe, for example, that if gays are permitted to join the armed forces there will be less discrimination against and hostility toward them. The scene should be a "fit container" for the act. For example, the Lincoln Memorial was a "fit" scene for Martin Luther King, Jr.'s, "I Have a Dream" speech—the setting helped make the speech memorable. Burke believed that persons favoring scene as a key element have a materialist philosophy of life. They think that the physical, social, and psychological environment in which action occurs can be the cause of good or bad outcomes.

Act in Burke's model refers to any motivated or purposeful action. In persuasive messages, the verb is the best indicator of the act. High comedy or high tragedy results when the act is not appropriate for the scene. For instance, a Charlie Chaplin film in which the snooty society hostess gets hit in the face with a cream pie is funny because the act doesn't "fit" the social scene. The assassination of a political leader while attending church is tragic because the act doesn't "fit" the physical scene.

Access InfoTrac College Edition, and enter the words "word choice" in the search engine. Examine the items regarding word choice in advertising; the item from *ETC,* the journal of general semantics; and the item in the *Journal of Direct Marketing* titled "The Future of 'force communication.'" What possible effects does the semantic dimension contain?

FIGURE 6.4 The agent is the focus of this ad, as can be easily seen, but other elements of the pentad are apparent also.

(Reprinted by permission of Southern Comfort Company.)

Surely an element that contributed greatly to the public outrage at Bill Clinton's affair with Monica Lewinsky is that it (the fellatio she performed) occurred in the anteroom to the Oval Office in the White House. If the act had occurred in the No-Tell Motel on "D Street," the hue and cry certainly would have been considerable, but not nearly to the extent as when a sacred symbolic setting was involved. Burke suggested that realism is the philosophy of life associated with an emphasis on the act. What is the act in Figure 6.4?

Agent is Burke's term for the person or group of persons who take action in the scene—they are the actors or characters (the police officer, the corrupt politician, the terrorist, Howard Stern, Saddam Hussein, and so on). Figure 6.4 expresses an agent focus. Motives (hatred, instincts, greed, or jealousy) sometimes act as agents. Countries and organizations (militia groups, UN peacekeeping forces, the National Rifle Association, pro-choice groups, and so on) frequently act as agents. We would not be surprised by the public antics of Dennis Rodman, but we would be if the antics were performed by Barry Bonds. Persuaders who emphasize agent as a key element tend to have idealism as their philosophy of life, according to Burke. They believe that strong, honest, and well-intended individuals determine the outcome of important events and even of history.

Agency is the tool, method, or means used by persuaders to accomplish their ends. For example, Arm & Hammer baking soda used "focus group research methods" as the agency to conduct the market research that resulted in the almost universal box of Arm & Hammer in the refrigerator. This practice was inspired by "refrigerator guilt" about not keeping it as clean as Mom did. Shakespeare's Hamlet used the play within a play as the agency to determine guilt. Energizer uses a mechanical bunny to send the message that its battery "keeps on going and going and . . ." Calvin Klein uses nudity and prepubescent, anorexic-appearing females as agencies to get attention for Obsession perfume. And Wheaties uses famous athletes to promote the brand as "the Breakfast of Champions." The tricks and gimmicks used by corporate executives in recent times are also kinds of agencies. The lessened rules of the Securities and Exchange Commission were agencies for the corporate fraud and looting that ruined highly respected companies and caused stockholders in and employees of these companies to lose billions of dollars in stock holdings and pension funds. But the lax rules made the fraudulent actions easy and practical ways for the CEOs and CFOs to "get rich quick." Communication strategies also act as agencies (such as intensifying one's own good points or others' bad ones). Persuaders who emphasize agency as the way to a goal tend to have pragmatism as a philosophy of life.

Purpose is the reason an agent acts in a given scene using a particular agency. Sometimes the persuader's purpose is quite apparent; other times, it is covert. The U.S. Army's old recruiting slogan,

"Be All That You Can Be in the Army," suggested a purpose for an individual to enlist. The U.S. government sends food and other humanitarian aid for the apparent purpose of preventing starvation and anarchy. Pro-life advocates have as a purpose the overturning of *Roe v. Wade*. These are all *apparent* purposes, but what are the *true* purposes? Why did the Boulder, Colorado, authorities suspect the parents of JonBenet Ramsey in the child's murder? Why did Michael Jordan decide to retire from pro basketball after winning the NBA championship six times? Why did President George W. Bush favor an enormous cut in estate taxes for the richest 1 percent of the population? Why did the passengers on Flight 728 decide to try to overpower the 9/11 hijackers, and was their purpose critical in preventing a crash into the White House? The purposes of such actions aren't always clear. Burke believed that persuaders favoring purpose as a key element tend to have mysticism as a philosophy of life—they believe that something greater than the individual (God, the Constitution, the American spirit) determines the outcome of human affairs.

These five elements can be used to develop a persuasive strategy. For example, if you were trying to get a date for a rock concert, you might emphasize the scene, describing the auditorium, crowd, sounds, costumes, lighting, colors, and so on. An alternative strategy would be to focus on the act, describing the kinds of music and the interactions between performers and audience. You might also choose to focus on the agent, describing the musicians, their reputations, and their appearance. If you chose to feature agency, you might mention the new digital sound system, the unique instruments, and special effects such as explosions on stage. Finally, you could feature purpose by telling your prospective date that "to be really 'in,' you shouldn't miss attending a live rock concert, and you might meet other interesting people, too."

In any situation, all of these elements of the pentad operate simultaneously to a greater or lesser degree (see Figure 6.5). Burke suggested that if we compare them in pairs, or ratios, we can identify a persuader's "key" emphases. In Hamlet, for example, the dramatic tension created in the scene–act

Your tomorrows depend on the consistent performance of your long-term investments. And that's why investors have made Kemper one of America's largest asset managers. For over forty years, the Kemper Family of Mutual Funds has been dedicated to the kind of steady, long-term performance that builds tomorrows today. To learn more, talk to your financial representative at this location.

FIGURE 6.5 The scene here is a childhood home. The agents are father and daughter. The act is nurturing, and the purpose is planning for the future. As is often the case, the product is the agency. This ad was designed in response to an ad Kemper ran in which a father is planning for his son to go to college. What might be the hidden purpose and agency here?

(Used by permission of Kemper Financial Services.)

ratio comes from the fact that Hamlet's mother has married his uncle following the mysterious death of Hamlet's father, the king. Worse, the marriage followed the funeral by less than one month, hardly the proper act for a scene in which extended mourning for a deceased king should be occurring. Disturbed by this imbalance in the scene–act ratio, Hamlet curses his mother and uncle in a soliloquy, saying, "She married. O, most wicked speed, to post with such dexterity to incestuous sheets!" Later, Hamlet teases his friend Horatio, asking whether he had visited court for the funeral or the wedding. Hamlet expresses his anger ironically in these bitter words, which reflect his reaction to the imbalance of the scene–act ratio: "Thrift, thrift, Horatio! The funeral baked meats did coldly furnish the marriage tables." We can almost hear him ready to use more damning language, yelling, "Whore! Slut."

We also frequently see the persuasive power of the scene–act ratio in advertisements. For example, in Figure 6.6, the scene—the state of Alaska—offers tourists great fishing with the words "If you like your fish wild" and "twelve native species, all of them pugnacious." It adds that the Alaska scene has "two oceans, two seas, and hundreds of bays," thereby furthering the scene–act balance—after all, where but in the largest state would you expect the biggest fight with a fish?

Scene can also interact with the other elements of the pentad. In the scene–agent ratio, balance or imbalance again can indicate potent persuasion or high drama—comedy, tragedy, or melodrama. In the film *Psycho,* one of Alfred Hitchcock's masterpieces, viewers instinctively note a scene–agent imbalance when Anthony Perkins tells Janet Leigh that he has stuffed all the taxidermic specimens in the office of the Bates Motel. The imbalance is intensified when we see him spy on her through a secret peephole in the eye of one of the specimens. The imbalance here implies the strong possibility of danger, and we may subconsciously whisper, "Don't stay at this motel—find another one down the road!" The tension caused by the scene–agent imbalance is increased when we hear Perkins and his "mother" arguing at the Victorian house near the motel—again, we want to warn Leigh to "close and lock the bathroom door whenever you take a

FIGURE 6.6 How are the scene and the act balanced in this ad?

(Used by permission of the Alaska Division of Tourism.)

shower!" Her murder is later "discovered" by Perkins, who is shocked at the scene–agent disparity of someone as kind as his "mother" stabbing a young woman to death. Hitchcock uses scene–agent tension throughout the rest of the film, as well as in his other films, to keep the audience on the edge of their seats.

Any of the other ten possible pairs of elements of the pentad (act–purpose, act–agency, scene–purpose, scene–agency, and so forth) might be examined to discover a persuader's key term or element. Burke believed that a persuader's key term infuses every aspect of life—home, family, job, political choices, and philosophy of life, to name but a few. As a result, identifying a persuader's key terms or elements can alert us to the underlying motives of the persuasion and help us predict future persuasive appeals. As you encounter persuasion in any of its many forms, try to listen for the key term being used, and process your response to the persuasion accordingly. Remember that the key term being used can prompt information processing in either the peripheral or the central channels.

Tools for the Thematic Dimension

As noted previously, the thematic dimension of language is that quality in certain words or sets of words that gives them a texture or "feel." Although the words do have a semantic meaning and a syntactical function, their most important persuasive aspect is their ability to set a mood, develop a feeling, or generate a tone or theme for the persuasion—hence the term "thematic." For example, Abraham Lincoln set the theme for his famous Gettysburg Address with these words:

> Fourscore and seven years ago our forefathers brought forth on this continent a new nation, conceived in liberty and dedicated to the proposition that all men are created equal.

How far less stirring the speech would have been if he had said,

> Eighty-seven years ago the signers of the Declaration of Independence started a new country designed to assure us of freedom and equality.

The two sentences have nearly equivalent semantic and functional meanings; the obvious difference between them lies in their texture.

Earlier, we also noted how the repetition of consonants (alliteration) or vowels (assonance) carries thematic meaning. The advertisements for Satin cigarettes, for example, used alliteration to create a thematic meaning for the brand—"Smooth. Silky. Satin Cigarettes." Or consider the slogan for Lexus: "The Relentless Pursuit of Perfection." Sometimes, parallel sentence structure communicates a thematic meaning. For example, consider the no-nonsense theme or texture contained in the parallel sentences used in the following print ad promoting MTV for a specific audience. The ad featured a male in his twenties slouching in an easy chair holding a TV remote control device. The headline reads, "Buy this

24-year-old and get all his friends absolutely free." The copy read as follows:

> If this guy doesn't know about you, you're toast. He's an opinion leader. He watches MTV. Which means he knows a lot more than just what CDs to buy and what movies to see. He knows what clothes to wear, and what credit card to buy them with. And he's no loner. He heads up a pack. What he eats, his friends eat. What he wears, they wear. What he likes, they like. And what's he never heard of . . . well . . . you get the idea. MTV. A darn good way to influence the MTV Generation. (*Advertising Age,* July 5, 1993, p. S-3)

We also noted earlier that thematic differences also come from the metaphors persuaders create or from the use of onomatopoeia (words that sound like their meaning, such as "swish" or "burp"). Let's turn now to several other tools for discovering the thematic meaning in persuasive messages. These include finding metaphorical themes; noting the use of sensory language; looking for god, devil, and charismatic terms; identifying the pragmatic and unifying styles; and using semiotics to determine the thematic meanings communicated by nonverbal symbols or "signifiers" in a text.

Metaphorical Style. Persuaders can convey a great deal of their message by setting the mood for persuadees and by repeatedly using certain sounds and images. As mentioned earlier, Michael Osborn (1967) studied the use of archetypal metaphors (universal and primal images consistent within and even across cultures), in particular the light–dark comparison, as in the Churchill war message. Osborn maintained that we traditionally identify light with the sun, warmth, growth, comfort, and so on; we associate dark with night, cold, mystery, and other uncomfortable and troubling things. Osborn pointed out that persuaders often use repeated references to this dichotomy. President John F. Kennedy, for instance, in his inaugural address, used this archetypal metaphor when he talked about passing a torch from one generation to another and predicted that the light from this symbolic torch could illuminate the world for freedom.

The light was depicted as good, warm, friendly, and virtuous, whereas elsewhere, the world was filled with dark and menacing shadows. Dan Hahn (1998), whom we met earlier, applies another of Osborn's metaphors—that of water as a dangerous image—to political communication. In the following excerpt from an address made by the late Senator Barry Goldwater, notice both the positivity and the negativity of the underlined water images:

> Due to <u>foggy thinking</u>, the <u>tide has been running against freedom</u> and we are sinking in a <u>swampland of collectivism</u>. Therefore, despite the detractors who say <u>don't rock the boat</u>, the <u>campaign we launch here</u> will <u>set the tide running again</u> in the cause of freedom. The past will be <u>submerged,</u> and we will <u>travel democracy's Ocean highway</u> where freedom will accompany the <u>rising tide of prosperity</u>.
> (p. 115)

Hahn goes on to remind us of other associations we have with the water metaphor. For example, it is cleansing, it is important in baptism, it is life giving, and it is the basic element from which life emerged (p. 115). Other powerful metaphors include references to wind and windstorms, blood and blood bonds, the locomotive as representative of the economy, the boxing ring as a stand-in for any of life's contests, and words as power.

To learn more about the power of metaphor, access InfoTrac College Edition, and type the word "metaphor" in the search engine. Peruse the more than fifty periodical titles, and choose some articles to read. Report your findings to your class.

Sensory Language. Courtroom communication expert Stephanie L. Swanson (1981) maintained that the most effective lawyers rely on words relating to the senses. She speculated that jurors can be influenced according to which sensory information channel they prefer. They might be auditorily dependent—that is, relating best to words that are tied to sound or sounds. They might be visually dependent—that is, relating best to words that are tied to sight. Or they might be kinesthetically dependent—that is, relating best to words that are tied to the sense of touch. How could a persuader

use these preferences? Suppose an attorney asks three witnesses to describe an automobile accident. The auditorily dependent witness might answer by saying, "I was walking down Oak Street listening to my Walkman, when I heard the screech of brakes, and then there was a sickening sound of crashing glass and metal, and someone screamed." The visually dependent witness might say, "I saw this brown Ford coming around the corner practically on two wheels. Then he must have hit the brakes, because it looked like the car slid sideways toward me, and then I saw the front end of the Ford make a mess of the little Geo." The kinesthetically dependent witness might say, "I had this feeling that something was about to happen, and when it did I felt frightened and helpless, and I cringed as the cars crumpled up like scrap paper." Swanson advised attorneys to "listen closely to the sensory language used by your clients . . . try to respond in kind—matching the sensory language of the other person" (p. 211). She urged them to carefully attend to the kinds of words used by prospective jurors during the voir dire process and then to "tailor your language to your listeners' primary sensory channel. You can 'paint a picture' for a visual person, 'orchestrate the testimony' for an auditory person, and 'touch the heart' of the kinesthetic individual. By using sensory language, you let the jurors feel that your discourse is directed toward them individually" (p. 211).

Thus, in trying to identify a persuader's use of the thematic dimension of language, another aspect to explore is the sensory language contained in the persuasion.

God, Devil, and Charismatic Terms. Another thematic or textural characteristic of style often used in persuasion is the development of families of terms. Persuaders like to divide the world into tidy categories that can be used to persuade others. One of these category sets is made up of god terms and devil terms, as noted by Richard Weaver (1953). According to Weaver, although terms or labels are really only parts of propositions, they are often linked with other terms or labels to shape a message or a persuasive argument. He defined "god term" as an expression "about which all other expressions are ranked as subordinate and serving dominations and powers. Its force imparts to the others their lesser degree of force" (p. 211). Weaver saw a god term as an unchallenged word (or phrase) that demands sacrifice or obedience in its name. He used three terms as examples of god terms: "progress," "fact," and "science." Progress still has persuasive power, but it is hampered by some of the things associated with it—pollution, for example. Science has lost some of its credibility, for science has produced, along with constructive marvels, nuclear weapons and technology that might destroy the earth. Devil terms are just the opposite. They are "terms of repulsion" and express negative values. As Weaver put it, "They generate a peculiar force of repudiation" (pp. 210–215).

The first *Newsweek* issue of 1988 declared, "The 80s Are Over: Greed Goes Out of Style." The magazine went on, in a long article, to describe the god terms of the "me generation/decade," as symbolized by Madonna's Material Girl, Sylvester Stallone's Rambo, and *Lifestyles of the Rich and Famous* with its "aptly named" host Robin Leach (Barol, 1988). These god terms were displaced by the god and devil terms of the 1990s—for example, "the environment," "green," "the family," "security," "terrorism," "deficit spending," "politically correct," "technology," "feminazis," "dittoheads," "surfing the Web," and "budget surplus." Such god and devil terms alert you to potential persuasive appeals that could persuade you or that you might use. And as we enter the twenty-first century, other god and devil terms are emerging. Some of the more recent devil terms include "cooked books," "Al Qaeda," "corporate fraud," "stock and real estate bubbles," "deflation," "terrorists," "aggressive accounting practices," "credit card fraud," and "CEOs and stock options." Some of the more recent god terms include "family/family time," "low fat," "rule of law," "air security," "financial security," "employment," "education," "phased retirement," "weight loss," "nutrition," "defense," "fuel cell," and "hybrid car."

The use of god and devil terms is evident in advertisements for consumer goods. For example, consider just a few recently popular god terms in ads for food: "lite," "light," "low sodium," "no sodium," "low calorie," "clear," "organically grown," and "with fiber." Candidates for devil terms include "artificial preservatives," "salt," "gas guzzler," "herbicides," "pesticides," "fat," and "toxic." You should be

able to discover many more as you search contemporary advertising texts for the thematic dimensions of words or terms.

Weaver pointed out that the connotations of certain negative terms can sometimes be reversed, making the terms neutral or even positive. Take, for example, the expression "wasted" or "getting wasted." Its use during the 1970s referred to killing Viet Cong or others perceived to be the enemy during the Vietnam War. Later, it referred to getting drunk or stoned. Today, "wasted" is equivalent to "squandered" and can refer to such varied topics as corporate trust, credibility, energy, and trust.

Weaver also described charismatic terms— "terms of considerable potency whose referents it is virtually impossible to discover. . . . Their meaning seems inexplicable unless we accept the hypothesis that their content proceeds out of a popular will that they shall mean something" (p. 48). His example is the word "freedom," which has no apparent concrete referent but which still seems, many years after Weaver discussed it, to have great potency.

Perhaps because so many things are being questioned in this first decade of the new century, we have fewer examples of charismatic terms, but there are some good candidates. For example, the terms "budget surplus" and "saving Social Security" became charismatic at the close of the 1990s. There was unanimity, regardless of one's political affiliation, that a "budget surplus" was a magnificent thing after decades of "budget deficits" (a devil term for those times, and more recently as well). And there was near unanimity on the wisdom of "saving Social Security" for the sake of the future—especially for the baby boomers who were in their early fifties at the time. Many of them had doubted that Social Security would be there for them at retirement, so naturally, the term became quite charismatic. Almost any policy could be justified if it would help "save Social Security."

Another candidate for a charismatic term was and remains "recycling." With the growing awareness of declining natural resources, the concept of recycling has been applied to a host of things—paper, plastic, aluminum, glass, and even people. A logo consisting of arrows acting as the three sides of a triangle is imprinted on grocery sacks, product containers, newspapers, aluminum cans, and a host of other items, indicating that they are recyclable. Thousands of communities, schools, corporations, churches, and other groups have gone on recycling kicks, even though some of the recycled material is either warehoused or discarded because there is now a surplus of the stuff. The term has nonetheless had the power to motivate impressive numbers of persons. It has convinced them that it is their duty to wash out and crush aluminum cans, collapse two-liter bottles and milk jugs, and carefully save miscellaneous paper, from used envelopes and junk mail to empty cereal boxes. "Patriot" and "patriotic" have become charismatic terms since the events of 9/11, and certainly "rescuer" stands out as well.

Pragmatic and Unifying Styles. Another characteristic that builds a thematic wholeness or that gives texture to persuasion is the reliance of a persuader on one of two kinds of styles—the pragmatic or the unifying. These styles can be thought of as signifying two separate strategies; however, persuaders can use the tactics of either strategy, or they can combine the two.

Pragmatic persuaders usually find it necessary to convince listeners who do not necessarily support their positions. As a result, these persuaders must try to change minds rather than reinforce beliefs, and they must choose appropriate tactics. A politician speaking at a public event (for example, a college convocation or a news conference) rather than at a party event (for example, a rally of supporters) will favor the pragmatic style. Unifying persuaders are in a much more comfortable position, because they talk to people who already believe what is going to be said. They don't need to change minds; they only need to reinforce beliefs—to whip up enthusiasm and dedication or to give encouragement. Thus, when Rush Limbaugh and Howard Stern speak to their television and radio audiences, they are likely to use the tactics of the unifying speaker—these audiences already believe what they are going to say.

These two styles demonstrate two opposing situations, and they describe the problems facing the persuader in these situations. The problems for pragmatic persuaders are clear—they must change opinion before they can expect action. Unifying persuaders can be much more idealistic—they can

usually afford to be more bombastic without offending the audience. The unifying persuaders thus can be more emotional and less objective than the persuader faced with a questioning audience.

What are the stylistic devices of these extremes? The unifying persuader is able to focus on the then-and-there—on the past or on the future —when things were ideal or when they can become ideal. The position of unifying persuaders is that things look better in the future, particularly if we compare them with the present. Because the audience will fill in the blanks, language choice can be abstract. It is usually poetic, emotional, and filled with imagery that excites the audience's imagination. Although there may be little that is intellectually stimulating or that requires logical examination in what unifying persuaders say, there is much that is emotionally stimulating. The words and images offered by such persuaders are precisely the words listeners believe they would have said if they were doing the talking. The unifying persuader is thus the sounding board for the entire group, providing them with the cues (the gist), but not the details, of the message. The audience can participate with the persuaders in the creation of the message; in fact, audiences sometimes participate actively by yelling encouragement to unifying persuaders or by repeating shibboleths to underscore their words—"Right on" or "Amen, brother" or "Tell it like it is."

Pragmatic persuaders, because they must win an audience, cannot risk appealing to abstract ideals. They must be concrete, focusing on facts instead of images and emphasizing what cannot be easily disputed or misinterpreted. They do not try to depict an ideal situation in subjective, then-and-there terms. Rather, they have to focus on real aspects of immediate problems familiar to the audience—problems of the here-and-now that are realistic, not idealistic. Their orientation is to the present instead of the future. Because pragmatic persuaders are forced to be specific and realistic, their language is concrete and prosaic. Lofty thoughts are of little value, especially if they are expressed in equally lofty terms. These persuaders tend to focus on facts and statistics instead of imagery, and their messages are processed via the central information-processing route.

Clearly, these two extremes are not an either/or proposition—persuaders may, on occasion, use the tactics of both perspectives. When they do, they are probably responding to their audience's level of doubt or acceptance. In the following excerpt, the author is using the pragmatic style. Note the use of here-and-now references, the prosaic language, and the concrete examples and references.

> I came here 26 years ago to teach, and like many of my friends, I really didn't expect to stay. I like to think we're all still here because we found a place that only asks us to be whatever we can manage. Call it refuge, an escape from the hurly burly of the rest of the country. Now the West is confronting epic changes. We're growing faster than any other region; people from . . . all over America. People who can are running to enclaves like Montana in search of an unthreatening life. . . . So it's no wonder that a lot of Montanans way down the economic ladder are feeling alienated. A few of them—the militant ones we're reading about—are furious. . . . In Montana, this wave of crazies is regarded as bad luck we don't deserve. On the other hand, some of us are guilty . . . of ignoring conditions that drove such folks to think they have to pursue their political objectives with guns and bombs. (Kittredge, 1996, p. 43)

This persuader is a Montana professor who is trying to convince his audiences (primarily Montanans, but also other readers of *Newsweek*) that his state is not as filled with militant lunatics as it appears and that such people need to be convinced that violence is unacceptable. With his audience spread out and divided, he needs to be down-to-earth, practical, and present oriented. Notice his use of common expressions such as "hurly burly" and "wave of crazies." He also uses concrete examples and references and focuses on what needs to be done now to salvage the situation. He has assessed his audience accurately as one that needs persuasion, not reinforcement—as a bipolar versus a unipolar one—and his style fits the audience's needs.

Consider what the following pragmatic persuader does in trying to change a doubtful audience. He is responding in a "Voice of the People" letter to the editor to an article that criticized a skydiving facility operator.

> When I stand in the door of an airplane in flight, I alone am responsible for the decision to jump. If the winds, clouds or any other conditions are unfavorable, I have the option of riding down in the plane—something I have done on several occasions. Neither the pilot nor the drop zone operator forces me to jump if I choose not to. Once a skydiver exits the plane there's no going back. One person and one person only has the responsibility of deploying the parachute . . . and executing a safe landing. . . . Skydiving is not a preprogrammed carnival thrill ride with simulated risk. . . . While the trend in American society is to find someone else to blame for your own mistakes, that is not the way it is in skydiving. To suggest otherwise indicates total misunderstanding of the sport on the part of your reporters. (Kallend, 2002, p. 8)

The pragmatic and unifying styles are a function of the audience and its needs, and not of the speaker. We can learn something about persuaders by observing which style they choose for which kinds of audiences. Persuadees can gain insight into how they are viewed by the persuader by identifying the style of the message.

Semiotics and Signifiers. We have briefly referred to the field of semiotics as a way to study meaning. Although the origin of this approach dates back to the works of Charles Morris and Charles Sanders Peirce in the 1940s and 1950s, its most important contemporary theorist is Umberto Eco, known for his best-selling novels *The Name of the Rose* and *Foucault's Pendulum*. Eco (1984) proposed that the process of "signification" (or the giving of meaning to a "sign") involves four elements: (1) the objects or conditions that exist in the world, (2) the signs that are available to represent these objects or conditions, (3) the set of choices among signs, or the repertoire of responses available for use, and (4) the set of rules of correspondence that we use to encode and decode the signs we make and interpret.

This final characteristic most directly relates to the goal of this course. The discovery of the various codes or sets of rules that are used by persuaders and understood by persuadees characterizes cooperatively created meanings. In other words, we participate in our own persuasion by "agreeing with" the code(s) persuaders use. Most importantly, we can become critical consumers of persuasion by continually striving to discover and reveal these codes (Eco, 1979). Semiotician and former circus owner and ringmaster Paul Buissac (1976) offered some fascinating examples of codes in his semiotic analysis of circus acts, illustrating this idea of an easily discernible code understood by "children of all ages" around the world:

> Wild animal, tightrope, and trapeze acts never occur back to back in the circus . . . they are always interspersed with clown acts, small animal acts, magic acts, or the like. If a daring act is canceled, the entire order of acts needs to be altered because of audience expectations, tension reduction, and the need to communicate that the world is alternately serious and comedic. . . . Death-defying acts also have a code—usually a five-step sequence. First, there is the introduction of the act by the ringmaster (a godlike figure able to control not only the dangers but the chaos of the circus). This introduction, with its music, lights, and revelation of dazzling and daring costumes, is followed by the "warm-up," in which minor qualifying tests occur: The animal trainer, dressed as a big-game hunter, gets all the animals to their proper positions; the trapeze artist, with his beautiful assistants, can easily swing out and switch trapeze bars in mid-air; the tightrope walker dances across the rope with ease. Then comes the major tests or tricks: getting the tiger to dance with the lion, doing double trapeze switches, and walking the wire blindfolded. Having passed these tests, the

circus performer then attempts the "glorifying," or "death-defying," test. It is always accompanied by the ringmaster's request for absolute silence and, ironically, by the band breaking the critical silence with a nerve-tingling drumroll. Then comes the feat itself: The animal tamer puts his head into the lion's mouth; the trapeze artist holds up a pair of beautiful assistants with his teeth, demonstrating his amazing strength; and the blindfolded tightrope walker puts a passenger on his shoulders and rides a bicycle backward across the high wire. Frequently, there is a close call: An unruly tiger tries to interfere with the "head-in-the-mouth" trick, there is a near miss on the trapeze or a stumble on the high wire, and so on. Once the glorifying test is passed, the ringmaster calls for applause as the act exits and then returns for a curtain call. This sequence is a "code" we all understand. (n. p.)

More subtle examples of codes are frequently found in advertising. For example, consider the ad for Bostonian shoes in Figure 6.7. What codes are operating in this ad? Some are rather obvious, but others are more subtle. In fact, some codes in the ad are embedded within other codes. The most obvious code is that the ad is trying to sell a product although the kind of product is not so clear. Finding out requires more detailed decoding, but we soon discover that the product is men's shoes. Another less obvious code is that the product is an upscale one, as indicated by the composition and copy of the ad and by the price of the shoes—$105. The ad is understated; there is little actual ad copy. Finally, the photograph is distinctively "fine art" in its composition.

Within these codes is an even more subtle code —one that is only implied and never directly stated. This code signifies the lifestyle that goes with the product. The shoes are merely an emblem of that lifestyle. What do we see in this photograph? Clearly, it is the "morning after" a satisfying night of lovemaking (notice the coffee cups and pastries on the bed, the negligee on the well-rumpled bedding, the indentations on both pillows). The lifestyle includes a fine home (notice the expensive furniture and the

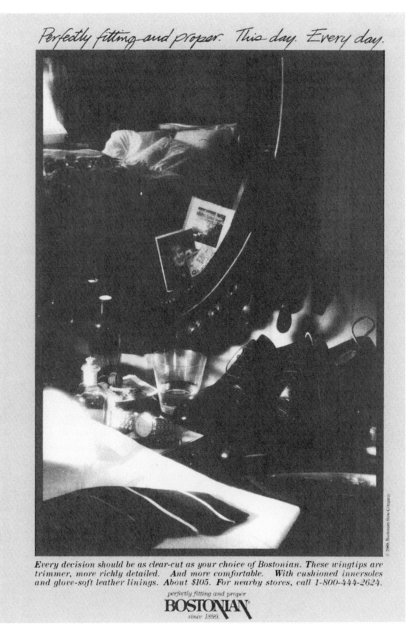

FIGURE 6.7 What messages are implied by the "code" of physical objects in this ad (theater tickets, rumpled bedclothes, articles of clothing that seem to have been hurriedly discarded, an empty cocktail glass, and so on)?

(Reprinted by permission of the Bostonian Shoe Company.)

framed photographs on the nightstand in the upper left corner). This lifestyle includes expensive accessories such as the Rolex watch and the Mont Blanc pen on the dresser. The stylish suspenders, the theater ticket stubs slipped into the frame of the mirror, and the picture of a beautiful wife under the tickets signal a lifestyle that values the arts, stylishness, beauty, and physical attractiveness (note the snapshot of the man, bare-chested and muscular). Clearly, this ad carries a lot of meaning, "signified" by the verbal and nonverbal symbols being used (or perhaps misused, depending on one's perspective). It is a persuasive message that must be cooperatively created by both persuader and persuadee based on their agreed-upon and shared semiotic code. It would be difficult to characterize the message as a "logical" one. The signifiers, or repertoire of objects in the room, probably trigger emotional values in which the persuader assumes the audience believes.

Although analyses like these may be intriguing, they are difficult to carry out without some kind of systematic methodology. The fields of theoretic semiotics and applied semiotics (for example, advertising and image/political consulting) are rapidly expanding, and as receivers we need a simplified way to pin down these uses (or misuses) of symbols. A methodology for doing this kind of semiotic analysis has been developed by communication scholar Arthur Asa Berger, whom we met briefly in Chapter 5. Berger (1984) provided a fairly simple checklist for doing such an analysis that my students find useful. First, consider the pieces of persuasion aimed at you as if they are "texts" to be read, and then put on your Sherlock Holmes hat and start looking for clues. Using the following steps, analyze the meaning of the ad for *Ms.* magazine in Figure 6.8.

1. Isolate and analyze the important signs in the text.
   a. What are the important signifiers?
   b. What do they signify?
   c. Is there a system that unifies them?
   d. What codes can be found (for example, symbols of status, colors, or music)?
   e. Are ideological or sociological issues being addressed?
   f. How are they conveyed or hinted at?

2. Identify the central structure, theme, or model of the text.
   a. What forces are in opposition?
   b. What forces are teamed with each other?
   c. Do the oppositions or teams have psychological or sociological meanings? What are they?

3. Identify the narrative structure of the text. (That is, if a "story" is being told, what are its elements?)
   a. How does the sequential arrangement of events affect the meaning? What changes in meaning would result if they were altered?
   b. Are there any "formulaic" aspects to the text (for example, hard work leads to success, justice prevails, or honesty gets its reward)?

4. Determine whether the medium being used affects the text, and how.
   a. How are shots, camera angles, editing, dissolves, and so on used?
   b. How are lighting, color, music, sound, special effects, and so on used?
   c. How do paper quality, typefaces, graphics, colors, and so on contribute?
   d. How do the speaker's words, gestures, and facial expressions affect meaning?

5. Specify how the application of semiotic theory alters the original meaning ascribed to the text. (You may want to do further reading in semiotics to complete this step effectively.)

Of course, this discussion of the semiotic approach to language and meaning is brief and necessarily simplified. Nonetheless, it gives us another tool for discovering the important first premises that emerge from our language preferences and the images molded from them.

To learn how semiotics is used in advertising and marketing, access InfoTrac College Edition, and enter the word "semiotics" in the search engine. Look at the article by Frank and Stark in the *Journal of Advertising Research.* Read the abstract, and then read the article and reference its footnotes through the InfoTrac College Edition system. You

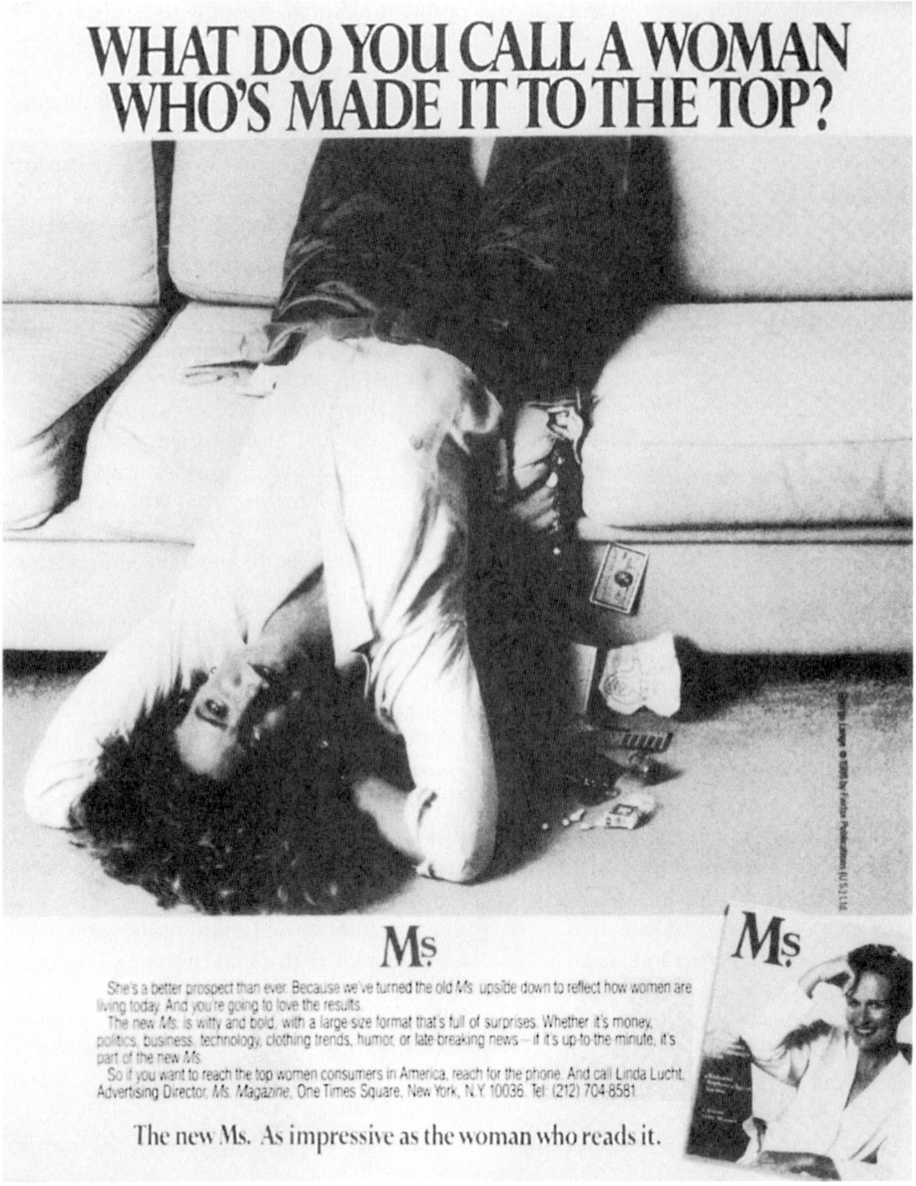

FIGURE 6.8 Using the semiotic approach to uncovering meaning as outlined by Berger, uncover the meaning of this ad/text. Note that the woman has "lost" items from her pockets—a passport, the keys to an Audi, credit cards, a picture of herself drawn by her child, jewelry, aspirin, a champagne cork, a $100 bill, and other signs. What do they signify? How old is this woman? Is she sentimental? Stressed? Busy?

(Used by permission.)

might also look under the related-subjects category and go to the discourse analysis option. Some fascinating titles can be found in the signs and symbols option as well.

GENDER AND STYLE

In an article titled "He: This Is an Okay (Lovely) Analysis (Emotional Investigation) of Our Words (Deepest Corridors of Meaning)," language critic and English professor Edwin Bruell (1986) considers how gender affects our use of language and style. As you may have guessed from the structure of the title, the words inside the parentheses represent the feminine mode of expression, and the words outside the parentheses represent the masculine mode. As Bruell notes, "There seems to be a form of poverty in America that is strictly a masculine phenomenon: poverty of expression" (p. 12). He goes on to point out some differences between male and female word choice. For example, women can characterize clothing, dolls, furniture, or sunsets with words like "lovely," "darling," "sweet," "adorable," or "cute," whereas men rarely use such words. Men might use the word "lovely" to express their assessment of a new dress on their spouse or another woman, but they would never use it to describe the new suit of clothes on another man. Bruell claims that "men shy away from all such usages because they passionately fear being labeled sissified. Their superlatives are likely to be far less flowery" (p. 12). Thus, men tend to limit their superlatives to words like "fine," "great," "good," and occasionally "grand" if they are talking about a sports event. Also, according to Bruell, "Women will speak of 'fragrance' and 'scent' and 'aromatic, seductive' concoctions. A man will speak of 'smell' . . . and . . . a shutout defeat just 'stinks.'" To men, locker room jokes are "dirty," whereas at cocktail parties, women listen to the same stories but label them "risqué." An orderly desk is "tidy" to a woman, but it is "neat and organized" to a man. An attractive, well-dressed, carefully groomed woman may be described as "dainty" or "fetching" by another woman, but she will be "nice," "okay," or "swell" to a man. Bruell recounts an encounter with a female confidante who exclaimed, "How stunning they are! How positively ravishing!" which he thought referred to stereotypes that "frighten me (no, make that 'scare the ———— out of me')." Actually, she was rhapsodizing about her first view of a pair of burly tag-team wrestlers (p. 12).

Other researchers have identified several additional gender-related characteristics of language use. For example, authors Diane Dunaway and Jonathan Kramer (1990) note that, because of their training, men avoid using more words than necessary and try to get to the point right away. As a result, many men view conversations between females as "superfluous chatter." Women see language as a kind of social glue, and they don't have to transfer information in their conversations. They view conversation as an aid to developing relationships. Dunaway and Kramer attribute this characteristic of what they call "malespeak" (which prevents men from being able to express affection and to forge satisfying intimate relationships) to gender training.

Another researcher in gender-related differences in language use, Deborah Tannen (1990), maintains that unless women are very direct in their conversations with men, they are likely to be misunderstood and perceived as manipulative. She advises women to avoid personal anecdotes and references when conversing with men, as men are likely to be uncomfortable with such references. Men are also likely to interpret interrupters such as "Uh huh" and "okay" as indicating agreement, so women should avoid those when conversing with men. More recently, researchers such as Michael Messner (1998) have held that, although the initial response of males to the women's liberation movement was either stunned silence or hostility, it may be that males are victims of language discrimination as well. Messner relies heavily on gender role theory in arguing that men have been victims of the same kind of gender stereotyping as females and that both have suffered because we all learn gender roles from modern media. These media typically depict males as successful, virile, and highly competent at a variety of tasks including seducing women. He quotes an early male feminist, Warren Farrell (1974):

> Women become objects of not only the male sex drive but a man's need to prove himself to other males. . . . He molds himself into an object he thinks will attract the woman . . . a woman becomes the sex object as the male becomes a success object. . . . they are even more restricted than women in the contempt they receive if they deviate into a feminine role or fail in a masculine one. Women can smoke a Marlboro, but no man dare smoke an Eve. . . . (p. 126)

With the advent of the World Wide Web and email, other differences between men and women in language use may be emerging. On my campus, men seem to be more assertive and more argumentative in a net chat group. A smaller proportion of women are members of and interact with this group, and those who do are frequently perceived as more assertive. Men also seem to send and forward more humorous messages than women. Scholar S. J. Yates (2001) looked at gender differences in computer-mediated communication in instructional interactions. Some educators hold that, because nonverbal cues are absent on the computer, inequality between males and females is a moot point. However, Yates found that inequality in instructional interactions could be greatly affected depending on social contexts and that the absence of nonverbal cues didn't guarantee equality of instructions.

Language choices can reveal much about persuaders: their cultural heritage, their political inclinations, their philosophy, the nature of their audiences, their gender, and a host of other kinds of meanings and interpretations. It becomes essential, therefore, for critical and ethical receivers of messages to look beyond the substance of the message for deeper indications of persuaders' attitudes and worldviews, as well as their potential future actions. How do we go about this?

TUNING YOUR EARS FOR LANGUAGE CUES

The basic message here is that consumers of persuasion should be vigilant when processing and responding to persuasive messages. In the course of this vigilance, one of the most important things persuaders can do is tune their ears to language for various clues to style and motives. Using some of the tools described in this chapter is one way. If you have thought about these tools or tried to apply them to the persuasion around you, you have already started the tuning process. Applying the study questions at the end of this and other chapters is another useful approach.

There are at least three specific strategies you might use to make yourself more critical of style and to "decode" or "psych out" persuaders:

1. *Role-play the persuader.* Assume that you are the persuader. How would you shape the persuasion you wish to present? For example, if you favor high salaries for baseball players, how would you frame a pragmatic message for half-hearted believers, those who are neutral, or others who are only moderately opposed? Would you mention the shortness of most players' careers (which means they receive a relatively low overall salary across a lifetime, despite high yearly salaries)? You might compare ballplayers to entertainers, who also make several million dollars per year for relatively little actual work time. If your audience happened to be the players' union, you could afford to bypass the numbers and use highly emotional and abstract language to motivate them. You might create images of club owners as filthy-rich bloodsuckers who blithely use up the best years of an athlete's life. Your language will probably be then-and-there—referring to new goals of the group or to past abuses.

2. *Restate a persuasive message in various ways.* Ask yourself, "What are other ways to say this?" Then try to determine how these alternatives will change the intent of the message and its

final effects. You might try using the parts of Burke's pentad. For example, take the following slogan for Grand Marnier Liqueur— "There Are Still Places on Earth Where Grand Marnier Isn't Offered After Dinner"—printed on a photo of a deserted island. The appeal is scenic. An agent-oriented version of this slogan might be, "People of Taste Offer Grand Marnier." A purpose-oriented version might read, "Want to Finish the Conference? Offer Grand Marnier." An agency-oriented version might say, "Grand Marnier—From a Triple-Sec-ret Recipe," stressing the method of production. The act might be emphasized by saying, "Make a Move—Offer Grand Marnier." Of course, each slogan would be accompanied by appropriate visuals.

3. *Attend to language features in discourse.* Don't allow yourself to passively buy into any persuasive advice that is being hawked. Instead, get into the habit of looking at each message's style. Analyze messages on billboards and in TV commercials, the language used by your parents when they try to persuade you, the wording on packages you purchase, or the phrases used in discussions between you and friends, enemies, or salespersons. In other words, start listening not only to ideas but to word strategies—the packaging of those ideas. Try it on me. What kinds of words do I use? Why? How does my style differ from that of other textbook writers?

Focusing on these features will give you an intriguing pastime, and you will develop an ear for stylistic tip-offs, a skill that will prove valuable in helping you predict and respond to the communication of others.

REVIEW AND CONCLUSION

Responsible receivers of persuasion relate to the language a particular persuader chooses. They gain general insight by looking at the semantic connotations of the words chosen. They look at word order, or syntax, and at the frequency of various parts of speech. The degree of ambiguity used by the persuader is often revealing, as in a dramatistic analysis such as that suggested by Burke. The motifs and metaphors chosen by a persuader often reveal motive. And persuadees can look at the god, devil, and charismatic terms used, as well as the choice of pragmatic versus unifying styles. Finally, they can apply the semiotic approach to the interpretation of persuasive messages, identifying as many of the signifiers in a persuasive message as possible.

All these critical devices are enhanced by role playing, restating, and developing awareness of the words, styles, and ideas used in a persuasive speech, TV documentary, film, political slogan, social movement, package design, or friend's request.

QUESTIONS FOR FURTHER THOUGHT

1. Transcribe the lyrics of a popular song. Now analyze them according to the functional tools presented in this chapter. Is there a preference for a certain word type? A certain sentence structure? Is the message ambiguous or concrete? Explain.

2. Describe several semantic tools. What do you think is the pentadic perspective of the president of the United States? Of your instructor?

3. Describe the tools for a thematic or textural analysis of language, and use some of them to analyze the persuasion occurring in a recent political campaign. What do these analyses tell you about the candidate?

4. What are the god terms of your parents? What are their devil terms? As an experiment, shape a request for something from your parents, expressed in their god terms.

5. How does a unifying persuader differ from a pragmatic one? Find examples of each type of persuader in your class, in persuasive attempts of the past, or in defenders of some persuasive issue being discussed in your community. Are there other differences between these two types? What are they?

6. What are the differences between semantics and semiotics? Which is more objective? When might it be appropriate to use each approach?

How do you use semantics and semiotics to both analyze and create persuasive messages?

7. What is the difference between a text and a symbol? What is the difference between a signifier and the signified?

8. How does gender affect how we use language? Can you give examples beyond those cited in this chapter?

 For online activities, go to the Web site for this book at http://communication.wadsworth.com/larson.

PART II

✳

Identifying Persuasive First Premises

As we saw in Part I, there are many ways to define, explain, and interpret persuasive messages and the symbols used to convey them. The critical question of ethics enters into every persuasive decision we make, whether as receivers or as persuaders. As we continue our study, you should refer to what you learned in Part I about the foundations of persuasion theory, the many theoretical explanations of persuasive phenomena, and the various means of analyzing the verbal and nonverbal symbols used in persuasive language and symbols, regardless of their source.

Underlying all means of analytically processing the symbols of persuasion is the ancient Aristotelian concept of the enthymeme, which we discussed in Chapters 1 and 3, where we examined Aristotle's triad of ethos, pathos, and logos. The enthymeme will serve as the analytical metaphor or organizational device for Part II. It is useful to think of Part II as a search for the types of major premises in enthymemes. In Part II, we identify those kinds of major premises that most audiences already believe and those that audiences can be convinced of to prompt the desired conclusion. We look at certain major categories of premises that audiences believe—we hunt for major premises.

The first category of major premise is the process premise, covered in Chapter 7. Process premises rely on psychological factors that operate in nearly all persuadees.

Persuaders tie their product, candidate, or idea to these process premises, which are then used as the major premises in enthymemic arguments that have wide appeal. In terms of the elaboration likelihood model, most process premises are dealt with in the peripheral information-processing path.

In Chapter 8, we look at the second category of major premises—content premises. Their persuasiveness lies in the audience's belief in the truth or validity of the argument, and they get processed centrally. For example, if the audience believes that history repeats itself and that, as a result, we can avoid the mistakes of the past, the persuader merely has to draw a convincing analogy between past and present. Then the persuadee processes the analogy to see if it truly fits the situation under consideration. This is done by processing the information in the central path.

You have probably noticed that there is considerable similarity between process premises and content premises. Process premises rely on psychological or emotional needs, whereas content premises rely on logical or rational patterns. We have been trained in these patterns of inference since early childhood, and they are reinforced throughout our lives. For instance, suppose we tell two-year-old children that if they continue to cry they will have to take a time-out or go without television or a particular toy. What we really are using is "if . . . then . . ." reasoning, or the rational pattern of consequences. A three-year-old understands this when a toy is no longer interesting or fun. When that happens, the toy takes a time-out.

The third category of major premises, discussed in Chapter 9, is the cultural premise. This kind of premise relies on patterns of behavior or beliefs that resemble articles of faith for audiences and that have been passed on to them by their culture or society. For example, Americans learn that when faced with a problem they must seek a solution to it, perhaps by establishing a task force or swallowing a pill. This seems so obvious that we are dumbstruck to discover that people from some other cultures prefer simply to accept the inevitable when faced with a problem. Problem solving is a culturally transmitted pattern for us. Knowing that, persuaders motivate us to take actions by portraying the actions as solutions. Even if we don't perceive that there is a problem, and thus are not searching for solutions, clever persuaders can create problems and then sell us a cure. Cultural premises consist of the myths and values our society holds dear. Because they operate almost by instinct, cultural premises are most likely processed in the peripheral information-processing route.

In Chapter 10, we explore nonverbal premises, which are similar to cultural premises in that they vary from culture to culture (and from subculture to subculture). These nonverbal premises are sometimes more potent than sophisticated verbal premises. Often, nonverbal premises contribute to the ultimate success or failure of persuasion. These premises are usually processed almost unconsciously following the peripheral path of the elaboration likelihood model.

As you read Part II, think of yourself as searching for major premises that you and an audience hold in common. By identifying these major premises, you can not only become a more skillful persuader but also, and more importantly, effectively evaluate the persuasion aimed at you.

7

✳

Process Premises

The Tools of Motivation

Some persuasion theorists distinguish between logical and emotional appeals, arguing that they represent opposite ends of a continuum and that the "better" appeals are the logical ones. Others characterize these two types of appeals along a continuum from rational to irrational and assume that rational appeals are "better." Both of these explanations assume that persuasive appeals are either one thing or another and that the two types of appeals operate separately and independently. "Rational" and "emotional" both carry with them the sense that persuasion occurs all at once as a result of some key phrases, statistics, qualities of the persuader, or other factors. It is true that some persuasion seems to occur all at once. For example, Patrick Henry's "Give me liberty or give me death" speech probably converted many members of his audience on the spot, but Henry's audience was probably already leaning toward his position.

In fact, most persuasion involves self-persuasion, usually occurs incrementally across time, and frequently involves many kinds of persuasive communication. One "emotional" appeal might accomplish a slight change in persuadees, which is then reinforced by a series of "logical" arguments, which lead to the final behavior proving that the persuasion was successful. For example, an automobile company trying to sell you a new car may use some clearly emotional appeals ("Bigger is better—Silverado is biggest"). But they will probably also use some clearly logical appeals ("Economical—up to 20 miles per gallon on the highway") and some hybrid—emotional and logical—appeals ("Now equipped with life-saving airbags on the driver's and the passenger's side, front and rear"). This unfortunate dichotomy between logical and emotional can be resolved easily enough using the elaboration likelihood model (ELM). The real question is not whether a persuasive appeal is logical or emotional but whether it is processed centrally or peripherally.

In this chapter, we examine appeals that tap into the psychological processes operating in persuadees and that rely on human emotions, drives, or instincts—appeals we rarely ponder. We call these appeals "process premises" because they target psychological processes that seem to operate in most people. For example, most of us have fears of some kind and will eagerly take action to dispel them. As a result, persuaders make appeals to alleviate fears about our health or grooming ("Now—with Fiber," or "Got halitosis? Listerine mouthwash makes your breath kissing sweet," or "The ONLY one [Arm & Hammer deodorant] that absorbs and eliminates odor instead of just covering it up—Arm yourself!") Arthur Asa Berger (2000) emphasizes American grooming paranoia by restating philosopher René Descartes' words "I think, therefore I am" as "I stink, therefore I am" (p. xi). Process premises are also operating when we buy a product because of brand loyalty, brand name, a memorable slogan, a catchy jingle, or even packaging. Process premises also operate in more serious situations, such as listening to political speeches or appeals from social activists. For example, pro-life advocates are using process premises when they show the film *The Silent Scream,* which claims that the tiny skulls of unborn fetuses are crushed during abortions.

And, of course, emotional appeals that rely on psychological processes are evident in interpersonal persuasion between spouses, parents and children, siblings, lovers, and bosses and employees. Psychological appeals are seen in business, marketing, advertising, sales promotions, and ideological advocacy on behalf of emotionally loaded issues.

NEEDS: THE FIRST PROCESS PREMISE

Each of us has a set of individual needs. Some of them are critical to us—we can't live without them (for example, food, water, clothing, and shelter). Others are not critical—we can get along without them, at least for a while. Not everyone's priorities are identical, but our needs resemble one another's enough that various theories of motivation can identify those that typify audiences. Some theories identify needs that are physiologically based, such as our needs for the staples of survival and physical security. Other theories focus on less concrete needs —those that lead to our overall sense of well-being (for example, success on the job or religious faith).

Without them or some substitute, we feel frustrated, anxious, afraid, and even angry. These needs are difficult to measure, so they are inferred from patterns of behavior that people exhibit. For instance, because people seem concerned about being successful, we quickly infer a need for physical symbols of success (for example, a Jaguar or a Rolex).

Such symbols become emblems of the fulfillment of that person's need to succeed. For the most part, persuasion in today's changing world focuses on promoting or selling symbolic ways to meet people's physiological and emotional needs. Although some products (such as self-improvement courses) really can help individuals make a better impression on the boss, for the most part what people buy and support doesn't have such a direct effect. They use Binaca breath spray not because it ensures a better impression but because they hope it prevents bad breath. They drive a BMW and enjoy the admiring looks they get from other drivers.

To be really effective, persuaders must successfully determine their audience's needs. If they analyze these needs incorrectly, persuasion can boomerang. For example, a well-known luggage manufacturer once spent thousands of dollars to produce an impressive and clever TV ad. The spot opens with luggage being handled roughly as it is loaded into the cargo bay of a huge airliner. The central piece of luggage was made by the ad's sponsor. The plane is next seen in flight, but someone has failed to latch the cargo bay door. As the plane banks, our star piece of luggage falls out of the now-open door. The camera follows the suitcase as it plummets 30,000 feet and lands with a huge thud on some rocks. The suitcase is then opened to reveal the undamaged contents. Now, that ought to be a fairly convincing ad. However, after the spot was broadcast in a test market, there was a tremendous drop in sales. Why? Showing the ad to typical viewers and following up using focus group interviews, researchers found that most people, even regular airline travelers, have a deep-seated fear that their flight might crash. They resented the implication that their luggage would survive them in the event of a crash.

Some of the motivation research done on behalf of advertisers appeared in a book titled *The Hidden*

Persuaders by Vance Packard (1964). It was promoted with sentences like these: "In this book you'll discover a world of psychology professors turned merchandisers. You'll learn how they operate, what they know about you and your neighbors, and how they are using that knowledge to sell you cake mixes, cigarettes, soaps and even ideas" (p. 5). Packard reported that a majority of the hundred largest ad firms in the country had been using psychoanalytic research. He noted that other professional persuaders—public relations executives, fund-raisers, politicians, and others—were turning to psychological theorists to discover customers' motives. They then tied their products, candidates, and causes to these motives. Packard quoted one ad executive as saying:

> Motivation research . . . seeks to learn what motivates people in making choices. It employs techniques designed to reach the subconscious mind because preferences generally are determined by factors of which the individual is not conscious. . . . Actually in the buying situation the consumer acts emotionally and compulsively, unconsciously reacting to images and designs which in the subconscious are associated with the product. (p. 5)

Another advertiser gave some examples of how the research was used: "The cosmetic manufacturers are not selling lanolin; they are selling hope. . . . We no longer buy oranges, we buy vitality. We do not buy just an auto; we buy prestige" (p. 5).

Clearly, psychology had entered the field of advertising. According to Packard, market researchers operating from this perspective had three basic assumptions about people: (1) They don't always know what they want when they make a purchase; (2) one cannot rely on what they say about what they like and dislike; and (3) they do not act logically or rationally. Packard gave several examples of how these assumptions operate. For instance, motivation researchers wondered what made people buy a certain brand of laundry detergent. Purchasers said they bought it because of its cleaning power. A sample group of consumers was given three boxes of detergent and asked to test the three types and report back. Actually, the three boxes contained the

same detergent—only the color of the boxes was different. The test group reported that the detergent in the yellow box was too harsh, the one in the blue box was too weak (it left clothes gray after washing), but the stuff in the yellow-and-blue box was great.

To learn more about the fascinating field of motivation research, access InfoTrac College Edition, and enter the words "motivation research" in the search engine. Read several of the articles listed there. The two articles by Jerry Thomas provide a thorough description of some of the techniques used to do this kind of research. You will also enjoy the article "21 Meaningful Motivational Messages."

The psychoanalytic approach to marketing most closely reflects the symbolistic tradition of psychology. Indeed, much of the in-depth research that Packard described resembles psychoanalysis. The researchers used focus group interviews that encouraged consumers to describe the fears, pleasures, nightmares, fantasies, and lusts they associated with the product or the ad for it. Other researchers used complex psychological tests like the Minnesota Multiphasic Personality Inventory. Still others used projective tests in which people completed sentences about the product, did word associations about the brand, or described the "real meaning" behind cartoon vignettes related to the product.

This trend continues, more than forty years after Packard first described it. In spite of the fact that Packard was seen as a popularizer, the "hidden persuaders" are still with us today. Now, however, ad agencies and others are using increasingly sophisticated methods to fine-tune their pitches via process premises. In fact, they are finding ways to combat the new technologies for "zapping" commercials with a fast-forward remote control:

> Advertisers aren't about to take this lying down. Desperate to keep you tuned to their pitches, they're trying some new tricks. If that's news to you, it may be because these new techniques are manipulating you in ways you're not aware of. "Many of these commercials have more impact on the subconscious level,"

charges New York University media professor Neil Postman. Perhaps more disturbing, ad agencies often enlist psychologists and neurophysiologists to make sure the pitches have the desired effect. (Freedman, 1988)

And, in a more recent development, a new kind of data is being examined to get into our heads. This cutting-edge offspring of motivational research is called "psychographic data and data-based marketing." For example, one marketing firm, Amherst Incorporated, has developed a research instrument called the Motivation and Attitude Profile (MAP), which has been used in the marketing of goods, services, and politicians and even in fund-raising for a children's hospital. The firm's creative director puts the philosophy of MAP this way: "People are driven by their emotions, it's not about fact or logic. Increasingly, the only button you press is an emotional one. You find out what their needs are and you discover how to reflect those needs" (Booth, 1999, p. 32).

Products as varied as Haagen Daz ice cream, Volkswagens, and life insurance rely on psychographics as a means of getting into the consumer's mind. Whether we call it motivational research, lifestyle research, hidden persuaders, or psychographics, it amounts to the same basic idea—find hidden or obvious needs, and develop the product and the persuasion to fulfill those needs. A Chicago-based company named Claritas used psychographics and lifestyle data to develop their PRIZM system, which identifies more than sixty market segments having names that reflect the inner needs of the consumers in each segment. For example, persons in the segment called "Pickups and Gun Racks" obviously have different needs from those of the people in the segment "Town and Gowns" (you may be living there right now), and these needs, in turn, differ from those of the people in the segment "Red, White, and Blue Collar." Specifically, persons in "Pickups and Gun Racks" are heavy users of generic or house brands of sweetened soda pop. If they purchase lingerie, it tends to be from Frederick's of Hollywood. Their most recent financial transaction is the purchase of a lottery ticket, and they tend to live in mobile home

parks. For persons in "Town and Gown," in contrast, the most frequent financial transaction is the use of an ATM. If they purchase lingerie, it is frequently at a department store or from Victoria's Secret, and most of them live in houses, apartments, dorms, or fraternity and sorority houses. Psychographic researchers know a lot about the residents in over sixty kinds of neighborhoods, so successful persuasion still relies on "hidden persuaders"—though they may not be exactly like those first described by Packard.

Packard's Eight "Compelling Needs"

In his research, Packard identified eight "compelling needs" that were frequently used in selling products. We still see them in use today, although with far more sophistication than in the advertisements that Packard studied. Advertisers have discovered new ways to tap the "hidden needs" by using the focus group interviews or projective tests to identify what they call "compelling needs." Merchandisers design their ads to promise that the product or service will provide some degree of real or symbolic fulfillment of the compelling need. You can almost imagine Freud himself probing even deeper into consumers' subconscious minds, looking for the "hot" buttons that will turn people on to products and avoiding the "cold" ones that will turn them against a product.

The Need for Emotional Security. We are living in one of the most insecure eras in human history. Terrorism seems unstoppable. Militia groups are heavily armed. Our environment is becoming more and more polluted. The protective ozone layer surrounding our planet is disintegrating. The world economy is poised on the edge of disaster. AIDS threatens many countries—in some parts of Africa, over half the population is infected. We wonder if the stock markets will crash, thus bringing on a worldwide depression. With corporate mergers and downsizing, many feel insecure about their jobs. Though the doomsayers were wrong about Y2K, many people worried that on January 1, 2000, the lights would go out, the banks would fail, and chaos would reign. Ours is an insecure and unpredictable world indeed. Little wonder that we search for substitute symbols of security. And the events of 9/11 did little to calm our fears. Neither did the corporate scandals that ruined companies and destroyed many persons' stock portfolios and, as a result, their plans for retirement.

Deodorants promise us "social security." Self-improvement courses promise better job security. Retirement planning programs offer financial security in our "golden years." And politicians promise economic security (and almost every other kind of security) if they are elected. All these examples serve as minor premises in enthymemes that begin with the major premise "Security or permanence is good" and that lead us to buy the product, adopt the service, or support the cause. Even in interpersonal relations, the need for security causes people to search for permanence in the relationship. In the 1970s, we first saw the phenomenon known as "living together" prior to marriage. As time passed, women in such relationships particularly wanted the reassurance of some kind of "commitment" even as many men tried to avoid it. At first, living together seemed to be a liberating lifestyle, and one that would contribute to future marital stability. But this is now being questioned by some. For example author Stephanie Staal (2001) points out that the divorce rate of those who live together before marriage is 50 percent higher than it is for those who did not cohabit prior to marriage. Staal calls this pattern the "cohabitation effect." At a time when we need permanence, we face unpredictable change, and that makes us vulnerable to persuasion aimed at assuring or reassuring us of some semblance of security—be it financial, social, physical, or interpersonal.

The Need for Reassurance of Worth. We live in a highly competitive and impersonal society in which it is easy to feel like mere cogs in a machine. Packard noted that people need to feel valued for what they do—whether it is in a factory, at a desk, in a classroom, or in a day-care center. Housewives, blue-collar workers, managers, and public sector workers all need to feel that they are accomplishing something of value, are needed by their families and organizations, and are appreciated by others. In

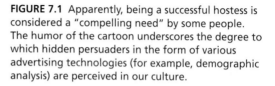

"GREAT PARTY! WHO DID YOUR DEMOGRAPHICS?"

FIGURE 7.1 Apparently, being a successful hostess is considered a "compelling need" by some people. The humor of the cartoon underscores the degree to which hidden persuaders in the form of various advertising technologies (for example, demographic analysis) are perceived in our culture.

(*Freeze Frame* cartoon from *Advertising Age*, December 28, 1987. Copyright Crain Communications, Inc. Reprinted by permission of Crain Communications and Bill Whitehead.)

other words, people need to feel that they make a difference. This need forms the basis of many persuasive appeals—from volunteer organizations, to groups pushing self-help tapes promoting self-esteem, to companies selling products that purportedly help us to be better parents (Bactine for those cuts and bruises) or better spouses ("Remember her with flowers"). Some promise to make us more successful at work (advertisements for career training). This latter need was demonstrated in an interesting study in which managers and workers were asked to rate ten factors in job satisfaction. Managers rated "wages," "fringe benefits," and "working conditions" as the top three. Workers placed those three at the bottom; their top three were "appreciation for work done," "my boss listens to me," and "fellow workers." As Figure 7.1 suggests, even hostesses need to be reassured of their self-worth.

This is also a time when skepticism is "in," and people don't seem to really communicate with one another. The recent corporate scandals, the 9/11 tragedy, and other events have led many people to believe that it is risky to trust people, the government, and other institutions. As one social critic put it, "They no longer live in a world of friends and neighbors and families, but [now live] in a world of associates, clients, and customers who will look them in the eye, smile—and lie like a rug" (Marquand, 1988, p. 5).

To learn more about how this new skepticism can affect brands and businesses, access InfoTrac College Edition, enter the words "corporate ethics" in the search engine, and examine some of the articles there.

Sociologist Robert Bellah and his colleagues (1985) interviewed hundreds of Americans about their lives and concluded that most contemporary Americans see themselves as in a race for material goods, prestige, power, and influence. And in this race, they separate themselves from others and find little emotional security in "the lonely crowd." Small wonder that we have become a "culture of consumption," seeking in the ownership of material goods the self-worth we can really only derive from being committed to and relating with others in our personal and public lives (Bellah et al., 1985). We also live in an era in which distrust and skepticism of others is increasing. For example, ethics author Kathleen Sibley (1997) notes the growing feelings of distrust felt by many employees over the issue of company monitoring of employee email. When we feel less and less important as individuals to our employers, our peers, and even our families, we become vulnerable targets for persuasion that promises Packard's reassurance of worth.

The Need for Ego Gratification. Packard found that many of the consumers he studied not only needed to be reassured of their basic worth but also needed their egos "stroked," as if they were really special—a step beyond mere self-worth (see Figure 7.2). This need for ego gratification can come from a variety of sources: friends, co-workers, neighbors, parents, groups, institutions, and, most importantly, ourselves. Packard cited the example of a heavy-

road-equipment manufacturer that increased sales by featuring the machinery operators rather than the machines in magazine ads. When contractors buy heavy equipment, they generally ask those who operate the machines for their opinions, and by stroking the operators' egos, the manufacturer could count on a positive recommendation.

Persuaders often target groups whose members feel that they have been put down for some time—teachers, police officers, fire fighters, postal workers, or social workers, for instance. The tragedy of 9/11 certainly brought many of these groups into a well-deserved public spotlight. It certainly must have been ego gratifying for such people to be featured on the front pages of newspapers and the covers of news weeklies, on posters and packaging, and in TV specials and a multitude of other media. Indeed, it is easy to sell products, ideas, and candidates by hooking into an out-group's ego needs in personal ways that appeal to their self-perception. The popular appeal of Congressman and, later, Speaker of the House Dennis Hastert depends in large part on the fact that he is a former high school teacher and wrestling coach. Large numbers of baseball caps, T-shirts, bumper stickers, and other paraphernalia featured police and fire department logos after 9/11, presumably so the ordinary citizens could identify with the newfound heroes.

Our ego needs can be met in other ways as well. Take family values, for example. For several decades, the traditional family was out of style; divorce rates soared, and many couples chose to cohabit instead of getting married. Those who remained committed to the ideal of the traditional family and its associated values felt like outcasts. Thus, it was the perfect time for a persuasive "pro-family" appeal, which is precisely what happened on both sides in the last three presidential campaigns, with the candidates all promising to restore the family to its prior place of respect.

If this issue interests you, go to InfoTrac College Edition, enter the words "living together" in the search engine, and peruse some of the related articles.

Ego gratification needs are potent. A good example of an ad based on this need is shown in

FIGURE 7.2 The Fluid Milk Promotion Board strokes the ego of average citizens by making them feel special, hinting that they are sophisticated, and suggesting that they can avoid health problems by drinking three glasses of milk a day.

(Reprinted by permission.)

FIGURE 7.3 Hyatt promises to fulfill the need for ego gratification.

(Used by permission of Hyatt Corporation.)

Figure 7.3. Note that the ad copy stresses the importance Hyatt places on the individual—in this case, the female executive, whose needs traditionally have been largely overlooked by the hotel industry. Hyatt offers her thoughtful extras—skirt hangers, shampoo, and even hair dryers in the room. She must be rather special to have a large hotel chain go out of its way to provide her with such amenities.

Similarly, politicians know how to stroke the egos of appropriate groups of potential voters. Consider how Elizabeth Dole used ego gratification while campaigning for the Republican Party nomination for governor of North Carolina. On one campaign day, she arrived by limousine at a GOP women's gathering wearing a conservative dark blue dress and scarf and had chicken salad for lunch.

Next, she donned a black leather jacket, boots, gloves, and leather pants for her visit to the Young Republicans club at Duke University. She arrived driving a Harley and ate pizza with the students. Little wonder that both groups gave her rousing rounds of applause (National Public Radio, 2002). If you look closely, you will see elements of Packard's ego gratification in almost any political campaign.

The Need for Creative Outlets. In our modern technocracy, few products can be identified with a single artisan. This was not always the case. For example, craftsmen such as cabinetmakers created a piece of furniture from beginning to end—it was their unique product. The same applied to housewives who did the weaving, knitting, sewing, and cooking, as well as to bakers, farmers, and so on. But with the advent of mass production in the late nineteenth century, more and more people became only a part of the production cycle—cogs in the machine. They had less and less that they could point to as their own unique product, and they felt less and less "creative" in many ways. Packard identified a need for expressing one's own unique creativity.

In today's quickly evolving world, the opportunity for creative outlets is further reduced as more and more people work in service occupations in which no actual construction of products occurs. In fact, the country's important product today is not automobiles, furniture, architecture, or fashion. Instead of tangible objects, our most important products are intangible—services and information—and frequently these are not the result of the work of a single individual but of groups of persons. And so we become more and more like stages in a process or cogs in a wheel while on the job. The financial scandals of 2002 showed how little CEOs thought of individual creativity, except perhaps in the world of accounting. Even supposedly supercreative Martha Stewart has been identified with the trend, at the expense of her presumed role as the "diva of domesticity" (Naughton, 2002). And this trend toward producing symbolic instead of real things and then using groups instead of individuals is likely to continue. Even a book such as this one is not the result of one individual's work and creativity.

Rather, reviewers make suggestions; editors alter the first, second, and third drafts for style and mechanics; artists create the diagrams and illustrations; designers choose fonts and formats; and so on. Most advertising, news releases, public relations efforts, films, TV programs, political speeches, and other familiar forms of persuasion are also the product of many hands.

Meanwhile, more and more work formerly done by people is now being done by technology—robots, computers, word processors, food processors, microwave ovens, and so on. And the trend seems to be growing, not lessening. Yet people still seem to need to demonstrate their own handicraft through gardening, cooking, home improvement projects, and other hobby-type activities. Even with prepared foods (from which the art of cooking has been almost totally removed), creativity still sells. For example, Hamburger Helper leaves room for you, the cook, to add your own touch; Noodles Romanoff makes you a chef worthy of the czar; El Paso taco dinner allows you to add all the toppings; and Budget Gourmet and Healthy Choice make being creative with a microwave a done deal. The need for creative outlets may be phrased differently from Packard's label, but the concept is as potent a persuader as ever.

To see how the need for creativity operates today, access InfoTrac College Edition, and enter the words "need for creativity" in the search engine.

The Need for Love Objects. Packard observed that people whose children have grown up need to replace the child love object—a situation called the "empty-nest syndrome." I recall noticing how quiet the house became when our last kid went off to college, for instance. No one needed me for much except when it came time to pay the bills. In fact, I used to tell my friends that the typical conditioned reflex for such fathers is to reach for their checkbook. Like other empty-nesters, I tried to fill the need in other ways—in my case, by devoting more time to teaching and research. For some, the replacement is a pet; for others, it might be a foster grandchild. Persuaders understand this need and strive to meet it in a variety of ways. Television pro-

ducers, for example, provide us with childlike entertainment personalities who may serve as "substitute" children—for example, Rudy and Theo on *The Cosby Show* or Kevin on *The Wonder Years.*

Many older persons have pets as substitute love objects. They coddle them, spoil them, and even dress them up. The pet food industry knows this and targets the "gourmet" level of their product lines to such persons. These pet lovers would never buy "generic" dog or cat food or even "standard" brands like Red Heart or Alpo, but they proudly bring home gobs of "Premium Cuts," "Tender Vittles," "Beef 'n Gravy," "Tuna Surprise," and "Chicken Spectacular." The food sounds like something a human would cook up, and it even looks appetizing. In ads, it is always served up with a piece of fine silverware and in bite-sized pieces. The substitute love object generates lots of sales these days.

The Need for a Sense of Power. If you have ever driven a motorcycle—especially a Harley Davidson—on the open road, or if you have ever used a chain saw, you know what it is like to feel powerful. We Americans, perhaps more than members of any other culture, seem to be programmed to chase potency and power and to gratify our need for them symbolically. The bigger the car engine or outboard motor is, the better. Snowmobiles, ATVs, jet skis, and dune buggies are marketed by promoting the sense of power they give to the user. Whether the product is a double-triggered chain saw or a garden tractor, power is the central issue. Stanley Tools doesn't sell wimpy, "light duty" hammers and wrenches—the consumer wants "heavy duty" tools. Similarly, Americans don't elect many nonmacho politicians. Remember Elizabeth Dole in her 2002 campaign? Riding that Harley is something that no "sissy girl" would do. In fact, every major candidate for the presidency has to demonstrate physical and psychological strength or power. An owner of a tow-truck business whom I know told me that over half his calls come from owners of four-wheel-drive SUVs—the very vehicles that are supposed to be able to go through anything and never get stuck. That, apparently, is the problem. The owners of these vehicles satisfy their need for power by finding impossibly tough terrain through which to take their vehicles. Unfortunately, they frequently get bogged down and have to call for a tow. Recently, the power need was used to market the $100,000 Hummer as the vehicle that can go through anything. The new Hummer campaign touts many new models and a variety of colors—in my town there is even a Hummer stretch limousine!

The Need for Roots. One of the predominant features of modern society is mobility. Individuals employed by a large firm will probably have to move several times during their careers, and most persons have three or more careers during their lifetime. In the decade following college graduation, the average American moves at least a dozen times; several of the moves involve crossing county lines, and at least one involves a move across a state line. For instance, IBM traditionally moved its young executives so frequently that the company has been referred to by employees as "I've Been Moved." When individuals do move, especially if it is some distance from home, family, and friends, there are several "pieces of home" they can bring along to keep them from getting too lonely. One is brand loyalty, and recent college graduates have one of the highest levels of brand loyalty. This helps explain why my university inked a deal with Pepsi to give the company exclusive "pouring rights" on campus, so that only Pepsi products (for example, Mountain Dew, Lipton Iced Tea, and Fruitopia) could be sold or served on campus. Further, all materials used to serve the products (cups, straws, napkins, and so on) had to have the Pepsi logo imprinted on them. Pepsi gave over $8 million to the school's scholarship fund for this right, because the company knows that college is the most important time for developing brand loyalty.

If you have ever moved to another state, you will have noticed how disconcerting it is to not find familiar supermarket, convenience store, or service-station chains. Advertisers appeal to these feelings. This need for roots and sense of brand loyalty also helps explain the concept of "line extension" in the development of new products. We feel more at home buying the new Quaker Oats Squares than another brand because of the familiar, old-fashioned face of the Quaker promising "An honest

taste from an honest face." He is an emblem of our tradition, our need for an "old-fashioned" hearty breakfast, and our need for a sense of roots. And brand names are portable—we can take them to a new home to remind us of our roots. Nabisco, for example, increased its nationwide shelf space by twenty miles by introducing an eighteen-item "New Stars" cookie and cracker line. The familiar name of the manufacturer helped establish the credibility of the new products (Friedman & Dagnoli, 1988). The need for roots can also be appealed to using emotional ties to "home." The Lane Furniture company, for example, offers newlyweds a Lane cedar chest to "take part of home" with them when they marry. Indeed, we see the appeal to roots in ads for the old-fashioned, whether it's apple pie, Heartland cereal, or stockbrokers who earn their money "the old-fashioned way." We've already noted the appeal politicians make to the value of the family. It is surprising how many politicians manage to hold their marriages together just until they win an election. In addition to providing us with symbolic roots, brands make us more noticeable, and hence more important feeling.

This trend of increasing mobility and fragmentation of our lives probably will continue into the future. As a result, the need for roots that Packard described many years ago remains an important touchstone. It is a responsive chord that advertisers, politicians, and ideologues will continue to strike in their many persuasive appeals to us.

Brand loyalty can be further investigated in InfoTrac College Edition by typing the words "brand loyalty" in the search engine. Examine a sample of the articles listed and some of the related subjects.

The Need for Immortality. None of us wants to believe in our own mortality. Studies have shown that only the fear of giving a speech exceeds the fear of dying. The fear of growing old and of dying clearly drives the healthy-living industry, which promotes such things as good nutrition, stress reduction, exercise, and a healthy lifestyle. Packard suggested that the fear of dying and the need to maintain influence over the lives of others underlie many kinds of psychological appeals. The bread-winner is made to feel that in buying life insurance, for instance, he or she obtains "life after death" in the form of financial security for the family. The buyer can help the kids go to college even if he or she isn't there.

Other products make similar appeals to the fear of death. For instance, Promise margarine will keep you healthy longer because "Promise is at the heart of eating right." And Nivea's Visage face cream will make your skin "firmer, healthier, and younger" for only pennies a day. As the ad execu-tive noted in an earlier quote, we aren't buying lanolin, we are buying hope—hope for a chunk of immortality. This need for immortality seems par-ticularly relevant in our modern technocracy. Per-haps people now feel even more helpless to control their lives than they did when Packard conducted his research. The much-talked-about "midlife cri-sis" is an example. This occurs when people get di-vorced, quit or lose their job, or confront other major life events. Many then buy a sports car, run off with someone half their age, and engage in ad-ventures such as bungee jumping or skydiving. These behaviors may be symptomatic of the fears people have as they realize that they have passed the probable midpoint of their lives. They want to be young again, or at least to enjoy some of the expe-riences they missed along the way. And there are many other persuasive appeals that succeed because they are somehow tied to the desire for immortality (Lafavore, 1995).

Maslow's Pyramid of Needs

Abraham Maslow (1954), a well-known psycholo-gist, long ago offered a starting point for examining people's needs. His theories about the power of human needs are as relevant for persuasion today as they were when he first described them. Nancy Austin (2002), a California management consultant, maintains that, though the theory may be over a half century old, "for modern managers looking to pump up performance, it still has zing." Robert Zemke (1998), the senior editor of the journal

FIGURE 7.4 Maslow's pyramid of needs.

Training, notes, "It's ironic that this 50's psychologist with no head for business played such a central role in the development of the psychology of manage-ment and the thoughts of modern managers." In 1998, Maslow's daughter, Ann Kaplan, published a revised edition of his work, titled *Maslow on Man-agement,* which was greeted with rave reviews (Rowan, 1998).

Maslow theorized that people have various kinds of needs that emerge, subside, and then reemerge. In his pyramid of needs, the lower levels represent the stronger needs, and the higher levels the weaker ones (see Figure 7.4). Keep in mind that this pyramid is only a model and that the lines be-tween needs are not as distinct as the graphic sug-gests. Note, too, that Maslow did not believe that higher needs are necessarily superior to lower ones; rather, they are merely different and, in all likeli-hood, weaker and less likely to emerge until stronger needs are met. In Maslow's pyramid of needs, the "center of the onion" is the base of the pyramid—needs or beliefs about which there is unanimous agreement. As we move up the pyramid or out from the core, we find needs or beliefs on which there may not be unanimous agreement and on which individuals may place varying degrees of value. So there is an upward or outward dynamic in Maslow's hierarchy of needs: As more powerful needs are met, less potent ones emerge.

As time passes, the earlier needs emerge again as they are or are not met. For example, the need for food or water emerges and then recedes as we eat or drink. Maslow argued that these needs have a *prepotency*—that is, they are tied together so that weaker needs, such as those for self-respect, emerge only after stronger needs, such as those for air, food, and water, have been filled. We probably could not persuade a dehydrated desert wanderer to clean up a little before drinking from our well, because he will want to fulfill the need for water first. The need to slake our thirst is prepotent; and until it is at least partially fulfilled, it is impossible for us to consider other needs.

Basic Needs. The bottom level of Maslow's pyramid contains the strongest needs we have—our basic needs. These are the physiological needs for regular access to air, food, water, sex, sleep, and elimination of wastes. Until these needs are met, we cannot concern ourselves with other, higher needs. At the same time, basic needs can be used to motivate behavior. For example, the person who is starving can be motivated to do all sorts of unusual things to secure food, ranging from stealing it to eating insects. And we know that the need for air can cause drowning victims to panic and drown not only themselves but their would-be rescuers as well (see Figure 7.5).

Security Needs. The second level of Maslow's pyramid contains the need for safety and security. There are several ways to look at these needs. We might want to feel secure in our ability to satisfy basic needs. If we fear losing our job, we have a strong need to obtain income security. We might want to get another, more secure job, or we might want to save money for hard times. We can also look at this need level in another light. Even if we have job security, we still might feel insecure because of the rising crime rate in our neighborhood. We might take drastic action to ward off thieves, such as installing a burglar alarm system or keeping a loaded pistol on the nightstand. Even

when we feel secure in our community, we still might feel insecure because of world politics. We might fear that our country is vulnerable to terrorists or that our leaders are considering military actions against some organization like Al Qaeda or some country such as Iran. In the interpersonal realm, we have a need for "social security," or acceptance by others. As a result, we spend money on self-improvement classes, hair transplants, face-lifts, or maybe something as simple as deodorant or mouthwash.

Those who are not technically trained to meet the requirements of the computer age realistically fear falling by the wayside. Global competition has eaten into the market share of U.S. industries, leaving many millions unemployed or underemployed. Political analysts have explained several recent election results as related to fears of economic displacement and the resulting loss of jobs. According to Maslow's model, this fear emerged in response to current economic conditions. In other words, the need for security emerges and reemerges as various threats to our security become evident and are met. Once the need is met, it redefines itself and thus is always present to some degree.

Today, insecurity, like change, is one of the few predictable things. Eight of every ten jobs that will be filled by tomorrow's college graduates do not even exist today. It's almost impossible to prepare for the future because the rate and pace of change is accelerating. New computer technology becomes obsolete in less than two years. No one can keep up with all the new (and frequently essential) information about jobs, health (as seen in Figure 7.6), communities, and a host of other personal and social issues. We live in a time when very little is secure. It is not surprising that so many security-oriented products, politicians, and organizations appeal to us on a daily basis.

Belongingness and Affiliation Needs. Once our security needs are met, at least in part, we become aware of needs on the third level of the pyramid—so-called belongingness or association needs and love needs. A number of options are open to us in meeting our need for association. Usually, individuals go beyond the family and

DEDICATED TO FINDING A CURE FOR AIDS. IN TIME.

The AIDS time bomb is still ticking. *SEARCH Alliance* is dedicated to finding a cure. Our physicians & scientists are at the vanguard of AIDS research. *SEARCH Alliance* knows that the best hope for progress lies in our fast-track approach.

WITH YOUR DONATION YOU CAN HELP US FIND A CURE FOR AIDS...IN TIME.

A Non-Profit AIDS Research Foundation 7461 Beverly Boulevard, Suite 304, LA, CA . 90036 (213) 930-8820

SEARCH

FIGURE 7.5 Using Maslow's hierarchy of needs, explain which of our needs this ad appeals to.

(By permission of Search Alliance.)

BREAST CANCER BEGINS EVEN SMALLER THAN THIS. THAT'S WHY YOU NEED A YEARLY MAMMOGRAM, ESPECIALLY AS YOU GET OLDER. MAMMOGRAMS CAN DETECT LUMPS TOO SMALL FOR YOU TO FEEL AND EARLY DETECTION MAY SAVE YOUR LIFE, SO CALL 1-800-ACS 2345.

GET A MAMMOGRAM.
EARLY DETECTION IS THE BEST PROTECTION.

A Public Service of This Publication AMERICAN CANCER SOCIETY

FIGURE 7.6 The need for security is the appeal used in this ad from the American Cancer Society.

(Reprinted by permission of the American Cancer Society.)

workplace and seek groups with which to fill this need, such as the PTA, bowling leagues, churches, golf clubs, and service groups. Generally, we limit the number of groups we join, and although we might be members of various organizations, we are active members in only a few. The flip side of belongingness and love needs is the trend toward isolation. A number of people and organizations are concerned about the tendency of people to "cocoon" or isolate themselves. In his article "Bowling Alone," Robert Putnam (1995) observes that more and more persons are joining what he calls "checkbook groups" such as the Citizen's Utility Board or the American Association of Retired Persons; all they have to do to belong is to write the check, because the groups rarely, if ever, actually meet. At the same time, membership is down in traditional groups like the Lions, Elks, and Rotary Club, and fewer people bowl in organized leagues, preferring to "bowl alone."

Like physiological and security needs, the need to belong often interacts with these other needs and continues to reemerge throughout our lives. Also, what fulfills our belongingness needs differs at various points in our lives. It may be important to belong to a fraternity or sorority when we are in college, but after graduation, these affiliations fade and are replaced by job-related associations. Later, when we have families, other affiliations tend to be more important to us, such as community group and church membership. In this context, a recent trend is the emergence of "mega-churches" like the Mariners Church of Newport Beach, California. This church offers programming for various market segments, grief therapy, Gen X activities, and seminars on a variety of topics like twelve-step recovery, divorce dynamics, and parenting of adolescents—all served up with cappuccino after services. The need to belong will always be with us, and going hand-in-hand with a need to be a part of some groups is the need to feel loved or esteemed by the members of those groups, be they family, fraternity, team, church, or political party. As persuadees, we need to recognize when this need is being appealed to by persuaders so that we can critically evaluate their appeals.

THE GRILLER: MARATHON MOM

No time to waste, right? So a gas grill has to perform quickly, easily. Enter MasterFlame². It's built with your schedule in mind: easy push button ignition, sturdy shelves for extra work space, a cooking system that virtually eliminates uneven heat, and multi-level cooking to prepare the main course and side dishes at one time. Give it a try... you'll find you've made a delicious dinner for your family and it wasn't a chore at all. In fact, it's our guess you'll find you even had fun.

To locate Char-Broil MasterFlame² gas grills, and find out about a free gift with purchase, just call

1-800-477-0118

THE GRILL: MasterFlame²™ FROM Char-Broil

FIGURE 7.7 Esteem needs are the key appeal in this ad.

(Reprinted by permission of Char-Broil.)

Love and Esteem Needs. Once we satisfy our belongingness needs, we feel the emergence of needs in the fourth level of Maslow's model: the need for love or esteem. Once we are part of a group, we want to feel that the group values us as a member and as a human being. We are happy when our families understand and admire the things we do. The esteem need is also a reemerging need. That is, if we find that we are needed, loved, and esteemed by our family, our need for esteem does not fade away; instead, its focus shifts. We now want to feel needed by our co-workers, our boss, and our friends. Many product appeals offer a kind of symbolic substitute for esteem. For example, as Figure 7.7 shows, the kids will hold Mom in high esteem if she uses a Char-Broil gas grill to whip up a great meal.

Cultural trends also influence our esteem needs. For example, at various times and in various places, esteem was rooted in conspicuous consumption or consumption engaged in for purposes of display. However, important things sometimes happen to change the way people satisfy esteem needs. For instance, recent political, financial, and religious scandals have shaken people's faith in traditional institutions. There also seems to be communal concern for the environment. Young and old, producers and consumers, conservatives and liberals—all are helping in a variety of ways to clean up our air, land, and water resources. People realize that working in community can help them meet their esteem needs. In fact, "community" has become a kind of god term.

Self-Actualization Needs. Although Maslow initially put the need for self-actualization at the top of his pyramid, thereby implying that it would rarely emerge, he later came to believe that, in one sense, the need to live up to their potential is an integral part of everyone's life. At first, Maslow believed that individuals could live up to their potential only when all four of the lower needs were met. In many ways, Maslow's initial ideas were accurate. It is hard for young people "on the way up" to think about self-actualization, just as it is difficult to meet love or esteem needs if individuals do not belong to some group that can offer love or esteem. Yet Maslow's later thinking about all these needs and their prepotency is valid, too. He came to see self-actualization as occurring through what he called "peak experiences"—events in which people can enjoy themselves, learn about themselves, or experience something they have only dreamed of previously. Thus, the person who ventures into the wilderness and learns to be self-reliant and not to fear isolation has enjoyed a peak, or self-actualizing, experience. The same might apply to people who learn something about themselves when they take their first job after high school or college and discover that they have abilities that are of value to a company or to fellow workers.

Cultural trends can affect the ways in which we seek to satisfy our self-actualization needs. Social critic T. J. Jackson Lears (1983) has noted that the search for ways of identifying ourselves and our potential came about when the United States shifted

from being a culture of production to a culture of consumption. That is, in moving from a secure farm existence to an unsettling urban isolation, we experienced a loss of traditional values and chaotic changes in our lifestyles. The result, Lears claimed, was the search for a "therapeutic ethos," or an identity that would let us be at ease with ourselves—that would permit us to self-actualize. To a large extent, this therapeutic ethos offered inner harmony, a reduction of feelings of emptiness, and a hope for self-realization through patterns of consumption. As we enter a new century, what will be the means for achieving self-actualization, or our own true potential? Certainly, persuaders will offer a variety of means for achieving this final prepotent need.

To examine the culture of consumption in which we live, access InfoTrac College Edition, and enter the words "consumption culture" in the search engine. Be sure to read the reviews of *Consuming Desires: Consumption, Culture and Happiness,* a book of essays on consumption edited by Ed Rosenblatt. They may make you want to read the entire book.

As you encounter various persuasive events and opportunities (public and interpersonal), apply Maslow's model to them. See whether it sheds light on the needs that people feel and that may motivate their actions. You may want to experiment with persuading another person using several levels of Maslow's model. If the person doesn't seem motivated by appeals to security, try appealing to basic or belongingness needs.

Uses of the Needs Process Premise

In our search for the first premises that serve as springboards for persuasion in enthymemes, psychological processes show us promising possibilities in the area of human needs. These needs, whether identified by Packard's list or Maslow's pyramid or some other model, are strongly felt by audiences. Persuaders frequently tie other minor premises to them to allow audiences to complete the argument by drawing the conclusion. For example, feeling the need for job security, a college student may decide to major in a field that holds the promise of job openings after graduation. It is only common sense. Yet what we call "common sense" is common only because so many of us have the same or similar needs.

We may wish to relabel our needs in terms other than those used by Maslow or Packard, but their categories serve as good general descriptions. As persuadees, we should consider the requests persuaders make of us from the perspective of our own needs. And as persuaders, we should examine the current needs of those we wish to influence. If we do that, not only are we more likely to succeed, we are more likely to do our audience members a service by giving them a means by which to satisfy their needs.

A good way to train yourself to evaluate appeals from this critical perspective—as persuadee or persuader—is to restate persuasive messages, such as TV commercials, from the perspective of the Packard and Maslow models. As first premises on which persuasion can be built, human psychological and physiological needs clearly are powerful motivators. As you will see, attitudes—the second type of process premise—operate in similar ways.

ATTITUDES: THE SECOND PROCESS PREMISE

When we surveyed the theoretical perspectives on persuasion, we looked at how various researchers explain attitudes using a variety of theories. One unifying element among these theories is that attitudes can serve as the unstated major premises in persuasive enthymemes. We noted in Chapter 4 that for a long time attitudes were considered to be predispositions to behavior. In other words, holding an attitude or a set of attitudes makes an individual ready to behave. Until recently, however, confusion existed about the degree to which attitudes reliably predict behavior. For example, psychologists Martin Fishbein and Icek Ajzen (1975) believed that a better predictor of behavior was what they called the "intention to behave."

Attitude Objects

Psychologists Alice H. Eagley and Shelley Chaiken (1993) define an attitude as "a psychological tendency that is expressed by evaluating a particular entity with some degree of favor or disfavor" (p. 1). In this context, evaluating includes all classes of responding—"overt or covert, cognitive, affective, or behavioral." The important word in this definition is "tendency," by which they mean "an internal state that lasts for at least a short time" (p. 2). Because it is internal, we cannot observe it directly, so we try to detect it in "evaluative responses." Examples of evaluative responses include expressing "approval or disapproval, favor or disfavor, liking or disliking, approach or avoidance, attraction or aversion, or similar reactions" (p. 3). According to Eagley and Chaiken, we make such evaluations concerning "attitude objects," which include "virtually anything that is discriminable" (p. 3).

Even more recently, several researchers have identified a social function served by attitudes. This "functional approach" to the study of attitudes resembles one discussed by communication theorists Charles Larson and R. Sanders (1975). They maintained that attitudes function to construct social "alignments" with other persons or in unfamiliar situations. Thus, if I want you to identify with me and to like me, I will articulate attitudes that I believe you prefer. If I want to distance myself from you, I will articulate attitudes that you disfavor. In an unfamiliar situation, I will monitor what other persons say and will try to mirror their attitudes or take actions that support those attitudes if I want them to like me. If after listening to the discussion, I want to distance myself from the group, I will articulate attitudes that are the opposite of theirs. So, one function of attitudes is to allow people to "take sides."

Take, for example, the attitudes surrounding vegetarian eating habits. Vegetarians usually justify their eating preferences in one or both of two ways: (1) Eating only vegetables and grains is healthier and more ecologically sound, and (2) vegetarian habits do not bring pain to animals—it is a "kinder" way of living. Both of those justifications are evaluative responses to the attitude object called "vegetarianism." We try to predict the behavior of vegetarians based on those evaluations if we want to align or identify with them. Thus, we won't offer steak tartar to them as an hors d'oeuvre because we predict that they won't try it and, in fact, will probably be insulted by the offer.

In another approach, ad researcher by S. Shavitt (1990) maintained that attitudes serve both social and utilitarian functions. In research on the reactions of subjects to advertisements, the social functions of attitudes in the ads told others what the respondents were like. For example, the ad might claim that discriminating persons prefer high-fiber diets to high-fat, low-carb diets such as those promoted by Dr. Atkins. Utilitarian functions of attitudes are used when the intent is to stress the features and benefits of the product. For example, an ad might claim that the new Honda hybrid automobile gets up to 60 miles per gallon and is extremely quiet, especially when in the electric-powered mode. And this fits with elements in the ELM. For example, psychologists K. G. De Bono and R. Harnish (1988), R. E. Petty and D. T. Wagener (1998), and others found that for persons they call "high self-monitoring" an attractive source of persuasion can trigger elaborate processing of the message. For "low self-monitoring" individuals, in contrast, elaborate processing is more likely to occur if an expert source conveys the message. This makes sense. If you are a high self-monitoring person, you do not want to make a mistake simply because the product is recommended by Jennifer Aniston—you are afraid you will be judged by the quality of your decision in the eyes of others. So, you will do serious investigation of the product in the central processing route of the ELM. If, however, you are a low self-monitoring individual, you care little about what others think of you, but you do care about living up to your "true inner self." As a result, you will elaborate on the information via the central route because the evidence comes from an expert source, and believing in experts is part of your decision-making process.

For our purposes, attitude objects are usually found in the persuader's request for action or offer of products, ideas, beliefs, and so on. For example, following the 9/11 tragedy, many American flags were flown, and many bumper stickers, yard signs,

and other expressions of patriotism were displayed. Flags and slogans (for example, "United We Stand" or "These Colors Won't Run") are symbols that reflect certain attitudes, and people can "announce" their attitudes by displaying them. This, in turn, causes alignment or identification with others and helps to foster interpersonal relations and interpersonal influence. The persuader who asks us to display our patriotism may use the attitude object of the Stars and Stripes as part of the appeal. If we evaluate the actions or offers positively, we will be more likely to act as requested or to accept the offer being made. The obverse is also true: If we want to distance ourselves from jingoistic patriotism, we won't follow the requested action and will express our attitudes about hyper-patriotism. This, in turn, will reduce the possibility of our forming interpersonal relationships with superpatriots, which is precisely the goal. So attitudes have an important social function in that they can foster social networking. Nelson (2001) notes that the social function of attitudes in organizations (especially businesses) can make or break the organization. And according to D. C. Schrader (1999), the social function of interpersonal influence is largely dependent on the goal complexity of the persuader's appeals. In other words, depending on the persuader's intent, his or her influence attempts are judged competent or incompetent, appropriate or inappropriate, and polite or impolite. As a result, the social function of attitudes can often affect persuasive outcomes.

To learn more about the importance of interpersonal influence on getting compliance from others, access InfoTrac College Edition, enter the words "interpersonal influence" in the search engine, and review a few of the many articles listed there.

Attitudes and Opinions

From another point of view, communication researcher Milton Rokeach (1968) pointed out that individual beliefs range from those that are primitive and strongly held to those that are based on authority and are not as strongly held. These belief sets cluster and form attitudes, which, according to

Rokeach, fall into two categories: (1) attitudes toward objects or issues and (2) attitudes toward situations. Both classes of attitudes can predispose us to action, but they can also confuse us, especially when they conflict with each other. Such conflict is evident when parents protest the presence of AIDS-infected students in public schools. Some parents' hold attitudes toward the object (the infected student) and toward the situation (the possibility that their own children will be infected). These two attitude objects can either conflict or converge. These attitudes, in turn, probably emerge from complex sets of beliefs about both the object and the situation. The parents may sympathize with the innocent victim and at the same time hold certain negative beliefs about the situation—the pandemic of sexually transmitted diseases (STDs) and the deadly outcome of the AIDS virus. A persuader on either side of this controversy would need to address both sets of beliefs.

Opinions resemble beliefs but are far more fickle; as opinion polls demonstrate, opinions change rapidly and often dramatically. We all have opinions about politicians and what they say in campaigns and do after taking office. These opinions can change, however, especially if the president makes a few key errors, makes a foolish statement, loses to Congress on a particular issue, or chooses to support a friend who turns out to be corrupt. The Gallup and Harris polls record such shifts of opinion on a regular basis. Sometimes, the errors lead to low voter ratings and even rejection at the polls. Remember, however, that opinions might not influence the behavior of the persons who hold them. This was the case with the impeachment trial of President Clinton in 1999. Despite his sordid, well-publicized affair with Monica Lewinsky, his ratings in the polls went to an all-time high. Why? Rokeach's theory might explain the riddle. People had a highly negative attitude toward Clinton's behavior (attitude toward object). But their highly positive attitudes toward the nation's economy, with its low unemployment, low inflation, budget surpluses, and bullish stock market (attitude toward situation), probably conflicted with their feelings about the affair. The economy won out. This is not to say that opinions do not affect behavior at all—

only that they sometimes exert a weak influence (Larson & Sanders, 1975). Given a sufficiently large change in opinion, however, we might not support a president in the next campaign; or, given enough small shifts in our opinions, we might change our overall attitude toward that president.

To learn more about the measurement and uses that are made of measures of public opinion, go to InfoTrac College Edition, and enter the words "public opinion" in the search engine. Peruse a few of the more tantalizing items listed under the periodical titles.

Philip Zimbardo, a prominent social psychologist, and his colleagues (1976, 1991) note that attitudes are "either mental readiness or implicit predispositions that exert some general and consistent influence on a fairly large class of evaluative responses" (p. 20). Notice that Zimbardo stresses the enduring quality of attitude shifts. There is even a school of advertising research, known by the acronym DAGMAR, which suggests that ad agencies ought to Define Advertising Goals for Measured Advertising Results (Colley, 1961). In other words, the goal of advertising might be only attitudinal change toward the brand, and not change in purchase behavior. The idea is that, if consumers have an improved image of a product—say, Rice Chex—they will buy more of it. Unfortunately, this attitude–behavior link has been difficult to demonstrate, perhaps because of the many intervening variables that can also affect consumer behavior. Simple product awareness, packaging, a display location, special offers, or background music may cause us to make the purchase. But, other factors, such as time of day or gender, might be the key. Even in carefully controlled experiments, with many of these causes filtered out, attitude and behavior do not consistently link up (Zimbardo, Ebbesen, & Maslach, 1976).

The Functions of Attitudes

Another way to think about attitudes is to focus on their various persuasive functions, dimensions, or effects. For one thing, attitudes have a cognitive function or dimension, in that they are learned. Consider the environment: Our attitudes toward air and water pollution, recycling, and endangered species are all part of what we know about these issues. Some advertisements are aimed at cognitions. For example, a mutual fund company advertises that it is "no load"—customers don't have to pay commissions when they purchase shares. This knowledge is learned, and it may persuade consumers to select this fund over others that do charge commissions. The same function is met by some political advertisements.

Attitudes also have an affective function in that they can influence our emotions and feelings. For instance, our attitudes toward recycling and air and water pollution affect how we feel about these issues. Again, some ads are aimed at the affective dimension, or at emotions. For example, how do you think the smash HBO series *The Sopranos* affects viewers' attitudes and perhaps emotions toward mob figures? Chris Seay, a Christian minister and television critic from Houston, was initially worried what his wife would think about his rushing home from church to watch the profanity- and nudity-filled episodes of the fourth season. His emotions were being affected by his wife's attitude toward the series and his own emotional dedication to it. He says he ultimately convinced her that the show was about "faith, forgiveness and family values," and that helped him out of his emotional or affective dilemma. But it took attitude change on his wife's part to set him at ease (Pinsky, 2002).

Finally, and most importantly, attitudes have a behavioral function in that they predispose us to take certain actions. Thus, because we hold certain attitudes about air and water pollution, we do or do not buy gas guzzlers, we do or do not use detergents, and we do or do not recycle. In other words, the behavioral function of attitudes affects what we do about these issues. Once he had convinced himself (and his wife) that *The Sopranos* was a positive series, Seay went on to author a book titled *The Gospel According to Tony Soprano: An Unauthorized Look into the Soul of TV's Top Mob Boss and His Family* (Pinsky, 2002). His attitudes functioned to prompt behavior—the act of writing the book. Some advertisements are aimed at promoting attitudes that lead to the behavioral function, prompting actual behavior change. One goal of advertising, for example, is to "induce trial," or to get consumers to try the brand. Such ads might include a free sample or might offer a rebate with purchase of the product.

Attitudes and Intention

The work of Fishbein and Ajzen (1975) has added the concept of behavioral intention to the research on attitude and behavior change. Behavioral intention relates to what individuals *intend* to do about something, regardless of what action they finally take. Here, a fairly consistent set of results emerges. For instance, attitude change does seem to precede what people say they intend to do about the environment. As a result of attitude change, we say that we intend to recycle, that we intend to conserve water, or that we intend to purchase, join, try, vote, or donate. When people describe what they intend to do, they have, in a sense, already symbolically enacted the behavior. Thus, the person who displays a bumper sticker in favor of a certain candidate is stating a behavioral intention, and it is likely that this person will vote for that candidate. Knowing this, politicians urge potential voters to display buttons, bumper stickers, and signs to guarantee their votes on election day.

Attitudes and Interpersonal Communication/Persuasion

There are several other dimensions to the attitude change and subsequent behavior puzzle. One of these dimensions is the degree to which attitudes function as tools of interpersonal communication or persuasion, or both. In other words, do expressions of attitudes have more to do with fitting ourselves into a comfortable position with those with whom we are interacting than they have to do with our ultimate behavior? For example, I have a hunting and fishing buddy who is much more politically conservative than I am. When I express political attitudes or even opinions about political issues of the day to him, I am very careful about the words I use. His friendship is worth more to me than my need to express my attitudes bluntly. R. J. Eiser (1987), a critic of much of the attitude research that has been conducted, puts it this way:

> One of the main shortcomings of many attitude theories is their emphasis on individualistic, intrapsychic factors to the relative neglect of the social and communicative context within which attitudes are acquired and expressed. Not only the expression but also the experience of attitude is shaped by how we have learned to anticipate what we say and do. For this reason, attitude is both a subjective experience and a social product, and the expression of an attitude is a social act. (p. 2)

In other words, we express attitudes in ways that help us get along with persons who are significant to us. As a result, there sometimes may be logical discrepancies between expressed attitudes and subsequent behavior.

Attitudes and Information Processing

The focus on human information processing is closely related to behavioral intentions. The key idea here is that we can't look at attitudes and behavior without also looking at what information in persuasive messages is processed by the audience and how it is stored and retrieved. When trying to look at this process, one of the first questions we must ask is this: Can the audience comprehend the message? The next step is to determine how the message is stored in audience members' long-term memory (LTM). It may be entirely new information to the audience, or it may fit with an existing network or several networks ("nets") of information already stored in LTM.

Take, for example, the "cents off" coupons that appear in newspapers, circulars, and magazines. As persuasive information, they fit with several memory nets in our minds: whether we already use the products, how often we use them, and whether the value of the coupons is sufficient to justify taking the time to clip them. To someone else, the coupons may mesh with different nets that might include totally different information. Interestingly, even the size and shape of the coupons can affect differing memory nets for different persons. Apparently, the best size is the same as a dollar bill, and more coupons will be clipped if they have a dotted line around them—and especially if there is a picture of a little scissors on the dotted line. (Well duh!) On a more serious level, Hispanics tend not to clip coupons because they associate them with welfare or food stamps—a social stigma.

Research into how information is stored in LTM is in its infancy, but most theorists agree that information is usually stored in networks and in the form of key words, symbols, and relationships. For example, I have remembered the names and other details of three very small towns in Arkansas—Flippin, Midway, and Cotter—for more than twenty years. Why? Because I associate them with fishing experiences on the nearby White River. But, more than that, the word "flippin" is also used to describe a kind of cast in fishing; Midway is halfway between Mountain Home and Bulls Shoals, Arkansas; and I lost the cotter key for the propeller on my outboard motor near Cotter. When I heard of the Whitewater scandal in the late 1990s, all these associations came to mind.

Another organizing device for LTM might be episodic in nature. That is, we remember things that are presented to us in episodic or dramatic segments; these then become integrated with LTM networks relating to one of many personal episode types such as being deceived, beating the odds, or revealing the culprit. Have you ever had the experience of being late for an appointment and rushing off only to find that you are stuck behind the slowest (and probably dumbest) driver on the road? This driver also seems to have a talent for missing all the stoplights. Further, this driver has the unusual luck of never facing oncoming traffic when in a no-passing zone and always facing it in a safe-passing zone. Suppose you made a television commercial of just such an experience and used it to promote Compoz, an over-the-counter drug that claims to settle people's nerves. If you can identify the episodic types that people have, these could serve as vital first premises in persuasive enthymemes. As we will see later, another theorist, Tony Schwartz, provides a model for resonating with or "evoking" such experiences from audiences.

To learn more about what affects our long-term memory, access InfoTrac College Edition, and type the words "long-term memory" in the search engine. Browse some of the more tantalizing titles.

At the behavior stage of the information-processing model (for example, voting, buying, joining, saluting, smiling, or expressing one's view), the critical concepts or episodes are retrieved from LTM and provide persuadees with good "reasons" for taking action.

As noted earlier, nearly two decades ago, social psychologists Richard Petty and John Cacioppo (1986) offered an insightful application of their information-processing model to persuasion. The model has prompted a multitude of research insights into the process of persuasion since its introduction. Researchers S. Booth-Butterfield and J. Welbourne (2002) suggest that the model "has been instrumental in integrating the literature on source, message, receiver and context effects in persuasion and has also been a springboard for new research in this domain" (p. 155). You will recall from Chapter 4 that Petty and Cacioppo presented an "elaboration likelihood" explanation for persuasion, particularly as seen in highly "logical" and "reasoned" persuasion rather than "emotional" or "affective" kinds. They postulate two routes of persuasion: (1) Logical/reasoned persuasion flows through a central processing path that requires much evidence and reasoning and that is frequently used when making major purchase decisions; and (2) emotional persuasion flows through a peripheral processing path and relies on simple cues (advertising, packaging, coupons, or other sales promotions). This path is usually associated with making less important decisions, such as whether to eat at Burger King or Subway. Their explanation rests on a set of basic assumptions:

- Although people want to have "correct" attitudes, the degree to which they will elaborate on an issue/decision will vary from individual to individual and from situation to situation.
- A variety of variables can affect attitude change and can act as persuasive arguments, peripheral

cues, or attitudinal positions (interests, motivation to research an issue or elaborate on it, and so on).

- When motivation or ability to elaborate decreases, peripheral cues become more important and carry the load of persuasion/attitude change (for example, "I don't know much about the Internet, and I'm not that interested anyway"). Conversely, as motivation or ability to elaborate on a claim increases, peripheral cues lose impact (for example, "After hearing that the Internet includes libraries, companies, and governmental groups, I wanted to get more info").

- The persuader affects consumers' motivation (or persuadees' ability to process information/arguments) by either encouraging or discouraging careful examination of the argument/claim. For example, the persuader might say, "April 15 is only a week away, so you'd better bone up on the new tax laws" versus "At your income level, you might as well use the short tax form 1040EZ or file online."

- Issues/arguments that flow from the central processing path are more likely to persist, predict actual behavior, and be resistant to counterpersuasion (deciding to purchase a camcorder after doing lots of research versus deciding which breakfast cereal to purchase based on brand preference).

For our purposes, persuasion relying on process premises is likely to be processed in the peripheral path, whereas persuasion that relies on reasoned premises (which we will discuss in Chapter 8) is likely to be processed in the central path. Petty and Cacioppo offer a flowchart depicting the various options and routes available and in any persuasive transaction (see Figure 7.8).

Notice that the various options in the model rest on the motivation to process a persuasive message. In the first step, we see that persuadees must want to investigate a given product, candidate, or cause. The process is short-circuited if the motivation isn't there. In the second step, we see that if motivated to process an offer/appeal/claim persuadees must also possess the ability to process the

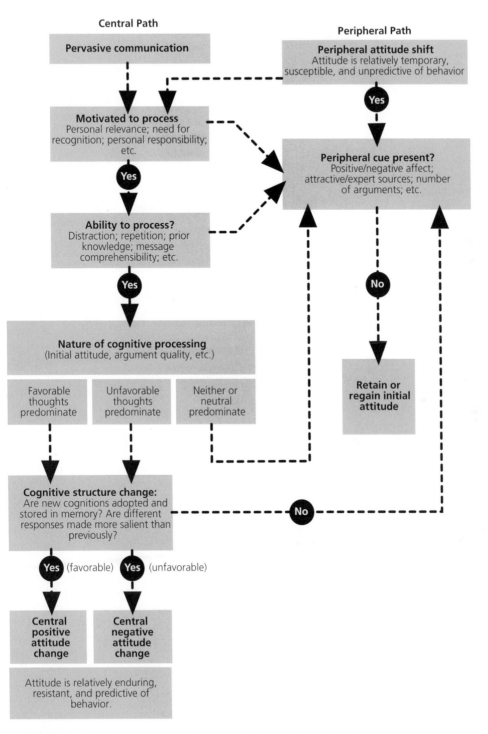

FIGURE 7.8 Decision flow in Petty and Cacioppo's elaboration likelihood model.

persuasion in one of the two paths. From that point on, the nature of the attitude change depends on which path is followed. If the peripheral path is used, the resulting attitude change will be weak, short-lived, and less likely to result in behavior; if the central processing path is used, the resulting attitude change will be potent, long-lived, and likely to lead to change in behavior.

There are several other approaches to studying the message–attitude–behavior chain, each of which has its strengths and weaknesses. But all researchers agree that attitudes have something to do with behavior, and attitudes can be altered via persuasive messages. The presumption, then, is that the suggested behavior will ultimately follow.

What does all this mean to us as persuadees who live in a world of doublespeak? What can we do to uncover persuaders' intentions toward and beliefs about the audience? Being aware of attitudes helps us to pinpoint what persuaders think of us. By seeking to identify the attitudes that persuaders assume we have, we become more critical receivers. We can become conscious of our attitudes and can see how persuaders use them to get us to follow their "program."

CONSISTENCY: THE THIRD PROCESS PREMISE

In Chapter 4, we looked briefly at one of the theories that explain human behavior in terms of people's need for balance. This theory posits that people feel comfortable when the world lives up to or operates consistently with their perceptions of or predictions about events. When this consistency is not evident, they are predisposed to change either themselves or their interpretations of events to bring the world into a more balanced state. Knowing where and when this phenomenon is likely to occur, persuaders can offer a means to return to consistency and thus comfort. For example, persuaders attempting to change public attitudes toward the health care issue usually try to create dissonance in health care users ("Your employer's group insurance plan won't begin to cover the costs

of major surgery" or "With an HMO, you don't get to go to the best surgeon").

If as humans we naturally seek out psychological equilibrium, it is valuable for us as receivers to try to identify what puts us into states of imbalance or inconsistency, thus making us vulnerable to persuasion. Conversely, if psychological equilibrium is our goal, we ought to identify those circumstances that make us comfortable and that can be targeted for persuasion that reinforces attitudes. A half century ago, congruency theory researchers Charles Osgood and Percy Tannenbaum (1955) put it this way: "Changes in evaluation are always in the direction of increased congruity with the existing frame of reference" (p. 43).

More recently, as Eiser (1987) pointed out, defining the "existing frame of reference" is a critical factor in predicting attitude shifts. That is, we must identify the receiver's current frame of reference to create the kind of incongruity or inconsistency that will prompt feelings of psychological "uneasiness," which will then lead to movement along an attitude scale. According to Eiser, these "evaluative frames of reference . . . are more general than the specific objects of judgment being evaluated" (p. 27).

Cognitive Dissonance Theory

We began to discover how these frames of reference worked in their most elementary ways when we discussed balance theory in Chapter 4. A problem for balance theory relates to the degree of difference between the two people or the two instances to be judged. In other words, although the theory accounts for *qualitative* differences between judgments, it doesn't deal with *quantitative* differences. At first glance, this may seem to be a minor problem. However, given the differences that might exist between persons or between concepts with regard to controversial topics such as creationism, abortion, or school prayer, it's important to take into account how far persons are from one another on a topic. Cognitive dissonance theory, first suggested over forty years ago by Leon Festinger (1962), addresses this problem of quantitative and qualitative differences between persons and ideas.

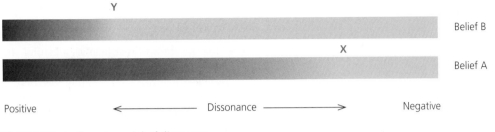

FIGURE 7.9 Festinger's model of dissonance.

Unlike balance theory, which predicts changes in attitudes, judgments, or evaluations, cognitive dissonance theory predicts that when we experience psychological tension we try to reduce it in some way. Tension reduction involves more than simply change; it has a quantitative dimension as well. In other words, we can change our evaluations or judgments a little, a moderate amount, a lot, or not at all. Another feature of cognitive dissonance theory is that tension is produced by dissonance within an individual's psychological system. Balance theory relies more on logical inconsistencies than on psychological or sociological ones. However, our attitudes and opinions reflect how we feel about various ideas and how those feelings relate to our prior experience, our idiosyncrasies, and so on. Cognitive dissonance theory allows us to take those things into consideration.

Festinger defined dissonance as a feeling resulting from the existence of "two nonfitting," or contrasting, pieces of knowledge about the world. As in balance theory, there are times when things fit, or "go together"—this is consonance (from the Latin for "to sound together, harmonize, agree"). For Festinger, balance existed when "considering a pair of elements either one [of which] does follow from the other." Consider this example: Although I may greatly dislike telemarketers as a group, I am also part owner of a small advertising agency that occasionally uses telemarketing. This disparity may create slight feelings of dissonance or imbalance for me. Thus, I need to find a way to reduce the tension caused by the disparity. Fortunately, I discover that telemarketing is a successful tool of marketing

and advertising. I also discover that when the telemarketing is "inbound" (that is, when the customer calls in to place an order or to learn more about the product) consumers like it. I further discover that when "outbound" telemarketing is used in business-to-business advertising the recipient of the call frequently appreciates getting the information and learning more about the product or service being marketed.

Festinger suggested that any two beliefs can be shown as two parallel lines, as shown in Figure 7.9. The bottom bar represents belief A, and the X above it marks a position on that belief. The top bar represents other information about belief A, and the Y above this bar represents our position on the new information, which we might call belief B. The distance between these two points—X and Y—is the amount of dissonance we feel. And reducing this dissonance provides the basis for many actions. Some persons change dissonant cognitions by moving their beliefs closer to one another. Others rationalize the problem away by discrediting the source of the cognitions. Still others escape from feelings of dissonance by the process of selective perception, selective retention, or selective exposure; that is, they choose to forget, to not receive/perceive, or to not be exposed to the information. In other words, we reduce tension or dissonance by moving either X or Y, or both, toward the center of the two bars. So, in reference to my telemarketing dilemma, I can reduce tension or dissonance by altering my negative attitudes toward telemarketers or by evaluating the information about inbound and business-to-business telemarketing much more positively than I would otherwise have done.

Recently, dissonance theory has been used to explain the new sense of "uneasiness" affecting sexually active individuals, especially if they have multiple partners. Most intelligent persons know that the main causes of infection by the AIDS virus are unsafe sex practices, the sharing of needles among drug users, and, to some degree, blood transfusions or accidental exposure to the blood of AIDS carriers. What can sexually active people do to reduce these feelings of psychological uneasiness about being sexually active and having more than one sex partner? They have a variety of options:

- They can devalue their initial beliefs about the most appropriate methods of birth control and use condoms.

- They can devalue the AIDS information by telling themselves that this media blitz is merely a scare tactic dreamed up to cut down on the promiscuity of the younger generation.

- They can selectively perceive the information, telling themselves that their sex partners are not likely carriers of the AIDS virus.

- They can try to forget the frightening information about AIDS through the process of selective retention.

- They can try to rationalize the problem away by telling themselves that a cure for AIDS is just around the corner.

- They can become celibate or have fewer partners.

- They can do more than one of these.

Although Festinger mainly dealt with the notion of consonance as a means of reducing dissonance, it seems clear that we seek it as a means of reinforcing our existing attitudes. Thus, we listen to the candidate of our choice but more often than not avoid listening to the person we do not plan to vote for. Similarly, conservative people read conservative newspapers and magazines whereas liberal people read liberal ones. The most avid readers of ads for Fords are persons who just bought a Ford. Chicago Cubs fans try not to expect a winning season so they won't feel disappointed—but what hap-

pens to these same fans now that the Cubbies are playing much better under new management? Or, if you decide to major in communication and then discover that the jobs in that field are plentiful and well paid, you will experience consonance.

Experiences like this are common; we find information confirming our position, and that makes our belief stronger. We can take many actions as a result of feelings of consonance:

- We can revalue our initial beliefs, making them stronger in all likelihood ("It really was a good idea to major in communication").

- We can revalue the source of the information input ("Boy! Those other communication students are really sharp and on the ball. They'll go far in this world!").

- We can perceive the information as stronger than it actually is and focus on the strongest parts of it.

- We can remember the most positive parts of the information and choose to highlight those that best support our belief (for instance, the high salaries).

- We can seek more supporting information (for example, by going to the placement office and looking up the starting salaries of communication graduates).

- We can do several of these.

The tactic of creating consonance, then, is used to strengthen and reinforce attitudes, to undergird existing cognitions, and to increase credibility. Consonance probably is used as frequently in persuasion as is dissonance, for persuaders often want to reinforce people's opinions, attitudes, beliefs, or behavior. Unfortunately, Festinger's theory and much of the myriad resulting research studies focus mainly on those cases in which dissonance arises, as the cartoons in Figure 7.10 suggest. Another shortcoming of the theory is that it oversimplifies the human situation. Recently, researchers in communication, psychology, and sociology have looked at a variety of other factors that enter in. For example W. Wood (2000) points out that social factors play a role in the process of reducing dissonance. The acquisition of new information is not the whole story

FIGURE 7.10 This car owner is obviously faced with a dissonance-producing situation. How might he go about reducing these feelings?

(Reprinted by permission of Matt Hansel.)

on dissonance and attitude change. People want to fit in with significant reference groups and engage in normative behavior to do so; they try not to sound or appear different from members of these significant reference groups. Further, receivers' internal states and psychological mechanisms determine the outcome of persuasive appeals at least as much as do the source's skill at designing and delivering the dissonance- or consonance-producing messages.

Another way to think about consonance and dissonance is illustrated in Figure 7.11. The horizontal axis of the model represents our initial attitude toward a topic or issue, which can range from highly positive to highly negative. The vertical axis represents any kind of input that we might receive

concerning the topic (something we read, a discussion we had regarding Internet access, an experience we had). Again, the input can range from highly positive to highly negative.

The arrows on both axes indicate the dynamics of the model. Notice that the positive end of the initial attitude axis has an arrow pointing toward the positive end of the input axis. For instance, if you have a positive initial attitude about inbound telemarketing, you will seek, agree with, or relate to information, experiences, and other evidence that support this point of view. Conversely, if you have a negative initial attitude about outbound and inbound telemarketing, you will seek, agree with, or relate to information, experiences, and other evidence that supports this point of view. Because of

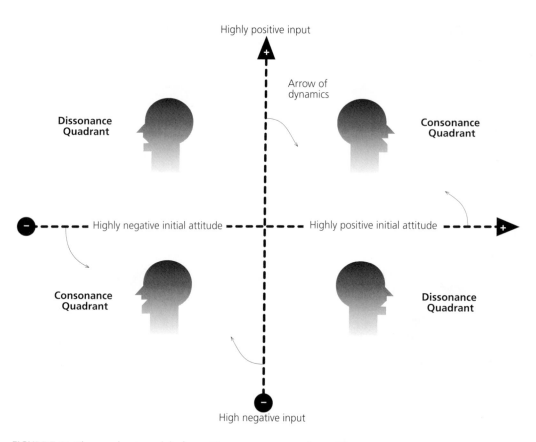

FIGURE 7.11 The quadrant model of cognitive consonance and cognitive dissonance. The advantages of this model over the one shown in Figure 7.9 are clear. Not only can we represent the *kind* of psychic comfort or discomfort being experienced, we can represent the *amount* of comfort or discomfort experienced, as well as the dynamics of dissonance and consonance.

the dynamics of the model, the upper-right and lower-left quadrants of the model each depict persuasion that relies upon consonance. Conversely, the upper-left and lower-right quadrants depict persuasion that plays on feelings of dissonance.

Try charting your own initial attitudes toward given topics—for example, the environment, vegetarian diets, or gun control. Then examine how you relate to various kinds of information or other input relating to the topic. For example, I recently received a mailing claiming that the Democratic candidate for governor in Illinois was dedicated to

banning handguns, increasing the cost of a gun ownership card from $7 to $500, and outlawing the sales of firearms at gun shows without a five-day waiting period. I am a gun owner and a hunter, but I also think that handguns are dangerous and too easily available. Would these inputs create either dissonance or consonance for me? You can determine the degree to which you are vulnerable to various kinds of persuasion by referring to the model in Figure 7.11. The model applies to such varied persuasive situations as voting for a candidate, switching brands, deciding to distance yourself from a person or group, and choosing to donate money to a good cause.

Sources of Dissonance

What kinds of situations or events can cause you to feel a sense of imbalance? Some of them are unique to you, of course, but many of them are similar—and even identical—for large groups of people. These are likely targets for persuaders because the predictable inconsistencies in life are potent first premises in persuasive arguments.

Loss of Group Prestige. One way for persuaders to make us feel dissonance is to cause us to perceive a loss of group prestige. For example, prior to the revelations of her insider trading of ImClone stock, Martha Stewart was highly regarded by many people who considered themselves persons with class and good taste. They wanted to emulate her, to try her recipes, to rewire antique lamps the way she did, and to have not only a flower garden like hers but a vegetable garden with Armenian cucumbers in it. One of her fans said, "We put a copy of Martha Stewart's *Living* magazine on a coffee table. It's the prettiest thing in the living room." Another said, "We want a little of what she's got—a scant teaspoon in Marthaspeak—of her taste and talent" (Rowell, 2002, p. 16). After the revelations, which surely must have dimmed Martha's sheen, one former fan said, "Even carving a Martha Stewart jack-o-lantern requires a nine piece pumpkin carving kit. . . . (Fortunately, this set is now on sale at a reduced price—$67—at marthastewart.com)." Another, obviously feeling put out by her loss of fan prestige, said, "There's nothing in her magazine that even hints at her virtue" (Rowell, 2002, p. 16). The loss of group prestige can apply to small and large groups alike—from a fraternity or sorority to an entire profession or region of the country. The loss can even cause dissonance for an entire nation, as was the case when the nature of President Clinton's affair with Monica Lewinsky was revealed in graphic detail. In such cases of a loss of group prestige, members of the concerned institution usually move quickly to reduce dissonance by such means as jokes, apologies, and explanations.

Economic Loss. Another kind of fear frequently exploited by persuaders is the fear of economic loss. When we perceive that our economic value (measured in savings, property, salary, or whatever) is in danger of being reduced, we suffer from psychic dissonance and feelings of insecurity. For example, following the events of 9/11 and the subsequent stock market nosedive, many persons were "downsized" or "merged" out of their jobs—jobs that they had assumed would be theirs until retirement. Others lost huge amounts of retirement savings. And for some, the failure of their companies meant that their retirement and company stocks became totally worthless. The obvious dissonance caused by such loss was dealt with in a number of ways. Some of the displaced workers "chose" to take early retirement, some had to postpone retirement, and some returned to school to improve their work skills. Many accepted jobs with much lower salaries, and still others went into business for themselves.

Persuaders can appeal to this fear of losing our job or retirement security to induce us to vote for politicians who promise to reform company retirement programs or to save Social Security. They can sell us investment schemes to shore up our financial security or induce us to join organizations or support causes to protect our economic well-being.

Loss of Personal Prestige. Whenever we perceive that we are losing the respect of others—our personal prestige—and feel helpless to do anything about it, dissonance is bound to emerge, regardless of the situation or the degree to which we feel responsible. This source of dissonance is used to appeal to parents whose children aren't achieving to their ability. For example, an ad for a series of motivational programs said, "If your child comes home with bad grades from school, refuses to practice the piano, watches too much television, and seems bored with school, then the responsible thing for a parent to do is to send the child to Chicago's Motivational Institute." In other words, parents could regain lost self-respect by being responsible and enrolling their child. Ads promoting hair restorers or weight reduction plans also play on the loss of personal prestige. And we are all familiar with ads warning that, if people see dandruff on your collar in the elevator on Monday morning, your standing at work will plummet. Other fears related to loss of prestige include the loss of youth, the loss of health, and deteriorating appearance.

Uncertainty of Prediction. We also feel discomfort when we are unable to predict people's behavior or the course of events with any degree of certainty. A dramatic example of this is recorded in Viktor Frankl's book *Man's Search for Meaning* (1962). Frankl reported that some former Nazi concentration camp inmates found it impossible to reenter the unpredictable, free world; they needed the predictability of the camp schedule and personnel in order to cope.

We find the same reaction in much less vivid but more personalized contexts. For example, whenever we move, change schools, take a new job, or break up with a spouse or lover, we feel uncomfortable because we can no longer predict probable outcomes. One of the most powerful weapons of terrorists is the unpredictability of their target selection. For example, the United States seemed insulated from terrorism, at least within its borders, prior to the 1990s. Then came the first bombing of the World Trade Center in the early 1990s, the 1995 bombing of the Federal Building in Oklahoma City, and the events of 9/11. Obviously vulnerable to terrorism, we will have to come to terms with a new kind of unpredictability, and the development of an Office of Homeland Security will not ease our national state of dissonance. Products that promise to "protect" us from some negative circumstance (illness, job loss, financial difficulties) use the inability to predict as a "hook" to persuade us. This inability to predict events with any certainty often serves as the missing premise in a persuasive enthymeme.

Guilt. A final source of dissonance is guilt, which springs from the potentially disapproving judgments of important others such as parents, peers, or fellow citizens. Media images of starving prisoners, genocide victims, and ruined homes in the Middle East can cause a national sense of guilt in Americans, prompting the government to send troops, food, medicine, and other forms of aid. Such self-imposed and internalized feelings of dissonance can be explained in various ways. Freudian psychoana-

lysts would say that we are afraid of reprimands from our symbolic parents, incorporated in our conscience, or superego. These fears lead to shame or self-hatred, as we noted in Chapter 4, and guilt is a symptom of that shame. Transactional psychology offers a similar explanation for guilt: The child in us fears a reprimand from the parent in us, which the adult in us handles by taking action to alleviate the feelings of guilt.

In any case, this source of dissonance is frequently used in persuasion. Kenneth Burke (1961) explained the process using a religious allegory. In the epilogue of his book *The Rhetoric of Religion,* Burke narrated an argument between God and the Devil about human motivation. God explains that he will ultimately win out over the Devil, who has introduced sin into the world. His explanation hangs on the development of guilt as an inevitable result of sinning, guilt that will have to be purged. The purgation will set things right with God, against whom mortals have sinned, and the result of the purgation will be a sense of redemption.

Of course, we have seen this pattern repeated in various religions, but we ought not overlook more mundane examples of this sin–guilt–purgation–redemption chain. Politicians who urge us to return to the principles that "made this country great" are using the religious model. Our sin lies in disregarding those principles. Our guilt is the sense of dissonance we feel. Our purgation is whatever action is suggested to return us to the tried-and-true principles—prayer in the schools, abolishment of affirmative action, or a constitutional amendment banning abortion on demand.

Numerous product pitches rely on the sin–guilt–purgation–redemption pattern. For example, most health-related products (such as nighttime cold medicines) show a sick child coughing and sneezing—the sin. Then the parent goes to the medicine cabinet only to discover that the Pertussin container is empty—the source of guilt. But the open-all-night supermarket has more on its shelves, so the parent goes out in the middle of the night to get some—the means of purgation. The next morning the child awakens refreshed and perky—the resulting redemption. The consumer is urged to avoid the sin, guilt, and purgation steps by making sure that there is enough medicine on hand. Auto manufacturers use a similar technique to persuade consumers to buy cars with air bags for both the driver and the passenger as well as side-door airbags. Advertisers even identify dull, drab, and dirty clothes as a sin that can be redeemed by using the right detergent, resulting in a whiter, brighter, fluffier, and better-smelling batch of laundry. You can no doubt identify numerous other examples of the use of guilt to sell products.

Sources of Consonance

On the other side of the coin, some appeals give receivers a sense of consonance, and these are made more frequently than those aimed at creating dissonance. Consonance-producing appeals are used to reinforce existing beliefs, attitudes, or behaviors and to activate receivers. What are some of the means used to create consonance?

Reassurance of Security. One of the ways to appeal to our need for equilibrium or balance is to reassure us that we are secure. As noted in both Maslow's and Packard's models, security needs are basic and can have several dimensions. To reassure us that we are somewhat secure from terrorist attacks, police stations, airports, courthouses, and other public buildings are now protected with metal detectors and even armed guards. Promises of job security are powerful persuaders for persons making career choices, and IRA and Keogh accounts offer retirement security. Politicians promise to stop the loss of factory jobs to foreign employers and to ensure the viability of Social Security and Medicare. Sometimes we see ideological persuaders use this tactic as well. Religious leaders convince their followers that by remaining true to the faith, by participating in rituals, or by increasing their donations they can avoid damnation. And various good causes also promise a kind of security: MADD will get drunk drivers off the roads, the church will offer salvation, and the Citizen's Utility Board will fight increases in utility costs.

Demonstration of Predictability. A consonance-producing tactic related to reassurance of security involves demonstrating that the world operates in predictable ways. Following the 1929 crash of the U.S. stock market, predictability went out the window, causing several other devastating drops in the value of the market. Only after the market had bottomed out and the government was able to demonstrate predictability by insuring savings through the FDIC did small investors reenter the market. Manufacturers also rely on the appeal to predictability when they offer guarantees or use slogans like "You Can Be Sure If It's Westinghouse." Any time we see warranties emphasized, we are probably being persuaded by a consonance-producing appeal regarding predictability. And we are supposed to feel more secure at airports when we see armed guards and metal detectors, and people being asked to take off their shoes. I confess to having felt that way when on one flight I was required to return to the check-in gate and send my jackknife as baggage instead of being allowed to carry it in my pocket. And it didn't bother me when a tiny combination screwdriver/penknife was confiscated from my key chain on another flight.

The Use of Rewards. A third consonance-producing tactic is the use of rewards, or positive reinforcements. You might remember from our discussion of learning theory in Chapter 4 that reinforcement increases the probability that a behavior will be repeated. Persuaders often use positive and complimentary statements to reinforce behavior. A half century ago in one of his most famous books, *How to Win Friends and Influence People,* Dale Carnegie (1952) offered this advice to his readers:

> Let's cease thinking about our accomplishments, our wants. Let's try to figure out the other man's good points. Then forget flattery. Give honest sincere appreciation. Be "hearty in your approbation and lavish in your praise," and people will cherish your words and treasure them and repeat them over a lifetime—repeat them years after you have forgotten them. (p. 38)

As you can see, Carnegie had put his finger on ways to make audiences feel good about themselves. This is a good approach to persuading audiences or, as Carnegie put it, influencing people.

Ads for products frequently use positive pitches to prompt feelings of consonance and thus reinforce behavior. Look at the travel section in the Sunday paper, and you'll find numerous examples, such as the ad for a midwestern ski resort that advises readers to "Go Ahead. This Year Give Yourself the Best Ski Vacation of Your Life—You Deserve It," or the American Express ad that promises, "Our London. Now You Can Afford to Be Penny Wise and Pound Foolish." These claims and others like them build feelings of psychological comfort in readers, who now perceive that they deserve the ski vacation they have wanted or that they can afford to go to London. These offers are persuasive because they reward people by convincing them that they deserve good treatment. Even something as simple as expressing appreciation for work done by an employee is rewarding and tends to increase the probability that similar behavior will occur in the future. That's why successful supervisors seem to be just as good at giving rewards as offering criticisms and why such things as "customer appreciation days" tend to reinforce brand and customer loyalty.

The old saying that "You will draw more flies with honey that with vinegar" is a key to why giving rewards is so consonance producing. Try to learn more about how persuaders use these techniques in persuading you. For instance, what are some consonance-producing appeals used in your world? Chances are, you can identify numerous examples of this kind of persuasion in your everyday life.

REVIEW AND CONCLUSION

In Part II of this book, we are searching for various kinds of unstated and widely held major premises that can serve in persuasive enthymemes. One of these kinds of premises, the process premise, relates to appeals to the emotions and the will—to the psychological processes operating daily in each of us.

One kind of process premise involves our needs and wants. We can see needs and wants operating in Maslow's hierarchy of needs and in Packard's (sometimes Freudian) listing of human needs. And though both of these models have been around for a long time, they still have applicability for us as their many rejuvenations demonstrate. There are other models of human need states as well, and learning about them will make you a more responsible receiver. A second kind of process premise that can predispose us to action involves our attitudes and beliefs. If persuaders change our beliefs and attitudes about, say, fuel efficiency, they predispose us to buy fuel-efficient autos, furnaces, and water heaters. If persuaders want us to continue voting for a certain party, they reinforce our existing beliefs and attitudes. Both of these persuasive types can be used with either attitudes toward objects/issues or attitudes toward situations. It may be important for persuaders to reinforce or change our behavioral intentions. If persuaders can get us to clip a product coupon, their job is more than half done, because we intend to buy the product when we clip the coupon.

Attitudes also have an impact on very important and less important purchases, voting, and joining decisions, as depicted in the Petty and Cacioppo elaboration likelihood model.

Finally, closely related to both attitudes and needs is the human desire for psychological consonance. We seek a world in which our predictions are verified, in which people we like approve of the same things we do, and in which our values and attitudes do not conflict with our behavior. If we feel a lack of balance, we actively seek ways to bring our world into congruity. If we perceive balance to exist, we experience a sense of ease and can be easily motivated to continue to act as we have been doing. Persuaders try to create dissonance if they want us to change our behavior and try to create consonance if they want us to maintain our behavior. Although each of us is unique, our need states, attitudinal clustering, and desires for psychological balance are similar enough that persuaders can use these processes as first premises for large groups of people.

QUESTIONS FOR FURTHER THOUGHT

1. What is a process premise? Explain.

2. What is the difference between an attitude and a need? Give examples.

3. What did Maslow mean when he called his hierarchy of needs "prepotent"?

4. Which needs described by Packard are the most ego involving or personal in nature?

5. What is an example of the need for emotional security?

6. What is an example of how advertisers use the need for ego gratification?

7. What is an example of the need for a sense of power?

8. What are three functions of an attitude?

9. What is the difference between an attitude and an opinion?

10. What is the difference between a behavior and a behavioral intention?

11. According to the elaboration likelihood model, which decision path will be used when we consider purchasing ice cream?

12. According to the elaboration likelihood model, what happens if the audience can't be motivated regarding the processing of information in a voting decision (such as reasons to vote for or against a school bond referendum)?

13. According to the elaboration likelihood model, what happens to a joining decision if the audience does not have the ability to respond?

14. Using the elaboration likelihood model as depicted in Figure 7.8, explain the flow of information regarding a current issue.

15. What are some sources of dissonance?

16. What are some sources of consonance?

For online activities, go to the Web site for this book at
http://communication.wadsworth.com/larson.

8

✳

Content Premises
in Persuasion

Another type of premise that frequently operates in enthymemes is based on people's ability to think logically or rationally. The elaboration likelihood model suggests that this kind of persuasion uses the central processing route and involves considerable analysis and intellectual activity. Premises relying on logical and analytical abilities are content premises. Many such premises are perceived as valid and true by large segments of the audience and hence serve as major premises in enthymemes. Some persuasion theorists call these premises "arguments," or "propositions"; marketers call them "offers." Whatever the label, this chapter examines persuasion that operates by using the persuadee's logical, reasoned, and intellectual abilities.

For example, suppose I want to persuade you to support legalized prostitution. What would you consider good and sufficient reasons for doing so? For some persons, there aren't any good (let alone sufficient) reasons for such a policy, so there would be no way to persuade this segment of the audience. For others, the policy seems so sensible on the face of it that you don't need to persuade them

—perhaps they have seen how well the system works in Holland or Nevada. But what about those who neither approve nor disapprove—the undecided members of the audience? They require more information, evidence, discussion, and debate on the issue before taking a side. In other words, they are asking for good and sufficient reasons for supporting the proposition. You might tell them about how legalized prostitution reduced the rate at which people contract AIDS in Holland. You might discuss the tax revenues that could be generated by having governmental licensing of prostitutes. And you might point out that such a policy would remove criminal elements from the practice of prostitution. The success or failure of any of these "arguments," "claims," or "propositions" relies on underlying premises held by the audience: that AIDS is epidemic and deadly, that tax revenues are needed, and that criminal elements in any activity are undesirable. Those widely held beliefs are content premises and serve as major or minor premises in persuasive enthymemes.

We have all learned certain logical patterns because we have encountered them repeatedly over time. Most of us believe, for example, that events have causes and that when certain things occur other things invariably follow. Problems also have causes, and when these causes are removed, the problem seems to be eliminated. This particular pattern of rational and intellectual reasoning—cause–effect reasoning—is a powerful first premise often used in persuasion. For instance, evidence could be presented that a certain baseball team's pitching staff had experienced many training camp and early-season injuries. A logical "effect" of this "cause" would be that the team would end the season with a poor record. It would not be necessary to convince an audience that injuries lead to losses, but only to list the various injuries and then rely on the cause–effect premise already operating in the audience's mind to draw the conclusion that a losing record was likely. As this example shows, the cause–effect pattern can be a potent first premise in a persuasive enthymeme.

This pattern is a type of content premise frequently used by politicians and government officials, in the courts, in business, and even in advertising. All major or first premises use assumptions already in the audience's mind as the implicit premise in an enthymeme. Content premises rely on the patterns by which the content of messages is connected with what are believed to be accepted patterns of logical or rational thought. In other words, content premises "sell" because they are assumed to be logical. The power of the content premise lies not in its ability to stir emotions, create psychic uneasiness, or appeal to hidden needs. Rather, its power lies in its ability to elicit a rational or logical response from or conclusion in persuadees.

WHAT IS PROOF?

Proof varies from situation to situation. What may "prove" a point to students in a fraternity meeting may not "prove" the same point to a university administrator. In recent decades, several books, documentaries, and films have tried to "prove" that President John F. Kennedy's assassination was the result of a complex conspiracy. They have successfully persuaded some people but failed with others. This tells us that "proof" varies from person to person as well. The Clinton administration tried to "prove" that cutting the deficit would spur economic growth. Their evidence convinced some people but not others. However, when the economy improved after the budget cuts and led to the longest bull stock market in U.S. history, many doubters became convinced. They needed more proof than the original believers did, and the economy provided it. What do you think the populace thought when the stock market bubble burst and President George W. Bush's administration ran budget deficits, especially after the administration instituted tax cuts for the wealthy? Proof can thus vary not only from person to person but also from group to group and from situation to situation. In general, though, we can say that proof consists of enough evidence that can be connected through reasoning to lead typical audience members to take the persuader's advice or to believe in what he or she says.

Aristotle identified what he called *topoi,* which means "places of argument," or logical locations where persuaders would be likely to find propositions or premises and evidence to support them. Sometimes, for instance, the topic might be some sort of precedent that the audience recognizes as the way things have always been done. The precedent sets the tone for the future, and, unless the audience is given many good reasons for breaking the precedent, the precedent controls future instances of similar issues.

For example, a precedent that you probably take for granted is that school, from the primary grades to high school, is typically a September-to-June affair. Why? From an economic standpoint, this schedule is foolish, given the expense of heating school buildings during the winter months in most of the United States. However, we all know that there is a precedent for the September-to-June model. It was originally devised during the heavily agrarian phase of our society, when young people's help was essential to get the crops planted, tended, and harvested. In fact, at the first high school I taught at, in a small farming community, vacation days called "rock days" were granted to students following spring plowing so that they could pick rocks out of the newly plowed soil and haul them away to make stone walls or fences. Today, a similar precedent operates, but with a slightly different twist, because farming now involves less than 1 percent of our population. The new precedent reflects how the summer months are used by most people. June, July, and August are months in which lots of construction and repair work takes place. People also go on vacation and need to be temporarily replaced. And many summer service industries (swimming pools, state and national parks, golf courses, and so on) need additional help to serve their customers. Students can fill these temporary jobs. For these and other reasons, the agrarian precedent still serves as our model, even though the need for young people's labor on the family farm is no longer critical.

Most contemporary theorists agree that proof is composed of two facets: reasoning and evidence. In the proper mix, these two elements will lead persuadees to adopt the changes a persuader advocates. There are several ways to look at evidence and reasoning. By examining how persuaders operate, we can infer motives and discover what they are up to. For example, suppose I wished to persuade you that smoking causes lung cancer. The thrust of my message is a cause–effect argument. I want to prove to you that a given effect (lung cancer) has a given cause (cigarette smoking). Along the way, I can engage in a variety of tactics. I might show slides of cancerous lung cells, or I might give vivid testimony of the pain and suffering involved in lung cancer deaths, or I might offer statistical correlations of the relation between smoking and cancer. Any of these approaches would be related to my general strategy or intention. These tactics are the source from which proof will ultimately emerge for you as persuadee. Somewhere along the line, I will reach the threshold for you and will have "proved" to you that smoking causes lung cancer. This might or might not persuade you to stop smoking. In other situations, other elements will persuade you to stop, and a persuader might not even plan the key evidence that leads to "proof." For example, my father, who was a heavy smoker, contracted lung cancer

and died an unenviable death. For my spouse and I, witnessing this event became the "proof" we needed to quit smoking.

Although the nature of evidence and reasoning has remained quite stable, their uses have changed dramatically in the information age and now include not only persuasive speeches but also the kinds and amount of evidence needed to induce change. Before the advent of electronic media, modern advertising, and contemporary propaganda, audiences were accustomed to receiving very specific, verifiable evidence. For example, if a person's testimony was used to prove a point, it was critical to tell the audience why that person qualified as a good source of evidence. Audiences were suspicious of some kinds of evidence, such as analogies. Today, however, we accept the testimony of a professional athlete when he endorses an investment plan even though he does not qualify as an expert on economics. And we frequently accept analogies as evidence—animated automobile tires depicted as having tigers' claws to grip the road, for instance. Or we see news footage of the planes crashing into the twin towers, followed by their collapse and the 3000+ resulting deaths; the pictorial evidence persuades us that we need to support the war on terrorism and to provide financial and other assistance to the victims' families. And other kinds of premises and evidence convince us through the central information-processing channel. For example, politicians offer us evidence in support of a policy or their own incumbency or candidacy, and government institutions offer data on some social phenomenon (see Figure 8.1). Parents supply what they think are good and sufficient evidence and reasons for not living with someone of the opposite gender, while students frequently counter with their own evidence and reasons in favor of such a living arrangement. In all these cases, proof varies from person to person and from situation to situation. Underlying all these examples, however, is a pattern of enough evidence combined with reasoning resulting in what we call proof.

To discover how proof operates in the law, access InfoTrac College Edition, type the word "proof" in the search engine, and select the

Return
to the BJS
home page

Crime &
Justice
Electronic Data
Abstracts

U.S. Department of Justice
Bureau of Justice Statistics

Key Crime & Justice Facts at a Glance

ı   **Crime trends**
ı   **Trends in Federal investigations and prosecutions**
ı   **Trends in felony convictions in State courts**
ı   **Corrections trends** including **Capital punishment trends**
ı   **Expenditure trends**

Small versions of the charts and brief statements of findings are presented here
with links to full size charts, additional information about the charts and findings,
and the data that support the chart. A complete **list of the trend tables** that support these
charts is available.

Full size versions of selected trend charts suitable for overheads or handouts also are
available.

Get the latest Federal Government social statistics from other agencies from the
Social Statistics Briefing Room at the White House Web site.

Crime trends
To more on crime and victims

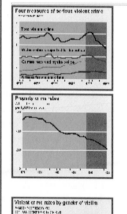

**Serious violent crime levels continued to decline in
1998.**

Additional facts and graphics about violent crimes including
homicide, rape, robbery, and assault and the involvement of
juveniles in violent crime and use of firearms

Property crime rates continue to decline.

Additional facts and graphics about the property crimes
including burglary, theft, and motor vehicle theft

**Violent crime rates declined between 1997 and 1998.
Rates for men and women are getting closer.**

Additional facts and graphics about the characteristics of crime
victims

FIGURE 8.1 The material in this figure from the U.S. Department of Justice
exemplifies the use of statistics as a form of proof.

(Courtesy of the Bureau of Justice Statistics.)

burden of proof option(s). Read a few of the items listed.

TYPES OF EVIDENCE

Different kinds of evidence vary in strength or persuasive power, depending on the context in which they are used. In some situations, for instance, statistics have a powerful effect; in others, pictorial evidence persuades us; and in yet others, vicarious or retold experience most effectively delivers the persuasive message of the content premise. In these and other cases, persuasion relies on the assumption that people can learn about and act on information gained indirectly and vicariously and processed via the central information-processing route. This is why stories about the experiences of others are such effective evidence and why they are favored as persuasive devices. Advertisers use testimonials from both ordinary people and celebrities to endorse products. The advertisers assume that consumers will vicariously absorb the experience that the ordinary citizen, movie star, or athlete relates and buy the product.

But even when we do not learn from or become swayed by the experiences of others, our own experience is usually enough to cause us to change. The Lakota were aware of this. As a Lakota baby crawled close to the campfire, no one pulled it away with shouts of "Hot! Stay away, baby! Hot!" as we do in our culture. Instead, they watched the baby's progress very closely and allowed the baby to reach into the fire and touch a hot coal, burning itself mildly. They then quickly pulled the baby away and treated the burn. The experience "persuaded" the child to be careful with fire. Or suppose a professor explains to you her very stringent attendance policy for a television production class, but you take the policy with a grain of salt and fail the class, necessitating taking it over. You hear the same lecture on attendance on the first day of the class the next semester. If experience is persuasive, you will never miss a class this semester. Or maybe you don't have to have the experience of failure yourself, but several communication majors tell you that "Scary Mary" has an attendance policy from hell and detail their own failure of the class. Their dramatic re-

counting of their experience with Scary Mary and her policy is enough to convince you to attend every class.

There are three broad forms of evidence: (1) direct experience, (2) dramatic or vicarious experience, and (3) rationally processed evidence. The first two usually are processed via the peripheral information-processing route without much forethought, whereas rationally processed evidence usually follows the central information-processing route. Direct experience demonstrates the major premise that "actions have consequences." Dramatic evidence relies on the human tendency to structure our lives in narrative or story form. Rational evidence relies on our innate ability to reason using logic and evidence. In previous chapters, we looked at some theorists who present the case for dramatic evidence convincingly. Burke and Fisher, for example, discuss the power of dramatic or narrative evidence. Aristotle's *topoi* or "places of argument" (which we shall visit shortly) will demonstrate the power of rationally processed evidence. Let us briefly examine these three broad categories of evidence.

Direct Experience

Most parents of more than one child will probably tell you that they have one kid who always had to learn "the hard way" by experiencing the "actions have consequences" principle. Actually, most of us learn the power of this principle after only a few experiences, but some seem never to catch on. The power of direct experience lies in the ultimate positive or negative reinforcement we receive, according to the Skinnerian model discussed in Chapter 4. That is, direct experience derives its powerful persuasiveness from outcomes. As a sixteen-year-old, for instance, I learned that even if you do not directly engage in a crime you still might be held accountable for it. On a "guy" vacation with some friends, we decided to save money by siphoning gasoline from cars parked near a dance hall. While the others did the dirty work, I stayed in the car to watch for the cops. However, one of the "victims" got our license number and reported it to the authorities. When charges were brought, they included me as one of the thieves. The lesson stuck with me

—you don't need direct involvement with a crime in order to be named as a participant. In this sense, direct experience persuaded me. You can probably identify some direct experiences in your life that provided a powerful form of evidence for you.

Dramatic or Vicarious Experience

All of us have learned or been persuaded by hearing about the experiences of others—that is, by vicarious experience. There are a variety of types of vicarious experience, most of them dramatic in nature.

Narratives. People have always been fascinated by stories, including myths, legends, and ballads, handed down in an oral/aural tradition. With the advent of literate society—writing and later print—other forms of narratives emerged, such as plays, poetry, novels, and short stories. Technology has brought us still other forms, including radio programs, movies, cartoons, soap operas, documentaries, evening news shows, game shows, talk shows, news stories, and athletic events—all with their roots in storytelling.

Evidence that is dramatic in nature invites and encourages vicarious involvement in an attempt to persuade people to a certain course of action. Such persuasion relies on the human ability to project themselves into the context or situation described by the persuader—to "feel" what others feel, to "live" the problem vicariously. This type of evidence encourages persuadees to cocreate proof with the persuader. The result is powerful, long-lasting persuasion.

Several types of evidence lend themselves to the dramatic approach. For example, a good way to use dramatic evidence is through the narrative. In his book *People of the Lie: The Hope for Healing Human Evil,* noted author and psychotherapist M. Scott Peck (1983) related "The Case of Bobby and His Parents." The narrative began with Bobby, who had been admitted to the hospital emergency room the night before for depression. The admitting physician's notes read as follows:

Bobby's older brother Stuart, 16, committed suicide this past June, shooting himself in the head with his .22 caliber rifle. Bobby initially seemed to handle his sibling's death rather well. But from the beginning of school in September, his academic performance has been poor. Once a "B" student, he is now failing all his courses. By Thanksgiving he had become obviously depressed. His parents, who seem very concerned, tried to talk to him, but he has become more and more uncommunicative, particularly since Christmas. Although there is no previous record of antisocial behavior, yesterday Bobby stole a car by himself and crashed it (he had never driven before), and was apprehended by the police. . . . Because of his age, he was released into his parents' custody, and they were advised to seek immediate psychiatric evaluation for him. (p. 48)

Peck went on to observe that, although Bobby appeared to be a typical fifteen-year-old, he stared at the floor and kept picking at several small sores on the back of his hand. When Peck asked Bobby if he felt nervous being in the hospital, he got no answer—"Bobby was really digging into that sore. Inwardly I winced at the damage he was doing to his flesh" (p. 48). After reassuring Bobby that the hospital was a safe place to be, he tried to draw Bobby out in conversation. But nothing seemed to work. Peck got "No reaction. Except that maybe he dug a little deeper into one of the sores on his forearm." Bobby admitted that he had hurt his parents by stealing the car; he said he knew that he had hurt them because they yelled at him. When asked what they yelled at him about, he replied, "I don't know." "Bobby was feverishly picking at his sores now and . . . I felt it would be best if I steered my questions to more neutral subjects" (p. 50). They discussed the family pet—a German shepherd whom Bobby took care of but didn't play with because she was his father's dog. Peck then turned the conversation to Christmas, asking what sorts of gifts Bobby had gotten.

Bobby: Nothing much.

Peck: Your parents must have given you something. What did they give you?

Bobby: A gun.

Peck: A gun?

Bobby: Yes.

Peck: What kind of a gun?

Bobby: A twenty-two.

Peck: A twenty-two pistol.

Bobby: No, a twenty-two rifle.

Peck: I understand that it was with a twenty-two rifle that your brother killed himself.

Bobby: Yes.

Peck: Was that what you asked for for Christmas?

Bobby: No.

Peck: What did you ask for?

Bobby: A tennis racket.

Peck: But you got the gun instead?

Bobby: Yes.

Peck: How did you feel, getting the same kind of gun that your brother had?

Bobby: It wasn't the same kind of gun.

Peck: *(I began to feel better. Maybe I was just confused.)* I'm sorry, I thought they were the same kind of gun.

Bobby: It wasn't the same kind of gun. It was the same gun.

Peck: You mean it was your brother's gun? *(I wanted to go home very badly now.)* You mean your parents gave you your brother's gun for Christmas—the one he shot himself with?

Bobby: Yes.

Peck: How did it make you feel getting your brother's gun for Christmas?

Bobby: I don't know.

Peck: *(I almost regretted the question: How could he know? How could he answer such a thing?)* No, I don't expect you could know. (p. 52)

Peck then brought the parents in for counseling. However, they seemed unable to realize what message they had sent their remaining son by giving him his brother's suicide weapon. Bobby continued therapy until he was sent to live with a favorite aunt.

By the time he was discharged to Helen's care, three weeks after his admission to the hospital, the sores on his arms and hands were only scars, and he was able to joke with the staff. Six months later I heard from Helen that he seemed to be doing well and that his grades had come up again. From his psychiatrist I heard that he had developed a trusting therapeutic relationship but was only barely beginning to approach facing the psychological reality of his parents and their treatment of him. (p. 59)

When I first read this dramatic example, I literally gasped as I discovered that Bobby's parents had given him a gun for Christmas, and I was totally dumbstruck to learn that it was *the* gun. Although the story was emotionally charged, we would be hard put to call it "illogical." In fact, it is probably totally logical to conclude that such behavior is harmful even though that conclusion is based only on a single case. If the evidence is dramatic enough or emotional enough, persuadees will not ask for more.

Most great preachers, orators, and politicians are also great storytellers. They use the narrative skillfully to capture an audience's attention and to draw them into a topic. This effect is reinforced with other evidence, and more narratives might be worked in to keep the audience interested. Chances are, you have heard speeches or sermons in which narrative was skillfully used. Such speeches seem to have the most impact and to be remembered the longest. Similarly, the storylike parables of the New Testament are easy to recall, whereas many of the other verses fade from our memory soon after we hear them. As a professor of mine once said, "The narrative will carry more persuasive freight than any other form of evidence."

Testimony. Another type of dramatic evidence is the testimony of a person who had seen, heard, and experienced events related to the topic. Here, the persuader might read an eyewitness account aloud or simply recount his or her personal experience. For example, if the issue is unemployment, persuadees might be swayed if they hear from out-of-work persons. The humiliation of having to wait in line for an unemployment check, the embarrassment of having to take government surplus food-stuffs, and other experiences of the unemployed will probably have dramatic persuasive power. As receivers, we vicariously live through what the witness experienced when we hear direct testimony.

Although eyewitness testimony is potent, studies have shown that it is often unreliable and even incorrect (Loftus, 1980). In many cases, as has been documented, persons have been wrongfully imprisoned on the basis of eyewitness testimony (Loftus, 1984). As Figure 8.2 illustrates, witnesses often see and hear what they want to see and hear, and give testimony from their idiosyncratic points of view.

As receivers, we need to carefully examine the testimony used to persuade us. We need to ask questions like these: Was the witness in a position to see what is claimed? Could the witness be mistaken in any way? Does the witness have a bias that might cloud his or her testimony? Might the witness have a motive for giving the testimony? Is the witness being paid for giving the testimony? What might he or she have to gain from testifying?

Anecdotes. Anecdotes are short narratives that make a point in a hurry—maybe in only a sentence or two. For example, there is the anecdote of the optimist who was asked to describe his philosophy: "That's simple. I'm nostalgic about the future." Anecdotes are often funny and are frequently hypothetical, so they are quite different from actual testimony. The key thing about anecdotes is that, unlike testimony, we rarely take them as truth. Instead, we tend to process anecdotes as if they are the exclamation points of persuasion. As a young lawyer, Abraham Lincoln was once arguing a case in which the opposing attorney was rather long-winded. Lincoln used this anecdote to make that point to the judge and jury: "My friend is peculiarly constructed. When he begins to speak, his brain stops working. He makes me think of a little old steamboat we had on the Sangamon River in the early days. It had a five-foot boiler and a seven-foot whistle, and every time it whistled, it also stopped" (Moore, 1909, p. 49). In discussing the NRA's opposition to the ban on assault weapons, President Clinton used the anecdote. He recounted the many hunting trips he had been on using standard hunting guns, not assault weapons, and ended by saying, "And you know something? I never saw a turkey or a deer wearing a flak jacket." The anecdote made the point very clearly: Assault weapons aren't needed for any legitimate purposes like hunting—they are intended for waging war and for killing people.

Participation and Demonstration. There are several other ways in which persuaders can dramatize evidence. At an antismoking presentation, for instance, audiovisual materials can show cancerous lung tissue. Smokers can participate by exhaling cigarette smoke through a clean white tissue and observing the nicotine stains left behind. Sometimes, persuaders dramatize a point by using visual aids to demonstrate the problem and solution. For instance, one of my students spoke on the need for people to be aware of when stress is building up and of how to use jogging to reduce it. He displayed a large, deflated balloon that he said represented an average student at Northern Illinois University. The "student" was inflated a little with the stress of settling into a new dorm room; another puff of air represented the stress of registration; and more air went in for the first exams and fraternity rush. Soon the balloon was ready to pop. The speaker then called on his audience to release their stress through exercise. He ended the speech by saying, "Or else, do you know what could happen?" Whereupon he popped the balloon with a pin. The audience's attention never strayed from the balloon, and they all got the point of the speech. The demonstrations that form the core of most direct marketing on television also use participation. The viewer sees the greaseless grill, the "guaranteed" bass bait, or the "quik-n-easy" food chopper at work, and they imagine what it would be like to use the product. Then viewers are advised to "act now!" by calling the 800-number shown them on the screen.

Rationally Processed Evidence

Not all evidence is dramatic. Sometimes evidence appeals to our logical processes in nondramatic, intellectually oriented ways. For instance, newspaper editorials frequently use evidence that appeals to readers' logical processes. A good example comes

FIGURE 8.2 Witnesses see events or persons from their own point of view.

(Reprinted by permission of John Jonik from *Psychology Today.*)

from a series of editorials in the *Chicago Tribune* that promoted early childhood education ("The Payoffs for Preschooling," 1984). The lead sentence of the editorial made the major claim that "early childhood education is the surest way to break the chain of chronic poverty." The case was developed with supportive claims like these:

> Early childhood education reduces the costs of welfare, special education, and the criminal justice system. . . . Early learning programs reduce the risks of mental malnutrition. . . . These children [attending preschools], then, need less special and remedial education. They are happier with themselves and their school environment. They get along better with teachers. . . . They are more likely to graduate from high school, get a job or go on to higher education. . . . They are less likely to get caught up in delinquency and crime. (p. 25)

Research was reported that at-risk students who had attended preschool had "better grades and fewer failing marks. They were absent less from school. They needed less special education. And they had a better attitude toward school than a group of similar youngsters who did not get the pre-schooling" (p. 25). And at age nineteen, the children with preschooling were "more likely to finish high school and to score average or above on competency tests. More of them had jobs or were involved in higher education. And they were less likely to have been arrested, to be on welfare, or to become pregnant" (p. 25). The editorial went on to cite the savings resulting from preschool education and the resulting cut in remedial programs:

> It actually cost less to educate the children who got the preschooling . . . even when the expenses of the early classes [were] included. . . . Preschool cut the cost per student of each succeeding year in school by about 20 percent—about $800 per child every year in savings.
>
> In terms of reduced crime alone, taxpayers will save $3100 for every one of the youngsters who got the preschool training. . . . These are the direct costs and don't count the anguish,

fear and suffering that criminals can inflict on victims. Nor does it attempt to measure the psychological benefits of a reduction in crime rate in a community. . . .

> Taxpayers have already saved seven times the cost of one year of preschool in the Ypsilanti project and 3½ times the tab for two years. And the savings resulting from reduced needs in welfare, from less crime, and from greater ability to earn will continue for the rest of the lives of these young people—even reach into the lives of the following generation. (p. 25)

Notice how these claims appeal to our logical, central information-processing channel. The writer knows that as receivers we have a major premise in our heads about costs versus benefits. We demand that any idea, product, or program have benefits that justify its costs. Knowing that we have this internal premise, the writer makes claims of great benefits for the preschool idea. The writer also knows that we expect to see some sort of evidence to back up such claims and that we will probably respect this evidence if it is reported "scientifically." There are no narratives in the editorial; there are no anecdotes. The only testimony is the report of the Ypsilanti project, which is not testimony from an eyewitness but rather is a statistical summary.

Appeals to our logical processes can be seen in other persuasive messages—in advertising, for example. Look at Figure 8.3. The Campbell Soup Company knows that persons concerned with health and nutrition are aware of the need to increase the amount of fiber in the American diet. Most of the literature on this subject has recommended eating high-fiber foods such as whole wheat bread and bran cereals. However, many people don't like dry cereal, let alone dry bran cereals. Campbell's offers similar benefits but with different costs—you can get fiber by eating Manhandler soups such as Bean with Bacon or Split Pea with Ham.

As you can see from these examples, the appeal to logical processes relies on a reasoning pattern such as "the past is a guide to the future" or "the cost is less than the benefits." What are some other logical patterns that persuaders often use?

MADE OF THE FINEST FIBER

If you're like most people who eat right, you probably give high fiber high priority.

And like most people, when you think of fiber, you probably automatically think of bran cereals.

Well, there's another good source of dietary fiber you should know about. Delicious Campbell's® Bean with Bacon Soup.

In fact, Campbell's has four soups that are high in fiber.

And you can see from the chart that follows exactly how each one measures up to bran cereals.

So now when you think of fiber, you don't have to think about

FIBER IN A SUGGESTED SERVING			
CAMPBELL'S SOUP		**BRAN CEREALS**	
Bean with Bacon	9g	100% Brans	11g
Split Pea with Ham	6g	40% Brans	6g
Green Pea	5g	Raisin Brans	5g
Low Sodium Green Pea	7g	Others	5-10g

This comparison includes soluble and insoluble fiber

having it just at breakfast.

Instead, you can do your body good any time during the day. With a hot, hearty bowl of one of these Campbell's Soups.

You just might feel better for it—right to the very fiber of your being.

CAMPBELL'S SOUP IS GOOD FOOD

Campbell's has a full line of low sodium soups for those people who are on a salt-restricted diet or have a concern about sodium.

FIGURE 8.3 This appeals to our logic. What rational argument does it present?

(Used by permission of the Campbell Soup Company.)

To see how many kinds of evidence exist, access InfoTrac College Edition, type the word "evidence" in the search engine, and sample the references listed.

TYPES OF REASONING

Recall our definition of proof as "enough evidence connected with reasoning to lead an audience to believe or act on a persuader's advice." We will now explore the second step in the process of logical persuasion: connecting the pieces of evidence by reasoning. Martin Fishbein and Icek Ajzen (1975, 1980) devised what they called a "theory of reasoned action," which led to a great deal of research into the process of reasoning.

Several patterns of reasoning seem to be deeply ingrained in our culture. One school of research suggests that there is a linguistic explanation for reasoning, that the "deep structure" of our language is accompanied by logical "deep structures" (Clark, 1969; Reynolds & Burgoon, 1983). This possibility is dramatically exhibited when people violate the accepted deep structure of logical reasoning and so are labeled as "off the wall" or "out in left field," or when a logical deep structure is violated and humor results. For example, the night before the Battle of the Little Bighorn (better known as Custer's Last Stand), Custer told his troops that he had good news and bad news and asked which they wanted to hear first. They decided to hear the bad news first. Custer proceeded to tell them that they would all be dead and scalped by the end of tomorrow, their belongings seized, and their bodies left to rot in the Wyoming sun. The troops then asked what the good news was. Custer replied, "We won't have to go back to that damned North Dakota." The violated deep structure of Custer's statement is what makes the story humorous. Sometimes, such violations of logical deep structure makes a potential persuader sound like a lunatic. Consider the following letter to the editor of a local newspaper regarding ways of removing nuisance deer from public parks in the area (Scott, 1989):

Let's look at some hard facts:

- It cost taxpayers $50,000 to shoot the deer at Rearson Woods.
- It would cost taxpayers $30,000 a year to shoot the deer at Rock Cut Park.
- The Department of Conservation made $20,000 a year from hunting at Rock Cut.
- Hunters already have won the right to hunt on public land in the Supreme Court.
- Hunters pay millions of dollars annually to buy state parks. (n. p.)

So far, so good, even if we don't agree with the writer's position. He begins with what appears to be an inductive line of argument using "effect-to-cause" reasoning (that is, citing a set of effects and then concluding by identifying a probable cause). He shows the varying degrees of effectiveness of several alternative plans used in the past (his first three points), and then goes on to state a fact about the law relating to hunting on public lands. Finally, he makes the claim that hunters pay for state parks. His logic is a little unclear, but he probably means that state parks are at least partially funded by revenue from hunting licenses, federal and state taxes on guns and ammunition, and the hunter's own property, sales, and income taxes. We anticipate that he is about to claim something like "Therefore, hunters are positive persons and deserve to hunt in state parks, especially when their hunting helps remove nuisance deer from these parks in economical and even revenue-producing ways." The fact that we anticipate such a "logical" conclusion is probably evidence of at least one type of deep logical structure. But notice what happens when our expectations are unmet in the conclusions the author actually draws from his five points:

If you were an animal, would you prefer to live ten years free, even if you died a slow death, or would you want to live it penned up, sleeping in your own manure? I think most Americans would want to be free. That's also the way God wanted it. That's why he said it is a good thing to be a hunter. For Jesus Christ is alive and well, but Bambi never was. (n. p.)

The conclusion is wacky: It seems befuddled and barely related to the evidence. What do living free and dying slowly have to do with the argument? How does sleeping in one's own manure relate to the issue? Where did God say that it was good to be a hunter? What does the Jesus-versus-Bambi comparison mean? None of these conclusions flow from the evidence.

Clearly, this letter writer's conclusion contains several serious violations of the deep structural logical expectations held by most people; our preference for a line of reasoning has been violated. But what does this example have to do with our study of persuasion from the receiver's point of view? Remember that we are looking for content premises—logical patterns that serve as the first premises in enthymemes. The deep structural logical preferences serve in this way: We believe and act on what we perceive to be logical arguments presented to us by persuaders. Fishbein and Ajzen's theory of reasoned action (TRA) is one such potential deep logical structure. The theory predicts that actions (or "volitional behaviors") are the effects of behavioral intentions. Behavioral intentions, in turn, are the results of people's attitudes on issues and on the social norms that they hold in high esteem. For example, if we were trying to persuade people to stop buying SUVs and to consider purchasing one of the new hybrid automobiles, we could give them evidence such as testimonials from hybrid owners as to the superiority of the vehicle's mileage performance (60 mpg). They might also testify to the quietness and smoothness of the ride. Further, we might compare this performance with the poor mileage of most SUVs and note that four-wheel drive isn't really necessary for most people's needs. This might change their attitude toward SUVs. Then we could point out that the hybrid owners are opinion leaders and innovators in many things besides automobile buying. Specifically, they tend to be better educated, to have better jobs, to earn more, and to be more socially conscious. According to TRA, if our audience believes that these traits are ones to be emulated, then the shift in attitudes toward SUVs and the audience's respect for the social norms of hybrid users will lead to a behavioral intention— the audience will consider buying a hybrid instead

of an SUV. And when the purchase is finally made, it will be the result or effect of the behavioral intention. Unfortunately, there are some problems with TRA. One is that, unless we measure the behavioral intention very close in time to the behavior, its power as a predictive measure dwindles. Communication scholar S. Sutton (1998), for example, points out that intentions are subject to change over time and are provisional in nature. And several researchers have found the predictive power of behavioral intentions to be either weak or negative as more and more time passes. Let us now turn to some traditional forms of reasoning that can serve as premises in enthymemes.

Cause-to-Effect Reasoning

Cause-to-effect reasoning is powerful in our culture; even our language depends on it. For example, we rarely say, "The ball was thrown, and the window was broken," which is a passive-voice sentence. Instead, we put the cause out front and let it "create" the effect. We say, "Johnny threw the ball and broke the window." This active-voice sentence tells us that Johnny caused the ball to fly through the air and break the window. This construction gives us much more information: It tells us who did what.

Persuaders frequently use cause-to-effect reasoning to identify events, trends, or facts that have resulted in certain effects. They tell us that if a cause is present we can expect certain effects to follow. If the effects are bad and we want to do something about them, we usually try to remove the cause. For instance, if you are allergic to garlic and eat some food that has garlic in it, we can predict that you are going to have an allergic reaction. Or, if you are carrying too much credit card debt, you should get rid of all but one of your credit cards. This argument assumes that cutting up all but one credit card (cause) will reduce your ability to accumulate consumer debt (effect). Both of these examples make perfect sense, and that is why cause-to-effect reasoning has such persuasive power.

Advertising frequently uses the cause-to-effect form of reasoning. Consider an ad for a cellulite-reducing complex. It identifies a cause for the effect of dimpled-appearing thighs—a weak skin support system—and then goes on to offer a way to remove the cause and with it the undesirable effect—regular use of the product. The advertiser knows that the audience has a deep logical structure for cause-to-effect reasoning and skillfully uses that structure as the first premise in the enthymeme underlying the ad. Politicians also use the cause-to-effect form of reasoning when they argue that cutting taxes will stimulate the economy and end the recession. Parents use this form of reasoning when they point out to their kids that spending too much time watching television will lead to poor grades in school. And we could make the argument that U.S. support of Israel was the real cause of the 9/11 and subsequent terrorist attacks. There are several types of causations as well. For example, communication scholar C. Hitchcock (2001) argues that there are at least two types of effect: component effect and net effect. Component effect causation involves effects that are linked to a cause, such that the cause initiates a change in the effects. Net effect causation involves a cause that contributes to overall changes in effects. In other words, it contributes to the final outcome, though there might be other causes. In this case, the cause is probably more properly thought of as an influence on the ultimate outcome. Again, this kind of reasoning is most often processed along the central route of the ELM.

To explore how others have viewed causation, access InfoTrac College Edition, and enter the word "causation" in the search engine. Read several of the over one hundred periodical articles.

Effect-to-Cause Reasoning

Another type of reasoning that is less frequently used (and sometimes flawed) is called effect-to-cause reasoning. Sources of food poisoning are identified this way. We know that some people who ate at a restaurant became violently ill, while others who ate at the same time did not, so we search for the one food item that the one group ate and the other did not. This was the cause of the observed effect. With this pattern, the persuader cites some known effects and tries to work back to the cause. The problem with this reasoning is that there might be an intervening cause or a contributing cause. For example, in the world of the TV commercial, Bob Garfield (1988), a staff writer for *Advertising Age,* gives high praise to a spot for Stokely's Singles, microwaveable single-serving vegetables. "Moms don't like heating and re-heating broccoli for their busy families' various dinner shifts," writes Garfield. "They hate trying to please four finicky palates with one frozen vegetable dish. And they despise the grimaces that greet their bowls of succotash." Those were the effects. How to identify the cause, remove it, and substitute Stokely's Singles was the problem. In a "slice of life" ad, the family members would come off as ingrates who were lucky to be getting a meal at all. So Stokely's did an exaggerated slice-of-life ad using humor. "When Mom dishes up the vegetables, Dad and the kids grimace outsize grimaces, Mom responds with an outlandish sneer and slings the whole bowl over her shoulder in disgust. The problem is real. The identification is immediate. The exaggeration is amusing. And the solution, lo and behold, is Stokely's" (p. 86). However, consider the possible intervening or contributing causes for the finicky vegetable-eating habits of the family. For example, maybe Mom has been too accommodating to individual menu requests over the years. Or maybe the life schedules of the family members have changed, causing Mom to have to heat and re-heat the veggies.

A recent change in my life schedule probably had such an intervening or contributing cause. For years, during the summer months between 5:00 and 7:00 each evening, we have had a standard "open invitation" to our friends to swim in our in-ground pool, provided they bring an appetizer and their own beverages. The group is called MSPP (My Summer Pool Party), and our common link is that we all are members of the same church. For years, we had regular visitors and contributors. This past summer, however, we had only one visitor, and she came only two times. We assumed that the effect (almost no visitors) had as its cause our criticism of the sermonizing of the new minister, and we said as much to the members of MSPP. But it turned out that the real cause was changes in the life schedules of our friends. For one, the number of her grand-children had doubled since the previous summer. Another person's work schedule had changed, and he couldn't make it during those hours. As you can see, intervening or contributing causes can lead to faulty effect-to-cause reasoning.

Reasoning from Symptoms

Persuaders sometimes identify a series of symptoms or signs and then try to conclude something from them. For example, politicians cite how much worse things are now than they were when their opponent took office. Unemployment is up, and the stock and bond markets have been ravaged. Business crime is rampant especially among top CEOs and accounting firms, and recent polls show that people have lost faith in their ability to control their own destinies. The hope is that the voters will blame the incumbent for the troubles. Watch for this sort of reasoning in the upcoming presidential election.

Returning again to Garfield's high-quality TV commercials, we find reasoning from symptoms in an ad for South Carolina Federal bank. The ad agency understood that "people pay no attention to disingenuous ersatz bankers. To persuade any-body that it is more human than the competition, a bank first must get his or her attention. Then it has to act more human" (p. 86). The usual bank ad relies on research to find out what people dislike about banking and then has some "bankerish-looking actor" claim, "Our bank is different because we value our customers." And because the ads all look alike, consumers overlook them. South Carolina Federal's approach was different. Instead of using humans, the bank used animals to react to the things consumers dislike about banking. One ad featured an orangutan in its opening spot. "How does your bank react when you ask for a home equity loan?" asks an off-screen wimpy voice. The orangutan yawns. Then the voice asks about bank hours: "Do they have all-day bank-ing?" The orangutan shakes its head "No!" "Free checking?" The orangutan blows a raspberry at the camera. And so it goes, with the voice eliciting other examples of disliked banking practices, fol-

lowed by a humorous look or gesture by the orangutan until the final line: "Well, if we were you, we'd bank with us." The persuasion works be-cause the audience recognizes that the orangutan's behavior is mimicking that of bank employees in limited-service banks. The symptoms of behavior (and the fact that they resonate with the audience's past experience) are persuasive in and of them-selves. The audience participates in and con-tributes to their own persuasion by recognizing the symptoms and linking them to their decision to change banks.

Criteria-to-Application Reasoning

Sometimes, persuaders establish what appears to be a reasonable set of criteria for purchasing a product, voting for a candidate, or supporting a cause and then offer their product, candidate, or cause as one that meets these criteria. For example, following the phone system deregulation that gave rise to the "baby Bells" (for example, Illinois Bell, Pacific Bell, and others), an ad for the Bell System established several criteria for good telephone service: (1) rea-sonable rates and reliable service, (2) free informa-tion services for long-distance areas, and (3) the ability to handle calls to all parts of the country, not merely those areas serviced by the system. The spokesman, a well-known TV actor, reminded viewers of the Bell System's past dependability and of its ability to reach anywhere in the country, as well as foreign countries. Finally, after noting the free information service Bell provides, he offered viewers the "ten-dollar hour." They could get sixty minutes of long-distance telephone time anywhere in the country for only ten dollars if they called a special number and made the request. Note that by presenting a reasonable set of criteria up front the persuader has already won half the battle. Re-ceivers, having accepted the criteria, then logically infer that Bell is a good choice when they get the reminders of past dependability, free information services, international dialing, and—the final hook—the ten-dollar hour. Remember the student who cut Scary Mary's classes and flunked because of his absences, only to have to retake the class and maintain perfect attendance, thus earning a passing grade? Reasoning from symptoms persuaded him.

Reasoning from Comparison or by Analogy

Sometimes, persuaders use comparison as their logical reason for some conclusion. In this form of reasoning, an example is analyzed and described, and conclusions are then drawn about that example or situation. The persuader then compares the example with another situation, pointing out similarities and identifying reasons conclusions about the example apply to the current situation. During a recent presidential primary, numerous candidates proposed revising the U.S. tax code to simplify its complex rate structure and to shift tax burdens. In arguments for various plans, argument by comparison was a frequent logical appeal. Tables, charts, and graphs were used to compare how much tax an individual would pay under the old system with how much he or she would pay under the new one. Supposedly, voters who saw their position improved as compared with their position under the old system would vote for the candidate whose plan seemed best. This was a literal analogy. A recent editorial in the *Chicago Tribune* titled "Season to Kill Enriches Some, Repulses Many" (Zorn, 2002) discussed hunters and ascribed certain beliefs and actions to them. In a 2001 editorial, the writer had depicted hunters as "sadists" and had gotten hundreds of letters of outrage as a result. In the 2002 editorial, hunters were portrayed as "more or less indifferent to animal suffering; they don't go out of their way to prolong it, but they're not particularly concerned with curtailing it either. Therefore they are not sadistic, merely depraved . . . calling themselves sportsmen. Here's a thought, It's not a sport when the 'opponent' doesn't know it's playing, doesn't want to play and can't fight back. It's just a disgrace." The "hunting is like a game" analogy is a figurative one.

We also frequently see argument by comparison in advertising, with competing products compared in terms of cost, effectiveness, safety, and so on. For instance, the big battle over the light beer market largely involves reasoning from comparison, with

one brand claiming fewer calories and better taste than others. The same thing is seen in ads for low-tar and low-nicotine cigarettes. And the Energizer Rabbit uses comparison to make the point that this brand is much longer lasting than, say, Duracell—after all, the little bunny keeps "going and going and . . ."

In the case of reasoning by analogy, something familiar is used to demonstrate something unfamiliar or complex. For example, in 2002, President George W. Bush went to war with Iraq in order to destroy their alleged weapons of mass destruction. Another reason for going to war was to replace the dictatorial regime of Saddam Hussein with a democratic form of government. Finally, the war with Iraq was supposed to further the other war—the war on terrorism—that had been so labeled by Bush following the events of 9/11. Opponents of Bush's action claimed that it would likely lead to a situation like that in Vietnam or the former Yugoslavia, in which all we achieved was the alienation of friendly nations. In argument by analogy, persons who disagreed with this view pointed out that in both earlier cases guerrilla warfare was the predominant mode of fighting, that governmental leaders were corrupt, and that the terrain in Vietnam and Yugoslavia was quite different from that of Iraq. This is another literal analogy. In other words, we are comparing familiar past wars (Vietnam and Croatia/Serbia) with an unfamiliar present (and possibly future) war.

Using a figurative analogy, we compare a familiar but unrelated and simple thing with something that is unfamiliar and complex. For example, political races are often compared with horse races through such expressions as "front-runners," "early starters," "latecomers," and "dark horses." Such persuasive means of comparison can help simplify the issue or example being discussed, but receivers need to ask if the comparison or analogy is appropriate. In the horse race analogy, there are numerous differences. For instance, in political races, there is only one winner, and those who "place" and "show" receive nothing; further, not all candidates start from the same "gate," and there are no early starters or latecomers. Figure 8.4 uses a figurative analogy. What is it?

FIGURE 8.4 What is the figurative analogy here?

(Reprinted by permission of Aaron Johnson.)

Deductive Reasoning

A familiar form of appeal to logic is deductive reasoning, which involves reasoning from the general to the specific. For example, in a legislative body, a persuader might support a bill or a motion by saying something like, "The legislation before us is desperately needed to prevent the state budget from going into a deficit situation," and then providing the specifics. An editorial might begin, "Sycamore needs to pass this school bond referendum in order to save its extracurricular sports, its music and art programs, its newspaper, and its dramatics program," and then go on to describe the details. One of the problems with the deductive approach is that receivers who feel the least bit negative about the persuader's general point may quickly lose interest and not pay attention to the specifics that are at the heart of the issue. Or the initial generalization might prompt rebuttal before the persuader has the opportunity to provide the details of the case.

Inductive Reasoning

Inductive reasoning gets the specifics out on the table before bringing up the generalized conclusion. For example, in the school bond case, the persuader might begin this way:

> Many of you know that it costs over $60,000 just to run the athletic program. The budget

for the marching band is over $12,000 for travel, instruction, and uniforms. I was surprised to learn that it cost over $2000 just to pay the royalties for the spring musical. We have cut and cut until there is nothing left to cut. The last referendum increase was fourteen years ago—inflation has risen over 200 percent since then. Unless we pass the referendum, the district now faces elimination of these valuable extracurricular programs.

With the specific evidence apparent, the generalization flows logically from it. Another example of inductive reasoning was made in the December–January 2002 issue of *Outdoor Life* (Zorn, 2002). The following facts were listed:

1. Deer typically kill more persons annually than the combined total of all commercial air, train, and bus accidents.
2. In 2002, drivers are expected to hit and kill 1.8 million deer.
3. This number is four times the number of whitetail deer in the country at the turn of the 20th century.
4. In spite of the 7.4 million deer killed annually by sportsmen and the 1.8 million killed by automobile drivers, the whitetail deer population had grown from 29.8 million in 1994 to 32.7 million in 2002. (p. 15)

And what conclusion was drawn from these facts and inductive reasoning? That hunting is necessary? No, it was to urge hunters to fill their doe tags. The readers of *Outdoor Life* probably know that most hunters pass up does early in the season hoping for a big buck. They also probably know that the best way to control the deer population is not to kill bucks but to kill does, because bucks can and do mate with multiple does. One buck is sufficient for several does. Therefore, using one's doe tag is the best way to control mushrooming deer populations.

To see the variations in the use of reasoning, access InfoTrac College Edition, type the word "reasoning" in the search engine, and look at the article by Brian McGee on the argument from definition. You will see how reasoning was used to define "race" in the early twentieth century. Also check the various articles from the journal *Argumentation and Advocacy* and the item on the conditional syllogism and deductive reasoning.

MISUSES OF REASONING AND EVIDENCE

Of course, logical persuasion can be exploited by intentionally or unintentionally misusing either evidence or reasoning, or both. Let's look at some examples of the misuse of reasoning and evidence so that we can spot it when it occurs.

Statistics

One of the mainstays of logical persuasion is the use of statistics. We tend to believe statistics without questioning them. But several questions ought to be asked when statistical evidence is offered. First, we need to ask, "Is the sample from which the statistics are drawn a representative one?" In other words, is the sample selected in a way that might bias the results? We need to know whether the sample is a reliable representation of the larger population. We might want to know how the sample was selected. Perhaps it was from the phone directory? But not everyone has a telephone, some people have several, and others have unlisted phone numbers. So, sampling from a phone directory is not truly representative. Perhaps the subjects were approached at a shopping mall and given a survey there. But, again, mall shoppers might not be representative of the population at large. Maybe the subjects were intercepted in front of the student union. Would we find any different results if we interviewed them in the morning rather than in the evening when most students are studying? These and other questions should be asked of any statistical proof used by the persuader. Another misuse of statistical evidence involves using a single instance as an example of all instances. Thus, we hear of an enormously wealthy person who pays no taxes and are led to believe that other enormously wealthy persons pay no taxes. Still, another misuse of statistics is biased sampling, which occurs when a nonrepresentative portion of the population is sampled. Responses from a sample drawn from subscribers to *The National Rifleman* will be very different from one drawn from subscribers to *Horticulture* or *The Organic Gardener.*

The mode of presentation can also misrepresent statistics. For example, the graph in Figure 8.5 was used to demonstrate the degree to which homosexuality exists in the general population. The shaded portion indicates persons who have had *at least one* homosexual encounter; the unshaded portion of the graph indicates heterosexual persons. The graph suggests that the proportion of the population that is homosexual is at least 50 percent when actual research indicates that it is far smaller—around 2 percent (Guttmacher, 1993). Clearly, the graph visually misrepresents the actual case and distorts the meaning of the statistics. What the graph fails to provide is information about the size of the sample in each segment.

There are many other ways to distort statistics using graphic presentations of the numbers, so receivers need to be alert not only to what statistics really mean—for example, the way the samples were chosen and the type of measurement used—but also to how they are presented.

Testimony

As noted earlier, one problem with the use of testimonials is that the person "testifying" might not be providing accurate information. Also, seemingly insignificant shifts in wording can "lead" witnesses to

Number of homosexual encounters reported

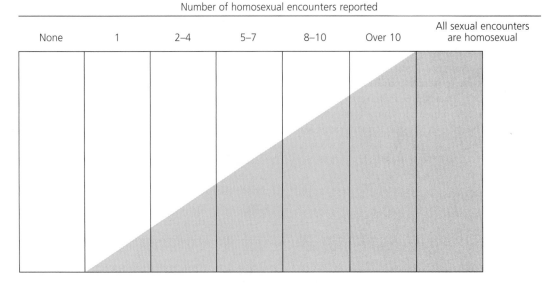

| None | 1 | 2–4 | 5–7 | 8–10 | Over 10 | All sexual encounters are homosexual |

FIGURE 8.5 This graph is misleading because it implies that half the population is homosexual when the statistics being represented are much lower than that.

certain answers. Most of the time, we don't have the opportunity to "cross-examine" the person giving the testimonial. Instead, when we see or hear a person endorsing a product, a candidate, or an organization, we are forced to make up our minds right away about whether the person is qualified to give the testimonial. When testimonials are used to persuade, we need to ask if the person giving the testimonial is an authority on the subject, and if so, how reliable he or she is. Was the person giving the testimonial close enough to have witnessed the evidence he or she is testifying about? Is it possible that the person giving the testimonial is biased, and if so, is the bias pro or con? For example, in Chicago, a female violinist was recently awarded nearly $30 million from METRA, the commuter train conglomerate. Her $500,000 violin got caught in the train doors, and she tried to save it. She testified at the trial, offering "dramatic detailed testimony . . . as she painfully recalled for jurors the winter day in 1995 when she became pinned against the doors of a commuter train and was dragged more than 360

feet before she fell under its wheels" (Deardorf & Finan, 1999, p. 1). She lost a leg as a result of the accident. Could her testimony have been biased? How well could you remember what happened if you were in that situation? Was she partially responsible for putting herself at risk? These and other questions are the kinds of issues to be raised when the testimonial is being offered as evidence.

As persuadees, we need to be alert to the ways in which testimonials can be distorted or misused. We know that in many cases the testimonial is being given only because the sponsor has paid the person to give it. So, the next time you see a sports personality endorsing a product, don't assume that he or she uses it on a daily basis. And try to determine the degree of authority the person has about the product.

Comparisons and Analogies

As also noted earlier, the misuse of comparisons and analogies (sometimes labeled the fallacy of faulty comparison or faulty analogy) is common in persuasion. For example, politicians frequently compare the national budget to the budget necessities of the individual family. They argue that the family has to live within its resources, so the government should do so as well. However, individuals can't create money the way governments can, they don't have to provide for the national defense, and they don't have to build the roads they drive on. If they did, there would be no money left for the necessities of life. Comparing the government's budget to the individual family's budget is like comparing apples to oranges.

The same thing applies to faulty literal analogies. For example, one father of a college freshman maintained that his college experience was analogous to that of his son: Because the father had gotten by on five dollars a week spending money, the son should surely be able to make it on ten dollars a week. This faulty analogy has several dimensions. Inflation has quadrupled, not doubled, in the years since the dad was in college, and dormitories no longer provide clean towels and linens. Further, athletic, theater, and concert tickets are no longer provided for a single low price but have to be purchased separately.

Figurative analogies like the political race as a horse race, described earlier, can also be confusing. Granted, there are some similarities, but the analogy is misleading taken in its entirety. Persuadees need to examine comparisons and analogies to see whether they do indeed lead to a certain conclusion or whether some faulty comparison or analogy is being used.

COMMON FALLACIES USED IN PERSUASION

Webster's Collegiate Dictionary defines *fallacy* as "deceptive appearance . . . a false or mistaken idea . . . an often plausible argument using false or invalid inference." It is this last definition that concerns us here: believable arguments or premises that are based on invalid reasoning. In spite of the fact that these fallacies have been identified for centuries, they still pop up frequently in advertisements, polit-

ical persuasion, interpersonal persuasion, and other arenas in which persuasion is used to influence beliefs, attitudes, and actions. Briefly, here are some of the more common fallacies that we encounter almost daily.

Post Hoc, Ergo Propter Hoc

Post hoc, ergo propter hoc, commonly called the "post hoc" fallacy, derives from the Latin meaning "after this, therefore because of this." As the translation implies, because one event follows another, the first event is assumed to be the cause of the second. We constantly run into this fallacy in the world of advertising. For example, in a recent radio ad for *TV Guide,* a salesman for computer hardware seated next to a French businessman on an airplane describes how his firm could modify the Frenchman's computer system. The Frenchman wants to know about American television, so the salesman gives him a spare copy of *TV Guide* and makes a $30 million sale—all because of *TV Guide.*

In political persuasion, the post hoc fallacy is often used to blame the current state of affairs on the incumbent. For example, political adversaries might charge that the reason the school system is out of money is that the superintendent and school board wasted all the money from the referendum eight years ago on unneeded frills. Not necessarily so.

When both Sammy Sosa and Mark McGwire broke Roger Maris's home run record in 1998, people attributed the renewed public interest in baseball in general to the race to break the record. That may be true, but interest could have come from other factors not related to the sluggers, such as both the Cubs and the Cardinals being in a pennant race for the first time in some years and the acquisition of new and exciting players by both teams. It would be fallacious to say, "After the home run race, therefore because of the race."

Ad Hominem

The Latin term *ad hominem,* meaning "against the man," refers to any attack against an individual instead of her or his argument. The purpose is to lead the audience to take certain actions simply because

FIGURE 8.6 These cartoons use the *ad hominem* fallacy.

(Reprinted by permission of Kevin Craver.)

of an alleged character quirk or other flaw in the person presenting the opposite viewpoint. The cartoons in Figure 8.6 are good examples of the ad hominem argument being used against yours truly. As faculty president of the policy-making body on my campus, I was responsible for implementing the recommendations of a task force on committee structure and size. One such recommendation was to alter the duties of the publication board of the student newspaper, *The Northern Star,* so that the board would become involved in the selection of the editor and would also be responsible for periodic review of editorial policy. The paper's editors and cartoonist felt that this was an infringement on their First Amendment rights and launched a campaign to attack me, not the proposed change, as can be seen in the cartoons. (By the way, the reform passed, and I rather enjoyed the temporary notoriety.) This tactic is not usually used in advertising because products, not people, are being promoted. However it is frequently used in ideological persuasion. Whenever attacks are made on a person's character instead of on his or her stands on issues, be aware that the ad hominem fallacy is probably at work. If persuaders have nothing substantive to debate, they frequently resort to attacking the personality of the opponent.

Ad Populum

As its name implies, the ad populum fallacy involves persuasion that relies on whatever happens to be in vogue at that time. There are many examples in our history of the use of ad populum arguments—some important, some tragic, and some trivial. For example, consider just a few trends that justified themselves at one time or another using the logic of the ad populum. These would include Prohibition, with its speakeasies and flappers, during the 1920s. The ad populum would also include the baby boom, rock 'n' roll, and suburbs in the 1950s. More recently, it would include the essentialness of personal computers, the fall of communism in Eastern Europe, recycling, rap music, virtual reality, interactive media, the World Wide Web, and the dot com bubble and bust.

Appeals using the ad populum also abound in the worlds of fashion, popular culture, and advertising and usually result in persuasion of the masses— for example, to wear one's baseball cap backward, own Air Jordan athletic shoes, get body piercings, use 900-number telephone "services," and join email erotica interest groups. Whenever someone urges us to "get on the bandwagon" or to "follow the crowd," the ad populum fallacy is probably operating.

The Undistributed Middle

The fallacy of the undistributed middle occurs in most cases of what we call "guilt by association," whereby the persuader argues that, just because an individual, group, or philosophy shares one or more aspects or attributes with another, it shares all other aspects or attributes. Consider the following argument: "Gut Malloy is a member of Tappa Kanna Bru fraternity, and fraternity boys are heavy drinkers, so he must be a heavy drinker, too." Common sense tells us that there is something missing here. The heart of the fallacy is in the phrase "fraternity boys are heavy drinkers," which is used to suggest that *all* fraternity members share *all* attributes beyond group membership. In other words, the argument assumes that heavy drinking is equally distributed among or practiced by all members of fraternities when, in fact, some members are moderate or infrequent drinkers or don't drink at all (Jensen, 1981).

Of course, this example is trivial, but persuaders use the guilt-by-association or undistributed-middle principle to sway opinion and alter behavior in significant ways. For example, I served on a committee to advise our Board of Trustees on a proposed Convocation Center. Because I served on the committee, many critics of the idea assumed that I must favor the project. Therefore, I was guilty by my association with the group even though I frankly didn't know whether I favored or opposed the building in a time of tight budgets. Or consider this example, which appeared in a small-town newspaper recently.

> Consider these facts: The Japanese eat very little fat and suffer fewer heart attacks than the British or the Americans. On the other hand, the French eat a lot of fat and suffer fewer heart attacks than the British or the Americans. The Italians drink excessive amounts of red wine and also suffer fewer heart attacks than the British or Americans. Therefore eat and drink what you like. It's speaking English that kills you. ("Consider the Facts," 2002, p. 10)

The fallacy of the undistributed middle also frequently persuades us to purchase products, vote for candidates, and support "good causes." The fallacy underlies any appeal suggesting that buying and using a certain brand will make us like others who buy and use it.

The Straw Man

In the straw man fallacy, persuaders set up a weak, or "straw man," case they know they can easily defeat. They then represent this case as the position of the other side in the debate, bring out their key evidence and reasoning, and defeat the bogus case, along with the opposition. Political persuasion is riddled with this tactic. For instance, candidate A might say that candidate B's position on defense spending is such-and-such and then promptly show how wrong the straw man position is by presenting impressive statistics, examples, and so on. Clearly, anyone holding such a weak position shouldn't even be considered for public office.

In the world of advertising, in which it is usually considered bad strategy to mention the competition, we occasionally see, read, or hear a straw man case. A good example is the TV ad in which the announcer says something like, "Do you think this Chevy pickup truck can climb this tough mountain carrying a Dodge pickup on its back?" Then we see the Chevy climb the mountain with the Dodge on its back. Of course, if the Chevy couldn't do the job, they would never have aired the ad. Most comparative advertising depends on the straw man fallacy. In the cola and burger wars, for instance, the opposition is often set up as a straw man waiting to be demolished by the advertiser's brand. The straw man fallacy is also commonly used in ideological arguments. Anti-abortion advocates frequently argue that abortion is an inhumane form of birth control and should thus be outlawed. However, pro-choice advocates have never recommended abortion as a means of birth control—that claim is a straw man argument that will naturally be demolished by pro-life advocates. Or consider the controversial antiabortion films *The Silent Scream* and *Conceived in Liberty*. The very titles seem to set up a straw man. In one scene, a fetus that is about to be aborted seems to be desperately trying to escape from a surgical instrument that has been inserted into the womb. The narrator, a medical doctor, uses powerful language to describe the struggle and the instrument. He relates what will happen when the fetus is removed, describing how forceps will crush its skull. Of course, the audience will feel revulsion at the thought of the brutal crushing of the fetus and will oppose abortion. What the narrator does not tell the audience is that they are seeing a third-trimester abortion, which accounts for only about 10 percent of all abortions. Again, a straw man argument has been set up so that it can be easily defeated.

Other Common Fallacies

Another type of fallacious reasoning involves using partial or distorted facts (such as only telling one side of the story or quoting out of context). Other types include substituting ridicule or humor for argument (such as depicting the opposition candidate as "a slow-dancing bureaucrat"), in appealing for sympathy, using prejudices or stereotypes (such as that college professors are absentminded, so they can't be counted on), appealing to tradition ("That's the way we've always done it around here"), begging the question or evading the issue ("National health care is nothing less than socialism!"), and using a non sequitur (an irrelevancy) or creating a false dilemma ("We either outlaw deficit spending or declare the country bankrupt") (Kahane, 1992; Thompson, 1971).

LOGICAL SYLLOGISMS

There are three major types of syllogism that commonly form the foundations of content premise persuasion: conditional syllogisms, disjunctive syllogisms, and categorical syllogisms.

Conditional Syllogisms

Conditional syllogisms use "If A then B" reasoning. Like other syllogisms, they have a major premise, a minor premise, and a conclusion. The major premise states a condition or relationship that is presumed to exist in the world. Receivers are assumed to accept the existence of the condition or relationship in most cases. The following is a conditional syllogism in its classical form:

If the U.S. government can't control terrorism with the present laws, then we need to give it new laws that are tough enough to stop terrorism. (major premise)

The Oklahoma City and World Trade Center bombings and the events of 9/11 are proof that the government can't control terrorism with the present laws. (minor premise)

Therefore, we need to give the government tougher laws to stop terrorism. (conclusion)

The first element in the major premise is called the antecedent, and the second element is called the consequent. In affirming the antecedent, which is what we did in the minor premise by referring to the attacks, we can draw a valid conclusion that tougher laws are needed.

I hope you are saying to yourself, "Hey! That's not necessarily the case." If so, you are making a distinction between truth and validity. The syllogism is valid, but the premises are not necessarily true. Validity depends on the general rules of reasoning, and not on the truth of the premises. Advertisers know this and frequently make perfectly valid arguments using false premises. A good example is this statement on a package of Trilene fishing line: "If you are seeking a world record, you should use one of the pound tests coded in the chart at right." You can detect the "if . . . then . . ." format in the sentence. We all know that using the right line—Trilene—won't assure anyone of a world record fish. But the advertiser used the conditional form on the package because receivers tend to accept it as logical and factual.

With conditional syllogisms, there are two valid forms of conclusion drawing. First, we can affirm the "if" part of the major premise and accept the "then" part of the major premise. A related but invalid procedure would be to deny the antecedent and conclude that the consequent has also been denied. Suppose, in the terrorism example, that we had affirmed the consequent instead of the antecedent in the minor premise. This could be done by saying, "We have given tougher laws to the U.S. government" (which did occur via the Anti-Terrorism Act of 1995 and with the establishment of the Office of Homeland Security in 2002). And

then we could conclude, "Therefore the U.S. government will be able to control terrorism." The fallacy becomes apparent immediately—the existence of tough laws doesn't necessarily indicate an ability to control terrorism. The reasoning here is invalid because there may be an intervening cause. In fact, there are several such intervening causes for the terrorist bombings, including the ready availability of fertilizer and diesel oil (the key ingredients for making a bomb) and lax security at commercial airports.

In a related but also invalid procedure, suppose we had denied the consequent in the minor premise by saying, "We have not given enough tough new laws to the U.S. government," and then concluded, "Therefore, the U.S. government will not be able to control terrorism." The fallacy is less apparent but is still there—the lack of tough laws doesn't necessarily indicate an inability to control terrorism. Again, there could be intervening causes, such as those previously noted. Although invalid, this form of syllogism is frequently used in advertisements. For instance, a romance is "saved" by a certain mouthwash or shampoo, or a family feels more loving toward Mom because she uses a certain product in her cooking.

Thus, although a conditional syllogism might be perfectly valid in a logical sense, it can be untrue. Be alert to this trap. Persuaders can use a logically valid syllogism to camouflage untrue premises. Ask yourself whether the premises are true and whether the argument is valid.

As you have probably noticed, the conditional syllogism is similar to the cause–effect linkage described earlier. To get a better idea of how conditional syllogisms can be used, access InfoTrac College Edition, and type the words "conditional syllogism" in the search engine. Then read the items on the various strategies for using syllogisms and on the order of information in them.

Disjunctive Syllogisms

The disjunctive syllogism has as its basic form "Either A is true or B is true." This is the major premise of a disjunctive syllogism and is usually accompanied by some proof or evidence that suggests the probable presence or absence of A or B. The conclusion is then drawn on the basis of these probabilities. For example, a school board could threaten to do away with extracurricular activities unless voters approve a referendum increasing property taxes, saying, "Either you vote to increase property taxes or you lose the extracurricular activities." The voters would provide the minor premise of the syllogism through their votes. This strategy is often effective because the issue is so clear-cut. In 2002, the United States and Britain stated, "Either Iraq gets rid of weapons of mass destruction or we will invade Iraq, destroy them ourselves, remove Saddam Hussein and the military from power, and set up a democratic form of government."

Most disjunctive syllogisms have a key weakness: Few situations present a clear either/or, even in cases of life and death. For example, politicians often state that, to deal with the problems of the national debt and deficit spending, we must either increase taxes or decrease spending, suggesting that there are no other workable solutions. However, many economists argue that increasing the gross national product will generate more income for the government and so reduce deficit spending, leading to a decrease in the national debt. Another solution might be to institute a national lottery (though some argue that this is nothing more than another form of taxation, albeit voluntary). Strict either/or logic cannot take into account other belief systems or more than two alternatives in a situation. Thus, you need to examine persuasion framed in the either/or mode to search for other alternatives or differing belief systems under which the disjunctive model will not work.

Categorical Syllogisms

Categorical syllogisms deal with parts and wholes or sets and subsets. Both the major and minor premises involve membership or nonmembership in one of two categories or clusters. The conclusion relates the clusters of both premises into a new finding or result, as shown in the following classic categorical syllogism:

All men are included in the class of mortal beings. (major premises)

Socrates is included in the class of men. (minor premise)

Therefore, Socrates is a mortal being. (conclusion)

Although this example is frequently used to demonstrate the categorical syllogism, it is not one that you will find many opportunities to use, and it is not likely to be brought up in any controversial arguments or debates. Its format, however, is frequently seen, read, or heard in various kinds of persuasion. Take, for example, the U.S. Marines' recruiting slogan: "We're looking for a few good men." The implied categorical syllogism is as follows:

All U.S. Marines are included in the class of good men. (major premise)

You are a good man. (minor premise)

Therefore, you should become a Marine. (conclusion)

Because you are a member of one category, it is assumed that you must or should be a member of another.

IBM used this technique when it ran a two-page public relations ad that features two pairs of baby booties, one pink and one blue, and the question "Guess which one will grow up to be the engineer?" The ad goes on to explain that boys are encouraged to excel in math and science whereas girls are not, thus accounting for the discrepancy in the numbers of male and female engineers. The ad then points out that IBM has supported over ninety programs to strengthen women's skills in these areas and intends to continue such support. Two uses of the categorical syllogism can be seen here. First, there is one concerning engineers: "Persons encouraged to excel in math and science are likely to become engineers" (major premise); "Males are encouraged to excel in math and science" (minor premise); "Males are likely to become engineers" (conclusion). On another level, the ad says: "Good companies encourage women to excel" (major premise); "IBM encourages women to excel" (minor premise): "IBM is therefore a good company" (conclusion). Although the first syllogism is valid (and probably true as well), the second is invalid. IBM uses the illusion of logical syllogism to make its case. Although good companies do encourage women to excel, simply doing that does not necessarily guarantee the label "good."

THE TOULMIN FORMAT

Most of us do not encounter persuasion that is overtly syllogistic. Instead, the syllogism often is the underlying structure in persuasive arguments. British philosopher Stephen Toulmin (1964) developed a model that identifies the kinds of logical persuasion we encounter in everyday events. According to Toulmin, any argument aimed at our logical reasoning processes is divided into three basic parts: the claim, the data, and the warrant.

Basic Elements

The claim, or the proposition that the persuader hopes will be believed, adopted, or followed, is the first element in Toulmin's model. Claims usually need to be supported by evidence, or data, the second part of the model. Data give the receivers reasons for following the advice of the claim. However, the relationship between the claim and the data is not always clear, so the persuader must explain the relationship; Toulmin called this the warrant. These three elements become clear as we examine persuasion at work.

Take, for example, the recent debate over cultural diversity, and the response of the educational system to non-English speaking students. The following letter to the editor, which appeared in the *Northern Star,* addresses the problem and demonstrates the use of the claim, the data, and the warrant of Toulmin's system:

Recent articles, editorials, letters to the editor, and other commentary have argued that there is a need/right to have courses taught in one's own native language. A better alternative would be to require all students to be proficient in at least two languages, one of which must be English. Let me point out some relevant facts.

1. English is the international language of diplomacy, science, commerce, politics, literature, travel, and popular culture. Ninety percent of all computer files are in English as are 100 percent of the indexes to them. A Chinese pilot flying a Chinese airliner into Chinese airspace and in contact with a Chinese air traffic controller must communicate in English, not Chinese—it's international law.
2. With the exception of Chinese, English is the first language of more native users than any other language, and its users as a second language outnumber native users. It is the first language of forty-five countries, and nonnative users claim it is the easiest (and most fun) language to learn and use.
3. A recent study in Houston showed that Southeast Asians who are fluent speakers of English earn three times more than nonfluent speakers. The same holds true for native speakers of other languages.

As the child of immigrants, I understand the need to preserve the language and customs of the "old country," but I also understand the economic and social necessity of becoming proficient in the language and customs of the "new country." To advise persons to do otherwise is a cruel hoax that will doom them to jobs at minimum wage or less and will make them social outcasts. We live in a global economy in which the universal language is now English. If one isn't fluent in English, he or she can plan on a career in the fast food industry.

The author's claim is that people should learn two languages, one of which must be English. His data are the various facts about English and fluency that he presents. His warrant is the statement that not teaching non-natives to be fluent in English will doom them to low-paying jobs and make them social outcasts, which he reasons from his own experience as the child of immigrants.

If the audience accepts the persuader's claim, there is no need to present any data and hence no reason for a warrant. If the audience rejects the persuader's claim, again there is no need for a data or warrant. However, if the audience is unsure or if

Claim: The U.S should become an international peacekeeper using military intervention and other assistance in world crises.

Option 1. Accept the persuader's claim, and the U.S. becomes globo-cop.

Option 2. Reject the persuader's claim and rely on other means of solving global crises.

Option 3. Request evidence to support the claim.

Data: Past crises have escalated into full-scale warfare and its resulting loss of life and property (Vietnam, Kuwait, Somalia).

Option 1. Accept the claim now supported by the data and work to institute global police power for the U.S.

Option 2. Reject the claim as unsupported by the data—work to keep the U.S. out of international conflicts.

Option 3. Request an explanation of how and why the data support the claim.

Warrant: The U.S. is the only remaining superpower capable of maintaining stability in a world that would otherwise lapse into total war, suffering, death, disease, and so on.

Option 1. Accept the claim now supported by the data and explained by the warrant.

Option 2. Reject the claim as unsupported by the data and the warrant.

Option 3. Ask the persuader to refine the claim, back up the data, or provide for possible exceptions in the warrant.

FIGURE 8.7 Toulmin's basic elements of an argument, applied to the example of U.S. intervention in world crises.

the persuader anticipates some skepticism about the claim, then data must be presented. If the data are accepted or rejected outright, again there is no need for the persuader to proceed to the warrant. However, if the audience isn't entirely convinced, or if the persuader anticipates some doubt about the claim now supported by data, then it will be necessary to present a warrant that explains the reasoning by which the data support the claim. In this letter to the editor, it is apparent that the persuader anticipates audience resistance at each step of the way and thus presents a complete, three-part argument with claim, data, and warrant all apparent.

This pattern of moving the logical argument from claim to data to warrant, and the resulting three kinds of responses (agree, disagree, and uncertain), is typical of almost every reasoned argument in the everyday marketplace of ideas. Figure 8.7

uses the claim that the United States must become a "globo-cop" to show how the flow of argument goes in the Toulmin system. Trace the stages of argument in the figure.

Substantiating Elements

Toulmin's system has a number of secondary terms. For example, a claim may be modified by a qualifier —usually a simple word or phrase like "In most cases" or "Probably" or "It is likely that." The concession qualifies or limits the claim. To continue our globo-cop example, you might ask the persuader to qualify the claim by pointing out the limits or boundaries beyond which the claim doesn't apply. For instance, the persuader might alter the claim to state, "In most cases, the United States should become an international peacekeeper using military intervention and other assistance in world crises." Qualifiers limit the claim, thus allowing for the possibility that this is not a simple case of the either/or argument.

Another minor term in Toulmin's model is the reservation, a statement related to the warrant that states the conditions under which the warrant is valid. The reservation features words like "unless" or "only if there is a reason to believe that." In the globo-cop case, the reservation might indicate that there are some conditions under which the warrant becomes non-operative or non-binding. For instance, suppose the warrant stated, "Except in the case of revolutions, the United States is the only remaining superpower capable of establishing and maintaining world stability." Another reservation is expressed with the word "Unless," in which case the warrant might state, "Unless the United States is not the only remaining superpower capable of establishing and maintaining world stability . . ."

Both persuaders and persuadees often overlook this aspect of the reservation. They assume that both parties begin from the same point, from the same frame of reference. Only when we begin at the same point or when we make allowances (such as reservations) for these differences can we really progress in any persuasive transaction. Coupled with the qualifier, the reservation allows for great flexibility in persuasion because both encourage dialogue; both provide the persuadee with an opportunity to object or agree to part but not all of the persuasion.

Advertisers are clever with the use of qualifiers. For example, the label on Cascade dishwasher detergent says that it will make your dishes, not spotless, but "virtually spotless." Who can say whether one spot or three spots or twelve qualifies as being "virtually spotless"? Thus, we need to be aware of two problems connected with qualifiers and reservations: (1) the absence of them, which can lock us into one course of action or belief, and (2) the too-vague qualifier, which allows persuaders to wriggle out of any commitment to a product, action, person, or idea. Persuaders may still try to interpret the qualifiers to their advantage, but it is much more difficult when details are given. We need to think twice when confronted with a lack of details and specificity in persuasive claims. If advertisers say that their tires will stop faster, we need to ask such questions as "Faster than what?" and "Under what conditions?" For all we know, they may be comparing the tires with wagon wheels or doughnuts.

The final element in Toulmin's system for showing the tactics of argument is the backing for the warrant. Suppose a persuadee does not consider a warrant to be valid or doubts some part of it. The persuader must provide proof that supports the reasoning expressed in the warrant. What we have then is a whole separate argument with a separate claim, data, and warrant to support the original warrant. Essentially, persuaders claim that the warrant is acceptable because of the support or data.

We can now see that the tactics of persuasion are not usually parts of simple syllogisms. Instead, persuaders make claims that persuadees can respond to by (1) accepting them outright with no questions asked, (2) rejecting them outright, or (3) asking for proof. Persuaders then can provide data, which again can be accepted, rejected, or questioned. If the persuadee continues to request more, the persuader ultimately must provide the warrant, or reason, for linking the proof to the request. Given enough time, three other elements may enter into the persuasive appeal: the qualifier, the reservation, and the backing. Finally, the job of persuadees is to dissect persuasion. What matters is that persuadees be aware, critical, and fairly sophisticated and systematic as they are exposed to persuasion. Toulmin's system for analyzing the tactics of persuasion provides us with a simple but discriminating tool that operates well with the kinds of persuasion we are exposed to every day.

RESEARCH ON THE EFFECTS OF EVIDENCE

Some researchers use the scientific method to determine the effects of evidence on receivers. In such studies, presumably typical persuadees (for example, several hundred college students) are given attitude tests. Then they are exposed to various degrees or types of persuasion and evidence (for example, emotional versus logical evidence, good versus poor delivery of the same evidence). Following this, the subjects' attitudes are reevaluated. The results are compared, by statistical methods, with pretreatment scores to determine the effects of varying types or amounts of evidence. Early studies demonstrated that, although the relationship between evidence and attitude change is elusive and sometimes even fickle, several patterns seem to be stable.

Communication scholars Rodney Reynolds and Michael Burgoon (1983) reviewed the relationships among belief processing, reasoning, and evidence. They determined that some of the previously fickle or negative findings could be interpreted from a different perspective, one suggesting that there is a positive relationship between datalike assertions and apparent attitude change. These patterns led them to make a series of propositions that support the evidence–persuasion relationship, especially in cases in which other variables are present (such as credibility of the speaker). Reynolds and Burgoon made the following assertions.

- Using evidence produces more attitude change than not using evidence.

- Using evidence produces more attitude change than using simple assertions.

- Using irrelevant evidence from poorly qualified sources produces counter-to-advocated attitude change (in other words, produces the opposite effect) regardless of an advocate's credibility.

- If advocates who have low-to-moderate credibility fail to use relevant evidence from qualified sources, the result might be counter-to-advocated attitude change.

- If advocates fail to cite relevant evidence in a message that follows an opposing message that does cite evidence, their credibility will be lowered.

- Citing evidence produces more attitude change when the evidence source and source qualifications are provided or when evidence is presented without a source citation than when

evidence is presented with only a source identification.

- If an advocate who has low-to-moderate credibility cites evidence clearly, the advocate's credibility and success in persuasion will increase.

- Using evidence from highly credible sources will, over time, increase an advocate's credibility.

- If an advocate cites evidence from less credible sources after, rather than before, other evidence, message acceptance will improve.

- Poor delivery of evidence citations by advocates who have low-to-moderate credibility reduces persuasive effects.

- Using evidence results in attitude change when receivers have no prior knowledge of the evidence.

- Using evidence increases attitude change over time, regardless of the credibility of the advocate.

- Using evidence results in attitude change over time only when receivers hold extreme attitudes on an issue.

- The credibility of an advocate increases the evaluation of message attributes.

- The clarity of evidence citations increases evaluations of the evidence and the advocate.

- Highly dogmatic people select persuasive messages containing highly documented, rather than undocumented, evidence.

- People tend to evaluate evidence from the perspective of their own attitudes, regardless of the quality of the evidence.

- Evidence that is inconsistent with the major propositions being advanced is more difficult to detect than is irrelevant evidence or evidence from unqualified sources.

These propositions make sense especially when applied to familiar persuasive events.

In a review of the past fifty years of research on the effects of evidence on persuasion, communication scholar John C. Reinard (1988) used Petty and Cacioppo's elaboration likelihood model (ELM) to identify a number of consistent trends. As you will recall, the ELM suggests that there are two information-processing modes in persuasion: the peripheral and the central processing paths. Topics or issues that are not personally involving typify persuasion in the peripheral path. The audience is often swayed by variables other than the message or good evidence. For example, persuasion can be affected by variables such as how attractive the source is and how discrepant the message is from the audience's own position. In the central processing route, however, persuadees are highly involved with the issue or topic and can be persuaded only with compelling arguments that are well documented by evidence. Using the model, Reinard was able to identify the following trends:

- Testimonials seem to be consistently persuasive as long as the source of the testimony is clearly documented.

- Factual information such as reports of events or examples seems to be persuasive, but it can be affected by the mode of presentation. For example, on issues regarding policy ("The United States should stockpile petroleum for the next five years"), specific facts are more persuasive than general facts.

- Despite the almost reverent attitude that many people have toward statistical evidence, such evidence is not as persuasive as other factual evidence. (Reinard speculates that this might be because statistics are not vivid or dramatic.) However, when powerful, involving, and vivid examples are backed up by statistics that show the examples to be typical, the examples become more powerful.

- Presenting audiences with evidence seems to "inoculate" or protect them against subsequent counterpersuasion.

- Evidence seems to have long-term effectiveness when an issue is processed in the central path, but there is little long-term effectiveness when the issue is processed in the peripheral path.

- A source's credibility has persuasive effects—that is, credible sources are more persuasive than less credible ones. (This is one of the most consistent patterns identified by Reinard.)

- Evidence that reinforces the receiver's beliefs is more persuasive than evidence that does not reinforce the receiver's position.

- Strong evidence is more persuasive than weak evidence, especially when an issue is personally involving to the receiver, who then uses the central processing path.

- Novel evidence is more persuasive than evidence the audience already knows.

- Unless a topic is personally involving, credibility seems to be more persuasive than evidence, but even credible sources can enhance their persuasiveness by using evidence.

- Evidence consistently increases speaker credibility.

- Good delivery enhances the effectiveness of evidence unless the audience is distracted.

- Evidence is most effective with highly intelligent receivers, those who are "hard-nosed about getting the facts."

- People who are highly analytical are more likely to be persuaded by evidence, and intellectually sophisticated receivers prefer technically oriented evidence.

Reinard's overall conclusion is that evidence is persuasive, especially if we look at the past fifty years of research from the perspective of the ELM. As with Reynolds and Burgoon's conclusions, the patterns Reinard identified (especially those related to the model) make real sense when used to analyze "real-world" persuasive examples.

More recently, Reynolds and Reynolds (2002) generated a listing of other facts that we know about the uses of evidence:

- Evidence must be cognitively processed. In other words, people have to process evidence in the central route of the ELM. However, in some cases, the narrative or anecdotal evidence seems to be more effective.

- Evidence must be judged as legitimate. In other words, the persuadee needs to view the evidence as authentic, high quality, and unbiased.

- Evidence needs to be evaluated by the audience. This evaluation of evidence leads to overall message evaluation, which, in turn, leads to postmessage beliefs. It then follows that these postmessage beliefs will lead to some sort of action.

In conclusion, several characteristics of the use of evidence in content premises in persuasion can be noted. First, evidence is probably most effective when it encourages audience participation. Earlier, we noted that, in using emotionally oriented evidence, persuaders are most effective when they present audiences with a dramatic scene or setting and then ask members to empathize with the character acting within that setting. By participating with their imaginations, members of the audience cocreate the proof—they incorporate the proof into their own frames of reference.

In using intellectually oriented evidence, effective persuaders present claims and perhaps data to support them. They hope that warrants will be provided by the audience, but even if listeners do not supply the necessary linkage and instead question the persuaders' conclusions, they are still participating in their own persuasion when they begin to play the game (that is, cocreate a proof with the persuaders).

Finally, effective persuaders who are using evidence for "logical" or content-oriented persuasion highlight the evidence—either as part of a narrative or in some form of analogy.

REVIEW AND CONCLUSION

Content premises do not necessarily rely as much on the internal states of persuaders as do process premises. Instead, they rely more on universally agreed-on norms or rules. Evidence tends to be either dramatically oriented, intellectually oriented, or experiential/participative in nature. Users of dramatically oriented evidence lead persuadees to a "logical" conclusion, drawn from a content premise, by creating a dramatic scene and then inviting the audience to join in the drama. Persuadees thus "prove" the validity of the premise to themselves. Users of intellectually oriented evidence, in con-

trast, lead their persuadees to "logical" conclusions by presenting them with a set of data in support of a certain claim or content premise. The persuadees provide the connection between these data and the claim in the form of a warrant. And experiential or participative evidence may prove to be the most persuasive because of persuadees' personal involvement in or experience of the evidence.

All three types of evidence rely on a kind of self-persuasion on the part of the persuadee. Persuadees ought to participate in some way in their own persuasion, whether the evidence is intellectual, dramatic, or experiential/participative. When we engage in self-persuasion, even if it runs counter to our own beliefs, the effect of the participation is powerful.

From a strategic point of view, the traditional syllogism usually forms the skeletal structure of an overall argument or content premise. Within this structure, the tactics or particular arguments or premises are represented by claims supported by data. Claims and data are linked by audiences through warrants.

Finally, of the types of evidence available to the persuader, several seem more important than others. Most important, probably, are those that support the three major linkages: cause–effect, symptoms, and congruency. Also, evidence that provides perspective for the audience is probably more effective than evidence that does not. We focused on two particularly effective methods of providing this perspective: the use of analogy, which provides a comparative perspective, and the use of narrative, which has the same ability to provide a perspective within a dramatic frame of reference. Both are also "artistic" in the sense that neither merely presents information; rather, both depict evidence in dramatic or visual formats.

In sum, we are most effectively persuaded by our own experiences—real, vicarious, or imagined. Successful persuaders try to shape content premises—their linkages, claims, data, and warrants—in terms of the audience's experience. If persuaders can invite audiences to participate in drawing conclusions or in the drama of the proof, audiences will share in their own persuasion, thus being affected by it.

QUESTIONS FOR FURTHER THOUGHT

1. What are the three types of syllogisms discussed in this chapter? Give examples of each from advertisements, political speeches, or some other source of persuasion.

2. Define proof. What constitutes adequate proof for you? Does it change from issue to issue? If so, in what ways?

3. Review some magazine commentary concerning a particular issue, and attempt to identify the data offered. What kinds of evidence are they? Are they dramatic? If so, in what ways? If not, are they persuasive? Why or why not? What is the underlying syllogistic structure inherent in the discussions of the issue?

4. What is the difference between intellectually oriented evidence and emotionally oriented evidence? Give examples and explain how they differ.

5. Give examples from your own experience of (a) opinion, (b) attitudes, (c) beliefs, and (d) values that affect behavior. Give examples that do not affect behavior. How do they differ?

6. Why was "The Case of Bobby and His Parents" so persuasive? Was logic involved? Was the example an illogical one to prove the point Peck wanted to make?

7. What is the difference between a figurative and a literal analogy? Which is being used when a political campaign is compared to a horse race?

8. What are some of the ways in which statistics can be misused? Give examples.

9. What are some of the ways in which testimony can be misused? Give examples.

10. What is a post hoc fallacy? Give an example.

11. What is an ad hominem fallacy? Give an example.

12. How has the ad hominem been used in recent elections?

13. What are some contemporary examples of the ad populum being used in advertising?

14. How does the undistributed middle fallacy operate? Give examples.

15. How does the straw man fallacy operate? Give examples.

16. What is the false dilemma fallacy? How does it operate? Give examples.

17. How does the ELM help to explain the differences between content and process premises?

 For online activities, go to the Web site for this book at http://communication.wadsworth.com/larson.

9

✳

Cultural Premises
in Persuasion

We are all prisoners of our own culture, and as a result, we often overlook patterns of behavior that influence how and by what means we are persuaded. Anyone who has visited another culture (even another Western culture) immediately becomes aware of significant cultural differences between his or her patterns of behavior and those of the foreign culture. Not only are values, languages, and customs different, but hundreds, even thousands, of little things differ from our familiar American ways. For example, only one-third of the world's people use our kind of flatware to eat. Another third eat with chopsticks, and the rest use their fingers. Even in England, differences are apparent. For example, the British wait at bus stops in neat, orderly lines, or queues, to board, whereas we Americans usually crowd around the bus door. The exact opposite is true of ski lift lines. In the United States, skiers line up in orderly fashion to wait their turn; in France, they will walk right over others' skis to get to the front of the line.

If you visit one of the formerly communist countries in eastern Europe, you will quickly un-

derstand the immense difference between "hard currency" and "soft currency." Even the hotel I stayed at in Prague refused to accept "soft" Czech currency; however, they were more than willing to accept "hard" currencies like the U.S. dollar. A friend recently told me that taxis in Moscow will stop only if you hold up a pack of cigarettes; they don't want rubles. In eastern European countries, many people always carry a shopping bag just in case they find something available. In fact, the slang term for a shopping bag is a "perhaps." They don't buy something because they need it; they buy it because it happens to be available—an idea that would never cross our minds here in the United States.

Although many aspects of any given culture are relatively permanent, cultures are also subject to constant change. In the United States, for example, the constant influx of different ethnic groups is reflected in a variety of ways, and diversity and multiculturalism are apparent everywhere. For instance, in supermarkets, you will find items not normally available until a short time ago, such as soybean curd, bean sprouts, wontons, corn and flour tortillas, and pita bread. You can also buy a wok or a futon at department stores. These minor cultural differences are, of course, only the tip of the iceberg. Our American culture is becoming multicultural, and it is happening very quickly. Look around you, and you will see lots of evidence of this trend that is altering the way we live in the twenty-first century.

To better understand the wide-reaching impact cultural diversity has on our lives, access InfoTrac College Edition, and type the word "multiculturalism" in the search engine. Explore the many articles that address various aspects of this phenomenon.

The important differences among cultures involve the values, beliefs, and behavior patterns that are instilled in us from early childhood through our language, the myths and tales we hear, and our observations of how those around us behave. As our discussion of activity theory in Chapter 4 revealed, many of these cultural perceptions begin in infancy as we learn language. Many of these values and beliefs are relatively permanent aspects of a culture, although over time they change in response to societal shifts.

CULTURAL PATTERNS

This cultural "training" forms some of the premises we have been discussing. The cultural preferences we have, the cultural myths we believe in, and the cultural values we embrace are all missing premises in enthymemes that persuaders can construct. This kind of persuasion occurs at a low level of awareness and is usually processed in the peripheral information-processing channel. Thus, we often react subconsciously to various stimuli based on our cultural training. Robert Cialdini (2001) calls these reactions "fixed action patterns" or "shortcuts," which are as automatic and instantaneous as the "click, whirr" of a camera taking a picture. These shortcuts are the heuristic found in the heuristic-systematic model discussed in Chapter 4. Cialdini observes

that "you and I exist in an extraordinarily complicated environment, easily the most rapidly moving and complex that has ever existed on this planet. To deal with it, we *need* shortcuts. . . . As the stimuli saturating our lives continue to grow more intricate and variable we will have to depend increasingly on our shortcuts to handle them all" (p. 7). And cultural patterning and cultural premises are just such "shortcuts" to being persuaded. Consider the following instance of cultural patterning.

Suppose you are a member of an Inuit tribe called "People of the Deer," whose sole food supply is caribou. You kill enough animals in the fall to last the tribe until the spring, when the animals migrate north following the food supply. The custom is to kill and preserve these deer in a period of a week or two. You have just finished your fall hunt, only to discover that you face a severe winter without having killed enough caribou to last until the spring migration. Death is certain without sufficient supplies of meat and fat. You attend a meeting called to consider the matter. What would you do?

In my persuasion classes, students brainstorm solutions to this problem and come up with the following suggestions, usually in this approximate order:

1. Let's follow the deer and kill enough of them, thus increasing the supply.
2. Let's seek an alternative food supply—we can eat berries or fish or birds.
3. Let's send a band of the young and healthy to get help.
4. Let's ration food to make it last longer.
5. Let's eat all the parts of the caribou—skin, horns, everything—to increase the supply.
6. Let's send some of the people away to another place where food is more plentiful and thus decrease demand.
7. Let's kill some of us to decrease demand.
8. Let's kill the most useless persons—the old first, and the very young next.
9. Let's resort to cannibalism; let's eat those we kill.

The most practical solutions emerge first, and then the ideas become increasingly desperate, to the point of cannibalism. In real life, the People of the Deer would do nothing—they would eat the food at their regular rates, knowing full well that they would not live through the winter. Then they would sit and wait for death. They simply do not enter into the problem-solving frame of mind typical of Western cultures. They accept a situation and do nothing, whereas we try to find solutions for all problems, even though some may be insoluble. We are trained to do something. In our culture, persuaders succeed if they outline a problem and suggest solutions.

The case of the People of the Deer reveals other cultural attributes that we have and that can be targeted by persuaders. Notice, for instance, that students' early solutions focus on positive and assertive steps. These are always suggested first, indicating an American cultural bias in favor of the "pull-yourself-up-by-your-bootstraps" approach. Americans have always valued individualism and individual achievements. This country has always been a place where immigrants could make a new life for themselves. And persuaders market a host of products and services based on this "bootstraps" belief.

Another appeal to the value or potential of individuals and their ability to succeed is the multilevel marketing plan for selling products. One example is Amway, which stands for the "American way." Such plans persuade people that they can go into business for themselves, not only by selling products to their friends and neighbors but by recruiting others to do the same and getting a percentage of each recruit's sales as well. The recruits, in turn, recruit others and get a percentage of what they sell, and so on down the line, until one develops a wide and complex "network." Success is measured by the individual's wealth and by the various symbols—pins, jewelry, or whatever—that the company awards. At Mary Kay Cosmetics, for example, persons at the top levels in the network get a pink Cadillac.

But there is a flip side to this individualism, as Robert Bellah and his associates (1985) point out in *Habits of the Heart: Individualism and Commitment in American Life.* As you might recall from an earlier chapter, Bellah and his colleagues did in-depth interviews with more than 200 Americans from vari-

ous walks of life. He was attempting to duplicate what Alexis de Tocqueville did in his book *Democracy in America,* written in the 1830s, in which he described core American values and mores as "habits of the heart." Key among them was the value of the individual. Bellah and his coauthors point out:

> The central problem of our book concerned the American individualism that Tocqueville described with a mixture of admiration and anxiety. It seems to us it is individualism and not equality, as Tocqueville thought, that has marched inexorably throughout our history. We are concerned that this individualism may have grown cancerous. (p. viii)

What they meant by "cancerous" is that individualism has become "me-ism," with emphasis on the individual at the cost of the community, thus drawing people inside themselves with little concern for others.

Many other observers have echoed this theme. For example, what we describe as "yuppie" values are those that Bellah and his associates see as the early signs of a cancerous individualism. This interest in feathering one's own nest was recently seen in the actions of CEOs of firms like Enron and WorldCom, which led to the collapse of their companies. The executives were charged with criminal actions, and the employees lost jobs and pension holdings. Further, the initial student responses to the dilemma of the People of the Deer are positive and action oriented, reflecting the good side of the American value of individualism. The middle responses are more reflective of a sense of community and cooperation, but the last three reflect the malignant side of American individualism.

How do we identify these patterns of cultural values? Where do they come from? How do persuaders appeal to them? Questions such as these are the focus of our search for cultural premises. To see how these premises relate to persuasion in general, we look first at how we get them—through cultural training and societal pressure. Then we look at two kinds of cultural premises: (1) cultural images or myths and (2) the American value system. Bear in mind that a value is an idea of the good or the desirable that people use as a standard for judging people's actions or motivating others. Examples of values are honesty, justice, beauty, efficiency, safety, and progress. Because our value system is a major source of persuasive leverage, you may be interested in discovering how persuaders link proposals and arguments to values.

CULTURAL TRAINING AND SOCIETAL PRESSURE

You may have heard stories about how the children of various Native American groups never cried because it was essential not to frighten off game. Anyone who has been around a newborn infant must doubt these stories. Children cry when they are lonely or hungry, or want exercise. How, then, did Native Americans train their children not to cry? During the first hour of life, whenever a Lakota baby cried, its mother clapped her hand over the child's mouth and nose. The hand was removed only if the child stopped crying or began to smother. If this was done within the first hour of life, the infant never again cried out loud (Santos, 1961). Of course, as children grew, they saw this pattern repeated over and over again. Parents and elders spoke of the power of silence, valuing quiet and stealth in stalking game. Young men were tested and proved their courage by experiencing pain and not crying out in a ritual dance. A leather thong was sewn into the young man's shoulder flesh. He was then tied to a symbolic tree at the center of a sacred circle or "medicine wheel." The test was to dance away from the pole until weariness and pain forced him to fall (typically after several days of dancing). The fall usually tore out the thong from the shoulder. The young man was then a full-fledged warrior. Later, he could do the sun-gazer's dance, which involved dancing while staring directly into the sun. Sitting Bull is supposed to have done this for three days, after which he had a vision of the future massacre of Custer and his soldiers at the Little Big Horn. Thus, the pattern introduced at birth was seen at work throughout life.

In less dramatic terms, perhaps, each of us is trained in the ways of our culture. This training forms the core of our values, which then become rules for governing ourselves as we interact. We do not even notice that they are there; we respond instinctively to them. In all likelihood, we process and apply these premises via the peripheral information-processing path. This training underlies our cultural premises and lurks beneath our surface thoughts and acts. Sophisticated persuaders appeal to these premises directly and cleverly. Persuaders can appeal to cultural and societal premises because they believe in them and expect that their audiences do as well.

CULTURAL IMAGES AND MYTHS

Every culture has its own myths and heroic figures who do things valued by the culture. For example, early Greek society developed a series of myths surrounding the sin of pride that eventually became institutionalized in such Greek dramas as *Oedipus Rex* and *Electra*. Parts of the myths related to physical acts (such as trying to control one's own destiny) that were discouraged. Greeks placed a high value on avoiding prideful action and on demonstrating modesty. We have similar beliefs. You probably know that the overly proud student is less likely to be elected to school office or chosen as team captain than the more humble person. We view the antics of pompous people with disfavor, and we ridicule needless pride.

What are some of the myths or legends or images underlying American culture and society, and how do persuaders use them? Can these images be changed, and if so, how? Are they being changed at present, and if so, how? Stereotypes and proverbs are good indicators of cultural myths. Let us consider a few of them.

Access InfoTrac College Edition, and type the words "cultural myths" in the search engine. Look at the review by Carl Stepp of the

"Of course, one of the more popular myths is that our 16th president was born in a little log cabin."

FIGURE 9.1 The wisdom of the rustic.

book *Slick Spins and Fractured Facts: How Cultural Myths Distort the News* by Caryl Rivers, which deals with how cultural myths put various kinds of "spin" on news events. If you find this review interesting, you can retrieve the entire item or buy Rivers' book.

The Wisdom of the Rustic

One of the legends in American lore that has great persuasive appeal is that of the clever rustic. No matter how devious the opposition, the simple wisdom of the backwoods wins out. Numerous folktales rely on this rustic image including the Daniel Boone tales, the stories about the inventiveness of Paul Bunyan, and many Abraham Lincoln stories (see Figure 9.1). We believe in humble beginnings, and we believe that difficulty teaches even the most uneducated of us to be wise and worldly. Thus,

politicians throughout American history have emphasized their humble origins. In fact, many have manufactured myths about their rustic origins even to the point of constructing log cabins that they claimed as their birthplace, as did William Henry Harrison in the nineteenth century. Ronald Reagan emphasized his humble origin in Dixon, Illinois, and Bill Clinton lets it be known that he was born in a small house in Hope, Arkansas. And if the politician cannot claim humble beginnings, he or she must find some substitute for them—usually hardship or suffering. Thus, patricians such as Franklin D. Roosevelt and John F. Kennedy are viewed as humble when the public learns of their physical disabilities, pain, or emotional suffering.

Products are frequently marketed using a rustic as the spokesperson—Wilfred Brimley, for instance, serves as a rustic when he endorses the value of good old-fashioned Quaker Oats. Even as we value the simple, commonsense rustic, our culture tends to devalue the intellectual or the educated. Tocqueville (1965), in *Democracy in America,* described this distrust:

> The nearer the people are drawn to the common level of an equal and similar condition, the less prone does each man become to place implicit faith in a certain man or a certain class of men [intellectuals]. But his readiness to believe the multitude increases, and opinion is more than ever mistress of the world. Not only is common opinion the only guide which private judgment retains . . . it possesses a power infinitely beyond what it has elsewhere. (p. 148)

Historian Richard Hofstadter (1963) also wrote about this anti–intellectualism. Persuaders often use this reverse side of our value in the wisdom of the rustic: The intellectual is the brunt of jokes, and the rustic wins out over the smart guy.

The Possibility of Success

The Horatio Alger myth is based on several novels written for boys by Alger in the nineteenth century. The protagonist of these novels was invariably a young man who, through hard work, sincerity, honesty, law-abiding behavior, and faith in the future, was able to make good. He might even rise to the top and own his own company, have a beautiful wife, live a fine life, and be able to do good for others. The myth was particularly appealing to immigrants, the poor, and the downtrodden. They passed it on to their children, admonishing them to work hard and thus to achieve success. More recently, the myth has been generalized to include women and has appeal for new groups of immigrants. These new immigrants, particularly those from Third World countries, often share living quarters to save money or go into business for themselves, and all members are expected to do their share of providing for the family. The myth of possible success is as alive in the new millennium as it was at the turn of the twentieth century, when immigrants came mainly from Europe.

Again, this myth was observed by Tocqueville (1965):

> No Americans are devoid of a yearning desire to rise. . . . All are constantly seeking to acquire property, power, and reputation. . . . What chiefly diverts the men of democracies from lofty ambition is not the scantiness of their fortunes, but the vehemence of the exertions they daily make to improve them. . . . The same observation is applicable to the sons of such men . . . their parents were humble; they have grown up amidst feelings and notions which they cannot afterwards easily get rid of; and it may be presumed that they will inherit the propensities of their father, as well as his wealth. (pp. 156–158)

You probably can see your grandparents and parents in this description—and you may also see yourself. Naturally, we are receptive to persuasion that promises the possibility of success. Products and services such as Internet access are marketed with the claim that they will result in success for the entire family, from Mom and Dad down to the toddlers. Politicians promise a bright future for voters who support a commonsense approach to problems. This promise probably will continue to be a part of our political vision. After all, who would vote for a politician whose campaign promises don't offer us a chance to improve ourselves? Expect to hear appeals made for the myth. Persuaders will promise success

"just around the corner" if only we will follow them and not the false prophets. They will offer the "big break" and the chance to have a better life for ourselves and our children. This possibility-of-success myth is probably what led many investors to buy Internet stocks. After all, the entire human race seemed to be going online, and marketing would never be the same again. When the dot.com bubble burst in 2002, the possibility-of-success myth went out the window for many. Still, whether it is a pyramid marketing scheme, a body-building machine, or a weight loss club, the carrot is always the same —try and you will succeed.

To learn more about the Horatio Alger novels on the possibility of success, access InfoTrac College Edition, and type the words "Horatio Alger" in the search engine. Explore the link to the Horatio Alger Society. Try reading one of the "Pluck and Luck," "Tattered Tom," or "Ragged Dick" novels.

The Coming of a Messiah

A cultural myth that is related to the possibility of success is that of the coming of a messiah. Here, the situational assumption is slightly different—society is approaching disaster or perhaps is already in a terrible mess, be it economic, religious, or political. It is a period of great uncertainty and pessimism; things are chaotic, confusing, and frightening. At such times, we expect to be rescued from the chaos and danger by some great leader who projects a sense of confidence and who we believe can turn things around. Historically, many leaders have filled this role. For example, Abraham Lincoln emerged from obscurity to save the Union, and Franklin D. Roosevelt saved the country from economic collapse. More recently, John F. Kennedy "rescued" the entire world for democracy; Ronald Reagan delivered the country from double-digit inflation and worldwide scorn; and Bill Clinton reversed the mounting deficits in the national budget. And the future will no doubt bring us other problems from which we need to be delivered. Rest assured that there will be a messiah (maybe more than one) promising us deliverance. Although circumstances may change, Americans seem always to be waiting for another messiah to come down the road and save them from one big bad wolf or another.

What makes us so receptive to the messianic? First, as noted previously, we are action-oriented. As shown by the values expressed in the People of the Deer solutions, we want our saviors to be doers, not thinkers. Second, our solutions had better not be too theoretical or intellectual—we prefer simple and practical answers to the most complex problems. The messiah should also be vigorous, witty, and charming, and not afraid to try the unknown or unproven.

The Presence of Conspiracy

Another cultural premise is the belief that big problems don't have simple causes. Hofstadter (1967) called this belief the paranoid style—the conviction that when problems appear large, the only reasonable explanation is that a powerful group has conspired to cause them. This conspiracy argument has recurred throughout our history. Most recently, the conspiracy argument has been used to explain the Oklahoma City bombing, the 9/11 tragedy, and other, more recent terrorist attacks. Some people believe that militia groups are conspiring to overthrow the government, and many in the militia movement believe that the government is in the hands of international conspirators. Many people believe that there is a conspiracy between Al Qaeda and "rogue nations" like Iraq, Iran, and North Korea, whose purpose is to destroy America's sense of security, its economy, and, ultimately, its system of government. Others believe that the Internet is really a government conspiracy to monitor the citizenry.

If Hofstadter is right, we can expect to hear conspiracy offered as an explanation for problems any time three factors are operating for the audience members:

1. They have something of value to lose—they are in possession of some kind of power, property, or privilege.

2. They see themselves as in danger of losing some or all of this power, property, and privilege or as already having lost some of it.

3. They see themselves as helpless to prevent the loss.

It is easy to see how belief in a conspiracy could give rise to a messiah: Only a messiah can defeat the evil conspirators and thus save the culture. One of the dangers of the conspiracy myth is that it invites mass hysteria and charismatic leaders. In times of trouble and confusion, we may see the rise of mass movements following leaders who are believed to be heroes or saviors combating those who conspire against us. Far-right fringe groups such as the Christian identity movement and individuals like Rush Limbaugh are examples.

The Value of Challenge

The myth of the value of challenge is fairly simple and parallels tribal tests of strength and character. It suggests that a kind of wisdom can be gained only through rigorous testing, that some rite of passage or initiation gives one power, character, and knowledge. You are probably now going through such a test in college. People say that college represents a test of endurance more than training for a specific job. By graduating from college, you show that you can meet a challenge and handle it, that you have matured, and that you have learned how to learn. Employers hire college graduates and then train them for a job after college. Boot camp offers another example of belief in the value of overcoming difficulty and meeting challenges.

The concept of the Outward Bound program rests on this myth. Somehow, it says, the most problematic children will be restored to good behavior if they get through a mountain-climbing expedition, a rafting trip down the Colorado River, or a wilderness canoe trip. Even corporate America believes in this concept and often sends its executives on such Outward Bound experiences to "shape them up."

Political persuaders frequently offer voters a dramatic challenge and present their election as of critical importance. For instance, Lincoln said that his election would decide whether the nation could exist "half slave and half free." Roosevelt maintained that the country had "a rendezvous with destiny." Kennedy said that with his election a torch had been passed to a new generation and that the light from the torch would "light the world." Clinton declared that under his administration there would be a "new covenant" between the governed and their leaders. And George W. Bush promised to win the war on terrorism and return America to a secure state of affairs. Product appeals frequently present consumers with a challenge—"Use the Soloflex machine regularly and lose 20 pounds in 30 days!" or "Get your MBA at Olivet College by attending classes one Saturday a month!"

In many cases, the value-of-challenge myth is presented as a rite of passage underscoring several cultural values that persuaders frequently use in their appeals. First, the myth suggests that there is something good about suffering or that nothing good was ever accomplished without pain. Second, the myth suggests that suffering begets maturity, humility, and wisdom—that individuals learn and grow as they meet challenges and surmount them. Finally, the myth suggests that all great leaders have become great because they were tested and found equal to the challenge. Thus, defeats and failures can be explained away as tests that prepare people for the future. As you begin to catalogue the persuasion aimed at you, you will find the value of challenge used frequently, whether for products, candidates, or ideologies (see Figure 9.2).

Access InfoTrac College Edition, enter the words "meeting challenges" in the search engine, and explore some of the ways this myth is used to persuade various constituencies.

The Eternal Return

Mercia Eliade (1971), a professor of history at the Sorbonne, identified a historical myth persistent not only in Western culture but in other cultures as well. He called it the "myth of the eternal return." He said that people reject concrete historical time and instead yearn for and often re-enact a "periodical return to the mythical time of the beginning of things, to the 'Great Time.'" American culture seems to embrace this myth, perhaps because our beginnings are so recent compared with those of other cultures. America was conceived with the perception that it was a "second Eden," a chance to start anew with no historical baggage to clutter up its purpose. According to the myth of the eternal

return, there was a time when things were perfect and harmonious, when events could be shaped or molded as they were meant to be. This time of creation is usually associated with a specific geographical "center," where things are assumed to have begun.

In the United States, this center is probably Philadelphia, where the Continental Congress signed the Declaration of Independence and where the Liberty Bell supposedly cracked while pealing out the chimes of freedom. Another potential symbolic center is Washington, DC, where our great historical documents are enshrined in the National Archives. Another is Boston, where the American Revolution began. At the creation, there were heroes (George Washington, Benjamin Franklin, Paul Revere, John Hancock, and so on) and there were villains (King George, the colonial governors, the British generals, and the redcoats). After suffering for some time, the heroes participated in some critical act that was redemptive—it released them from their former enslavement and permitted them to create the "Great Time" or the "Golden Age."

Included in the myth is the notion that society has lost sight of this archetypal beginning and must find its way back if we are to rid ourselves of the corruption, misplanning, and confusion that have developed since then. We accomplish this through reenactment of the original act in a ritual, usually held at the center where everything began. This periodic return to the origins of our beliefs reestablishes these values for us and serves as an act of redemption. The ritual freezes us in a mystical time that has power to transform us. As Eliade noted, "Time, too, like space is neither homogeneous nor continuous. On the one hand there are the intervals of a sacred time, the time of festivals (by far the greater part of which are periodical); on the other hand there is profane time, ordinary temporal duration" (Beane & Doty, 1975, p. 33). Our contemporary language reflects this belief in the cyclical nature of things and in the two types of time. For example, when we say, "What goes around comes around," we mean, "This will come back to haunt you," "What ye sow, so shall ye reap," or "History repeats itself." We have a reverence for certain "sacred" times—historical holidays, ritualistic meals (such as

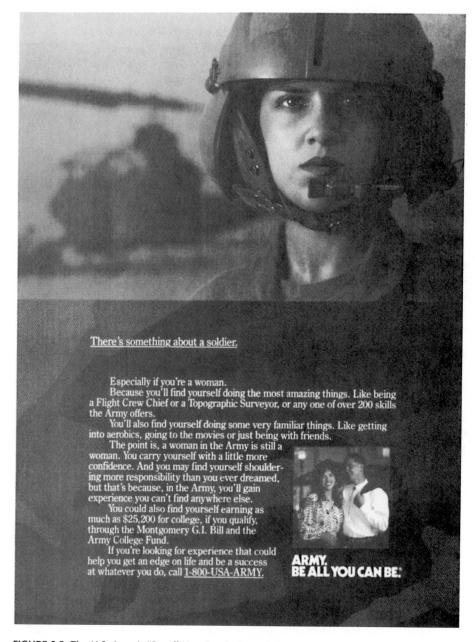

FIGURE 9.2 The U.S. Army's "Be All You Can Be" campaign exemplified the persuasiveness of the value-of-challenge myth, especially for women in this advertisement.

(Army photograph courtesy of U.S. Government, as represented by the Secretary of the Army.)

Thanksgiving or Passover), and governmental rites (such as the inaugural address, the oath of office, or the State of the Union Address). At the same time, we disdain persons who waste time, who are just "passing the time," or who are "couch potatoes" living through "profane" time. Recessions are profane times, as are losing seasons for athletic teams.

Commercial persuaders are aware of the importance of sacred time. They have special sales on historical holidays—a "Hatchet Days Sale" on Washington's birthday, an "Independence Day Sale" on the Fourth of July, and, in recent years, a "Super Bowl Sale" in mid-January. And every four years, the Olympics provides numerous instances of sacred time being celebrated. Politicians are skilled at challenging us to return to an earlier time—to reestablish and renew ourselves. Not only is this apparent in their speeches, but the inaugural ceremonies themselves are acts of renewal that promise to return us to the untainted past.

In ideological campaigns and mass movements, the return-and-renewal theme is also persistent. Martin Luther King, Jr., used it in his "I Have a Dream" speech. We hear strains of the myth in the pro-life, anti-abortion movement; one leader said, "People are going to look back on this era the way they look back on Nazi Germany. They'll say 'Thank God there were a few sane people'" ("America's Abortion Dilemma," 1985, p. 21). This reference to profane time was echoed by "moral majority" leader Jerry Falwell, who said of abortion, "This criminal activity . . . sets us back to the Stone Age" (p. 22). In the anti-abortion case, the focus is on the profane ground of the abortion clinics and the profane time following *Roe v. Wade* and on symbolic acts such as the bombing of clinics. One pro-lifer called the protest bombings of clinics "a gift to Jesus on his birthday" (p. 23).

Even in product ads we can detect appeals to the new beginnings or to the return-and-renewal myth. NEC Corporation says, "The new information age is built on the merging of computers and communication . . . you deserve no less. NEC, the way it will be." The famous Virginia Slims "You've Come a Long Way, Baby" ads are based on a new beginning, which is contrasted to a tainted past. Mercedes-Benz reminds us, "This year, as for ninety-nine years, the automobiles of Mercedes-Benz are like no other cars in the world." In fact, one of the most frequent advertising appeals is a renewal idea: "New and Improved!"

This myth of the eternal return and the cyclical reenactments of some Golden Age—with its heroes, villains, and sacred and profane time—is a powerful tool that persuaders use in a variety of circumstances (see Figure 9.3). It is reflected in a set of cultural myths or parables described next.

REICH'S CULTURAL PARABLES

In his book *Tales of a New America,* Robert Reich (1987) contends that the future appears chaotic for a variety of reasons: rapidly advancing technology, rising expectations for prosperity throughout the world, and general confusion about where we are headed as a nation. Reich and his Harvard colleagues have identified what they call basic cultural parables for the United States. These parables convey

> lessons about the how and why of life through metaphor [which] may be a basic human trait, a universal characteristic of our intermittently rational, deeply emotional, meaning-seeking species. . . . In America the vehicles of public myth include the biographies of famous citizens, popular fiction and music, feature stories on the evening news and gossip. . . . They anchor our political understandings. . . . What gives them force is their capacity to make sense of, and bring coherence to, common experience. The lessons ring true, even if the illustration is fanciful. (p. 7)

Reich's work often echoes what has been emphasized earlier in our study of persuasion: Human beings are fascinated with and driven by the power of the dramatic or the narrative.

Reich's myths are rooted in the vignette of a man named George, the son of immigrant parents who worked hard to provide a good home. George did well in school and worked long hours to bring home a few dollars for the family. He was good in sports although he didn't have much time to participate. He never picked a fight, but on one occasion

FIGURE 9.3 This ad by Danner boots appeals to the myth of the eternal return with its reference to a "Golden Age" when men were men and their boots stood the test of time.

(Reprinted by permission of Danner Shoe Manufacturing Co.)

he did step in to stop the town bully and banker's son, Albert Wade, from beating up on the smallest kid in class. He let Albert have the first swing and then decked him with a single punch. George went off to fight in Europe in World War II and saved his squad by single-handedly destroying a machine gun nest, but he was too humble to wear or display the medal he received for heroism. After the war, he returned to his hometown, married his childhood sweetheart, and built successful construction business. He gave his spare time to good causes and lived modestly. George kept to himself until his old nemesis, Albert Wade, inherited his father's bank and began to squander the depositors' savings by making shady loans to his buddies and buying himself into the office of mayor. The only person to stand up and challenge the corrupt election was George. Then Wade's bank refused to loan any money on houses built by George. In a showdown town meeting, one of Wade's corrupt councilmen finally broke down under George's accusatory gaze and spilled the beans on Wade, who ended up in jail while George went back to his modest life. It is the American morality play, according to Reich.

This brief story has been told over and over again in various versions, including Horatio Alger novels, films such as Frank Capra's *It's a Wonderful Life,* and biographies of famous Americans. It contains Reich's basic cultural parables. As you read about these parables, note some of the similarities between them and what we have been calling cultural myths.

The Mob at the Gates

The basic idea in this parable is that America stands alone as the last, best hope for a good, moral, and affluent life in a world filled with perilous possibilities and awesome problems. This parable creates an "us versus them" mentality or mind-set. The mob at the gates may be drug traffickers, illegal aliens, or terrorists; or it may be environmental polluters, the militia movement, or foreign or slave labor that can provide goods at prices much lower than American companies. The mob may also be the greedy corporate executives who exploit workers by insider trading, outrageous salaries and perks, and outright

cheating. Or the mob may be secular humanists, minorities, and do-gooders. The parable has at least two sides—a liberal one and a conservative one. Both sides may defy the mob at the gates on one issue, such as foreign competition; on other issues, however, the mob may be acceptable for one side but not for the other. Such a case might be the issue of illegal aliens, which liberals see as far less threatening than conservatives do.

Reich (1987) cites several events of central importance to our nation that rested on the mob-at-the-gates parable. One example he gives is Franklin Roosevelt's "rotten apple" metaphor—several "rotten" nations could ruin the "whole barrel" of nations. Reich argues that the post–World War II "domino theory," in which nation after nation fell to the communists, was also an appeal to the mob-at-the-gates myth. The rotten apples at the top of corporate America have ruined the trust and confidence so essential for a healthy and growing economy. We also have seen this myth applied to George W. Bush's "rogue nations" that form an "axis of evil" that condones, supports, and even trains terrorists.

Advertisers base many of their ads for products on this parable. Thus, millions of germs are lying in wait to infect you, but if you use Listerine mouthwash, you'll knock them for a loop. Hordes of mosquitoes will ruin your picnic unless you are vigilant enough to spray the area with long-lasting Raid insect fog. And Orkin products can exterminate the swarms of termites and carpenter ants that are destroying your home.

The mob myth is a natural for ideological campaigns as well. For example, the secular humanists are supposedly ready to taint America's moral fiber with their approach to questions of morals, so it is absolutely essential to join the "moral majority." And, of course, politicians use the image in a variety of ways: The mob may be the other party, the threat of uncontrolled terrorism, or runaway national debt.

The Triumphant Individual

This parable has as its subject the humble person who works hard, takes risks but has faith in him- or herself, and eventually reaches or even exceeds goals of fame, honor, and financial success. It is the story of the self-made man or woman who demonstrates what hard work and determination, combined with a gutsy approach to problems and a spunky style, can do. Usually, the individual is a loner, and sometimes even a maverick, who is willing to challenge the establishment and try to do something on a shoestring.

A modern example is Steven Jobs, the inventor of the Apple computer. Not only did Jobs begin building the Apple empire in his garage, but he went out and started over again when he left Apple to form NEXT. He was self-reliant and hard-working, and he believed in himself. And when Apple nose-dived after he left, he returned, the triumphant individual who put the company back on course. Bill Gates is another example of the triumphant individual. Another example from the corporate world is Lee Iacocca, the maverick at Ford who bucked the odds and the office politics, fighting long and hard for a product he believed in and finally persuading the company to bring out its most successful product ever—the Mustang. After he was fired by Ford, Iacocca took over the nearly bankrupt Chrysler Corporation and turned the company around, paying off a $1.2-billion government "bailout" loan early; innovating with front-wheel drive and the minivan; instituting customer rebates, driver and passenger airbags, and the seven-year/70,000-mile warranty; and bringing back the convertible. This myth strikes the same chord as the wisdom-of-the-rustic and possibility-of-success myths discussed earlier.

We frequently see the triumphant individual in a variety of persuasive arenas. In politics, self-made men or women are the ones to put your money on—they made it this far on guts and a belief in themselves, and as a result, they will come out winners on election day as well.

The Benevolent Community

The myth or parable of the benevolent community reflects the essential goodness of people and their willingness to help out the other guy in time of need. An ad for Miller beer portrayed this myth in action. A small town in Wisconsin was struck by a tornado that demolished several homes and nearby farms. But the men and women of surrounding communities joined forces and within two weeks had nearly rebuilt all that had been destroyed. Of course, at the end of a hard day of raising walls and rafters, they enjoyed drinking the sponsor's product. Groups of students help victims of flooding in the Midwest. Though recent events have soured our taste for corporate executive officers, Corporate America regularly enhances its image after various disasters by advertising that they have donated money and products to the victims, and thus the corporation becomes part of the benevolent community. The U.S. Marines are a part of the benevolent community when they sponsor their annual "Toys for Tots" campaign around the holidays.

We find this cultural myth recurring throughout our history in struggles like abolition, women's suffrage, the civil rights movement, and pro-life demonstrations. As Reich notes, "The story celebrates America's tradition of civic improvement, philanthropy, and local boosterism" (p. 10). We can be sure persuaders will continue to use the lesson of the benevolent community to market products, candidates, and ideologies.

Rot at the Top

The "rot at the top" parable or myth has conspiratorial aspects and revolves around a number of subthemes: corruption, a lack of morals or ethics, decadence, and the malevolence of persons in high places. Like the presence-of-conspiracy myth, it seems to follow a cyclical pattern, which Reich calls "the cycles of righteous fulmination." First, we trust the elite; then we find them lacking in trust or goodwill; and finally, we end up distrusting or unseating them. Reich traces the myth to the Founding Fathers' sensitivity to the abuse of power experienced under King George of England and his designees, the colonial governors and English soldiers. There always exist abuses of power by elites who buy their power with money and favors (as did our George's archenemy, Albert Wade) or who have been corrupted by power.

Our history features numerous and varied types of rot at the top, but Reich believes that the myth usually has one of two main targets: political corruption and economic exploitation. Politically, we have seen it in Teapot Dome in the 1920s, Watergate in the 1970s, the Iran–Contra and savings and loan scandals of the 1980s, Bill Clinton's Whitewatergate in the 1990s, and, most recently, the fiscal scandals in corporate America. Economically, we often hear that big business has exploited the common man; Teddy Roosevelt was a "trust-buster" on behalf of the common man, and Franklin Roosevelt in his first inaugural address promised to "throw the money changers from the temple." And we still see numerous Wall Street scandals based on insider trading by "stock market jackals" and "corporate barracudas"—all examples of rot at the top.

The lesson of this myth is simple: "Power corrupts; privilege perverts." And the power of this myth is considerable, especially in politics: "When in doubt, vote the scoundrels out."

Go to InfoTrac College Edition, enter the words "corporate scandal" in either the subject or the key word search engine, and read a few of the titles listed. See if they incorporate elements of the rot-at-the-top cultural myth.

THE "MAN'S MAN" AND THE "WOMAN'S WOMAN"

Another popular myth is that for a male to be a success he must be a man's man—a real macho guy. Schools, family, and television tell children that important males are those who do macho things: compete in "manly" activities, use colognes with names like "Iron," are involved in sports, talk tough, and own guns and SUVs. They never show their emotions, and they die with their boots on. In contrast, the ideal woman is soft spoken, kind, and nurturing. She may work, but she is also the perfect wife and mother, and is immaculately groomed. However, she is also vain, rarely has meaningful thoughts, and never wastes time on serious things.

These myths, of course, affect the way we treat our children—valuing certain things they do and devaluing others. Until recently, it was "unfeminine" for girls and women to engage in any sport except tennis, golf, gymnastics, and swimming. On the other side of the coin, it was "unmasculine" for boys and men to take up gourmet cooking, needlepoint, or flower gardening (vegetables were okay). Further, males weren't very nurturing or emotional, and they talked about important things like jobs, the economy, cars, and sports.

This myth of the distinctions between the sexes is obviously changing, however. High schools and colleges boast women's field hockey, basketball, and baseball teams. In many towns, you will find girls' softball leagues for seven-, eight-, and nine-year-olds. In fact, we now place great emphasis on athletic ability and health in both men and women. Further, female executives are featured in ads for hotels, and female pilots are shown using deodorant. At the same time, men are now expected to contribute their fair share of housework.

Old myths do not die easily, however, and we still see many examples of the stereotypical "macho" man and the "perfectly feminine" woman. Beer ads feature retired athletes engaged in a man's world, bragging to one another over beers. The makers of perfume know that Cindy Crawford, for example, epitomizes femininity. One look at any current magazine will show advertisers pitching their products at people who buy into these images of men and women.

Although gender-bound and stereotypical representations of men and women are changing, these images still have persuasive power and are still used to advertise products, push candidates, and promote ideas. Despite reductions in gender differences in job and political candidacy and in gender-related language use, the old stereotypes are still potent persuaders. The major change in attitude toward gender-related issues has occurred in young, college-educated, upper-middle-class, nonminority populations. But the far greater proportion of our population still seems to buy into the "man's man" and "woman's woman" myths. And "thin" is still in for women who openly discuss the physique of attractive males. We still see ads for SUVs, assault weapons, and chain saws. And we continue to see ads for Victoria's Secret (sort of a prudish but sexy name), *Elle* magazine, and Emeraude perfume, along with their advice: "Want Him to Be More of a Man? Try Being More of a Woman."

Persuaders will adapt as Americans shift their values regarding gender and other human characteristics, such as age, single parenthood, and economic status, but their persuasion will reflect the premises that the audience believes. Persuasion is more often a reflection of a culture's values than a shaper of them (see Figures 9.4 and 9.5).

Others have identified and labeled myths that are similar to those we have just discussed. For example, sociologist Murray Edelman (1967) noted that one myth that emerges when problems arise is that "All problems are caused by outgroups," which resembles the mob-at-the-gates myth. His "Our leaders are benevolent heroes who will lead us out of danger" myth is similar to the coming-of-the-messiah myth. And his "The function of the citizen is to sacrifice and work hard and do the bidding of the leader" myth has some similarities to the value-of-challenge myth (pp. 217–228). Writer Michael Parenti (1994) identifies several other myths that are fairly self-explanatory: "You can't fight city hall," "Our leaders know best," "You can't legislate morality," "All politicians are the same," and "The more things change; the more they stay the same" (pp. 2–13). And communication scholar D. Hahn (1998) has identified several other political myths, such as the "myth of progress" (which we shall see reflected in our core American values), the "myth of youth," and the "myth of love and openness," which is epitomized in encounter groups, various kinds of therapy, and help and twelve-step programs (pp. 128–129).

There is a broad literature on gender stereotypes. Explore it by accessing InfoTrac College Edition and entering the words "gender stereotypes" in the subject search engine. Browse the periodical selections.

IMAGE AS A CULTURAL PREMISE

Sometimes, persuaders are successful because of their image or charisma. Somehow they seem to have a special presence, and they command the public's attention. We believe them because their presentations are convincing and dynamic, or because they have a reputation for being truthful or knowledgeable. You will recall that this kind of proof was recognized by Aristotle, as well as others. He called it ethos, or ethical proof. More recently, researchers have worked at identifying exactly what causes or creates high ethos in some persons and low ethos in others. One research technique is to have audiences rate various speakers on a variety of scales that have sets of opposing adjectives at either end. For example, the scales may have words like "fast/slow," "strong/weak," "hot/cool," "active/inactive." Researchers have discovered in repeated tests that the choices seemed to cluster around three traits or three dimensions of source credibility: expertise, trustworthiness (sincerity), and dynamism. Together, they accounted for more persuasion than the rest of the dimensions combined. Let us explore these dimensions of source credibility more fully.

Expertise

The expertise component of source credibility means that highly credible sources are perceived as having knowledge and experience regarding the topic they address. This makes sense; we tend to put more store in the ideas and advice that come from experts than those that come from nonexperts. Whom would you listen to for advice on auto racing—the winner of the Indy 500 or the kid down the block who drag-races on Friday nights? The clustering of items related to expertise has been

FIGURE 9.4 Here are examples of the myth of the "man's man" done tongue in cheek.

FIGURE 9.5 The myth of the "Man's Man" has always revolved around sexual potency, as can be seen in this Big Stinky cartoon.

verified by experiments in which a variety of groups listened to the same tape-recorded speaker giving the same speech. The speaker was introduced to some of the groups as an expert—the surgeon general—while to others the speaker was introduced as a college senior. The listeners found the "expert" much more believable than the nonexpert. Many advertisements use expert testimony from doctors, financial advisors and analysts, and journalists because they are deemed to be credible, and consumers feel that they can rely on these experts' advice.

Over thirty-five years ago, researchers reported that three believability factors emerged from audience-generated words describing credible sources: safety, qualification, and dynamism (Berlo, Lemmert, & Davis, 1969). Qualification is similar to expertise. This dimension has been identified under various conditions repeatedly since then and seems to be one of the more stable factors in determining whether we believe someone.

Trustworthiness

Another dimension that recurs in studies of image, credibility, or charisma is trustworthiness or sincerity. More than fifty years ago, researchers at Yale identified this factor in their studies, concluding

that the credibility of any source is tied to "trust and confidence" attributes (Hovland, Janis, & Kelley, 1953). This dimension has reemerged in numerous studies over the years, although at times it may have been labeled as "safety" or "personal integrity" (Baudhin & Davis, 1972).

An interesting indicator of trustworthiness occurs in situations in which a biased source testifies against his or her own self-interest or bias. This may give us a clue to what is really involved in the trust dimension. Psychology researchers Herbert Kelman and Carl Hovland (1953) wanted to know who would be believed in the following situation: A message promoting the need for stiffer penalties for juvenile delinquents was attributed in one case to a juvenile court judge and in another case to a drug-pushing juvenile delinquent. The audience believed the judge because of his expertise in dealing with juvenile cases, but their belief in the delinquent came from their trust in testimony that was obviously against the speaker's self-interest.

Trust involves receivers analyzing speakers' motives or hidden agendas, and their motivation is a key to their sincerity. The etymology of the word "sincerity" gives us some insights. It comes from the Latin *sincerus,* which literally means "without wax." This had a dual meaning in ancient times. The first meaning referred to the use of wax coatings as preservatives; to be without wax was to be fresh, pure, or unadulterated. The second meaning referred to a practice of unethical pillar carvers, who used wax to cover up blemishes in an otherwise perfect pillar that had been ruined by the carver's mistakes. Only after decades of weathering did the wax fall out to reveal the deception practiced by the long-gone carver. So a sincere person was without wax, or uncamouflaged.

Audiences may believe speakers are sincere when they maintain good eye contact, don't shift back and forth on their feet, and lack a tremor in their voices. Or audiences may judge sincerity from speakers' reputations. Trustworthiness or sincerity is also a fairly stable factor in credibility, as has been repeatedly demonstrated in research studies. Although its effects vary from situation to situation, receivers believe persons they trust, whether because of their reputation, delivery, or supposed motivation.

Dynamism

A final dimension of credibility that has been demonstrated through experimental research is not as easy to define or even describe. This factor has been labeled "dynamism," "compliance," "charisma," or "image" by various researchers. It is the degree to which the audience admires and identifies with the source's attractiveness, power or forcefulness, and energy. The following word pairs have been linked in testing for the dynamism factor: "aggressive/meek," "emphatic/hesitant," "frank/reserved," "bold/passive," "energetic/tired," and "fast/slow."

Dynamism is clearly related to charisma, and although it is influenced by speakers' attractiveness, unattractive persons can be charismatic or dynamic, too. Dynamic speakers don't necessarily move about or wave their arms to give off dynamism cues. They simply seem to take up a lot of psychological space. They enter a room and people expect them to be in charge. Their voices seem to be assured and confident. Their word choices are eloquent and sometimes border on the poetic. They seem to know just what to say in tough or even tragic moments, and the audience lingers on their words. Dynamic persuaders populate important and crisis events across

American history. Their names are familiar to most —Thomas Jefferson, Benjamin Franklin, Abraham Lincoln, William Jennings Bryan, Elizabeth Cady Stanton, Winston Churchill, Franklin and Eleanor Roosevelt, John F. Kennedy, Martin Luther King, Jr., Malcolm X, and Ronald Reagan.

There are other dimensions of source credibility that could be investigated, and some already have been. A tall speaker, for example, is generally more likely to be believed than a short one. Timid or shy and reserved persons are likely to have low credibility, whereas authoritative and self-assured ones have high credibility. Bossy and egotistical persuaders lose credibility, whereas pleasant and warm persuaders do not. These and many other dimensions of source credibility interact and affect the three fundamental dimensions of trust: sincerity, expertise, and dynamism, or potency.

These elements of source credibility are not shared by all cultures. In cultures in which the *baksheesh* (bribe) is the order of the day, people actually are admired for being untrustworthy. The popular practice of haggling over prices in bazaars and markets is based on insincerity, not sincerity. In some cultures, a religious leader who lacks expertise in economics and diplomacy becomes the head of state while the experts are ejected from government.

THE PRESENCE OF AN AMERICAN VALUE SYSTEM

The myths and parables we have examined are actually fantasy forms of deep and enduring values that most Americans hold. They are expressed in myths in order to simplify them and make them seem less lofty. For example, Americans have a belief or value that all persons are to be treated equally and that in the eyes of God they are equal. This value has been debated for more than two centuries in the context of such issues as slavery, women's suffrage, civil rights, desegregation, and affirmative action. The value is acted out or dramatized in the possibility-of-success myth. We see the myth portrayed in print and TV ads. For example, a recent print ad for the

DuPont Chemical Company featured a black man who was still able to play basketball even though he had lost both legs in Vietnam. This was thanks to the good folks at DuPont, who sold the raw materials for making the artificial limbs that now enable him to succeed in the world of amateur sports (see Figure 9.6).

One of the early speech communication studies that explored values was conducted by Edward Steele and W. Charles Redding (1962). They looked at the communication in several presidential election campaigns and tried to extract core and secondary values. Their work has been replicated numerous times since then with very similar outcomes, thus suggesting that these core American values have great durability, longevity, and persistence. And they are frequently articulated by the media as the values that relate to various social issues (Kosicki, 2002). You will be able to see them in current times if you look around. The following are descriptions of the core values observed by Steele and Redding and since verified by other communication researchers.

Puritan and Pioneer Morality

This moral value involves the willingness to cast the world into categories of foul and fair, good and evil, and so forth. Although we tend to think of this value as outdated, it has merely been reworded. The advocates and foes of marijuana laws and of legal abortion both call on moral values such as just/ unjust, right/wrong, and moral/immoral to make their cases. And, of course, this value came to the forefront following the 9/11 attacks. The injustice of the event, the immorality of the terrorists, and the loss of innocent lives led Americans and others to see the event as having a major moral dimension.

The Value of the Individual

This value involves the ranking of the rights and welfare of the individual above those of the government or other groups. This value seems to persist as well. All politicians claim to be interested in the individual, and our laws ensure and protect individual rights over all others. Further, each person has the right to succeed or fail on his or her own.

Although no one is an island, no one is tied to the will of others, either. In the world of advertising, most products are marketed with "you" in mind. Cosmetics are made "especially for you," and Burger King lets you "Have It Your Way." In politics and government, according to this value, the real power of a democracy lies within each individual.

Achievement and Success

This value entails the accumulation of power, status, wealth, and property. In the 1960s and 1970s, many young Americans rejected this value, favoring communal living and refusing to dress up for school, church, or even job interviews. Many of those same young people are now the upwardly mobile, achievement-oriented, and graying yuppies. People today seem to evaluate others by symbols or emblems of success—whether it's BMWs or Mercedes-Benzes, Rolex watches, Mont Blanc pens, or even pinky "success" rings.

Persuaders frequently appeal to this need for achievement or success. Most of the military recruitment posters, advertisements, and slogans promise that by starting a career in the Army, Navy, Air Force, or Marines you will be able to climb the ladder to success faster. If you read the *Wall Street Journal,* success and status will be yours. First impressions count, so be sure to "dress for success" by shopping at Neiman Marcus. Self-help books and programs will help you to be an achiever and will contribute to your success. The achievement and success value, like the cultural myths, seems to ebb and flow with time. Thus, self-improvement courses and pyramid schemes will continue to be marketed even when the values of achievement and success seem most dormant.

Change and Progress

This value is typified by the belief that change (of almost any kind) will lead to progress and that progress is inherently good for us. This is the appeal of any product that is either "new" or "new and improved." The product life cycle theory almost dictates "change" and "progress" in the form of "improvement" to delay a decline of product sales. From a legal point of view, the producer of a

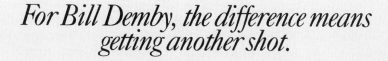

For Bill Demby, the difference means getting another shot.

When Bill Demby was in Vietnam, he used to dream of coming home and playing a little basketball with the guys.

A dream that all but died when he lost both his legs to a Viet Cong rocket.

But then, a group of researchers discovered that a remarkable DuPont plastic could help make artificial limbs that were more resilient, more flexible, more like life itself.

Thanks to these efforts, Bill Demby is back. And some say, he hasn't lost a step.

At DuPont, we make the things that make a difference.

Better things for better living.

FIGURE 9.6 This ad enhances DuPont's ethos by implying that the company is responsible for Bill Demby's "getting another shot" at life.

(DuPont Company photograph. Used by permission of DuPont.)

laundry product, for example, can claim that its product is new and improved merely by changing the color of the "beads of bleach" or by slightly altering the ratio of ingredients.

Because we as a culture value change and progress, we go for so-called new and improved products the way trout go for worms. Indeed, General Electric once had as its slogan "At GE, Progress Is Our Most Important Product." This is not to say that all such products are bad—only that the appeal has great power. The word "new" is one of the most powerful words in advertising, surpassed perhaps only by "free" and "more." Indeed, many changes obviously have been beneficial, such as the downsizing of the American automobile and the increase in its fuel efficiency—at least, prior to the SUV boom. And few would disagree on the value of the new generations of home and business computers, or digital audio and video, or the many new medical technologies. Further, the Internet has made available an enormous quantity of information on any and every topic, as well as making communication with people all over the globe instantaneous.

Ethical Equality

The equality value reflects the belief that all persons ought to be treated equally. They should have an equal opportunity to get an education, to work and be paid a fair wage, to live where they choose, and to hold political office. But we all know that, although this value may be laudable, the reality is that not everyone is born equal, nor do they all have an equal opportunity for jobs, education, or decent housing. Nonetheless, since the nation's founding, through the abolition, women's suffrage, civil rights, and other movements, attempts to create a situation of equality have been a part of the American cultural landscape. The words "All men are created equal" best capture the power of this value.

Effort and Optimism

This value expresses the belief that even the most unattainable goals can be reached if one works hard enough and "keeps smilin'." The myths of the triumphant individual and the possibility of success are examples of these values in action. The many self-help books and programs are further evidence of the ongoing belief in these values. And in today's business world, it is important to be a "striver" or a "self-starter." Nuggets of folk wisdom such as "Every cloud must have a silver lining," "If at first you don't succeed, try, try again," "Keep on the sunny side," and "Lighten up" serve as cultural metaphors of the value we place on effort and optimism. And phrases such as "a hard worker," "nothing ever gets them down," and "the eternal optimist" reflect how we much we believe in the value of effort and optimism. If you don't let the world get you down and keep plugging away, things will work out.

Efficiency, Practicality, and Pragmatism

Americans are a practical people. The key question often asked of any piece of legislation is "Will it work?"—whether it be a new set of tax revisions, a new cabinet office such as the Office of Homeland Security, or new immigration statutes. This value extends to other parts of our lives, too. Over twenty-five years ago, my family was one of the first purchasers of a microwave oven, at a cost of $400. Before making the purchase, we wanted to know whether a microwave oven would be energy efficient, practical, and handy, and not merely another fad. Similarly, we want to know whether our schooling will lead to a job. We are fascinated by questions of efficiency—fuel efficiency in our cars, energy efficiency in our appliances, and efficiency of movement on the job. And we go for practical solutions, as was demonstrated in the film *Apollo Thirteen,* in which the crew was able to use various pieces of equipment and supplies to jerry-rig a repair of their malfunctioning spacecraft. In other words, we value what is quick, workable, and practical.

Even though these values were catalogued more than forty years ago, they still have a great deal of relevance. This, if nothing else, suggests their basic validity. The fact that political position has less to do with the strength of these values than with the method of enacting them underscores the probability that they are core values for Americans. Our culture is effective in instilling these values in nearly all its members; radicals, moderates, and reactionaries may believe in the same things but tend to apply them differently. The power of a social system or culture to train its members is immense, even though they do not often realize this as they react to the dictates deeply ingrained in them.

Does this mean that values remain essentially static and cannot be changed? Not necessarily. It means only that they are so deeply ingrained in a culture that its members often forget how strong they are.

Access Infotrac College Edition, and enter the words "American values" in the key word search engine, and examine a few of the many articles devoted to the topic. How closely do they resemble the Redding and Steele list of core values?

REVIEW AND CONCLUSION

By this time, you know that the world of the persuadee in an information age is not an easy one. There are so many things to be aware of—the persuader's self-revelation using language and stylistic choices, the internal or process premises operating within each of us, and the interactive rules for content premises. In addition, societal and cultural predispositions for persuasion can act as premises in persuasive arguments. Persuaders instinctively appeal to values that rely on the societal training in the target audience. On at least three separate levels, this training has an effect on each of us—in the cultural myths or images to which we respond, in the sets of values we consciously articulate, and in the nonverbal cues to which we react (artifacts, space, and touch, to mention a few).

QUESTIONS FOR FURTHER THOUGHT

1. What are the three types of culturally or socially learned predispositions for persuasion? Give examples of each from your own experience.

2. How does a culture or society train its members? Give examples from your own experience.

3. How do you rank the core values mentioned in this chapter? How do you put them into practice? Are there other values in your value system not mentioned here? What are they? Are they restatements of the core values? If so, how? If not, how do they differ?

4. Considering today's headlines, is there a mob at the gates present? Explain.

5. To what degree can you identify a benevolent community in your life? Explain.

6. In the popular Harrison Ford film *Patriot Games,* there clearly is rot at the top. At what

critical moment does the "narrator" of the film discovers the "rot"? What does he do about it?

7. Explain the ethos of the hosts of the various TV talk shows. How does their ethos differ from the others'—for example, does Jay Leno seem more or less sincere, expert, or dynamic than David Letterman?

8. How have the core values described by Steele and Redding operated on your campus? In your own life?

9. How have American values changed since September 11, 2001? What examples can you give?

10. The slogan "These Colors Don't Run" that appeared in many places following the events of 9/11 clearly articulate an American value. What is it?

 For online activities, go to the Web site for this book at
http://communication.wadsworth.com/larson.

10

✹

Nonverbal Messages
in Persuasion

Videotapes of persons shopping in stores during the devastating 1989 earthquake in the San Francisco Bay Area show that the first thing people did after checking the environmental symptoms of the earthquake—whether objects fell from shelves, windows broke, and walls cracked—was to check out the nonverbal behavior of the people around them. They looked for facial expressions, movement, and a host of other cues of impending danger. During the Gulf War of the early 1990s, Saddam Hussein tried to win worldwide public approval for his invasion of Kuwait by being photographed and filmed talking with young Western children who were being "detained" (or held hostage) in Iraq (see Figure 10.1). During his interviews, he stroked the children, prompting widespread criticism and even outrage. Fictional hero Jason Bourne, in Robert Ludlum's best-seller *The Bourne Ultimatum,* is able to identify the disguised assassin and terrorist named "Carlos the Jackal" by the way the villain walks. Advertising researchers observe and record the dilation of the pupil and the eye's path as it surveys a print advertisement to

determine the ad's effectiveness. And *Saturday Night Live* performers like Dana Carvey and Darrel Hammond mimic the nonverbal gestures, facial expressions, and vocal qualities of politicians and celebrities.

These are but a few of many examples of nonverbal communication that occur every day. You and I produce and process hundreds—perhaps thousands—of nonverbal messages daily. In fact, researcher Albert Mehrabian (1971) once estimated that nonverbal communication accounts for over 80 percent of the meaning transferred between people. Usually, these nonverbal messages are part and parcel of the appeals we process in our world of persuasion.

Nonverbal premises in persuasion resemble cultural premises in that both are culturally taught and both are consistent across and within cultures. A major difference between cultural and nonverbal premises is that the latter seldom are carefully examined and analyzed. We may sense that a certain persuader seems disreputable and that it may have something to do with his or her shifty eyes. How-

FIGURE 10.1 What kinds of meaning do you derive from this photograph?
How is the meaning communicated?

(Photo by AFP. © 1990 Newsweek, Inc. Reprinted by permission of *Newsweek*.)

ever, we rarely dissect the interaction to find out exactly what causes us to distrust the other person. A major difference between cultural premises and nonverbal ones is that nonverbal premises usually occur at a very low level of awareness and so aren't readily apparent. They are almost certainly processed in the peripheral route of the elaboration likelihood model. One of the more valuable strategies persuadees can use to deal with the barrage of persuasion aimed at them is to sensitize themselves to some of the nonverbal factors that enter into the equation. This sensitivity serves a dual purpose: (1) It increases the amount of information on which to base decisions, and, more importantly, (2) it provides tip-offs to persuaders' hidden agendas and ultimate goals. Communication researcher Donald Orban (1999) points out the power of these tip-offs when he asks, "When a person glares at you, forms a fist, invades your space, [or] uses a harsh and loud voice to accompany a verbal argument demanding that you do it his way instead of your way, are you intimidated? Are you more likely to be influenced by the manner of the argument behavior or the validity of the argument?" (n.p.) Most nonverbal communication occurs almost instinctively or automatically. It is hard to fake, and even when faked, the persuader's intent seems to "leak" through nonverbal channels.

NONVERBAL CHANNELS

There are several channels through which we can communicate nonverbal meaning. Communication researchers J. K. Burgoon, N. E. Dunbar, and C. Segrin (2002) have identified three classes of nonverbal appeals that seem to be used when trying to influence others: (1) appeals to attractiveness, similarity, intimacy, and trust, (2) dominance and power displays, and (3) expectancy signaling and expectancy violations. With regard to appeals to attraction and similarity, we have long been aware that physical attractiveness is strongly correlated with persuasiveness, regardless of the expertise or sincerity/trustworthiness of the persuader. And we have also long known that the degree of similarity between persuader and persuadee is a powerful pre-

dictor of attractiveness and hence of persuasiveness. Recall the discussion of Heider's balance theory in Chapter 4. There we learned that people like and believe in persons who hold opinions similar to their own and may find those individuals attractive for this reason.

Since Heider's time, a variety of other persuasion theories have confirmed his predictions—congruency and dissonance theories, to name two. More recently, cognitive valence theory (CVT), proposed by P. A. Andersen (1985, 1999), predicts that the nonverbal immediacy of the persuader (if it is noticed by the audience members) leads to what he calls "arousal," which, in turn, can lead to relational nearness or closeness between the two. Another theory, proposed by H. Giles, N. Coupland, and J. Coupland (1991) and called communication accommodation theory (CAT), predicts that people will respond more positively to the persuader whose nonverbal communication style is similar to their own. This is particularly true when their vocal qualities are similar (tone of voice, articulation, volume, and so on) although other nonverbal channels have influence as well. Both theories link similarity and attractiveness with persuasiveness. Acting and thinking like a physically attractive source is seen as socially rewarding. Both theories (and others) also recognize the various channels or cues of attractiveness and similarity identified by earlier theorists in nonverbal communication. These include physical movements of the body (kinesics), the use of interpersonal space (proxemics), the use of touch (haptics), the way one looks (physical appearance), the use of time (chronemics), and the use of objects (artifactual communication).

Another communication researcher, Dale G. Leathers (1986), has identified seven nonverbal channels including facial expression, eye behavior, bodily communication, proxemics, personal appearance, vocal factors (voice stress, timbre, volume, and so on), and tactile communication (the use of touch). Earlier, communication researcher Mark Knapp (1978) identified eight channels: the environment (including architecture and furniture), proxemics and territoriality, physical appearance and dress, physical behavior and movement, touching, facial expression, eye behavior, and vocal cues. Other researchers have noted similar categories, with some, such as P. Ekman and W. V. Friesen (1975), focusing only on various aspects of facial communication. Orban (1999) has identified nine channels that impact argumentation. They include eye contact, facial expression, gesture, and bodily movement, of which there are five types: emblems, illustrators, regulators, affect displays, and adaptors. Gender differences are the focus of study for some researchers (Hall, 1984), whereas others study nonverbal cues of deception and the nonverbal behavior of liars (Knapp & Comendena, 1985). We can't begin to examine all these fascinating topics in a single chapter, but we can focus on some of them, especially those that affect persuasive messages. For our purposes, let's use the categories suggested by Orban and Leathers, as well as considering gender differences in nonverbal communication.

Facial Expression and Eye Behavior

The first nonverbal message channels identified by Leathers (1986) are facial expression (sometimes called "affect displays") and eye behavior. According to Leathers, the face is "the most important source of nonverbal information" (p. 19). Facial expression is familiar and readily noticed, and subtle nuances in facial expression can make a world of difference in perceived meaning. Such variables as the amount and rate of dilation of the pupils or eye blink rates can communicate a great deal of information about individuals' attention, emotion, and interest. Orban (1999) defines eye contact as "visual interaction with the eyes of listeners" and facial expression as "variations of facial muscles that convey perceptual stimuli to listeners." He claims that these two channels can team up to "create emotional and credibility cues that can ignite or diffuse argument potential" (n.p.).

For more detailed information about how facial expressions and gestures affect credibility, access InfoTrac College Edition, and type "nonverbal" in the search engine. Click on the periodical option, enter the words "nonverbal communication" in the subject guide search engine, and explore the over two hundred periodical sources. Also explore the twenty-five subdivisions and eight related topics.

Knapp (1978) noted that, correctly or not, people often use the face as a measure of personality—for example, judging high foreheads to indicate intelligence, thin lips to indicate conscientiousness, a bulbous nose to indicate drunkenness, and close-together eyes to indicate low intelligence. Leathers identified ten general classes or categories of facial expression (and many more specific kinds of facial meaning): disgust, happiness, interest, sadness, bewilderment, contempt, surprise, anger, determination, and fear. Among his more specific kinds of expressions, Leathers also included rage, amazement, terror, hate, arrogance, astonishment, stupidity, amusement, pensiveness, and belligerence, to name but a few.

Leathers (1986) also identified six functions that the eyes serve. One is the attention function, indicated by mutual gazing. You have probably noticed persons who continually look over your shoulder and past you as if they are looking for more interesting conversational possibilities. Some eye behavior serves a regulatory function, by indicating when a conversation is to begin or stop. When speakers look back at a person or audience, this is generally taken as a signal for listeners to take their turn talking. Eyes can serve a power function as well, as when a leader stares at an audience. Many have remarked on the power expressed in the eyes of cult leader and convicted murderer Charles Manson. Eye behavior also serves an affective function by indicating positive and negative emotions. You probably know what your parents' eyes look like when they are angry with you or what the eyes of someone "in love" look like. Both are examples of the eyes' affective function. Further, eyes are used in impression formation, as when persons communicate a winning image or a lack of self-esteem. Finally, Leathers noted the persuasive function of eye behavior. We rate speakers who maintain eye contact as credible, and we are suspicious of those whose gaze is continually shifting about. If people avert their eyes when talking to us, we assume that they are either shy or hiding something. Orban (1999) puts it this way: "Through our eyes we reflect cognitive and emotional behavior. We project impressions of penetrating thought, confusion and inattentiveness. We show our emotions of fear, anger, happiness, and sadness. We do not realize the hidden messages eye contact reveals" (n.p.).

Bodily Communication

Bodily communication has several dimensions, one of which is kinesics, or physical movements of the body, such as how a person holds her or his body (tense or relaxed posture) and how she or he uses it in given contexts. Powerful persuaders are physically or perceptually "above" their audience. They also demonstrate relaxed but erect posture, dynamic gestures, good eye contact, and variations in speaking rate and inflection. Powerless persuaders, in contrast, behave more submissively and exhibit lots of body tension, little direct eye contact, "closed" postures (for example, legs and arms crossed), and few gestures.

Knapp (1978) identified several head movements that convey meaning, including cocking, tilting, nodding, shaking, and thrusting out the jaw. And, of course, other bodily movements convey meaning, such as clenching a fist, putting hands on hips, and standing in an "open" stance with legs spread apart. These movements can indicate anger, intensity, and degree of commitment or dedication. In some cases, gestures and bodily movements are emblematic—they stand for a particular meaning. For example, stroking the index finger while pointing it at someone is emblematic of "shame on you," crossed fingers indicate "good luck," and the hitchhiker's closed fist and extended thumb are emblematic of wanting a ride (although the same gesture means "hook 'em" to students at Texas A&M). Orban (1999) points out several others including the "A-OK" sign (which conveys the same meaning to Latin Americans as "the bird" does to us), the "be quiet" sign, and the "peace" sign. Such emblems can perform a function ("shush"); communicate positive, negative, or neutral values (thumbs up, thumbs down, or shoulder shrugging); and provide an evaluation (as the "A-OK" emblem does in the United States). And many obscene gestures can quickly provoke anger or other emotions.

For some fascinating insights into how gestures and bodily communication communicate, access InfoTrac College Edition, and type the word "bodytalk" in the key word search engine. Explore the article by Donovin. Then enter the words "nonverbal communication" in the subject search engine. Select the eight related topics, and read about flirting, eye contact, hugging, and much much more.

Proxemics

Proxemic communication (or how people use physical space) is the fourth category of nonverbal channels in Leathers' system. You have undoubtedly noticed, for example, how most people fall silent and don't look at one another when they are in crowded elevators or public restrooms. Edward T. Hall (1959) identified several kinds of space in his book *The Silent Language,* which have been confirmed by numerous researchers since then:

- *Public distance.* This type of distance is often found in public speaking settings in which speakers are 15–25 feet or more from their audiences. Informal persuasion probably will not work in these circumstances. Persuaders who try to be informal in a formal situation meet with little success.

- *Social or formal distance.* This type of distance is used in formal but nonpublic situations, such as job interviews or committee meetings. The persuader in these situations, although formal in style, need not be oratorical. Formal distance ranges from about 7 to 12 feet between persuader and persuadee. Persuaders never become chummy in this context, but they do not deliver a "speech," either. You probably select this distance when you go to your professor's office for a conference.

- *Personal or informal distance.* Two colleagues might use this distance when discussing a matter of mutual concern—such as roommates discussing a class or a problem they share. In these situations, communication is less structured than in the formal situation; both persuadee and persuader relax and interact often with each other, bringing up and questioning evidence or asking for clarification. In our culture, informal distance is about 3½–4 feet—the eye-to-eye distance when sitting at the corner of a teacher's desk as opposed to the formal distance created when you sit across the desk.

- *Intimate distance.* People use this distance when they whisper messages they do not want others to overhear or when they are involved in a conspiratorial or other "secret" conversation. Persuasion may or may not occur in these instances. Usually, the message is one that will not be questioned by the receiver—he or she will nod in agreement, follow the suggestion given, or respond to the question asked. When two communicators are in this kind of close relation, their aims probably are similar. The distance ranges from 6 to 18 inches.

How do persuaders use these distance boundaries? Are we vulnerable to persuasion using proxemics? Actual examples of such persuasion often escape our notice because proxemic communication is transmitted at such a low level of awareness. Take automobile sales. When customers come into a showroom, imagine the results if the salesperson rushes over to them and, within personal or even intimate distance, asks something like, "What can I do for you folks today?" The customers will probably retreat from the showroom or at least from the salesperson, saying something like, "Well, we're just looking around." Clever salespeople stay within public distance of customers until they perceive an indication of interest or a verbal or nonverbal signal that the customers want help. Only then will they move into informal or even formal distance.

Look at the advertisements in any popular magazine, and you will notice the use of proxemics as a persuasive device (see Figure 10.2). The young adults who "go for it" in beer ads are having fun and enjoying one another in personal or intimate space. Recently, people in the real estate business have become interested in the communicative power of the strategic use of space. Industry publications have discussed such questions as how close a real estate agent should be to prospective buyers during a tour of a home and whether the agent should lead or follow the buyers. In many other contexts—offices, hospitals, banks,

prisons, and factories—serious consideration is given to the use of space as a communicative device or a communication facilitator. Try to be alert to the uses of space in your life. How have you arranged your room or apartment? Does the arrangement facilitate or deter communication? How do various people with whom you interact use space? Do foreigners use space differently than you do? You will soon discover how important this nonverbal channel of communication is to persuasion.

To understand how powerful proxemic communication can be, access InfoTrac College Edition, and type the words "proxemic behavior" in the subject search engine. Select the personal space option and then the periodical option, and peruse the articles listed.

Physical Appearance

During a recent faculty externship at a major advertising agency, I learned that the agency had just fired a female employee because of her appearance; they simply couldn't expose their clients to her unprofessional and sloppy looks and grooming. At my school, it is always easy to guess what's going on toward the middle of the spring semester when my students come to class "dressed to kill." It is job interview time on campus, and everyone knows that appearance sends a message to interviewers. But physical appearance involves much more than simply good grooming and proper attire, according to Leathers (1986). For example, his sources maintain that larger-than-normal facial features—nose, ears, and lips—are generally considered unattractive.

Knapp (1978) reported other interesting findings regarding physical appearance. For instance, first-born females who are attractive tend to sit toward the front of the class, to make more comments during class, and to get better grades. Attractive females are also more likely to persuade male audiences than are unattractive females. You may wonder what is meant by "attractive" in these cases. The research used the same female in both the attractive and unattractive conditions, but in the unattractive condition, she wore loose-fitting clothing,

FIGURE 10.2 Which of Hall's four types of communication distance seems to be operating in this ad? Why do you suppose this distance was used?

(Reprinted by permission of Hotel Intercontinental, Chicago.)

had no makeup on, had messy hair, and appeared generally ungroomed (p. 155).

Another element in physical appearance is bodily attractiveness, according to Leathers (1986). Specifically, slenderness is considered attractive in females, whereas larger-waisted and hippier females are perceived as less attractive. A recent fashion trend called "heroin chic" features attractive but emaciated-appearing female models who should be taken to an "all you can eat" buffet as soon as possible. For males, broad shoulders, a well-muscled upper body, and a tapering upper trunk correlate positively with attractiveness ratings. Leathers also found that self-image has a lot to do with ratings of attractiveness; that is, if you feel good about yourself, you will probably engage in good grooming and keep your body in good physical condition.

Clothing and adornments such as jewelry also contribute to people's physical appearance (see Figure 10.3). The dismissed ad agency employee tended to dress too casually for the workplace, and her clothing wasn't always clean or pressed. With regard to jewelry, think of the different evaluations you might make of a person wearing a Rolex as opposed to a Timex watch or the degree to which gold jewelry can attract your attention. Eastern European businessmen appeared threadbare and shabby to me when I first saw them just after the fall of the Soviet bloc, and I wondered what triggered that evaluation. After some analysis, I realized that all of them carried imitation leather attaché cases and that the quality of their suits and shoes rated below that of the specials at discount stores.

Artifacts

Although birds feather their nests with bits of string, straw, hair, and wood, they do it for purely functional reasons: to keep their nests intact and cozy. We humans feather our nests not only for these reasons but also for highly symbolic ones. To illustrate, look at your work area or at that of a roommate or friend. You will find that it is arranged not only for work. People feather their nests with objects—artifacts—that symbolize their sense of self. For example, think of the many things that you have on or near your desk or that you use to "deco-

rate" your living space at school and at home. Artifactual arrangement is also symbolic (some people have messy desks, whereas others have extremely neat desks, with each pencil sharpened and papers stacked in neat piles). Our culture has taught us to react in certain ways to the artifacts of others and the way they are used. These patterns of responses form premises for persuasion.

A common type of artifactual communication is revealed in the objects surrounding a persuader in a message situation. For example, in a public speech, the banners, bunting, flags, and insignias all contribute to the ultimate success (or failure) of the persuasive attempt. Clothing is another type of artifact. What people wear sends signals about what they are like and what they believe or represent (for example, a priest's collar or an army officer's uniform).

Another type of artifact is exemplified in the personal objects surrounding persuaders. Consider how you feel when you go into a doctor's office that has diplomas on the walls—no art, no colorful posters, no other kind of decoration, just diplomas. What kind of person is the doctor likely to be? Compare that with the feeling you have when you enter a college professor's office that has posters and art on the walls. These artifacts symbolize the kind of persuasion you are likely to hear—in the one case, professional, concrete, and prescriptive; in the other, abstract and informal.

Large objects such as furniture also send signals. We expect a certain kind of communication to occur when we are told to sit down at a table and the persuader sits on the opposite side. Persuaders who put a lectern between themselves and the audience will probably engage in a certain kind of communication—formal. If they step out from behind the lectern or walk around while talking, they will come across as more informal. Types of furniture can also symbolize certain characteristics. What kinds of persuasion and what kinds of persons would you associate with French provincial furniture? What kind of persuasion is likely to occur in a room with metal office furniture? Consider how artifactual communication is discussed by the characters in Figure 10.4. These artifactual messages vary among cultures and even subcultures. Frequently, artifactual communication makes the difference

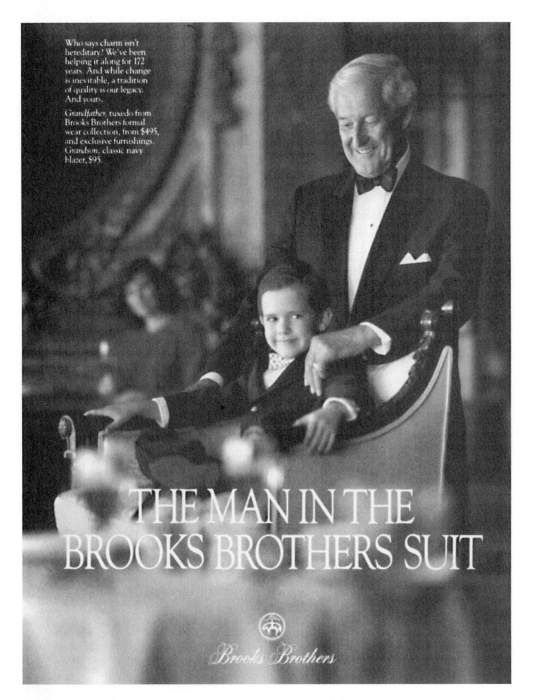

Who says charm isn't hereditary? We've been helping it along for 172 years. And while change is inevitable, a tradition of quality is our legacy. And yours.

Grandfather, tuxedo from Brooks Brothers formal wear collection, from $495, and exclusive furnishings. *Grandson,* classic navy blazer, $95.

THE MAN IN THE
BROOKS BROTHERS SUIT

Brooks Brothers

FIGURE 10.3 Clothing is used to communicate. What message is being communicated in this ad?

(Reprinted by permission of Brooks Brothers Clothing.)

FIGURE 10.4 What message(s) are sent by purposely altering one's hair color? What about piercing parts of one's body?

(Reprinted by permission of Nick Jeffries.)

between successful and unsuccessful persuasion. Try to identify the most effective kinds of artifacts for persuading you.

You will find some fascinating information about the effects of furniture and room layout in InfoTrac College Edition. Type "proxemic" in the search engine, select the personal space option, and select the related subjects option. Then select the room layout option and examine the articles listed.

Vocal Features

Each of us has had the experience of answering the phone and not being able to figure out who is calling. We listen carefully and ask innocuous questions until something the person says triggers recognition of his or her vocal patterns; then we breathe a sigh of relief and carry on as if we knew who was calling all along. Leathers (1986) notes that a semantics of sound affects how we respond to persuaders' messages. The factors he identified include volume or loudness, pitch, rate, vocal quality, clarity of pronunciation, intonation pattern, and silence. These elements enable you to recognize the voice on the phone. More importantly, these vocal factors influence whether you are persuaded by a given source, and they frequently indicate a lot about persuaders and their emotions, goals, and sincerity.

Monotonic persuaders bore their audience and lose most of their persuasiveness. High-pitched voices can indicate excitement; low-pitched but tense voices can indicate anger; and rate of speech can indicate nervousness or confidence. Vocal quality communicates a number of things; breathy voices in females, for example, communicate a stereotype of simplemindedness and shallowness, whereas breathy voices in males may indicate that the speaker is effeminate. Screeching or tense voices indicate stress and concern, and nasality is often associated with arrogance. Persons who articulate poorly and who mispronounce words generally lose some of their credibility and effectiveness (see Figure 10.5). Knapp (1978) reported on research indicating that people can fairly reliably identify certain stereotypes from vocal cues. These stereotypes include such characteristics as masculinity/femininity, age, enthusiasm/apathy, activeness/laziness, and attractiveness/ugliness. He also reported on research that identified the following correlations: (1) Breathiness in males indicates youthfulness and an artistic nature; (2) a "thin" voice in females indicates social, physical, and emotional insecurity; (3) vocal flatness indicates sluggishness for both males and females; and (4) nasality is associated with a number of undesirable traits in both males and females. Krapp further noted that most listeners are quite sensitive to vocal cues. In sum, one feature of oral

FIGURE 10.5 Here Malaprop Man demonstrates how mispronunciation can damage credibility and persuasive effectiveness.

(*Frank and Ernest* reprinted by permission of NEA, Inc.)

persuasion that receivers must pay attention to is the vocal qualities of the communication coming from persuaders.

Tactile Communication

Some of the more important nonverbal message carriers involve the ways in which and degree to which people touch one another. We know that infants need to be touched and cuddled. We also know that this need doesn't diminish as the child matures but that in our culture the number, type, and duration of touches the growing child gets are greatly reduced. Children may substitute other kinds of physical contact for the touches they received from their parents: socking or shoving someone, tickling a pal, holding hands, and so on.

There are gender-related differences in the use of touch, with women more likely to use touch to communicate than men. In fact, the average woman touches someone else about twelve times per day, whereas the average man touches someone only

eight times a day (Kotulak, 1985). Touches by both males and females are more likely to involve a person of the opposite sex, which is the reverse of what occurs in some other cultures. In Western culture, touch between men generally is limited to shaking hands or backslapping, with the occasional manly hug. Leathers (1986) observes that we live in a "noncontact" society, with touch noticeably absent in public places, particularly between men. We probably would not accept the vice president hugging and kissing the president on the president's return from abroad, yet such behavior is perfectly acceptable in many countries and cultures. These norms for the use of touch, Leathers notes, usually relate to two general factors: (1) the part of the body that is touched and (2) the demographic characteristics of the interactants (age, gender, social class, race, and status). The head, shoulders, and arms are the most frequently touched parts of the body, with other parts being more or less "off limits" to public touch. The use of touch is also more frequent among minorities. Further, persuaders who touch persuadees are the most successful (Kotulak, 1985). Yet persuaders who are too "touchy" probably offend not only the people being touched but also those observing the touch. Credibility can be drastically undermined if persuaders misread a relationship and respond inappropriately to touch.

Touch seems to be a good way to convey special kinds of emotional persuasion, such as empathy, warmth, and reassurance. Among firefighters, the only acceptable touch from another male is a handshake or backslap. However, firefighters must sometimes calm frantic men, women, and children to get them out of a burning building, so willingness to touch varies depending on the situation. The laying on of hands used in some religions is sometimes given credit for conversions or even faith healings.

Touch can be extremely important in facilitating certain kinds of communication. Terminal cancer patients, for example, need more touch than less ill patients, according to some experts. Touch helps to express sympathy at a funeral service. In another study, strangers were asked for information by a researcher posing as an ordinary citizen. In half of the cases, the researcher lightly touched the stranger before saying, "Excuse me, but I'm sort of lost. Can you tell me where . . . ?" The researcher got much more information and even conversation when using the light touch. Look at the kinds of touches used in magazine ads. You will discover that the persuasive potential of touch has many dimensions.

Some touches are taboo. These include (1) the touching of strangers; (2) touching that inflicts pain, as when someone touches someone else's sunburn; (3) touching that interferes with another's activities or conversation; (4) touching that moves others aside; (5) playful touching that is too aggressive, as in mock wrestling or pinching; and (6) "double-whammy" touching, in which touch is used to emphasize a negative point (as in touching someone's belly when mentioning that they have put on weight) (Kotulak, 1985).

As you continue to improve your abilities as a receiver, one of the nonverbal channels of communication to observe closely is the use of touch, whether it occurs at the first meeting with a stranger, punctuates the closing of a business deal,

expresses empathic sensitivity toward another person, or provides the assurance that can help move people out of a dangerous situation.

To find some more examples of the communication power of touching, access InfoTrac College Edition, and type the word "haptics" in the subject search engine. Select the periodical option, and review the articles under the touch option.

Chronemics

Solid evidence suggests that our use of time sends many signals about how we evaluate others. A popular saying in our culture is, "Time is money." Indeed, the use (and misuse) of time can communicate many messages to others. Suppose you have set a time and reserved a place for a meeting of a work group. Because you are arranging the meeting, you show up ten minutes early to make sure things are in order. A few minutes before the meeting is to start, two members of the group arrive and begin to chat. Right on time, to the minute, comes another group member. Now only two people are missing. You probably will say something like, "Let's wait a few minutes before starting." After five minutes, one of your missing members shows up, and you start the meeting. Nearly half an hour later, the final member arrives. What messages were sent by each member of the group? In our culture, it is permissible to arrive at a meeting a few minutes late, but arrive later than that and you'd better have a good excuse, such as a flat tire, a stalled elevator, or a speeding ticket. By coming late, you "persuade" the others that you don't care about the appointment, that you are a thoughtless person, and that you are a prima donna.

If, however, you are invited to a party, be sure to show up at least forty-five minutes late if it is a college bash and at least twenty minutes late if it is a dinner party. If you show up on time, the host and hostess might still be grooming themselves or putting the final touches on the place settings.

If you really want to put people in their place, make sure they have to wait to get in to see you—a favorite trick of some police officers, corporate executives, and even college professors. On one campus, students must wait at least five minutes for an "instructor" to arrive at class, ten minutes for a "professor," and twenty minutes for a "Doctor" before assuming there will be no class. So time is not only money; it is often also status. And there are important cultural and subcultural factors related to chronemics. The most famous of these might be the way time is handled by African Americans— what has come to be called "CPT" (colored people's time). In a scene in the 1999 play *OO BLA DEE,* the story of an all-black women's jazz band during the 1940s, the members of the band discuss CPT. One character traces the concept to being freed after the Civil War. Before that, he says, slaves had to work from "cain't" until "cain't" six days a week, or from when you "cain't" yet quite see the sunrise until you "cain't" see the sun because it has set. Free of this grueling schedule, he goes on, made flexibility of time use one of the prime features of the new-found freedom for the ex-slave. Quite naturally, the idea carried on across generations. Begin to observe how time works in your culture or subculture, but don't be surprised if it doesn't operate the same way in other cultures or even in subcultures within our culture.

GENDER DIFFERENCES IN NONVERBAL COMMUNICATION

Recently, researchers have investigated gender differences in nonverbal communication. For example, in a 1989 study of attitudes toward the use of touch, researchers found that women are significantly more comfortable with touch than are men and that higher levels of "touch comfort" are signs of a greater level of socialization (Fromme et al., 1989). Communication scholar Brenda Major (1984) noted significant gender differences in how individuals touch others and in how they receive such touches, and she found that these differences are exhibited shortly after birth. Whereas men tend to initiate touching in cross-gender encounters, they are less likely to initiate touch in same-gender encounters. Women, in contrast, are less hung up about touching other women. Although touch often expresses warmth and intimacy (especially among women), it can also communicate power or

status relationships. In this latter case, men tend to use touch more frequently, indicating that they perceive themselves to be superior.

Major also reported gender differences in reactions to touch. If, for example, the toucher is of the same status as the touchee, women react more positively and men more negatively, particularly when the toucher is a woman. Major concluded that, overall, women tend to react more positively to touch than do men and that this probably stems from the fact that girls are touched more frequently from birth on and are perceived as being more fragile and passive than boys.

Scholars N. Porter and F. Geis (1984) wondered whether gender and nonverbal communication are related to leadership in small groups. They found that, in both all-male and all-female groups, physical placement at the head of the table is the best predictor of leadership. In mixed-gender groups, males emerge as the leader if they sit in the leadership position, but women do not.

Researchers S. Ellyson, J. Dovidio, and B. J. Fehr (1984) investigated dominance in men and women as it relates to visual behavior. They found that dominance is usually indicated by what they called "look/speak" rather than "look/listen" behavior (that is, attempting to dominate by speaking rather than listening when catching the eyes of others). Further, they found no gender-related factors. Thus, if women use the "look/speak" strategy, they are just as likely to be evaluated as dominant as are men who use the same strategy.

Communication scholar Judy Hall (1984) found that women have more expressive faces than men and smile and laugh more often than men, especially when they are in all-female groups. She speculated that smiling and laughing may be seen as unmasculine, which tends to discourage males from exhibiting these behaviors.

Regarding "gaze" and "gaze holding," Hall found that women tend to gaze more at other persons than do men and that they are more uncomfortable than men when they cannot see the person being spoken to. They also seem to be gazed at more frequently than men (which makes perfect sense to me). Hall hinted that gaze differences between men and women exist because females are perceived as having more warmth than males. Also,

FIGURE 10.6 There are some verbal gender differences in this cartoon, but notice some of the nonverbal differences, including facial expressions or affect displays, the use of touch, and the use of proxemics.

(Reprinted by permission of Todd Michael.)

males avoid the gazes of other males to avoid the potential sexual implications of such gazing.

Regarding proxemics, Hall observed that men maintain greater distances from others when in conversation and that women are approached more closely than men are. Women tend to face more directly toward the person with whom they are interacting. When given the choice of sitting adjacent to or across from others, men tend to occupy the "across" position, whereas women prefer the "adjacent" position. Finally, females are more approachable than males, which Hall attributed to real or perceived "warmth, affiliativeness, and/or size," rather than to any perception of lower status, as is the case when gender is not a variable. She also found that women initiate touching more than men. Hall speculated that this may be due to women's appreciation for being touched more and that there may be gender-related differences for various kinds of touch (for example, where on the body and how emphatic the touch).

Regarding body movement and position, Hall found little research on which to base generalizations. However, it does appear that men are more relaxed than women, more physically expansive (for example, spreading their arms and legs and leaning back in chairs with their legs forward), and more restless (for example, fidgeting, playing with objects, and shifting

their bodies in various ways). Another difference is that, whereas women tend to carry things in front of their chest, men carry things at their side.

Hall reported several gender-related differences in the use of the voice in nonverbal ways. Men, for example, are less fluent than women, make more verbal errors, and use more vocalized pauses such as "uh" or "um." Women's voices tend to have higher pitches even though their vocal mechanisms permit them to use lower ones. At the same time, women's voices have more variability in pitch, are more musical, and are more expressive than men's voices. Women's voices are also softer than men's and are judged to be more positive, pleasant, honest, meek, respectful, delicate, enthusiastic, and anxious and less confident, domineering, and awkward. Men's voices, in contrast, tend to be demanding, blunt, dominant, forceful, and militant. Consider the verbal gender differences in Figure 10.6. Are there any nonverbal differences?

Using an entirely different perspective and methodology, Jean Umiker-Sebeok (1984) studied women as they appear in magazine advertisements. Among other things, she found that, in ads showing women in a professional role (for example, wearing a doctor's smock and taking someone's blood pressure, or dressed in a suit at a business conference), their hair is always in place, they always wear makeup, and their posture and gestures are feminine. Also, the setting is usually "feminized" by the use of houseplants, floral arrangements, flouncy curtains, and mirrors. The result is women who are dressed for someone—usually a man—and defined, in the words of Roland Barthes, as "entirely constituted by the gaze of man." So there are important gender differences in nonverbal communication beyond dress and vocalic features. The successful persuader is aware of these and plays on them when attempting to persuade.

To discover more about gender differences in nonverbal communication and how to use them better, access InfoTrac College Edition, and type the words "nonverbal communication and gender" in the key word search engine. Select the periodical option, and peruse some of the articles you find there.

DIALECT

Dialect, or patterns and styles of pronunciation and usage, is culture bound and often indicates individuals' socioeconomic or regional background. We learn dialect culturally. It can communicate many things about us and can affect our persuasion, too. Many of my students come from Chicago or its suburbs—often from the South Side. They get angry with me when I tell some of them to stop "talking like steelworkers." They do not hear themselves saying "dis" for "this" and "dat" for "that" and "dem" for "them." Yet they will be discriminated against if they keep their dialect. Students from the North Side and some suburbs have another dialect that may cause equal problems for them. They say "Dubbie" for "Debbie," "Shovie" for "Chevy," and "newahth" for "north." And it would be easy to document the kind of discrimination that occurs when African American or Hispanic dialect is used. Be aware of your responses to various dialects, and see whether people respond to your dialect in certain ways. I still have a Minnesota dialect and get certain responses because of my frequent use of "Yup" and "You betcha." People start looking for hayseeds in my hair.

Communication professor Norman Heap (1976) observed that we tend to regard dialect as signaling educational background and communication context, resulting in a four-category system:

1. *Formal context/educated speaker.* This category is typified by proper pronunciation and usage, such as that used in the courtroom, in governmental bodies, and on TV news programs.

2. *Informal context/educated speaker.* This category includes proper pronunciation accompanied by slang usages, which signal the informal context. It includes localisms like my "You betcha" or profanity. Once this usage is exposed in formal contexts, it is sometimes viewed as unacceptable.

3. *Formal context/uneducated speaker.* This category is marked by attempts at proper pronunciation and usage, such as might be heard when an uneducated person testifies in court or at a government hearing. The speaker tries too hard to sound correct.

4. *Informal context/uneducated speaker.* This category includes pronunciation and usage such as we might expect in steel mills—the "dese" and "dem" and "dose" pronunciations. These vary from locale to locale but usually are associated with blue-collar job or informal settings. Educated speakers can lose credibility by being too formal or correct in such contexts.

THE USE OF NONVERBAL TACTICS

Nonverbal message carriers can be manipulated by persuaders in a process that scholar Erving Goffman (1957) called "impression management." This involves using powerful verbal and nonverbal signals to convince the audience that the source is a certain kind of person. One candidate for the 1996 GOP presidential nomination wore red-and-black-checked "lumberjack" shirts when he campaigned in New Hampshire and hip boots when his opponents began to engage in mudslinging. Bill Clinton managed our impressions of him by wearing jogging suits and other casual clothing in the White House.

The use of clothing to communicate nonverbally in impression management is a popular topic in the corporate world. In her book *The Power of Dress,* Jacqueline Murray (1989) provides a number of case studies to demonstrate the communicative use of dress. For example, at Electronic Data Systems, everyone has a military look: clean-shaven face; shiny, black, plain-toed shoes; white shirts and dark suits; and army haircuts.

Murray identifies three categories of business dress: (1) "corporate dress," which is used by bankers, attorneys, and executives; (2) "communication dress," which is used by persons in sales, marketing, education, personnel, and high-tech industries; and (3) "creative dress," which is used by interior decorators, commercial artists, people in advertising, boutique owners, and entrepreneurs. Corporate dress is simple in line, shape, and design; tends to be tailored; and features gray and blue colors for suits and off-white or light blue for shirts and blouses. Corporate dress also uses fabrics such as silks, herringbones, tweeds, and flannels in suits or dresses and plain cottons, wools, or linens in shirts and blouses. Communication dress features suits and dresses that are practical, relaxed, and semitraditional, as well as blazers and sports coats. Communicators use a mix of colors for their blouses and shirts, are willing to wear stripes or relaxed prints, and choose fabrics such as knits, loose or bulky weaves, and those preferred by the corporate types. Creative dress tends to be loose fitting, with elongated lines and exaggerated design in both suits and dresses and blouses and shirts. The preferred colors in this category are striking, dramatic hues, as well as understated taupes, peaches, and basics. Although some may question Murray's conclusions, few would argue that dress is unimportant as a nonverbal channel of communication.

OTHER NONVERBAL MESSAGES

Eye movements and other movements of the head can also communicate. We are all aware of the negative impression we have of persons whose eyes are continuously darting about or who can't look us in the eye for more than a brief moment. Completely different meaning can come about from what is called "gaze holding," or maintaining eye contact with another person. Usually, this conveys sexual interest. Even the rate of eye blinks can communicate. Vance Packard (1964) reported in *The Hidden Persuaders* that grocery shoppers' eye blinks slow down as they proceed up and down the aisles—to the point that they are almost mesmerized, approaching the early stages of hypnotism.

Other movements and uses of the body carry nonverbal meaning as well. Albert Scheflen (1973), a researcher in the use of gestures during psychotherapy, found that when a psychiatrist uses the "bowl gesture" patients often open up and reveal more about themselves and their problems. We are familiar with the use of this gesture in persuasion: It is the logo for a large insurance company—"You're in good hands with Allstate."

People can use their bodies to invite or inhibit communication. Notice the two configurations in Figure 10.7. In triad A, the body positions of the three persons would inhibit a fourth person from joining in the conversation, whereas in triad B, the body positions invite participation. The use of the body to discourage communication or interaction could be called "blocking" behavior, and the use of the body to encourage communication or interaction could be called "inviting" behavior. Scheflen (1973) came to call these and other nonverbal invitations or blocks "quasi-courtship behavior" when he observed the behaviors in pairs of persons of the opposite sex.

Related to the use of the body to block or invite communication is the use of objects such as furniture, piles of books on a library table, or a podium to either encourage or discourage communication. The incidence of violence on the New York City subway system increased radically when the folio newspaper then being published went on strike. Apparently, many persons had been using the newspaper to "block" themselves from fellow passengers by holding it up in front of their faces. When the paper was no longer available to discourage interaction, there were more opportunities for confrontation to occur, which resulted in the increase in violent interchanges.

Top view

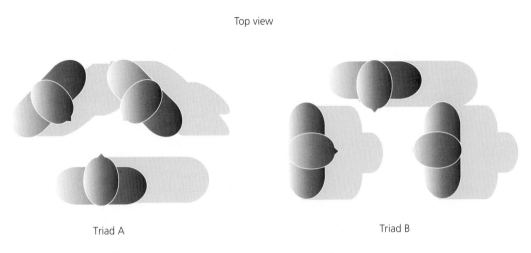

Triad A   Triad B

FIGURE 10.7 Notice the difference between the body positions of the persons in each triad. Which is involved in "blocking" behavior?

Other types of body movement send nonverbal messages as well. For example, research has shown that lifting or lowering the chin at the ends of sentences serves as a signal that the person intends to continue to speak or that he or she is done speaking and someone else can join in. And, of course, we are all aware of the communicative power of head nodding, winking, and various obscene gestures, which vary in meaning from culture to culture. Orban (1999) and others call these nonverbal indicators "regulators." Among the regulators are those that involve turn taking, turn requesting, and turn yielding or "back channeling," whereby the listener encourages the speaker to continue instead of taking his or her turn. Orban says this indicates full attention and interest, which means back-channeled persuaders will advocate longer and with more enthusiasm.

As you begin to observe the nonverbal messages occurring around you, you will discover an almost infinite number of potential nonverbal message carriers. What about the color of a room or of a person's clothing? How do seating and furniture arrangement communicate? Who reaches for the check at a restaurant first? What do nervous gestures or twitches, volume and tone, and pauses commu-

nicate? How do you interpret curious habits, such as cracking the knuckles or doodling, which may communicate subconscious tensions?

Even the sense of smell seems to be an important carrier of information. We are all aware, for example, of the person who uses too much cologne or after-shave lotion or of the person with body odor; apparently, we can detect more subtle odors as well. For instance, some persons claim to be able to smell hostility or tension upon entering a room. In the popular film *Scent of a Woman,* Al Pacino's character bases his judgments about women on the scent of their perfume and other olfactory cues, and he uses scent to plan his strategies of romance. Many homes have unique and characteristic odors caused by the kinds of food cooked in them, the kinds of cleaning solutions used, or the kinds of wood used in their construction. The fragrance of a new car is now available in aerosol cans to spray in used cars, thus making them seem newer and "fresher." And a real estate agent I know advises those listing a house with her to have a loaf of raised bread dough in the refrigerator ready to pop in the oven so the house will smell of baking bread when the agent shows up twenty minutes later with a potential buyer.

REVIEW AND CONCLUSION

By this time, you know that the world of the persuadee in an information age is not an easy one. You need to be aware of so many things: the persuader's self-revelation using language and stylistic choices, as well as the internal or process premises operating within each of us. You need to recognize the interactive rules for content premises. In this chapter, we also learned about the world of nonverbal premises. The responsible receiver recognizes the variety of channels, including facial expression, eye behavior, and bodily communication. You need to be aware of the ways in which gestures and posture, proxemics, physical appearance, and artifacts can communicate. You also need to realize that vocal communication, tactile communication (the use of touch), chronemics (the use of time), and gender and life-stage differences all send messages. These premises do not make receivers' tasks any easier, especially given that they operate at particularly low levels of awareness and frequently are overlooked as we analyze persuasion. That's probably because they are processed in the peripheral channel, where we don't really give them much analysis. You will have to train yourself to be more sensitive to nonverbal elements in the persuasive process, not only so you can skillfully use these channels in your own communication, but, more importantly, so you can more accurately decode the real meaning of the messages aimed at you every day.

QUESTIONS FOR FURTHER THOUGHT

1. What are some of the facial expressions you find easiest to identify? Which are most difficult?

2. What is kinesics? Give some examples, and explain how and what they communicate.

3. Which of your friends uses gestures most effectively? What does he or she do that makes the gestures so effective?

4. What are some examples of how physical appearance sends messages in your world? What are some examples of how physical appearance identifies a contemporary musical artist or group?

5. With what artifacts do you surround yourself? What do they mean to you? (Some students have reported that the first thing they do after unpacking for dormitory living is to purchase "conversation pieces" or artifacts that symbolize themselves.) What about your roommate? What artifacts does he or she use? What do they symbolize about him or her? What about your family members' artifacts?

6. How often do you touch others? Try to increase the number of touches you use, and observe the responses of others. Does the increase have any effect? If so, what?

7. What are some examples of how chronemics operates in your life—on campus, in the dorm, in the classroom, and at home?

8. What are some of the gender differences in nonverbal communication as they appear in contemporary advertising?

9. What is the predominant dialect where you live? Are there any other dialects that you can identify in your community? What effects do they have on people's attitudes and behaviors?

10. What is "blocking" behavior? Give examples from your everyday life.

 For online activities, go to the Web site for this book at http://communication.wadsworth.com/larson.

PART III

✳

Applications
of Persuasive Premises

I n Part I, we examined some of the definitions of persuasion and the underlying
theoretical foundations for persuasion, with a special emphasis on language. We
focused on receivers and noted how they could use a knowledge of persuasion to
critically process the persuasion that bombards us every day. In Part II, we explored
sources for the various premises that persuaders use to develop their pitches. These
are the unstated but powerful first premises in the enthymeme, a form of argument
in which persuadees provide a missing part (usually a major premise), thereby participating in their own persuasion.

In Part III, we look at applications of these theories and audience-held premises in
a variety of contexts. We maintain the receiver focus, always asking how our
analyses of these applications can assist us to make critical judgments about
whether to buy, elect, join, quit, give, believe in, or support.

Chapter 11 explores a familiar application, the persuasive campaign or movement
—a series of messages designed to lead receivers to specific ends. Chapter 12 focuses on the source of persuasion and discusses how to become a persuader. In addition to helping you persuade others, what you learn enables you to critically
process the persuasive messages aimed at you. Knowing what kind of proof or organization a persuader uses helps you judge the validity of his or her message.

In Chapter 13, we explore the most dominant channels for persuasive messages: the mass media. Mass-mediated messages range from the brief but influential TV or radio commercial to more extensive advertisements, speeches, documentaries, and news reports. We will discover that the media of our time may be the determining factor in deciding which problems we, as a culture, should concentrate on. In some cases, media take over the role of the family or parent in shaping values.

Finally, Chapter 14 investigates a particular form of persuasion—print and electronic advertising—and discusses how they have come to dominate contemporary American society.

11

✹

The Persuasive Campaign or Movement

For many years, the study of persuasion focused mainly on the public speech and the "single-shot" or "hypodermic needle" perspective on persuasion. As a result, persuaders, researchers, students, and teachers overlooked the impact of artistically coordinated multiple messages that ultimately lead to product adoption, voting decisions, or support for movements. The single-shot or hypodermic needle model placed a receiver at a certain position—favorable or unfavorable—on an issue prior to an "injection" or "shot" of persuasion. Following the persuasion, the researcher either speculated about or tried to statistically measure any changes that might have happened to the receiver. This makes for simple models for persuasion, but it hardly matches reality. After all, it is difficult to name an instance in which a single persuasive message changed the outcome of events. Of course, it has happened. Shakespeare (relying on the historical "facts" set down by Plutarch) dramatized the funeral oration given by Marc Antony. The speech supposedly turned the Roman crowd from an anti-Caesar to a pro-Caesar sentiment, which resulted in the

stoning and deaths of Brutus, his coconspirators Casius and Casca, and the families of all three men. But such occurrences are rare indeed.

Most persuasion is incremental and cumulative. We change our attitudes and opinions a bit at a time in response to message bits in both the peripheral and central information-processing routes of the elaboration likelihood model. For instance, if you were considering whether to buy a digital camcorder, or to vote for a candidate for office, or to give money to a charity, or to join a cause, the decision would not be instantaneous. Rather, it would be the result of a series of messages. Some would be processed in the peripheral path—the advertisement for the camcorder, the candidate's appearance, your history with the particular charity, or the stirring words of the leader of the movement or cause.

Until the 1990s, marketing, advertising, and public relations campaigns were dominated by the single-shot approach. The ad campaign and the public relations campaign were both seen as periods of time when messages were being sent, but it was still assumed that a single ad or news release could sell a product, candidate, or cause. Then a new term came into vogue—integrated marketing communication (IMC)—which refers to more carefully coordinated activities of marketing, advertising, public relations, sales promotion, packaging, personal selling, Web sites, branding, brand contacts, and event staging. Each element works with the others and leads to synergies that make the whole far greater than the sum of the parts. All these elements were part of many successful campaigns, but now theory has caught up with practice and dramatically altered the marketing world.

For a long time, political scientists also ignored the communication dimensions of political campaigns, with the possible exception of research on campaign financing and public opinion polling. They remained focused on the nature and structure of government and ignored "politics." Meanwhile, most of the research done on campaigns occurred in advertising or marketing departments and was proprietary. In other words, it belonged to the client, candidate, or cause leader, who naturally were reluctant to make it public. The fact that candidates used focus groups to determine how to, say, comb their hair was best kept secret. Remember the example of Elizabeth Dole changing her form of dress and mode of transportation when she shifted from a GOP women's luncheon audience to a college campus one? No doubt, her campaign committee wished those changes hadn't seen the light of day.

Until the first edition of this book, no text on persuasion even had a chapter on campaigns. Since then, campaign and movement theory has come a long way, and the literature on campaigns, especially political campaigns and mass movements, is extensive. Most persuasion textbooks now have sections and even chapters devoted to campaigns and social movements. And this is appropriate, given that the persuasive campaign is probably the most prevalent form of persuasion today. In this chapter, we look at three general types of persuasive campaigns: product oriented, person or candidate oriented, and idea or ideologically oriented. Of course, there are other types of campaigns but these three categories account for the bulk of persuasive campaigns to which we are exposed.

Of course, a single chapter can't possibly cover all there is to say about persuasive campaigns. All that can be hoped for is that you become more aware of campaign persuasion as you receive it and as you produce it. Yes, as you produce it, because as an individual you wage your own persuasive campaigns—for the purchase of a new piece of technology, for a desired change in the behavior of someone you know or love, on behalf of some organization, or on other public and interpersonal issues.

We shouldn't underestimate the impact of advancing technology in computers, the Internet, digital audio, video, and graphics on campaigners' ability to convey powerfully persuasive messages. Consider what a changed world we face in the new millennium. The number of persuasive campaigns will surely increase, and so will their sophistication. With satellite and cable television, direct marketing, and Internet options increasing, costs for media time will drop, and market segmentation will become much easier to accomplish. In fact, market segmentation experts predict that within the foreseeable future segmentation will become so precise that our individual needs, circumstances, patterns, and idiosyncrasies can be targeted and advertising tailored so specifically that each of us becomes a segment of one person. In fact, the theme of the 2002 Direct Marketing Conference was "One-to-One."

To learn more about how sophisticated market segmentation has become, access InfoTrac College Edition, and enter the words "market segmentation" in the subject search engine. Browse a few of the periodical items, and then go to the related subjects listing and select "students as consumers." Finally, go to the related subjects option, where you will find research about yourself under "college students as consumers."

CAMPAIGNS AS SYSTEMATIC COMMUNICATION

Campaigns and mass movements are classic examples of communication systems at work. The first communication system discussed in this text was

Shannon and Weaver's SMCR model, which includes a feedback loop (see Figure 1.3). This model is a good example of a communication system because it produces a predictable flow of symbolic information and a means of evaluating the success or failure of the attempted communication. All communication systems have some means of feedback or evaluation. In campaigns, the systematic and predictable flow of persuasive information includes all the auditory and visual symbols—both verbal and nonverbal. Campaign communication consists of words printed on a sign, page, or screen; graphics, typeface, pictures, symbols, or scenes in an ad; auditory words; and auditory "pictures" created by music, words, sound effects, and silence. Campaigns thus represent complex and rather challenging sets of messages for persuadees to process.

An example of a visual symbol within the systematic flow of campaign information comes from the initial ad campaign for the Infiniti automobile. The vehicle was never actually shown in the campaign. Instead, the advertiser used various visual symbols of the concept of infinity—a flock of geese migrating or rushing water in a stream, accompanied by classical music. Then the scene faded to the word "Infiniti" printed on the screen—nothing else. Understandably, the campaign created a lot of curiosity related to the unveiling of the first models. An example of a nonverbal but auditory symbol might be the sound of crickets in a radio drama to signify that it is night.

In both cases, the systematic flow and evaluation of persuasive information had measurable effects on either the audience or the environment. In most integrated campaigns, teams of experts carefully research their target audience. Using the research, they plan campaign messages in such formats as press releases, print and electronic ads, and Web pages, painstakingly testing them at each stage in their development. Using research on the audiences of various media, the teams schedule time or space in magazines, newspapers, and radio and TV networks and stations. When the nationwide "rollout" of the campaign finally takes place, its systematic nature shifts to an evaluation mode using sophisticated polling techniques, focus groups, and other means of measuring the effect of the campaign. The results

of the evaluation are then fed back to the campaign staff, and midflight corrections are made, tested, tried, and evaluated in an ongoing process that doesn't cease until long after the campaign is over.

The rule of thumb in advertising agencies is that it takes at least three exposures for an ad to create brand awareness. The first exposure passes by almost unnoticed by consumers. The second exposure alerts consumers to the existence of the product and triggers their unconscious memories of the first exposure. It also creates curiosity about the product. If it is well designed and timed, the third exposure either prompts a preexisting need for the product or begins to create a new need for the product. The consumer, voter, donor, or joiner now is aware of the product, candidate, or cause, and if the campaign is properly orchestrated, she or he will begin to evaluate the appeal and may ultimately buy, vote, donate, or join. The final push may come from subsequent ads, news stories, coupons, staged events, packaging, or special promotions.

CAMPAIGNS VERSUS SINGLE-SHOT PERSUASIVE MESSAGES

How do campaigns differ from other kinds of persuasion? Campaigns are not merely series of messages sent to audiences over time about some product, candidate, or cause—though they once were thought of that way. For example, political campaigns used to start on Labor Day and end on election day. Now they might begin years in advance of election day. Nor are campaigns debates over specific issues, though they may employ the debate format as a means of communication. Campaigns differ from single shots of persuasion or from "collections" of persuasive messages delivered over time in several ways:

- Campaigns systematically create "positions" in audience members' minds for the product, candidate, or idea.

- Campaigns are intentionally designed to develop over time; that is, they are composed of stages for getting the audience's attention, preparing the audience for action, and, finally, calling the audience to action.

- Campaigns dramatize the product, candidate, idea, or ideology for the audience, inviting members to participate in real or symbolic ways with the campaign and its goal(s).

- Campaigns deliberately use a multitude of sophisticated communication technologies to reach target prospects, voters, or joiners in systematic ways.

Starting in the late 1980s, the computer became increasingly capable of handling large amounts of information about potential voters, customers, donors, and joiners. In some cases, this capability dovetailed with the newly emerging technology of the Universal Product Code bars imprinted on packages and with newly developing research and advanced statistical techniques. These technological advances led to what is called "data-based marketing" whereby the seller tries to capture as much information about customers as possible and updates it regularly. As noted previously, another result was the rise of integrated marketing communication (IMC), in which all elements in selling something are coordinated, including packaging, advertising, public relations, trade promotions, events, consumer sales promotions, personal selling, and even the costumes worn by store clerks. And academic programs in advertising and public relations began to migrate in unprecedented numbers from departments of marketing and journalism to departments or colleges of communication, where more than 60 percent of advertising and public relations courses now are taught.

To learn more about IMC, access InfoTrac College Edition, and enter the words "integrated marketing" in the search engine. Look at some of the articles that were included in the special 1997 issue of the *Journal of Advertising Research*. The entire issue was devoted to the topic.

Following movements or campaigns is like watching a TV series. Although the episodes can stand alone (each has its own beginning, middle, and end), they rely on one another to form a collage of messages that meld together until an entire image or picture of the campaign is perceived and stored in the minds of the consumer, voter, or joiner. If it is well designed, large segments of the population will have been exposed to enough "episodes" that a similar image of the product, candidate, or idea emerges by the end of the campaign.

TYPES OF CAMPAIGNS

As noted earlier, three kinds of movements or campaigns predominate: (1) the product-oriented advertising campaign, (2) the politically oriented campaign for office, and (3) the ideological, or cause-oriented, campaign (sometimes called a mass or social movement).

These three campaign types have many similarities. For instance, several high-profile individuals can be prominent in both the second and third types. However, the person-oriented political campaign centers on the individual's name. The focus of such campaigns may be on electing someone to office, freeing someone from prison, or raising enough money to pay for someone's organ transplant. The slogan might feature a candidate's name—"Be Sure to Vote for John Countryman" —or it may feature a person needing financial support—"Dollars for Jimmy, Our County's Liver Transplant Candidate." In issue- or "cause"-oriented campaigns, in contrast, the slogan or theme always features the cause—"Guns don't kill. People kill."

Often, the kinds of campaigns overlap, making it difficult to draw precise distinctions among them. A good example is Jesse Jackson's 1988 campaign for the Democratic Party nomination for president, in which he promoted the idea of establishing a "rainbow coalition" of the poor, minorities, and the underprivileged to influence government. Thus, an idea-oriented subsidiary campaign was embedded in his political campaign.

GOALS, STRATEGIES, AND TACTICS IN PRODUCT, PERSON, AND IDEOLOGICAL CAMPAIGNS

The successful campaign is not a case of "salesmanship in print," as it has sometimes been defined. Campaigns don't "sell" anything. Instead, they deliver a prospective consumer, voter, or joiner to the point of sale, the voting booth, or the headquarters of the good cause. And if the campaign is to succeed, it must educate and prepare the consumer, voter, or joiner to be ready to take action—be it purchasing, voting, or joining/donating behavior. To accomplish this task, campaigns must (1) zero in on well-defined goals, (2) create appropriate strategies to accomplish the goals, and then (3) use various tactics to put the strategy into action.

This pattern of goals/strategies/tactics applies to advertising and election campaigns and to campaigns for causes or ideologies. For example, the advertising agency for Claussen's pickles, in conjunction with the manufacturer, might set as a goal to "increase sales in specified test markets by 10 percent in the fourth quarter of the year." The campaign staff and the manager then work out a promising strategy. In the case of Claussen's, one actual strategy was to use television spot advertisements to emphasize the unique feature of the brand: It is refrigerated rather than cooked. The benefit to the consumer is that Claussen's pickles are crisper and crunchier than the competition's. The product had previously been advertised only in print media—not a very effective way to communicate crispness or crunchiness. As a result, Claussen's hadn't been successful in communicating this brand benefit. To implement the strategy, the agency used the tactic of comparative advertising, matching Claussen's against the main competition, Vlasic's, in TV spots. The agency prepared several ads in which the competitor's cooked pickle was bent in half without breaking, whereas Claussen's pickle couldn't be bent without snapping in two, giving off a spray of brine and cucumber.

The goal of any primary election campaign is to win the party's nomination from opposing candidates. A strategy for achieving this goal might be to ignore the opposition, taking the high road on the issues and simply letting them attack one another. A tactic for implementing the strategy might be to stage a debate against several empty chairs, with each labeled with the name of one of the opponents.

A church music committee had as a goal to raise $100,000 to rebuild a fifty-year-old pipe organ. Their strategy was to educate the congregation about the wisdom of rebuilding a pipe organ instead of purchasing a new electric one and to challenge the congregation's sense of pride. The tactics included several presentations during services plus postservice demonstrations of the difference in sound between a pipe organ and an electric one. Further, the music committee offered individual members of the congregation the opportunity to "buy" or sponsor variously priced parts of the organ (a rank of pipes, an octave of pipes, the console, the keyboard, the high-speed motor, and so on). A final tactic was to sell the pipes that were being replaced, for a nominal sum. They made decorative conversation pieces to hang on members' walls and raised some cash at the same time.

As we have noted, product, person, and ideological cause campaigns are similar in some ways and quite different in others. These similarities and differences are highlighted in the following survey of models or explanations for successful and unsuccessful campaigns. In some cases, only one or a few elements of the model apply to more than one of the types of campaigns. Your task is to use these models (or subelements of the models) to help you make decisions about whether to make a purchase, cast a vote, or join/support a cause or ideology.

DEVELOPMENTAL STAGES OF SUCCESSFUL CAMPAIGNS

All three types of campaigns are developmental—they pass through a series of predictable stages as they grow and mature and adapt to audience feedback, the competition, the issues, and the demands of the persuasive situation. One campaign goal of a

FIGURE 11.1 Many devices are used to gain product, person, or idea identification in campaigns. Logos such as this one are one kind of device. Why is the winged foot of Mercury used? What does it communicate? Why put it between "GOOD" and "YEAR"? Answers to these questions help explain how product image or identification develops.

(Used by permission of the Goodyear Tire and Rubber Company.)

new product, candidate, or idea is to establish itself in the audience's consciousness. A variety of strategies can be used to accomplish this identification. For instance, the product maker could give out free samples; the candidate could announce his or her candidacy at a press conference; and advocates could stage a dramatic protest in some highly symbolic location. This initial stage might succeed or fail, but no matter what the outcome, the campaigner learns about the audience. Perhaps the customers seem to be buying the brand because of its warranty, and not its price. Maybe the voters don't want to hear much about increasing taxes on gasoline but do respond to the issue of deficit reduction. And some animal rights supporters may respond to some issues but not others. So, in all three types of campaigns, strategies are tried and kept, altered, or dropped as the campaign develops.

The Yale Five-Stage Developmental Model

Most campaigns pass through at least some of the stages of a model developed by researchers at Yale University (Binder, 1971). Although the model was originally used in the international political context, it is highly applicable to product, person, and ideological campaigns in other contexts as well. The five functional stages noted by the researchers are identification (including but not limited to name identification), legitimacy, participation (real and symbolic), penetration, and distribution.

Identification. As we've briefly noted, one thing all campaigns must do is develop an identity in the minds of consumers, voters, and potential converts or donors. Many products and causes use a graphic symbol or logotype to create identification in the audience's mind. For example, in the well-established logo of the Goodyear Tire and Rubber Company, shown in Figure 11.1, the winged foot of Mercury is inserted between the two syllables of "Goodyear," probably to suggest that the company's products are swift and safe. Another well-known product logo is McDonald's parabolic Golden Arches, but what they are supposed to communicate is less obvious. Some have suggested that they signify shelter, structural strength, and home. Freudians liken them to female breasts, thus making them a mother symbol. And, of course, there are those who say they signify . . . golden arches! The lowercase "e" used to identify the environmental movement was inserted inside the capital "C" to create the logo of Commonwealth Edison electric company, suggesting that the company is environmentally conscientious, a good identification for an energy monopoly. A series of arrows in a triangle with the point of each arrow bent to point at the next arrow is the logo for any kind of recycling and is used by many cause campaigners. And you will notice hundreds of other logotypes that are supposed to communicate something about the product or cause.

The name associated with the product, candidate, or cause is closely related to the logo in creat-

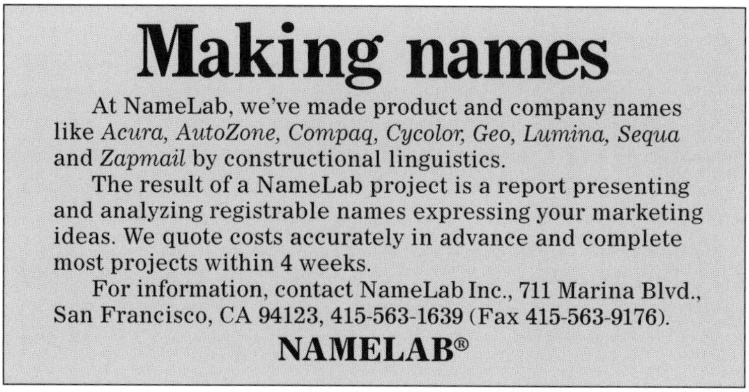

Making names

At NameLab, we've made product and company names like *Acura, AutoZone, Compaq, Cycolor, Geo, Lumina, Sequa* and *Zapmail* by constructional linguistics.

The result of a NameLab project is a report presenting and analyzing registrable names expressing your marketing ideas. We quote costs accurately in advance and complete most projects within 4 weeks.

For information, contact NameLab Inc., 711 Marina Blvd., San Francisco, CA 94123, 415-563-1639 (Fax 415-563-9176).

NAMELAB®

FIGURE 11.2 The name of a product, political entity, or cause is part of the mix of factors that create identification for the campaigner.

(Used by permission of NameLab.)

ing identification. For example, the name of the magazine *Newsweek* suggests that it contains the news of the past week, and the name of Cadillac's "Escalade" SUV is probably meant to suggest good taste, classiness, and European distinction. The name of the fast-food franchise Burger King also communicates something about the quality of the food you will find there—it will be "fit for a king." Some candidates for office label themselves "The People's Candidate" or a similar term to create identification. In the abortion controversy, anti-abortion advocates selected a particularly strategic label—"pro-life"—for their cause, and the label is persuasive. It suggests that advocates are in favor of life—something everyone could agree with. It also implies that opponents of the movement are either "anti-life" or "pro-death," neither of which is very positive. Upstaged by the "pro-life" label, abortion rights advocates had to settle for the less effective "pro-choice."

Try this experiment to demonstrate the potency of a good name. Ask a sample of people to name three brands of turkey that are available for Thanksgiving dinner. The name "Butterball" will be on everyone's list while competitors' names will not come up as consistently, if at all. Then ask them what the key benefit of a Butterball turkey is, and they will tell you that it is the moistest turkey on the market. Its name is the key to this

perception. And there are other examples of the persuasive power of the name selected for a product, political organization, or cause. Figure 11.2 shows an ad for NameLab, a company that designs and tests various names to help organizations establish an identity for a product, political entity, or cause.

Another device that helps identify a product, candidate, or cause is color coding. The campaigner picks a color or colors and consistently uses them in packaging, in advertising, on letterheads, and perhaps in uniforms. For instance, United Parcel Service carriers wear dark brown uniforms, and their trucks are painted dark brown. Political candidates usually select some combination of red, white, and blue. Camouflage and drab olive green are associated with the "Be All You Can Be—In the Army" campaign. And Century 21 real estate agents wear gold blazers. Further identification can be achieved by using the same color and typeface in all ads, signs, buttons, and bumper stickers. The successful "Stop ERA" movement to defeat the Equal Rights Amendment adopted the color red, probably to associate with its connotations of "Danger" and "Stop!" among others.

Slogans also help promote identification and frequently become part of our cultural heritage if they are catchy enough. "Folgers—The Mountain Grown Coffee," "When You Care Enough to Send the Very Best," "You're in Good Hands with All-state," "We Try Harder," and "Smart. Very Smart" are all good examples.

Consider how coordinated and successful the campaign for State Farm Insurance Company has been over the years. Their slogan and jingle—"Like a Good Neighbor, State Farm Is There"—is the central theme from which all other communication flows. Agents are urged to live in the community they service, join civic organizations in those communities, and be visible and active in them. They are instructed to include not only the slogan but their pictures in all advertising. They are told to write congratulatory cards to customers and members of their families on birthdays, graduations, and other important days. The agents (or their designees) must be available by phone 24/7. National advertising usually includes a feature on a specific agent with testimonials from his or her customers telling how State Farm was there when needed. The campaign has wiped out the former image of the company as a heartless corporate giant that canceled auto policies when a driver had an accident, grew old, or got more than two traffic tickets.

Finally, jingles, uniforms, salutes, and all sorts of campaign paraphernalia (balloons, buttons, hats, and so on) can help establish name and purpose identification. Logos, slogans, jingles, color codes, and other identification-producing devices are then communicated to the target market or audience using a variety of media ranging from simple signs, to electronic spot advertisements, to sophisticated home pages on the Web.

Legitimacy. The second functional stage entails the establishment of legitimacy. Candidates usually achieve this by gaining the party endorsement or by winning primary election battles. Legitimacy can be thought of as a power base. Candidates might choose to demonstrate how power works using rallies, appearing with well-known supporters (who are usually celebrities), or being photographed in front of some national symbol of legitimacy, such as the U.S. Capitol building, the Lincoln Memorial, or the White House. In political campaigns, incumbents have automatic legitimacy (unless they have bumbled and botched the job), so challengers have a

major task. They must try to discredit the legitimacy of the incumbent and develop their own. Further, they might have to do this while running in primary elections against fellow party members who are also emphasizing the shortcomings of the incumbent. A favorite tactic is getting endorsed by local newspapers, politicians, and well-known and respected citizens. Another is to list their experience in government or community groups (school or library boards, community-oriented task forces and so on), their church affiliations, their family accomplishments, and so on. Remember our old friend "ethos" and its elements? Expertise, sincerity, and activity/charisma are all elements that the candidate emphasizes when trying to establish legitimacy.

Mudslinging in political campaigns usually represents an attempt to destroy another candidate's legitimacy. For example, a challenger charges that the incumbent gave government contracts to friends, whereupon the incumbent points out the nasty tactics of the challenger. The real question is which candidate the voters will consider the most legitimate.

Products can demonstrate legitimacy in several ways. One way, of course, is to show the product in use. Historically, patent-medicine shows used the testimony of persons who swore that they had been cured using the product. More recently, model Cindy Crawford symbolized the legitimacy of the "New Generation" of Pepsi drinkers, and professional athletes demonstrate the legitimacy of various shoes; they act as testimonials for the product. Established endorsements can also help products demonstrate legitimacy—the Underwriter's Laboratory seal of approval is an example, as is the Good Housekeeping seal. Demonstrations can create legitimacy by showing how effective the product is at solving consumers' problems. Brands can also develop legitimacy by associating themselves with good causes, such as by sponsoring community events (see Figure 11.3).

In ideological campaigns, large numbers of participants or amounts of money are used to demonstrate legitimacy. Such tactics as newspaper ads with the names of known supporters who endorse the movement can establish legitimacy. Large numbers of angry citizens show up at a council meeting and

She makes it look effortless.
Reflecting the thousands of hours she's practiced and honed her skills, until every muscle responds in unison to the command for perfection. It is this dedication, this courage to face competition boldly and without compromise, that has inspired Phillips Petroleum to proudly sponsor United States Swimming since 1973.

And we'll be national sponsor for years to come. Because we believe that with every leap of grace and form, we are watching the future of our nation take shape.

PHILLIPS PETROLEUM COMPANY

FIGURE 11.3 Phillips Petroleum established its legitimacy by sponsoring U.S. Olympic teams.

(Reprinted by permission of the Phillips Petroleum Company.)

demonstrate their displeasure. In one high school, a group of students who objected to the school lunch program demonstrated the legitimacy of their movement by using nonviolent protest tactics. One day, several hundred students boycotted lunch, leaving the school with tons of leftovers. The next day, all students bought the hot lunch, leaving the school short of supplies. The following day, everyone paid with a large bill, running the cashiers out of change. The next day, they paid in pennies, creating havoc in the checkout lines as cashiers counted each cent. On the fifth day, school officials negotiated with student representatives about improving the lunch program.

Participation. The legitimacy stage of campaigns usually blends so smoothly with the participation stage that it is almost impossible to tell when one ends and the next begins. In the legitimacy stage, the participants are known supporters. In the participation stage, the leaders seek to involve previously uncommitted persons. There are many techniques for doing this. Some involve effort by participants; others require minimal or only symbolic participation.

The distributors and users of products participate in the use of and profit from the products. In some instances, stores are paid to allow some of their space to be used for special displays of soaps, wines, and so forth. Dealers may get an extra discount for pushing certain products. Dealers also are urged to participate in contests to win prizes and trips by increasing monthly sales. They are given "dealer loaders," which are valuable display containers that they can keep for their own personal use after the campaign is finished (such as wheelbarrows or garden carts in which to display the brand). And both dealers and customers can "earn" prized items such as an NBA Championship warm-up jacket with the logo of the favorite team. Customer rebates are another form of participation. The customer has to fill out the rebate form and mail it in with the receipt. All these activities are forms of participation in order to "share" the profits. All these items encourage real and symbolic participation with the brand to the point that some of them even advertise the brand (for example, T-shirts,

caps, or other clothing with the brand name imprinted on them).

Coupon offers are one way to promote participation. Clipping coupons represents a kind of symbolic purchase or "behavioral intention," to use a term discussed in an earlier chapter. Some coupon offers are made to product users, who buy and use the product and receive money or gifts. Various brands provide merchandise (T-shirts, caps, coolers, and so on) imprinted with the logo, slogan, or name of the brand, again producing both walking advertisements and audience participation with the brand. Getting a free sample is another way to prompt participation.

A movement may urge participation in real or symbolic ways. People might be asked to wear armbands or badges, to yell slogans at rallies, or to put signs on their lawns or bumper stickers on their cars. Candidates running for student body president may ask others to canvass dormitory floors or student groups. This kind of activity gets people involved in the campaign or movement and guarantees further active support. People who put bumper stickers on their cars are more likely to show up at the polls and will usually vote for the name on the sticker. Movements ask supporters to do something, even if it is only symbolic. Supporters can march, hold a vigil, or salute. The effect of these activities is to increase commitment to the cause.

As new technologies develop, they are used to encourage participation. Examples include holograms and "scratch and sniff" perfume strips in magazine ads. Seagram's ads often have a supposedly "subliminal" message embedded in them, and readers are told where in the ad the message is located, thus prompting participation with the ad. (See Chapter 14 for examples.) Photographic enhancement or alteration, such as the new digitally enhanced 3-D "moving" signs by Kodak, also increases audience participation. Other signs, mousepads, and so on depict several images that shift and move while customers walk around the sign or shift the mousepad, altering the line of sight, which also increases audience participation. And we will surely see participation on the Web. Of course, there are always the old reliable techniques for prompting participation—giving free samples, offering trial use of the product, getting people to canvass their precinct on behalf of the candidate, or enlisting people to sign a petition supporting the ideological campaign or good cause. All these devices are designed to get the audience involved with the product, candidate, or cause, as even symbolic behavior represents both commitment and participation. This fits nicely with the idea of persuasion as a process of "cocreation," as discussed in Chapter 1. As Figure 11.4 demonstrates, participation can include "playing" with the ad.

Penetration. The penetration stage can be thought of as the point at which a person, product, or idea has "made it" in the market; that is, it has earned a meaningful share of the market, electorate, or constituency. For products, gaining a significant share of the market is enough to achieve the penetration stage. Crest and Gleem dominated the toothpaste market for years by offering fluoridation as a product feature and decay prevention as the resulting product benefit. Then new toothpastes such as MacLeans, Pearl Drops, and others offered the benefits of whiteness and sexiness in place of decay prevention, thus segmenting and penetrating the market. This resulted in several other "me-too" toothpaste campaigns that offered the whiteness and sexiness benefits, while both Gleem and Crest lost sales.

Chrysler's innovations enabled it to penetrate the auto market, with front-wheel drive in 1980, the minivan in 1984, and the seven-year/70,000-mile warranty in 1988. Then came the four-passenger Dodge Ram pickup, new versions of the four-wheel-drive SUV, a second side door for passengers, and passenger airbags in the 1990s. Other innovations such as the return of the convertible were to follow. The share of the market that these innovations captured was significant enough to force the competition to follow suit; front-wheel-drive cars, minivans, extended warranties, and convertibles were being marketed by several other automobile manufacturers by the mid-1990s. A successful penetration stage in campaigns for products usually prompts a response from the competition. You can be fairly certain that the competition

will begin to market their own versions of the newly dominant innovation.

In presidential politics, especially early in the primaries, candidates don't have to win the most delegates to establish penetration. Running third might be enough. Other indications of political penetration include higher ratings in public opinion polls, increases in the number and size of financial contributions, increases in the number of persons volunteering to help, and larger crowds showing up for campaign events. Communication scholar T. A. Borchers (2001) reports that one of the keys to Jesse Ventura's winning the Minnesota governorship in 1998 was his use of email and his Web site to turn out large crowds on short notice—for example, seven hundred in the small town of Willmar within an hour. Just as in product campaigns, penetration of the market in political campaigns usually prompts a response from the competition, or the other candidates in the race.

In ideology-oriented campaigns, penetration is achieved when those in power find that they are hearing about a campaign often enough or when it is "costing" them a lot. This might happen when legislators are barraged by mail or have to repeatedly answer questions about the campaign topic at news conferences. Other indicators of penetration in these campaigns include rally crowds that are large enough to seriously inconvenience those supporting the status quo, an increase in the number of persons joining the cause, increased financial and volunteer support, and significant responses from the competition.

Distribution. In the fifth and final stage of development—distribution—the campaign or movement succeeds and becomes institutionalized. Having achieved the control, votes, or market share they sought, the campaign or movement leaders must now live up to their promises in some way. They must signal their supporters or customers that social change is going to occur or that things like rebates and frequent user points will be forthcoming. Typical actions in movement campaigns involve the designation of subgroups of the campaign staff or the movement's leadership to positions of power with tasks to complete. These tasks fit with the

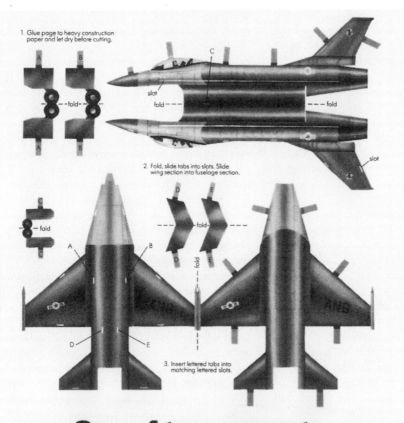

FIGURE 11.4 This ad for the Air National Guard encourages real, not symbolic, participation by cutting out the model F-16 and gluing it together or by joining the Air National Guard.

(Courtesy Air National Guard.)

promises made in the campaign and with the goals of the movement. Patronage jobs are used to distribute the "winnings" achieved in the campaign. The penetration stage does not always occur in product campaigns. However, devices such as rebates, money-back coupons, and incentives to store owners (such as discounts, prizes for most sales, and premiums or other gifts) are some of the kinds of distribution that we see in product campaigns.

One problem with ideology-oriented campaigns and, to some degree, political campaigns is that the persuaders don't always live up to their promises. For example, Fidel Castro never enacted the land reforms that he promised once the Cuban Revolution was over. The populace then becomes cynical about the movement or the leaders. This is how many people come to believe that all politicians are crooks. As Cicero put it, "Politicians are not born; they are excreted."

Product-Focused Models

Although some campaign models can be used to describe all three types of campaign, other models are more focused on one of them. Let's examine several models that are more appropriate for and focused on product-oriented campaigns.

The Hierarchy of Effects Model. Advertising and marketing experts Robert Lavidge and Gary Steiner (1961) suggested a model that for many decades has been the basis for setting goals in many marketing departments and advertising agencies. It is a developmental model in that it assumes that potential customers must pass through a series of stages in roughly sequential order, from initial awareness to ultimate purchase. Their hierarchy of effects model has subsequently been altered and adapted by various theorists, but it remains as valid today as when first suggested (Schultz & Barnes, 1991). The model comprises seven distinct stages or phases, and various communication, advertising, research, and promotional strategies and techniques can be used at each stage.

At the bottom of the hierarchy, consumers are completely unaware of the product, brand, or service being promoted or of the benefits being prom-

ised. As a result, the persuader's first task is to learn about consumers' current patterns of use of similar products, brands, or services before spending time or money on advertising. So consumer research precedes the entire campaign and is the first step the advertiser takes, using focus groups, surveys, and other research methods. For example, suppose the makers of Oreo cookies are considering adding a new product to the Oreo and Double Stuffs brand family but wonder what the consumer response might be to a third Oreo cookie. They do research using focus groups and observe people eating the regular Oreos and the Double Stuffs. A pattern emerges—many people start eating the Oreo or the Double Stuff by splitting the cookie in half and eating the filling, then they eat the chocolate portion —behavior that had originally inspired Double Stuffs (Fortini-Campbell, 1992). Consumer attitude tests reveal that the filling is rated as the "best" part of Oreos and Double Stuffs and that a cookie with a different-flavored filling would sell. Voilà! The Double Chocolate Stuff by Oreo.

Now, with a "consumer-driven" product to promote, the hierarchy of effects model suggests that the persuader move on to creating consumer awareness of the product and developing consumer knowledge about it. The advertiser can begin to create product or brand awareness in a variety of ways. For example, the product/brand gets a name. The agency creates a slogan and jingle, and public relations specialists send out press releases inviting the media to the premiere taste-testing press conference. Then "teaser" ads communicate that "Double Chocolate Stuff is coming soon! Watch for it on your grocer's shelves!" Descriptive copy is prepared, and various promotional devices are used (free samples, events, coupons, and so on). Researchers continue testing brand awareness, and as the awareness stage merges with the next step in the model—developing knowledge—the advertiser informs and "teaches" consumers about the product or brand using print, electronic, and direct-marketing techniques. Researchers then test consumers' knowledge level using surveys, mall intercepts, and unaided and aided recall.

In the fourth and fifth steps—liking and preferring—the advertiser uses image ads that communicate, say, status and glamour as being associated with the product or brand. Spokespersons appear and tell why they like and prefer the brand. If the brand has competition, the advertiser might use comparative ads to demonstrate how Double Chocolate Stuffs are better than the competing cookies. Consumers are now aware of the product/brand and have reason to like and even prefer it. The only task remaining is to convince them to purchase the brand and try it.

One of the important goals of many persuasive campaigns is to "induce trial," and it is in the final two stages of the hierarchy—conviction and ultimate purchase—that this goal is accomplished. Researchers might measure "intention to purchase" among potential consumers to determine whether they are convinced that they want to try Double Chocolate Stuffs and merely need that final nudge to store shelves. Marketers encourage retailers to feature the product/brand in retail advertising. Testimonial ads are continued in the hope that conviction will increase if consumers become confident that the testimonial is sincere. Price appeals are usually made during this stage (two for the price of one, cents-off coupons with a tight expiration date, cross-couponing with another product), as are "last-chance" offers. This is the time to prepare and distribute promotional materials such as in-store coupons, free end-of-aisle displays for retailers, shelf or shopping cart signs, premiums, and in-store samples. A combination of these tactics should not only deliver prospects to the retail outlet but also prompt them to make that first purchase. Repeat purchase and ultimate brand loyalty now become the focus of the advertising/promotion activities, using on-package coupons, brand image advertising, and special prices to induce continued use of the brand. Lavidge and Steiner's hierarchy of effects model is but one of several models that help us to understand the goals, strategies, and tactics of product-oriented campaigns. Let's examine some others.

The Positioning Model. In their best-selling book *Positioning: The Battle for Your Mind,* marketing experts Jack Trout and Al Ries (1986) offer their positioning model as a way to attract prospects to a campaign. The model begins with the premise that consumers are swamped with information and can

maintain "top of mind" awareness of only a few brands in a product category. Research has shown that, depending on the complexity of the product, consumers can usually remember only five to nine brands. The campaign's goal is to establish such a level of awareness for the brand in prospects' consciousness. Trout and Ries advise searching for unoccupied niches in the marketplace and then positioning the brand in that psychological space. These niches and appeals to them are almost always processed in the peripheral information-processing channel of the ELM. Here are some ways to position a brand in the marketplace.

Be the First. The first brand to appear in a product class has a natural advantage of being the "pioneer" in that class. Lunchables by Oscar Meyer, now a fifteen-year-success product, are such a brand and were initially positioned in "first" niche throughout their introductory and subsequent campaigns. Other snack-pack brands followed, but none could claim pioneer status. Lunchables were subsequently able to offer "line extensions" or "new and improved" versions of the product/brand (for example, "Now new and improved lunchables with Dijon mustard packet and chocolate mint dessert"). (At your age, you may even have been one of the first users of Lunchables and its line extensions.) Similarly, as noted earlier, Chrysler Motors innovated several brand features, so the company was able to position itself and its products as being first.

Be the Best. Consumers repeatedly shop for quality and are usually willing to pay a reasonable price for high-quality brands. In fact, one indicator of quality is price. This niche is filled by the brand that can claim to be the "best" in the product category. As noted earlier, Swift's Butterball turkey, one of the most expensive brands, claims to be best because a full pound of butter is injected into each turkey, resulting in "butter basting" throughout the roasting process. This feature is associated with the benefits of juiciness, moistness, and good taste. The brand name is also fortunate in that it is linked to the feature being promoted and the resulting benefits to the consumer. Not surprisingly, Swift's can ask a premium price for their "best" brand. Further, research has shown that the typical Butterball consumer spends more time in the supermarket and buys more premium accoutrements (cranberry relishes, bakery pies, and so on) than consumers selecting a different brand. Retailers are glad to prominently display the brand. Over the years, several imported car brands have tried to claim the "best" position. At one time, Mercedes-Benz seemed to be the permanent occupant of the position. Later, other existing brands (Jaguar and BMW) and several new brands (Infiniti and Lexus) also claimed to be "best," resulting in a crowded niche. Gold and, later, Platinum credit cards, Rolex watches, and Mont Blanc pens are examples of other brands positioning themselves as being the best on the market.

Be the Least Expensive. Besides shopping for quality, consumers often shop for price, so being able to claim that one's brand is the least expensive in the product category is a definite advantage. Not surprisingly, as a product class becomes crowded, some brands will be offered as the least expensive. A good example can be seen in the burger and cola wars that have typified the fast-food marketplace. Another is Walmart's EDLP (every-day low pricing). Even with high-ticket items such as cars, computers, and camcorders, price wars proliferate. The Geo, the Hyundai, and other brands in the automobile market compete to offer the best value for the price. The introduction of generic branding for such products as napkins, facial tissue, sugar, and flour prompted grocery store chains to come up with their own versions of generic branding. Many service products also claim the "least expensive" slot. The airline industry goes through regular cycles of fare wars, with different carriers claiming to have the lowest fares. More recently, various bank and credit cards have engaged in price wars related to annual fees and low initial finance rates. The least expensive I've seen is zero percent interest rates for the trial period—sometimes more than a year! No doubt we will continue to see price wars as the wholesale and retail business markets become increasingly price competitive.

Be the Most Expensive. Status in relation to others is critical to some people, and one way of demon-

strating status is by buying the most expensive brand on the market. The Visa Gold card could claim that its steep annual fee and high finance rates are worth the highest price in the credit card market because Visa Gold is the most universally accepted form of credit. Coco Chanel, the French clothing designer and perfumer, made it a point to sell the most expensive brand in the marketplace. With most products involving fashion (designer clothes, perfumes, shoes), one or more brands eagerly claim to be the most expensive and hence the best indicator of status.

Tell What You're Not. Another means of positioning a brand is by telling consumers what the brand is not. For example, the makers of Seven-Up, on the brink of bankruptcy at one time, were saved by claiming that the soft drink is the "Uncola." Dr. Pepper imitated this strategy and was also able to capture a portion of the cola market. Claussen pickles claim to be "uncooked" and hence crisper and crunchier. With the recent interest in various health issues, numerous brands claim to be "fat free," which suggests that they will also be low in calories—which is not necessarily the case. Not having artificial ingredients such as dyes is another way to claim "what we're not." And now we see many brands of "clear" products—clear cola, clear dish detergent, and even clear gasoline—to communicate purity.

Position by Gender. Many brands compete by purposely appealing to only one gender, by positioning themselves as the woman's brand or the man's brand. Few right-thinking males would ever smoke Virginia Slims or Eve cigarettes, and few women smoke Camel or Lucky Strike nonfilter cigarettes. One company considered marketing a male version of pantyhose after learning that pro football players and many males who work outdoors wear pantyhose for warmth. Among the company's strategies of positioning by gender were the brand's name (Mach-Hose), testimonials from construction workers and firemen, and "six packs" of hose. Calvin Klein's Obsession for Men and the magazine *Gentleman's Quarterly* are obviously positioned by gender, as is the brand shown in Figure 11.5. A risk

FIGURE 11.5 In this ad, Lincoln Financial promotes its product by appealing to the independent woman, thus positioning Lincoln's services by gender. Considering the increased number of women in the labor force and in various kinds of investment plans, the strategy seems to be a good one.

(Used by permission of the Lincoln Financial Group.)

is involved in offering a brand only for males or only for females, but if the strategy is well executed, a brand can capture a huge segment of the market.

Communication researcher A. N. Valdivia (1997) analyzed product advertising for women's lingerie and discovered that both gender and class position brands. After looking at catalogues for Victoria's Secret and Frederick's of Hollywood, she concluded that Victoria's is targeted at the upper middle class while Frederick's is targeted at the lower middle class. The brand names are just the beginning of the tactics used to achieve this targeting. Victoria's Secret sounds discreet, old-world, and Victorian, whereas Frederick's of Hollywood sounds male dominated, voyeuristic, and glitzy. Victoria's lists its address as "London" and uses a prerecorded voice with an English accent as its introduction to placing an order. Frederick's models are unknowns photographed against fabric backdrops; Victoria's models are well known and are usually photographed in indoor and old-world settings suggesting elegance and class. Surprisingly, though quality is far lower in Frederick's, prices for similar items in the two catalogues are remarkably close.

Position by Age. Advertisers often target a given cohort as the most likely prospect for a product or brand. Cohorts can be defined either as those born in the same year or those born in a certain set of years. That is what Trout and Ries mean by positioning by age. Targeting a specific set or group of potential consumers has many advantages. For example, one of the most targeted and fastest-growing cohorts remains the baby boom generation —a segment sometimes labeled as "the aging" though they would more likely think of themselves as "mature." The baby boomers were born between 1946 and 1964. They are joining another highly targeted age group—senior citizens—many of whom belong to the American Association of Retired Persons (AARP). Benefits of joining include lobbying efforts on behalf of retirees, discounts on certain products (such as motel rooms and car rentals), group activities (such as travel), and information about such topics as retirement programs and exercise equipment. And you can join the AARP at age 45! Joiners also receive a subscription to *Modern Maturity* magazine, which has the largest circulation among U.S. magazines, making it an ideal advertising vehicle for targeting this affluent and growing cohort in our population. Gen Xers are another cohort that advertisers have decided to target. Positioning by age is used to market such disparate products as soft drinks, designer jeans, book bags, hair tints, and medicines. You can imagine how the targeting of cohorts focuses advertisers' packaging, slogans, message strategies, media buys, and other communication efforts in product-oriented campaigns.

Politically Oriented Campaigns

Although they share some characteristics with product-oriented campaigns, politically oriented campaigns differ in many ways from the marketing of products or brands. For example, the research data available to candidates are much more limited than that for brand marketers, and politically oriented campaigns usually must communicate much more sophisticated information than that used for selling brands. Let us now turn to developmental models that help explain political campaigns.

The Communicative Functions Model. Communication researchers Judith Trent and Robert Friedenberg (1995) describe four stages that a political campaign must achieve if it is to be successful. They call their model the communicative functions approach.

In the first stage, the candidate lays some groundwork by mapping out the district, organizing financial committees, developing contacts in key areas of the district, and so on. This process is usually accompanied or preceded by a formal announcement of candidacy. This stage is called the "surfacing" or "winnowing" stage. The main campaign themes are floated and focused, the candidate's image is tested and promoted, issues are addressed, position papers are issued, and, with luck, adequate funds are raised. In presidential politics, this process may begin for the out-of-power party as early as the day after losing the election.

In stage 2 of this model, the primary election campaigns serve to narrow the field of candidates and to focus issues. More people get involved, as in the participation stage of the Yale model. These persons may pass out leaflets, attend rallies, sponsor fund-raisers, or perform some other overt activity that gets them involved.

In presidential politics, this stage is extremely expensive, even with the matching funds the government gives to candidates. As much as $45 million would not be an unbelievable sum to spend in pursuing a presidential nomination (National Public Radio, 1999). Of course, the costs are smaller with lower offices, but even senate primaries can cost several million dollars. This is a dangerous stage for candidates because they might make promises that they later can't fulfill, might reveal plans that later come back to haunt them, and might make mistakes, misstatements, or "gaffes" that can topple their candidacy.

During stage 3—the nomination—the candidate is legitimized in the eyes of the media and potential voters, and so are the party's platform and themes. The final stage—the election—is that period between nomination and election day when candidates wear themselves to a frazzle going from crowd to crowd saying basically the same thing, over and over again. Here, the use of the press is critical in both paid-for political promotions (billboards, signs, bumper stickers, buttons, TV ads, radio spots, newspaper ads, and so on) and unpaid media coverage (interview programs, short "sound bites" on the evening news, and so on). Candidates need press coverage to get key items broadcast or quoted. They must also purchase their TV and radio times carefully to get the messages to the target audience at the right time, in the right way, and in a cost-efficient manner.

The advent of the Internet in national politics during the 1996 presidential primaries means that candidates at all levels must also use this method of communicating with their constituencies. This interactive and highly personal medium will only increase in importance in campaigns in the new century. In 1998, for instance, both candidates for mayor of my small town (population 11,000) had Web pages with multiple links, just as most brands and many retailers have at present. It remains to be seen how much this new technology will alter political and other types of campaigns. As we will see in Chapter 13, this use of media is sophisticated and complex. In all likelihood, political campaign messages are processed in both the central and the peripheral information-processing routes. Issue-oriented messages probably use the central path and require rational thinking and preparation. Image-oriented messages, though they may be rationally thought out, are probably processed peripherally.

In the third edition of their *Political Communication in America,* Robert Denton and Gary Woodward (1999) focus on the strategies and tactics used in political campaigns. Strategies are the various plans a campaigner forms in hopes of achieving the campaign goal or goals; tactics are the means used to implement the strategies or to put them into action. In political campaigns, of course, there is but one goal—to win election to office—but several strategies could be used to meet that goal (such as win the primary, raise money, or get favorable voters registered). Referring to R. Faucheux (1998), Denton and Woodward identify four strategy types that are needed in any political campaign. The first is a "message sequence strategy" that addresses the order in which various campaign messages should be sent out. These could be messages about issues, the candidate or opponent, qualifications for office, personal beliefs, and so forth. Second, a "timing and intensity strategy" involves when messages should go out, and how much effort, money, and other resources should be dedicated to that phase of the campaign. Third, a "mobilization and persuasion strategy" focuses on how to reach and convince certain groups of voters who might be favorable to the candidate and his or her positions on the issues (for example, first-time voters, homeowners, minority voters, the party faithful, or gun owners). Finally, an "opportunity strategy" relates to finding ways to respond to the unexpected events, opportunities, or threats to the campaign that inevitably seem to arise. Examples might include revelation of the amount of money being spent or the source of the funding, negative advertising, and a sexual scandal involving the candidate or his or her opponent.

Several message sequence strategies are possible. The ignore-the-opposition strategy usually means being positive in speeches, news releases, interviews, and comments from the beginning of the campaign until election day while rarely or never referring to the opponent. The aggressive message sequence tactically begins the campaign on a positive note but then quickly turns to negative campaigning focused on the opponent's shortcomings. In the final days of the campaign, this strategy is implemented by using a "dual track" approach of both positive and negative or comparative appeals. With the frontal attack strategy, the candidate begins with negative and comparative ads focusing on the opponent's shortcomings, turns positive in the middle portions of the campaign, and then closes using the same dual-track approach as in the aggressive strategy.

Several message timing and intensity strategies are available as well. With the tortoise strategy, the candidate begins slowly, communicating and spending only modestly, and then builds momentum until election day, when a message and spending blitz happens. The bookend strategy involves a big, flashy, and expensive opening with a steady buildup and the same blitz strategy used to close the campaign the day before election day. With the Pearl Harbor strategy, the candidate starts very slowly and is barely noticeable. This is intended to lull the opposition into underestimating the candidate's strength, which then allows him or her to "sneak attack" the opponent at an opportune moment. Former U.S. Senator Carol Moseley-Braun used this strategy in her primary campaign by letting her two better-financed opponents outspend one another on negative campaigning. Then, in the closing days, she used her limited resources to focus her blitz on the fact that she was black and female. Voters were so turned off by the weeks of negative campaigning used by her opponents that this was a fresh and welcome approach. She won the nomination.

Opportunity strategies might include setting a trap, whereby the candidate attacks the opponent over a minor shortfall to set the opponent up to respond in such a way as to lead to a much larger criticism. For instance, the candidate might accuse him or her of being financed by an enormously rich father who is trying to buy the election for his spoiled son or daughter. The opponent responds by saying that it is no sin to be successful and to spend money on what one truly believes in. Then the candidate springs the trap—dear old Dad amassed his fortune by exploiting slave labor in China and avoiding paying taxes by locating his corporation in the Cayman Islands. The candidate concludes by charging, "The average blue-collar voters are the ones who are really being forced to finance your election!" The technological advantage strategy was used in the 1996 presidential campaign by numerous candidates who were aware of the newly emerging Internet and who used skilled technicians to formulate Web pages, which surprised their uninformed opponents. Of course, such an advantage is only good for a brief time, so candidates need to be alert to these opportunities. Three's a crowd is a strategy that takes advantage of a crowded field by financing a minor third or fourth opponent who will siphon off votes from the real opponent. The lightning rod strategy involves getting a controversial person to endorse the opponent or introducing a controversial issue to which the opponent can respond in only one way—a negative, controversial, and highly visible way.

Persuasion and mobilization strategies relate to how the candidate deals with voter groups—the party faithful, undecided voters, and those favoring the opponent. I used the classic formulation strategy in an election campaign in which I was a precinct captain. I had my candidate's supporters go door-to-door telling homeowners their names and stating that they were from the Democratic Party. If the door got slammed in their face, supporters were told to record that fact. If the homeowners listened and took a brochure, we made sure they were telephoned during the campaign, received literature weekly, and were reminded to get out and vote on election day. We made no such attempts with door slammers. We identified our voter base and the undecided voters and then reinforced them with messages and turned them out to vote. Using the base strategy, we would have relied on lists of registered Democrats and made sure they turned out early and often, a famous Chicago tactic. In the Marion Barry strategy, the candidate identifies a base and then expands it until election day, when these voters are urged to turn out and vote. Pro wrestling celebrity Jesse Ventura used this strategy in 1998 to win the Minnesota governorship over two well-financed opponents.

Denton and Woodward also identify several tactics that can be used in implementing strategies including advertising, opinion polling, direct mail and telemarketing, and fund-raising. You can observe these and other strategies being used in the local, state, and national elections.

To learn more about political campaign communication, access InfoTrac College Edition, and enter the word "campaign" in the search engine. Select the political campaigns in mass media option, and browse the selections.

Idea/Ideological Campaigns

In a third kind of campaign—the idea/ideological campaign—neither a product nor a person/candidate is being promoted. Instead, the persuader is trying to get an audience to engage in or change some behavior or to embrace some religion or other ideology. For example, some campaigns promote preventive measures that individuals might take to avoid contracting sexually transmitted diseases. Other campaigns solicit donations to various not-for-profit charities or other good causes. Idea campaigns are also used to urge people to help the environment, such as by recycling aluminum, glass, tin cans, plastic containers, and so on. A protest campaign might persuade people to wear black armbands on a certain day to indicate their displeasure with a policy or law. In early 2003, the group Women Against Military Madness (WAMM) protested the saber-rattling rhetoric of various members of the second Bush administration directed toward Iraq. They held rallies, sold yard signs and bumper stickers reading "Say No! to War with Iraq," and used other tactics to implement their strategies for avoiding a U.S. invasion of Iraq, which was their ultimate goal. Any of the elements in the Yale model help explain the strategies of such campaigns, and some elements of the product/person campaign models can also apply. But other models have originated specifically to explain idea/ideological campaigns, sometimes called "social movements."

The Social Movements Model. Communication researchers Charles J. Stewart, Craig A. Smith, and Robert E. Denton, Jr. (1989) define and describe the social movement model of idea/ideological campaigns. They maintain that social movements have seven unique characteristics that set them apart from product- or person-oriented campaigns. First, social movements are organized groups of people, with leaders who usually act as spokespersons for the movement. Second, although they are organized, they are not "institutionalized" or recognized by those in power. Third, social movements attract large numbers of persons and are large in scope either geographically or historically. Thus, "pro-lifers" would qualify as a social movement, whereas those promoting radon-free drinking water probably wouldn't because of the limited scope.

Fourth, social movements either promote or oppose social change. Stewart, Smith, and Denton identify three subtypes of groups promoting or opposing change. The innovative movement wants to totally replace existing social values and norms (for example, gay liberation or radical feminism). The revivalistic movement seeks only partial change in society and a return to past values (for example, breakaway religious sects). The resistance movement seeks to block instead of oppose change (for example, the pro-choice movement wants *Roe v. Wade* to remain the law of the land, and the NRA opposes limitations on the right to own handguns and also opposes the use of background checks to assure that convicted felons cannot acquire guns). Fifth, social movements are moralistic, preaching about good versus evil, right versus wrong, or patriotism versus treason. Sixth, social movements encounter opposition from those in power. The power may be held by formal groups (the military, police, a regulatory body), officeholders (senators, judges), or "beneficiaries" of the status quo (small business owners, religious or patriotic groups). This opposition often leads to symbolic and then real violence, such as initially sending movement members to "havens" or "enclaves" and then starving, raping, or killing them—as has happened in a number of dramatic cases. For their part, those promoting change might begin by shouting slogans, then move to violence against property, and finally end up doing physical violence to people. Finally, persuasion is the essential tool for attracting new converts, changing people's minds, and ultimately motivating those supporting the movement to take action. The persuasion may be verbal or nonverbal, it may attempt to use mass media, and it usually involves a call to action on the part of the persuadee.

Social movements also have their own set of developmental steps or "stages" through which they seem to pass, according to Stewart, Smith, and Denton. Their model of social movement outlines five stages: genesis, social unrest, enthusiastic mobilization, maintenance, and termination. In the genesis stage, ideologues preach about perceived shortcomings or injustices in the status quo. These early prophets might go unheard for a long time, as did those who warned that terrorism would spread to the United States. Finally, like-minded persons are drawn to these prophets, and the first stage creates a core of devoted supporters. Then, usually, a dramatic event (like the attacks of 9/11 on the World Trade Center in New York City) catapults the issue into the public spotlight.

In the second stage—social unrest—growing numbers of people identify with the movement and feel displaced by the shortcomings described by the prophets, who now agitate these frustrated people by identifying the devils and gods of the movement and its sacred and profane grounds and acts. This leads to the third stage—enthusiastic mobilization—in which the true believers begin to convert more and more people and to encounter opposition from those in power. These are active converts now, not merely persons who identify with the movement, as in the social unrest stage. Sometimes, competing organizations promoting similar ideas spring up, and bickering and disagreements result. The overall message of this stage is that there is a "we–they" world out there and "you" had better join "us" so "we" can take care of "you" and defeat "them."

Fourth, in the maintenance stage, the movement adopts a lower profile as the media turn to other events and some success is perceived by converts. These successes may dull enthusiasm for and drain energy from the movement, so it must bide its time until a significant event occurs or a charismatic spokesperson emerges to rekindle enthusiasm. In some cases, the movement achieves its goal(s), or it may merely wither and die in the termination stage. Perhaps supporters lose faith and patience, or the movement is outlawed or becomes outmoded, or its leaders are co-opted by or assimilated into the establishment, or it achieves its goals and thus becomes irrelevant.

The Agitation and Control Model. In their book *The Rhetoric of Agitation and Control,* John Bowers, Donovan Ochs, and R. J. Jensen (1993) describe several stages through which most ideological movements pass before ultimately failing or succeeding. In the first stage, agitators petition the sources of power (the government, a corporation, a school district), making demands that slightly exceed what the power source can or will give up. This makes the power source appear unreasonable and assists the agitators in their second stage—promulgation, or the marketing of the movement. Using handbills, leaflets, and rallies, the agitators develop their movement by informing outsiders of the unreasonableness of the power source. At this stage, the movement leaders hope to gain recruits and to get publicity that will attract even more recruits, as was the case in 2003 when WAMM became a nationally publicized social movement. If this stage is successful, the movement moves into a third stage—solidification. Now the newly recruited members are educated and hyped up through rallies and protest songs (for example, "Solidarity Forever," "We Shall Overcome," or "We Shall Not Be Moved"). They may use salutes (for example, the Nazi "Heil," the "V" for victory or for peace, and the Black Power salute) and symbols (for example, the swastika, the picture of a fetus with the "forbidden" symbol superimposed on the picture, or the uniforms worn by militia members or some groups of terrorists).

In the fourth stage, with a now-committed and educated following, the movement leaders seek polarization of the uncommitted population. They do this by focusing on a flag issue or person. The reason they are called "flag" issues or persons is that they epitomize the ultimate enemy or are the most easily recognized symbol of what the movement or ideology hates. Past flag issues have been the aborting of fetuses, the use of napalm on civilians, the mistreatment of refugees, and the bombing of civilian targets. Flag persons personify the issue. Past flag persons have included Iraqi dictator Saddam Hussein and Israeli leader Ariel Sharon. In local politics, flag persons might include mayors, councilpersons, senators, representatives, or any other leaders who are depicted as the root of the problem. The polarization stage forces the onlookers to choose between "us" and "them."

In the fifth stage, nonviolent resistance is used. For instance, police call in sick with the "blue flu," or students occupy a building and claim that they have "liberated" it, or renters go on strike, or a militia stages "war games." Some militia members and others on the far right refuse to obtain driver's licenses or license plates for their vehicles, pay taxes, or enter a plea when charged with crimes because they do not acknowledge the legitimacy of the government. These and other devices call attention to the mass movement and are meant to prompt some sort of response from the power source. Agitators may hope that the power source will call out the army or police and that the media will cover the confrontation. Then agitators may claim repression or "Gestapo" tactics. Usually, this leads to the sixth stage—escalation—which is intended to increase tension in the power source. Perhaps threats are made, such as rumors of planted bombs or public displays of weapons. Perhaps some violent act occurs, such as a strike with fights, a killing or kidnapping, or the bombing of an important building or landmark, as in the attacks of 9/11.

If the power source tries to repress the movement at this time, there usually is a split within the movement between those who favor violence and those who favor nonviolence. Bowers, Ochs, and Jensen call this stage Gandhi versus guerrilla. Usually, the nonviolent segment goes to the power source and argues that, unless the power source gives in, the guerrillas will take over and the violence will escalate. Depending on the response, the final stage may or may not emerge. This last stage is revolution. We saw social movements and the rhetoric of agitation and control lead to revolutions in a variety of places in recent decades and will undoubtedly see the same pattern in some of the social movements in the decades to come.

In the 1990s, a number of ideological campaigns followed this sequence of stages, including both the pro-life and the pro-choice movements, the gay liberation movement, and many religious movements. With the end of the cold war and the new role of the United Nations as a global police force, we have seen (and will very likely continue to see) such agitation and control tactics used throughout the world and in ideological campaigns here at home as well. The ability of the agitation and control model to describe, explain, and even predict stages in movements across time testifies to both its validity and its reliability.

The Diffusion of Innovation Model. Some idea campaigns do not seek to promote an alternative ideology. Rather, these campaigns hope to induce people to adopt new practices or change their behaviors, such as instituting safer procedures in a factory, reducing the intake of red meats and fats, or conserving energy. Everett Rogers (1962) studied the stages through which people approach the adoption of any new technology (computers, cell phones, email, the Web), practice (recycling various kinds of waste), or value (gays in the military). His diffusion of innovation model also has some applicability to product- and person-oriented campaigns. He outlined four stages through which people must pass on the way to adopting change.

In the first stage—information/knowledge—the potential adopter acquires or actively seeks information about the innovation. How does it work? What are its features and benefits? How much will it cost? How have other adopters rated it? When people first became aware of the practice of recycling—a time-consuming activity with little direct payoff—few rushed out and got containers for aluminum, glass, tin cans, newspaper, and mixed paper. However, being made aware of recycling drew people's attention to various pieces of information (the life expectancy of local landfills, the effects of deforestation on climate) that increased their knowledge about the value of recycling.

In the second stage—persuasion—the potential adopters process persuasion aimed at inducing them to actually try the new practice. With major changes in practice, this takes longer than when the change is only minor. Those advocating the change might use testimonials from well-known persons who have adopted the new practice. When the Beef Council, for example, wanted to change the frequency of people's use of their product, they hired TV stars Cybill Shepherd and James Garner to appear in television commercials. Both testified that, contrary to popular opinion, beef isn't necessarily high in calories if people choose lean cuts and prepare them in new and exciting ways. The Beef Council further promoted beef by running full-page ads in gourmet magazines, featuring recipes and appetizing pictures, and noting the low level of fat and calories in each serving. Overall, the campaign was successful, although it did run into difficulty when Shepherd made it known that she really didn't eat much beef and when Garner had a heart attack.

In the third stage in Rogers' model—decision, adoption, and trial—the potential adopters decide to try the new practice. They get the recycling containers, go to a trade show to try the new model of the Palm Pilot, or order prescriptions, groceries, books, and even pets from Amazon.com. Then they actually use the new technology, product, or practice. A key element in most innovation campaigns is to "induce trial," which is why in the initial stages of such campaigns free samples, free trial periods, low prices, and other techniques are used to get prospects to try the product or service. Sometimes, marketers request that users respond to the product/brand/practice by completing a rating survey. This technique moves potential adopters into the next stage in the model.

Finally, in the confirmation and evaluation stage, the new adopters reconsider the adoption and measure its performance against their expectations. They ask, "Did it deliver what it promised?" "Did I like it?" "Was it worth the price?" and similar questions that, if confirmed, cement the adoption decision. If they decide to continue usage, they then search for information that confirms or "okays" the adoption. As adopters of innovations, we seek confirmation of our decision.

If the diffusion model interests you, access InfoTrac College Edition, and enter the words "diffusion of innovation" in the search engine. Browse some of the periodical selections.

The Rogers model is helpful in considering campaigns that offer new and innovative practices to consumers. With the rate of change accelerating in our technocracy in the new millennium, we will undoubtedly go through these stages ourselves or observe them in others many times. Most recently, we have seen the process at work in getting people to try online shopping or digital camcorders. Knowing what is happening in such situations helps put decisions to adopt new practices into a clearer perspective that should result in wiser choices.

Besides these developmental models of campaigns, several other theories help explain the ultimate success or failure of a given product-oriented, person-oriented, or idea/ideological campaign. We now examine one of these explanatory tools or characteristics.

Symbolic Convergence Theory

Most of us like to affiliate with people with whom we agree and who are like us in "substantial" ways (to borrow and adapt terminology from Burke). This means that we seek to find "communities of agreement," or groups of people who share the same basic values and who have the same lifestyle as we do. Such agreement necessitates the merging of my meanings for events and values with your meanings for those same things. We don't need to be identical twins, just similar persons. Having similar values and lifestyles identifies us as a "particular audience"—or, to use the marketing term, "a market segment"—to whom advertisers, politicians, and ideologues try to appeal.

A theory developed by E. G. Bormann (1985), his students, and other researchers helps explain how shared meanings begin, develop, continue, and finally motivate us to action. The theory is known as symbolic convergence theory, and its methodology or technique of analysis is fantasy theme analysis. This theory and technique of analysis was initially applied to small-group communication. After witnessing the power of the theory and methodology in the analysis and explanation of group communication, Bormann and his followers applied them to interpersonal, corporate, institutional, and organizational communication. For our purposes as students of persuasion, the theory and methodology are ideal for doing audience analysis for product, idea, and political campaigns. When combined with focus group interviews and a statistical technique called Q-sort analysis, the theory and method have great power for analyzing the kinds of dramas to which specified groups of consumers and voters respond (Cragan & Shields, 1994, 1995).

A basic premise of symbolic convergence theory is that reality is socially based and socially constructed. That is, the way each of us perceives the world is the result of our interactions with others and our adoption of and addition to the meanings of these interactions. Because we share our inputs and interpretations with others in our social groups, we come to believe them even more devotedly than if we had been told what to believe from some respected authority. When this sharing occurs fully, we have a "symbolic convergence" of meaning.

The first clues to the power inherent in the social creation of realities came from the work of Robert F. Bales (1970), a professor of sociology at Harvard. His initial interest was in identifying the kinds of interaction that occurred in small, task-oriented groups. He noticed that in one category of interaction tension was released through the telling of stories in which the group participated. He called this category "dramatizes." He began to describe the way these stories or minidramas seemed to develop or, as he put it, "chain out" in the group, resulting in what he called "fantasy themes."

At this point, Bales' work caught the attention of Bormann and, later, Bormann's students and colleagues. They, too, had noticed the sharing of fantasies in small groups at the University of Minnesota and thought that the process of reality building in small groups had a wider application. In hundreds of studies, Bormann and his followers identified the operation of symbolic convergence in political and other campaigns. Using a variety of techniques, they discovered that "a number of communities of voters shared differing configurations or dramatizations and thus shared statistically different visions of the campaign" (Bormann, 1985). These visions were later checked against actual voting behavior and were found to be reliable predictors of voter behavior. This pattern replicated itself in studies of purchasing and joining behavior.

The researchers also discovered that the reporters covering the campaign developed their own "rhetorical vision" of the campaign, in which the role of the reporter was to dig out the "real" truth. In this process of investigative reporting, "fantasy types," or favorite topics, themes, or images, were discovered by reporters trying to dig out the "truth." One fantasy theme is that of "the frontrunner," the candidate who, according to the polls or because of incumbency, has the kind of legitimacy discussed earlier in the Yale five-stage campaign model. This candidate is focused on by the media, which cover such issues as whether the candidate is showing signs of stumbling, is hiding something, or is acting as a stalking horse for other candidates. This dramatic presentation of the "truth" about the campaign makes for good reporting, as well as bonuses and other perks for the press.

Another political campaign fantasy theme is that of the baseball game, with the candidates being in "the early or final innings" or unable to "get to first base" with the electorate. Another theme makes use of boxing images, with candidates "being on the ropes" or delivering "knockout blows" to the opposition, which is "just a lightweight" and not a real "contender."

In politically and product-oriented advertising, the ad agency or an advertising huckster puts "spin" on the product by issuing press releases about the product, by getting press coverage for giving the product away to some worthy group, or by emphasizing the product's astounding benefits. Bert Metter (1990), chairman of the J. Walter Thompson USA advertising agency and part-time columnist for *Advertising Age,* puts it this way: "We are in the age of spin. The art and science of creating images is out of the closet. . . . As spin becomes more common . . . we've got to deliver more effectiveness. . . . The agencies with the answers will succeed. Others will have a lot of spinning to do" (p. 36). Naturally, this kind of spin doctoring for people and products is bound to earn criticism from those who believe that the ad industry is responsible for conspicuous consumption and its accompanying ills: pollution, easy credit, desperate attempts to "keep up with the Joneses," and so on. Spin operates in idea/ideological campaigns as well. For example, pro-life advocates use interpretations of when life begins that have a pro-life spin. We shouldn't forget that symbolic convergence is not limited to political campaigns. For example, consider the effects of the bombings of the Word Trade Center and the Pentagon with commercial airliners flown by Middle Eastern pilots trained in U.S. flight schools. Following those events, the public meaning of the word "terrorism" took on new dimensions. Now it was not merely a lone nut or two as was the case in the 1995 bombing in Oklahoma City. Instead, terrorism was associated with an intricate and highly secretive series of small "cells" of individuals around the world coordinated by Osama Bin Laden and the leadership of other "rogue nations" that formed an "axis of evil," which needed to face a "War on Terrorism." Those key words got picked up by the press initially and shortly thereafter by the public and ultimately emerged into a fantasy type—the terrorist conspiracy/threat—which later developed into a rhetorical vision—worldwide terrorism.

REVIEW AND CONCLUSION

All persuasion involves self-persuasion. We must agree to be persuaded and then find good reasons for deciding. Many of these good reasons are already embedded in our conscious or subconscious memory. Clever persuaders identify ways to cue these memories and connect them to a product, candidate, or idea/ideology. Persuaders tune persuadees' ears to the kinds of messages that will be communicated in campaigns seeking new buyers, new voters, or new joiners. Person/candidate, product, and idea/ideology campaigns demonstrate both permanence and change. The formal and functional characteristics of campaigns that we have explored seem to persist over time, forming permanent patterns. The ever-shifting issues and increasingly sophisticated technologies of product testing, public opinion polling, media production, and direct marketing are the elements of change. Among the recurring aspects of campaigns are a systematic flow of communication from persuader to audience and back to the persuader via a feedback loop (something that typifies all communication systems); the establishment of formal goals, strategies, and tactics; the creation of a "position" or "niche" in the audience's mind; stages through which most campaigns must pass; a participatory dramatization of the product, candidate, or idea/ideology in which the audience is invited to participate in the campaign drama in real or symbolic ways; the kinds of appeals that unify and recruit zealots for the mass movement; and the "chaining out" of rhetorical visions in campaigns/social movements that ultimately involve mass audiences.

You need to become a critical receiver who makes responsible decisions about which product to buy, which candidate to vote for, and which ideas or ideologies to endorse. These decisions are appropriate only after thorough analysis of the campaigns. Ask yourself how the campaign responds to feedback; what its objectives, strategies, and tactics are; how the campaign positions the product, person, or idea; what developmental stages emerge; and in what kind of drama you are being invited to participate. When you have answered these questions, you will be ready to make a responsible decision.

QUESTIONS FOR FURTHER THOUGHT

1. Choose a present-day campaign for a product, person, or idea/ideology. What appear to be its objectives, strategies, and tactics?

2. Define each of the Yale developmental terms. Can you identify examples of the first three stages in a magazine or newspaper campaign?

3. In the agitation/control model, what stage of a campaign or movement is represented when we vote for or against a particular candidate or proposition? Why?

4. What are some ways now being used to position products you use? Candidates running for office? Idea campaigns requesting your active or financial support? Mass movements seeking converts?

5. Identify a social movement that is either going on or seems to be developing. Use the social movements model and agitation/control model to trace its development. Which most accurately describes what is happening?

6. Using Bormann's symbolic convergence theory, explain the same social movement identified in question 5. Which of the methodologies seems most message oriented? Which is most audience related?

7. Identify several "fantasy types" in a campaign for a product made popular in the previous decade. Are they similar to those for today's products?

For online activities, go to the Web site for this book at
http://communication.wadsworth.com/larson.

12

✳

Becoming a Persuader

Thus far, we have focused on receiver skills: how to be a critical, responsible, and ethical consumer of persuasion. However, some times, we become persuaders. Luckily, the knowledge gained in our role as persuadee can be applied to our occasional roles as persuader. We can use tactics of intensification and downplaying; we can mold our persuasion using process, content, cultural, and nonverbal premises; and we can apply our knowledge of what is ethical in persuasion.

As a persuader, your first steps in preparing your message involve learning about your audience and shaping your message. Here, considerations such as patterns of organization, kinds of proof, and styling of messages will be important. Finally, you must choose how to go about delivering your message. This will involve not only the physical characteristics of how you speak (eye contact, posture, and so on) but also the channel through which to deliver the message, the timing of the delivery, and so on. Finally, you want to be aware of some common persuasive tactics. Throughout this entire process, you need to ask whether what you are doing is ethical in

terms of the models presented by Richard Johannesen in Chapter 2. Sometimes, you need to ask questions about the lasting, larger issues in life. One such question is, "Is what I am doing or persuading about likely to have a more negative or more positive effect on my listener's lives? For that matter, will it make for a better or worse world?" Being an ethical persuader means being a part of a community in which your persuasion has a positive effect on relationships in that community. Your persuasion must not undermine the idea of community.

KNOWING YOUR AUDIENCE

It is easy to assert that persuaders should know as much as possible about their audience, but it is not so easy to prescribe specific ways you can get to know your targets. One of the best ways is to listen to them as they persuade. When they persuade, they use tactics that would be persuasive to them. For example, I am most persuaded when a source uses narratives and examples. I often use the narrative example to get you to take my advice. And if you want to persuade me, fill your message with narratives and examples. I served three terms as president of our faculty senate. During my first term, I observed those key persons whom I knew I would need to persuade—the president of the university, the provost, the chair of the board of trustees, and faculty senators. I watched them in their attempts to persuade others for about a semester before trying to persuade them of many things. I realized that whereas some wanted the facts—just the facts—others wanted to know the story behind the story or to be complimented profusely before becoming open to persuasion. I became a better persuader by observing my audience carefully, but was this sort of snooping and amateur mind reading really ethical? After some reflection, I decided that the analysis was ethical. Nothing illegal or immoral had been done, and the analysis helped the audience make much needed decisions. My actions furthered the goals of the community.

I also look at my audience's patterns of processing information in terms of the elaboration likelihood model (ELM). I want to use the central information-processing route when that is appropriate, and I want to allow the audience to use the peripheral information-processing route when that is called for. The basic goal is to know the audience so that you can shape messages that will appropriately and ethically persuade them. Study audience members, observe them, listen to them, and analyze what they say and how they say it. When your parents try to persuade, how do they go about it? What kinds of evidence do they use? Some people, for example, are most easily persuaded when they think that they are the ones who came up with the idea for change. It is best to give such persons several alternatives and let them make the choice. Then they "own" the idea or innovation. Others are most satisfied with a decision if they see that significant others have made or are making the same or similar decisions. Best-selling author Robert Cialdini (2001) calls this tool of influence "social proof," which means viewing a behavior or decision as correct "to the degree that we see others performing it" (p. 100). If others whom we respect and trust are

doing it, then it must be wise and good. Most of the time, that is a reliable way of thinking. But is it ethical for the persuader to use social proof to win the day? It depends on the issue, the costs, and the potential benefits of following the decision or action. It is far more important for us as persuadees (sensing that a persuader is using social proof to convince us) to ask ourselves if we should decide or act simply because others are acting or have acted in a certain way. Sometimes, the masses are wrong, and we need to be the ultimate catalysts for change. Thus, the ethical issue reverts back to where it should be—with us as receivers of persuasion. We need to be on guard and not be hoodwinked by affinity appeals such that we follow the advice of persons who only seem to be like us.

To learn how important knowing your audience is, access InfoTrac College Edition, and type the words "social proof" in the subject search engine. Examine the items published in *Direct Marketing*. Then type in the words "audience analysis" in the key word search engine. Explore the many ways being used to analyze the invisible audience going to locations on the Web.

DEMOGRAPHICS AND AUDIENCE ANALYSIS

When persuasion is aimed at larger audiences, persuaders can use demographics to analyze the audience. In demographics, people are grouped via their shared attributes—their likes, dislikes, habits, and values. A good indicator of demographic clustering is the magazine subscriptions people have. If you subscribe to *Outdoor Life, Field and Stream,* and *Sports Illustrated,* you likely differ from the person who subscribes to *The Atlantic Monthly, Horticulture, Organic Gardening,* and *Bon Appétit.* Both of you would be good bets for catalogues featuring outdoor clothing. In all likelihood, only one of you is interested in hunting or fishing gear and would be a good candidate for a catalogue for lures, rods and reels, ammo, and decoys. Probably neither of you is interested in rock music or MTV.

Your affiliations (church, fraternal, or community groups) are another demographic index, as are your credit cards. Although some credit information is held in private, other elements are shared with firms that specialize in doing demographic research. Based on these databases, census data, DMV records, returned warranty cards, and many other sources, all of us have been identified demographically as good candidates for certain pitches. What do you think about having all that information about you available to anybody wanting to sell you something? Is it ethical for the government, periodical publishers, and others to sell that information?

Most of us don't do this kind of elaborate analysis of a potential audience, but we can do a lot even with limited time and resources. For example, suppose you have been asked to make a presentation to the governing board of your college or university. Your goal is to get the board to provide enough funding so that each student can have access to the Internet and the Web via computer labs, computers in dorm rooms, or board-subsidized home computers and modems. You need to find out who the board members are, what they do for a living, and where they live. How have they voted or acted in the past? What kinds of past funding have they used? What kinds of alternatives have they allowed? Why? These are the kinds of questions that can help you analyze your audience.

What are some of the demographic factors to look at in preparing a formal persuasive presentation? The first step is to decide which factors will be significant for your audience. Audience factors that make a critical difference vary with the goal of the persuader. Age is important if you are discussing tax planning for retirement, but not if your topic is recycling. Gender is important for some topics, like pay equity, but not for others. The same thing goes for your audience's level of income, their religion, or their political affiliations.

Let's return to our Web access situation. Which of the following will you want to explore about your audience?

- *Average age.* Will it matter if they are all over fifty or if they are all under thirty-five? Probably.

- *Income.* Will it matter if they are well-to-do or struggling to get by? Yes.

- *Gender.* Are the board members likely to be male or female, and does that matter? Maybe.

- *Religion.* This factor is one you can probably ignore. However, if your proposal was to have board approval for conducting abortions in the student health center, it clearly would be important.

- *Family size.* Will it matter if your audience members have two or five children? Probably, because children frequently influence parents on matters of technology.

- *Political party.* In this case, political affiliation would have little bearing.

- *Occupation.* Will the board members' occupations affect their persuasibility? Probably. If the audience members are white-collar workers, they might be convinced by a solid set of statistics and a formal, tightly reasoned presentation. Plan to use graphs, charts, and informational handouts, and remind them of the importance of technology and computer literacy on the job. Your request is not designed to provide students with access to merely useless, "fun," or "erotic" materials. Rather, it will provide hands-on training that will make students better employees and citizens upon graduation.

Once you know the key demographic factors for your group/topic/context, the next stage is to explore them. The president will be able to tell you about some of the board members. The public relations people at your school can provide information about where they live, which can cue you to income and age. If they have turned down past requests from students, you need to know why. Sometimes, merely talking to one or two typical members of a group before you attempt to persuade can be helpful. Any characteristics they share as a group can be useful in shaping your message for that audience. Much of this information will be used in the central information-processing route, but don't ignore the possibility that some elements will carry emotional meanings. These will be processed without much conscious investigation.

Would it be ethical for you to do this kind of demographic research for your presentation? Why or why not?

Determining Audience Needs

Some audience touchstones are emotional, some logical, some cultural, and some nonverbal. We can do some fairly sophisticated analysis of our target to determine their needs. We might focus on the human need for self-improvement and confidence to sell our idea. Or we could talk about the need to constantly keep up with technology. Or we might use appeals based on the Rank model, discussed in Chapter 1. Fear appeals might also prompt the audience to action. Most of the touchstones that help persuade others can be traced back to emotions, memories, and experiences that are common to large percentages of the population.

All audiences have some sets of shared experiences. We all remember where we were when we first heard about the attack on the World Trade Center. Some of you may remember hearing about and/or watching the explosion of the *Challenger* spacecraft, though as the years pass fewer and fewer college-aged persons remember the event. Why? They weren't in school when the accident happened, and most schoolchildren were compelled by their teachers to watch the liftoff because a schoolteacher—Christina McAuliffe—was on board the spacecraft. It was intended to be a historic first. However, most of you recall seeing a similar explosion of the space shuttle *Columbia*. You probably weren't in a schoolroom watching the reentry, but the image was broadcast often enough to stick in your memory. You are, as a result, part of a certain cohort by dint of having seen the 2003 space tragedy.

An interesting example of such shared experiences and emotions for college students is the classic examination dream first identified by Freud. Apparently, it is common for college graduates to dream about showing up for a final exam only to be unable to recall anything about the class. In other variations, students cannot find the examination room or realize that they have not studied for the exam or perhaps never even went to class or purchased the

texts. Most college graduates remember the stress of their college years. All these stored memories can be persuasive building blocks. What might be some of these stored experiences for the members of the governing board? They probably all can remember getting their first PC and trying to learn how to use it. The value of getting hands-on training is an argument that will resonate with them. They probably all also remember coming to the realization that people will not have to learn how to use the PC just once. Instead, they recognize that using and learning about computers will be a lifelong process given that the "half-life" of technology is constantly shrinking. Thus, in the process of audience analysis, the persuader should try to locate the key experiences that relate to the topic or goal. The next time you need to persuade someone, try to list the experiences he or she likely has had. Can some of these be tied into your message?

Tony Schwartz (1973) suggested another factor in audience analysis is in his book *The Responsive Chord*. Schwartz designed messages built for specific times and places. For example, suppose you are trying to send a message to people telling them to vote for someone, and you know that they will hear it on Labor Day weekend. How will you design the message? You will want to plug into the picnic mood, the out-of-doors experience, and the family fun that people are having on that weekend. You might have the candidate talk about the importance of conservation for parents and their children or about the need to make it easy for friends to get together. Schwartz called this the "task-oriented" approach to persuading. You can use it, too.

Ask yourself whether your goal fits with the audience's ability to follow your advice. If you are going to ask them to quit smoking, you'd better do it in such a way as to make it easy for them. Give them brochures that offer helpful hints on quitting. Try to find out the state of mind of your audience—the board, the sales force, or the job interviewer. What is the likely mood? Will they be relaxed? Will they have doubts? Take these things into account, and design your message accordingly. With regard to the Web access example, remind them of the good feeling they get from knowing that they are computer literate. Then tell them that there is a chance to make that kind of feeling available to more students through universal access to the Web.

Once you know something about your target group and how its members feel about your topic, you can shape the message. There are many steps in the shaping process. First, you need to organize the message in the most useful way. People are more likely to recall messages that are well organized.

FORMS OF ORGANIZATION

There are a number of ways to organize messages to make sure they are memorable and persuasive. We will look at five such formats here: (1) the topic format, (2) the space format, (3) the chronological format, (4) the stock-issues format, and (5) the motivated sequence format. For the first three of these formats, we will use the following example: A student group on my campus wanted to bring Bob Zemeckis, the highly successful filmmaker and a former student, back to school as a guest speaker to discuss the challenges of film production. Zemeckis was willing to donate his honorarium to the sponsoring student group to be used for field trips, travel to national conferences, and funding for a career day. The persuasive presentation to the student government committee could be organized in several ways.

Organization by Topic

The topical format is most useful when the message that you want to convey covers several topics or issues. Here is a list of topics that might be used in the Zemeckis example:

- His fame and success as a reason to bring him to campus

- The kind of role model he would provide

- The special offer of previewing his latest film

- The degree to which he is in demand on the speaking circuit

- His generosity in donating his fee to the student group in the department

- The other benefits to be derived from his presence on campus: publicity for the school, the added programming made possible by his donation, and the career counseling he might be able to give to aspiring student filmmakers

By presenting these topics with supporting evidence, you give the student government a variety of good reasons to fund the speaker. The topic format is a good choice when presenting specific reasons for some suggested action.

Organization by Space

The spatial format is a good choice when you want to compare your topic to the larger picture. The spatial idea relates to the comparative size of the proposal. In the Zemeckis example, you might compare his relative cost to that of speakers invited by other groups. His fee might be only a quarter of that asked for by another student group and for a less well known speaker. Further, his fee might represent only 5 percent of the total guest speaker budget for the semester. And your student group may be only one of more than forty similar groups in the university, so the fee is not out of line. In the spatial format, you might draw several pie graphs. In one, you could visually depict your speaker's fee as one-twentieth of the pie and label the remainder "Other Speaker Fees." Another graph might show your 5 percent share as only a fraction of the funds allocated to other student groups. In all of these examples, you would be using space as an organizing principle.

Organization by Chronology

Sometimes, the essential message in persuasive communication is best relayed to the audience by taking them through the issues in historical sequence. You might relate Zemeckis' career as follows:

1. In 1975, he became a major in our department and took his first media classes there.

2. Two years later, he transferred to the USC film school. But he still values the basics of filmmaking he learned while he was with us.

3. He made his first picture, *Caddy Shack,* as an independent a year later.

4. It was released the next June, and as a minor summer hit, it recaptured the initial investment plus a small profit.

5. Later that year, the film got several "honorable mentions" at film festivals, and he then signed a contract to make pictures for Stephen Spielberg and one of the largest film studios.

6. In the next few years, he turned out several moneymakers, such as *Romancing the Stone.*

7. Then, in 1982, he made his first blockbuster, *Back to the Future,* which went on to win several Academy Awards.

8. Since then, he has been independently turning out hits like *Back to the Future II, Who Framed Roger Rabbit?, Forrest Gump,* and *Contact.*

9. He is now one of the best-known writer/producers in Hollywood.

Organization by Stock Issues

The stock-issues organizational format is most frequently seen in cases in which a major policy change is being considered. Its name refers to the fact that there are several universal issues that need to be addressed when major policy changes are considered. Our Bob Zemeckis example doesn't involve a policy change, so we will look at a different example.

In the recently revived Broadway musical comedy *The Music Man,* band instrument and band uniform salesman Harold Hill sells an entire town on a need for a boys band complete with uniforms on the flimsiest of logical appeals. He points out numerous symptoms of trouble in the town (kids are smoking, reading "dirty" books, cussing, dressing outrageously, and so on). He then concludes with these words, "There's trouble, my friends, right here in River City. I said trouble, and that starts with *T* and that rhymes with *P* and that stands for 'Pool'!" He goes on to point out that with a band to keep them busy the boys will make no more visits to the pool hall, where the bad habits are all learned. In this example, an overkill of symptomatic evidence

enables the persuader to short-circuit the reasoning process. Hill's "proof" relies on a rhyme scheme—*P,* the first letter in "pool hall," rhymes with *T*—therefore, the pool hall means trouble. However, the letter *P* also rhymes with *B, C, D, E, G, V,* and *Z*—a fact Hill conveniently ignores.

Hill is successful because he plays on the stock issues expected whenever a policy such as supporting a city band is addressed. In a stock-issues approach, two sides debate an issue: One side wants change, and the other prefers the status quo. Think of the stock issues using the metaphor of a trial in our law courts. The side wanting change is the prosecutor, who wants to convict the defendant. And obviously, the side favoring the status quo is the defense attorney, who wants the defendant found innocent. In our legal system, you are presumed innocent (the status quo) unless the prosecution can show beyond a reasonable doubt that you are guilty (change). We say that the burden of proof rests with the prosecution, the side that wants to change the status of the defendant. The status quo is presumed to be wise or true until proven otherwise. If the prosecution's case is a weak one, the defendant's lawyer will move for a directed verdict of innocent as soon as the prosecution rests its case. If the prosecution's case is a good one, the judge will refuse to direct a verdict, and the case proceeds because the prosecution has met its burden of proof. The defense now has the burden of proceeding.

The side having the burden of proof must show serious shortcomings with the status quo, usually by indicating symptoms of a problem. These symptoms are then tied to a supposed cause to create a cause–effect or problem–solution frame of reference. In the trial, the prosecution must show several things: that a crime has been committed, that the defendant had a motive for and a means of committing the crime, and that a convincing linkage of forensic physical evidence to the defendant exists. The political persuader might tie the high unemployment rate to deficit spending and say that reducing the deficit will increase investment and hence employment. Or she or he may link unemployment to corruption among top CEOs and move to enact legislation forcing independent outside audits of businesses at least once a year and making public any sale of company stock by any top corporate officer.

Once the persuader has presented an adequate need for change, the focus of the argument shifts to the necessity for some plan of action that we can reasonably assume will somehow solve a problem. In other words, effective persuaders can't merely point out shortcomings in the status quo and leave it at that. Neither can they offer a ludicrous plan of action that obviously cannot solve the problem or that has no possibility of being enacted. Thus, a critic of the status quo can't offer to solve the federal deficit problem by having the government print trillions of dollars in unbacked paper money. Such a plan would never pass Congress; further, it would create runaway inflation. The critic might suggest legalizing marijuana and taxing its manufacture and sale, thus generating $30 billion in revenue. Or the persuader might suggest a national lottery, like the Irish Sweepstakes, that could generate another $20 billion to be set aside for debt service and deficit reduction. Having shown a need for change and a realistic plan for change, the persuader can now move to the final stage of stock issues—demonstrating that the need shown can be dealt with through the suggested plan.

This third stage, the plan-meets-need stage, involves demonstrating that the suggested plan could be enacted, produce the needed results, and would not create other problems that would be worse than the status quo. With regard to marijuana legalization the side defending the status quo might bring up such issues as the possible side effects of such a move, such as increased drug-related automobile and other accidents. The critic of the status quo might point out the realistic nature of the plan and its supposed effects by citing the example of Holland, where the legalized marijuana plan has worked. The persuader might even go further and point out added benefits, such as reduced costs for the criminal justice system. The defender of the status quo may grant that there is a need for change and move directly to this plan-meets-need stage, comparing a repaired status quo with the proposed plan or offering a totally different plan, and then debating the comparative advantages and disadvantages of the two.

We see stock issues frequently used as content premises in the world of politics and business, and in other policy-making forums as well. As a receiver, you should also be aware of the stock issues. Any time you are the target of persuasion focused on policy change, identify the side suggesting change and the side supporting the status quo. That will tell you which side has the burden of proof.

As a persuader attempting to bring about a change in policy, you need to begin by demonstrating a strong need for a change. Like Harold Hill, you need to be specific about the "trouble" being caused by the status quo. You have the burden of proof. Start by citing lots of symptoms of the problem. You should research specific instances that demonstrate to the audience that they are suffering something, are losing something, or are in danger of losing it. In terms of the FUD model mentioned earlier, you need to create fear, uncertainty, and/or doubt. Tie the symptoms to a cause that, if removed and replaced, will solve the problem. Then present a reasonable alternative to the status quo—the plan or the new policy. Finally, show that "plan meets need." One way to do this is to show that the plan has been successful in other places. Another way is to point to historical events, such as the repeal of Prohibition and the resulting positive effects on the economy in the Great Depression. This is arguing from precedent. Still another way is to use expert testimony to the effect that the plan for change has a reasonable chance of succeeding.

At each stage of the stock-issues format, expect some kind of rebuttal. In some cases, it will be openly stated, as in a policy debate in your student government. If you are giving a speech covering all three stock issues—need, plan, and plan meets need—anticipate such rebuttals and be ready to counter them. You might also short-circuit anticipated rebuttals by presenting a two-sided message stating the anticipated rebuttals and answering them then and there, depriving the opposition of an opportunity to impress the audience with its rebuttal.

The stock-issues format is useful for persuaders who are proposing a change in policy from the status quo. Just remember the steps of the stock-issues format. Remember that Harold Hill was able to persuade the citizens of River City to fund a boys band simply because the letter *T* rhymed with the letter *P*, but only after he made them aware of troublesome symptoms in the actions of the young people of the town.

Organization by the Motivated Sequence

Another organizational pattern that resembles the stock-issues approach is the motivated sequence format, suggested by communication scholars Alan Monroe, Douglas Ehninger, and Bruce Gronbeck (1982). This format involves five steps used by persuaders to get persuadees to attend to their message, to feel a need to follow their advice, and, most importantly, to take action related to the advice. The motivated sequence is a good pattern to use in sales, recruitment, politics, and many other contexts.

The first step in the motivated sequence—the attention step—aims at capturing the attention of the audience. There are hundreds of ways to do this. You could begin your message with a question, a startling statistic, or a fear appeal. For example, you might ask, how clean is your mouth? You could then point out that there are over three hundred kinds of microorganisms that thrive in the human mouth, and most persons brush their teeth only once or twice a day. Further, they "clean" their mouth with the same toothbrush for months without ever thoroughly cleaning it and while storing it in warm, moist conditions a few feet from the toilet! Thus, people need to change their toothbrush every two weeks and at the beginning and end of any infection or respiratory disease (Woods, 1993). Or you could use a quotation (for example, Will Rogers said, "I ain't got no philosophy—I calls 'em like I sees 'em"), a joke, or an anecdote. Another approach is to make an important announcement in the first few moments of the message. Our old friend the narrative can also capture audience attention, as can visual aids that arouse curiosity. In all of these examples, the attention-gaining step may initially be processed emotionally or in the peripheral channel of the ELM, but you want your audience to centrally process more of your claims.

In the second step of the motivated sequence, you try to convince the audience that they are losing something, are about to lose something, or could be gaining something but aren't. This is the need step. You might use a real or hypothetical case to show the need. For example, consider the following:

> How would you like to get out of college and have a sizable nest egg? In his sophomore year, Bill Smith used his student loan as a down payment on a student rooming house. He lived there all four years rent-free and was able to charge rent for the other nine rooms. Smith used the rents to make mortgage payments and to pay tuition and fees. After selling the rooming house on graduation, he paid off his student loan and had a $50,000 profit on his investment. You can follow his example and not only graduate debt-free but end up with a nest egg.

This need step could easily be tied to the attention-getting step—for example, using a "reward poster" that offers a $50,000 nest egg—thus creating a smooth flow from step to step for the audience.

Steps 3 and 4 are the visualization and satisfaction steps. In these steps, the persuader gives examples, data, testimony, or some other form of proof to induce the audience to visualize what life will be like for them if they follow the persuader's advice—for instance, if they go ahead and invest part of their student loan in student housing. Or the persuader might take the opposite tack pointing out what life will be like if they don't invest in the rooming house. She or he might say that you will graduate with the debt of student loans, without the experience of being in business for yourself, and, most importantly, without the $50,000 nest egg to build your future on. Following this visualization step, the persuader can then offer some way to satisfy the positive need or to avoid some negative consequences—for example, showing them how easy getting a student loan is and how little is needed for a down payment on income property.

Finally, the persuader needs to give a definite, specific, and realistic action step. It probably will do no good to ask audience members to alter their attitudes on the topic. Attitudes are fickle, as we have seen, and, further, it is hard to know whether an audience has changed. It is far better to give the audience specific things to do to avoid tooth decay, save energy, make wise investments, graduate with no debt and a handsome nest egg, or earn good grades. In one research study, people given a booklet with specific action steps to cut electricity consumption registered less use of electricity on their meters in the following two weeks than did those not given the specific action steps (Cantola, Syme, & Campbell, 1985). If you want the audience to write to their elected representative, it is a good idea to have a petition on hand that members can sign or to announce the phone number and email address of the legislator's local office. After all, phoning or emailing is much easier than writing a letter. In effective persuasion, it is essential to give persuadees a realistic action step, whether it is signing a sales contract, phoning a friend who has used the product, or boycotting a certain food. Build such steps into your persuasive attempts, and you will find your chances of success increasing dramatically.

A related model for making a persuasive appeal is called the AIDA approach—short for attention, interest, desire, action. In this model, as in the motivated sequence, the first step is to capture the audience's attention using any of the tactics cited earlier. In the second step, the persuader's goal is to heighten the audience's interest in his or her topic or proposal. This might be done using a satisfaction or a visualization process, as in the motivated sequence. Or the persuader might tell how many persons have already tried the product or used the new procedure and found it to be useful, or point out unforeseen problems with continuing the present practice.

Once attention and interest have been gained, the next task is to create a desire in persuadees to purchase the product or service, vote for the candidate, or follow the advice. There are several ways to create such desire. In product-related persuasion, it usually is done by providing some product benefit or product promise. For example, Chrysler advertised a safety feature that was standard in their cars: built-in air bags for the front seat and sides. The obvious benefit of this feature was that it could save lives in an accident. By mentioning research that proved how well the bag cushioned the driver's body, Chrysler created a desire for the product in the audience. In their action step, they asked the

FIGURE 12.1 Rank's model for ways to create desire in audiences.

customer to go to their nearest Chrysler dealer to learn more about the air bag and to take a test drive.

Hugh Rank (1982), whose intensify/downplay model was introduced in Chapter 1, has offered a simple four-part model for creating desire. In addition to promoting products, it also can be used in a variety of other persuasive situations. Persuaders can use four kinds of desire-stimulating tactics with this model (see Figure 12.1). First, they can promise the audience security or protection by demonstrating that their advice will allow the audience to keep a "good" they already have but might be in danger of losing. Crest and other fluoridated toothpaste brands, for example, promise that regular use of their toothpaste will help keep your teeth free from decay—you keep a "good." Politicians frequently point out all the funding they have brought to their districts and then claim that their reelection will mean keeping this "good." The other approach to motivating persons via various kinds of "good" is to point out that, although they are not going to lose something they already have, they are not taking advantage of an available "good." It might be an inexpensive online account for buying and selling stocks and mutual funds or something as simple as Jell-O's no-bake cheesecake. If audience members have not tried the new "good," telling them about it might motivate them to acquire it.

A second set of desire-stimulating tactics relates to "bad" or uncomfortable symptoms or feelings. Persuaders who use these tactics promise that by following their advice people can either avoid a "bad," get rid of a "bad," or experience relief from it. Rank called these two approaches the "prevention" and "relief" appeals. Advertisers often promise that their products will prevent the embarrassments of bad breath, body odor, or dandruff or will provide relief from headaches, heartburn, flyaway hair, or acne. Such "scare and sell" approaches can also be used in nonproduct persuasion. For example, a persuader can promise that by passing the school bond referendum we can "avoid" losing athletic and music programs and other extracurricular activities. More recently, school districts have been reassuring students and parents that their school buildings are "safe" because of the presence of security devices and personnel. The idea is that these precautions will prevent killings such as occurred in Littleton, Colorado, in 1999. You will discover ways to use any or all of these desire-creating tactics when you choose to become a persuader.

FORMS OF PROOF

People want good reasons for changing their attitudes, beliefs, and decisions. The proof requisites for taking action steps are even more demanding. Even if the advocated change is a good one, people still need proof to motivate them to act. Let's look at the forms of proof available to persuaders and discuss how they can be used to prompt audiences to change attitudes or take action.

Statistical Evidence

Sometimes, the most effective proof or support is statistical. For instance, an important goal of some car buyers is to get good gas mileage. In this case, EPA data will probably persuade them to choose a car model more than a salesperson's reassurances that the car is a real gas saver. Statistics persuade best when they are simple and easy to understand. When you decide to use statistics, make them clear,

and provide a reference point for the numbers. If you are warning persuaders about the severity of the national debt, make it real to them. Tell them that the interest on the debt amounts to $1800 per year for every man, woman, and child in the country and that the average family has to pay taxes from January 1 until March 15 to pay their share of the interest on the debt. In the case of the student landlord, going through the statistical details of buying the rooming house would probably be persuasive.

Narratives and Anecdotes

Earlier, we noted the power of drama, stories, and jokes. Narratives make examples come alive and make them easy to recall and relate to. The story of a person rising from rags to riches probably persuades more than any set of statistics does. I tell potential clients for my advertising firm about the power of the word "Free" in making an offer to prospective customers. Then I back this up with a narrative and an anecdote. The narrative I tell is of the success of the Cabela family, which has not only its widely distributed outdoors catalogue but several retail outlets around the country. Mr. Cabela began in the 1950s by purchasing hand-tied trout flies from Japan at a fraction of a penny each. He advertised them in newspapers in trout country—Wyoming and Montana. His initial offer was "Five Hand-Tied Trout Flies—Only $.25!!! Free Shipping and Handling," and he got some orders. But the venture didn't really take off until he changed his ad to read, "Five Hand-tied Trout Flies—Absolutely Free!!! Shipping and Handling—Only $.25" The offer is identical, but it doesn't seem that way. The anecdote I use to back up the narrative is about Cracker Jacks, which have been around for over a hundred years Whether they are four years old or ninety-four, the first thing people do when they buy the product is to look for the free prize inside. And in all those years, there has never been a worthwhile prize. At stadiums, the people who clean up after ballgames find lots of caramel corn, peanuts, and Cracker Jack's boxes, but they never find a discarded prize.

To discover the power of the narrative and statistical evidence, access InfoTrac College

Edition, and type the word "persuasion" in the search engine. Select the persuasion/rhetoric periodicals option, and find the article titled "Persuasive Effects of Story and Statistical Evidence." There you will find the details of an interesting research study on the topic implied by the title.

Testimony

We usually suspect people who attempt to persuade us using only their own feelings or opinions. This is why the testimony of another person is valuable. Even unqualified testimony has influence. Of course, it is much better to have an expert witness testifying about the value of a person, product, or idea. I follow up my narrative and Cracker Jacks anecdote by referring prospective clients to other retailers that have had success with the "Free" offer, and I carry testimonial letters avowing to the various successes these retailers have had using the services of my ad agency. In a way, the testimonials act as a kind of social proof, to use Cialdini's term.

Visual Evidence

Walk into a department store where a salesperson or a videotape is demonstrating a food processor or a pasta machine, and you will see the power of visual evidence. The many television offers for various kinds of cooking equipment also testify to the power of the demonstration. Ron Popeil has made millions of dollars using the technique, beginning with his Pocket Fisherman and continuing with his Ronco glass and bottle cutter and various other unlikely devices. Much of the information offered in the demonstration is processed in the peripheral channel of the ELM. Visual persuasion also can be used—and misused—in political news coverage and advertising (Simons, 2001).

Of course, actual demonstrations of products are not always feasible, but persuaders can develop various kinds of visual evidence (such as graphs or charts) to help the audience understand the problem. Visuals should be large enough that everyone can see them. They should also be simple, because complex charts will only confuse the audience. For example, a student promoting a trip to Jamaica

sponsored by the student association effectively used travel posters, large pictures of local cuisine, easily seen cutouts from magazines depicting sandy beaches, and other images of tropical life to motivate her audience.

Keep visual evidence unobtrusive. For instance, it may be better to use drawings of how to fend off an attacking dog than to bring your dog to class and have it pretend to attack you while you demonstrate how to fend it off. One student who did so was embarrassed when his dog relieved itself instead of attacking on command.

You will find three very interesting articles about the use of visual evidence by accessing InfoTrac College Edition and typing "persuasion" in the search engine. Select the persuasion/rhetoric periodicals option, and explore the articles you find there, as well as related subjects. Then enter the words "visual evidence" in the key word search engine. There you will find some fascinating articles on the uses and power of visual evidence.

Comparison and Contrast

Sometimes, it is difficult to put problems in perspective. People tend to see issues from single viewpoints and to not judge them accurately. For instance, how big is the problem of disposing your old cell phone batteries in landfills? How does it compare with the problem of the disposal of auto or flashlight batteries? It is a little hard to know, so persuaders should provide something with which to compare or contrast their point about cell phone battery disposal. Comparisons should help the audience see the difference between two sides of the issue or between two cases. It doesn't help them much to know that OPEC decided to increase crude oil production by 550,000 barrels per day. It will be more meaningful to mention that this is an increase of 20 percent over previous production levels. Make your comparisons and contrasts meaningful by elaborating on them and by explaining the relative difference in the things being compared. Tell your audience that the increased production will reduce the price of a gallon of gas by as much as 25¢—that will mean more to them than the number of barrels of oil. Or compare the gas mileage of the new gasoline/electric-powered hybrids with that of other fuel-efficient car models.

Analogy

We have discussed analogies as a form of proof and noted that, although they can be effective, a risk is involved in using analogies—particularly figurative ones—because they can be turned around on the persuader. Analogies thus must be chosen carefully.

BUILDING YOUR CREDIBILITY

All the evidence in the world, organized perfectly and delivered well, will not persuade if listeners do not trust the persuader. In matters such as persuading the boss to give us a raise or our parents to let us marry before graduation, credibility is a key factor. What makes some people credible and others not? How can we build our own credibility before and during persuasion? In earlier chapters, we discussed the idea of credibility using Aristotle's ideas about the reputation of the speaker, the speaker's delivery during the speech, and the audience's response to the speaker's image. In more modern times, this has translated into several dimensions of credibility. Reputation is roughly equated with the known expertise of the speaker. For example, when an identical speech is attributed to experts in some cases and to novices in others, the "expert's" speech is always rated as more persuasive than the "novice's." Effective delivery is related to sincerity, dynamism, and charisma. We don't believe speakers who cannot maintain eye contact, and tall speakers have more persuasive potential than do short ones. Further, speakers with an animated delivery persuade more effectively than do speakers who are frozen at the podium. Exciting language usually helps make the speech more credible, and a well-groomed speaker is more credible than an unkempt one.

Most of these points seem obvious, yet they are overlooked daily by sales reps, politicians, spouses, teachers, students, and parents. Here are some examples from everyday life in which the elements of credibility can be used.

Trust

We trust people for many reasons. We trust them because they have been trustworthy in the past, because they have made direct eye contact, and because they have a calm voice. We also try to give off trust cues. We look at our persuadees directly; we try to sound sincere; we remind our audience of our past record for trust; and we refer to times when it would have been easy to break that trust. You might, for example, remind your boss of the many times when she was out of town and you could have slacked off but didn't. Or you might remind your parents of the many opportunities you had to party but studied instead. All these devices and others help build credibility.

Expertise

How do we know whether someone is a true expert on something? Generally, we look for past success at a task. If a person was a good treasurer for the fraternity or sorority, he or she will probably be a good treasurer for the student government. Sales representatives who did well in the Midwest should also do well on the West Coast. A person who has had experience in many areas of the company—shipping, sales, and so on—is much more credible to co-workers than the person who has had experience in only one area. Even if you do not have direct expertise on a given topic, you can "borrow" it by referring to known experts in your presentation. It is always useful and ethical to refer to your sources' background so receivers can judge the credibility of their testimony.

Clothing consultant John Molloy (1977) argued that individuals can create credibility by giving off competence cues. He has written several books and a syndicated column dealing with how clothes can send messages that say, "I am competent and in charge," or "I am a threat." Molloy suggested that the color of clothing communicates, too. And other nonverbal signs can further augment your credibility. In addition, you can signal expertise by being well prepared and by demonstrating knowledge about the topic. And being willing to engage in question-and-answer sessions when you have finished speaking also communicates credibility.

Dynamism

The dynamism factor of credibility is elusive. It is sometimes related to physical appearance, in that attractive people tend to hold attention better than less attractive persons. Dynamism or "charisma" probably cannot be developed much. However, other factors can. Many people who aren't particularly attractive are nonetheless persuasive and dynamic. Dynamic speakers seem to take up a lot of psychic space—they have "stage presence." You can project a dynamic image in several ways. One is to speak with authority—project your voice, maintain appropriate volume, and choose words that indicate certainty. Posture, good grooming, and appearance also signal dynamism, as do gestures, facial expressions, and eye contact.

WORDING YOUR MESSAGE

Stylistic speeches and exciting language choices persuade better than dull speeches. How do persuaders develop style in their presentations? What kinds of factors make some speeches, advertisements, or other persuasion memorable while other presentations are quickly forgotten or even ignored?

Variety in Word Choice

Most of us need to improve our vocabularies. You should try to rewrite your speeches using word variety to make them livelier, flashier, sexier, more dramatic, or more humorous. It helps to develop an interest in puns and other wordplays, as they can help you get the attention and earn the goodwill of your audience. Study the eloquence of other people, such as the great addresses of Abraham Lincoln (Selby, 1902). Pay attention to the language used in

government news releases, speeches by politicians, and various advertisements. Use the thesaurus feature on your computer.

Figures of Speech, Alliteration, and Assonance

Enhance your style by using proper figures of speech at the right time. Metaphors and similes help your audience visualize a point. The audience ties the information to the metaphorical structure and then remembers the information better as a result. Alliteration—the repetition of consonant sounds—and assonance—the repetition of vowel sounds—also enliven style. Both create a kind of internal rhythm in the message, which makes it more lively and memorable. We see this device used in advertising frequently to aid in brand name recall. Satin cigarettes are "smooth, slender, and sensuous," and the Parker pen is "wrought from pure silver and writes like pure silk." Both alliteration and assonance can be heard in "A portable phone system? Gee! No, GTE." Both devices help improve your style.

Vivid Language

Choose vivid words to catch your audience's interest. Although vividness can be overdone, it is more frequently overlooked in favor of dull and uninteresting language. Which of the following is more vivid?

> I'm offended by your representation of lutefisk. It is not rubbery!

> Lutefisk may be "a rubbery and repulsive ethnic dish" to the socially deprived, but to the properly initiated, it is the nearest thing to ambrosia this earth has ever produced.

Vivid and colorful language helps make a persuasive presentation memorable and effective. Developing your vocabulary arms you with more vivid and persuasive language.

Concise Language

Be as economical with your words as possible. Go over your presentation and pretend you are paying fifty cents per word to send it by telegraph. Then see how much excess baggage you can cut. Often, a straightforward statement is most effective. You can state your point in a short introductory declaration and elaborate on it later if necessary. Once, when Lincoln was trying to justify a pardon he was granting to an army deserter, he said, "I think the boy can do us more good above ground than under ground," thus stating his case concisely. You don't have to say everything in one sentence; you have an entire speech. Make your major point as a concise assertion or frame it in a provoking question. Then follow up with elaboration. If you try to say everything in the opening sentence, you will confuse your audience.

Parallel Structure

Parallel structure involves using similar or even identical wordings or sentence structures. For example, in a speech to the American Legion, Bill Clinton once said,

> I am not the only American whose life has been made better by your continuing service here at home. From baseball to Boy Scouts; from keeping veterans hospitals open to keeping kids off drugs; from addressing homelessness to preventing child abuse to instilling a deep sense of patriotism into still another generation of Americans, a grateful nation owes you a debt of gratitude.

His repeated use of the "from . . . to . . ." format provides parallel structure and symmetry in the speech.

Imagery

Imagery appeals to our senses, experiences, and impressions. Perhaps you can't bring the smell, taste, touch, sight, or sound of something to the audience, but you can use words that conjure up sensuous memories. It might be of a "tall, cool glass of chilled beer dripping with beads of perspiration" or the "fragrant smell of Mom's pot roast, ready to fall apart, with its juices making a savory gravy that starts your mouth watering." Think about the sensory experiences your audience has had that you can evoke, and state your points so that they appeal to one or more of the senses. A good way to develop this skill is to take a given product and try to restate its appeals in terms of the various senses. For instance, Campbell's soups are "Mmm, Mmm, Good." How might they be described using the other senses? As an insurance salesperson famously put it, "Don't sell the steak; sell the sizzle."

Humor

The use of humor in persuasion is an obvious stylistic asset if handled properly. But a word of warning is necessary here: If a persuader uses humor that is inappropriate, in bad taste, or just plain unfunny, there will likely be a boomerang effect. If you are going to use humor in your persuasion, test it out with friends and relatives. How can you develop humorous examples, comparisons, anecdotes, and stories? People who regularly engage in public speaking usually have a ready supply of humorous material with which to embellish their speeches. They develop the humorous aspects as they work up other materials for their speeches. You may be the kind of person who can never remember a story or joke. If so, keep a file of stories or jokes or maybe just punch lines. When you need the material the file will trigger your memory, and you will be able to retrieve those to-the-point humorous examples. Sources for humorous examples and anecdotes include *Reader's Digest;* browse through it while you're waiting at a doctor's office. Collections of stories or jokes are available from the library. Television shows such as *Saturday Night Live, David Letterman,* and *The Tonight Show* can provide you with humorous examples, as can your daily newspaper and people who frequently tell jokes (bartenders, barbers, and others). Amass a supply of humorous material to improve your style; it will make your persuasion more effective and memorable.

DELIVERING YOUR MESSAGE

Usually, we think of delivery as a source- or persuader-produced factor in influencing others. To some degree, this is true. However, several other factors can affect the delivery of your message, including the appropriate channel and the means of audience involvement. Persuaders often overlook these. In the following consideration of delivery, we will look both at those things that the source does during delivery and at those that are not tied to delivery.

The Persuader

Among the factors that persuaders adjust before and during delivery are their posture, eye contact, body movement and gesture, articulation, and vocal quality. Other factors under their control are the use of visual aids and other nonverbal cues. Some persuaders are so nervous that they cannot stop pacing back and forth. And when they do stop, they stand ramrod stiff, looking as if they might freeze into statues. Former Vice President Al Gore had this problem—people thought he was too "stiff." Since the 2000 election, he has seemed more relaxed and even hosted *Saturday Night Live*. Other speakers are so relaxed that they seem uninterested in their own messages. They slouch over the podium or slide down into their chairs during a meeting. They rarely look up and sometimes even nod off. Clearly, posture can signal the audience that you are either too relaxed or too nervous. The ideal posture lies somewhere in between. You should be alert and erect, and your shoulders should not tense or slump. Avoid looking nervous or tense (I wiggle my toes, but no one can see that). Overall, the message should communicate confidence. Observe persuaders in differing contexts—interviews, speeches, arguments—and you will see that the effective ones avoid both the nervous and the "nearly asleep" extremes.

Most people believe that a person cannot lie to you while looking you straight in the eyes. You will be more believable if you maintain eye contact with your audience. You don't need to look at everyone individually. Instead, look at various areas in the room. In a one-on-one context, establish repeated eye contact with the other person. Politicians make sure to look directly into the TV camera and so seem to make eye contact with each viewer. In a meeting, establish eye contact with as many participants as possible.

Body movement and gestures liven up a speech, as long as they don't distract. Using gestures during a speech keeps audience attention. However, it is a mistake to overrehearse gestures, body movements, and facial expressions. These nonverbal elements in delivery must appear natural, not staged, to have a positive effect. We all use gestures every day without thinking about them. Let your natural impulses guide you in your use of gestures in formal and interpersonal exchanges. Nothing can add more to your message than a natural gesture, movement, or facial expression (Scheflen, 1964).

Articulation and vocal quality also affect your delivery. Everyone has heard people who pronounce words incorrectly. As a result, the audience focuses on the error and not on the message. Successful persuaders listen carefully to themselves and work on articulation, pronunciation, and vocal quality. Listening to yourself on tape will help you pinpoint your mistakes and focus on your vocal quality. Some persons, especially females, think that a breathy or "thin" voice makes them sound sexier, but there is no evidence to support this belief. In fact, some suggest that just the opposite is true. If you are interested in persuading others, spend some time working on your voice and your articulation.

The Channel

Choosing the correct channel for sending your message is another key element in delivery. In one rural political campaign for the U.S. House of Representatives on which I worked, the candidates put most of their money into billboard space—which was rather surprising in this TV age. In this case, however, the candidate's district was large, stretching nearly half the length of the state, and no single TV network reached all of it. Using TV would have meant having to pay a triple load to get a single message across. But because the district was so large, all residents had to drive to shop, do business, socialize, worship, and farm. Thus, the billboard was the one channel that could touch nearly all voters in the district.

Similarly, recent presidents have returned to using radio for regular weekly persuasive talks. Why is radio such an appropriate channel for political persuasion? People listen to the radio while they are doing something else—driving, reading, mowing the lawn, exercising, and so on. It is estimated that Americans listen to the radio an average of four hours a day, and more than half of all persons listen to the radio at work, especially females (Russell & Lane, 1999). People also usually do these things during the daylight hours, so by choosing the relatively inexpensive medium of daytime radio, presidents are able to reach people they otherwise might not, and at a reasonable price. The same is becoming true of the various cable television outlets that are available.

On a more personal level, ask yourself what is the best way to inform your boss that you will look for another job if you don't get a raise or promotion. Perhaps tapping the grapevine might be best, or sending a straightforward memo, or asking her to be a reference so she will not get an out-of-the-blue inquiry. In general, start by listing all the potential channels that could be used to send your message. Then try to match them with your audience. Sometimes, persuaders encourage audience participation, which can increase audience energy and activity. Get your audience involved by asking direct questions and addressing people by name. You can also get the audience involved by leaving sentences incomplete and letting them supply examples. One speaker got audience involvement right away by asking them to stand up before he even began his speech. He then asked them to become aware of the muscles they were using in their feet, ankles, calves, and thighs at that moment and tied this awareness to his topic—the need to develop communication awareness on the job.

One word of caution: Don't distribute any printed material until the end of the speech. Audiences start reading right away, so you will lose their attention and interest.

COMMON TACTICS OF PERSUASION

Successful persuaders spend time finding out what the audience already believes and then use various tactics to link their points to audience beliefs. Depending on who you are reading, the tactics vary from author to author. Dale Carnegie (1952), for instance, emphasized the importance of remembering persuadees' or audience members' names and giving them honest credit for their accomplishments instead of false flattery.

The Foot in the Door or Door in the Face

Robert Cialdini (2001) describes several tactics including the foot-in-the-door and the door-in-the-face techniques. The foot-in-the-door technique involves getting a potential customer, joiner, contributer, or convert to make a small initial commitment that starts what will become a long-term relationship resulting in ever larger sales, contributions, and commitments. He traces the use of the technique to the Chinese communists' successful "brainwashing" of prisoners of war.

To illustrate, some time ago I signed a protest petition from the Citizens' Utility Board (CUB), which promised to use the petition to prevent price increases by Illinois utilities—Commonwealth Edison, Ameritech phone services, and the gas company, for example. Soon after, I received a newsletter explaining that CUB had stopped one of the utilities from instituting a 15 percent price increase. But the battle was not over, because the utility was appealing. Could I donate $50, $25, or even $10 to help carry on the fight. I donated $10. Next, a letter from CUB informed me of another victory, warned that the other utilities were suing CUB, and asked that I become a full-fledged dues-paying member of the organization for only $25. My signature on the petition was merely a foot in the door, and I continue to receive requests for donations.

In the retail field, this tactic may involve getting a prospective retailer for an entire product line to agree to initially carry one item in the line. That commitment may become the foot in the door to finally agreeing to carry the entire product line exclusively. As Cialdini puts it, "You can use small commitments to manipulate a person's self-image; you can turn citizens into 'Public servants' prospects into 'customers,' prisoners into 'collaborators'" (p. 67). Cialdini relates how the technique is used by the highly successful Amway Corporation. Staff members are asked to set themselves specific sales goals and then to write them down: "There is something magical about writing things down. So set a goal and write it down. When you reach that goal, set another and write that down. You'll be off and running" (p. 71). The written commitment somehow translates into motivation and action. That's the idea behind the required twenty-five-word written testimonial about a product in order to enter a contest or sweepstakes. The written testimonial is the foot in the door to lifelong brand loyalty. This tactic is also the idea behind the partial commitment sought by evangelists to spur religious conversions. Raising your hand in the air if you are becoming a believer is a small commitment, but it is a foot in the door to much more serious commitments.

The door-in-the-face tactic involves getting turned down on a request for a significant commitment, and then settling for an initial small commitment, or engaging in what Cialdini calls the rejection-then-retreat strategy. If a salesperson tries to get the prospect to go for the top-of-the-line or "loaded" version of the brand but is rejected, he or she can always retreat by offering a stripped-down version of the brand. Cialdini attributes the effectiveness of this strategy to feelings of responsibility and satisfaction on the part of customers, joiners, or donors. By settling for less, they feel as if they are in control and responsible for having "dictated" the deal. Because they believe that they have forced the concessions, they are more satisfied with their decisions. Another approach with this strategy is to "sell up" after retreating to a position of concession. Thus, once you've signed the contract to buy the new car, a good salesperson will offer you the extras —the undercoating and soundproofing, the extended warranty, the upholstery Scotchguard protection, and so on. Others have suggested similar tactics using somewhat different terms.

Here are some tactics suggested by Drs. William Howell and Ernest Bormann (1988). They may overlap with some of the other techniques discussed previously. Examine your world of persuasion for examples of these tactics in action.

The Yes-Yes Technique

A common tactic in sales and other persuasive appeals is called "yes-yes." The source attempts to get the target group or person to respond positively to several parts of the appeal, withholding the key request until last. Having agreed to most parts of the appeal, the persuadee is likely to say yes to the key and final request. For example, suppose you are trying to sell a lawn service. You might ask the homeowner, "You would like to have a beautiful lawn, wouldn't you?" The answer is going to be yes unless the receiver is a goofball. Then you ask, "And you'd like to get rid of the weeds?" Another yes is likely. "And wouldn't it be nice if these things could be effort free?" A yes answer is likely again. Now that the homeowner has accepted all your points in favor of the service, it is nearly impossible to respond with a no to "Then you'll want to sign up for our lawn service, won't you?" By accepting the yes pattern, the buyer accedes to your final request. The same technique is useful in a meeting in which a persuader gets the participants to agree to all but the final point in favor of, say, a change in work schedules. They agree that flexibility is good, that more free time for workers is good, and so on. They are then likely to agree that the change is a good one. Persuaders use the yes-yes technique to lead their target buyer, voter, donor, or convert through stages to a final yes answer.

The Tactic of Asking Not If but Which

It is easier to make a choice between two alternatives than from among many. This is the strategy behind the "don't-ask-if-ask-which" persuasive tactic. I learned as a parent of young children that the worst thing to ask them on Saturday mornings was, "What would you like for breakfast today?" I got all kinds of requests. It was better to say, "Which would you like for breakfast today—Dad's blueberry pancakes or Dad's blueberry coffee-cake?" The same thing applies in persuasion. Don't ask your audience to choose from too many options; ask them to choose from only a few or maybe between only two—"Would you rather have us undercoat your new car, or do you want to take it elsewhere?" or "Would you rather meet on your promotion this week or next?" or "Do you want guns or butter?"

Although this tactic can be manipulative, and hence can be used unethically, it has the distinct advantage and value of forcing some decision or action when buyers, voters, or others are stubbornly trying to avoid making decisions. When we present proposed ad layouts or scripts to prospective and existing clients, we always bring a small number of alternative layouts or scripts—usually two or three.

A Question for a Question

A tactic that some people use to throw others off guard is to respond to a request by asking a question. For example, they say, "Why do you think I would like to do that?" or "What gave you that idea?" We are expecting them to come to the point, to make a statement that relates to the discussion or the request. The tactic of responding with another question is useful because it usually catches other people off guard and gives the questioner time to think. Even asking people to repeat themselves or to elaborate can have these effects. This puts the ball back in their court. People who question you sometimes are trying to discredit or annoy you. Turn the tables—answer with another question. Suppose a prospect for advertising services asks, "Who else has used your services? Maybe I could check with them before deciding to go with your agency." A good response is, "I can bring you written testimonials about how successful we are in creating traffic for businesses like yours from across the country. Or I can give you names and phone numbers for local businesses that might be slightly different than yours, and you can call. Or I can do both. Which would you prefer?" Many people like to have things simplified and prefer fewer rather than more choices.

The Partial Commitment

This tactic resembles the door-in-the-face or rejection-then-retreat strategy. Evangelists often close their pitches by asking people in the tent or auditorium to bow their heads and close their eyes for prayer. This gets a partial commitment from the audience. The preacher then asks the Lord to enter the hearts of all and asks those who want God to come into their lives to raise their hands. The final request may then be, "Those of you with your hands up come to the front and be saved." The tac-

tic is seen elsewhere, too. Trying a sample of a product represents a partial commitment, as does clipping a coupon. The smart auto salesperson won't ask you to sign a sales agreement right off the bat. Instead, he or she will suggest that you look around and see if you find anything that appeals to you and then take it for a test drive. Merely by looking around, you are partially committing to the sales pitch, and the test drive is usually the clincher. After all, the salesperson knows you are going to buy an automobile. He or she simply needs to lead you bit by bit to choose one of that dealer's. Once you are partially committed, you are a good prospect for full commitment.

Of course, other kinds of commitment are used to persuade. When a politician asks you to sign a petition to put his or her name on the ballot, the act is a form of commitment to that politician. A favorite way to generate "qualified leads" in the marketing of some products is to run a sweepstakes. Anyone who submits an entry for the free version of the product has already made a partial commitment to it and thus is a good lead to follow up on. The tactic resembles the yes-yes technique but uses acts instead of words to lead the prospect to the final request. Persuaders can use it with neutral or negative audiences.

The Tactic of Asking for More
So They Settle for Less

This tactic is almost identical to the door-in-the-face or rejection-then-retreat strategy. Asking for more so they settle for less involves setting a price or level of commitment in people's minds that is higher than what they are probably willing to pay or do. When the persuader backs off, the buyers or voters think they are getting a special offer. For example, suppose I bring in a set of test scores to my class and sketch on the board the grading curve that the computer suggests. When I distribute the answer sheets, students moan because the curve is so high. Then I say that, because I think the computer's curve is unreasonably high, I am making my own curve, and I record a lower curve on the board. Students cheer and sigh with relief. I set a high expectation and then back off from that high level; my curve, compared with the machine's curve, is like a gift from Santa Claus. And I think I get better student evaluations of my teaching to boot!

Contemporary retailing is built on the notion of setting prices that can be marked down. No one buys anything at the regular price nowadays. It's always "marked down." And who would think of buying a car without either a great financing rate or a hefty rebate—or maybe even both! Persuaders can use this tactic when they have a product or goal that is hard to sell. Better to ask for more than your audience will stand for so that, in compromising, you will persuade.

Planting

The tactic of planting involves using one or more of the five senses to open a channel to the audience's experiential memory. The idea is to get the target group or person to recall how the product, idea, or candidate was experienced. This kind of memory is almost certainly processed in the peripheral information-processing channel. Memory responds best, it seems, to messages that have sensory data as raw material. Restaurant ads often appeal to several senses, and not just the sense of taste. They describe the "crisp and crunchy garden salad" to appeal to the sense of touch. They offer "sizzling hot steaks seared on a grill" to appeal to the sense of hearing. They describe the "thick red tomato sauce" to appeal to the sense of vision and use the words "a steaming fragrance of garlic and spices" to appeal to the sense of smell. In a classic case of using the sense of touch, Mr. Whipple of Charmin toilet tissue fame was regularly caught squeezing a pack of Charmin when he thought no one was looking. An ad for an automobile may have someone slam the door so audience members hear the solid "thunk" and mentally compare it with experiential memories of the rattles of their own five-year-old cars. Tie your persuasion to one of the five senses, and you'll find that the audience will remember your message better and longer.

The IOU

Sometimes called the reciprocity tactic, the IOU technique involves trying to get listeners to feel that they owe you something. For instance, the insurance salesperson spends several hours doing a complex assets-and-debts analysis for a prospect to prove to the prospect that he or she needs more insurance. The sales rep then spends several more hours explaining the figures to the spouse, perhaps taking the couple out to lunch or dinner. By the end of all the special treatment, the couple may feel that they really ought to buy something even though they may not need it or cannot afford it. They respond to the obligation—the IOU—that was created by the salesperson's effort. After observing how reciprocity works in various cultures, Cialdini (2001) notes that the need to reciprocate—the IOU—transcends "great cultural differences, long distances, acute famine, many years, and self interest" (p. 21).

Persuaders find this tactic useful when it is hard to make a first contact with buyers, voters, or joiners. You can place your audience in your debt by giving them free samples or offers of help. The old adage "There's no such thing as a free lunch" is a good warning in our double-speak world.

REVIEW AND CONCLUSION

We all have to persuade at some point. To be effective, we must plan how our format will affect the message. We must develop our forms of support and think about which will be most persuasive. We must control factors in delivery. We need to use source factors, such as posture, eye contact, and dress. Channel factors are subject to our control as well. Receiver factors can be used to get the target group involved in its own persuasion. As you are called on to persuade, use these skills in preparing. Rely on the audience analysis that the receiver-oriented approach teaches—listen to your audience. Get messages out of them, not into them.

QUESTIONS FOR FURTHER THOUGHT

1. What demographic clusters can you identify for the people in your class? In your dorm? In a club? Elsewhere?

2. What is a task-oriented message? Give examples from ads in which persuaders used this technique effectively. Give other examples from ads in which they failed.

3. What are the forms of organization? How do they differ from the forms of support? What might be other ways to organize a message?

4. What is AIDA, and how does it differ from the motivated sequence?

5. What are Rank's desire-building tactics? How do they work?

6. What are the factors in credibility? Give examples of people who have them. Find ads that rely on each factor. Describe the person and the ad in terms of the factors.

7. Where does humor fit into the persuasion process? Give examples of sources who use humor. Does it relate to the audience? How?

8. How can a persuader get his or her audience more involved? What are some examples you have seen or heard recently?

9. What is the difference between the forms of proof discussed here and those discussed in Chapter 8?

10. How does "planting" work? What about "getting an IOU"?

 For online activities, go to the Web site for this book at
http://communication.wadsworth.com/larson.

13

✳

Modern Media and Persuasion

We live in a media-rich society and are not fully aware of how many mass-mediated messages we receive each day. Many of them are informational, such as directions to places, instructions for assembling some product, news stories, and weather reports. But many—perhaps most—mass-mediated messages are aimed at persuading the audience to vote, join, purchase, donate, or change attitudes and behaviors. Recall from our discussion of language in Chapter 5 that prior to the invention of language we were cave-dwelling brutes. Since that time, other media of communication have been developed, and each of them has made communication and hence persuasion easier and more far reaching. Let's explore how these media affect persuasion and how they have changed the scale and pace of life.

MEDIA INNOVATIONS

There have been five major communication innovations in human history, each tied to the development of a new medium or technology for commu-

nicating with others. Each innovation, medium, or technology has shaped and changed the world and the destiny of humanity. And each has allowed humans to see the world in vastly different ways and to interact with one another more efficiently and with varying degrees of permanence. Of course, we are uncertain about all the changes the most recent of these media innovations will bring in the future. These media innovations or technologies are (1) the spoken word, (2) the written word, (3) the printed word, (4) the electronic word, and (5) the interactive electronic word. The first three innovations took us thousands of years. The fourth began only 150 years ago and began to rise to dominance only a half century ago—the 1952 presidential campaign was the first to really put television to use. The fifth is but a few years old.

The Spoken Word

When we were still only hominoids, or humanlike creatures, we used grunts and gestures to communicate. Over thousands of years, we developed the first communication innovation in human history: the power to speak and to symbolize. This permitted humanity to gather into groups or tribes. Speech also led us to develop labor specialization, rituals and religions, and a kind of history, embodied in myths, ballads, and legends. We sense the immense power of this development in the reverence with which the spoken word is held in the realms of religion, commerce, and politics and in our everyday lives. For example, in the Book of Genesis, the story of the creation indicates that with each creative act God spoke. Speaking was the catalyst for the creation of night and day ("Let there be light"); the land and seas; the fishes, animals, and birds; and, ultimately, man and woman. Later in the Old Testament, God again speaks to the various characters: Jacob, Moses, and David. In the New Testament, the speaking of words by Christ brings about almost all of his miracles. Christ is also referred to as "the Word." The Gospel of John begins, "In the beginning was the word, and the word was with God, and the word was God . . . and the word was made flesh and dwelt among us." In our daily social life, this reverent attitude toward the spoken word continues. At baptisms, the child's name must be spoken, and at weddings, the vows must be said aloud. We must be sworn in to testify, or to speak to the court, and the judge must speak the sentence before the defendant can be taken to prison. Even in death, we speak words of absolution and commit the body to the grave using the spoken word. We rely "on a person's word," actions "speak for themselves," and we look for "the final word" on various issues of life. We swear in political officials using the spoken word, and when we confer citizenship, we require that the applicants speak a similar oath.

The spoken word permitted humans to become social animals and to work together for the common good. It allowed one generation to pass down the history and knowledge of the tribal society in the form of myths or legends. It provided a means for the society to pass information down from generation to generation, thus allowing progress to occur: The wheel didn't have to be reinvented in each generation. In a sense, the development of the spoken word led to the organization of information

that could be shared by everyone. In oral/aural cultures, such as Native American tribes, information or knowledge is most frequently and fully held by the old and is passed down by "word of mouth." Thus, age is valued and honored. And because wisdom or knowledge increases with age, the older one becomes, the more important he or she is to the tribe. Among the Lakota, it was the custom to give every newly married couple an "Old One," perhaps a relative, to live in the couple's tepee to do the simple chores of tending the fire, comforting the babies, and being available for advice. Not only did this help the young couple, but it provided the Old One with a home. There were no "bag ladies" among the Lakota.

The spoken word still exists, of course, but not in the same way it did in an oral/aural world, as Father Walter J. Ong (1982) has pointed out. In the oral/aural culture and even after, the spoken word was an experience—an event. It occupied time, not space. It was ephemeral; the beginning of the word was gone before the end of the same word was uttered. Its only permanence was in the human mind and memory, and people reexperienced it only by reuttering it. The spoken word has always been essential for leaders. And it has always had "magical" qualities and continues to have them today. The tribal medicine man or voodoo doctor spoke words over the ill or over effigies of the enemy and worked his magic with spoken language. And even the stage magician uses the spoken word—"abraca-dabra" or "hocus-pocus-filiocus"—as a catalyst for performing magic tricks.

The Written Word

The next major communication innovation was the development of the phonetic alphabet, an alphabet tied to speech sounds, and not an ideographic one tied to vision (for example, Egyptian hieroglyphics or Chinese pictographs). It had different but equally profound effects on human history as the spoken word. With the alphabet, people could collect knowledge and store it. Advances of various kinds could be based on these stored records of what others had tried to do and how. The written word allowed societies to develop complex legal systems and to assign or deed land and other possessions, which led to the centralization of power. Knowledge was power and could be obtained and held only by those who controlled the written word: kings, emperors, feudal lords, and church leaders. Unlike the ephemeral knowledge "stored" via the spoken word (in ballads, legends, or myths), the knowledge stored in the written word could be recalled perfectly and long after the author was dead.

In ancient Greece and Rome, few people could read or write, and only the rich could afford scribes. Thus, information came to be thought of as individual property that could be "owned" and not necessarily shared with others. The great ancient libraries (such as the Greek library at Alexandria in Egypt) were the repositories of these societies' knowledge and information. But they weren't "lending libraries" as we know them—that would have to wait until Benjamin Franklin invented them in the eighteenth century. These libraries were private, so not everyone had access to the knowledge or information. Without this access, the average person remained ignorant of much of society's knowledge and thus remained at the bottom of the social order as fief, peasant, or even slave.

Not long after writing made the "ownership" of knowledge possible, the concept of ownership was applied to other property—land, cattle, horses, jewelry, buildings, and so on. Such ownership could be officially recorded in deeds to property, for example, which made lawyers, or official interpreters of the deed, a necessary evil. No such concept existed in the oral/aural cultures of Native Americans, for example. As a result, they had no concept of land ownership. This accounts for much of the misunderstanding associated with the land treaties of our history. To the white man, these treaties represented the legal contracts through which land ownership was transferred; to the Indian, the treaties were "worthless scraps of paper."

Ong (1967) pointed out that, whereas the spoken word took up time, the written word took up space and was not ephemeral—it lasted across generations—making people more likely to rely on written records for the "last word" on an issue. Indeed, the written word came to be thought of as more trustworthy and more "magical" than the spoken word. Even if they couldn't read, people wanted to see things "in writing" before they would believe them.

Ownership of knowledge as property also made knowledge a key ingredient for establishing and maintaining power. The written word allowed powerful persons to develop "nations" over which they ruled. It is no accident that the Romans attacked and destroyed the great library at Alexandria. In a certain sense, they "destroyed" the Greek nation by destroying its knowledge base. This might seem far-fetched, but imagine what the results would be if some country developed a weapon that could momentarily negate or "wipe out" magnetism. This could destroy all computer information, digital data, batteries, and so on.

Yet the spoken word as an experience persisted even in the societies in which writing was invented. As Ong (1967) observed:

> Ancient Hebrews and Christians knew not only the spoken word but the alphabet as well. . . . But for them and all men of early times, the word, even when written, was much closer to the spoken word than it normally is for twentieth-century technological man. Today we have often to labor to regain the awareness that the word is still always at root the spoken word. Early man had no such problem: he felt the word, even when written, as primarily an event in sound. (p. ix)

So the word remained an experiential phenomenon even when it was written. And it was to continue to be so perceived.

The Printed Word

The third major communication innovation was Johannes Gutenberg's invention of the printing press using movable type in the late 1400s. The effects of spreading the power of the written word to the common people were immense. Within a short time, the release of this power led to the Renaissance. Because information could be spread and shared, science developed rapidly. Scientists could read about one another's work and build on what others had done. Knowledge was no longer limited to clerics, although religion itself was greatly affected by the printing press. Before the printing press—the Dark Ages—few people outside the church could read or write. Books were expensive, and knowledge was power, held mainly by the church. But when it became possible to cheaply and accurately reproduce the Bible and other books, pamphlets, and tracts, this power became diffused.

The Reformation, like the Renaissance, was the inevitable outcome of this diffusion of knowledge and thus resulted in individual power and ownership. The notions of serfdom were superceded by ideas of owning land or businesses. People could read the writings of Martin Luther, and because the printing press was available, his objections to certain features of Catholic Church practices were duplicated and spread to many people. Many decided to start their own churches. The process continued with factions breaking away to form various Protestant religions. Governments weren't immune to this diffusion of knowledge, either, and soon most of them set up a censorship policy to help them control information and thus maintain power. Not until John Peter Zenger, a German printer in the American colonies, was tried for sedition because he had printed a tract criticizing a British colonial governor did the notion of freedom of the press gain credibility. Curiously, Zenger was tried not for *writing* the criticism but for *printing* it. The British government held all printers responsible for what they published, in effect making every printer an unofficial censor. Zenger may never even have read the pamphlet.

Like the power of the spoken word, the power of the printed word has diminished to some degree. Although the number of newspapers published in the United States has risen since the advent of television, readership of newspapers and newsmagazines is down. Nearly 30 percent of the U.S. population is functionally illiterate, which means they can't read such simple things as menus, labels, and street signs (Kaplan, Wingert, & Chideya,

1993). Some estimates indicate that those who do read newspapers devote only about eight minutes a day to the daily paper. The per capita consumption of books is down to less than a third of a book per year per person.

Still, the printed word gave us the Renaissance, the Reformation, and their many effects. These included the "New Science," because scientists could share the results of experiments in learned societies. The "New Art" developed because artists did not need to devote their energies to religious subjects alone. And the "New Music" emerged because musical scores could be printed accurately and cheaply and exchanged among composers, who learned from one another's works. But most importantly, in terms of persuasion, the printed word gave us *literacy,* which was to greatly influence the way people formulated and shared their thoughts and ideas. It led to a conception of humans as unique because they could think and reason and write down their thoughts and logic. Logic became the password of literacy, and the emotions of experience were demoted.

Literacy led to great discoveries and inventions in Europe and America. As noted earlier, Benjamin Franklin invented the lending library—a remarkably generous concept when you think of it. He also invented the postal service, the fire department, bifocals, central heating, the battery, the lightning rod, the rocking chair, the harmonica, and *The Saturday Evening Post,* among many other things. It is probably no accident that Franklin's background was as a printer's apprentice. Literacy opened the remarkable door of opportunity for Franklin and for many others, but it also enslaved us to some degree. We had to set aside a certain number of years of our lives to "learn" all the things that literacy had led to, and as a result we had to invent "childhood" —that time when a person gets an education. Naturally, we have had to expand the length of childhood several times as the amount of information to be learned has increased. Today, we talk of "lifelong learning" and frantically try to read as much as we can, falling further and further behind all the while. And the Internet hasn't made things any easier. Even as the sheer amount of printed and published material has mushroomed, nearly all of the Internet Web sites require literacy of some sort on the part of the user.

The Electronic Word

The electronic word appeared in 1844 with the first demonstration of the telegraph. The telegraph used electrical impulses that were turned on and off by the telegrapher's key to signal the various letters and spaces. This allowed words to be sent as a series of dots and dashes, via Morse code. Then, in 1876, came the telephone, which transformed the spoken word into electronic impulses. Shortly thereafter came the radio, or wireless telegraph, which transformed written and later spoken words into electronically produced sound waves. We looked briefly at the changes brought by the electronic word when we discussed technological determinism in Chapter 4. As noted there, we are only dimly aware of the influences of all these electronic words—the telegraph, radio, and telephone—but it is possible to get a glimmering of their effect with a hundred-year perspective. For example, the telegraph greatly sped up the communication process. Instead of relying on the Pony Express to get a message across the country (which took ten days), people could telegraph the message in minutes. In a sense, the electronic word wiped out not only space but time as well. For example, with telegraphs, people could learn the results of the game or horse race almost immediately—think what that means to bookies. The same was true of election results, the news of catastrophes, joyous and sad family events, and a host of other aspects of social life.

Of course, there exist other versions of the electronic word—television, personal computers, video games, the telephone and cell phone, VCRs and DVD players, CDs, and more. Most of them have been developed only recently, and the changes they are effecting in society probably pass unnoticed. For example, consider the changes wrought by the cell phone alone. Many students on my campus no longer have a land-line telephone and rely instead on their cell phone for local and long-distance communication—you see them communicating while they drive, walk, ride a bicycle, or work out at the Rec Center. When the first edition of this book was published, dormitories at many colleges had but one phone to service an entire floor of occupants. The immense changes attributed to the electronic word are there even if they go unnoticed. And the critical consumer of persuasion should be alert to the ways the electronic word influences our culture and ourselves.

Some people are concerned that this explosion of electronic media adversely affects us. For example, many critics worry that the home computer will drive Western culture inward, making us unable to interact with others on an interpersonal level. Anyone who has used a PC knows that time can flash by in the twinkling of an eye—you think you started on the document just a few minutes ago and now three hours are gone. People regularly complain about the way society is becoming depersonalized in an era of electronic technology. People are offended by voice mail and resent automated answering systems; they want to talk to a real person. The phrase "playing phone tag" is but one example of how electronic media have changed life as it was known only a few generations ago. Likewise, many people are concerned about the amount of television being watched each day by the average American child—and adult (see Figure 13.1). We worry about the effects of television violence. We wonder whether America's youths may go prematurely deaf because of the volume used on radio headsets, tape players, and compact disc players. And many parents are concerned about their children's access to pornography on the Internet. A researcher on the effects of television on children and the family whom I know recently entered the words "teens," "anal," and "sex" in the search engine and got a list of nearly 1.5 *million* Web sites where that kind of material is available.

The most common kind of electronic persuasion that we receive is advertising—in TV and radio spot commercials. As noted before, most college freshmen have seen more than 22,000 hours of TV

FIGURE 13.1 Certain aspects of modern electronic media are causes of concern, as this cartoon demonstrates.

(*Frank and Ernest* reprinted by permission of NEA, Inc.)

programming and who knows how many commercials. We live in a world in which electronic and print messages literally surround us—on billboards and in newsletters, magazines, catalogues, signs on shopping carts, banners, unwanted spam and pop-ups on the Internet, electronic catalogue kiosks in airport terminals, videos in supermarkets, email "opt-in" lists, and so on. The mass media are the most effective channels to persuade large numbers of people. They persuade us to buy products, to vote, and to take up causes. Why is this? One reason may be that there is only limited feedback in mass message systems (you cannot question, applaud, or respond very easily), so certain ploys work that would usually fail in an open, face-to-face context.

We are all annoyed by unwanted telemarketing calls. If they are so universally disliked, why are they still in such wide use? Because they work—they sell products, candidates, and good causes very effectively. Another reason that modern mass media, particularly electronic media such as radio, television, the Internet, digital audio and video, and the personal computer, are able to persuade so effectively is that they are inherently oral/aural in nature. That is, in the same way that spoken words are fleeting, electronic signals or images are also fleeting. We hear or see them for only an instant, and then they disappear from the screen or speaker, never to be recalled unless someone "saved" them on an audio- or videotape, a CD, a DVD, or a computer disc. These electronic signals are "experienced" more than they are logically thought out, reasoned with, or subjected to tests of proof. The greater portions of them are probably processed in the peripheral information-processing channel and pass by without much serious investigation. For example, we can't ask whether the actors on *General Hospital* are "true" or "false" in their roles in various settings or as spokespersons for some product. They are neither and they are both. Our experience with this week's episode or ad is not necessarily logical. In fact, it is more likely to be emotional, and neither truth nor logic has anything to do with it. As the controversy over the alleged presence of weapons of mass destruction in Iraq suggests, in this oral/aural age, truth is increasingly irrelevant, and logical persuasion is giving way to experiential or emotional persuasion, largely in the peripheral channel of the elaboration likelihood model (ELM).

The same holds true of many other electronic media messages: Like the spoken word, they are events meant to be experienced before being recorded or analyzed. Technological developments suggest that such messages will become even more emotional—perhaps not as experiential as the "Feelies" of Aldous Huxley's *Brave New World,* in which people went into a booth, touched electrodes mounted there, and then experienced what was happening on the screen. They felt what it was like to swim in the ocean, to make love, to be strangled, to eat shark, and so forth. In other words, in the Feelies, people really "lived" movies.

The Interactive Electronic Word

We are just beginning to deal with a new kind of communication innovation—the interactive electronic word. To date, the electronic word has affected us mostly as receivers—we consume more of these media than we produce. With interactive electronic media, however, the receiver gets into the act much more. Although only in its infancy, one such experiential medium beginning to affect society is virtual reality. In one form, it resembles a video battle game and costs about a dollar per minute to play. A player either enters a "cockpit" or dons a helmet and glove, whereupon the battle begins. Unlike traditional video games, in which the player "looks in" at the battle occurring on a video screen, virtual reality puts players "inside" the battle. The players each have the equivalent of 360-degree vision (that is, the picture seems to surround them). As they turn their heads, they can "see" the full 360-degree battlefield by either "revolving" their cockpits or turning their heads. In some versions, as many as eight players divided into "teams" can fight it out with the enemy for ten minutes. At the end of the session, each player receives a printout that gives a blow-by-blow description of what happened plus scores for all the players. As a result, the battle seems to be almost real.

Such game versions of virtual reality have little practical applicability. However, the potential uses of virtual reality technology are breathtaking. For example, surgeons can now conduct "virtual operations" for training purposes; then laser scalpels might be programmed, using the virtual operation, to perform the real one—after, of course, redoing the mistakes. In retailing, virtual reality might replace the showroom floor or retail outlet. Charles Madigan (1993), a researcher into potential applications for the technology, describes a potential "virtual purchase":

> A customer in his or her own living room facing a bigger-than-life fully digitized television

screen will say, "Shop Ralph Lauren." After a pause of only a few seconds, the image of Ralph Lauren will come, smiling to life on the screen. . . . Ralph will ask for some particulars. . . . Perhaps price will be discussed. . . . It won't really be Ralph Lauren. . . . More accurately, it will be virtual Ralph having a virtual conversation. (p. 14)

Other possible uses for virtual reality technology include virtual golf lessons at home taught by a virtual Tiger Woods. Or how about virtual concerts after dinner by famous string quartets, or virtual physical therapy, or psychiatry in the privacy of your own home. Virtual exercise could be led by a holographic three-dimensional Cindy Crawford. You could experience virtual holidays in foreign countries. Not surprisingly, virtual reality has spawned "teledildonics," a term coined to describe virtual sex with holographic lovers—not far from Huxley's "Feelies" (Madigan, 1993).

The potential implications of this new medium are awesome. Imagine virtual TV spot advertisements, virtual propaganda, or virtual politicians and virtual elections. Does this sound like some far-fetched fantasy? Perhaps, but Madigan poses an important question when he asks, "Who could have anticipated the impact that television would have on a society back when it was still a novelty? Information technology is moving so rapidly, developing so exponentially, that no one knows quite where it will lead" (p. 16). Research into virtual reality technology is largely being funded by the military and the pornography industry. Most of the air sorties flown in Operation Desert Storm and Iraqi Freedom had been rehearsed using virtual reality technology. Some surgeons practice doing surgical procedures using the technology. These and other uses of the technology raise interesting philosophical, economic, political, and ethical questions such as we have never had to face before. Can or should the surgeon charge for the practice operations he or she performs? Will insurance companies cover practice operations? Could we elect a virtual president? Is theft or murder using virtual reality a true crime? Is adultery in virtual reality grounds for divorce?

If you think these examples of the potential of virtual reality technology seem far-fetched, go to InfoTrac College Edition, and type the words "virtual reality" in the subject search engine. Explore just a few of the nearly one thousand periodical titles listed there. Also go to some of the commercial applications listed there. If you are really interested in this technology, the listings will give you locations where you can go and actually experience it. Report back to your class what you have discovered.

We have just begun to process the implications of this new kind of electronic word through phenomena such as militia movements or the stalking of crime victims on the Internet. Consider the possibilities of interactive fraud on the Internet or terrorist uses of the Internet. What are the ethical implications of porn or gambling online, and what are the implications of protecting privacy in cyberspace? And we need to consider what is going on with regard to the new interactive technologies in research labs around the world (most notably in Japan, Germany, and England). They are delving into possible technological innovations that will certainly expand the interactive electronic word. Consider Stewart Brand's (1987) description of some of the developments at the Media Lab at MIT that occurred while he was there on sabbatical almost twenty years ago. The $45-million lab was established and funded by the leading corporations in three communication fields: the print industry, the film/video/audio industry, and the computer industry. Each corporation and industry realized that phenomenal changes in communication technology were imminent and that the ability to develop them effectively and prudently was far beyond the financial and research capabilities of any single corporation or industry. So they pooled their resources, sought out the brightest and best media researchers, technicians, engineers, and theorists in various communication fields, and asked them to literally "invent the future" in the various communications industries. The Media Lab's director, Nicholas Negroponte, knew that the three industries were already beginning to converge, as shown in Figure 13.2. Some examples of this convergence include

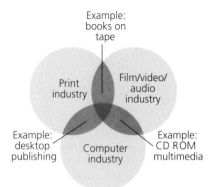

FIGURE 13.2 The convergence of the print, film/video/audio, and computer industries and technology today.

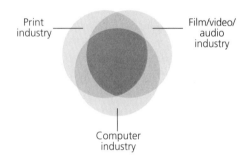

FIGURE 13.3 The convergence of the print, film/video/audio, and computer industries and technology in the future.

print that is computer typeset and enhanced visually by digital video technology; computer-generated and -produced video graphics; electronic mail, faxes, and digital audio; print ads that incorporate appropriate electronic music; and 3-D IMAX theaters. Negroponte foresees a much broader convergence of the three technologies, which will look more like Figure 13.3 in the new millennium. And the predicted changes exceed our wildest dreams. A brief example demonstrates the immensity of these changes: Negroponte bases all of his plans on the growing computer intelligence of the TV set itself.

"Twenty years from now your TV set will probably have 50 megabytes of random access memory and run at 40 to 50 MIPS [millions of information pieces per second]. It'll basically be a Cray computer" (Brand, 1987, pp. 77–78).

It is not my intent here to hypothesize about future developments of the interactive electronic word, but rather to illuminate how they might affect us and try to persuade us. Here, the work of two important media theorists, Tony Schwartz and Marshall McLuhan, can help us understand the experiential nature of the current technology and prepare us for the developments we will encounter in the next decade.

To find out how Hollywood is taking to the new interactive electronic word, access Info-Trac College Edition, and enter the words "media innovations" in the search engine. Find the article titled "Traffic Jam" by Laura Stevens.

SCHWARTZ'S PERSPECTIVES ON MEDIA USE

Although thirty years old, the ideas in Tony Schwartz's book *The Responsive Chord* (1973) have been used by sources ranging from presidential media staff to firms and ad agencies selling everything from baby powder to booze. Schwartz offers two competing models for explaining the way media work to persuade: (1) the evoked recall, or resonance, model and (2) the transportation, or teaching, model. Schwartz favors the first approach and offers reasons for this.

Resonance and Experiential Meaning

The evoked recall (or resonance) model rests on the idea that it is better to get a message out of receivers than to try to put one into them. In other words, it relies on the set of experiences and memories that people have stored inside them. Schwartz's initial interest was in how various sounds could trigger responses in radio listeners. For example, an early client wanted the sound of a newborn crying in order to cue feelings of fear, concern, and even guilt in expectant mothers in order to sell the client's baby powder. The sound of crying resonated with real experiences that the expectant mothers had had with their other children or with infants of family and friends. There is nothing quite so piercing as the cry of a newborn—and remember, they cry, on average, for four hours a day. When and if you have children, you will understand just how effective the strategy was in persuading the mothers to make a purchase. Later, Schwartz's interests expanded to television, which he felt closely resembled radio and the oral/aural means of communication in its ephemeral nature and its reliance on cuing experiential meaning out of receivers.

Using this approach, persuaders might address the problems people have with, say, a stalled car. Aware that the potential buyer of the product—an AAA membership—knows what a stall is like, the source can build a message around the feelings people have when their car stalls. Actors in an ad might show frustration, signaling the anxiety motorists have felt when they knew a stall would make them late for an important appointment. The music or score can heighten the feelings. The voice-over might then say soothingly, "When you've got to be there, Triple A gets you there." Schwartz observed that most experiential meaning is not cued symbolically because it is not stored as a symbol. Instead, it is stored as a feeling—a sense of ease or dis-ease. And the best way to cue these feelings is through drama: The source acts out the feeling in the target's head. Many times, the cuing occurs through music, color, sound effects, the actors' facial expressions or tone of voice, the acoustics, or some other nonverbal and usually visual image or message.

What are some stored experiences and emotions that are common to large numbers of people and that media can cue in them? The examination dream mentioned in Chapter 12 is one example; frustration over a traffic jam is another, as is car trouble. Any event or situation to which people respond with something like "Boy, are you touching a nerve there" or "You're getting awfully close to home" probably resonates with large numbers of people. Mass media persuaders, especially advertisers, have identified many of these resonating experiences and use the media to cue them in us. For instance, an automobile company advertised its sporty convertible on billboards. The boards showed a teal-colored model heading off into an unclear "future," represented in the background, and the words on the board read, "Go Ahead—Have a Midlife Crisis." The ad was targeted at baby boomers approaching midlife. Teal was a popular "boomer" color; the convertible resonated with experiences in their youth; and the unseen future resonated with their fears of mortality. The words were merely the action step offering a "cure" for the dis-ease being experienced by the target market. The baby boomer could purchase the vehicle instead of divorcing his wife, finding a twenty-something girlfriend, and going to California to sell hot air balloon rides on the beach.

As you examine the media persuasion aimed at you in magazine ads, TV and radio spots, and billboards, try to identify the common experiences being targeted. In all likelihood, they are being processed in the peripheral channel of the ELM without much intellectual evaluation and consideration. Instead, they simply "feel right." In Schwartz's words, they are "resonating" with a "responsive chord." You probably won't find many of these experiential or emotional roots for media persuasion in the verbal script of an ad or other persuasive message, which usually contains the logical and discursive part of the message. The messages that tug at the heartstrings instead of the mind probably occur elsewhere. One place is in the auditory script, which goes beyond verbal symbols. This involves such things as the musical score, the lyrics, the sound effects, and maybe even subliminal cues. Another place where common experiences might be identified is in the visual script—the images, montages, camera angles, pictures, colors, and other visual effects such as computer graphics. Each of these media "languages" can be critical in plucking a responsive chord.

The Verbal Script

Of course, Schwartz's idea runs counter to what many ad agencies believe. It is also counter to much of the theory about persuasion, which emphasizes specificity, logic, and cleverness with words. In this view, the verbal script is the message. And when ad agencies test their ads, they do just that: They ask people to look at ads and then to respond by recalling the words, images, numbers, and names in the ad. Rarely are respondents asked about their feelings or about the characters in the ads. Often, a quirk of fate brings out such data, as in the case of the people who resented the idea that their suitcase would survive a plane crash when they would not. However, if the verbal script resonates and cues experiences from the audience, powerful results usually occur. For example, a recent radio ad for a brokerage firm cued the experience of being trapped by an automated answering message: "If you want to check your balance, press 1 now. If you want to get a quote, press 2 now. If you want to talk to a real financial advisor, press 8 now and start over. Or try calling Financial Expertise at 1-800-MONEYAID." This persuasive message probably is carefully considered in the central channel of the ELM even though it was probably initially processed via the peripheral channel.

The Auditory Script

The typical TV spot includes more than just its verbal script. It usually has a sound script—things you hear that are not words. The "language" of sound—sizzles, pops, grinds, klunks, plops, and buzzes—can sometimes cue powerful, unconscious emotions. For instance, good feelings about parties are cued by the sounds of beer being poured. The gurgle of the first mug being filled triggers the memory of good times. Then the advertiser simply adds words: "We've got beer in a can that's as good as beer from a keg—Hamm's draft in the new aluminum can." The can is shaped like a barrel or keg to reinforce the good feelings most people have about past keg parties. This auditory-script message can be reinforced by the musical score and sound effects.

We have all had experiences cued out of our collective storehouses of memories in the same way that small cues prompt what we call a déjà vu experience. For example, take an ad for Diet Coke titled "Break Time," which was targeted at working women ages 18–34—the typical cola drinker. We see a group of attractive women gathered at the drinking fountain at break time and looking out the window. One says something like, "Okay, it's time," and a handsome, muscular male construction worker across the street peels off his T-shirt. The women ogle him and sigh as he pops a Diet Coke and swigs it down. His muscles ripple as he shakes his sweaty head, and more sighs are heard. The words are practically irrelevant—it is what the women look like and what the man looks like, accompanied by the sighs, that make the ad work. These act as cues for the experience of voyeuristic lusting in the minds of the target market—something most of us recognize. There is nothing logical about the ad or the response it cues from viewers, nor is the ad particularly true or false in any way. It simply "is."

The same kinds of experiences can be cued in an entertainment program, a radio spot ad, or a foldout 3-D print ad. They all rely on stored experiential memories associated with a particular cue—a sound effect, a musical score, and so on. In fact, some of the scores for jingles have been so effective that they have become popular songs. For instance, the Coca-Cola jingle "I'd Like to Buy the World a Coke" was transformed into a popular song titled "I'd Like to Teach the World to Sing."

The Sight Script

The sight script also serves as an important source of cues. The keg-shaped beer can and the drum-shaped cleaner bottles, which convey the feeling of heavy-duty power, are examples. Another way the sight script cues feelings is by camera angle. A low angle distorts size somewhat and "says" that this person is someone to be looked up to—a cut above most people. A wide-angle shot showing crowds of people thronging to see a person sends the message that this is a great leader of an important movement. Hitler used this technique in the famous Nazi propaganda film *Triumph of the Will*. It was outlawed in Germany for many years after World War II because its wide-angle shots and musical score retained the power to stir emotions and feelings in the audience.

Close-up or zoom-in shots of people convey the idea that we need to take a closer look, to find out what they are made of. Editing can evoke feelings that are then used to persuade. Quick-cut edits convey a sense of action. A camera that pans from left to right expresses the immensity of a scene or crowd. Frequently, when there are few people in a crowd, the camera hides that fact by dollying (moving or rolling forward) up to the last row of spectators, giving the illusion of a crowded room when actually there are many empty seats. If news editors want to show the sparsity of a crowd for a certain politician, however, they can take a shot from behind the speaker and pan the empty seats.

The quick-cut edit builds excitement and gives a sense of speed. For example, in one ad, a snowmobile cutting through a huge snowdrift suggests action and excitement. The view then cuts quickly to downhill racers carving their way through a tough slalom course, and a final quick cut shows ice-boat racers zooming across a frozen lake. Only at the end of the ad is there any verbal script— "Warm Up Winter This Year. Come to the Winter Wonderland of Lake Geneva." The ad then closes by showing an attractive couple snuggling in front of the fireplace in the ski lodge. The visual script does most of the work here. It builds the excitement and cues the experiential memories from the audience's subconscious. The verbal script merely tells viewers where the memories can be brought to life.

Other aspects of the sight script continue the job of evoking responses from us. Many newscasts convey a "newsroom atmosphere": Printers churn out copy, people rush around the set carrying pieces of paper meant to be news flashes, and so on. The anchorpersons are then superimposed on the scene to give the visual impression that they are in the middle of the hustle and bustle of the newsroom. You feel that you won't miss any news if you stay tuned to that channel. Similarly, the background shots for political candidates can signal sophisticated nuances of meaning. If the candidate is standing in front of the Lincoln Memorial with the president, he or she must be devoted to issues of equality and justice.

Props, jewelry, furniture, artworks, costumes, and other visible effects are part of the sight script, too. See the ad for *Ms.* magazine in Figure 13.4. Each visual element adds a new layer of meaning,

FIGURE 13.4 Here is the ad for *Ms.* magazine that prompted the angry letter to the editors of *Advertising Age.* Is the ad true or false? Is it realistic or unrealistic? At whom was the ad probably targeted? What do you think would be Tony Schwartz's response to the ad, to our semiotic analysis of it in Chapter 6, and to the letter to the editors?

(Used by permission.)

suggesting that the *Ms.* reader is a sophisticated and attractive woman, approaching middle age, a well-dressed, bejeweled world traveler and mother. She uses cosmetics, carries cash, and drives an Audi, all the while being sentimental but open to new technologies. These elements are all part of the sight script. Are they true or false? One reader had some strong feelings about the ad, which she put in a letter to the editors of *Advertising Age* magazine, where the ad appeared:

> [The] ad on behalf of *Ms.* magazine is one of the most unrealistic, off-target ads I've seen in a long time, and probably succeeds in irritating, if not aggravating, the very reader it was targeted at. No woman of any note, especially one who's "made it to the top" would ever carry around most of the objects "falling" out of her pocket. . . . Guys gimme a break: A passport? Champagne cork? A $100 bill? Not to mention "cute" kid drawings, credit cards and pills or breath mints. Why do you think women carry purses? . . . Women are lucky to find velvet pants with pockets in the first place. . . . My second objection is that any woman worth her gender and deserving of making it to the top would never find herself in this "falling out of pockets" position in the first place if she DID have stuff in her pockets. Any reader of *Ms.* magazine would have been prepared and removed this stuff before becoming comfy in an upside-down mode. (Victory, 1988, p. 20)

The tone of the letter and several phrases in it make it clear that the author assumes that the intended targets of the ad are the readers of *Ms.* magazine (for example, "any woman worth her gender" and "any reader of *Ms.*"). The criticisms she raises in her letter would probably be accurate if that was the intended target. However, the target was potential advertisers in *Ms.* magazine. *Ms.* had been sold to the same company that publishes *Sassy.* They tried to reposition *Ms.* by shifting its image from that of a magazine for ardent feminists to one for successful, upscale women in their middle years—baby boomers, yuppies, and muppies

(mature urban professionals). They hoped to get airlines to advertise in the new *Ms.* magazine—hence the passport. They wanted cosmetics companies to advertise—hence the lipstick. They wanted computer companies to advertise—hence the calculator. They wanted companies that market sentimental products to advertise—hence the champagne cork and the florist's card with her husband's name on it. Of course, the ad was unrealistic; it was intended to be that way in order to be explicit about the readership of the new *Ms.* magazine.

Thus, the most effective advertisements are those that resonate most closely with the experiences of the audience. The title of Schwartz's book, *The Responsive Chord,* reflects that relationship between the audience and the persuasive message, whether the message is the advertisements, the articles printed in magazines, or the programs heard on radio or seen on TV. The degree to which they resonate with the experiences stored in the conscious or unconscious minds of the audience predicts their success or failure. In fact, Schwartz noted that the issue of truth is irrelevant in examining the programming or the advertising of electronic media. And he would probably say the same thing about many of the print ads in contemporary magazines and newspapers. In a sense, they have become more like the video medium in the past decade. Today, we see ads with little or no copy that present a potential dramatic script that could be brought to life on a television screen. A good example of the resonance principle being used by advertisers can be seen in the storyboard for an ad for the 1994 Acura Integra, shown in Figure 13.5. The ad aims at graying baby boomers who can recall having played with Hot Wheels, a racetrack toy by Mattel, as youngsters. The Integra runs on a giant Hot Wheels track and negotiates the loop-the-loop part of the track just as the boomers' old toy did. In a bit of clever humor at the end of the ad, an announcer says, "Track sold separately."

Or take the Chivas ad in Figure 13.6. The visual script is effective because it resonates with the experiences of many parents of young children. The couple in the Chivas ad are treating themselves to

FIGURE 13.5 This ad for the Acura Integra taps into men's experience of having played with a Hot Wheels racetrack, thus resonating with the experiences of its target audience—male baby boomers born in the 1960s and early 1970s.

(Reprinted by permission of American Honda Motor Co.)

Sometimes life begins
when the babysitter arrives.

What are you saving the Chivas for?

FIGURE 13.6 Despite the fact that only a select number of critical words are used, this ad presents a visual script that is very clear. What is the script? What is the plot? What will happen after dinner?

(Courtesy of Joseph E. Seagram & Sons, Inc.)

the best restaurant dinner, the finest scotch whiskey, and probably a night of lovemaking. Many consumers identify with the plot, characters, and setting in the visual script. In other words, the script resonates with the experiences consumers have stored in their conscious or unconscious minds. Persuaders need to identify such common experiences and then design print or electronic messages that prompt the audience to recall the experience while also mentioning the product, candidate, or organization seeking support.

What if the audience doesn't have such a stored experience? Schwartz recommended "planting" the experience in ads early in the campaign. For example, show macho guys in whitewater rafts being bounced up and down as they navigate the Colorado River. Then they reach a slack pool, paddle to shore, and open their cooler to enjoy a cold can of Bud or Miller. Even someone who has never whitewater rafted now has the experience planted in his or her mind. The next step is to reinforce that experience in print ads, focusing on the final scene, and with shorter TV and perhaps radio ads. Then, at the point of purchase, voting, or joining, some cue prompts the recall. The product's packaging (for example, a picture of whitewater rapids), the candidate's name on the ballot, the organization's logo on a billboard or package—all help cue meanings at the point of purchase.

As it is used in contemporary advertising, Schwartz's resonance principle presents receivers of persuasion with several challenges. They need to identify common experiences that the persuasion aims to prompt in them, and they need to identify persuasive messages used to "plant" experiences that are to be triggered later, at the point of purchase. They also need to be aware of the symbiotic relationship between the verbal, auditory, and visual elements in any mass-mediated persuasion.

To learn more about Tony Schwartz, access InfoTrac College Edition, and type the words "Tony Schwartz" in the search engine. Read Kostelanetz's interview with Schwartz, and see what you learn about this media master.

McLUHAN'S PERSPECTIVES ON MEDIA USE

The Modern Media Revolution

Marshall McLuhan (1963) was another theorist who studied media use in our times. He was remarkably accurate in his predictions on media effects, as his forty-year-old prognostications are now coming to pass. His ideas resemble Schwartz's in many ways. McLuhan believed that we relate to media in two ways. First, every medium is an extension of one of our senses or body parts. For example speech is an extension of our ears and print is an extension of our eyes. Second, media can change our way of thinking about our world, as when the telegraph gave people the idea that they could communicate quickly across distances, thus "destroying" space. The invention of the wireless helped bring David Sarnoff to power as president of NBC. As a young man, he was broadcasting and receiving wireless Morse signals from high atop a Wannamaker's department store on the night of April 14, 1912. He picked up a message from sea: "*S.S. Titanic* ran into iceberg, sinking fast." He relayed the message to the news media and for the next several hours remained in contact with the ship, serving as a key liaison between powerful people aboard the ship and their families, business associates, and attorneys. Essential directions about where wills were located, what to buy and sell, and so on were communicated through Sarnoff, thus providing him with an entré to the rich and powerful. They helped him promote radio and radio programming—the arenas that gave Sarnoff both wealth and influence, and ultimately led to his creation of the RCA corporation and its network, NBC.

Radio revolutionized the reporting of news and helped create what we call "popular culture." Its entertainment programming (dramas and variety shows) enthralled the public. Its news reporting (national, state, and local coverage; on-the-spot reporting; play-by-play sports reporting; and coverage by foreign correspondents) made news seem immediate. Its cultural offerings (the Metropolitan Opera, documentaries, radio adaptations of great works of literature, and classical music) brought high culture to the masses. And its broadcasts of several types of music (big bands, country/western, rock 'n' roll, and rhythm and blues) created a large part of "pop culture." Television changed and expanded popular culture in similar ways. Instead of reading a newspaper account or listening to a radio report of a news event, we are transported via television to see and hear the actual story unfolding anywhere in the world. TV news announcers (such as Dan Rather, Connie Chung, Peter Jennings, and Tom Brokaw) have become universally recognized icons. Investigative television journalism changed the concept of what is newsworthy and what is credible in news reporting. Take, for example, the reporting of national scandals beginning with Watergate and continuing to Iran–Contra, Whitewater, the Clinton impeachment hearings, and corporate piracy at Enron, WorldCom, and Arthur Andersen, as well as local scandals or issues. Today, most Americans report that their primary source of news is television —not the newspaper or news weeklies.

Television news has been further diluted by "fluff" journalism, in which "nonstories" and pseudoevents are reported as if they had earth-shattering importance. Television has even effected changes in the world of sports. Take the two-minute warning in football. It didn't exist in the days of radio or even in television's early years but was "invented" by the networks to create more opportunities to run spot advertisements. Now, all NFL games are stopped by the officials for an "artificial" time-out two minutes before the end of each half. Teams can use this "free" time-out, in conjunction with their other time-outs, to "control the clock" and get quick, game-saving scores.

Television also changed the nature of family and individual lifestyles—think of the "TV dinner" instead of regular meals, and of models of "good" or "typical" families in sitcoms such as *The Brady Bunch* and, more recently, *Roseanne, The Simpsons,* or *Home*

Improvement. The medium gave us new ways of organizing our lives around its programming: the six o'clock or the ten o'clock news at night, *The Today Show* and its clones in the morning, and *Sesame Street* in the afternoon. Some people schedule their lives around certain shows, such as *Monday Night Football, Oprah Winfrey,* or *Jerry Springer.* In many homes, television serves as a "clock" used in determining the time of day and the day of the week ("If *Everybody Loves Raymond* is on, it must be seven o'clock on Tuesday"). Television has surely altered our sense of community and belonging as well. With TVs on more than seven hours a day in the average American home, there simply is not enough time for the socializing that occurred prior to its existence. Sixty-five percent of children above the age of eight have a television set in their bedrooms, further fracturing family relations (Kaiser Family Foundation, 1999). This has created what one critic labels "the lonely crowd," in which people in neighborhoods and apartment complexes rarely know one another. You probably experience the feeling of the lonely crowd both on and off campus. In some Third World countries, in contrast, televisions and VCRs are owned by the entire village or community and serve as entertainment, a political debate forum, a source of education, and more.

Because television has an easy "access code" (that is, we don't have to learn to watch television in the same way we have to learn to read a book), it may have contributed to the growing illiteracy in our country. MTV clearly altered American pop culture and provided new and sometimes disturbing role models (Madonna, Beavis and Butt-Head) and actions (violence against women). And there have been many other changes wrought by television in the past fifty years. Most of these changes have important implications for persuasion, and they demonstrate that McLuhan was right when he wrote, "The medium is the message." For example, computers have transformed our culture in revolutionary ways, creating a new "information society." The computer has changed the way we think about literacy. People must now be "computer literate," which means being conversant in several computer "languages." The computer has certainly changed

Table 13.1 Hot and Cool Media

Medium	Source of Information	Definition	Participation	Type of Medium
Television	Lighted dots	Low	High	Cool
Books	Completed letters	High	Low	Hot
Cartoons	Dots on paper	Low	High	Cool
Photographs	Image on film	High	Low	Hot
Telephone	Low-fidelity sound wave	Low	High	Cool
Movies	Moving image on film	High	Low	Hot
Telegraph	Dots and dashes in sound	Low	High	Cool
Digital audio	High-fidelity sound wave	High	Low	Hot
Personal computer and Internet	Lighted dots	Low	High	Cool

our language, giving new or changed meanings to such words as "backup," "boot," "mouse," "hacker," "menu," "window," and "virus" (Lederer, 1991). The half-life of computer technology (the "power" you get for your money) is now less than eighteen months, creating a marketing and advertising gold mine. Further, the computer drives us inward to a world occupied only by the self, the machine, and the task at hand—thereby altering our sense of community and isolating each of us. For example, someone at the computer usually resents being interrupted, especially merely to "shoot the breeze" even if they are only using the computer to play solitaire. More and more, computers are making us members of the lonely crowd and simultaneously determining the scale and pace of our lives.

One of the ways in which media tend to affect the way we look at our lives, according to McLuhan, is by the quality or "fidelity" of their signals. He distinguished between the "signal" and the "message." The signal is what stimulates our information-processing receptors—our corneas, our hearing organs, and in some cases, our senses of touch, taste, and smell. The message is the meaning intended and interpreted via the signal. Some media signals come to us in a complete, or high-fidelity, form; others come to us in an incomplete, or low-fidelity, form. High-fidelity forms require little from our information-processing senses (seeing, hearing, smelling, tasting, and touching) in as-

sembling the signals into complete messages. Low-fidelity forms require us to stretch our senses and to convert incomplete signals into complete messages. The telegraph was such an incomplete, low-fidelity form or signal (that is, the message was encoded in long or short electronic impulses that translated into letters and words using Morse code). The signal of radio is complete words and sentences, so we don't have to "decode" them to get their meaning. According to McLuhan, the same message sent via the two forms would have somewhat different meanings. The high-fidelity form, by requiring little participation, results in little physiological or sensory involvement. The low-fidelity form, requiring much participation, results in high physiological or sensory participation. McLuhan called the high-fidelity, or complete, message signals "hot" and the low-fidelity, or incomplete, ones "cool" (see Table 13.1).

Hot Media

As noted above, McLuhan used "hot" to refer to media whose signals have high fidelity, completeness, or "definition" as he called it. As a result, these signals are easy to perceive and process using one of our five senses. Their images are well drawn or recorded, and we do not have to work very hard to complete the "signal," image, or sound. It is like the difference between the old wind-up phonograph that scratched out the sounds of the 1920s and today's digitized sound that makes you feel as if you are right in the middle of an orchestra. The digital sound is "hot" because it has high fidelity or definition. Hot messages (not signals) have the same quality. A good example is the hard-sell advertiser who comes on during the late movie and tries to sell three rooms of carpeting for only $599.99. The message is distinct—it comes through crystal clear or hot. The *Jenny Jones* show is a hot message whereas *Oprah Winfrey* is a cool one. Or consider the hot political candidate who "says it like it is" and promises to halt crime and violence in the public schools by arming the teachers and administrators and by reintroducing corporal punishment as a means of discipline. Another example of a hot persuader on a "cool" medium is Jerry Springer, who regularly invites controversial guests to his show and then prompts the audience to get into verbal combat with them, and vice versa. Jerry sits on the sideline fanning the flames with his commentary. In contrast, Jay Leno is a cool spokesperson on a cool medium, and the audience is less "fired up" by his program format, style, and guests. Other hot persuaders include Rush Limbaugh and Howard Stern.

Cool Media

The signals we perceive and process in cool media have low fidelity or definition, so we must work to process their signals. Consider television, for example. At any given instant, only half of the lines of resolution on the screen are lit. We must put together these "half-images," just as we had to imagine a lot of sound quality with the old wind-up phonograph. These media that require work on our part to be decoded are "cool." Cool media, according to McLuhan, produce lower-fidelity signals—those that come out of a telephone receiver—than those that come from a radio, for example. And a cartoon's "signals" are far less complete or defined, and hence far cooler, than a digital photograph. What kinds of messages are best for these media? McLuhan said that cool media breed cool messages, or vague and ill-defined images. He saw the politician of the TV-dominated future as abstract, fuzzy, shaggy around the edges, and not needing to say everything at the

gut level. Instead, the candidate would let the voter fill in or put together a meaning or image.

With some exceptions (such as Jesse Ventura), McLuhan was right, judging by the growth in image politics since his theory first appeared. Forty years ago, McLuhan predicted that someday a movie star would be elected president. Today, the politicians who catch on are easy-going and "cool," like Bill Clinton and George W. Bush. Likewise, we see more and more TV commercials relying less on words or scripts and more on creation of a mood or feeling. Viewers add to or subtract from such commercials and arrive at a final meaning. Think of the many commercials that create a sense of anticipation through the use of music or sets or lighting. We hear the sounds of a love ballad. Then we see a well-dressed man and woman slowly walking down the stairs from the opera house. The man asks the valet to get his car. Up drives a Volkswagen Passat. Only then does the voice-over tell us that the Passat is in good taste anywhere. Another recent ad for Miller Genuine Draft begins with two well-endowed and attractive females who are obviously displaying their wares seated at a poolside table having the familiar "tastes great versus less filling" debate. As the debate heats up, they throw one another into the pool and tear away each other's already scanty clothing until both are clad only in panties and bras. The camera cuts to two guys at a bar watching the ad. One says, "Boy that's an ad I'd like to watch. Who wouldn't?" The camera pans left to reveal two attractive but angry-looking women. The ad closes by cutting to the original two females still fighting, but now in a bed of mud. The cool content of the message is not very obvious and so matches the cool quality of the television signal.

So cool media have low fidelity or signal quality and high audience participation. The participation is usually physiological—we use our senses to "complete" the message. The message itself may be insipid and not worth processing, but it still results in high levels of physiological interaction between signal and receiver. The cool media also tend to result in cooler messages. McLuhan further noted that we spend an increasing portion of our days involved with cool rather than hot media. In addition to the hours we spend watching TV, we may spend hours in front of a computer terminal and screen. Many people report that they spend a great portion of their workdays on the telephone, another cool medium. And most homes have video recorders, computers, and DVD players that involve family members with the cool medium of television. In addition, as cellular technology increases, we will be processing more and more cool signals. If you use a cell phone, you know that the signals can break up depending on your location. When that happens, you are experiencing the further cooling down of an already cool medium. It may get so cool that both parties agree to hang up and try again later when reception improves.

McLuhan predicted that this great increase in the use of cool media and the corresponding increase in audience participation, coupled with satellite transmission of television, radio, and telephone signals, would lead to a "global village" in which everyone was interested in everyone else's business. For the most part, his prediction has come true, and it is demonstrated most dramatically with Internet chat groups, electronic mail, and the Web. Here, McLuhan and Schwartz overlap and enhance one another. The involving and participatory trend, coupled with the notion of identifying experiences that can be prompted by minicues allowing people to add their own meanings, provides a powerful set of tools in the hands of creative and insightful persuaders.

To discover how much impact Marshall McLuhan's ideas have had on the information age, access InfoTrac College Edition, and enter the words "Marshall McLuhan" in the search engine. Read a few of the articles listed there.

AGENDA SETTING
BY THE MEDIA

One explanation of how mass media persuade relates to the agenda-setting function of mass media (McCombs & Shaw, 1972). According to this theory, the public agenda—the kinds of issues people discuss, think about, and worry about (and some-

FIGURE 13.7 Although media may not tell us what to think, they can tell us what to think about.

(*Berry's World* reprinted by permission of NEA, Inc.)

times ultimately press for legislation on)—is powerfully shaped and directed by what the news media choose to publicize. As theorists put it, mass media do not tell us what to think; but they do tell us what to think about (see Figure 13.7). How many of us would have followed the O. J. Simpson trial if the media hadn't continually reported on it, thus putting it on the "front burner" of the American agenda? Would we be thinking about the militia movement if the media hadn't kept running stories about various bombings involving persons affiliated with militia-type groups? Would there be such concern over the amount of violence on television if the media hadn't focused on the school shootings in Littleton, Colorado, and elsewhere? Would we be engaged in a "War on Terrorism" if we hadn't all seen the airliners crash into the World Trade Center and then repeatedly watched the towers collapse? Would we have invaded Afghanistan or Iraq if we hadn't seen another airliner crash into the Pentagon and still another one, presumably targeted at the White House, crash in an open field in Pennsylvania after the passengers took on the terrorists? Deciding what to focus on and, equally important, what not to focus on in reporting the day's news falls to a small number of "gatekeepers."

How do gatekeepers make programming decisions, and by what criteria? Not much is known about this process, but there are some hints as to how and why the decisions are made. Media scholar J. Meyrowitz (1985) refers to one criterion called "least objectionable programming." This means that "the key is to design a program that is least likely to be turned off, rather than a program viewers will actively seek out" (p. 73). Some media critics note that, although media advertisements purportedly sell products to viewers, the economic design of mass media is to sell audiences to advertisers. With television, for example, we tend to think of programs as "products" for which we pay a price—we have to watch ads from the programs' sponsors. In reality, however, what is really being sold is an audience. In other words, we are the "products," and we are being "sold" to the advertisers. Therefore, the goal is to design programming that will capture and "hold" the attention of the largest number of people or of a certain segment of people, such as upscale spenders, gourmet cooks, outdoorsmen, or sports fans.

So another criteria for determining what sort of news to present is the nature of the known audience that the broadcast or publication will reach. Audience members who read *U.S. News & World Report,* for example, will be more conservative than those who read *Newsweek.* The gatekeepers will usually select stories that put a conservative slant on an issue, thus setting a different agenda for the conservative readers than for the liberal ones.

Another criterion for deciding what is to be broadcast on television news is whether or not a piece can be delivered as a 20- to 30-second "sound bite" or "news bite." Communication scholars Kathleen Hall Jamieson and Karlyn Kohrs-Campbell (1996) define a news bite as a piece of news less

FIGURE 13.8 The 30-second news bite is one criterion that affects gatekeepers' decisions about what is newsworthy and what is not. As this cartoon implies, the news bite might even be affecting our conversational styles.

(*Berry's World* reprinted by permission of NEA, Inc.)

than 35 seconds long, delivered by a credible source in an energetic way. Meyrowitz (1985) explains that viewers actually might prefer short "bites" because they report whether anything important has happened that day (see Figure 13.8). For example, if the first story or "bite" in the broadcast is not earth-shattering, then it hasn't been an important news day. However, if the first story is of a crisis nature, viewers know that an in-depth report will follow.

Because they generally provide us with yesterday's news tomorrow, newspapers frequently follow the gatekeeping decisions of television. They are practically compelled to run stories that TV news programmers chose the day before. Weekly news-magazines are caught in the same bind, presenting last week's news in this week's issue. Both the newspaper and the news weekly can do in-depth coverage of issues, but fewer and fewer people are reading them, and those who do are spending less and less time doing so. In fact, people are spending less and less time reading anything other than a computer screen at all. At the time he published *The Responsive Chord,* Schwartz (1973) reported that the average rate of consumption of books was about one book per person every three years.

Another criterion used to determine which story gets broadcast and subsequently printed is the expressiveness or dramatic quality of both the video and the audio elements in the message (Meyrowitz, 1985). "Newsworthy" stories include the instantaneous reactions of a mother who has just heard that her son has been kidnapped. A mike is shoved under her chin, the camera zooms up to her face, and the audience supposedly "experiences" how she must feel at that moment. McLuhan once observed of newspapers that the only good news in them was advertising and public relations and that it took an awful lot of bad news to sell all that good news.

As critical receivers of persuasion, you need to diversify your reading of, listening to, and viewing of news and information to expose yourselves to as many divergent sources as possible. You might want to listen to the news as reported on public television or National Public Radio. Try adding *Morning Edition* and *All Things Considered* to your radio selections and *Washington Week in Review* or the *News Hour with Jim Lehrer* to your TV viewing. Above all, don't let one medium—such as TV—so dominate your awareness of the world that you overlook other sources of news and information. Even if you watch as much TV as the student in Figure 13.9, delve into other sources such as radio, books, periodicals, and newspapers. Widen the range of the agenda being set for you. With several sources telling you what to think about, you can decide both what to think and what to think about.

To see how gatekeepers can promote their advertisers through news selection, access

FIGURE 13.9 The hours we spend watching TV strongly influence our agenda. Note also that the average seventeen-year-old now might have watched 20,000 or more hours.

(*Berry's World* reprinted by permission of NEA, Inc.)

InfoTrac College Edition, and enter the word "gatekeeper" in the search engine. Find the selection titled "Now the Editor As Marketer," and speculate how you might have been affected by editorial selection.

ROLE MODELING AND THE MEDIA

In earlier times, people learned to model themselves after those with whom they worked or lived. Girls learned to be homemakers by watching their mothers; boys learned to be farmers by watching their fathers and the other farmers in the community. Today, the media exert a much more potent influence on role modeling than the immediate world around us does. Cultivation theory offers a good explanation for this media-centered role modeling. The media "cultivates" or "grows" favorable predispositions to preferred lifestyles, personal images, patterns of acceptable and unacceptable behavior, and value systems, among other things. As a result, we learn what it is like to be a parent, child, lover, employee, and so on from media, and then we model our behavior on those examples.

We adopt such roles in two ways. Sometimes, we take on a certain role because the scene or setting demands it of us. For example, people expect certain roles at funerals and others at weddings—these are assigned roles. The scene assigns our president the role of leader, and shows of emotion are not called for in our leaders. Bill Clinton's behavior with White House intern Monica Lewinsky did not fit with the assigned role of "U.S. president," but it was even more objectionable to most people because of the scene or setting of the Oval Office anteroom. Other times, the setting demands a role that we reject, and we choose another role. For example, pro football players must make a show of proving that they are "all man"—big, tough, burly he-men don't hurt, and they don't cry. The football field scene assigns this role. However, suppose the players know that a teammate is dying of some disease. Now the tough guys show emotion and cry at the end of the final game of the stricken player's final season. These actions come from roles dictated by the players, not the scene. These are assumed roles. They are taken on at the will of the role player and often run counter to the demands of the scene.

Again and again throughout our lives, we choose between these two options—assumed and assigned roles. We have varying degrees of success and failure in playing roles, and we learn from them. How do we learn which roles to emulate and which to reject? Here is where mass media come in. Ask yourself what a working mother is like. Your responses might come from watching your own working mother, but they will also come from characters in ads, films, situation comedies, or other TV and radio programs. This explains why critics of the mass media express such concern about TV shows, ads, and other media messages that feature sex or violence. One study reported that by the time the average child has finished grammar school he or she has seen an average of 8000 murders and 100,000 other acts of violence (Levin, 1998). Even though current programming does present characters and situations that more closely approximate the real world, there are still major objections to what is referred to as "jiggly programming." Such programming usually involves spandex-clad or scantily clad and well-endowed females running up and down stairs or across beaches. Examples are *Baywatch* and *Baywatch II*—the most popular programs in the world even in reruns. And there is also concern over the glamorizing of teenage motherhood on many soap operas. Successful women don't always have to be beautiful, shapely, and ready to tumble into the sack. Successful men don't look like Tom Cruise. These are media illusions.

When *The Simpsons* first debuted more than fifteen years ago, many parents wouldn't let their children watch it. Why not? After all, it was all in good fun, and the barrage of Simpsons paraphernalia (T-shirts, lunch boxes, stickers, and so on) on the market showed the program's popularity. Communication researcher Mary Larson observed that parents' objections related to the role models depicted by the Simpson family members (Ramhoff, 1990). Bart is an underachiever with an "attitude problem," which means that he is disrespectful of parents and authority figures. He also uses smart-aleck slang words and phrases such as "dude" and "Don't have a cow!" Marge Simpson yells at her kids and sometimes uses earthy language: "Get your butts down here: we're going to be late for church!" and Homer Simpson is a glutton and a lout who is incompetent at his job.

NEWS MANIPULATION AND PERSUASION

In his book *Don't Blame the People,* Robert Cirino (1971) observed that the role of the news industry is to do business with business. After all, the media stand to profit from the success of their clients and customers. Does news manipulation really occur, or are people such as Cirino simply supersensitive and paranoid about the power of the networks, the wire services, and the major newspapers and news-magazines? If there is any manipulation, we ought to acquaint ourselves with the possible tactics that can make or unmake news. That will allow us an extra safeguard against possible "hidden persuasion" in news programs. Let us look at some of these tactics and at our news system.

Key News Sources

Three major wire services (AP, UPI, and Reuters) supply most of the news we see, hear, and read. Go through your daily newspaper and see how many stories are run from each service. In a way, we are all getting the same news. There is nothing wrong with that, as long as the news is accurate and as long as the key news items get printed or broadcast. And this is the problem: The key items *don't* always get on the front page. The problem is more severe with broadcast news. The evening TV news contains only about 22 minutes of news. Further, the messages are sent through the aural/oral channel. Speech speed on broadcast news is about 125 words per minute, or about 3000 total words in an average 30-minute news broadcast (22 minutes of news and 8 of spots). The average 400-words-per-minute reader can cover that in only 7 to 8 minutes, and that, in fact, is about the average time spent per day by newspaper subscribers. And we know that newspaper subscription rates are falling. There is no telling how much information the average person gets from the daily newspaper. So we miss a lot of important information if we rely only on electronic media for news, and even this truncated news becomes diluted by the pressure of the ratings. The news as "show business" began with male and later female anchors, and continued with slick "news teams" and now "fluff" journalism. A generation ago, Ron Powers (1978) wrote that the result was news that caters to audiences instead of educating or informing them:

> People did not want complicated, disturbing newscasts any more. . . . People were sick of

unpleasant news. The new "mood of the country" . . . was no longer "issue-oriented" but "people-oriented." The very term "Pee-pull" to denote a news genre became oracular; it was spoken in hushed italics; it bore the tintinnabulation of cash register bells. (p. 2)

The result was a news *program,* not a news *broadcast.* The news was manipulated, selected, shaped, and massaged to attract the largest share of the audience —to please the most and offend the fewest.

Since 1980, with the advent of *Nightline* (which grew out of the hostage crisis in Iran), television news has seen great change. All-news channels such as CNN, all-sports channels such as ESPN, special-interest channels such as the History Channel, the Weather Channel, and a major new network—Fox —have all come online in recent times and provide viewers with more in-depth coverage of not only news but also other areas of interest. Barbara Matusow (1983) agrees in her book *The Evening Stars.* There, she says, "The triumph of the Anchor is, in fact, the logical outgrowth of a system almost totally unfettered by any consideration except the need to maximize profits" (p. 40). Her account of the struggle by CBS to land Dan Rather to replace retiring Walter Cronkite makes the point clearly. After lots of bumping and shoving among CBS management, Rather, and other networks, CBS offered Rather the anchor spot for a salary of approximately $25 million, spread over ten years, plus other perks. Matusow quotes Roone Arledge of ABC News, which was competing for Rather's services, as saying, "It's hard to put a value on Dan Rather. If he . . . brings viewers to the *World News Tonight,* how much he is worth over ten years is incalculable."

When you are trying to gain a certain segment of the market, the temptation is to manipulate the news, to make it more interesting, sexier, more sensational, and more entertaining. Your tactics are limitless, and bias is bound to creep in. As Edward R. Murrow, the first electronic news star, put it:

> One of the basic troubles with radio and television news is that both instruments have grown up as an incompatible combination of show business, advertising and news. Each of the

three is a rather bizarre and demanding profession, and when you get all three under one roof, the dust never settles. (Matusow, 1983, p. 304)

The show-business aspects of today's news distort electronic news just as yellow journalism distorted print news. Here are some specific ways news can be manipulated.

Methods of Manipulation

Ignoring.   One way gatekeepers distort the news is by simply ignoring it. Officials ignored the danger of buildings containing asbestos until one school district in Virginia finally brought suit. Asbestos without a lawsuit apparently wasn't an interesting story. More recently, the news media ignored warnings about the breakup of the former Yugoslavia until it was too late to shape public opinion and influence U.S. and UN policies regarding the breakup. The resulting public ignorance later led to widespread terror, violence, ethnic cleansing, and wholesale mayhem in Serbia, Croatia, and Albania. Until the events of 9/11, few persons could tell where Afghanistan was located, and fewer knew who Osama Bin Laden was and why he mattered.

Favoring the Sponsor. Because every commercial news program has sponsors, news reporters and editors may soft-pedal any negative news about these sponsors. For example, it took broadcasters years to refuse advertising from cigarette manufacturers and the ongoing campaign to keep beer and wine ads from being banned. It is always wise to ask who the sponsor is for a newscast. Getting news from several sources helps us to avoid sponsor-favoring editing. However, this is getting more complicated as a few large corporations buy up communication outlets and the companies owning such outlets; now, General Electric owns NBC, Westinghouse owns CBS, and Disney owns ABC, to give just a few examples.

The Pseudoevent. Although there is an overabundance of news each day, not all of it is interesting or entertaining, so news reporters are often drawn to highly dramatic or bizarre events. Historian Daniel Boorstin (1961) called these "pseudoevents" or "planned news." This occurs with the announcement of stock dividends, contract settlements, or grand openings. Such stories fall somewhere between public relations and "soft" news, such as reporting a celebrity's coming out of retirement (for example, Michael Jordan). Various mass movements use pseudoevents to draw media attention to their causes by holding marches, rallies, or vigils or even using violent tactics such as bombings or lootings. Most corporations, banks, major not-for-profits, and so on maintain sophisticated public relations offices that employ "events" coordinators whose job it is to plan pseudoevents to "make news" for the organization.

Bias: Verbal and Nonverbal. We previously noted several kinds of bias, such as gatekeeping and ignoring; there are numerous others. A skillful interviewer can make an interviewee seem to be quite different from his or her real self. Larry King is an expert at drawing out interviewees in selective ways. News reporters can make a candidate seem controversial by dubbing an audio track of booing on a video track of cheering and then having the announcer say that the candidate faces opposition from left and right. Or editors might superimpose two or more conflicting images: angry farmers and grain dealers, or college students and loan officers, or homemakers and supermarket owners, or starving children and people wasting food or gorging themselves. They can select who is featured, choosing only pro or only con advocates. And reporters can say that so-and-so refused to comment on the issue, thus making it seem that so-and-so must be guilty.

Finally, news can be biased by the media's taking things out of context or by misquoting sources. As Black Muslim leader Malcolm X put it, "I don't care what points I made . . . it practically never gets printed the way I said it" (Cirino, 1971, p. 147). You can't possibly look at and listen to all the print and electronic news available. But you can diversify your exposure, not relying on any one medium such as television or on any one network, newspaper, or magazine.

THE INTERNET AND PERSUASION

The bursting of the dot.com bubble continues to dampen the speculative mania for Internet start-up companies. Advertising revenue for the Internet has plummeted as well. As a result, many dismiss the importance of the Internet as a persuasive channel. Yet those in the know point to the sweeping effects the Internet continues to have on Western society and the global economy. Unquestionably, the Internet is changing the structure of communication and persuasion as no other medium has since the introduction of television. It is not merely a major incremental step in the evolution of technology, as with the introduction of fax machines and cell phones, but a major technological revolution that is changing the structure of our communication practices. There are now new ways for persuasion to be delivered. The Internet is also changing the persuasive process by altering the power structure of the participants. Let's review how the Internet is changing the way we practice persuasion.

Changes in the Information Power Structure

Perhaps the most significant contribution of the Internet is to the redistribution of the control of information. Recall that automobile salespersons do not like the Internet because dealer costs for vehicles are available to customers. The Internet also allows consumers to solicit bids from dealers on new cars or mortgage rates to find competitive prices more easily. One of my colleagues purchased a new car in another state and saved a few hundred dollars; the dealer even provided transportation to pick up the vehicle.

Travel agents were previously the major source of information for long-distance trips, but no longer. The large number of travel agencies closing their doors is due, in part, to competition from the Internet. The Internet carries information about flights and prices for most airlines, hotels, and car rental companies. Reservations can now be made without direct human assistance, and some carriers provide additional incentives for using the Internet such as fares available only there. Southwest Airlines, the most profitable airline over the past decade, uses the Internet as a primary source of booking trips and no longer pays travel agents a commission for booking passage for customers. This means that customers actually pay a fee for using a travel agent when flying with Southwest. Companies such as Priceline.com, Travelocity.com, and Expedia.com enable consumers to find bargain fares. They are so successful that the airline industry has started its own discount Internet travel agency, Orbitz.com. Most airlines now maintain their own Internet sites.

The Internet is changing the lodging industry as well. Through the Internet, travelers can stay in luxury hotels such as the Crowne Plaza, Hotel Inter-Continental, or Swisshotel for prices as low as one would pay at a Hampton Inn. The Internet is a boon to bed-and-breakfasts as well, enabling them to publicize their presence. The Internet makes it easy to book lodging in bed-and-breakfasts for vacations to Louisiana, Maine, and Nova Scotia and to decide what sights and attractions to visit. Quite simply, the Internet reduces the number of gatekeepers of information that were required in the past. The challenge for persuaders is to frame persuasive messages in a way that attracts visitors to their property, and not the dozens of competitors.

Information on Demand

A major selling point of the Internet is its ability to deliver information immediately around the clock. Traditional businesses struggle to find hours to accommodate customers across time zones, but the Internet provides and collects information regardless of the hour. Of course, in complex situations that involve many issues, it's still preferable to deal with a person, but many routine transactions are well suited to the Internet, just as automatic teller machines can handle most of our banking needs.

Direct-to-Consumer Markets
Without Geographic Boundaries

The Internet provides direct market access to people in developed countries and easier access to those in developing countries. Farmers growing crops find the best markets more easily using the Internet. Small, independent coffee growers possess the means through the Internet to sell their crops internationally for better prices by cutting out the processors in the middle—a process called disintermediation. Many artists take advantage of the Internet's direct-to-consumer capability because art dealers often take a 40–50 percent cut when items are sold through galleries. People use eBay to buy and sell across national boundaries, so that an individual can now complete a sale from, say, Hungary to the United States with minimal difficulties.

Increased Access and Convenience

The Internet offers convenience for those limited by geography, time, or special requirements. The Internet provides individuals in remote parts of the world with access to many of the amenities available to those living in or near cities. Amazon.com sells books to those who have great distances to travel to get to a bookstore. Internet grocery shopping services such as Peapod are convenient for the elderly and those who are limited by physical disability. Even city dwellers find that the Internet provides great convenience for gift-giving tasks. It's easy to send flowers through companies like Flowers.com—and you get to see a picture of what you are sending. The Internet also provides many more choices than are generally available locally. For example, people with very narrow or very wide feet have more shoe options through the Internet than in their neighborhood stores. So the Internet provides special opportunities for persuaders who

wish to focus on niche or specialty markets. For example, CDW, a leading technology supplier, couples its Web presence with a massive inventory that ships very quickly. Friendly sales representatives are available to answer questions by email or by phone (see Figure 13.10). The Internet is also a great source for parts to repair discontinued items. Recently, for instance, OfficeMax.com delivered toner cartridges for a discontinued printer model on the next business day, and they were cheaper over the Internet.

The Immediate Transfer of Information
and Financial Resources

Many customers need information immediately, and the Internet provides this capability. Fax machines share a lot of these tasks, but they do not provide the person on the receiving end with the editable information needed for inclusion in estimates and procurement documents. The use of email attachments simplifies the immediate transmission of information. Many types of financial payments are available on the Internet, and the seller is paid immediately. Electronic deposits and withdrawals are available through systems such as PayPal.com.

Linkage Between the Real World
and the Virtual World

A dichotomy need not exist between a physical entity and the Internet. Barnes & Noble effectively uses the fact of its having many physical locations and a Web presence to compete against Amazon.com—its major Internet rival. Many business experts see the benefits of the joint strategy.

Companies with an Internet presence maximize the convenience for shoppers because Internet stores offer different conveniences than physical stores. The Internet allows busy people to shop at any time—they are not limited by store hours. It also permits those who can't physically get to the store to make their purchases. Yet there is comfort in a physical presence—we believe the

CDW has everything you need to find the right technology for your business. Like more than 50,000 products in stock. And hundreds of brands. And account managers who are free to recommend the best technology out there—not just the best from any one manufacturer. So you get objective advice and plenty of choices. Which may be why so many businesses nationwide turn to CDW. To find out what we can do for you, call or visit our Web site.

FIGURE 13.10 CDW combines a massive physical inventory with efficient Internet technology to serve 69,000 Web customers daily.

company is less likely to be gone the next day. In addition, some items like shoes are difficult to fit without trying them on in the store. We expend more time and money when we return something by mail. When we look at the bottom line, Barnes and Noble's joint strategy has been more profitable. In contrast, the history of financial performance of Amazon.com is summarized by one word: losses.

A Global Library for Products and Services

Many people overlook the fact that persuasion often has many steps. One of those steps involves gathering information about various products and services. Many companies do not sell directly to the public, such as automobile manufacturers (although they are contemplating it and have tested it). Yet they maintain sites on the Internet to provide information about their products. Visit a few of these sites, such as www.ford.com, www.chrysler.com, and www.gm.com. Not only do these Web sites provide information about the nearest dealers, but the sites help consumers narrow their choices before they actually visit these dealers. Listings of the technical specifications save consumers a lot of time. No longer do they have to visit three or four dealers to build an adequate information base about the vehicle they want. A useful function of these Web sites is to show the many vehicle options available. Dealers often do not mention these options until a customer does not find an acceptable vehicle on the lot.

Many industries offer extensive details of their products on the Internet to help consumers select which products best meet their needs. Retailers, however, often provide even more help because they carry competing brands, and their Web sites may offer comparisons among products. Thanks to the Internet, consumers are more informed when they meet their persuaders—which means that persuaders must be better informed than ever before.

The Opportunity for Maliciousness

Ethical use of the Internet is a big issue. Despite the many wonderful opportunities the Internet provides, its unseemly underbelly brings opportunities to exploit others. Children are particularly vulnerable to adult predators. The Internet makes it easy for persuaders to misrepresent themselves and the items they are selling. Consumers must always be on guard when assessing ads in newspapers and on television, and there is even less regulation of the Internet for truthfulness. As with mail-order houses, consumers must always question whether a persuader is trustworthy. So a key issue for you as a persuader on the Internet involves establishing your credibility. Many merchants and persons doing business on the Internet are forming associations that provide some level of assurance of trustworthiness. Privacy issues continue to arise regarding the protection of customers' personal information by businesses on the Internet.

REVIEW AND CONCLUSION

The average eighteen-year-old American has seen tens of thousands of hours of television and hundreds of thousands of commercials. And TV is just one media channel being used for persuasion. Billboards, films, magazines, and newspapers affect most of us. Labels, bumper stickers, T-shirts, and other paraphernalia persuade us. When we happen to read them, books can persuade us, too. All in all, we live in a highly persuasive, media-rich environment. We need to be persuaded about some things, and media persuasion is sometimes the best way to get information about alternatives. You can protect yourself from persuasive attempts made by the media by looking beyond the surface meanings in media messages. Look for the responsive chords being plucked, and decide whether the messages that elicit them are hot or cool. Look for the agenda being set. Also consider the immense changes we are facing because of the development of new communications media such as the Internet and virtual reality (Gumpert & Drucker, 2002; Larson, 2002; Postman, 1996; Zettl, 1996). Establishing trustworthiness remains important across all of these media innovations, but it is particularly important with regard to the Internet.

QUESTIONS FOR FURTHER THOUGHT

1. What are some similarities between primitive oral/aural cultures and the electronic culture in which we now live?

2. Why is information associated with power? Give examples.

3. How was the concept of "ownership" associated with the development of writing?

4. What changes in society resulted from the development of print?

5. How did literacy both free us and enslave us?

6. What are some of the developments at the Media Lab at MIT? How will they affect us in the future?

7. Which media type—hot or cool—dominates our times?

8. What are some examples of the criteria gatekeepers may be using to determine what to put on the evening news?

 For online activities, go to the Web site for this book at http://communication.wadsworth.com/larson.

14

✳

The Use of Persuasive Premises in Advertising and IMC

The dominant, and perhaps the most effective, forms of persuasion in contemporary culture are print and electronic advertising. Although we might feel smug about not running out and buying every product we learn about from advertisements, product ads still have a dramatic impact on us. They shape not only our purchasing behavior but other behaviors as well (for example, becoming aware of a product's existence, developing attitudes toward products, and even making changes in our values and preferred lifestyles). The field of advertising has a long and frequently sordid history, but it is also a fascinating area of persuasion to study. In previous chapters, we discussed innovations such as the increased use of various approaches to direct and interactive marketing, the use of the Internet, market segmentation, and data-based marketing. Of special importance is the development of what is called "integrated marketing communication," or IMC. Its fundamental premise is that successful marketing involves more than traditional advertising. Other elements in the IMC mix include direct marketing, public relations, event planning, sales promotion,

and personal selling. All these activities must be integrated with one another to create unified messages, with the ultimate goal of targeting each individual with a unique appeal. This chapter will focus on advertising as the key (but not the only) element in successful IMC.

Despite recent cutbacks because of a recession, massive advertising spending continues. To give you an idea of how much is being spent on advertising, consider the following statistics, reported in *Advertising Age* in June 2002:

- Advertisers spent $231 billion on advertising in the United States in 2001, or $822 per person. This includes all kinds of print and electronic advertising.

- General Motors spent $12 on advertising in 2001 for every man, woman, and child in the United States. Even the U.S. government spent $3.76 per person on advertising in 2001.

- At $2.2 billion versus $900 million, Pepsi outspent Coke on advertising in the United States in 2001. Coke, however, spent $1.4 billion versus Pepsi's $1.0 billion outside of the nation on advertising in 2001. So, Coke spent 155 percent more on advertising outside of the United States, and Pepsi spent 220 percent more on advertising within the nation. This tells us something about the respective strategies of each company.

It is impossible to dismiss the importance of global marketing any longer. Several surprising trends were noted in the special report that appeared in *Advertising Age* in November 2002:

- The United States no longer dominates the advertising strategy of many U.S. companies. Coke, Mars, and Colgate-Palmolive spend more on advertising in Europe than in the United States.

- The world is being divided into global marketing territories, and fierce battles are being fought to establish dominance. Procter & Gamble spent $102 million in advertising in China, far outdistancing its competitors. Yet its competitor Unilever spent $373 million in India in 2001—outspending Proctor & Gamble by a 4:1 ratio. Major battles are building for these two largest nations. The two companies are in close advertising battles in the Philippines, Taiwan, Belgium, Germany, Ireland, Hungary, Poland, Latvia, and Turkey, and even on Unilever's home turf in the United Kingdom.

- Advertising aimed at Hispanic Americans continues to grow. Now that Hispanics rank as the number one ethnic minority, at 13 percent of the U.S. population, advertisers direct more attention toward them. McDonald's devotes 10 percent of its general-market ads to Hispanic spots, with most non-Latino viewers noticing the Hispanic cues that are not meant for them (see Wentz & Cuneo, 2002).

The Internet is another force changing the face of advertising. Despite the recent lackluster performance of Internet companies, advertisers see the Internet as playing a major role in the coming years (Cuneo, 2002). For example, in an advertising market in which the average Internet expenditure is in the 1–2 percent range, Frito-Lay devotes 9 percent of its product marketing budget to Internet ads in the belief that it helps them tap into the teen market (Thompson, 2002). With research showing that as many as 92 percent of teens are online, Frito-Lay sees the Internet as the way to reach this most coveted market segment. Apparently, teens are attracted to Frito-Lay's practice of placing commercials on the Internet before they air on television. Moreover, it provides a way of testing ads before larger release. A major goal is to build a one-to-one dialogue with its consumers. Thus, a promotion with Microsoft's Xbox garnered 700,000 registrations for Doritos.com. In this sense, advertisers see the Internet as a way to make more personal connections with consumers.

To gain an appreciation for the many facets of advertising, access InfoTrac College Edition, and enter the word "advertising" in the search engine. Select the advertising campaigns option and then the case studies. Read and report on any of them.

ADVERTISING AND WESTERN CULTURE

As we analyze the "world's second-oldest profession" (as advertising has been referred to by some of its critics), you will find yourself evaluating our culture in various ways, too. No matter when or where you look in human history, there have been sellers and promoters of one kind or another, but there has never an advertising blitz to compare with that in the United States in the first decade of the new millennium. And even though we Americans aren't unique in our use of advertising, we are the world's most effective producers and consumers of it. Some of it ranks as pop art and is extremely creative and entertaining. Some of it isn't even good enough to rank as schlock.

The real lesson to learn from studying the persuasive appeals of advertisers is how they affect human society and behavior and whether those effects are bad or good, and ethical or unethical, for humankind in general and for individuals in particular. An additional benefit of studying advertising, and a key element of IMC, is that it can help us understand ourselves as consumers.

Also keep in mind that any discussion of the topic is really an interpretation of events as seen through the eyes of the beholder. Thus, Marxist critics see advertisements as tools of the upper classes used to exploit the lower classes. Advertising executives see ads as better or worse than those of the competition. Consumers see them as either just so much "clutter" or as a kind of entertainment (consider what is really watched on Super Bowl Sunday). My perspective is both as a teacher of persuasion (especially as seen in principles of persuasion and advertising) and as a practitioner of various advertising techniques (I am a partner in a small ad agency). But my perspective also contains a concern for consumers as they face the cluttered world of advertising in their lives. This chapter should make you a much more critical, insightful, and selective consumer of today's barrage of advertising appeals.

ADVERTISING, SALES PROMOTION, AND POSITIONING

We all are targets of advertising and sales promotion at various times in our lives. We ought to be aware of the kinds of appeals that are targeted at us so we can make wise purchase decisions. We are usually only aware of brand advertising, and even then, we are usually only conscious of the big picture—the slogan or jingle, the spokesperson, the main "pitch." We often overlook numerous smaller yet persuasive details such as the nature of offers, brand naming, packaging, sales promotions, the tasks that advertising addresses, and positioning.

One thing to keep in mind is that a product is not a brand, though the terms are often used interchangeably. Brands compete with one another within a product category (for example, Folgers and Maxwell House in the coffee category). Products compete with one another across product categories according to the need they are supposed to fill (thus, coffees also compete with teas, cocoa,

and spiced ciders, among hot drinks). As already noted, in the newest approach to marketing—IMC—advertising is intimately connected with personal selling, direct marketing, sales promotion, and public relations, among other things, to achieve the ultimate marketing goal—sales of goods and services.

Branding, Brand Names, Slogans, and Logos

Contemporary advertising grew out of the establishment of branded, packaged foods in the late nineteenth and the early twentieth centuries. Nabisco was the first. In 1899, they put their crackers not in barrels but into tin boxes and labeled the boxes with the company name. Lifesavers became the first branded hard candy in the early 1920s. Before that, people went to the general store and bought unbranded candy, flour, sugar, coffee, saltines, beans, salt, and other products. With the growth and development of brands, producers had to differentiate their version of a product from the competition to promote recognition in consumers' eyes. One way to differentiate was via packaging (for example, the tin boxes for Nabisco crackers were handy for a variety of purposes—people bought the brand just to get the package). Another way was to vary the means of distributing the brand (such as mail order catalogues or multilevel marketing networks). And, of course, advertising was used to promote the brand in memorable ways, emphasizing its distinctiveness from other brands in the same product class. Until the 1920s, advertising was limited to the print medium—newspapers, magazines, in-store signs, packages, and (with the emergence of the automobile) outdoor billboards.

The mid-1920s brought radio on the scene. Consumers adopted the new medium slowly at first because of limited programming and the high price of a receiver. By the 1940s, however, most homes had a receiver, and the family gathered around it to listen to dramatic programming like *Superman, The Lone Ranger,* and *Little Orphan Annie* and daytime romantic serials like *Stella Dallas.* These came to be known as "soap operas" because they provided soap manufacturers with an ideal audience for their brands—stay-at-home moms and housewives—virtually all married women. The radio commercial became ubiquitous, and soon radio slogans and jingles were part of the daily routine. Children could sing the jingles and repeat the slogans. Now branding really took off. And with the emergence of television in the 1950s, advertisers not only could talk and write about the brand but could also demonstrate it using print, visuals, special effects, animation, and various audio techniques.

Several strategies emerged in those early years to market the brand more effectively. For instance, the naming of a brand makes a big difference in how it is perceived and is embedded in consumers' memories. For example, one of the earliest facial soaps was named "Palm Olive," suggesting that the product contained a combination of coconut and olive oils. An early hand soap contained a fine grit to increase scrubbing power and so was named "Lava," suggesting that it contained volcanic sand and was good at getting out ground-in dirt. Consider the case of Allegheny Airlines, a regional brand, as the name implies. When Allegheny wanted to change its image to that of a national carrier, its marketers researched various new names and ultimately settled on USAir. That name was already trademarked by an air freight company, so Allegheny bought the brand name. Another way of differentiating a brand from the competition is to make an attractive offer and tie it to a company logo or emblem. Consider an old favorite—Cracker Jacks—which came up with a novel way to differentiate itself from other popcorn snacks. Each box offered consumers a "Free Prize" in the package. The response to the brand is fairly universal: Regardless of their age, the first thing consumers do is go for the free prize. In over 100 years, there has never been a good one, yet everyone wants to find (and usually keep) what they know is a worthless prize.

Consider other brand names to see whether they persuasively communicate their differences from competing brands. For instance, compare the competitors in the frozen turkey market. If you ask friends and acquaintances to name a brand of frozen turkey, most will say "Butterball," the brand with the greatest name recognition. Note that not only is the name memorable, but it says something about

the brand's attributes and benefits: Butterball turkeys have the reputation of being the moistest brand because they are basted with a pound of butter (Dollas, 1986). A few other examples will get you going: DieHard auto batteries, Easy Off oven cleaner, No Pest Strip insecticide, Taster's Choice instant coffee, and Duracell and Energizer batteries. How do these brand names compare with those of their competitors in the product category?

Several criteria can be used as guides in brand name selection. Among other things, a good brand name should describe product benefits, fit with company image, and be memorable, "trademarkable," easy to promote/advertise, unique among the competition, easy to pronounce, suited to the package, contemporary, understandable, and persuasive. Research on shopping lists demonstrates that consumers frequently list brand, not product, names (Rothschild, 1987). Closely related to and sometimes interchangeable with the brand name is the slogan that goes along with the name. Virtually every reader can tell me which coffee is "Mountain Grown." If you said "Folgers," you are wrong—all coffees are mountain grown. Which coffee is "good to the last drop?" I don't really know—there could be several brands that keep their flavor even when reheated, but I do know that Maxwell House's slogan and logo (a coffee cup with the last drop) claim that their brand does. Slogan infringement has been a problem for Enterprise Rent-a-Car. Do you know its slogan? Advantage Rent-a-Car, a locally owned firm in Austin, Texas, sued Enterprise for infringing on a slogan—"We'll Even Pick You Up" —that they had been using for several years.

Go to InfoTrac College Edition, and enter the words "slogan" and "logo" in the key word search engine. Review any of the case studies cited there, and report back to the class. The one titled "Branded!" talks in a humorous way about branding yourself. It's a stitch.

Packaging

Packaging persuades, reinforces the brand name, builds brand equity or value, and provides another "brand contact" or impression. Not only does the package protect the product, but also it makes the brand more attractive, recognizable, and easy to see, and it should make it easier to store and display. Most importantly, packaging "says something" about the brand and is a cost-efficient way to make "impressions" on consumers. The goods have to be packaged anyway, so why not make the package attractive and memorable in as many ways as possible? Showing the package in advertising also helps consumers recall brand characteristics and advantages at the point of purchase (POP). The package can also carry a sales promotion, such as a coupon for future purchases of the brand, and can be valuable in and of itself. For example, many people keep the unique Grolsch beer bottles with the ceramic stopper for storing other things, and the L'Eggs plastic "egg" containers have been used in a variety of "craft" items. As noted earlier, Nabisco crackers once were packaged in a metallic box that consumers usually kept to store a variety of things. Recently, packaging has made a brand impression through product placement in movies, sit-coms, sports events, and so on. Is it effective? Communication scholar T. Borchers (2002) reports that sales of Red Stripe beer jumped 50 percent after Tom Cruise sipped from a can of the brew in *The Firm*. Thus, the critical receiver needs to be alert to the kinds of brands and packages that are included in programming.

Packaging also interacts with and boosts the impact of brand naming. Consider the case of Taster's Choice instant coffee in terms of its naming, advertising, and packaging. Instant coffees have been around for a long time (soldiers in World War II got packets of instant coffee in their K-rations, and Sanka and Nescafé have been on the market since just after the war), but they never did well because they didn't taste like brewed coffee. In the late 1960s and early 1970s, "freeze-dried" instant coffees came on the market and demonstrated that an instant coffee could taste almost like the real thing. The brand positioned as being "first" with a real coffee taste was Maxim by Maxwell House, an established brand already known for being "good to the last drop." Maxim maintained an early market share, but in 1971, Taster's Choice came on the market and soon replaced Maxim as the market leader.

Taster's Choice was made by Nestlé, which had no identification with the coffee market, yet the brand succeeded. Why? It obviously had a better name than Maxim (which sounded modern and technological but said nothing about the brand or its benefits). The name "Taster's Choice" was also unusual and made a claim about the brand's benefits —it was a good-tasting one. Further, the jar, unlike Maxim's (which was cylindrical and pear shaped), was almost square, and its wide "shoulders" communicated a sense of masculinity, another attribute reinforcing the claim that the brand had "robust" and "stronger tasting" benefits. Taster's Choice labels further underscored the masculinity message by picturing a man "tasting his choice" from a steaming mug. Also, the label was smaller than the competition's and thus allowed consumers to see the "coffee crystals," which appeared significantly different from powdered instant coffees. In its early electronic advertising, the Taster's Choice jar was magically fitted with a handle and spout to resemble an old-fashioned coffeepot. Consumers could see the "pot" giving off wonderful-smelling aromas, which enticed a masculine fellow to pour and savor a cup of the stuff. Perceptual maps of the brand showed that it was perceived as "easy to use" and as having a "strong, rich taste." In contrast, Maxim was perceived as "easy to use" but with a "weak taste." Proof positive of the effectiveness of the brand name, brand packaging, and brand advertising were Taster's Choice's capture of a significant share of the market and the fact that Maxim soon changed the shape of its jar and used a smaller label.

As a critical consumer, try to identify the effects of brand naming, packaging, and labeling and how they interact with brand advertising. A few examples will get you started here, too—look at the naming and packaging/labeling of Janitor in a Drum, Paul Newman's spaghetti sauce, and Mrs. Butterworth's and Log Cabin pancake syrup.

Sales Promotion

As consumers, we are usually more aware of POP advertising and sales promotion appeals than we are of the details of naming, slogan and logo design, packaging, and labeling. POP appeals include signs telling us that the brand is available at that location, and they frequently announce special "in-store" bargain prices. Other POP approaches include displays showing the product in use, signs on shopping carts, free samples, "free" taste testings, promotional buttons or signs, "shelf-talkers," in-store coupons, fliers, in-package "gifts," and reduced-price premiums (appliances, dish sets, or sets of books/tapes/CDs in end-of-aisle or checkout counter displays). All these methods are aimed at reinforcing the brand name, "teaching" consumers about brand benefits, and providing another brand contact, as well as increasing purchase behavior, particularly impulse purchasing. Research has shown that POP displays and signs can increase sales by 20–90 percent, depending on product category. This is not so surprising when you consider that research has also shown that almost half of all supermarket purchases are unplanned (even when consumers are shopping with a list) and that 65 percent of all purchases are based on in-store decisions (Rothschild, 1987).

Sales promotion can be defined as "temporary inducements to encourage immediate purchase decisions" Consumer-targeted sales promotions include special sale pricing ("two for the price of one") and short-term price reductions ("special six-hour sale!"). They also include coupons, rebates, "extra" product in the package ("Now 25% More Pepsi in the 20-ounce Bottle," "Free Steak Knife in Every Package"), contests, sweepstakes, recipes on the packaging, and bonus packs, to name a few. Because it makes logical sense to save money, or to get something for free, or to get "more" of a product, or to be entered into a sweepstakes, most POP promotional offers are probably processed in the central route of the elaboration likelihood model (ELM).

Another thing to remember is that all sales promotional offers are designed to increase demand. They try to "pull" the product through the supply pipeline using artificially pumped-up consumer demand for the brand as the "carrot" and short-term appeals (coupon expiration dates or limited supplies) as the "stick" to prompt purchase. If the demand increases sufficiently, the store manager must stock and shelve the brand. The manager has been "pulled" into moving the brand. After all, the store

manager is interested in moving *goods*—not *brands* —off the shelves while manufacturers are interested in moving brands onto the shelves. The store manager uses "push" to move goods and usually relies on pricing and displays to encourage purchase. All these sales promotions work hand-in-hand with brand advertising, brand naming, packaging, and other practices to form the IMC that causes us to buy certain brands and not others.

Positioning

Finally, marketers believe that every brand should occupy a "position" in consumers' minds. We live in a world filled with too many products and brands to remember. Research has shown that we are able to remember only a finite number of brands in each product category. Some theorists speculate that this "top-of-mind" awareness (TOMA) is limited to five to nine brands. For complex product categories such as computers, most consumers can recall only about five brands, whereas they can recall as many as nine brands in less complex product categories such as beer or breakfast cereal (Ries & Trout, 1986). As a result, a brand needs to stand out so it will be remembered at the point of purchase, when TOMA most significantly affects purchase behavior. TOMA is most likely created through information processed in the peripheral channel of the ELM— slogans, jingles, packaging, and so on.

Most contemporary professionals in the field agree that advertising is a tool of marketing. In other words, companies don't come up with a product and then try to sell it to consumers using advertising messages. Rather, the successful marketer begins with the minds of consumers, tries to identify potentially unmet needs, and then designs a brand or "redefines" an existing product to fill the need. This approach of beginning with consumers was made popular by Al Ries and Jack Trout. In their articles, speeches, and best-selling book *Positioning: The Battle for Your Mind* (1986), they deal with the concept of positioning. The idea is to find a niche in the minds of consumers that a given product might fill. For example, the designers of a snack food asked consumers to open bags of potato chips, pour them into serving dishes, eat a few, and imagine what each of their five senses was processing. Then they were asked to comment on the chips and tell what they liked and disliked about them. They said that the chips were hard to store, were sometimes burned or had parts of the green peel on the edge, smelled and felt greasy, and broke easily. In response, the company designed an alternative—Pringles, chips that were easy to store, never burned, weren't greasy (because they were baked, not fried), were all the same size, and rarely broke. Pringles was positioned as the "easiest" chip to store and serve.

Once a position is established for a product, advertising is used to prepare customers for trial and purchase. It lays the groundwork for sales by increasing product or brand awareness (for example, repeating slogans or jingles) and by communicating and improving the product image or personality. For example, Double Stuffs by Oreo are positioned as the cookie made to be eaten from the inside out. All that is needed is advertising that makes an offer attractive enough that it will move consumers to the point of purchase. Once consumers are at the grocery store, the auto dealership, or the clothing store, sales promotion and/or personal selling are used to close the deal.

PROBLEMS OF AN OVERCOMMUNICATED SOCIETY

One of Ries and Trout's (1986) main contentions is that we live in an overcommunicated society. They claim that the usual defense of consumers in our overcommunicated society is to develop an "oversimplified mind," by which they mean a mind that largely ignores most of the information to which it is exposed. Most people select the brands they think are most appropriate for their purposes and then stick with those preferences. We call this "brand loyalty." Brand loyalty makes it easier to live in an overcommunicated society, because you never have to change your mind, and you can easily ignore the ads for competing brands in that product category.

Interestingly, brand loyalty is most strongly developed in consumers between the ages of eighteen and thirty-four. Brand loyalty is portable—you can take it with you wherever you go (Pizza Huts are found across the country, and you can get Coca-Cola anywhere in the world). Besides being portable, brand loyalty helps consumers predict quality and value from place to place. This is appealing to those in the early years of their careers facing frequent job changes and moves.

Advertising agents and agencies often face the criticism that they sell people products/brands that they don't need or that might even be harmful (such as tobacco, alcohol, and foods high in sodium or fat). As Michael Schudson notes in his book *Advertising: The Uneasy Persuasion* (1984), advertisers defend themselves by claiming that their aim is "not to change people's product choices but to change their brand choices. Advertising . . . is a competitive war against commercial rivals for a share of a market" (p. 54).

To break through to oversimplified minds, advertisers must find something that is already in the audience's mind and then "retie the cords" to their products in ways similar to Schwartz's evoked recall model, which gets messages out of audiences, not into them. Ries and Trout (1986) suggest that the best way to do so is to use an "oversimplified message." They report the results of a 1980s survey of name recognition in which only 44 percent of supermarket shoppers recognized a photo of then-Vice President George Bush while 93 percent of them recognized Mr. Clean. Mr. Clean was a much simpler message than Bush.

The overcommunication problem is exacerbated by what Ries and Trout call the media explosion, which we looked at in Chapter 13. The media explosion includes TV, cable, satellites, AM and FM radio, morning and evening newspapers, news weeklies, magazines, catalogues, direct mail, billboards, bus signs, and interactive media, but there are other message carriers at work as well (see Figure 14.1). Even the human body carries trademarks including Calvin Klein, Gucci, Benetton, and Guess. Some of the brands insist that salespersons wear the brand while at work.

Besides the overcommunication problem and the media explosion, we also have what Ries and Trout call the "product explosion." For example, the

FIGURE 14.1 One of the major problems for advertisers today is what Ries and Trout call the advertising explosion, by which they mean not only the increased volume of advertising but also the new advertising "vehicles," or places where advertising can occur.

(*Freeze Frame* cartoon from *Advertising Age,* April 25, 1988. Copyright Crain Communications, Inc. Reprinted by permission of Crain Communications and Sidney Harris.)

average supermarket contains 12,000 products or brands; in Europe, and now in the United States, there are super-supermarkets that contain more than 60,000 products or brands from which to choose. To further complicate the situation, each year 25,000 new trademarks are registered at the U.S. Patent Office, with "hundreds of thousands of products and brands being sold without trademarks" (Ries & Trout, 1986, p. 14).

More branded products coming on the market means more advertising. Ries and Trout call this the "advertising explosion," reflected not only in the sheer increase in the volume of brand advertising but also in the many new types of professionals (lawyers, dentists, doctors) and institutions (hospitals, nonprofit organizations, governments) now advertising. Another aspect of this advertising explosion is the many new places where advertising is appearing—the Internet, rest rooms, grocery carts, and a host of others. No wonder brand loyalty develops early and persists over the years—there is simply too much advertising clutter for us to process.

Breaking Through the Clutter

How do advertisers overcome the triple whammy of exploding media, products, and advertisements? In other words, how do they break through the clutter? The techniques of positioning provide one way to do so. We encountered some of these tactics in Chapter 11, which covered market segmentation in persuasive campaigns. "Being first" has helped products such as Jell-O, Kleenex, and Xerox copiers break the clutter. These products have become "imprinted" in consumers' minds to the extent that the brand names are virtually generic terms for the product category. As Ries and Trout (1986) note, "You build brand loyalty in a supermarket in the same way you build mate loyalty in a marriage. You get there first and then be careful not to give them a reason to switch" (p. 21). Not only were Apple personal computers the first in the PC market, but they were also first at being "user friendly." This let them get the jump on IBM and thus gave consumers reason to remain loyal to Apple. Later, Apple lost its competitive edge to a variety of other brands that offered newer and sometimes better versions of user-friendly software. Consumers saw these improvements as reasons to change.

For brands that are not first in the market, positioning becomes even more important. They don't want to be "me, too" brands. In earlier advertising eras—the product benefit era of the unique selling proposition, led by Rosser Reeves, and the product image era, led by David Ogilvy—the competition wasn't nearly as fierce as it was in the 1990s. And the level of competition in the new millennium will dwarf that of the 1990s. With more and more "me, too" products on the market, neither product benefits nor product images are sufficient. Products have to be unique in the marketplace, and usually advertisers rely on simple but distinctive copy to communicate uniqueness.

The poetry of product benefit or product image ad copy still works. The familiar "99 and 44/100% Pure—It Floats" was among the earliest. A worker at the Ivory soap factory accidentally pumped too much air into the bars of soap (air has always been a "filler" for various brands). It was not long after the batch was on the store shelves that reports began to come in from store managers that consumers wanted the floating version of Ivory—it was easier to find in the bathtub. Other examples of convincing ad copy include "Magnavox. Smart. Very Smart," "At Ford Quality Is Job #1," "Introducing the Smell of Luxury," and "Dermatologist Recommended." We still encounter colorful "poetic" ad copy, as Figure 14.2 demonstrates. And just as effective was the slogan "First Class Is Michelob," which positioned Michelob as "unique" in the market—a premium-priced beer actually produced in America.

A variety of techniques can be used to make a product seem to be the only brand in the category with a certain benefit. You are exposed to these kinds of pitches every day. Remember which coffee was "mountain grown"? Chances are, you said, "Folgers." Folgers preempted that product claim, thus carving out its unique niche in the coffee market. It would be advertising suicide to say, for example, "Maxwell House is mountain grown, too." Instead, other brands of coffee need to find different niches.

But there aren't many niches in a given product category. So, if the competitors are firmly entrenched in the audience's mind, what can be done? One possibility is to go up against one of them with comparative advertising. Ries and Trout (1986) give an example of this approach in the Avis Rent-a-Car campaign, whose slogan was, "Avis is number 2 in rent-a-cars, so why go with us? Because we try harder." After thirteen years of losing money, Avis made $1.2 million the first year after admitting to being second, $2.6 million the second year, and $5 million the third year, before being acquired by ITT, which ditched the number-two idea and promptly began losing money. Interestingly, the

Granted. There Are Some Similarities
Between Other Fishing Lures And A Rapala.

This year, we crafted the 100 millionth Rapala. It was attached to a testing rod and
pulled by hand through a tank to inspect and perfect its swimming action. For over
50 years, only Rapala has taken the time to hand tune and tank test every
lure. Only Rapala. Which is why we have no equal among our many imitators.

Rapala. Celebrating 100 Million Hand-Tuned, Tank-Tested Lures.

© 1989 Normark Corp.

FIGURE 14.2 How did this hard-hitting product ad by Rapala break through
the clutter?

(Reprinted by permission of Normark Corp.)

"We're number 2, so we try harder" campaign didn't hurt the market leader, Hertz—in fact, it increased their business. Rather, the campaign took business away from the third- and fourth-place brands in the market—National and Budget.

One way a brand can break through clutter is by telling consumers what it "is not." In 1968, Seven-Up was near bankruptcy. Its advertising agency, J. Walter Thompson, came up with one of the most successful "Tell 'em what you're not" campaigns in history with the "invention" of the word "un-cola," which the agency then used in very creative ways. The Seven-Up delivery trucks were labeled "The Man from Un-cola," which played on the title of the popular TV series *The Man from U.N.C.L.E.* And there was a series of ads in various languages in which the only word most viewers could understand was "un-cola." The campaign positioned Seven-Up as third in the soft-drink market behind Coke and Pepsi. The only way to come up with an idea such as "un-cola" is to get into consumers' minds: "You won't find an 'un-cola' idea inside a Seven-Up can. You find it inside the cola drinker's head" (Ries & Trout, 1986, p. 34).

Another approach is to take advantage of one's existing image or reputation. For example, Arm & Hammer is known for producing baking soda, but did you know that it also makes and sells sodium bicarbonates to cattle raisers? Arm & Hammer took advantage of its already established reputation to market, in a very competitive marketplace, a new product—cattle feed supplements that aid digestion and result in increased rates of weight gain. This is called line extension. So, relying on one's strengths and reputation can be an effective means of breaking through the clutter.

Many "me, too" products claim to be "better." The problem is that it's hard to convince consumers that a product is better. A company may waste inordinate amounts of time and money trying to increase demonstrable product quality, thus allowing the competition to catch up and outadvertise and outsell the new "me, too" product. This happened when Volkswagen broke into the U.S. compact-car market in the late 1950s. Because few compact cars were available in the market at the time, VW preempted the niche using the simple words "Think

small" as its slogan. U.S. automakers countered by making smaller cars than they had been making, but none were as small or as successful as the VW "Beetle." When the Beetle was brought back in the late 1990s, dealers could not keep up with demand. Volkswagon's positioning had survived for almost fifty years!

Price can be another clutter breaker. A product can find a lower-priced niche, such as that filled by the Hyundai, or it can find a high-priced one like that of Mont Blanc pens, Rolex wristwatches, and BMWs (see Figure 14.3). Other clutter breakers are gender and age. The largest-selling perfume is not Arpege or Chanel No. 5 but Charlie—the first perfume to advertise using a masculine brand name. Examples of products occupying the age niche are Geritol, *Modern Maturity* magazine (which has the nation's leading circulation), and high-fiber foods. Distribution and packaging can break clutter, too. L'Eggs was the first hosiery to be distributed in supermarkets. That fact and its packaging gave it a unique position in the market (Ries & Trout, 1986). Hosiery is usually packaged in a thin, square envelope with a window in it to show the shade of the hose. There are high labor costs involved in folding the hose around a cardboard sheet inside the envelope. L'Eggs hosiery, in contrast, can simply be "stuffed" into the container, thus eliminating this labor cost and bringing the price down. And the egg-shaped container is not only visually unique but also appealing for secondary uses, such as storage of small items and various crafts (Dollas, 1986).

Advertisers can also break through the clutter by repositioning an existing brand—for example, changing Cheerios from a "children's" product to an "adult" product by stressing its high-fiber content. Further, choosing the right name or slogan for the product can cut through the clutter. A powerful bathroom cleaner named "The Works" fits with the idea of trying the ultimate—"Give It The Works!" Compare the clutter-breaking abilities of Buick's bland slogan "Buick Builds It Better" with Ford's much more reassuring claim "At Ford Quality Is Job # 1."

All these examples of clutter-breaking techniques grow out of various kinds of advertising research that permit advertisers to get into consumers'

The Purdey firearm. Created by James Purdey and Sons, the fabled London firm that has been gunmaker to the royal family since Queen Victoria's reign.

Today, the company's impeccable traditions are scrupulously maintained under the direction of The Honourable Richard Beaumont, son of the Second Viscount Allendale.

For more than 170 years, Purdey has produced sporting guns so distinctive, no two are exactly alike. The barrel of one cannot be interchanged with the stock of any other.

Purdey and Rolex: The most refined expressions of their respective arts.

So meticulous is their construction, only 70 are produced in a year. So artful is

Hand-engraving is a hallmark of Purdey guns.

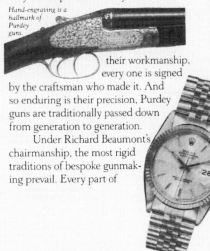

their workmanship, every one is signed by the craftsman who made it. And so enduring is their precision, Purdey guns are traditionally passed down from generation to generation.

Under Richard Beaumont's chairmanship, the most rigid traditions of bespoke gunmaking prevail. Every part of

every Purdey is custom-made. Distances between the owner's eye, cheek, shoulder and trigger finger are calibrated. The measurements are designed into the stock to ensure that each gun is precisely fitted to its owner.

Richard Beaumont is a man who maintains standards of craftsmanship that speak

Purdey utilizes the finest craftsmen in the world.

of a more civilized time. Which makes his choice of a Rolex understandable.

ROLEX

Datejust Oyster Perpetual Chronometer in stainless steel and 18kt. gold with Jubilee bracelet. Write for brochure, Rolex Watch U.S.A., Inc., Dept. 435, Rolex Building, 665 Fifth Avenue, New York, New York 10022-5481. World headquarters in Geneva. Other offices in Canada and major countries around the world.

FIGURE 14.3 This product image ad breaks through the clutter using a copy-heavy strategy to tell Rolex's product story. The comparison between Rolex watches and Purdey shotguns relies on both the price and quality niches.

(Reprinted by permission of Rolex Watch U.S.A., Inc.)

heads and resonate with their needs. Let's explore some research of this kind.

GETTING INTO THE CONSUMER'S HEAD: ADVERTISING RESEARCH

Three kinds of advertising or integrated marketing research are most frequently used: (1) demographics (which we discussed in Chapter 12), (2) psychographics, and (3) geographics or sociographics. Sometimes, one is used alone; other times, two of them are used in conjunction; still other times, all three are used.

Specific ways of conducting these kinds of research include census data, surveys, and questionnaires; focus group interviews; the pupilometer, which measures the dilation of the pupil of the eye as it scans a printed ad; and the tachistoscope, which gives viewers "miniglimpses" of ads, after which they are asked to recall the visuals and copy. Researchers also measure people's galvanic skin response—the electric resistance (sweat) in the palm of the hand when a person becomes excited. All of these techniques have the same purpose: to identify consumers' "hot buttons" and "cold buttons." Ad expert Terry Gallonoy (1970) noted that successful commercials have to "make people shut up or stop eating or freeze on the way to the bathroom. . . . 'Stop the lady with the full bladder for just one full minute' is the order of the day" (n. p.).

Demographics

Demographics are used in the study of groups of consumers, or market segments, on the basis of quantifiable variables including annual income, religious affiliation, political preferences, age, family size, gender, purchase patterns, or any combination of such factors. Based on these data, advertisers design ads that feature certain kinds of characters or have certain settings, props, and so on. One demographic pattern involves the growing number of DINK ("double-income, no-kids") households (see Figure 14.4). DINKs comprise two subgroups:

"WOW! We're DINKS — a double-income, no-kids couple!"

FIGURE 14.4 Demographics identified one segment of DINKs as older couples with no dependent children. Advertisers need to appeal to this group in different ways than they advertise to other groups.

(*Berry's World* reprinted by permission of NEA, Inc.)

(1) those who intentionally have no children and are largely self-indulgent, and (2) those whose children have left home and are now independent of their parents (formerly called "empty nesters" before Mom decided to go back to work). This second group is sometimes called "muppies" (mature urban professionals)—the now-aging front edge of the baby boomers. Obviously, advertisers need to appeal to these two subgroups in very different ways, using very different characters, settings, music, props, and so on.

The muppie segment is increasing at the rate of 5500 persons per day, which adds up to more than 2 million new consumers a year—one every twelve seconds. Advertisers know a lot about this segment. There are about 157 women for every 102 men in this age group, and the average age of group members is increasing—they now have a 76.8-year average life expectancy. Their rate of divorce is increasing at three times the national rate. Persons in this segment tend to get up earlier in the day and to retire earlier at night—perhaps just after the evening news. They have more discretionary income available than previously, but they spend a good amount of it on their children and, especially, their grandchildren. They are concerned about health issues and are exercising more. They travel more than the average person does. About half of them live in seven states—California and New York (with more than 2 million each), and Florida, Illinois, Michigan, Ohio, and Pennsylvania ("Happy 65th," 1988).

Now, *you* play advertising executive with these data and tell when, where, and how you would appeal to this market segment. Your product is a nationwide travel network that permits older persons to travel in groups at special low rates during the off-season. Would you advertise in *Modern Maturity,* or would you make your appeal during local evening news shows, which have a much smaller "reach" or population that can potentially see or hear the message? How about using the History Channel or *Moneyline* as an advertising vehicle? Or would you use direct mail to persons over the age of sixty in the seven major states? Could you use public relations, sales promotional materials, or special "events" to promote the network? Whom would you pick to be your spokesperson—Angela Lansbury, Burt Reynolds, Mike Ditka, or Tina Turner? And there are a host of other factors that could make a difference with one segment and not another. As you can see, even the dullest demographic facts can lead advertisers to target someone and to design ad copy, choose appropriate media, and select spokespersons, among other things. Thus, demographic consumer research is a part of successful IMC.

To learn how demographics can predict such diverse things as trends in purchasing products online and immigration patterns, access InfoTrac College Edition, and enter the word "demographics" in the search engine. Select the "Demographics 2000" article, and you will discover what children as consumers in 2010 will be like. Report back to the class.

Psychographics

Psychographics is the study of consumers' lifestyles. It provides quantitative data about how consumers spend their time (and money), what kinds of activities they engage in, what their interests are, and what their opinions are on any given set of issues. The shorthand term for these factors is AIO, or activities, interests, and opinions.

Activities, Interests, and Opinions. Examples of activities are work, social events, vacations, hobbies, entertainment, club membership, community activities, shopping, and athletics. Even these categories of activities can be subdivided into more narrowly focused market segments. For example, there can be sports and leisure activities (golf, bowling, tennis, and sports viewing on TV). Another subcategory might be labeled good-life activities (cultural events, gourmet cooking, investing, or wine tastings). Advertisers could look at outdoor activities (skeet shooting, fishing, or motorcycling) or at high-tech activities (video games, home computers, photography, or science channels on cable TV). In each of these categories, IMC and advertising need to be tailored to specific consumers. The golfer who is interested in gourmet cooking, skeet shooting, and photography is a different consumer from the bowler who is interested in the same things. Thus, the two need to receive their own idiosyncratic advertising messages, tailored to them specifically. This is the aim of data-based integrated marketing, the newest development in the field.

Examples of interests include the family and home, achievements, recreation, fashion, technology, food, and media. Opinions can be held about oneself, social and political issues, business and economics, religion and culture, education, and the future. A psychographic study is done by having large numbers of persons respond to questions about their activities, interests, and opinions in relation to a particular product. From these answers, the advertiser infers what the respondents' lifestyles are like and how they are likely to respond to the product. In some cases, the results may dictate points to include in the ad copy—and even specific language to be used.

The items in psychographic questionnaires can be general or specific. For example, a study could be conducted to determine what type of consumer would be most likely to bring a malpractice suit against a physician. Items in the questionnaire might look like these:

- I have a great deal of confidence in my own doctor.
- Many physicians are out of date.
- Physicians are overpaid.
- Malpractice is hard to prove.
- You are your own best doctor.

Responses can range from "strongly agree" to "strongly disagree." Trends in responses are then correlated to persons actually bringing malpractice suits.

In an example directly related to product advertising, persons strongly agreeing with the following items are highly likely to use Listerine mouthwash rather than Listermint mouthwash and are more likely to use mouthwash in general (Rothschild, 1987):

- I do not feel clean without a daily bath.
- Everyone should use a deodorant.
- A house should be dusted three times a week.
- Odors in the house embarrass me.
- The kind of dirt you can't see is worse than the kind you can see.
- I am a very neat person.
- Dirty dishes should be washed after every meal.
- It is very important for people to wash their hands before eating each meal.
- I use one or more household disinfectants.

Several effective advertisements could be developed based on the knowledge that Listerine users respond this way to cleanliness. Appeals could be made to the germ-killing and antiseptic qualities in the

product. An ad could justify Listerine's antiseptic taste by intimating that "clean doesn't mean 'good tasting' in mouthwashes" and go on to point out that "flavored mouthwashes" compromise cleanliness for the sake of taste. So, knowing about the activities, interests, and opinions of consumers provides advertisers with critical psychographic data about potential customers. Keep in mind that, no matter how ineffective you think a given print or electronic advertisement is, it probably had to pass rigorous research tests before ever going on the air or into print.

Another psychographic model widely used in advertising and marketing is known as VALS (short for "values and lifestyles"), developed by Arnold Mitchell (1983) at the Stanford Research Institute. It is very relevant for the implementation of IMC. Mitchell described three general lifestyles and then broke them down into subcategories having certain values, demographics, and buying patterns (Engel, Blackwell, & Miniard, 1986). The three general categories are (1) persons who are need driven, (2) persons who are outer directed, and (3) persons who are inner directed (see Table 14.1). Although the following data on the people in these three categories are several decades old, the related concepts still have relevance.

Need-Driven Consumers. These consumers are living on the edge of or in the midst of poverty. They represent only 11 percent of the population, and advertisers rarely target them because they have little discretionary income. They are forced to use most, if not all, of their income to buy the minimum essentials. There are two subcategories of need-driven consumers: survivors (4 percent) and sustainers (7 percent). Survivors struggle to provide the daily necessities of life, tend to mistrust people and products, and are usually social misfits. They live in slums, have limited education and poverty-level incomes, and most likely are members of a racial or ethnic minority. As you would expect, survivors' buying patterns are dominated by price and immediate needs.

Sustainers are a little better off. They are very concerned with security and safety; they really want

Table 14.1 VALS Segmentation

Percentage of Population (age 18 & over)	Consumer Type	Values and Lifestyles	Demographics	Buying Patterns
NEED-DRIVEN CONSUMERS				
4%	Survivors	Struggle for survival Distrustful Socially misfitted Ruled by appetites	Poverty-level income Little education Many minority members Many live in city slums	Price dominant Focused on basics Buying for immediate needs
7	Sustainers	Concern with safety, security Insecure, compulsive Dependent, following Streetwise, determined to get ahead	Low income Low education Much unemployment Live in country as well as cities	Price important Want warranty Cautious buyers
OUTER-DIRECTED CONSUMERS				
35%	Belongers	Conforming, conventional Unexperimental Traditional, formal Nostalgic	Low to middle income Low to average education Blue-collar jobs Tend toward noncity living	Family Home Fads Middle and lower mass markets
10	Emulators	Ambitious, show-off Status conscious Upwardly mobile Macho, competitive	Good to excellent income Youngish Highly urban Traditionally male, but changing	Conspicuous consumption "In" items Imitative Popular fashion
22	Achievers	Achievement, success, fame Materialism Leadership, efficiency Comfort	Excellent income Leaders in business, politics, etc. Suburban and city living	Give evidence of success Top of the line Luxury and gift markets "New and improved" products
INNER-DIRECTED CONSUMERS				
5%	I-am-me	Fiercely individualistic Dramatic, impulsive Experimental Volatile	Young Many single Student or starting job Affluent background	Display one's taste Experimental fads Source of far-out fads Clique buying
7	Experiential	Drive to direct experience Active, participative Person-centered Artistic	Bimodal income Most under 40 Many young families Good education	Process over product Vigorous outdoor sports "Making" home pursuits Crafts and introspection
8	Socially conscious	Societal responsibility Simple living Smallness of scale Inner growth	Bimodal low and high incomes Excellent education Diverse ages and places of residence Largely white	Conservation emphasis Simplicity Frugality Environmental concerns
2	Integrated	Psychological maturity Sense of fittingness Tolerant, self-actualizing World perspective	Good to excellent incomes Bimodal in age Excellent education Diverse jobs and residential patterns	Varied self-expression Esthetically oriented Ecologically aware One-of-a-kind items

SOURCE: Reprinted with permission of Macmillan Publishing Company from Arnold Mitchell, *Nine American Lifestyles: Who We Are and Where We Are Going* (New York: Macmillan, 1983). Copyright © 1983 by Arnold Mitchell.

to get ahead and think they can because of their "street savvy." Like survivors, they have limited education and low income levels, but they may live in the country as well as the city and aren't necessarily members of minority groups. Although price is important to sustainers, they also want warranties and are cautious. But their desire to get ahead may make them targets for get-rich-quick schemes such as multilevel marketing (for example, Amway or Mary Kaye). They might also engage in illegal activities such as selling marijuana or be hooked on buying lottery tickets.

Outer-Directed Consumers. This category makes up 67 percent of the marketplace and is an important target for all advertisers. Outer-directed consumers are divided into three subcategories. Belongers (35 percent) are very conventional and traditional. They do not usually experiment with new products or services, and they conform to traditional patterns. They tend to be blue-collar workers with low to middle levels of education. They are family oriented, focusing on products with domestic appeal. Belongers are also nostalgic and are good targets for direct-response television ads for "Great Music of the 50s" or "Patsy Cline's Greatest Hits" and other nostalgic products ("Bread like Grandma used to make—from a machine!!"). They are also affected by fads.

Emulators (10 percent) are upwardly mobile, ambitious, status conscious, and competitive. Sometimes, they try to project a macho image. They have good incomes, tend to be young, and live in urban areas. They have traditionally been males, but that is changing as more and more women enter the workplace. Emulators are into "conspicuous consumption" and purchase "in" products that represent popular fashion. They are good targets for the newest (and most expensive) styles in clothing, automobiles, and leisure activities (health clubs, cross-country skiing, fly-fishing schools and camps, and so on).

Achievers (22 percent) have "made it" in today's world. They are interested in efficiency, leadership, achievement, success, fame, comfort, and conspicuous consumption. They have excellent incomes and high degrees of education. They live in suburbs and "trendy" parts of large cities. They tend to be leaders in politics, business, and community activities. Achievers' buying patterns reflect their success—they always buy top-of-the-line products. They are willing to try "new" products and are good targets for luxury items such as Rolex watches, BMWs, "success rings," and Coach briefcases.

Inner-Directed Consumers. These consumers represent a small but distinctive slice of the market (22 percent) and are divided into four subcategories. I-am-me consumers (5 percent) are very individualistic and reject traditional possessions or ways of behaving. They are experimental and impulsive and tend to be dramatic and volatile (see Figure 14.5). I-am-me's come from affluent backgrounds, even though they themselves may not have much discretionary income. Many are students or are just starting to climb the occupational ladder. Their buying patterns are more related to "taste" than high price—just the opposite of emulators and achievers. In fact, I-am-me's may be "far out" as consumers and usually don't go for faddish items.

As their name implies, experientials (7 percent) want to have many and varied experiences. They participate in many activities, are introspective, and are frequently artistic. They may have high or low incomes depending on their decisions about living standards. They have good educations and are likely to have families and to be under forty years of age. Experientials' buying habits focus on vigorous outdoor sports—mountain climbing, backpacking, wilderness camping, and whitewater rafting. They are also into "do-it-yourself" projects if they relate to the home. Experiential consumers are good targets for products from L. L. Bean and they support the arts.

Societally conscious consumers are into simple living and are concerned with environmental issues. They have a strong sense of societal responsibility and are likely to join the Sierra Club, Greenpeace, the nuclear freeze movement, or the Green Party. They are interested in smallness of scale and inner growth. They are mainly white and have excellent educations but bimodal incomes (that is, they cluster around the low and high ends of the income scale). These consumers are as likely to live in cities

FIGURE 14.5 I-am-me's resent being labeled and want to be individualistic. They are also volatile and dramatic, as this cartoon shows. They usually are "early" baby boomers (born between 1946 and 1955).

(*Arlo and Janis* reproduced by permission of NEA, Inc.)

and towns as in villages or the country. Their buying habits have a conservation orientation, focusing on simplicity and frugality. They are good targets for energy-saving devices, cars that get good gas mileage, solar heating, and the human potential movement. They might be interested in organic gardening, wine making, and freezing home-grown produce.

Integrated consumers (2 percent) feel good about themselves and their niche in life. They are tolerant and have a sense of psychological maturity. They are also self-actualizers who take a broad view of the world, so they are concerned with issues like acid rain and might boycott products that pollute. They have good-to-excellent incomes but they vary in age. Like societally conscious consumers, their residential patterns are variable and their occupations are diverse. They express themselves in their buying habits, focusing on the uniqueness of the product in the marketplace, and are good targets for products that allow for self-expression (for example, pottery throwing). They might be interested in restoring historic homes, refinishing antiques, or collecting unique things. They are aesthetically inclined and so are good targets for "artistic products" (statuary, art, music, drama, and so on). Integrated consumers are usually "early" baby boomers—that is, born between 1946 and 1955. This market segment is growing rapidly, whereas the percentage of

need-driven consumers is declining and the proportion of outer-directed consumers is stable.

How do advertisers use such research models and results to target us, the consumers of this country? Consumer experts J. Engel, D. Blackwell, and P. Miniard (1993) offer an illuminating case study of how VALS was used to shape not only advertising and sales promotion but brand image as well. As they report it, a midwestern chain of restaurants called Max and Erma's analyzed more than four hundred of their frequent customers (customers who visited the chain twice or more a month), using the VALS categories. Their core customers fell primarily in the inner-directed group (38 percent compared with 20 percent for the overall population). They were typical DINKs who ate out frequently and who were willing to try anything. They were sophisticated nonconformists who liked to express themselves and favored personal tastes rather than status or other people's opinions of them. They were also success oriented, hardworking, and interested in quality versus price, which meant they probably wouldn't ever choose Wendy's, Bob Evans, or Shoney's. Based on these and other data, Max and Erma's reoriented its public relations, advertising, sales promotion, and even menus by featuring ways in which the inner-directed consumer could express his or her individuality. Menus now carried such items as "Name your own burger," "Top your own pasta," and "Build your own sundae." Local franchises offered various promotions, including coupons and special events, using direct-mail lists of potential customers. In one case, local television ads featured a well-known, successful attorney and his spouse, a well-known, inner-directed community leader who was also an attorney. The couple was shown eating at Max and Erma's on occasions when they wanted or needed such benefits as "time convenience," "informality," "fun times," and "quality items on the menu," all of which had been rated high by the VALS subjects/participants. Max and Erma's also provided sales training for franchise managers and staff. The result of the new approach was a turnaround in sales at a time when the industry as a whole was experiencing either further losses or at best flat levels of profits. New locations for the chain were established even as competing chains experienced essentially no growth or even losses.

To better understand how psychographics can help segment markets, access InfoTrac College Edition, and enter the words "psychographics" in the key word search engine. Read both of the articles listed there. Share them with the class.

Sociographics

Sociographics is the study of how, why, and where people live. Its basic assumption is that "birds of a feather flock together"; that is, people choose to live with or near persons whom they find to be similar to themselves. It is something of a combination of geographics (the places people live), demographics (the clusterings of variables associated with them), and psychographics (their lifestyles). Research in sociographics is done by sampling persons from a zip code area that resembles the kind of neighborhood to which the advertiser believes a product will appeal. Then the ad researchers bring subjects together in focus groups to answer a survey about the product and its competitors. A leader directs the groups to discuss the product, its competitors, the advantages and disadvantages, and their attitudes toward it. The researchers then analyze the data and look for patterns in the survey responses and in the focus group comments—for instance, recurring words, phrases, or images. These results are then turned over to the ad agency's creative staff, who design messages around the consumer-generated copy points. Sometimes, the exact language of the participants is used for the ad copy.

Some market research companies compile demographics about a variety of "typical" neighborhoods and sell these data to advertisers. For example, the ACORN (a classification of residential neighborhoods) system identifies forty-four residential types and then categorizes subsets of each. Market segment A2, for instance, is composed of "newer suburbs, professionals, and middle-aged families," with demographics "similar to A1's but with slightly younger families. Middle-aged and older white families. Children are in their teens." The housing in A2 is "newer than in A1, but still has extremely high values. Almost exclusively single family, owner occupied." The lifestyle and marketing implications are as follows:

> Households in market segment A2 are second only to A1 in terms of investments, leisure activities, and travel. They are heavy spenders on their children, home furnishings, and clothing. They are the heaviest consumers of imported wines and mixed drinks. They drive expensive cars which are sportier than those of A1 households; the second car tends to be a mid-size American car, sometimes a station wagon. They are high on fitness and travel to warm climates.

Knowing all this about a market segment tells the advertisers which of its products and brands should be marketed to the segment.

Sociographics also show media-use patterns, the parts of the day devoted to various media, radio format preferences, and so on. All of these data fall into place in designing an IMC campaign using sophisticated research techniques. Think how much research goes into ads that are nationally broadcasted or printed. Sophisticated persuaders using demographics, psychographics, and sociographics know a great deal about us and our consumer behavior.

Another psychographic/sociographic system is based on Michael Weiss's 1989 book *The Clustering of America* and is marketed by the Claritas Corporation under the brand name P.R.I.Z.M. The system has identified sixty-two distinct psychographic/sociographic neighborhood types. P.R.I.Z.M. gives segments catchy names that suggest what the neighborhood is like. For example, one is called "Two More Rungs," for the young emulators on their way up the corporate ladder. "Pools and Patios" refers to achievers who are enjoying the good life as they approach retirement. "Shotguns and Pickups" refers to high-school-educated blue-collar workers who live in modest homes or mobile homes that feature a large-screen TV, a dusty pickup in the driveway, and off-brand soft drinks in the refrigerator. They are frequently overweight and, when eating out, usually go to "all you can eat" buffet restaurants.

Companies like Claritas know an amazing amount about such clusters. For example, take "Towns and Gowns," or typical college towns—maybe like the one in which you are now living. They are populated largely by white singles who are college grads or students who vote Republican and jog. They make frequent use of ATM machines, and they are unlikely to have a van, toy-sized dog, mutual funds, or burglar alarm systems. However, they do have personal loans, like to water and snow ski, read *Modern Bride* or *Gentleman's Quarterly,* and drive Sables, Subaru DL4s, Toyota Tercels, Nissan Altimas, or Volkswagen Jettas. They like watching *David Letterman* but hate Sunday morning interview programs.

Imagine what knowing this kind of detail can do for advertisers in terms of targeting audiences, designing ads, selecting the media, and so on. And these are but a few of the details available through P.R.I.Z.M. You can imagine the various IMC messages that can be tailored using such detailed information—public relations, advertising, sales promotions, and so on. As critical consumers of persuasion, you need to be alert to the degree to which advertisers have psychographically designed ads aimed at you or your market segment.

Go to InfoTrac College Edition, and enter the words "demographics," "sociographics," and "psychographics" one at a time into both of the search engines—key word and subject. Which of the three yields the most entries? Why do you think that is the case?

FROM RESEARCH TO COPY: THE LANGUAGES OF ADVERTISING

Once the research department has done its job, the results are brought to the agency's creative staff for conversion into attention-getting and "memorable" ad and PR copy. It must not only be believable but should also "sell" the brand amidst the sea of ads that clutter the print media and the airwaves. Here is where our interest in persuasion should be greatest. If you have been fine-tuning your ability to analyze persuasive appeals of various types and have become more aware of the nuances of meaning that both verbal and nonverbal communication can carry, you should have a sense of what copywriters are doing to us each and every day.

John O'Toole, former chair of the board at Foote, Cone, and Belding (the eighth largest ad agency in the world) makes some interesting observations about reaching the audience in believable ways in his book *The Trouble with Advertising* (1985). His basic idea is that the consumer is at the center of the process. O'Toole believes that the only kind of language—verbal and nonverbal—that can effectively persuade in an advertisement is that which is targeted at the consumer as an individual and not merely one of the masses. At Foote, Cone, and Belding, the first task with a new product or account is to develop a "personal profile" of the consumer. The consumer is considered a unique individual with whom the client carries on an interpersonal dialogue using IMC. To quote O'Toole, "Advertising works best when it most closely approximates a dialogue between two human beings" (p. 122). He also says, "Regarding the other party as a person rather than as people . . . making that person know you recognize him as an individual rather than as a face in the crowd, is going to cause him to respond more positively to you" (pp. 110–111).

O'Toole gives several examples of this kind of personal language and copy, including, "Aren't you glad you use Dial? Don't you wish everyone did?" This slogan addresses the consumer much more personally than the one for another deodorant: "Get off the can. Get on the stick." Or take the Sears DieHard battery ad copy that follows a demonstration of the battery in action: "The DieHard. Starts your car when most other batteries won't." What about, "You're not getting older; you're getting better"? These copy lines are aimed at an individual, not at merely another cipher in the masses. They fulfill agency partner Fairfax Cone's memo to O'Toole: "Let us make every advertisement that we make personal. Let us aim it at just one person, just as we would in face-to-face contact."

That kind of ad copy gets what O'Toole calls "the nod of agreement." This phrase is close to what Tony Schwartz meant by resonance: Consumers recognize some part of themselves or their experiences in the words or visuals of the ad. The nod of agreement is part of what O'Toole calls "the implicit contract" between advertiser and consumer. Although the contract is unwritten, it is clearly understood by even the most naive consumer. The implied contract is that advertisers will promote a product but won't tell you about their competitors. They will try to present their product in its best light, but they won't mislead you, lie to you, or bore you. In return for the opportunity to promote their product, they will subsidize programs, journalism, documentaries, the news, music, sports events, entertainment, and more.

Sometimes, we are fooled and purchase a product that is not all it has been "puffed up" to be and does not perform as promised. In that case, we can return the product or never buy it again, and we can warn other consumers not to buy the product. O'Toole admits that there have been misleading and even outright false advertisements across the years, but he is quick to point out that consumers soon identify those ads and then ignore the products. O'Toole also contends that "American consumers are the canniest of creatures. . . . And they are powerful [because of] their refusal to repurchase" (p. 21). That is why 80 percent of the new products brought out on the market in any given year fail.

Although O'Toole's assurances are sincere, consumers should still be aware of some of the kinds of appeals advertisers make that do not actually lie or that are not obviously fraudulent, but that bend the truth without actually fracturing it. Several of the more interesting, useful, and lively discussions of the topic of misleading advertising are found in the works of Carl Wrighter and Hugh Rank.

WEASEL WORDS IN ADVERTISING

We have been looking at how advertisers use words in media messages. We know that symbols are the basic raw material of persuasion, and we know that words are central carriers of symbolic meaning. So we need to look at how clever persuaders use words and at how these words work in ad messages. Carl Wrighter, a former adman, in his book *I Can Sell You Anything* (1972) focused on some of the key words that are used to deceive us. He called them "weasel words" because they allow persuaders to seem to say something without ever really saying it. These words let sources weasel their way out of a promise. They are key tip-offs to the kind of pitch we need to guard against. Here are some to watch for.

"Helps"

The word "helps" is a clever one in that it seems to offer aid or perhaps even a cure. We hear that Listerine mouthwash helps prevent colds. Even if you get a cold, it helps you feel better right away. What is the promise here? Can you expect that you will feel better in a few days if you use Listerine? If you did, could you say that your improvement resulted from the help Listerine gave? These questions point out the problem with a word such as "helps."

"Like"

Another weasel word frequently used in ads is "like." For instance, a famous tennis star tells us that driving a Nissan Maxima is like driving one of those expensive European cars—but costs a lot less. Or the house brand is like the expensive name brands—"we just don't advertise." You can easily see the deception that can be floated with a word that has as many loopholes as "like." Cindy Crawford is supposed to be like women all over the world. A prepared food tastes just like homemade. A jug wine tastes like the expensive French wines. Geritol will make you feel like you are a kid again. A BMW hugs the road like a cat.

"Virtually"

The weasel word "virtually" resembles "like," except that it seems to promise even more. The new cotton chamois shirts are virtually indestructible. Leatherette feels virtually like cowhide. Cascade leaves your dishes and glassware virtually spotless. The promise seems so specific, and there is only a tiny loophole. But that loophole widens as much as is needed when the customer says that the leatherette wore out after several months or when we find a few spots on the dishes and stemware washed with Cascade. If the product did what is claimed, the word "virtually" would not be needed.

DECEPTIVE CLAIMS IN ADVERTISING

Another kind of deception to which we are exposed in ads is found in claims. Clever promoters use claims to attract our attention and to prompt us to buy products, to vote for candidates, or to adopt certain practices. Let us look at several kinds of claims identified by Wrighter (1972).

The Irrelevant Claim

Some persuaders use ad messages to make claims that sound impressive but are irrelevant if you look at them closely. You are exposed to such claims whenever you turn on your TV, open a magazine, or tune in your radio. The basic tactic is to make a truthful claim that has little to do with the purpose of the product, plan for change, or idea. Then that claim is dramatized in such a way as to link the claim with the product, candidate, or movement. J&B scotch claims to be "rare" and "natural." Why would you want "rare" scotch? What is "natural"

about J&B? Are other scotch whiskeys unnatural? If you can't find an answer, chances are you have identified an irrelevant claim.

The Question Claim

Wrighter noted a kind of claim often directed at us through the media: the claim that is hidden by a question. "If you can't trust Prestone, who can you trust?" "Why not buy the original?" "Why not send the best?" "Would a bunch of guys really go at it this hard just for a Michelob?" and "Why not catch a lunker—with Stren monofilament?" are all examples of the question claim. Notice that the product advantage is only implied. Trusting one's antifreeze is okay, but the question implies that dependability is to be found only in Prestone, and we know that other brands of antifreeze are also dependable. Why buy the original? It may be overpriced. Maybe the Michelob is just an afterthought. Will using Stren guarantee that you'll catch a lunker? When you see or hear a question claim, the best response is to ask for details and guarantees.

The Advantage Claim

Wrighter also noted the type of claim that seems to offer some advantage for a product or idea. Mother's noodles claim to be made with 100 percent semolina wheat—but so are all the other brands. If you compare the levels of vitamins in several types of breakfast cereal, you will discover that they are all about the same. Most of the protein comes from the milk you add and not from the cereal. Thus, there is no advantage in Corn Chex's claim that it is "fortified with six important vitamins and minerals." These are advantages that aren't.

Politicians often claim to have come from humble beginnings, which is supposed to be an advantage. It may be a real disadvantage from one perspective: People who had humble beginnings might be insecure. They probably had to compete for everyday things, which might limit their educational sophistication, sense of diplomacy, social skills, and ability to communicate with leaders in higher social strata. Whenever you are faced with a person, product, or idea that claims some significant

Dannon Yogurt may not help you live as long as Soviet Georgians. But it couldn't hurt.

Bagrat Topagua, age 89.

His mother.

There are two curious things about the people of Soviet Georgia. A large part of their diet is yogurt. And a large number of them live to be well over 100.

Of course, many factors affect longevity, and we are not saying Dannon Yogurt will help you live longer. But we will say that all-natural Dannon is high in nutrients, low in fat, reasonable in calories. And quite satisfying at lunch or as a snack.

Another thing about Dannon. It contains active yogurt cultures (many pre-mixed or

Swiss style brands don't). They make yogurt one of the easiest foods to digest and have been credited with other healthful benefits.

Which is why we've been advising this: If you don't always eat right, Dannon Yogurt is the right thing to eat.

By the way, Bagrat Topagua thought Dannon was "dzelian kargia." Which means he loved it.

Dannon Milk Products. 22-11 38th Ave. Long Island City, N.Y. 11101

FIGURE 14.6 The hazy claims about longevity and yogurt may confuse the persuadee enough to try the product, just to be on the safe side.

(Used by permission of Dannon Milk Products.)

advantage, you need to ask whether the advantage is real; whether it is exclusive to that person, product, or idea; and whether certain disadvantages accompany it.

The Hazy Claim

The hazy claim confuses the buyer or voter. If persuaders can confuse us, we will follow their advice just to be on the safe side. Consider the ad for Dannon yogurt shown in Figure 14.6. It confuses readers by implying that yogurt eaters live longer. As you read more of the ad copy, you see that the only health claim Dannon can make is that its yogurt, unlike some others (how many? which brands?), has active cultures. But is it good to eat Dannon Yo-

gurt, yogurt of any kind, or no yogurt? Out of this confusion, Dannon persuades through its slogan: "If you don't always eat right, Dannon yogurt is the right thing to eat." You need to ask, "Why is it right?" "Who says?" and "With what proof?" when a hazy claim appears.

Again, we can see hazy claims widely used in the world of politics. For example, a politician says that she supports the economic policies of free trade and protective tariffs. These policies, however, are 180 degrees apart, so the result for voters is confusion. If voters watch images, the problem becomes worse. What does it prove when a politician kisses babies or talks about the price of pork? These activities do not tell us much about an elected official's ability to construct policies on education, trade, or the environment. They are likely to confuse voters and draw attention away from the issues.

The Magic Ingredient Claim

Wrighter called this the "mysterious claim" because it refers to a mysterious ingredient or device that makes a better product. I prefer to call it the "magic ingredient claim." Noxzema, for example, has a product called "Acne 12," which supposedly contains a secret ingredient that dermatologists prescribe most. Oxy-Clean contains "a powerful yet gentle medication no ordinary cleanser has." If the manufacturers really had a secret ingredient, they probably would not tell us about it.

Many other kinds of claims are made through the mass media. Wrighter's book points out several. You will discover others as you begin to evaluate advertising messages you receive. The important thing is to maintain a critical attitude. Ask key questions of the claim.

Rank's 30-Second-Spot Quiz

Hugh Rank, who originated the intensify/downplay model discussed in Chapter 1, outlined an easy-to-apply set of key questions to ask about advertising appeals. His system, "The 30-Second-Spot Quiz," is based on his book *The Pitch* (1982).

Rank began by pointing out that any advertisement, but especially a television spot advertisement, is a synthesis of complex variables—research, script, settings, camera angles, acting, props, costumes, colors, and so on. Any analysis of such a complex synthesis demands that consumers look at the spots in a sequential way. This can be accomplished, Rank suggested, by listing, in order, the "shots" or visual frames that make up a 30-second spot, keeping in mind that there might be as many as forty quick-cut shots. For example, most spots have an "establishing shot," or the shot that "sets the stage" for the ad. Various versions of an ad for Miller's Reserve lager and ale used images of some familiar sight in the city in which the advertising was tested. The San Francisco version used the Golden Gate Bridge, and the Chicago version used the Sears Tower. Other shots further the "story" of the ad. A medium shot showing a couple from the waist up involved in an argument tells us that conflict is central to the story. The audio comes up, and we discover that they are arguing about whether to buy an American or a foreign-made automobile. The camera moves in for a close-up shot of the man's face, and we hear musical tension increasing as we see and hear the tension in his face and voice. Then the close-up shifts to the woman's face, and we hear her say, "You know, you're cute when you're serious like this." Then we hear a giggle and see a nuzzle. The shots tell the story. Your job as a receiver using Ranks' 30-second-spot quiz is to continue listing the shots in order until the ad is completely described. Try to distinguish the "surface variations" that occur and the "underlying structure" of the spot. For example, the underlying structure of the ad just described is conflict resolution, but a surface variation could have used two males for the argument. This surface variation would alter the dialogue, tension, drama, and, finally, meaning of the ad.

Rank also suggested the importance of recognizing the audience's involvement in the spot. What benefits are we seeking, and what benefits are being promised by the brand? For example, the Ford Escort initially advertised that it had "aerodynamic styling," "independent wheel suspension," and "rack and pinion steering." These are *features* of the Escort, and not *benefits*. Features should offer some benefit to the consumer. For instance, "aerody-

namic styling" offers the benefits of better handling, less wind resistance, better gas mileage, and a quieter interior. This is the key kind of question to ask.

Once these preparatory steps are taken, Rank suggests asking five basic analytical questions:

1. *What attention-getting techniques are being used?* Most ads appeal to one or more of the five senses (see Figure 14.7). Most also appeal to consumers' emotions and often use the unexpected, the interesting, and the noticeable (such as famous athletes) to capture consumers' attention.

2. *What confidence-building techniques are being used to convince consumers that they can trust the brand?* The use of authority figures, repetition, references to the number of years the brand has been successful, appeals to trust and sincerity, the use of expert testimony such as from a doctor or other authority, satisfaction and service guarantees, warranties, and a host of other techniques help build consumer confidence.

3. *What desire-stimulating techniques are being used to motivate consumers to try the brand?* Rank suggested that identifying the benefits being offered is a good way to discover these techniques. He noted that most ads offer one or more of the following as desire-stimulating reasons to try the brand: Use the brand to prevent or avoid some bad thing (disease, discomfort, embarrassment), to protect or keep some good thing (health, status, appearance, wealth), to gain relief or get rid of some bad thing (bad breath, dandruff, financial worry), or to acquire or get some good thing (a new car, a cash card, a no-load mutual fund).

4. *What urgency-stressing techniques are being used to get consumers to "act now"* (for example, expiration dates, deadlines, or "while supplies last" warnings)?

5. *What response-seeking techniques are being used to tell consumers what kind of action is being sought* (for example, try the brand, purchase it, shift to a new brand, join the organization, or call the 800 number)?

FIGURE 14.7 Using Rank's 30-second-spot quiz, explain how this ad gets consumer attention.

(By permission of Search Alliance.)

CHANGES IN OUR WORLD: IMPLICATIONS FOR ADVERTISING

Since the first edition of this book was published nearly thirty years ago, a number of societal changes have occurred that have had enormous effects on how we behave as consumers and how critics of persuasion—especially in the field of advertising—have come to look at this field. Consider the trends noted at the beginning of the chapter. Markets are becoming more global and more diverse. Some companies like McDonald's have few new markets to enter in the United States without cannibalizing sales at other locations. More families than ever now rely on two incomes per household, a trend that has led to many new products. For example: Campbell's "Soup for One" is a single-sized serving of the product, just as Stokely's Singles are servings of vegetables for one person, and many frozen entrees contain single servings.

Who are the targets of such products? Widows and widowers? Single persons? Divorced persons? To some extent, all of these, but research demonstrated to Campbell's that the eating habits of Americans were rapidly changing. Because of the two-income family pattern and children's increased activity, meals were not the traditional "family around the dinner table" anymore. Perhaps Dad had a late meeting, and Mom was not yet home from work; Bobby was at soccer practice, and his sister Susie had to rehearse for the high school play. The solution? Give both Bobby and Susie their choice of a sandwich and their favorite "Soup for One." At the same time, more and more families are dining out, bringing home meals from restaurants or delicatessens, or having home delivery. Eating out is a time-saver, and as a result, fast- and specialty-food establishments have proliferated. Recent research has shown that the average American eats more than half of his or her meals out.

Another change has been the introduction of 800, and later 900 and 888, dialing, which makes it much easier to purchase anything from clothing to phone sex. For two-income families, time is a commodity to be "spent" carefully, and mail-order and

online purchasing for themselves or for gifts for others saves time. Thus, we have an explosion in cataloguing—shopping by catalogue saves time. Amazon.com is typical of Web sites that save consumers shopping time.

An additional trend that has implications for advertising and IMC is that retail square footage has increased while disposable consumer income grew at a much slower rate in the same period. Simply look at the many new strip malls and mega-malls built in the past decade. This resulted in a very competitive marketplace, especially given the amount of disposable income being spent on catalogue, online, shopping channel, and other direct-marketed products. We now see "pre-Christmas sales," as well as the traditional "post-Christmas sales." The number of large discount chains has increased as well, which has important implications for advertising and IMC. For one thing, the amount of advertising will increase simply because one way to try to beat the competition is to outadvertise them. There will be more sales promotions—coupons, rebates, sweepstakes, celebrities at point of purchase, shelf-talkers, product demonstrations, displays, and so on—a persuasion approach closely related to advertising.

A new video-equipped grocery cart is being tested in several markets by Information Resources, whose chair says that, whereas most "in-store selling techniques are aimed at selling something without providing any benefits to the consumers, Videocart makes shopping more informative and fun for consumers" (Storch, 1988, p. 5). The local supermarket's satellite dish antenna receives a new product's advertisement, which replaces the old ad on the store manager's computer. This new ad is transmitted to the shelf space where the product is on display. When the video cart passes the transmitter, it triggers the ad on the cart's screen. At the checkout counter, the cash register/computer tells which ads triggered a purchase and what path the cart took through the store.

In short, in the years to come, there will be still more clutter for advertisers to try to break through and for us to try to sift through. And we are only on the front edge of interactive computer and Internet advertising. As people spend more and more time on their computers, advertisers will increasingly use the new technology as an additional way to promote their brands. *Advertising Age* began to include an "Interactive" section in its weekly issues in the early 1990s, and ad executives and others took notice. Today, no successful corporation would think of operating without a home page even though few knew what a home page was only a short while ago.

ACADEMIC ANALYSIS OF ADVERTISING

From an academic viewpoint, it has finally been recognized that advertising is a topic worthy of study and criticism. Even the lowly TV spot is a kind of "rhetoric" that needs to be critically analyzed, not simply being dismissed out of hand (Diamond, 1984; Leiss, Kline, & Jhally, 1986; Postman, 1987; Williamson, 1977). In the early 1970s, an academic journal rejected one of my articles because it focused on political TV advertisements. Since then, advertising has become acceptable grist for the communication scholar's mill. Let's explore some examples.

The Language of Advertising by Torben Vestergaard and Kim Schroeder (1985) is an excellent resource for analyzing the language used in advertising and IMC. They point out that advertising is pointless unless goods are overproduced to the point that sellers need to "beat the competition." They note that material needs and social status are frequently communicated through habits of consumption. In other words, the purchased objects have become semanticized. The kinds of clothing, cars, audio equipment, and so on that we buy have a "meaning" to us and others with whom we socialize. This permits advertisers to exploit our needs for group affiliation, self-identification, and status.

Vestergaard and Schroeder define advertising as a "text" that is meant to be "read" in all its verbal and nonverbal nuances. They describe it as having several specific dimensions:

■ It exists in a particular communication situation.

■ It is a structured unit and has texture.

■ It communicates meaning.

Perhaps the most difficult dimension to understand is the idea of a text having structure and texture. Vestergaard and Schroeder provide helpful examples. Take the structure or sense of the information content of this copy from an ad in *Cosmopolitan*. An automatic applicator gently "smooths on soft cream or high-shine colour, for a smooth, silky finish that lasts. And lasts. And . . . colours that look lastingly tempting. Longer." Here, we have two sentence fragments—"And lasts" and "Longer"—which could just as easily have been included in the sentences that precede them. Why split them up? Because in doing so the advertiser has cut two sense-making units into four, thus encouraging readers to focus on the product benefit—long-lasting—four times instead of two.

Another technique that can give an ad structure or texture is the drama implied. Vestergaard and Schroeder cite the work of A. J. Griemas and his pairs of terms, which are used to describe a fundamental drama in folktales and myths:

> subject–object
>
> helper–opponent
>
> giver–receiver

To see how this model can be used to analyze the verbal and nonverbal language in ads, consider an ad for Avon. The visual (or nonverbal) part takes up the upper two-thirds of the page. It shows a mature woman standing behind a younger woman who is trying to put on makeup. The headline reads, "I enjoy helping other women to look good," and the copy explains that by being an Avon representative you can bring all of the wonderful Avon products into customers' homes. Further, Avon products have a "no quibble guarantee." The "subject" is the young woman, and her "object" is to look good. Her "opponent" is her uncertainty. The "helper"—the Avon representative—solves this problem by bringing a "giver"—Avon products—to her door. The "receiver" is thus "rescued" from the opponent by the product.

Vestergaard and Schroeder point out several other concepts that contribute to the structure and texture of advertisements. The important thing is to try to take the ad apart, bit by bit, verbally and nonverbally, and see what it is really saying and how it works—to "deconstruct" or to "discover" the ad, in other words. They go on to point out that the traditional task of the ad copywriter has five steps; let's examine these in detail.

Attracting Attention

The easiest way to attract attention is to put the product's name next to a visual of the product and then to describe a product benefit. Another way to attract attention is to ask a question of the reader/viewer ("Why don't you come back to Folgers?") or to use the word "when" (as in "When the day is done, have a cold one—Coors, the Rocky Mountain reward"). Naming the user also captures attention ("Contact lens users—Now you can have all-day comfort with Comfortdrops"). Naming the consumer is even more effective when coupled with some kind of flattering statement about the user ("For the outdoorsman who has everything: give him a Schrade knife").

Certain words are attention getters—"free," "new," "more," "now," "you," "save," and "act" are just a few examples. An interesting example of the power of the word "free" is the case of the Cabela's catalogue for outdoor sporting gear. As discussed in a previous chapter, Cabela got his start by offering fishing flies via mail order and advertising them in newspapers in Colorado, Wyoming, and Montana —states famous for their trout fishing. His initial offer was for "5 hand-tied dry flies for $.25! Free shipping and handling!" After getting only a few orders, he revised his offer to read, "FREE!! 5 hand-tied dry flies—you only pay $.25 shipping and handling!!" The orders began to pour in, and he simply increased the handling charge as the cost of the flies went up to make his profit. Today, not only are millions of Cabela's catalogues sent out, but there are numerous Cabela's retail stores around the country.

Ads that have people in them pull better than those that merely show the brand, and attention improves if children, puppies, or kittens are shown. Recipes included in the ad also help attract attention and promote consumer involvement. Seductive and sexy models boost readership, and other attention-getting and -maintaining devices are be-

ing developed almost daily at the advertising agencies of the new millennium.

Creating Interest, Desire, and Conviction

Vestergaard and Schroeder also say that a good way to attract audience attention and then to create interest is to ask a question that the reader or viewer probably cannot answer. This provokes curiosity and usually leads the audience to interact with the advertisement in some way: reading the copy, looking at the visuals, or even physically interacting with it (scratch 'n' sniff, for example). One example of this tactic is to ask a question that leads to a true/false "quiz" that the reader is supposed to answer. For example, the headline of a full-page, four-color ad by General Motors asks, "Do you know where your next fender is coming from?" GM satisfies the reader's curiosity by answering, "America's body shops are being flooded with imitation parts. Look-alike doors. Copycat hoods. Imitation bumpers, grilles, fenders and more. . . . These not-so-exact replicas seldom measure up to General Motors original specifications. . . . Insist on genuine GM parts." This ad copy is designed not only to answer the attention-getting headline but also to create interest, desire, and conviction in the reader/viewer by pointing out product benefits—the unique selling proposition (USP) mentioned earlier. Again, notice the use of sentence fragments— "Look-alike doors" and "Copycat hoods"—to give the advertiser extra "shots" at the reader.

A problem in today's crowded marketplace is that most products are "me, too" imitations of the original, and so most of the USPs tend to be aesthetic. All dog food, for instance, looks pretty much alike—either like gravel if it is dry or like glop if it is canned. But look at what Gaines Burger did. In the first place, the name sounds like and the product looks like hamburger—the all-American food. Of course, its redness is not natural—it comes from an iron oxide additive. It won't hurt your dog, but it will cause you to make a link with a past experience: buying fresh hamburger meat (which is also not naturally red). Another tactic used to create interest, desire, and conviction in a "me, too" product is to stress the "high quality" of the product. High quality is a slippery thing to prove, which is why the word "quality" is used so often in ads. If an advertiser says its product is the lowest priced in town, that can be verified as true or false, which is why you do not often see that statement. Instead, advertisers more frequently say that they will "meet or beat" any price. But if they claim that the product has the best quality for the price, they are not likely to be called on to prove their claim. We all know that quality is not "Job #1" at Ford—productivity and resulting profit are the real priority. Another approach is to appeal to the reverence we hold toward anything scientific by including some scientific-sounding ingredient such as "Platformate," "Retsyn," or "DZM-21." An advertiser can also make a "scientific" claim: "The pain reliever recommended most by doctors and hospitals" is one example. Or the spokesperson might be dressed in a laboratory coat and standing in a lab with microscopes, test tubes, and so on in the background. This "scientist" then tells us about the product benefits.

Getting Action

Any salesperson will tell you that the critical, and usually the hardest, thing to do is to "close" the deal —in other words, to get action. The successful salesperson must be able to "ask for the order." "Buy now" would seem to be the most direct call to action, but Vestergaard and Schroeder found the word "buy" in only two advertisements in their analysis of the ten magazine issues on which their book was based. However, there are other ways to say "buy now" without using the word "buy," which scares prospects off. For example, "act now," "phone now," and "send now" say the same thing but avoid the possible negative connotations of the word "buy." Other urgency-stressing words and phrases can be the call to action: "While supplies last," "Offer good until . . . ," "24-hour sale," and so on. These are what Vestergaard and Schroeder call directive language. They found that 32 percent of the ads they studied used one form or another of this type of language. Directive language falls into several categories:

- *The imperative clause, which gives an order.* "Get one today" is one example. Another can be found in an ad for a fishing lure supposedly in short supply—the Shadrap. The ad copy for it reads, "The Rapala company was only able to send 125,000 Shadraps to the U.S. That's enough for every serious fisherman . . . as long as they only take one each—If you see one, grab it!" On one fishing trip, I bought three. I asked a passing canoeist if he had been having any luck with the Shadrap. He informed me that he had and that he had purchased nine.

- *Other less directive and more suggestive language that encourages the reader/viewer to buy.* An example is the "negated interrogative," as in "Isn't it time you tried Dial?" A softer version is "Why not try Dial?" Even less directive is "Dial is worth a try." And in the weakest version, the directions are attributed not to the reader or viewer but to a reference group: "For people who believe a deodorant bath soap should also be gentle on the skin, there's Dial with lanolin."

- *Directive language that invites the reader/viewer to send for details, use the trial sample, or remember the product.* Sometimes, these appeals are designed to get a sale, but more often, they are used to create "qualified leads" that can be followed up by a telephone call or a visit by a salesperson. If a consumer sends in for a free pamphlet on energy saving, for example, he or she is probably a good prospect—a "qualified lead"—for storm windows, aluminum siding, solar panels, and energy-efficient furnaces.

Altogether, only two of the ads investigated by Vestergaard and Schroeder used the word "buy"; seventeen other verbs made up most of the directive appeals. They were "try," "ask for," "take," "send for," "call," "make," "come on," "hurry," "come," "see," "give," "remember," "discover," "serve," "introduce," "choose," and "look for."

SEXUAL APPEALS AND SUBLIMINAL PERSUASION IN ADVERTISING

The issues of sexual appeals and subliminal persuasion in advertising are controversial ones. Criticisms of these practices arise from diverse constituencies. For example, feminists are concerned about advertising's exploitation of the female body. Others are concerned about increases in sexually transmitted diseases, high rates of teenage pregnancy, and increasing promiscuity at all levels of society. And still others question the ethics of subliminal appeals and maintain that such appeals violate individuals' right to know what messages are being targeted at them.

Sexual appeals in advertising range from the obvious and blatant ones that virtually promise sexual success for users of the product to the less obvious and more symbolic ones that seem only to suggest instead of promise sexual success. In addition, there may be subliminal ads that seem merely to suggest sexual success on the surface but that promise it at the unconscious or subliminal level.

Of course, the work of Sigmund Freud and his followers is applicable here. Freud maintained that sexual impulses and the procreative urge are among the most powerful motivators of human action. Not only do they alter physical behavior, they also affect symbolic behavior, giving sexual meanings to a wide variety of objects and actions. For example, the Freudians saw cylindrical objects (pens and pencils, cigars, bottles, guns, and so on) as being symbolic of an erect phallus, and they saw round or open objects (goblets, vases, bowls, open windows and doors, flowers, and so on) as symbolic of the vagina. Thus, all sorts of ordinary everyday activities (smoking a cigar, cupping the hands, or fiddling with objects) might be symbolic substitutes for human sexual activities—intercourse or masturbation. Freud's work was ridiculed by many, but it was taken very seriously by a number of psychologists and, more importantly for our purposes, by many people in the field of advertising, as we learned from Vance Packard back in Chapter 7.

Even putting Freudian explanations aside, simple observation of the power of the human sexual impulse makes the reason for the use of sexual appeals in advertising apparent. After all, one of the main goals of advertising is to gain and maintain the attention of prospective users, so why not use one of the most powerful and hence "interesting" topics in the world? The question facing advertisers is not whether to use sexual appeals in advertising but how to use them. We'll examine some obvious, some more sophisticated and not so obvious, and

some unconscious and possibly subliminal uses of sexual appeals in advertising in deriving some idea of how such appeals work on us. We are limited to print examples in this book, but electronic advertising obviously uses sexual appeals as well. For instance, in a TV commercial for Pepsi, two young boys make apparently suggestive comments about Cindy Crawford as they ogle her from afar while she buys a drink from a vending machine; they turn out to really be talking about the Pepsi. Obviously, these kinds of appeals are processed in the peripheral channel of the ELM.

Enter the term "sexual social marketing" in InfoTrac College Edition to find the article on sexual social marketing by Reichert, Heckler, and Jackson. What conclusions are drawn there about the impact of sexual appeals on processing?

As touched on previously, communication researcher A. N. Valdivia (1997) deconstructed two very different kinds of sexual appeals in lingerie catalogues. In comparing the appeals in the Frederick's of Hollywood and the Victoria's Secret catalogues, she found that although the merchandise was priced almost the same on an item-for-item basis the appeals were not nearly equivalent. For example, the name "Victoria's Secret" connotes an old world and almost prudish meaning whereas "Frederick's of Hollywood" connotes a kind of leering and glitzy meaning. The settings for the photos in Victoria's Secret connote wealth, leisure, class, and an English country house atmosphere—yachts, gardens, leather sofas, and so on. In Frederick's of Hollywood, the photos are mostly shot against fabric backdrops, and the only items of furniture in them are beds, cloth couches, and poolside lounge chairs. Victoria's Secret models look demure, and they frequently look away from the camera into a mirror. Frederick's of Hollywood models stand more often than they recline, and they stare at the camera, hands on hips, eyes closed, and jaws clenched. The Victoria's Secret catalogue is published twelve times a year, carries a price of $3 (though no one pays for it), and has a home address in London with the words "North America" added on to the recipient's address. The Frederick's of Hollywood catalogue is published less often, and pages frequently have a "This will be your last catalog if you do not order" message on them. These are just a few of the differences detailed by Valdivia in her article, but they do point out how much meaning can be read in an ad. Try to become aware of how pervasive and persuasive sexual appeals are in all kinds of advertising—whether they are blatant, sophisticated, or subliminal.

Obvious Sexual Appeals

In the use of obvious sexual appeals in advertising, the advertiser usually promises sexual success or satisfaction to the person using the product. The promise is carried in both the verbal (words, phrases, sentences) and the nonverbal (pictures, layout, typeface) elements in the ad. For instance, consider the ad for Royal Copenhagen Cologne for Men shown in Figure 14.8. The appeal is quite obvious: Use the product, and you will experience sexual success and satisfaction. With the exception of the play on the words "wildest storms," the reader would have to be rather slow not to get the meaning here. Some more subtle sexual appeals are at work as well. A Freudian would immediately point to the phallic prow of the ship and the bottles of cologne. The use of two bottles—one boxed and one unboxed—might also suggest intercourse. And the fact that we are seeing the nude couple in a love scene through a secret window makes us all voyeurs. You might try to do some analyses of other obvious sexual appeals in advertising in such magazines as *Vanity Fair, Cosmopolitan,* and *Gentleman's Quarterly.*

More Sophisticated Sexual Appeals

In more sophisticated sexual appeals, the advertiser seems only to suggest that the product will lead to sexual satisfaction instead of virtually promising sexual success. Such appeals may also contain subtle cues to indicate sexual prowess. For example, consider an ad by Tiffany for a sterling silver flask pendant by Elsa Peretti. A close-up photo shows the pendant, dripping water, hanging by a silver chain and resting in the cleavage of a well-endowed, wet, and nearly nude woman. Inserted in the flask is the

stem of an orchid on which a praying mantis is perched. Aside from naming the product and the stores where it is available, the ad contains no verbal appeals—no promise of sexual success, prowess, or satisfaction. Yet the ad clearly uses the sexual urge as an appeal to consumers. Again, Freudians would be quick to point out the symbolism of the phallic orchid stem inserted into the vaginally shaped flask. They would also see the abundance of water as symbolic of completed intercourse. But why put a praying mantis on the orchid? What do you think it symbolizes or communicates?

Subtle Appeals to Attractiveness

Many ads simply show an attractive person in modest attire. The sexual appeal is evident but not exploitative. Some believe that ads with more fully clothed persons are more appealing than ones with scantily clad models. Such ads can be placed almost anywhere without concern for appropriateness, and they can be shown to others without any question of impropriety. For example, one could show a colleague a suit on an attractive male in a prominently featured ad by Giorgio Armani in the *Wall Street Journal* without creating much notice. A big change in society is that women now openly comment on the appearance of attractive males.

Subliminal Appeals

Subliminal appeals are a highly controversial topic (Phillips & Goodkin, 1983). In fact, many people doubt their very existence, and some reviewers of this book have suggested that this section on subliminal persuasion be dropped. Why should this topic stir up so much controversy? Probably because it runs counter to the idea that human beings are by nature logical, not emotional, and are certainly not totally preoccupied by sex. Then, too, the controversy may arise because subliminal persuasion smacks of sensationalism and the kind of "witch-doctory" of which the Freudians often are accused. Let us examine the arguments of those who claim that subliminal messages do exist and the controversy over whether the technique works. We will also look at some ads that seem to be using subliminal or nearly subliminal appeals.

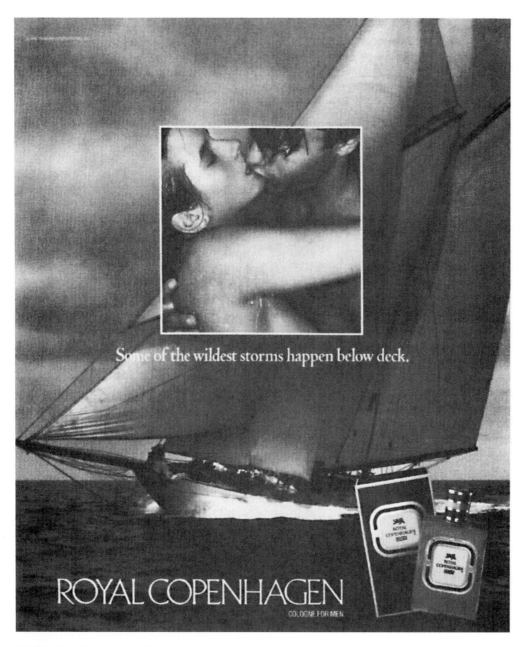

FIGURE 14.8 Blatant uses of sexual appeals in advertising promise sexual success to the user of the product.

(Reprinted by permission of Tsumura International.)

Support for the Existence of Subliminal Messages. The basic premise underlying subliminal persuasion rests on Freud's notion of the id, a component of personality that is completely unconscious. Freud saw the id as powerful and creative but as unruly and full of antisocial impulses. In his view, the impulses of the id are so powerful that they must be enacted in conscious life, even if in only symbolic ways. Freud also believed that the unconscious mind is constantly working at processing "information" that the conscious mind simply ignores, and that it stores this information from birth on. Those who believe in the existence of subliminal appeals maintain that such appeals are sometimes so short-lived or so disguised that the conscious mind ignores them, yet at the subconscious level of the id, they are extremely powerful.

The interest in subliminal persuasion dates back to the late 1950s. James Vicary, the owner of a failing research business, claimed that he had increased Coca-Cola and popcorn sales at a local theater by flashing the words "Drink Coke" and "Eat Popcorn" on the movie screen during a film. He claimed that the messages bypassed the conscious mind but were embedded in the unconscious. Sales of Coke and popcorn supposedly increased by more than 50 percent. Although his results could not be replicated, the technique seemed to be so powerful that it was barred from use in the radio and television industries by the Federal Communications Commission (FCC).

However, this ruling did not forbid the use of subliminal messages in print and film media. In 1972, a company marketing movies to airlines announced that it would be selling spots for subliminal ads. Over a dozen commercial research firms in Chicago and New York still offer services in producing subliminal messages to advertisers. Subliminal messages were used in the film *The Exorcist,* leading to a personal injury lawsuit against Warner Brothers over an alleged accident during a screening that was attributed to an embedded message (Goodkin & Phillips, 1983). The issue reemerged in the presidential election of 2002. A negative television ad was commissioned by the Republican National Committee criticizing Al Gore's prescription drug proposal, with the word "RATS" flashed over the images. Subliminal researcher Hal Becker used auditory subliminal messages to treat a number of psychological problems. Becker argued that subliminal persuasion could be used nationwide to reduce alcoholism, drug abuse, dangerous driving, and various phobias. He also recommended using subliminal messages to discourage shoplifting in stores by mixing messages about honesty and consequences with the piped-in music (Becker & Glanzer, 1978). The CIA has an ongoing interest in how subliminal communication might be used in intelligence work, especially in espionage and counterespionage (Goodkin & Phillips, 1983).

Beginning in the mid-1970s, researcher and professor of advertising Wilson Bryan Key popularized the issue in three books: *Subliminal Seduction* (1973), *Media Sexploitation* (1977), and *Clambake Orgy* (1980). All the books claimed that subliminal cues—usually erotic ones—were "embedded" in magazine ads that appealed to subconscious and repressed sex drives. The messages usually occurred in ads for liquor and cigarettes. These "embeds," as he called them, were faintly airbrushed into ads in the final stages of production and were subconsciously "remembered" some time later when cued by a chance to buy the product or brand.

Key was originally struck by the need to retouch photos in certain magazine advertisements. For example, Key noted that most liquor ads need airbrushing because the ice cubes in the glasses melt under the hot lights needed for magazine-quality photos. As long as the persuaders were airbrushing in the ice cubes, Key reasoned, why wouldn't they consider airbrushing in a subtle message such as the words "buy" or "good"? Advertisers need to get maximum effect for their dollar. They know that basic human needs are the most motivating and that themes of sex and combat are central in most people's fantasy worlds. Key tested his hypothesis by studying a Gilbey's gin ad; he found what seemed to be the word "sex" airbrushed into the ice cubes, and he thought he detected phallic symbols, reflections that depicted various stages in seduction, and so on. To counter potential claims that these vague airbrushed words and symbols were all in his head, Key tested a thousand people by showing them the ad and asking them to put into words the feelings they had while looking at it. None were told what to look for, and none had heard of or knew of subliminal techniques. Although 38 percent did not respond at all, the remaining 62 percent reported that the ad made them feel "sensual," "aroused," "romantic," "sexy," and even "horny." It is possible that this finding was accidental, but Key reported having replicated the test with several ads with similar results. It is also possible that advertisers do not consciously put subliminal messages into ads—that they are accidental. And perhaps it really does not matter as long as receiver effects occur.

Of course, if advertisers really were trying to persuade by manipulating the subconscious, that would raise some ethical issues. However, an agency that did use subliminal techniques would probably deny it (as many agencies have done since the publication of Key's books). So, whether or not the messages are there as a deliberate strategy of the source, they have effects that seem to correlate with Key's hypothesis that symbolic embeds (usually sexually oriented) affect audiences.

Key advised consumers to become critical receivers by looking beyond the surface message in an ad and searching for elements in the background, the lighting, and the potential symbolic messages. This will alert you to an ad's hidden meaning and may train you as an "embed spotter." He suggested that the ad copy, layout, and characters should tip you off to any potential embeds. Whether or not you see the embedded sexual symbols, you can be cued to possible subliminal persuasion by looking at ads more critically and by trying to determine what they imply without explicitly stating.

Some Possible Subliminal Ads. Let's explore some advertisements that may indeed use subliminal or near-subliminal persuasion. In all cases, their appeals seem to promise sexual prowess, success, and satisfaction.

Consider the two perfume ads in Figures 14.9 and 14.10. The first is called "The Promise Made," and the second is called "The Promise Kept." Observe what has changed between "The Promise Made" and "The Promise Kept." The champagne bottle is empty, the phone is off the hook, the fire has died down, the woman's shoes are on the dais, the flowers on the left seem to have blossomed and

opened in the heat, and the woman's earrings are off, as is her stole. Use Key's technique to see whether you find any subtle messages here. First, note the actual words included in the ad. Do they imply any dual meanings? If so, search for visual clues in the ad that would substantiate the implied meaning. Subliminal persuasion devices are being marketed as aids in self-improvement, as seen in Figure 14.11.

Now turn your attention to Figures 14.12, 14.13, and 14.14. They are part of an ongoing series of ads on behalf of Seagram's gin called the "Hidden Pleasure" campaign. The ads use embeds, but instead of hiding them, the folks at Seagram's point them out to you. They are, in a sense, spoofing Wilson Bryan Key's claims. The appeals in them are not directly sexual but rather are only benignly romantic.

In the ad in Figure 14.12, the key words turn out to be "HIDDEN PLEASURES," "Serve one," and "It's a hit" because, embedded in the ice cubes and drops of moisture on the glasses, are images of two tennis players, one male and one female. The one at the left has his racquet lifted as if serving a tennis ball; the one on the right has her racquet in the ready position. In Figure 14.13, the ad designers have once again given a clue for finding the embed: The words "Hint. It's as smooth as a moonlit waltz" are at the left of the goblet, and an arrow points to a waltzing couple emerging out of the air bubbles in the martini glass. In Figure 14.14, you'd have to be blind not to see a couple sitting next to one another, holding hands, embedded in the ice cube.

Consider a two-page ad for Bordeaux Fine Wines. In the first ad, there is an apparent perfect "hour glass" female figure, with her back to the reader. The headline reads, "Bordeaux Fine Wines. Be Seduced." In the second ad, we see only the headline "Bordeaux Fine Wines. Be Seduced." But now the female figure has turned to face the reader, exposing her genital area. On closer inspection, however, the curves that make up the female form in both ads are actually made by wine goblets. Are the visuals actually subliminal messages that have been cued by the words "Be Seduced," or is it simply that you are always thinking about sex?

Are Subliminals Effective? If subliminal messages are used, can they be effective in persuasion?

FIGURE 14.9 What kind of promise is being made?

(Courtesy Lanvin Parfums Co., New York.)

FIGURE 14.10 What differences imply that the promise was kept?

(Courtesy Lanvin Parfums Co., New York.)

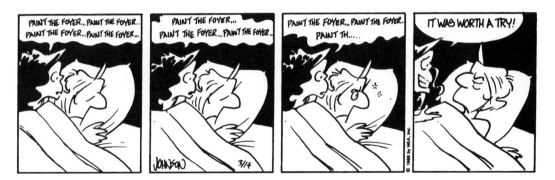

FIGURE 14.11 Subliminal behavior modification is now a multibillion-dollar business, with many users testifying to its effectiveness.

(*Arlo and Janis* reprinted by permission of NEA, Inc.)

The president of the American Psychological Association's Division of Consumer Psychology says, "Absolutely. . . . The controversy has always been over changing people's attitudes. That you can't do. What you can do is trigger a prior attitude or predisposition" (Lander, 1981, p. 45). Note how familiar to us that statement is—the most effective persuasion taps information that receivers already possess. Effective persuaders get messages *out of* their audiences, not *into* them.

There are several sides to the subliminal persuasion controversy. The ad people claim that they never use the technique, whereas people such as Key argue that our world is loaded with subliminal seducers. Interested observers also differ. Some say that Key is like the man who responded with the word "sex" to every inkblot presented by the psychiatrist. When accused of being preoccupied with sex, the patient countered that it was the doctor who collected all the "dirty" pictures. My position is that if it is possible to persuade through subliminal messages—sexual or otherwise—then someone is probably doing it.

I am not alone in my belief. A University of Utah professor of chemistry and president of Innovations Consulting has tested the use of subliminal suggestion during sleep and recently advised Oak Ridge, Tennessee, nuclear scientists that they could use the method to increase productivity and creativity. Subliminal tapes have become a multibillion-dollar business, with many users being "true believers" in the method ("Success," 1987). In another case, after

checking it out with the FCC, Dallas radio station KMEZ regularly broadcast subliminal messages to "stop smoking" as part of the American Cancer Society's "Great American Smokeout." The FCC views paid announcements containing subliminals as not exactly illegal but as "against the public interest." In the Dallas case, however, the message was considered a socially desirable one ("Subliminals Used," 1987).

Of course, certain ads that use sex aren't at all subliminal about their messages. The Calvin Klein ads for Obsession for Men are good examples. Others border on the subliminal: The message is hazy but clear enough to give you the idea the advertiser wants you to get. A good example is the campaign to promote Travel Fox sneakers. With a tiny budget and in competition with giants such as Nike and Reebok, the company hired a Swedish agency, Hall & Cederquist, to create ads for Travel Fox sneakers that had little ad copy. The visuals showed various permutations of a man and a woman wearing the shoes and posing in various suggestive positions. In the ad shown in Figure 14.15 the man and woman are clearly in a suggestive position. Sales in the New York test market tripled in a year.

For a good analysis of whether subliminal persuasion exists and works, access InfoTrac College Edition, and enter the words "subliminal advertising" in the search engine. Go to the subliminal projection option, and select the view 38

FIGURE 14.12 Can you see the "hidden" image?

(Reprinted with permission from Ogilvy & Mather.)

*Hint. It's as
smooth as
a moonlit
waltz.

CAN YOU FIND THE HIDDEN PLEASURE*
IN REFRESHING SEAGRAM'S GIN?

FIGURE 14.13 What hidden picture can you find in this ad?

(Reprinted with permission from Ogilvy & Mather.)

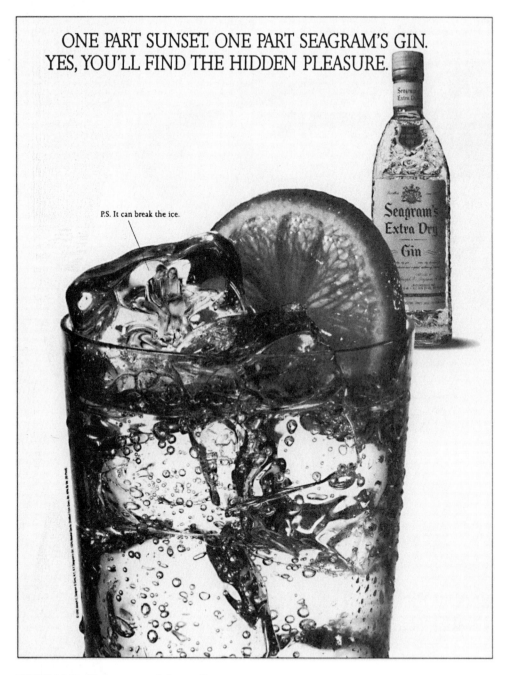

FIGURE 14.14 Obvious enough for you?

(Reprinted with permission from Ogilvy & Mather.)

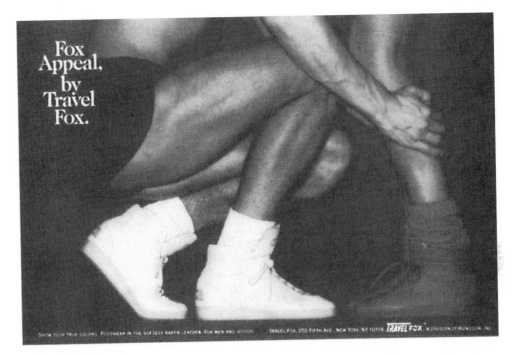

FIGURE 14.15 In this ad for Travel Fox sneakers, the words "Fox" and "appeal" tell you what is going on as we see a man and woman obviously in a sexual position.

(Used by permission of Hall & Cederquist Advertising, Inc.)

periodicals option. Explore a few of the articles reviewed there. Of special interest is the article by Stuart Rogers titled "How a Publicity Blitz Created the Myth of Subliminal Advertising." Report your findings back to the class.

REVIEW AND CONCLUSION

As noted earlier in this chapter, Americans live in a world exploding with new products and brands. This world is even more cluttered with advertising for those products and brands—probably many times more cluttered than other Western democracies. Yet advertisers continue to try to catch our attention; they then educate us about their brands' benefits and advantages; and finally, they use clever cues and sales promotions to prompt us to buy at the point of purchase.

These advertisements and sales promotions are but two elements in what is now termed "integrated marketing communication," in which many elements are integrated with the advertising to make "impressions" on consumers about brands. These elements include public relations, packaging, imprinted items (such as clothing, napkins, wrapping paper, and cups), and special events that feature the brand (for example, the Pepsi challenge or the Virginia Slims tennis tournament), consumer trade sales promotions, and direct marketing. IMC specialists use sophisticated kinds of research, including demographics, sociographics, and psychographics. Based on this research, they develop ad copy, layouts, and scripts to appeal to various needs and desires. As Carl Wrighter pointed out in his 1972 book *I Can Sell You Anything,* they often use misleading and even deceptive "weasel" words and claims, as well as sexual and subliminal appeals, to hype their products and brands. As consumers, we need to be on guard, for there is an ethical dimension to advertisements, and they can easily be used to our detriment. According to John Chaffee (1998), the positive side of advertising is that it provides consumers with valuable information about brand benefits in important areas like safety, health, nutrition, and cleanliness, as well as about more mundane issues like being attractive, sexy, and successful. He also argues that advertising as a tool of competition inevitably leads to lower prices. One could point to numerous examples, such as the costs of a mechanical calculator—$2500 in 1970—and that of a solar-powered pocket calculator in 2004—sometimes as little as nothing if imprinted with advertising. At the same time, author Russ Baker (1997) points to such questionable practices as brand manufacturers trying to manipulate the editorial content of the media in which their advertising runs. They warn media executives that they intend to withhold advertising if editorial content is critical of the brand or even the industry. They have been successful in censoring programming and articles to their benefit, and in some cases, they have managed to spike certain programs or articles. You might want to take a look at advocates on both sides of the issues in A. Alexander and J. Hanson's (2003) provocative book *Taking Sides: Clashing Views on Controversial Issues in Media and Society.*

QUESTIONS FOR FURTHER THOUGHT

1. How much money is spent for advertising in the United States per person compared with that spent in other countries?

2. How might advertising reflect the values and norms of a culture?

3. What might a Marxist critic say about the purpose of advertising?

4. What is "positioning," and how does it relate to the niche?

5. What product features can serve as niches?

6. What are some of the problems of an "over-communicated society"?

7. What is the "product explosion," and how does it affect us?

8. What does "breaking through the clutter" mean?

9. Why is "American-made" an example of positioning?

10. What are the difference between demographics, sociographics, and psychographics?

11. What is the "muppie" market segment?

12. What is a DINK?

13. What is VALS, and how does it work?

14. What are focus groups, and what is their purpose?

15. What is the ACORN system, and how does it work?

16. What are some of the "languages" of advertising? Give examples.

17. How does advertising research lead to advertising copy? Give examples.

18. What are "weasel words"? Give examples.

19. What are some deceptive claims? Give examples.

20. What is meant when we say that a product has become "semanticized"? Give examples.

21. What differentiates blatant sexual appeals in advertising from sophisticated ones? Give examples.

22. How are subliminals used in advertising? How effective do you think they are?

 For online activities, go to the Web site for this book at http://communication.wadsworth.com/larson.

Epilogue

One recurring phenomenon that I have noted while revising *Persuasion: Reception and Responsibility* over the past three decades is the continually increasing rate of change. Not only have we seen the rise of terrorist networks across the globe, but many of them seek to destroy the American economy and our sense of security. After the events of 9/11, no one can travel by air with the same sense of confidence that this is the safest mode of transport. Another ongoing change involves the "boomer" effect. The baby boomer generation that opposed the Vietnamese War as "hippies" and "yippies" have moved beyond their trend-setting (and frequently greedy) years as "yuppies" (young urban professionals). Some are now past their highest-earning years as "muppies" (mature urban professionals) and well into their "ruppie" (retired urban professionals) stage of life. They continue to impact our society enormously. Since the last edition of this book, we have seen the dot.com bubble burst and the economy go from boom to bust. And following the corporate scandals and bankruptcies of the 1990s, our faith in the integrity of CEOs of major corporations and large accounting firms is shot. We have become an incredibly diverse nation as compared to just a few years ago, and this diversity will have sweeping effects in the new millennium.

Technology continues to affect us in unexpected ways. For example, the wreckage of the space shuttle *Columbia* was scattered over rugged terrain of Texas and the Gulf of Mexico. Much of it was recovered by mountain hunters in East Texas forests and by Gulf fishermen using inexpensive but sophisticated GPS (Global Positioning Satellite) devices. They didn't have to lug pieces out of the woods or waters or even guide investigators to the site of the wreckage. They simply recorded the coordinates of the wreckage and reported that to the authorities, sometimes using their cell phones or marine radios. And, of course, use of the Internet, email, e-commerce, and so on has grown exponentially. When I revised the ninth edition of this book, the Internet contained about 10,000 pornographic sites; it now carries hundreds of thousands.

And there are other technologies yet to be introduced. Undoubtedly, they will involve persuasion and will be used to persuade.

As all of these and other changes unfold, the number and sophistication of persuasive messages continues to mushroom. Thus, it's more important than ever for us to become critical receivers of persuasion? My feelings are reinforced by Rod Hart (1999), a noted communication researcher and professor of communication at the University of Texas at Austin. He describes the dramatic appeal he makes to his students each term:

> On the first day of class, I observe to my students that all persuaders ask to borrow just a bit of their minds just for a little while. . . . I tell my students that my course will return their minds to them. I tell them that the cups-full of themselves they willingly loan out to teachers and preachers and cheerleaders in the bleachers can lead to an empty cupboard. I tell them that if they keep giving portions of themselves away that there will be nothing left when they need themselves most—when confused, when frightened, when pressed for a decision. I tell them that persuasion is a science that moves in increments, that it happens most powerfully when it least seems to happen at all. . . . I try to instill a kind of arrogant humility in my students, a mindset that gives them the courage to disassemble rhetoric but also the wisdom never to underestimate it. . . . The persuasion course is the most important course they will take in college. (n. p.)

As you conclude this course, I hope you will not cease practicing the critical reception skills discussed here. I hope you will try to expand your skills and ability to critically disassemble rhetoric. I hope you will continue to recognize the complexities of the world in which we live and the many persuasive messages we receive. I trust your instinctive suspicion of persuasive appeals. Together with Professor Hart, I "trust, mostly, in the critical mind's wondrous capacity to call a spade a spade and a rhetoric a rhetoric, to depuff puffery and to make mortals of gods and to maintain a tenacious resolve that we shall not all fall, lemminglike into the sea."

References

Chapter 1

Alter, J. (2002). "The Body": So Jesse's act is suddenly very old. We've learned that wrestlers can govern until government has to wrestle with something truly important. *Newsweek,* July 1, p. 37.

Beckett, J. (1989). Ad pitches popping up in unusual places. *San Francisco Examiner,* July 17.

Berger, A. A. (2000). Ads, fads, and consumer culture: Advertising's impact on American character and culture. Oxford: Rowan & Littlefield.

Brembeck, W., & Howell, W. S. (1952). *Persuasion: A means of social control.* Englewood Cliffs, NJ: Prentice-Hall.

Brembeck, W., & Howell, W. S. (1976). *Persuasion: A means of social control* (2nd ed.). Englewood Cliffs, NJ: Prentice-Hall.

Burke, K. (1970). *A grammar of motives.* Berkeley: University of California Press.

Fotheringham, W. (1966). *Perspectives on persuasion.* Boston: Allyn & Bacon.

Gearhart, S. M. (1979). The womanization of rhetoric. *Women's Studies International Quarterly, 2,* 195–201.

Jamieson, K. H. (1992). *Dirty politics: Deception, distraction and democracy.* New York: Oxford University Press.

Marwell, G., & Schmitt, D. R. (1990). An introduction. In J. P. Dillard (Ed.), *Seeking compliance: The production of interpersonal influence messages* (pp. 3–5). Scottsdale, AZ: Gorsuch Scarisbrick.

McLuhan, M. (1964). *Understanding media: The extensions of man.* New York: Signet.

Petty, R. E., & Cacioppo, J. T. (1986). The elaboration likelihood model of persuasion. In L. Berkowitz (Ed.), *Advances in experimental social psychology* (Vol. 19, pp. 123–205). Orlando, FL: Academic Press.

Postman, N. (1981). Interview. *U.S. News & World Report,* Jan. 19, p. 43.

Postman, N. (1985). *Amusing ourselves to death: Public discourse in the age of show business.* New York: Penguin Books.

Rank, H. (1976). Teaching about public persuasion. In D. Dieterich (Ed.), *Teaching and doublespeak.* Urbana, IL: National Council of Teachers of English.

Roberts, R. (1924). *The works of Aristotle.* Oxford: Clarendon.

Shannon, C. E., & Weaver, W. (1949). *The mathematical theory of communication.* Urbana: University of Illinois Press.

Simon, H. W. (1976). *Persuasion: Understanding, practice, and analysis.* Reading, MA: Addison-Wesley.

Sullivan, P. A. (1993). Signification and Afro-American rhetoric: A case study of Jesse Jackson's "Common ground and common sense" speech. *Communication Quarterly, 41,* 1–15.

Toffler, A. (1980). *The third wave.* New York: Bantam Books.

Chapter 2

Alter, J. (1987). The search for personal flaws. *Newsweek,* Oct. 19, p. 79.

Bailey, R. W. (1984). George Orwell and the English language. In E. J. Jensen (Ed.), *The future of nineteen eighty-four* (pp. 23–46). Ann Arbor: University of Michigan Press.

Baird, R. M., Ramsower, R., & Rosenbaum, S. E. (2000). *Cyberethics: Social and moral issues in the computer age.* New York: Prometheus Books.

Baskerville, B. (1967). Joseph McCarthy: Briefcase demagogue. In H. Bosmajian (Ed.), *The rhetoric of the speaker.* New York: Heath.

Bate, B. (1992). *Communication and the sexes.* (Reissue). Prospect Heights, IL: Waveland Press.

Beck, J. (1998). Clinton's character under siege once again. *Chicago Tribune,* Jan. 25, sec. 1, p. 19.

Borger, G., & Kulman, L. (1996). Does character count? *U.S. News & World Report,* June 24, 35–41.

Bosmajian, H. (1983). *The language of oppression* (rpt. ed.). Lanham, MD: University Press of America.

Bovee, W. G. (1991). The end can justify the means—but rarely. *Journal of Mass Media Ethics, 6,* 135–145.

Bradley, B. E. (1988). *Fundamentals of speech communication* (5th ed.). Dubuque, IA: Brown.

Buehler, E. C., & Linkugel, W. A. (1975). *Speech communication for the contemporary student* (3rd ed.). New York: Harper & Row.

Buursma, B. (1987). Do-or-die deadline rallies Roberts' flock. *Chicago Tribune,* Jan. 17, pp. 1, 10.

Chapman, S. (1987). How seriously has Joe Biden hurt his presidential effort? *Chicago Tribune,* Sept. 20, sec. 4, p. 3.

Chase, S. (1956). *Guides to straight thinking.* New York: Harper & Row.

Christians, C., Rotzoll, K. B., & Fackler, M. (1991). *Media ethics* (3rd ed.). New York: Longman.

Cooper, M. (2002). Covering tragedy: Media ethics and TWA flight 800. In R. L. Johannesen (Ed.), *Ethics in Human Communication* (5th ed.) (pp. 319–331). Prospect Heights, IL: Waveland Press.

Courtright, J. A., & Perse, E. M. (1998). *Communicating online: A guide to the Internet.* Mountain View, CA: Mayfield.

Cunningham, S. B. (2002). *The idea of propaganda: A reconstruction.* Westport, CT: Praeger.

DeGeorge, R. (1999). *Business ethics* (5th ed.). New York: Prentice-Hall.

Dobel, J. P. (1999). *Public integrity.* Baltimore, MD: Johns Hopkins University Press.

Ermann, D. M., Williams, M. B., & Shauf, M. S. (1997). *Computers, ethics, and society* (2nd ed.). New York: Oxford University Press.

Ewbank, H. L., & Auer, J. J. (1951). *Discussion and debate* (2nd ed.). New York: Appleton-Century-Crofts.

Foss, S. K., & Griffin, C. (1995). Beyond persuasion: A proposal for an invitational rhetoric. *Communication Monographs, 62,* 2–18.

Freund, L. (1960). Responsibility: Definitions, distinctions, and applications. In J. Friedrich (Ed.), *Nomos III: Responsibility* (pp. 28–42). New York: Liberal Arts Press.

Froman, L. A. (1966). A realistic approach to campaign strategies and tactics. In M. K. Jennings & L. H. Ziegler (Eds.), *The electoral process.* Englewood Cliffs, NJ: Prentice-Hall.

Garrett, T. M. (1961). *An introduction to some ethical problems of modern American advertising.* Rome: Gregorian University Press.

Gearhart, S. M. (1979). The womanization of rhetoric. *Women's Studies International Quarterly, 2,* 195–201.

Goodwin, H. E. (1987). *Groping for ethics in journalism* (2nd ed.). Ames: Iowa State University Press.

Green, M., & MacColl, G. (1987). *There he goes again: Ronald Reagan's reign of error* (rev. ed.). New York: Pantheon Books.

Greenberg, P. (1992). Character and other details on the Clinton watch. *Chicago Tribune,* March 20, sec. 1, p. 25.

Griffin, E. A. (1976). *The mind changers: The art of Christian persuasion.* Wheaton, IL: Tyndale House.

Hamelink, C. J. (2000). *The ethics of cyberspace.* London: Sage.

Hauerwas, S. (1977). *Truthfulness and tragedy.* Notre Dame, IN: University of Notre Dame Press.

Johannesen, R. L. (1971). The emerging concept of communication as dialogue. *Quarterly Journal of Speech, 57,* 373–382.

Johannesen, R. L. (1985). An ethical assessment of the Reagan rhetoric: 1981–1982. In K. R. Sanders, L. L. Kaid, & D. Nimmo (Eds.), *Political communication yearbook 1984* (pp. 226–241). Carbondale: Southern Illinois University Press.

Johannesen, R. L. (1991). Virtue, ethics, character, and political communication. In R. E. Denton, Jr. (Ed.), *Ethical dimensions of political communication* (pp. 69–90). New York: Praeger.

Johannesen, R. L. (1997). Diversity, freedom, and responsibility. In J. Makau & R. C. Arnett (Eds.), *Communication ethics in an age of diversity* (pp. 155–186). Champaign: University of Illinois Press.

Johannesen, R. L. (2000). Nel Noddings' uses of Martin Buber's philosophy of dialogue. *Southern Communication Journal, 65,* 151–160.

Johannesen, R. L. (2002). *Ethics in human communication* (5th ed.). Prospect Heights, IL: Waveland Press.

Johnson, D. G. (2001). *Computer ethics* (3rd ed.) Upper Saddle River, NJ: Prentice-Hall.

Kass, J. (1998). Blame for crisis lies not in the stars but in our apathy. *Chicago Tribune,* Jan. 16, sec. 1, p. 3.

Kecskemeti, P. (1973). Propaganda. In I. de S. Pool, W. Schram, F. W. Frey, N. Maccoby, &

E. B. Parker (Eds.), *Handbook of communication* (pp. 844–870). Chicago: Rand McNally.

Klaidman, S., & Beauchamp, T. L. (1987). *The virtuous journalist.* New York: Oxford University Press.

Langford, D. (Ed.). (2001). *Internet ethics.* Boston: St. Martin's Press.

Lebacqz, K. (1985). *Professional ethics.* Nashville, TN: Abingdon.

Lester, P. M. (1991). *Photojournalism: An ethical approach.* Hillsdale, NJ: Erlbaum.

Lester, P. M. (2003). *Visual communication* (3rd ed.). Belmont, CA: Wadsworth.

Levitt, T. (1974). The morality (?) of advertising. In J. S. Wright & D. S. Mertes (Eds.), *Advertising's role in society* (pp. 278–289). St. Paul, MN: West.

Ludwig, A. (1965). *The importance of lying.* Springfield, IL: Thomas.

Luthin, R. (1959). *American demagogues* (rpt. ed.). Gloucester, MA: Peter Smith.

Merrill, J. C., & Odell, S. J. (1983). *Philosophy and journalism.* New York: Longman.

Miller, C., & Swift, K. (1981). *The handbook of nonsexist writing.* New York: Barnes & Noble.

Minnick, W. C. (1968). *The art of persuasion* (2nd ed.). Boston: Houghton Mifflin.

Niebuhr, H. R. (1963). *The responsible self.* New York: Harper & Row.

Nilsen, T. R. (1974). *Ethics of speech communication* (2nd ed.). Indianapolis, IN: Bobbs-Merrill.

Oliver, R. T. (1957). *The psychology of persuasive speech* (2nd ed.). New York: Longman, Green.

Opotow, S. (1990). Moral exclusion and injustice: An introduction. *Journal of Social Issues, 46,* 1–20.

Oran, D. (1975). *Law dictionary for nonlawyers.* St. Paul, MN: West.

Pennock, J. R. (1960). The problem of responsibility. In C. J. Friedrich (Ed.), *Nomos III: Responsibility* (pp. 3–27). New York: Liberal Arts Press.

Perelman, C., & Olbrechts-Tyteca, L. (1969). *The new rhetoric.* Notre Dame, IN: University of Notre Dame Press.

Pincoffs, E. L. (1975). On being responsible for what one says. Paper presented at Speech Communication Association convention, Houston, TX, Dec.

Porter, J. E. (1998). *Rhetorical ethics and internet-worked writing.* Greenwich, CT: Ablex.

Qualter, T. H. (1962). *Propaganda and psychological warfare.* New York: Random House.

Rakow, L. (1994). The future of the field: Finding our mission. Address presented at Ohio State University, May 13.

Ross, R. S., & Ross, M. G. (1982). *Relating and interacting.* Englewood Cliffs, NJ: Prentice-Hall.

Samuelson, R. J. (1994). Clinton: Passionate hypocrite. *Washington Post National Weekly Edition,* Jan. 24–30, p. 28.

Samuelson, R. J. (1995). Clinton, the deficit and the truth. *Washington Post National Weekly Edition,* Nov. 27–Dec. 3, p. 5.

Samuelson, R. (1998). Clinton's problems with the other L word. *Chicago Tribune,* Jan. 30, sec. 1, p. 17.

Schwartz, T. (1974). *The responsive chord.* Garden City, NY: Anchor.

Shorris, E. (1977). The fourth estate. *Harper's,* Oct., p. 106.

Singer, J. B. (2002). The unforgiving truth in the unforgivable photo. *Media Ethics, 13,* 30–31.

Stewart, J., & Zediker, K. (2000). Dialogue as tensional, ethical practice. *Southern Communication Journal, 65,* 224–242.

Thompson, W. (1975). *The process of persuasion.* New York: Harper & Row.

Toulmin, S. (1950). *An examination of the place of reason in ethics.* Cambridge: Cambridge University Press.

Wallace, K. R. (1955). An ethical basis of communication. *Speech Teacher, 4,* 1–9.

Wellman, C. (1988). *Morals and ethics* (2nd ed.). Englewood Cliffs, NJ: Prentice-Hall.

Werkmeister, W. H. (1957). *An introduction to critical thinking* (rev. ed.). Lincoln, NE: Johnson.

Wheeler, T. H. (2002). *Phototruth or photofiction? Ethics and media imagery in the digital age.* Mahwah, NJ: Erlbaum.

Williams, H. M. (1974). What do we do now, boss? Marketing and advertising. *Vital Speeches of the Day, 40,* 285–288.

Wood, J. T. (1994). *Gendered lives: Communication, gender, and culture.* Belmont, CA: Wadsworth.

Chapter 3

Allred, J. (1999). Go for the greed. *Newsweek,* Jan. 25, pp. 30–31.

Andrews, J. (1980). History and theory in the study of the rhetoric of social movements. *Central States Speech Journal, 31,* 274–281.

Aristotle. (1984). *Rhetoric.* (W. R. Roberts, Trans.). New York: Modern Library.

Bowers, J. W., & Ochs, D. J. (1971). *The rhetoric of agitation and control.* Reading, MA: Addison-Wesley.

Buckley, W. F., Jr. (2002). Burying Wellstone. *National Review Online,* Nov. 1. Accessed Dec. 19, 2002, at http://www.nationalreview.com/buckley/buckley110102.asp.

Burns, S. (1990). *Social movements of the 1960s: Searching for democracy.* Boston: Twayne.

Campbell, K. K. (1998). Inventing women: From Amaterasu to Virginia Woolf. *Women's Studies in Communication, 21,* 111–126.

Fairhurst, G. T., & Sarr, R. A. (1996). *The art of framing: Managing the language of leadership.* San Francisco: Jossey-Bass.

Fisher, W. R. (1987). *Human communication as narration: Toward a philosophy of reason, value, and action.* Columbia: University of South Carolina Press.

Foss, K. A., Foss, S. K., & Griffin, C. L. (1999). *Feminist rhetorical theories.* Thousand Oaks, CA: Sage.

Foss, S. K., & Griffin, C. L. (1995). Beyond persuasion: A proposal for an invitational rhetoric. *Communication Monographs, 62,* 2–18.

Foss, S. K. (1996). *Rhetorical criticism: Exploration and practice* (2nd ed.). Prospect Heights, IL: Waveland Press.

Golden, J. L., Berquist, G. F., & Coleman, W. E. (1989). *The rhetoric of western thought* (4th ed). Dubuque, IA: Kendall/Hunt.

Griffin, L. M. (1952). The rhetoric of historical movements. *The Quarterly Journal of Speech, 38,* 184-188.

Kilbourne, J. (1979). *Killing us softly.* Cambridge, MA: Cambridge Documentary Films.

Kilbourne, J. (2001). *Deadly persuasion: Why women and girls must fight the addictive power of advertising.* New York: Free Press.

McGee, M. C. (1980). The ideograph: A link between rhetoric and ideology. *Quarterly Journal of Speech, 66,* 1–16.

Plato. (1937). The dialogues of Plato (Vol. 1). (B. Jowett, Trans.). New York: Random House.

Schwartz, T. (1973). *The responsive chord.* New York: Anchor.

Scott, R. L. (1993). Rhetoric is epistemic: What difference does that make? In T. Enos & S. C. Brown (Eds.), *Defining the new rhetoric* (pp. 120–136). Mahwah, NJ: Erlbaum.

Chapter 4

Allen, M. (1998). Comparing the persuasive effectiveness of one- and two-sided messages. In M. Allen & R. W. Preiss (Eds.), *Persuasion: Advances through meta-analysis* (pp. 87–98). Cresskill, NJ: Hampton Press.

Allen, M., & Stiff, J. (1998). The sleeper effect. In M. Allen & R. W. Preiss (Eds.), *Persuasion: Advances through meta-analysis* (pp. 175–188). Cresskill, NJ: Hampton Press.

Aristotle. (1984). *Rhetoric.* (W. R. Roberts, Trans.). New York: Modern Library.

Bandura, A. (1977). *Social learning theory.* Englewood Cliffs, NJ: Prentice-Hall.

Blumler, J. (1979). The role of theory in uses and gratifications studies. *Communication Research, 6,* 9–34.

Blumler, J., & Gurevitch, M. (1974). Uses of mass communication by the individual. In W. D. Phillips & F. Yu (Eds.), *Mass communication: Major issues and future directions* (pp. 11–35). New York: Praeger.

Bornstein, R. F. (1989). Exposure and affect: Overview and meta-analysis of research, 1968–1987. *Psychological Bulletin, 106,* 265–289.

Chaiken, S., & Eagly, A. H. (1976). Communication modality as a determinant of message persuasiveness and message comprehensibility. *Journal of Personality and Social Psychology, 34,* 605–614.

Chaiken, S., Giner-Sorolla, R., & Chen, S. (1996). Beyond accuracy: Defense and impression motives in heuristic and systematic information processing. In P. M. Gollwitzer & J. A. Bargh (Eds.), *The psychology of action: Linking cognitions and motivation to behavior* (pp. 553–578). New York: Guilford Press.

Chaiken, S., & Trope, Y. (Eds.). (1999). *Dual-process theories in social psychology.* New York: Guilford Press.

Cody, M. J., Canary, D., & Smith, S. (1987). Compliance-gaining strategy selection: Episodes and goals. In J. Daly & J. Wiemann (Eds.), *Communicating strategically.* Hillsdale, NJ: Erlbaum.

Cromwell, H. (1950). The relative effect on audience attitude of the first versus the second argumentative speech of a series. *Speech Monographs, 17,* 105–122.

Dillard, J. P. (Ed.). (1990). *Seeking compliance: The production of interpersonal influence messages.* Scottsdale, AZ: Gorsuch Scarisbrick.

Eagly, A. H. & Chaiken, S. (1993). *The psychology of attitudes.* Fort Worth, TX: Harcourt Brace Jovanovich.

Falk, E., & Mills, J. (1996). Why sexist language affects persuasion: The role of homophily, intended audience, and offense. *Women and Language, 19,* 36–43.

Festinger, L. (1962). *A theory of cognitive dissonance.* Stanford, CA: Stanford University Press.

Fishbein, M., & Ajzen, I. (1975). Belief, attitude, intention, and behavior. Reading, MA: Addison-Wesley.

Fishbein, M., & Ajzen, I. (1981). Acceptance, yielding and impact: Cognitive processes in persuasion. In R. E. Petty, T. M. Ostrom, & T. C. Brock (Eds.), *Cognitive responses in persuasion* (pp. 339–359). Hillsdale, NJ: Erlbaum.

French, J. & Raven, B. (1959). The bases of social power. In D. Cartwright (Ed.), *Studies in social power* (pp. 150–167). Ann Arbor: University of Michigan Press.

FUD-Counter. (2001). How does FUD relate to Linux? Nov. 1. Accessed Dec. 17, 2002, at http://fud-counter.nl.linux.org/rationale.html.

Grush, J. E., McKeough, K. L., & Ahlering, R. F. (1978). Extrapolating laboratory exposure research to actual political elections. *Journal of Personality and Social Psychology, 36,* 257–270.

Heider, F. (1946). Attitudes and cognitive organization. *Journal of Psychology, 21,* 107–112.

Heider, F. (1958). *The psychology of interpersonal relations.* New York: Wiley.

Hovland, C. I. (1957). *The order of presentation in persuasion*. New Haven, CT: Yale University Press.

Hovland, C. I., Janis, I. L., & Kelley, H. H. (1953). *Communication and persuasion*. New Haven, CT: Yale University Press.

Janis, I. L. (1967). Effects of fear arousal on attitude change: Recent developments in theory and experimental research. In L. Berkowitz (Ed.), *Advances in experimental social psychology* (Vol. 3, pp. 166–224). New York: Academic Press.

Janis, I. R., & Feshbach, S. (1953). Effects of fear-arousing communications. *Journal of Abnormal Social Psychology, 48,* 78–92.

Katz, E. (1957). The two-step flow of communication: An up-to-date report on an hypothesis. *Public Opinion Quarterly, 21,* 61–78.

Kellermann, K., & Cole, T. (1994). Classifying compliance-gaining messages: Taxonomic disorder and strategic confusion. *Communication Theory, 4,* 3–60.

Kipnis, D., Schmidt, S. M., & Wilkinson, I. (1980). Intraorganizational influence tactics: Explorations in getting one's way. *Journal of Applied Psychology, 65,* 440–452.

Lazarsfeld, P. F., Berelson, B., & Gaudet, H. (1944). *The people's choice.* New York: Duell, Sloan, & Pearce.

Lefrançois, G. (1980). *Of children* (3rd ed.). Belmont, CA: Wadsworth.

Leventhal, H. (1970). Findings and theory in the study of fear communications. In L. Berkowitz (Ed.), *Advances in experimental social psychology* (Vol. 5, pp. 119–186). New York: Academic Press.

Lund, F. H. (1925). The psychology of belief, IV: The law of primacy in persuasion. *Journal of Abnormal Social Psychology, 20,* 183–191.

Marwell, G., & Schmitt, D. R. (1967). Dimensions of compliance-gaining behavior: An empirical analysis. *Sociometry, 30,* 350–364.

McGuire, W. J. (1968). Personality and attitude change. In A. G. Greenwald, T. C. Brock, & T. M. Ostrum (Eds.), *Psychological foundations of attitudes.* New York: Academic Press.

McLuhan, M. (1964). *Understanding media.* New York: Signet.

Microsoft (2001). *Linux in retail & hospitality: What every retailer should know.* Seattle: Author.

Miller, G. R., Boster, F. J., Roloff, M. E., & Seibold, D. R. (1977). Compliance-gaining message strategies: A typology and some findings concerning effects of situational differences. *Communication Monographs, 44,* 37–51.

Mongeau, P. A. (1998). Another look at fear-arousing persuasive appeals. In M. Allen & R. W. Preiss (Eds.), *Persuasion: Advances through meta-analysis* (pp. 53–68). Cresskill, NJ: Hampton Press.

Newcomb, T. (1959). Individual systems of orientation. In S. Koch (Ed.), *Psychology: A study of science* (Vol. 3, pp. 384–422). New York: McGraw-Hill.

Palmgreen, P., Donohew, L., Lorch, E. P. Rogus, M., Helm, D., & Grant, N. (1991). Sensation seeking message, sensation value, and drug use as mediators of PSA effectiveness. *Health Communication, 3,* 217–227.

Petty, R. E., & Cacioppo, J. T. (1986). *Communication and persuasion: Central and peripheral routes to attitude change.* New York: Springer-Verlag.

Petty. R. E., & Wegener, D .T. (1999). The elaboration likelihood model: Current status and controversies. In S. Chaiken & Y. Trope (Eds.), *Dual-process theories in social psychology* (pp. 41–72). New York: Guilford Press.

Raven, B. H., & Kruglanski, A. W. (1970). Conflict and power. In P. Swingle (Ed.), *The structure of conflict* (pp. 69–109). New York: Academic Press.

Rogers, E. (1995). *Diffusion of innovations* (4th ed.). New York: Free Press.

Rogers, R. W. (1975). A protection motivation theory of fear appeals and attitude change. *Journal of Psychology, 91,* 93–114.

Rokeach, M. (1973). *The nature of human values.* New York: Free Press.

Rule, B. G., Bisanz, G. L., & Kohn, M. (1985). Anatomy of a persuasion schema: Targets, goals, and strategies. *Journal of Personality and Social Psychology, 48,* 1127–1140.

Ryan, B., & Gross, N. C. (1943). The diffusion of hybrid corn seed in two Iowa communities. *Rural Sociology, 8,* 5–24.

Schenk-Hamlin, W., & Wiseman, J. (1981). A multidimensional scaling validation of an inductively-derived set of compliance-gaining strategies. *Communication Monographs, 48,* 251–270.

Schiffman, B. (Ed.). (2002). Top-earning dead celebrities. Aug. 12. Accessed Jan. 6, 2002, at http://www.forbes.com/home/2002/08/12/0812deadintro.html.

Shaw, M. E., & Costanzo, P. R. (1970). *Theories of social psychology.* New York: McGraw-Hill.

Sherif, M., & Hovland, C. I. (1961). *Social judgment: Assimilation and contrast effects in communication and attitude change.* New Haven, CT: Yale University Press.

Skinner, B. F. (1957). *Verbal behavior.* New York: Appleton-Century-Crofts.

Vygotsky, L. S. (1978). *Mind in society.* Cambridge, MA: Harvard University Press.

Weimann, G. (1994). *The influentials: People who influence people.* Albany, NY: SUNY Press.

Wilson, S. R. (2002). *Seeking and resisting compliance: Why people say what they do when trying to influence others.* Thousand Oaks, CA: Sage.

Witte, K. (1992). Putting the fear back into fear appeals: The extended parallel process model. *Communication Monographs, 59,* 329–349.

Zajonc, R. B. (1968). Attitudinal effects of mere exposure. *Journal of Personality and Social Psychology, 9,* 1–27.

Zuckerman, M. (1979). *Sensation seeking: Beyond the optimal level of arousal.* Hillsdale, NJ: Erlbaum.

Chapter 5

Berger, A. A. (1989). *Signs in contemporary society: An introduction to semiotics.* Salem, WI: Sheffield.

Berube, M. (Ed.). (1985). *The American heritage dictionary.* Boston: Houghton Mifflin.

Burke, K. (1950). *A rhetoric of motives.* Berkeley: University of California Press.

Burke, K. (1966). *Language as symbolic action: Essays on life, literature, and method.* Berkeley: University of California Press.

Burke, K. (1986). *Language as symbolic action.* Berkeley: University of California Press.

Hahn, D. (1998). *Political communication: Rhetoric, government and citizens.* State College, PA: Strata.

Korzybski, A. (1947). *Science and sanity.* Lakeville, CT: Non-Aristotelean Library.

Langer, S. K. (1951). *Philosophy in a new key.* New York: New American Library.

Lederer, R. (1991). *The miracle of language.* New York: Pocket Books.

National Public Radio. (1999). *Morning Edition,* Feb. 3.

Postman, N. (1992). *Technopoly: The surrender of culture to technology.* New York: Vintage Books.

Suplee, K. (1987). Semiotics: In search of more perfect persuasion. *Washington Post,* Jan. 18, Outposts sec., pp. 1–3.

Chapter 6

Andrews, L. A. (1984). Exhibit A: Language. *Psychology Today,* Feb., p. 30.

Barol, B. (1988). The 80s are over. *Newsweek,* Jan. 4, pp. 40–48.

Berger, A. (1984). *Signs in contemporary culture.* New York: Longman.

Black Elk. (1971). *Touch the earth.* New York: Outerbridge & Dienstfrey.

Broder, D. (1984). The great American values test. *Psychology Today,* Nov., p. 41.

Bruell, E. (1986). He: This is an okay (lovely) analysis (emotional investigation) of our words (deepest corridors of meaning). *Chicago Tribune,* Dec. 31, sec. 7, p. 12.

Buissac, P. (1976). *Circus and culture: A semiotic approach.* Bloomington: Indiana University Press.

Burke, K. (1960). *A grammar of motives.* Berkeley: University of California Press.

Cialdini, R. (2001). *Influence: Science and practice.* Boston: Allyn & Bacon.

Dillard, J. P., & Pfau, M. (2002). *The persuasion handbook: Developments in theory and practice.* Thousand Oaks, CA: Sage.

Domzal, T., & Kernan, J. (1993). Mirror, mirror: Some postmodern reflections on global marketing. *Journal of Advertising,* Dec., p. 20.

Dunaway, D., & Kramer, J. (1990). *Why men don't get enough sex and women don't get enough love.* New York: Pocket Books.

Eco, U. (1979). *The role of the reader.* Bloomington: Indiana University Press.

Eco, U. (1984). *Semiotics and the philosophy of language.* London: Macmillan.

Eisenberg, E. M. (1984). Ambiguity as a strategy in organizational communication. *Communication monographs, 51,* 227–242.

Farrell, W. (1974). *The liberated male.* New York. Random House.

Follett, K. (2001). *Jackdaws.* New York: Random House.

Hahn, D. (1998). *Political communication: Rhetoric, government and citizens.* State College, PA: Strata.

Hosman, L. H. (2002). Language and persuasion. In J. P. Dillard & M. Pfau (Eds.), *The persuasion handbook: Developments in theory and practice.* Thousand Oaks, CA: Sage.

Kallend, J. S. (2002). Skydiving responsibility lies solely with jumper. *Chicago Tribune,* Aug. 11, sec. 2, p. 8.

Kittredge, W. (1996). The war for Montana's soul. *Newsweek,* April 15, p. 43.

Koenig, P. (1972). Death doth defer. *Psychology Today,* Nov., p. 83.

Lederer, R. (1991). *The miracle of language.* New York: Pocket Books.

Lewis, C. (1999). The athletes are the games. *Newsweek,* Feb. 15, p. 56.

Marshall, D. (1999). An Olympic-size problem. *Newsweek,* Feb. 15, p. 20.

Messner, M. R. (1998). *Politics and masculinity: Men in movements.* Thousand Oaks, CA: Sage.

Nimmo, D., & Combs, J. (1984). *Mediated political realities.* New York: Longman.

Osborn, M. (1967). Archetypal metaphors in rhetoric: The light-dark family. *Quarterly Journal of Speech,* April, 115–126.

Seigel, B. (1989). *The healing power of communicating with your body.* New York: Weider.

Swanson, S. L. (1981). Sensory language in the courtroom. *Trial Diplomacy Journal,* Winter, pp. 37–43.

Tannen, D. (1990). *You just don't understand: Men and women in conversation.* New York: Morrow.

Weaver, R. (1953). *The ethics of rhetoric.* Chicago: Regnery.

Yates, S. J. (2001). Gender, language and CMC for education. *Learning and instruction, 11,* 23–34.

Chapter 7

Austin, N. (2002). The power of the pyramid: The foundation of human psychology, and thereby motivation; Maslow's hierarchy is one powerful pyramid. *Incentive,* July, p. 10.

Bellah, R. N., Madsen, R., Sullivan, W. M., Swoder, A., & Tipton, S. M. (1985). *Habits of the heart: Individualism and commitment in American life.* New York: Harper & Row.

Booth, E. (1999). Getting inside a shopper's mind: Direct marketers are working out how and why consumers arrive at decisions, in order to satisfy their needs. *Marketing,* June 3, p. 32.

Booth-Butterfield, S., & Welbourne, J. (2002). The elaboration likelihood model: Its impact on persuasion theory and research. In J. P. Dillard & M. Pfau (Eds.), *The persuasion handbook: Developments in theory and practice* (pp. 155–173). Thousand Oaks, CA: Sage.

Burke, K. (1961). *The rhetoric of religion: Studies in logology.* Boston: Beacon Press.

Carnegie, D. (1952). *How to win friends and influence people.* New York: Simon & Schuster.

Colley, R. H. (1961). *Defining advertising goals for measured attitude results.* New York: Association of National Advertisers.

De Bono, K. G., & Harnish, R. (1988). Source expertise, source attractiveness, and the processing of persuasive information. *Journal of Personality and Social Psychology, 55,* 541–546.

Eagley, A. H., & Chaiken, S. (1993). *The psychology of attitudes.* New York: Harcourt Brace Jovanovich.

Eiser, R. J. (1987). *The expression of attitude.* New York: Springer-Verlag.

Festinger, L. (1962). *A theory of cognitive dissonance.* Stanford, CA: Stanford University Press.

Fishbein, M., & Ajzen, I. (1975). *Belief, attitude, intention, and behavior: An introduction to theory and research.* Reading, MA: Addison-Wesley.

Frankl, V. (1962). *Man's search for meaning: An introduction to logotherapy.* New York: Washington Square.

Freedman, D. H. (1988). Why you watch some commercials—Whether you want to or not. *TV Guide,* Feb. 20.

Friedman, J. L., & Dagnoli, J. (1988). Brand name spreading: Line extensions are marketers' lifeline. *Advertising Age,* Feb. 22.

Lafavore, R. (1995). From here to eternity: Men's desire for immortality. *Men's Health,* Nov., p. 74.

Larson, C. U., & Sanders, R. (1975). Faith, mystery, and data: An analysis of "scientific" studies of persuasion. *Quarterly Journal of Speech, 61,* 178–194.

Lears, T. J. J. (1983). From salvation to self-realization: Advertising and the therapeutic roots of the consumer culture. In *The culture of consumption: Critical essays in American culture, 1880–1980.* New York: Pantheon Books.

Nelson, R. (2001). On the shape of verbal networks in organizations. *Organization Studies,* Sept.–Oct., 797.

Marquand, R. (1988). Needed: Curriculum with character. *Chicago Tribune,* Jan. 24, p. 5.

Maslow, A. (1954). *Motivation and personality.* New York: Harper & Row.

National Public Radio. (2002). *All things considered,* Aug. 30.

Naughton, Robert. (2002). More headwind for Martha: As investigators run out of patience, the diva of domesticity may be ordered to testify in Washington. *Newsweek,* Sept. 2, p. 45.

Osgood, C. E., & Tannenbaum, P. H. (1955). The principle of congruity in the prediction of attitude change. *Psychological Review, 62,* 43.

Packard, V. (1964). *The hidden persuaders.* New York: Pocket Books.

Petty, R., & Cacioppo, J. (1986). *Communication and persuasion.* New York: Springer-Verlag.

Petty, R. E., & Wegener, D. T. (1998). Attitude change: Multiple roles for persuasion variables. In D. T. Gilbert, S. T. Fiske, & G. Lindsay (Eds.), *Handbook of social psychology.* Boston: McGraw-Hill.

Pinsky, M. S. (2002). Houston minister views Gospel according to the Sopranos. *Orlando Sentinel,* Sept. 4.

Putnam, R. (1995). Bowling alone: America's declining social capital. *Journal of Democracy 6,* 65–68.

Rokeach, M. (1968). *Beliefs, attitudes, and values: A theory of organization and change.* San Francisco: Jossey-Bass.

Rowan, J. (1998). Maslow amended. *The Journal of Humanistic Psychology,* Winter, 84.

Rowell, R. (2002). Martha's taste, not her ethics lures fans. Knight Rider/*Business News,* Oct. 2.

Schrader, D. C. (1999). Goal complexity and the perceived competence of interpersonal influence messages. *Communication Studies,* Fall, 188.

Shavitt, S. (1990). The role of attitude objects in attitude functions. *Journal of Experimental Psychology, 26,* 124–148.

Sibley, K. (1997). The e-mail dilemma: To spy or not to spy. *Computing Canada,* March 31, p. 14.

Staal, S. (2001). Warning: living together may ruin your relationship. *Cosmopolitan,* Sept., p. 286.

Wood, W. (2000). Attitude change: Persuasion and social influence. *Annual Review of Psychology,* 539.

Zemke, R. (1998). Maslow for a new millennium. *Training,* Dec., 54.

Zimbardo, P. G., Ebbesen, E. E., & Maslach, C. (1976). *Influencing attitudes and changing behavior.* Reading, MA: Addison-Wesley.

Zimbardo, P. G., & Leippe, M. R. (1991). *The psychology of attitude change and social influence.* New York: McGraw-Hill.

Chapter 8

Clark, H. H. (1969). Linguistic processes in deductive reasoning. *Psychological Review, 76,* 387–404.

Consider the facts. (2002). *Pine County Courier,* July 25, p. 10.

Deardorf, J., & Finan, E. (1999). Barton wins $29.6 million. *Chicago Tribune,* March 2, p. 1.

Fishbein, M., & Ajzen, I. (1975). *Beliefs, attitude, intention and behavior: An introduction to theory and research.* Reading, MA: Addison-Wesley.

Fishbein, M., & Ajzen, I. (1980). Predicting and understanding consumer behavior: Attitude-behavior correspondence. In I. Ajzen & M. Fishbein (Eds.), *Understanding attitudes and predicting social behavior.* Englewood Cliffs, NJ: Prentice-Hall.

Garfield, B. (1988). Ad review: Good commercials finally outnumber the bad ones on TV. *Advertising Age,* March 14, p. 86.

Guttmacher, A. (1993). Social science and the citizen. *Society,* July–Aug., p. 2.

Jensen, J. V. (1981). *Argumentation: Reasoning in communication.* New York: Van Nostrand.

Kahane, H. (1992). *Logic and contemporary rhetoric: The use of reason in everyday life.* Belmont, CA: Wadsworth.

Loftus, E. F. (1980). *Eyewitness testimony.* Cambridge, MA: Harvard University Press.

Loftus, E. F. (1984). Eyewitness testimony. *Psychology Today,* Feb., p. 25.

Moore, C. (1909). *A short life of Abraham Lincoln.* Chicago: Houghton Mifflin.

The payoffs for preschooling. 1984, *Chicago Tribune,* Dec. 25, p. 25.

Peck, M. S. (1983). *People of the lie: The hope for healing human evil.* New York: Simon & Schuster.

Reinard, J. C. (1988). The empirical study of evidence: The status after fifty years of research. *Human Communication Research,* Fall, pp. 25–36.

Reynolds, R., & Burgoon, M. (1983). Belief processing, reasoning and evidence. *Communication Yearbook, 7,* 83–104.

Reynolds, R., & Reynolds, J. L. (2002). Evidence. In J. P. Dillard & M. Pfau (Eds.), *The persuasion handbook: Developments in theory and practice* (pp. 427–444). Thousand Oaks, CA: Sage.

Scott, B. (1989). *Rockford Register Star,* Nov. 8, editorial page.

Thompson, W. N. (1971). *Modern argumentation and debate: Principles and practices.* New York: Harper & Row.

Toulmin, S. (1964). *The uses of argument.* Cambridge: Cambridge University Press.

Zorn, E. (2002). Season to kill enriches some, repulses many. *Chicago Tribune,* Nov. 11, sec. 2.

Chapter 9

America's abortion dilemma. (1985). *Newsweek,* Jan. 14, pp. 20–23.

Baudhin, S., & Davis, M. (1972). Scales for the measurement of ethos: Another attempt. *Speech Monographs, 39,* 296–301.

Beane, W. C., & Doty, W. G. (1975). *Myths, rites, and symbols: A Mercia Eliade reader.* New York: Harper Colophon.

Bellah, R. N., Madsen, R., Sullivan, W. M., Swidler, A., & Tipton, S. M. (1985). *Habits of the heart: Individualism and commitment in American life.* New York: Harper & Row.

Berlo, D., Lemmert, J., & Davis, M. (1969). Dimensions for evaluating the acceptability of message sources. *Public Opinion Quarterly, 33,* 563–576.

Cialdini, R. (2001). *Influence: Science and practice* (4th ed.). Needham Heights, MA: Allyn & Bacon.

Edelman, M. (1967). Myths, metaphors and political conformity. *Psychiatry, 30,* 217–228.

Eliade, M. (1971). *The myth of the eternal return: Of cosmos and history.* Princeton, NJ: Princeton University Press.

Hahn, D. (1998). *Political communication: Rhetoric, government, and citizens.* State College, PA: Strata, pp. 128–129.

Hofstadter, R. (1963). *Anti-intellectualism in America.* New York: Knopf.

Hofstadter, R. (1967). *The paranoid style in American politics and other essays.* New York: Vintage Books.

Hovland, C., Janis, I., & Kelley, H. (1953). *Communication and persuasion.* New Haven, CT: Yale University Press.

Kelman, H., & Hovland, C. (1953). Reinstatement of the communicator: Delayed measurement of opinion changes. *Journal of Abnormal and Social Psychology, 48,* 327–335.

Kosicki, G. M. (2002). The media priming effect: News media and considerations affecting political judgments. In J. P. Dillard and M. Pfau (Eds.), *The persuasion handbook: Developments in theory and practice* (pp. 63–82). Thousand Oaks, CA: Sage.

Parenti, M. (1994). *Land of idols: Political mythology in America.* New York: St. Martin's Press, pp. 2–13.

Reich, R. (1987). *Tales of a new America.* New York: Times Books.

Santos, M. (1961). *These were the Sioux.* New York: Dell, p. 19.

Steele, E. D., & Redding, W. C. (1962). The American value system: Premises for persuasion. *Western Speech, 26,* 83–91.

Tocqueville, A. de. (1965). *Democracy in America.* New York: Mentor.

Chapter 10

Andersen, P. A. (1985). Nonverbal immediacy in interpersonal communication. In A. W. Seligman & S. Feldstein (Eds.), *Multichannel integrations of nonverbal behavior* (pp. 1–36). Hillsdale NJ: Erlbaum.

Andersen, P. A. (1999). *Nonverbal communication: Forms and functions.* Mountain View, CA: Mayfield.

Burgoon, J. K., Dunbar, N. E., & Segrin, C. (2002). Nonverbal influences. In J. P. Dillard and M. Pfau (Eds.), *The persuasion handbook: Developments in theory and practice* (pp. 445–473). Thousand Oaks, CA: Sage.

Ekman, P., & Friesen, W. V. (1975). *Unmasking the face: A guide to recognizing emotions from facial expression.* Englewood Cliffs, NJ: Prentice-Hall.

Ellyson, S., Dovidio, J., & Fehr, B. J. (1984). Visual behavior and dominance in men and women. In C. Mayo & N. Henley (Eds.), *Gender and nonverbal behavior.* New York: Springer-Verlag.

Fromme, D., Jaynes, W., Taylor, D., Hanhold, E., Daniell, J., Rountree, R., & Fromme, M. (1989). Nonverbal behavior and attitude toward touch. *Journal of Nonverbal Behavior, 13,* 3–13.

Giles, H., Coupland, N., & Coupland, J. (1991). Accommodation theory: Communication, context, and consequence. In H. Giles, J. Coupland, & N. Coupland (Eds.), *Contexts of accommodation: Developments in applied sociolinguistics* (pp. 1–68). Cambridge: Cambridge University Press.

Goffman, E. (1957). *The presentation of self in everyday life.* New York: Anchor.

Hall, E. T. (1959). *The silent language.* Garden City, NY: Doubleday.

Hall, J. A. (1984). *Nonverbal sexual differences: Communication accuracy and expressive style.* Baltimore, MD: Johns Hopkins University Press.

Heap, N. A. (1976). Personal correspondence.

Knapp, M. L. (1978). *Nonverbal communication in human interaction.* New York: Holt, Rinehart & Winston.

Knapp, M. L., & Comendena, M. E. (1985). Telling it like it isn't: A review of theory and research on deceptive communication. *Human Communication Research, 5,* 270–285.

Kotulak, R. (1985). Researchers decipher a powerful "language." *Chicago Tribune,* April 7, sec. 6.

Leathers, D. (1986). *Successful nonverbal communication: Principles and applications.* New York: Macmillan.

Major, B. (1984). Gender patterns in touching behavior. In C. Mayo & N. Henley (Eds.), *Gender and nonverbal behavior.* New York: Springer-Verlag.

Mehrabian, A. (1971). *Silent messages.* Belmont, CA: Wadsworth.

Murray, J. (1989). *The power of dress.* Minneapolis, MN: Semiotics.

Orban, D. K. (1999). The integrative nature of argument and non-verbal communication in different communication contexts. Unpublished paper delivered to Midwest Basic Course Directors Conference, Feb. 4–6.

Packard, V. (1964). *The hidden persuaders.* New York: Pocket Books.

Porter, N., & Geis, F. (1984). Women and nonverbal leadership cues: When seeing is not believing. In C. Mayo & N. Henley (Eds.), *Gender and nonverbal behavior.* New York: Springer-Verlag.

Scheflen, A. (1973). *Communicational structure: Analysis of a psychotherapy session.* Bloomington: Indiana University Press.

Umiker-Sebeok, J. (1984). The seven ages of women: A view from American magazine advertisements. In C. Mayo & N. Henley (Eds.), *Gender and nonverbal behavior.* New York: Springer-Verlag.

Chapter 11

Bales, R. F. (1970). *Personality and interpersonal behavior.* New York: Holt, Rinehart & Winston.

Binder, L. (1971). *Crisis and sequence in political development.* Princeton, NJ: Princeton University Press.

Borchers, T. A. (2001). *Persuasion in the media age.* Burr Ridge, IL: McGraw-Hill, p. 312.

Bormann, E. G. (1985). *The force of fantasy.* Carbondale and Edwardsville: Southern Illinois University Press.

Bowers, J. W., Ochs, D. J., & Jensen, R. J. (1993). *The rhetoric of agitation and control.* Prospect Heights, IL: Waveland Press.

Cragan, J. F., & Shields, D. C. (1994). *Applied communication research: A dramatistic approach.* Washington, DC: Speech Communication Association.

Cragan, J. F., & Shields, D. C. (1995). *Symbolic theories in applied communication research: Bormann, Burke, and Fisher.* Cresskill, NJ: Hampton Press.

Denton, R., & Woodward, D. (1998). *Political communication in America* (3rd ed.). Westport, CT: Praeger.

Faucheux, R. (1998). Strategies that win! *Campaigns and Elections,* Jan., pp. 24–32.

Fortini-Campbell, K. (1992). *The consumer insight book.* Chicago: Copy Workshop.

Lavidge, R. J., & Steiner, G. A. (1961). A model for predictive measurements of advertising effectiveness. *Journal of Marketing, 24,* 59–62.

Metter, B. (1990). Advertising in the age of spin. *Advertising Age,* Sept. 17, p. 36.

National Public Radio. (1999). *All things considered,* April 2.

Rogers, E. (1962). *The diffusion of innovation.* New York: Free Press.

Schultz, D. E., & Barnes, B. (1999). *Strategic advertising campaigns* (4th ed.). Lincolnwood, IL: N.T.C. Business Books.

Schwartz, T. (1973). *The responsive chord.* New York: Anchor/Doubleday.

Stewart, C. J., Smith, C. A., & Denton, R. E., Jr. (1989). *Persuasion and social movements* (2nd ed.). Prospect Heights, IL: Waveland Press.

Trent, J. S., & Friedenberg, R. V. (1995). *Political campaign communication* (3rd ed.). New York: Praeger.

Trout, J., & Ries, A. (1986). *Positioning: The battle for your mind.* New York: Harper & Row.

Valdivia, A. N. (1997). The secret of my desire: Gender, class, and sexuality in lingerie catalogs. In K. T. Frith, (Ed.), *Undressing the ad: Reading culture in advertising.* New York: Peter Lang.

Chapter 12

Cantola, S. J., Syme, G. I., & Campbell, N. A. (1985). Creating conflict to conserve energy. *Psychology Today,* Feb., p. 14.

Carnegie, D. (1952). *How to win friends and influence people.* New York: Simon & Schuster.

Cialdini, R. (2001). *Influence: Science and practice.* Boston. Allyn & Bacon.

Howell, W. S., & Bormann, E. G. (1988). *The process of presentational speaking.* New York: Harper & Row.

Molloy, J. T. (1977). *The dress for success book.* Chicago: Reardon & Walsh.

Monroe, A., Ehninger, D., & Gronbeck, B. (1982). *Principles and types of speech communication.* Chicago: Scott, Foresman.

Rank, H. (1982). *The pitch.* Park Forest, IL: Counter Propaganda Press.

Russell, J. T., & Lane, W. R. (1999). *Kleppner's advertising procedure* (14th ed.). Upper Saddle River, NJ: Prentice-Hall.

Scheflen, A. E. (1964). The significance of posture in communication systems. *Psychiatry, 27,* 316–331.

Schwartz, T. (1973). *The responsive chord.* Garden City, NY: Anchor.

Selby, P. (1902). *Lincoln's life story and speeches.* Chicago: Thompson & Thomas.

Simons, H. (2001). *Persuasion in society.* Thousand Oaks, CA: Sage.

Woods, M. (1993). Toothbrush tips for wellness. *Chicago Tribune,* Sept. 12, sec. 5, p. 3.

Chapter 13

Boorstin, D. (1961). *The image: A guide to pseudo-events in America.* New York: Harper & Row.

Brand, S. (1987). *The media lab: Inventing the future at M.I.T.* New York: Viking Penguin Books.

Cirino, R. (1971). *Don't blame the people.* Los Angeles: Diversity.

Gumpert, G., & Drucker, S. J. (2002). From locomotion to telecommunication, or paths of safety, streets of gore. In L. Strate, R. Jacobson, & S. J. Gibson (Eds.), *Communication in cyberspace: Social interaction in an electronic environment* (2nd ed.). Cresskill, NJ: Hampton Press.

Jamieson, K., & Kohrs-Campbell, K. (1996). *The interplay of influence* (4th ed.). Belmont, CA: Wadsworth.

Kaiser Family Foundation. (1999). *Kids and media at the new millennium.* Menlo Park, CA: Author, p. 11.

Kaplan, D., Wingert, P., & Chideya, F. (1993). Dumber than we thought. *Newsweek,* Sept. 20, pp. 44–45.

Larson, C. U. (2002). Dramatism and virtual reality: Implications and predictions. In L. Strate, R. Jacobson, & S. J. Gibson (Eds.), *Communication and cyberspace: Social interaction in an electronic environment* (2nd ed.). Cresskill, NJ: Hampton Press.

Lederer, R. (1991). *The miracle of language.* New York: Pocket Books.

Levin, D. (1998). *Remote control childhood?* Washington, DC: National Association for the Education of Young Children, p. 13.

Madigan, C. M. (1993). Going with the flow. *Chicago Tribune Magazine,* May 2, pp. 14–26.

Matusow, B. (1983). *The evening stars: The making of a network news anchor.* New York: Ballantine Books.

McCombs, M., & Shaw, D. (1972). The agenda-setting function of the media. *Public Opinion Quarterly, 36,* 176–187.

McLuhan, M. (1963). *Understanding media: The extensions of man.* New York: Signet.

Meyrowitz, J. (1985). *No sense of place: The impact of electronic media on social behavior.* New York: Oxford University Press.

Ong, W. S. (1967). *The presence of the word.* New Haven, CT: Yale University Press.

Ong, W. S. (1977). *Interfaces of the word.* Ithaca, NY: Cornell University Press.

Ong, W. S. (1982). *Orality and literacy: The technologizing of the word.* London: Metheun.

Postman, N. (1996). Cyberspace, schmyberspace. In L. Strate, R. Jacobson, & S. J. Gibson (Eds.), *Communication and cyberspace: Social interaction in an electronic environment.* Cresskill, NJ: Hampton Press.

Powers, R. (1978). *The newscasters: The news business as show business.* New York: St. Martin's Press.

Ramhoff, R. (1990). Bart's not as bad as he seems: Simpsons as positive as other family. *Rockford Register Star,* Oct. 18, sec. 2, p. 1.

Schwartz, T. (1973). *The responsive chord.* Garden City, NY: Anchor/Doubleday.

Victory, V. B. (1988). Pocket veto. *Advertising Age,* April 25, p. 20.

Zettl, H. (1996). Back to Plato's cave: Virtual reality. In L. Strate, R. Jacobson, & S. J. Gibson (Eds.), *Communication and cyberspace: Social interaction in an electronic environment.* Cresskill, NJ: Hampton Press.

Chapter 14

Alexander, A., & Hanson, J. (2003). *Taking sides: Clashing views on controversial issues in mass media and society.* Burr Ridge, IL: McGraw-Hill/Dushkin.

Baker, R. (1997). The squeeze. *Columbia Journalism Review,* Sept.–Oct.

Becker, H., & Glanzer, N. (1978). *Subliminal communication: Advances in audiovisual engineering applications. Proceedings of the 1978 Institute of Electronical and Electronics Engineers: Region 3.* Atlanta: Institute of Electronical and Electronics Engineers.

Berger, A. (2000). *Ads, fads, and consumer culture: Advertising's impact on American character and society.* Lanham, MD: Rowan & Littlefield.

Borchers, T. (2002). *Persuasion in the media age.* Burr Ridge, IL: McGraw-Hill, p. 374.

Chaffee, J. (1998). How advertising informs to our benefit. *Consumers' Research,* April.

Cuneo, A. (2002). Creative execs stress the importance of the Internet. Accessed Nov. 13, 2002, at www.adage.com using QuickFind Id: AAO20F.

Diamond, E., & Bates, S. (1984). *The spot: The rise of political advertising on television.* Cambridge, MA: M.I.T. Press.

Dollas, C. (1986). Butterball turkeys: An examination of advertising theory and practice. Unpublished starred paper, Department of Journalism, Northern Illinois University, De Kalb.

Engel, J., Blackwell, D., & Miniard, P. (1993). *Consumer behavior.* Chicago: Dryden.

Gallonoy, T. (1970). *Down the tube: Or making television commercials is such a dog-eat-dog business, it's no wonder they're called spots.* Chicago: Regenery.

Global marketers spend $71 billion. (2002). *Advertising Age,* Nov. 11, 1–18.

Goodkin, O., & Phillips, M. (1983). The subconscious taken captive. *Southern California Law Review, 54,* 1077–1140.

Happy 65th birthday to 5,500 Americans—daily. (1988). *Chicago Tribune,* April 20, sec. 8, p. 10.

Key, W. B. (1973). *Subliminal seduction: Ad media's manipulation of a not so innocent America.* New York: Signet.

Key, W. B. (1977). *Media sexploitation.* New York: Signet.

Key, W. B. (1980). *The clambake orgy.* New York: Signet.

Lander, A. (1981). In through the out door. *OMNI,* Feb., p. 45.

Leiss, W., Kline, S., & Jhally, S. (1986). *Social communication in advertising: Persons, products and images of well-being.* New York: Methuen.

Mitchell, A. (1983). *Nine American lifestyles: Who we are and where we're going.* New York: Macmillan.

O'Toole, J. (1985). *The trouble with advertising.* New York: Times Books/Random House.

Phillips, M., & Goodkin, O. (1983). The subconscious taken captive: A social, ethical, and legal analysis of subliminal communication technology. *Southern California Law Review, 54,* 1077–1140.

Postman, N. (1987). *Amusing ourselves to death: Public discourse in the age of show business.* New York: Penguin Books.

Rank, H. (1982). *The pitch.* Park Forest, IL: Counter Propaganda Press.

Ries, A., & Trout, J. (1986). *Positioning: The battle for your mind.* New York: McGraw-Hill.

Rogers, S. (1992). How a publicity blitz created the myth of subliminal advertising. *Public Relations Quarterly,* Winter, pp. 12–18.

Rothschild, M. (1987). *Advertising: From fundamentals to strategies.* Lexington, MA: Health.

Schudson, M. (1984). *Advertising, the uneasy persuasion: Its dubious impact on American society.* New York: Basic Books.

Subliminals used to fight smoking. (1987). *De Kalb Daily Chronicle,* Nov. 18.

Success through the subconscious: Subliminal tapes help people improve. (1987). *Chicago Tribune,* Oct. 1, sec. 1, p. 28.

Storch, C. (1988). Humble grocery cart now a video ad vehicle. *Chicago Tribune,* May 1, Tempo sec., pp. 1, 5.

Thompson, S. (2002). Frito-Lay reports Doritos online ad success. Accessed Nov. 18, 2002, at www.adage.com using QuickFind Id: AAO21A.

Valdivia, A. H. (1997). The secret of my desire: Gender, class, and sexuality in lingerie catalogs. In K. T. Frith (Ed.), *Undressing the ad: Reading culture in advertising.* New York: Peter Lang.

Vestergaard, T., & Schroeder, K. (1985). *The language of advertising.* London: Basil Blackwell.

Weiss, M. J. (1989). *The clustering of America: A vivid portrait of the nation's 40 neighborhood types —Their values, lifestyles, and eccentricities.* New York: Harper & Row.

Wentz, L., & Cuneo, A. (2002). Double-digit Hispanic ad growth continues. Accessed Sept. 16, 2002, at www.adage.com using QuickFind Id: AAN95S.

Williamson, J. (1977). *Decoding advertising: Meaning and ideology in advertising.* London: Marion Boyers.

Wrighter, C. (1972). *I can sell you anything.* New York: Ballantine Books.

Epilogue

Hart, H. P. (1999). Teaching the undergraduate persuasion course: Why? In A. Vangelesti, A. Daly, & G. Friedrich (Eds.), *Teaching communication: Theory, research, and methods* (2nd ed.). Hillsdale, NJ: Erlbaum.

Index

A

Abstract words, 111
A-b-x theory, 91–92
Abzug, Bella, 43
Academic viewpoint of advertising,
    361–363
Acceptance
    ego-involvement and, 88
    stage of persuasion, 80, 81
Achievement in American value system,
    234
Achievers, 351
ACORN system, 353
Acquiescence, 14
Act and communication, 130
Action plans, 291
    in motivated sequence organization,
        292
Action stage of persuasion, 81
Activity theory, 77–80
Adams, John, 123
Adaptation
    audience adaptation, 54–56
    to context and purpose, 54
Additivity, 96
Ad hominem fallacy, 203–204
Adjectives, use of, 126–127
Adler, J., 6
Ad populum fallacy, 205
Advantage claims, 356–357

Adverbs, use of, 127
Advertising. *See also* Campaigns
    academic analysis of, 361–363
    attention-attracting, 362
    brand-scan marketing research, 8
    cause-to-effect reasoning, 196–197
    codes in, 139
    comparison, argument by, 199
    deceptive claims in, 356–358
    demographics and, 347–348
    diversion in, 23
    drama in, 361–632
    ethical standards for, 40–42
    exposure to, 7
    female image and, 70
    god and devil terms, 136
    intentional ambiguity in, 43
    languages of, 354–355
    legal perspectives of, 41
    meanings in, 108–109
    proxemics, use of, 243
    psychographics, 348–353
    research, 347–354
    self-protection method, 24
    semiological approaches, 114–115
    sexual appeals in, 363–375
    social changes and, 360–361
    sociographics, 353–354
    subliminal appeals in, 365–375
    television advertising, 9

    30-Second-Spot Quiz, 357–359
    weasel words, 355–356
    Western culture and, 336–337
Advertising explosion, 342–343
Affective function
    of attitudes, 169–170
    of eyes, 241
Affiliation needs, 162, 164
Affinity scams, 92
Age
    of audience, 287
    positioning by, 275
Agency and communication, 131
Agendas
    media, agenda-setting by, 324–326
    revelation of, 16
Agents for communication, 130–131
Agitation and control model, 279–280
Agitation process, 66
Agrarian precedent, 185–186
Ahlering, Robert, 88–89
AIDA approach, 293
Ajzen, Icek, 89–90, 167, 170,
    195–196
Alexander, A., 376
Alexander the Great, 53
Allen, Mike, 81, 84
Alliteration, 122, 297
    thematic meaning and, 134
Alter, J., 50